An Intellectual
and Cultural History
of the Western World

CONTRIBUTING AUTHORS FOR VOLUME TWO

Art

BERNARD MYERS
Editor-in-Chief, Art Book Department,
McGraw-Hill Book Company, Inc.

JOHN C. GALLOWAY
Oakland University

Literature (In Part)

WALTER B. SCOTT
Northwestern University

EDWARD HUBLER
Princeton University

WILLARD THORP
Princeton University

Music

MARTIN BERNSTEIN
New York University

An Intellectual
and Cultural History
of the Western World

by

HARRY ELMER BARNES

THIRD REVISED EDITION

IN THREE VOLUMES
VOLUME TWO

From the Renaissance through the Eighteenth Century

Dover Publications, Inc., New York

This new Dover edition, first published in 1965, is a revised and enlarged republication of the second edition published by Reynal and Hitchcock, Inc., in 1941. The first edition of the work was published by the Cordon Company, Inc., in 1937. The work, originally in one volume, now appears in three volumes.

Library of Congress Catalog Card Number: 63-21675

Manufactured in the United States of America

Dover Publications, Inc.
180 Varick Street
New York 14, N.Y.

TABLE OF CONTENTS

VOLUME TWO

XIII. THE TRANSITION TO MODERN TIMES: HUMANISM AND
    PROTESTANTISM   546
    I. The Historical Background   546
    II. The Renaissance Myth   549
    III. The Growing Interest in Classical Literature and Civilization   551
    IV. The Humanist Temper   555
    V. Philosophy during the Humanist Movement   562
    VI. Humanism and Education   566
    VII. Advances in Natural Science from Regiomontanus to Copernicus   568
    VIII. Printing Becomes a Practical Art   574
    IX. Political Theory under the Spell of Humanism   579
    X. The Protestant Revolution as an Intellectual Movement   582
    XI. The Witchcraft Epidemic   591
    XII. The Hangover of Medieval Intellectual Interests in Modern Times   595

XIV. LITERATURE, ART, AND MUSIC: 1450-1600   598
    I. The Rise of National Literature   598
    II. The Idealistic Art of the Sixteenth Century   623
    III. "The Golden Age" of Music   639

Part Four: The Origins of the Modern Age

XV. EUROPE EXPANDS AND A NEW ERA DAWNS   653
    I. From River to Ocean   653
    II. Economic Changes Resulting from the Expansion of Europe   657
    III. Social Transformations   658
    IV. New Political Developments   659
    V. Novel Legal Tendencies   661
    VI. Religious Readjustments   662
    VII. Intellectual Effects of the Expansion of Europe   662

XVI. NATURAL SCIENCE IN THE SEVENTEENTH AND EIGHT-
EENTH CENTURIES   668

   I. Progressive Intellectual Patterns in Early Modern Times   668
   II. Intellectual and Cultural Trends Encouraging and Accompanying
     the Progress in Scientific Research   670
   III. The Rise of Scientific Societies   671
   IV. New Scientific Instruments   674
   V. The Revolution in Celestial Mechanics   676
   VI. Some Important Advances in Natural Science in the Seventeenth
     Century   681
   VII. Leading Aspects of Scientific Development in the Eighteenth Cen-
     tury   694

XVII. THE IMPACT OF THE NEW INTELLECTUAL ORDER ON PHI-
LOSOPHY AND EDUCATION   707

   I. Introductory   707
   II. Giordano Bruno and the New Universe   708
   III. Montaigne Incarnates Urbanity and Serenity   711
   IV. Francis Bacon Assaults Scholasticism   717
   V. Descartes and the Mechanistic Universe   722
   VI. Hobbes Founds Scientific Materialism and Ethical Hedonism   725
   VII. Spinoza and the All-Embracing Naturalistic God   727
   VIII. Leibnitz Formulates a New Scholasticism in Terms of Mathemati-
     cal Physics   729
   IX. John Locke Makes Experience the Basis of Reality   732
   X. Hume Enthrones Skepticism   734
   XI. Main Trends in Education   737

XVIII. THE GROWTH OF TOLERANCE AND FREEDOM OF
THOUGHT   744

   I. Some Major Causes of Intolerance   744
   II. The Intolerance of the Catholic Church   746
   III. Protestant Intolerance   751
   IV. The Rise of Censorship of the Press   753
   V. The Growth of Tolerance   756
   VI. The Case for Free Thought   760
   VII. The Attack on the Censorship of the Press   766
   VIII. The Triumph of Tolerance and Freedom of the Press   769
   IX. The Struggle for Civil Liberties   771
   X. Later Forms of Intolerance   778
   XI. Cultural Lag and Civil Liberties   780

XIX. THE REVOLUTION IN RELIGIOUS AND ETHICAL THOUGHT   783

   I. Rationalistic Supernaturalism   783
   II. The Course of Deism   787

III. The Rise of Skepticism 804
IV. Mechanistic Materialism and Atheistic Doctrines 813
V. The Rise of Biblical Criticism 815
VI. The Secularization of Ethics 817

XX. THE KINGDOM OF MAN AND THE VISION OF PROGRESS 823

I. Cycles and the Golden Age 823
II. Fragmentary Contributions to the Theory of Progress in Early Modern Times 825
III. The Age of Rationalism and Ideas of Progress 828
IV. Romantic Philosophy and Theories of Progress 836
V. Early Sociology and Theories of Progress 840
VI. Present-Day Reservations Relative to the Theory of Progress 842

XXI. THE REACTION AGAINST REASON AND THE CRITICAL SPIRIT 844

I. The Reaction in Philosophy 844
II. The Religious Revival 852
III. Reactionary Political Theory 865
IV. Romanticist Conceptions of the Past 868
V. Conclusion 871

XXII. LITERATURE AND THE ARTS IN THE SEVENTEENTH AND EIGHTEENTH CENTURIES 874

I. Growth and Decline of the Classic Ideal in Literature 874
II. Baroque and Rococo Art 911
III. Application of Music to the Drama: New Instrumental Forms 929

An Intellectual
and Cultural History
of the Western World

XIII

The Transition
to Modern Times:
Humanism and Protestantism

1. Renaissance and Reformation

In this chapter we shall continue the study of those intellectual forces whose origins and developments were described in the chapter on the decline of medievalism. Indeed, the beginning of a new chapter at this point must be justified mainly on a physical and pedagogical basis. It would have been both logical and desirable to treat as a unit the intellectual and cultural trends from Roger Bacon to Francis Bacon. Few periods in human history are better knit together. The tempo of development was, to be sure, accelerated in the late fifteenth and the sixteenth centuries, and the cultural products were more impressive and diversified, but they all had their roots in the era from 1250 to 1450.

Such an interpretation is far different from that which dominated the historical writings of a generation ago and still remains approved in many conventional historical circles. The period from 1450 to 1600 has usually been regarded as an age of highly novel and unique developments; in particular, the so-called Renaissance and the Reformation. These were pictured as rather sudden cultural and institutional explosions, and little attempt was made to trace their antecedents back to the Middle Ages.

This approach is in disrepute among up-to-date historians of our generation. In fact, even the terms Renaissance and Reformation are being dropped on the valid ground that they are unhistorical and misleading to students of history. Both the Renaissance and Reformation, as they are called, were the logical and inevitable outgrowth of intellectual and cultural tendencies which began in the twelfth and thirteenth centuries.

Interest in Greek and Roman classics steadily increased after Fulbert of Chartres established his great cathedral school in the twelfth century. If the universities halted the Latin revival for a time they accelerated the Greek revival by glorifying and concentrating upon Aristotle. If they read him in Latin, this did not affect the fact that he was the greatest of Hellenic scholars. The efforts involved in procuring Greek texts of Aristotle for translation into Latin promoted a cultural and linguistic interchange with the East which led to the introduction of other Greek authors, at first in Latin versions and later in the original. Roger Bacon in the thirteenth century was a true intellectual forerunner of Petrarch in his desire to become acquainted with ancient authors in their original language and in the most accurate manuscripts. The Latin classics reappeared with new vigor in the secondary schools of the fourteenth and fifteenth centuries. This Latin revival, together with the growth of towns, commerce, wealth, and the middle class, produced a cultural milieu which welcomed those writings which expressed the unparalleled urbanity of literate Greeks and Romans. Literary and artistic trends which accompanied the decline of medievalism unfolded in the efflorescence of the humanistic period which we used to call the Renaissance.

In the same way, the so-called Protestant Reformation of the sixteenth century grew out of late medieval tendencies. Mounting discontent with scholastic obscurities and wranglings, the satire directed against relics and magic, the increasing popularity of mysticism in philosophy and religion, the growth of the middle class and its restiveness under the economic restrictions imposed by the Catholic church, the trend towards nationalism, the rifts and abuses in the church, the rise of new heresies—all of which we described in the preceding chapter—came to a head with Martin Luther, Heinrich Zwingli, John Calvin, and John Knox. In other words, the so-called Reformation had come to birth in the latter part of the Middle Ages. By the time of Luther the critical forces could not be so easily suppressed as they were in the days of Wycliffe and Huss. Better statesmanship on the part of the Catholic leaders in the sixteenth century would have countenanced sweeping reforms and prevented the catastrophe of a permanent schism in the church.

Hence, it is fairly clear that the so-called Renaissance and Reformation had their roots in the later Middle Ages and were in no sense catastrophic in origin. The chief novelty in the dawn of the modern age was the mastery of oceanic navigation and the expansion of Europe, which we shall treat in our Chapter XV. But even this was not wholly unique or separated entirely from medieval developments. Expansion and exploration began as early as the Crusades, were encouraged by Far Eastern traders and made possible by new nautical instruments and preliminary explorations already described.

These cogent facts, very briefly assembled, will suffice to indicate why up-to-date historians have radically modified their attitude towards the later Middle Ages and early modern times, a subject with which we shall deal more thoroughly below.

We need not describe at length the institutional background of the thought and culture of the late fifteenth and sixteenth centuries, which was much the same—

with an accentuation and acceleration—as those impulses we surveyed in the chapter on declining medievalism, namely, the expansion of city life, the growth of commerce and wealth, nationalistic trends, and symptoms of marked discontent with the doctrines, policies, and administration of the Catholic church. At the height of the humanistic period the discovery of oversea routes to the Far East and West undermined the commercial ascendancy of Italian cities. But this only meant an increase in the number and prosperity of northern and western cities, especially in the Netherlands. An important result of the discovery and exploitation of the New World was the enhanced power and prestige of the middle class in western Europe.

Nationalism became more pronounced in the fifteenth and sixteenth centuries. Strong monarchies were created in Spain by Philip II, in England by the Tudors, and in France by the Bourbons. Strife within the Catholic church produced a breach which was never healed, a subject to which we will devote some attention later on.

2. *Italy Takes the Lead*

Before considering why Italy pointed the way in literary and artistic growth, it is illuminating to look at some of the underlying causes of the mundane or secular philosophy of life which appeared in Florence and other Italian cities about the middle of the fourteenth century. The primary cause was the revival of the classics. But we must look further than this. When the collapse of finance and administration had undermined Roman civilization, it devolved upon the rude but vigorous semi-barbarians of the North to act as a regenerating cultural agency. This assimilation of barbarian blood and classical culture required a long time before it could bear full fruit. Christianity had to be diffused among the backward transalpine tribes. The basic conception of the medieval church which was, as Goethe put it, "the divine worship of sorrow," had to be revised. The old ideas that ignorance was pardonable, that pleasure was sinful, and that salvation depended upon the "mortification of the flesh" had to be undermined. New nationalities had to be blocked out, a national spirit developed, a reasonable degree of peace secured, town life revived, considerable wealth accumulated, a secular spirit stimulated, and learning divorced from the complete dominion of the church.

Because Italy first fulfilled many of these conditions, she plucked the fruits of the new or secular era before the rest of Europe. Italy enjoyed a favorable climate, commercial prosperity, a fair degree of political freedom, and considerable intellectual emancipation from scholastic dogmas, at a time when northern Europe was relatively backward culturally and engaged in endless internal turmoil and foreign warfare. The Hundred Years' War, for example, checked the promising intellectual revival in France. The city-states of Tuscany and Lombardy fostered culture and art, individual expression and civic pride, much as did ancient Hellenic and Hellenistic cities.

Italian communes were usually ruled by a powerful family, and the dominion of benevolent tyrants, from the time of Gelon of Syracuse to Louis XIV, has often stimulated an efflorescence of culture. Furthermore, when the intellectual tide turned towards paganism, Italy found abundant inspiration in her numerous classical remains. Italian trade with the East incidentally imported the Hellenized culture of the Byzantines, while many Byzantine refugees settled in southern Italy. Lastly, the presence in Italy of such men as Petrarch, Aurispa, and Chrysoloras, promoters of classicism or instructors in the classics, hastened the advent of a new era.

The intellectual revival, a natural outgrowth of late medieval trends, was in a measure communicated from Italy to the North. Nevertheless, the new era would have come to the North regardless of Italy, since similar forces of cultural evolution were at work throughout western Europe.

The significance of the revival of art and letters in the West and North is almost too obvious to deserve comment. It was the fruition of the medieval promise that out of the ruins of Greece and Rome would arise a new and more vigorous civilization. It signified that the Greeks and Romans had not lived in vain, and that the barbarians who destroyed the immortal city in 390 B.C., threatened it in the time of Marius, and finally overcame it under Alaric and Theodoric, had shaped a new civilization. The new virility of the German peoples had finally borne fruit.

II. THE RENAISSANCE MYTH

Few historical notions have undergone more of a change in the last generation than the conception of a "Renaissance" of thought and culture between 1350 and 1600. A generation ago it was fashionable to assign transcendent importance to the Renaissance in the development of modern civilization. Jules Michelet, John Addington Symonds, and Jacob Burckhardt, for instance, developed the thesis that the Middle Ages were a period of uniform stagnation, and that the paralyzing shell or envelope of medievalism was burst asunder by potent forces associated with the new appreciation of classical literature and the remarkable developments of chromatic and plastic art between 1350 and 1550. A vernal green spread over Europe in this cultural springtime when civilization emerged from the snow-blanket of a thousand years of desolate medievalism. To this cultural "rebirth" were assigned the most diverse results, including the rise of natural science, rationalism, and the national-state system.

The facts described in a preceding chapter suffice to show how erroneous is such a view of European intellectual and cultural development. Nearly all aspects of European culture steadily improved from the middle of the twelfth century onward. There was even more of an advance from 1200 to 1300 than in the century after 1350, the dawn of the so-called Renaissance. In fact, not until the expansion of Europe following 1492 did there emerge novel forces of relatively sudden and overpowering significance.

Many historians who accepted the idea of a renaissance after 1350 came, nevertheless, to apprehend the fact that it rested upon developments in preceding centuries.[1] Some stressed its relation to the revival of Latin literature in the later Middle Ages. Others emphasized the influence of Francis of Assisi and the growth of mysticism. Still others saw in it a continuity of Hellenic civilization, transmitted

[1] See Barnes, *History of Western Civilization*, I, 837 ff.

by the Byzantines. Finally, especially in the last generation, historians of philosophy and science, particularly in Germany, have revealed the remarkable scientific antecedents of the era of Leonardo da Vinci, Copernicus, and Bruno.

In thus making clear the multifarious ways in which the so-called Renaissance depended on antecedent developments, scholars, whether they understood the fact or not, actually destroyed the theory of a renaissance or "new birth" of civilization. If there was nothing really new about it there could have been no renaissance, for this is what the term means. If there was a revival, it took place in the twelfth and thirteenth centuries rather than in the fourteenth or fifteenth. And we showed in the chapter on the Dark Ages that culture made continuous progress from the tenth to the twelfth centuries.

In time, historians came to see the implications of scholarly researches into the background of what used to be called a renaissance. They concluded that there never was any such thing. This newer conception of the history of European civilization from the Dark Ages to the sixteenth century is admirably expressed by Professor Thorndike:

> The old slurs and disparaging generalizations at the expense of the middle ages are now repeated only by mechanical creatures of habit, by those who stopped thinking and reading twenty or thirty years ago, and who refuse to give up any catchword or prejudice that was instilled into their minds in childhood. Candid inquirers are becoming increasingly convinced that the true Renaissance occurred around the twelfth rather than the fifteenth century, that medieval Latin and scholasticism possessed great merits, that Gothic painting had been neglected just as Gothic architecture and sculpture once were, that democracy and popular education declined rather than advanced in early modern times, that organized charity and care for public health received much attention in medieval towns, whose unsanitary streets seem largely a figment of the modern imagination. Every intelligent person should, if necessary, revise his former estimate of the middle age and think of it, at its height and best, especially in the life of the towns, as having much closer and more vital connections with our present civilization and way of looking at things than used to be held.[2]

Especially difficult has it been to relinquish the idea that the period from 1350 to 1600 gave birth to a unique and unforeseen literature and art. This hypothesis, however, must also be surrendered. Interest in the pagan classics goes back to Gerbert of Aurillac and to Fulbert of Chartres, indeed to Lupus of Ferrières. And what has been said about art in the preceding chapter demonstrates just as clearly the complete continuity of aesthetic growth. There was no renaissance of letters and art, any more than of philosophy and science.

The specific facts about the philosophical thought, scientific discoveries, literary achievements, and artistic triumphs of the era from 1350 onward are, to be sure, about what they were represented by authorities who wrote a generation or more ago—Burckhardt, for example. But the historical perspective or setting of the age has been completely revolutionized. The fanciful notion of a cultural explosion has been superseded by that of a demonstrable evolution. Continuity has replaced

[2] *Science and Thought in the Fifteenth Century*, pp. 9-10.

catastrophe as the key to an interpretation of the period. Therefore, it is best that the word Renaissance be dropped from historical phraseology. If we use it quali-fiedly from time to time in this book, it is only as a pedagogical convenience in order to relate the age to the conventional historical nomenclature and chronology. The renaissance of the twelfth and thirteenth centuries is more of a reality, if taken with proper qualifications; that of the fifteenth and sixteenth centuries is a myth. With this brief introduction, we may profitably examine the cultural and intellectual achievement of the era.

III. THE GROWING INTEREST IN CLASSICAL LITERATURE AND CIVILIZATION

It has long been recognized that the humanist age was characterized by a revival of classical literature, but the conception of the genesis and nature of that revival used to be quite different from what it is today. The old view was consonant with the hypothesis of a unique and abrupt acceleration of culture between 1350 and 1550. The Latin revival used to be attributed primarily to the personal enthusiasm of Petrarch, who was called "the first modern man of letters." The Greek revival was formerly assigned to the capture of Constantinople which suddenly forced Greek scholars to migrate to Italy. The rôles of Chrysoloras and Aurispa, particu-larly, were emphasized, the former having come from Constantinople to Italy and the latter having gone to Constantinople to study and returned with a large num-ber of Greek manuscripts.

The tendency today is to stress the fact that both the Latin and Greek "revivals" may be traced back far beyond Petrarch and Chrysoloras, and that there were a multiplicity of personages who stirred interest in the classics.

The study of Latin classics inaugurated at the cathedral schools of Chartres, Orleans, and the like, never died out. Petrarch (1304-1374) and his followers simply widened the interest thus aroused. The pedagogical reforms of Paulus Vergerius, Vittorino da Feltre, and the Guarinos built the secondary school cur-riculum around Latin authors. Even before the establishment of these humanistic schools, wandering scholars like Giovanni da Ravenna (1346-1406) and Gasparino da Barzizza (1370-1431) evoked enthusiasm for Latin literature among many students. Finally, the search for lost Latin manuscripts, initiated by Petrarch, Coluccio Salutato, and Poggio Bracciolini, and the study of Roman antiquities originated by Flavius Blondus, recovered the full force of Latin culture.

Western enthusiasm for Greek culture, although of a later date than the Latin revival, began in the Middle Ages. In the thirteenth century, there was not only a zeal for reading Aristotle in the original, but men like Robert Grosseteste and Roger Bacon revived the study of Greek grammar in order to read and translate Aristotle. The enthusiasm for Greek literature in Latin translations grew apace as the Middle Ages moved along. The revival of Neoplatonism by Christian mystics and the return to Plato by philosophers like Nicholas of Cues added new sources of Greek influence in Western civilization.

It did not require the Turkish advances upon Constantinople to force Greek culture on Italy and the West. Many cultivated Greeks began to reside in Sicily and southern Italy after the seventh century, migrants who escaped from the ravages of the Persian and Muslim wars. The Iconoclastic controversy in the eighth century also forced many Byzantine scholars to seek shelter in Italy. Thus many oases of Greek culture existed in southern Italy from the seventh century. As Professor Vasiliev remarks, "thus the Italians of the fourteenth century did not need to appeal to Byzantium for elementary technical acquaintance with the Greek language and the beginnings of Greek literature; they had a nearer source, in southern Italy." The importance of south Italian Greeks in the Greek renaissance in the West has not been sufficiently appreciated by historians, save for Professor C. H. Haskins and a few others. The work of Chrysoloras, Aurispa, Bessarion, and Johannes Argyropulos in the fourteenth and fifteenth centuries merely intensified and widened an existing Hellenism which had been relatively quiescent for centuries. These few facts will suffice to show that the classical revival was as dependent upon medieval antecedents as all other phases of the so-called Renaissance. With this preliminary statement, we may examine in some detail various phases of the revival of Greek and Latin culture.

It has often been said that Aristotle passed into eclipse in the fifteenth and sixteenth centuries. But it is more accurate to say that he had new rivals for popularity, especially Plato, Plotinus, Cicero, and the Jewish cabala. Aristotle lost his ascendancy but not his popularity in this era. The interpretation of his doctrines became multiform instead of uniform. Various factions claimed him for their own and fought about his ideas.

The orthodox scholastic Aristotelians, led by the Dominicans, still a powerful order, were loyal to Thomist traditions, and regarded the better Latin texts of, and commentaries upon, their Greek master as wholly adequate.

The humanistic admirers of Aristotle, chiefly George of Trebizond (Trapezuntios, 1396-1484), Theodore Gaza (d. 1487), Pietro Pomponazzi (1462-c. 1525), Rudolph Agricola (1442-1485), and Jacques Lefèvre d'Étaples (1455-1537),[3] read him in the Greek and attempted to discover what he really said, undistorted by scholastic commentaries. Their work represented the first contact of western Europe with the true Aristotle—Aristotle for his own sake and not as a buttress to Catholic Christianity. They took delight in showing how Aristotle had been misconstrued and hushed up by the scholastics. There were followers of Averroës' pantheistic Aristotle—the university of Padua was their stronghold—and there were some who accepted the naturalistic Aristotle of Alexander of Aphrodisias (A.D. c. 200). Protestants like Philipp Melanchthon (d. 1560) even attempted to adapt Aristotle to their purposes and to create a Protestant scholasticism.

The revival of Plato, like that of Aristotle, had its medieval background. We have noted the persistence of Neoplatonism as such, and as clothed in mystical Christian garb, throughout the Dark and the Middle Ages. The Platonism of the fifteenth and sixteenth centuries was overwhelmingly Neoplatonism. The dialectical, logical, and rationalistic Plato was, for example, scarcely known to the mystical Platonic cult of the Florentine Academy, founded by the Medici under the influence of Gemistus Plethon (1355-1450) in the fifteenth century, the mem-

---

[3] Lefèvre d'Étaples also had a weakness for Neoplatonic mysticism.

bers of which liked to feel that they were reviving the old Platonic Academy of eighteen hundred years ago. Keeping in mind the Platonic heritage from the Middle Ages, we may nevertheless say that the leading popularizer of Plato at this time was Plethon, a Byzantine who migrated to Italy. Another influential fifteenth-century Platonist was Bessarion of Nicea (1403-1472), a Byzantine scholar and ecclesiastic who came to Italy to attend the Council of Ferrara-Florence. Remaining in Italy, he made his home in Rome and was created an Italian cardinal. He knew Latin and Greek well, assembled a large library, and was host to many of the leading humanists, such as Poggio and Valla. Bessarion's wide knowledge of Platonic and Neoplatonic literature was eagerly absorbed by the new Platonic cult.

Among native Italian humanists the most ecstatic Platonist was Marsilius Ficinus (1433-1499), who went so far as to suggest the Christianization of the Platonic system, in the same way that Albert and Aquinas had turned Aristotle into a scholastic. Ficinus made Latin translations of some of Plato's mystical dialogues, of the works of Plotinus, and of the *Celestial Hierarchy* of Dionysius. He looked upon Plotinus as the perfect expositor of Plato, for the obvious reason that Neoplatonism resembled Christianity far more closely than did Platonism. Ficinus greatly stimulated the tendency to confuse Plato and Plotinus.

To John Pico of Mirandola (1463-1494) not even Neoplatonism satisfied the mystical yearnings of his soul. He also relished the theurgy and magic of the cabala,[4] enthusiasm for which, common since the Middle Ages, Pico shared with scholars like John Reuchlin (1455-1522) and Cornelius Agrippa (1487-1535). Reuchlin carried the Platonic cult into Germany. He was also one of the leading Hebrew scholars of the period and the hero of the most biting of all humanist satires, *The Letters of Obscure Men*.

The growing enthusiasm for Greek philosophy was not limited to Plato and Aristotle. There were earnest Stoics, Epicureans, Skeptics, and Eclectics. The overwhelming popularity of Cicero, the great Roman authority on post-Aristotelian Greek philosophy, augmented the catholic interest in Greek thought.

In discussing the recovery of Greek literature by the West, it is well to correct the older view that this movement was started by, and was the result of, the Turkish conquest of Constantinople. We have pointed out that there was considerable Byzantine emigration to Sicily and southern Italy throughout the medieval period. We must also correct the assertion that the Byzantine introduction of the Greek classics after 1350 preceded the Western zest for them. The Byzantine visitors simply stimulated a revival that was already under way.

---

[4] The cabala was the most popular collection of Jewish mysticism, magic, and cosmogony. Into its composition went Babylonian myths, Zoroastrian theological dogmas, the Platonic mysticism of Philo, Neoplatonic mysticism and cosmogony, Pythagorean superstitions and number lore, and many Jewish fancies, elaborated in the centuries between the pre-Christian Era and the later Middle Ages. On its religious side, it was akin to the Christian mysticism which had also drawn on Neoplatonism and Pythagoreanism. It promoted a more spiritual view of religion than Jewish legalism and ritualism. Its effect on science and philosophy was wholly disastrous. As Professor Emil Hirsch writes: "It encouraged the belief in magic and in demons, and opened the door to many grotesque and even noxious superstitions. Its adepts came to put faith in signs and constellations, and otherwise naturalized in Judaism many conceits and customs of non-Jewish origin and significance." On Pico's intellectual interests, see Paul Kibre, *The Library of Pico della Mirandola*, Columbia University Press, 1936.

The first Greek texts were obtained by Italians from Eastern Greeks resident in Italy. Furthermore, Byzantine scholars were spreading a knowledge of Greek literature in Italy by the close of the fourteenth century, or long before the Turkish capture of Constantinople in 1453.

The first important Hellenizer was the erudite Byzantine classicist and teacher, Manuel Chrysoloras (1350-1415), who was sent to Italy on a mission by the Eastern emperor. He taught in most of the important Italian cities, receiving an especially enthusiastic reception in Florence. While not possessed of an original mind, Chrysoloras was well read in Greek literature and had considerable talent for transmitting his knowledge to crowds of eager students. The Platonists, Plethon and Bessarion, the Aristotelians, George of Trebizond and Theodore Gaza, whom we have already mentioned, Johannes Argyropulos (1416-1486), and Chalcondyles of Athens (1424-1511), all carried further Chrysoloras' Hellenizing mission.

Italians also visited Constantinople in search of manuscripts. Giovanni Aurispa (1369-1460) went to Constantinople to study Greek in 1418 and returned four years later with 238 Greek manuscripts, including poetry, drama, and philosophy. About 1427 Francesco Filelfo (1398-1481) returned from Constantinople with many manuscripts. Leonardo Bruni (1309-1444), the pupil of Chrysoloras, began to translate Greek manuscripts into Latin. Aldus Manutius of Venice and others at this time began to print them.

That the revival of the Latin classics first centered around Cicero is not surprising. Cicero had been the most esteemed of Latin prose writers in the Middle Ages. The urbane and comprehensive character of his writings, and his tolerance towards all pagan philosophies, permitted him to become the intellectual hero of an increasingly literate world. This position Cicero owed in some measure to the enthusiasm of Petrarch. The adoption of Cicero by the humanistic secondary schools, in particular by Johannes Sturm, carried the Ciceronian cult into northern Europe.

The admiration for Cicero's florid and involved style created an unfortunate revolution in European prose literature. For one thing, it put an end to the respectability of medieval Latin, a language mainly used by scholars, but a far more serviceable vehicle than the prolix and complicated Ciceronian Latin. As Professor Waugh remarked:

> Medieval Latin, largely because it differed considerably from classical Latin, was an excellent medium of both written and oral expression. Having a much richer vocabulary, it would give voice to a much wider range of ideas than the Latin of the Augustan age. For the clergy and the educated laity it was an established vehicle of communication all over central and western Europe. Then came the Humanists damning it as barbarous because it was not identical with the Latin used by Cicero 1,500 years before. . . . How much the advance of knowledge has been retarded through the consequent necessity of spending time and energy on the study of foreign tongues it is impossible to compute.[5]

5 W. T. Waugh, *History of Europe from 1378 to 1494*, Putnam, 1932 (3rd ed., Barnes and Noble, 1949), p. 492.

As Professor Waugh implies, had Cicero not been revived, medieval Latin might have remained to our day the international language of literate men.

The recovery of Ciceronian manuscripts by Petrarch stimulated a search for other ancient Latin literature. Monasteries and church libraries were ransacked for copies of these works transcribed in the Dark Ages and forgotten. These labors were richly rewarded. Many important works, such as the *Germania* and some of the historical books of Tacitus, the letters of Pliny, the writings of Ovid, the *Institutes* of Quintilian, Lucretius' great poem, Celsus' treatise on medicine, and the like, were brought to light.[6] But a good deal of Latin literature has never been recovered. Most of the historical work of Livy, and the voluminous books of Varro, for example, were never unearthed. Yet, nearly all the Latin literature we possess today·was recovered in the humanist period. Save for fragments on *papyri* and archaeological inscriptions, relatively little has been recovered since. Scholarship was promoted, and in the editing, collating and analysis of recovered manuscripts the science of textual criticism was created.

By the second half of the fifteenth century the enthronement of the ancient classics and the enthusiasm for Greek and Roman literature was quite general in western Europe, particularly in Italy. To be sure, Hellenists and Latinists continued their rivalry. As already observed, Cardinal Bessarion, above all others, first successfully fused the two currents of Greek and Latin ardor into one general stream of classical exaltation. Of Bessarion, Lorenzo Valla said he was "the best Greek of the Latins and the best Latin of the Greeks."

IV. THE HUMANIST TEMPER

Humanism is the term generally applied to the predominant social philosophy and intellectual and literary currents of the period from 1400 to 1650. The return to favor of the pagan classics stimulated the philosophy of secularism, the appreciation of mundane pleasures, and above all intensified the assertion of personal independence and individual expression. Zeal for the classics was a result as well as a cause of the growing secular view of life. Expansion of trade, growth of prosperity and luxury, and widening social contacts generated interest in worldly pleasures, in spite of formal allegiance to ascetic Catholic doctrines. Men thus affected welcomed classical writers who revealed similar social values and secular attitudes. After this preliminary statement we may examine a little more in detail the genesis and nature of the humanist mind.

Historians now fairly well agree on the general outlines of those mental attitudes and scholarly interests which may be regarded with some semblance of accuracy as the humanist outlook. The most fundamental point of agreement is that the humanist mentality stood at a point midway between medieval supernaturalism and the modern scientific and critical attitude. Medievalists regard it primarily as the terminal product of the Middle Ages. Students of modern history, especially those who have not yet come to understand the cultural import of

---

[6] For a partial list of the manuscripts recovered, see E. M. Hulme, *The Renaissance, the Protestant Revolution and the Catholic Reformation in Continental Europe,* Century, 1915, p. 87.

European expansion, are more likely to regard it as the germinal period of modernism. Professor Groethuysen graphically describes the relation of humanism to modernism:

> . . . it is best to characterize the period of the Renaissance not as a wholly distinct cultural epoch, but rather as a transition period between the mediaeval and modern ages in which old and new, religious and profane, authoritarian and individualistic principles and concepts existed side by side, while at the same time certain marked transformations and changes in ideas and ways of living took place in Italy, the Netherlands, Spain, France, Germany and England.

.   .   .   .

> The man of the Renaissance lived, as it were, between two worlds. The Christian world of the Middle Ages, in which the significance of every phenomenon was ultimately determined through uniform points of view, no longer existed for him. On the other hand, he had not yet found in a system of scientific concepts and social principles stability and security for his life. He was suspended between faith and knowledge. The Renaissance may be interpreted in different ways, depending upon whether this epoch is more closely associated with the world of faith of the Middle Ages or with the scientifically grounded approach of modern times.[7]

As the grip of medieval supernaturalism began to loosen, secular and human interests became more prominent. The facts of individual experience here on earth became more interesting than the shadowy afterlife. Reliance upon God and faith weakened. As one writer expressed it, Fortuna (chance) gradually supplanted divine Providence as the universal frame of reference. The present world became an end in itself instead of a preparation for a world to come. Indeed, as the humanist age wore on, the very distinction between this world and the next tended to disappear.

Beauty was believed to afford at least some glimpse of a transcendental existence. This goes far to explain the humanist cult of beauty and makes plain that humanism was, above everything else, fundamentally an aesthetic movement. Human experience, man himself, tended to become the practical measure of all things. The ideal life was no longer a monastic escape from society, but a full participation in rich and varied human relationships.

The tendency to substitute the cult of beauty and humanity for the supernatural obsession created an aristocratic trend among humanists. A new aristocracy, based upon cultural appreciation and achievement, was substituted for the old feudal aristocracy, founded upon status and privilege, and for the hierarchy of the church, resting on supernatural assumptions.

The dominating element in the finest pagan culture was aesthetic rather than supernatural or scientific. In the later Middle Ages urban intellectuals were well on the road to the recovery of an aesthetic and secular view of life even before the full tide of the classical revival was felt. It was only natural, then, that pagan literature, with its emotional and intellectual affinity to the new world-view,

---

[7] B. Groethuysen, article "Renaissance," Encyclopedia of the Social Sciences, XIII, 279, 284.

should accelerate the existing drift towards secularism and stimulate the cult of humanity, the worship of beauty, and especially the aristocratic attitude.

Almost everywhere, humanism began as a rather pious, timid, and conservative drift away from medieval Christianity and ended in bold independence of medieval tradition. Erasmus of Rotterdam (1466-1536), one of the greatest of humanists, occupied a position midway between extreme piety and frank secularism. Petrarch represented conservative Italian humanism. Robust secularism and intellectual independence appeared in the writings of Pomponazzi, Bembo, Machiavelli, and Guicciardini. Rudolph Agricola may be fairly regarded as a German Petrarch, while the secular and critical spirit emerged fully in Conrad Mutian, Crotus Rubianus, Ulrich von Hutten, and their circle. In England, Colet and More were early or conservative humanists, Francis Bacon represented later or agnostic and skeptical humanism. In France, pious classicists like Lefèvre d'Étaples were succeeded by frank, urbane, and devout skeptics like Montaigne and bold anticlerical satirists like Rabelais. Just how far critical and secular humanism might have gone had it not been checked or obliterated by the Protestant revolt and the Catholic Counter Reformation, it is difficult to say.

While the humanists were noted for their scholarship and for literary ability, it is not proven that the recovery of Greek and Roman classics produced an intellectual revolution.[8] Least of all did it measurably stimulate scientific curiosity.

Humanistic contributions to science consisted mainly in the recovery of Greek scientific literature which evinced a more accurate and acceptable body of facts and ideas than most medieval scientific works. But even this service should not be exaggerated. Everything of value, for instance, in Galen had long been incorporated into medieval medicine. The scientific treatises of Aristotle, Euclid, and Ptolemy were translated into Latin and known to scholars before the humanistic period. Moreover the Muslims had already introduced most Attic and Hellenistic science into western Europe, often with great improvements on the original.

The humanists were more attracted by the rhetorical and mystical than by the scientific treatises of antiquity—in other words, by books that did no violence to the Christian and aesthetic outlook. Cicero, Plato, the Neoplatonic writers, and the cabala were accorded a far more enthusiastic reception than Aristarchus, Archimedes, or Hipparchus.

It is clear, then, that humanism embodied the mystical and aesthetic temper of a prescientific age. It did not free the mind from subservience to ancient authority. If the humanists revered Aristotle less than the schoolmen did, they worshiped Neoplatonism, the cabala, and Cicero more. They shifted authorities rather than dismissed them. Even Aristotle, the greatest of scholastic authorities, did not, as we have seen, lack humanist admirers. The great libraries assembled by rich patrons of literature like Cosmo de' Medici, Pope Nicholas V, and the Duke of Urbino, devoted much space to the church fathers and the scholastic philosophers. The humanists did, however, read their authorities for aesthetic pleasure as well as moral uplift. In brief, according to James Harvey Robinson:

[8] Cf. *Cambridge Modern History*, Vol. I, chap. xvi; and Waugh, *op. cit.*, chap. xxi.

The so-called Renaissance offers nothing comparable to the [intellectual] achievements of the twelfth and thirteenth centuries. It is true that in the fourteenth and fifteenth centuries the Italian towns developed an interesting civilization and a marvellous art different from that which went before. These have perhaps blinded us to the relatively slight contributions of the period to general change. To one who is intent upon establishing the continuity of history the men of letters, the philosophers, and even the artists of the Renaissance, exhibit an extraordinary intellectual conservatism. They transcended relatively few of the ancient superstitions, contributed but little to the knowledge of the world, and readily yielded to the fascination of Neoplatonic mysticism, as is illustrated by Ficino, Pico, and Reuchlin.

As has been said elsewhere, it was quite possible to read the classics without becoming forthwith Hellenic in one's attitude of mind. It may be safely said that as one's acquaintance with the Middle Ages, as well as his appreciation of our own time, increases, the Renaissance seems to grow more and more shadowy as a distinctive period; and yet many writers use the term as if the Renaissance were a bright spirit hovering over Europe, touching this writer and that painter or architect, and passing by others who were in consequence left in medieval darkness. . . .

It is . . . a grave mistake to assume that this renewed interest in the Greek and Roman authors betokens a revival of Hellenism, as has commonly been supposed. The libraries described by Vespasiano, a Florentine bookseller of the fifteenth century, indicate the least possible discrimination on the part of his patrons. Ficino, the translator of Plato, was an enthusiastic Neoplatonist, and to Pico della Mirandola the Jewish Cabbala seemed to promise infinite enlightenment. In short, Plato was as incapable in the fifteenth century of producing an intellectual revolution as Aristotle had been in the thirteenth. With the exception of Valla, whose critical powers were perhaps slightly stimulated by acquaintance with the classics, it must be confessed that there was little in the so-called "New Learning" to generate anything approaching an era of criticism. It is difficult to determine the numerous and subtle changes which made them possible at the opening of the sixteenth; and it is reckless to assume that the Humanists were chiefly responsible for these changes.[9]

The intellectuals of antiquity, in contrast to the Christians, were relatively unconcerned about the supernatural world and the eternal destiny of the soul. They were primarily interested in a happy, adequate, and efficient life here on earth. Hellenic philosophy was designed to teach man how to live successfully rather than how to die with the assurance of ultimate salvation. This pagan attitude had been lost, theoretically at least, for about a thousand years, when Europe followed the warning of Augustine against becoming too engrossed in earthly interests, lest assurance of successful entry into the New Jerusalem be jeopardized. Humanism directly and indirectly revived the pagan scale of values.

When men like Petrarch and his fellow humanists read pagan literature, they were infected with the secular outlook of the Greeks and Romans. Even rather pious humanists became enamored of what Augustine branded as the City of the Devil. Petrarch, a devout Christian, worshiped the pagan eclecticism of Cicero.

⁹ Robinson, *The New History*, pp. 157-58, 116-17.

Erasmus suggested that such titles as St. Socrates and St. Cicero were not inappropriate or sacrilegious, and openly preferred the pagans to the schoolmen:

Whatsoever is pious and conduces to good manners ought not to be called profane. The first place must indeed be given to the authority of the Scriptures; but, nevertheless, I sometimes find some things said or written by the ancients, nay, even by the heathens, nay, by the poets themselves, so chastely, so holily, and so divinely, that I cannot persuade myself but that, when they wrote them, they were divinely inspired, and perhaps the spirit of Christ diffuses itself farther than we imagine; and that there are more saints than we have in our catalogue. To confess freely among friends, I can't read Cicero on Old Age, on Friendship, his Offices, or his Tusculan Questions, without kissing the book, without veneration towards that divine soul. And, on the contrary, when I read some of our modern authors, treating of Politics, Economics, and Ethics, good God! how cold they are in comparison with these! Nay, how do they seem to be insensible of what they write themselves! So that I had rather lose Scotus and twenty more such as he (fancy twenty subtle doctors!) than one Cicero or Plutarch. Not that I am wholly against them either; but, because, by the reading of the one, I find myself become better, whereas I rise from the other, I know not how coldly affected to virtue, but most violently inclined to cavil and contention.[9a]

As we observed, humanism encouraged the mystical and aesthetic, rather than the scientific and rationalist, spirit. At its best humanism produced the scholarly learning of a Scaliger and a Casaubon, the urbanity of an Erasmus, or the tolerant skepticism of a Montaigne. It could do even less to create the modern scientific era than it could to restore fully the Greek and Roman culture it admired. The science of the humanist age was mainly a direct heritage from the later Middle Ages. Moreover, whatever indirect impulse humanism may have given to secular studies and science was quickly obstructed by the revival of intolerance and persecution during the Protestant revolt and Counter Reformation. By the time scholarship had recovered from this blow, the explorers and the scientists had uncovered a new world of facts and ideas quite foreign to Petrarch, Alberti, Valla, Pico of Mirandola, Erasmus, Melanchthon, Baronius, and Loyola alike.

The leading intellectual trait of the era was the recovery, to a certain degree, of the secular and humane philosophy of Greece and Rome. Another humanist trend which cannot be ignored was the rebirth of individualism, which, developed by Greece and Rome to a remarkable degree, had been suppressed by the rise of a caste system in the later Roman Empire, by the church and feudalism in the Middle Ages. The church asserted that rampant individualism was identical with arrogance, rebellion, and sin. Medieval Christianity restricted individual expression, fostered self-abnegation and self-annihilation, and demanded implicit faith and unquestioning obedience. Furthermore, the church officially ignored the world of nature and man.

In other ways, also, medieval civilization suppressed the ego. In the feudal regime the isolated individual had little standing. He acquired status and protection mainly as a member of a definite group, whether lordly or servile. The manorial system revolved around the community rather than the individual.

9a Cited by Karl Pearson, *The Ethic of Free Thought*, 2d ed., Macmillan, 1901, pp. 165-66.

When the cities threw off the yoke of feudalism, they promoted collective and corporate liberty rather than individual freedom. In commercial relations group life was paramount, both in the town guilds and the peasant villages on manorial estates. Everything was regulated by law and custom down to the most minute detail. The individual who attempted to challenge authority and tradition, in matters of thought or action, was either discouraged or crushed.

The period from the fourteenth century to the seventeenth worked in favor of the general emancipation of the individual. The city-states of northern Italy had come into contact with the diversified customs of the East, and gradually permitted personal expression in matters of taste and dress. The writings of Dante, and particularly the doctrines of Petrarch and humanists like Machiavelli and Ulrich von Hutten, emphasized the virtues of intellectual freedom and individual expression. In the essays of Montaigne the individualistic view of life received perhaps the most persuasive and eloquent statement in the whole history of literature and philosophy.

Architects, sculptors, and painters broke away from Byzantine and Gothic patterns and indulged in sweeping independence and self-expression. Intellectual curiosity and self-expression were stimulated by the crusades, by Muslim science and philosophy, and by the growing interest of Christian scholars in the actual observation of nature and the objective study of human conduct. The rise of vernacular languages to a position of literary eminence destroyed the universality of Latin and although the humanist revival of Ciceronian Latin delayed the ultimate triumph of the vernacular, self-expression received a great impetus. The remarkable growth of self-expression and the sense of individuality under humanism aided the cult of humanity and beauty.

Individualism and the instinct of curiosity were vigorously cultivated. Honest doubt began to replace unreasoning faith. The skeptical viewpoint proposed by Abelard reached high development and wide acceptance among the humanists. Finally, the spirit of individualism to a certain degree incited the Protestant revolt, which, in theory at least, embodied a thorough application of the principle of individualism in religion.

In politics, individualism had less opportunity for expression than in philosophy, culture, and art. This was the age of despots and rulers by divine right. But even here Italy was temporarily freed from the dominion of the secular empire. The economic system stimulated the rise of the middle class, which ultimately challenged absolute monarchies and inaugurated an age of representative government and political individualism. Finally, growth of capitalism meant the inevitable triumph of individualism in business enterprise.

It need not be supposed that the emancipation of the ego was wholly beneficial to the human race. Yet, that aspect of humanism which combated the sovereignty of tyrant, feudal lord, class, corporation, and tradition, has, for better or worse, had a tremendous influence upon the course of modern history. Indeed, it was during the humanist era that the freedom of individual expression and opposition to authority got thoroughly under way for the first time in Western Europe.

Individuality meant freedom in worldly endeavor. But self-expression could not be wholly aimless and anarchical. Some framework of values was needed. The supernaturalism of the Middle Ages was no longer wholly adequate or valid. The scientific background, which anchored the deists and rationalists to reality in the seventeenth and eighteenth centuries, was not yet available. The cultured individual of the fifteenth and sixteenth centuries therefore turned to aesthetics for guidance and expression. Professor Groethuysen expresses this point admirably:

> This explains the cultural significance of art and poetry in the Renaissance. Only in poetic and artistic representation and invention could man realize the multiplicity of phenomena not yet subjected to systematic knowledge. Poetry and art were conceived as the actual organs of world understanding. The artist or the poet of the Renaissance found his world in that intermediate realm of potentiality which was limited neither by a dogmatically determined faith nor by the rigid systematization of scientific data.[10]

The freedom begotten of this attitude—even its extreme manifestations of violence, indulgence, and intrigue—formed the background for the remarkable efflorescence of art.

> From our picture of the Renaissance [says Thomas Craven], its rapacity and crime, its bewildering profusion of baseness, bloodshed and unsettling violence, the reader may well wonder why it was that art flourished so magnificently. There is no absolute explanation. No one knows precisely why art is produced, why Michael Angelo, at such a terrific cost of mental agony, forfeiting all the pleasures of companionship and good living, sold himself to endless creative toil, why Donatello and Brunelleschi, penniless and starving, went off to Rome in their youth to spend their days and nights digging among the bones of antiquity. But this we do know: art inheres in the human soul and under certain conditions manifests itself with extraordinary fertility. Impulses, which, for want of a more definite name, are called spiritual, demand fulfilment, and the artist, viewing the gross activities of life with reason and contemplation, finds order in lawless violence, significance in all experiences and permanence in transitory events. What circumstances are favorable to art is a question we will not attempt to decide. It is, I think, beyond dispute that when man is most free, when no artificial restraints are imposed upon him and it is possible for him to develop his individuality to its fullest capacities, that art is most likely to thrive. Does anyone suppose for a moment, considering the incomparable wealth and variety of Italian art, that such monumental records of imaginative power could have been produced by a civilization that ran along with the humdrum regularity of a Swiss village? The grandeur of Michael Angelo has its analogue in the grandeur of Julius II; we remember Cesare Borgia for his appalling brutality, but the frescoes of Andrea del Castagno contain similar qualities of terrible energy and vengeance; the fanaticism of Savonarola is matched by Ucello's obsession with the scientific problems of perspective; the sexual proclivities of Alexander VI are not more notorious than those of Cellini; the spirit of mysticism and simple faith, before it was extinguished in the hearts of the ineffectual minority, found its perfect spokesman in Fra Angelico; at the other end of the scale, the elegant and sophisticated tastes

[10] Groethuysen, *loc. cit.,* p. 285.

of Leo X created a congenial atmosphere for the classical decorum of Raphael. Today we demand more stability and less art, and we may be assured that whenever life is secure and uneventful, art in the aggregate is bound to be a reflex of commonplace experiences.[11]

V. PHILOSOPHY DURING THE HUMANIST MOVEMENT

We have already suggested that every type of philosophy known to classical antiquity, the Dark Ages, and the Middle Ages found expression and devotion in this period. We need mention here only some of the outstanding representatives of the leading schools.

One of the foremost philosophers of the period, and the leading Aristotelian of his age, was Pietro Pomponazzi (1462-c. 1525), professor of philosophy in the university of Padua. He took his interpretation of Aristotle from Alexander of Aphrodisias (known also as Alexander Exegetes) who, as we have seen, flourished around A.D. 200. Relying upon a persistent and unflinching analysis of Aristotle's physics, Pomponazzi concluded that Aristotelianism could not prove the independent existence of the soul. This doctrine he set forth in his book *On the Immortality of the Soul* (1516).

Pomponazzi did not deny the immortality of the soul. He claimed that the question is insoluble, and that therefore we cannot establish a theory of ethics on the assumption of rewards or punishments after death. We must relate ethics to earthly considerations—seeking good for its worth here and now: "The reward of virtue is virtue itself, while the punishment of the vicious is vice." This, he thought, should be the governing principle of our moral code.

Pomponazzi was discreet enough, however, to distinguish between faith and knowledge and to point out that what might be true for the philosopher might not be true for the theologian. Thus he was able to conform outwardly to the orthodox creed. Yet his work was burned by the Inquisition and he might have suffered a similar fate but for his friendship with the famous admirer of paganism, Cardinal Pietro Bembo (1470-1547). One of Pomponazzi's leading followers, Lucilio Vanini (1584-1610),[12] was actually burned at the stake for his doctrines.

Pomponazzi also vigorously attacked the mysticism of the Neoplatonic and cabalistic cults. In his tract *On Fate* he defended the doctrine of determinism in natural phenomena.

As for the Platonism of this era, we have already noted that it really meant Neoplatonism and that its foremost propagandist was Ficinus. The most distinguished exponent of the Neoplatonic attitude was none other than Giordano Bruno (1548-1600), put to death for his unorthodox cosmological theories which he based in part on Copernicus. This has led many to believe that Bruno was a hard-headed naturalist and an expositor of empiricism. We shall deal more thoroughly with Bruno later in connection with the reaction of science on philosophy. But nothing would be more erroneous than to assume that Bruno was a fore-

[11] Craven, *Men of Art,* Simon and Schuster, 1931, pp. 61-62.
[12] See below, p. 813.

runner of Newton, Locke, and Voltaire. His chief spiritual and philosophical forerunner was Nicholas of Cues, the Neoplatonic mystic and pantheist. He also shared the hylozoism of the ancient Greek cosmologists in believing that all nature is animated—is alive. Even Bruno's famous doctrine of the plurality of worlds and universes was based upon the Neoplatonic belief in the infinity of God. And his interest in the universe was motivated as much by his admiration for the Neoplatonic concept of the order and beauty of the universe as by his appreciation of the astrophysical views of Copernicus. Indeed, he advocated the latter chiefly because they seemed to offer mathematical and scientific proof of Neoplatonic doctrines. No other humanist philosopher so perfectly exemplified the fusion of mysticism, rationalism, theology, and aesthetics. That so devout a man could have been slain by the church is one of the most ironical paradoxes of history.

One of the most interesting developments in philosophy was the skeptical note sounded in the writings of Erasmus, of Crotus Rubianus (1480-1540) and his collaborators in the *Letters of Obscure Men,* and in the doctrines of Peter Ramus (1515-1572), Michel de Montaigne (1533-1592), Pierre Charron (1541-1603), Francisco Sanchez (1562-1632), and Blaise Pascal (1623-1662). However, one must not regard this skepticism as similar to that of Bayle, Hume, or Voltaire. Except for the essays of Montaigne, the fundamental verities of the Christian religion were not questioned. Urbanity is probably a better description of the mental attitude of Erasmus, Ramus, Sanchez and the like than skepticism, as the latter term is known in our day. They were skeptical about, indeed, disgusted with, the devious scholastic disputations, the pedantry of scholars, the dogmatism of theologians, the parading of metaphysical authority, and the vulgar superstitions of mystics and magicians, a state of mind which caused Erasmus to exclaim that it made him angry and weary to read Duns Scotus.

Erasmus was the most famous as well as the mildest of skeptics. His travels and writings made him the great international humanist, as Aquinas was the leading scholastic and Voltaire the outstanding rationalist. Erasmus was an extraordinary linguist and textual scholar and one of the finest Latin stylists of the humanistic period. His *Adages,* a collection of Latin phrases and allusions designed to polish and illuminate the sermons of Catholic priests, illustrate the fusion of Christianity and humanism. His *In Praise of Folly* (1511) reveals a gift for urbane but telling satire, and offers a gentle but devastating rebuke to mankind for its weaknesses, and to his age for its excesses. He took particular delight in exposing the superstitions of the Catholic masses and the pedantry and arrogance of Catholic scholars, especially Dominican scholastics. His book took the form of an oration delivered by Folly to an imaginary audience. Folly is portrayed as a female whose parents are wealth and youth and whose nurses are drunkenness and ignorance. Her servants are self-love, flattery, oblivion, laziness, pleasure, madness, wantonness, intemperance, and sloth. She recommended herself heartily to her listeners. The work enjoyed a tremendous popularity.[18]

In his *Handbook of the Christian Knight* (1503) Erasmus drew a sharp con-

---

[18] More vigorous satire appeared in his *Julius Excluded from Heaven,* Erasmus' closest approach to the sarcastic rather than the urbane temper.

trast between spiritual and institutional Christianity, the former resting upon
sincere piety, loyalty, devotion, and altruism, and the latter upon a multitude of
formal rites and artificial ceremonies. In his *Familiar Colloquies* (1518) he ridiculed the superstitions, quasi-paganism, and pedantry of pre-Reformation Catholicism simply by calmly describing them. He argued that the "yoke of Christ" was
made heavy because of Catholic formalism, ritualism, and intolerance, which
obscured the purely spiritual message of the Saviour who "commanded us nothing
save love for one another."

Far more spirited and devastating than Erasmus' satire were the famous
Letters of Obscure Men written by Crotus Rubianus, Ulrich von Hutten, and
other radical German humanists. This work, ironically praising intolerance, persecution, bigotry, and ignorance, reduced to absurdity the less lovely aspects of
sixteenth-century Catholic Christianity, and of the Dominicans in particular.

The occasion of this book, perhaps the best satire before Bayle and Swift, is
so significant as to warrant a brief summary. A Jew by the name of Johann Pfefferkorn had adopted Christianity and developed all the fervor and ferocity of a
new convert. Hence he proposed that Jews be forced to attend Christian churches
and listen to Christian sermons and be prevented from lending money at interest.
Furthermore he suggested the burning of all Jewish books except the Old Testament. Accordingly, the opinions of prominent German clerics and scholars were
sought. John Reuchlin, when approached, took his responsibility seriously and
went deeply into the subject. He praised Jewish literature as a whole, condemning only certain works devoted to witchcraft or abuse of Christianity. Instead of
approving Pfefferkorn's suggestion, Reuchlin recommended that a chair of
Hebrew be established in each university in order that Gentiles might become
better acquainted with, and therefore more tolerant of, Jewish literature.

This enlightened view enraged the anti-Semites. Reuchlin's attitude was declared heretical and his reply was publicly burned. The case aroused bitter controversy. Reuchlin's distinguished friends wrote him many letters of praise and
encouragement, and in order to justify his position Reuchlin published a selection of them under the title, *Letters of Eminent Men*. This suggested to the daring German humanists, Crotus Rubianus and Ulrich von Hutten, the idea of
satirizing the persecutors of Reuchlin, and in particular one of their leaders, a
German Dominican named Ortuin Gratius.

The *Letters of Obscure Men,* published in 1515, was ostensibly a collection of
epistles written by monks, lesser priests, and ignorant churchmen to Ortuin
Gratius, extolling his persecution of Reuchlin and indirectly exposing the ignorance and bigotry of the ecclesiastics who supported Pfefferkorn's anti-Semitism.
In this way the contrast between the enlightened scholars who praised Reuchlin
and the ignorant who supported Gratius was bitingly drawn.

> Writing in the most barbarous Latin [says Professor Preserved Smith], they
> [the writers] express their admiration for his attack on Reuchlin and the cause of
> learning, gossip about their drinking-bouts and pothouse amours, expose their
> ignorance and gullibility and ask absurd questions, as, whether it is a mortal sin
> to salute a Jew, and whether the worms eaten with beans and cheese should be

considered meat or fish, lawful or not in Lent, and at which stage of development a chick in the egg becomes meat and therefore prohibited on Fridays. The satire, coarse as it was biting, failed to win the applause of the finer spirits, but raised a shout of laughter from the students.[14]

The *Letters of Obscure Men* is a landmark in the history of philosophy as well as in the literature of satire. This work represented the most devastating, if indirect, assault ever made upon scholasticism and its Dominican expositors. Scholasticism never regained its prestige outside of orthodox Catholic circles.

Peter Ramus is known chiefly for his formal attack on Aristotelian logic, in which he foreshadowed Francis Bacon. He drew more students to his lectures than any other teacher in Paris since Abelard, whose popularity had been based upon the defense of Aristotle's logic. When, however, Ramus published his work on *Dialectic* it appeared that he scarcely differed from Aristotle in fundamentals; his repudiation was more verbal than actual. Ramus pretended to go back to nature and find her rules, but he sought nature in pre-Aristotelian philosophy rather than in the world about him. Ramus' attack on Aristotle aroused the fierce hatred of Catholic scholastics. He was murdered in the massacre of St. Bartholomew's Day and his corpse was torn to pieces by Catholic students.

Of Montaigne, the supreme exponent of tolerance and urbanity, whom we shall treat at length later, suffice it to say here that his chief significance in the growth of skepticism was his spirited defense of free thought in the face of the current dogmas of philosophers and theologians. Freethinking did not, however, lead Montaigne astray on fundamental principles. At the most, it made him an enthusiastic devotee of urbanity.

His disciple, Pierre Charron, was an earnest defender of Catholicism against Protestantism. He warned his generation that they should stick to the basic dogmas of the church lest they become entangled in new and less defensible ideas. Yet, with strange inconsistency, Charron attacked the orthodox association of religion and ethics. One should live right because it is the rule of nature and reason. "I will that a man be a good man," says Charron, "even though there be no Heaven and no Hell. It seems to me detestable when a man says: If I were not a Christian, if I did not fear damnation, I would do this or that. I will that thou shouldst be good because Nature and Reason so will it."

Francisco Sanchez moved closer to Bacon and Descartes. He wrote skeptical essays as well as tracts advocating observation and experimentation as the way to truth. In this he anticipated Bacon. But he also resembled Descartes in asserting that there can be no intellectual certainty without an understanding of, and command over, our mental states. He was unable, however, to go as far as Descartes in establishing a metaphysical basis for this philosophical attitude.

Blaise Pascal, a follower of Descartes and the mathematical method, employed skepticism to justify his mysticism and to attack Jesuit ethics. He held that mathematics can solve only problems of space. To understand reality and solve the problems of life, we must fall back upon the emotional assurance derived from religion.

14 Preserved Smith, *The Age of the Reformation*, Holt, 1920 (2 vols., Collier Books), p. 55.

A more robust skepticism appeared in the brilliant, if erratic, Tommaso Campanella (1568-1639), who attempted to create a philosophy based on experience. Yet he felt keenly what he regarded as the limitations of knowledge derived from sense impressions. The latter do not accurately reveal external reality. They merely record subjective perceptions. In this way, Campanella anticipated the viewpoint of Hobbes, and, in a different degree, of Kant.

We shall treat the philosophy of Francis Bacon at length in connection with his eulogy of the observational method and the prospects of natural science. In one sense, however, Bacon summed up humanist skepticism. He divorced humanism from theology and scholastic philosophy, secularized ratiocination, and turned its resources against scholasticism with unparalleled skill. This he accomplished more as a clever lawyer drawing up a rhetorical brief than as an experimental scientist. No one before or since has so effectively arraigned the deductive method of scholasticism before the bar of human reason. A master of style and an able dialectician, he ridiculed the old order of human thinking. But these very virtues became weaknesses when he posed as an advocate of the scientific method. As Sir William Harvey remarked in Bacon's own time: "Verulam [Bacon] writes about science like a Lord Chancellor."

VI. HUMANISM AND EDUCATION

The educational developments of this age reflected its intellectual and literary trends. The language and literature of pagan antiquity became the basis of academic education, a position from which they have never yet been dislodged in much of Europe and only in the twentieth century in the United States.

In the universities the theological and philosophical curriculum still dominated, although scholasticism lost its monopoly through the intrusion of Platonists, Stoics, Epicureans, Neoplatonists, eclectics, and the rival camps of Aristotelians, all spewed up by the Hellenic revival.

But enthusiasm for the classics was contagious among learned men and permeated the universities in spite of the vested interests of scholastics. Before humanism had spent its force, the classics were installed in most institutions of higher learning in Europe. The classical curriculum was first accepted by the Italian universities, whence it spread to the universities of Paris, Heidelberg, Erfurt, Leipzig, and Wittenberg, and finally to Oxford and Cambridge. The humanistic curriculum was introduced to Cambridge by Erasmus, to the Italian universities by the Italian classicists we have already mentioned, to the universities of Germany by men like Agricola, Reuchlin, Melanchthon, and Jacob Wimpfeling (1450-1523). The latter's teaching at Heidelberg was so infectious that this university became the center of German humanistic studies. Erasmus advocated the classical curriculum all over Europe. Thomas More, John Colet, Roger Ascham, and Sir Thomas Elyot were its crusaders in England; Le Fèvre d'Étaples, Guillaume Budé, and Ludovicus Vives in France and Belgium. In addition to adopting the classics, the universities became somewhat more tolerant of science, particularly mathematics and medicine. Early modern science, however, developed mainly outside the universities.

We have already observed that the classics entered the lower schools, as in Vittorino da Feltre's at Mantua, before they were welcomed by the universities. On the whole, secondary education, as in the German gymnasia and the French upper-class schools, was deluged by the sterile pedantry of Ciceronian classicism. An exception were the schools established by the Brethren of the Common Life—there were over 150 scattered throughout northern Europe by 1550—which utilized the classics as a guide to life and emphasized vernacular languages and the Bible.

In England, the so-called "public" schools, supported by private or royal endowments, expensive and exclusive at the same time, also borrowed the humanist curriculum, which became as narrow and lifeless as that of the German gymnasium. Winchester was founded in 1379, Eaton in 1440, St. Paul's in 1512. The English public school was transplanted to the American colonies in the form of the grammar school, the first of which was the Boston Latin School (1635). These American schools, however, were supported by the commonwealth and became public in regard to supervision if not in accessibility to the masses.

Influenced by the Brethren of the Common Life, the Jesuits created an educational system of their own. Later they tended to absorb most of the schools of the Brethren. The Jesuit order was incorporated in 1540. It became one of the chief educational influences in western Europe by the seventeenth century.[15] In the second quarter of the seventeenth century it is estimated that it had 40,000 students in its schools in France alone. The curriculum was essentially that prescribed by the scholastic tradition of the Middle Ages, to which was added instruction in Greek and Latin and in Aristotelian natural science. While vigorously opposing intellectual independence and originality on the part of students, the Jesuits encouraged studiousness by stimulating the competitive spirit rather than by relying on the customary brutal whippings of the time. The educational activities of the Jesuits were limited by the expulsion of the order from France in 1761 and temporarily ended through its suppression by the church in 1773. This termination of Jesuit education made all the more necessary the secular education provided by the state.

In the humanistic period, then, the so-called liberal education came to be identified, for the first time, almost exclusively with the classics. The fact that this did not take place until three centuries after universities were established shows the lack of historical validity in the often-advanced claim that the Bachelor of Arts degree is debased and distorted unless awarded for proficiency in the classics.

Among intellectual influences assignable to humanism, probably the most disastrous was its effect upon the educational curriculum of the Western World. It fatally limited for centuries the range of instruction for the best or most fortunate minds, prevented them from obtaining a grasp on the realities of life or public affairs, save as this was attained outside the schools, lessened their mental agility and flexibility, and turned education as a whole into a decided liability to

[15] See Smith, *History of Modern Culture*, I, 323 ff.; II, 429 ff.; and *St. Ignatius and the Ratio Studiorum*, ed. by E. A. Fitzpatrick, McGraw-Hill, 1933.

the human race. A deep appreciation of classical civilization is an invaluable component of a truly liberal education and might with profit be required today of every college graduate. But the arid pedantry of classical grammar, syntax, and wooden translation may fairly be called one of the great intellectual calamities of modern times.

The classical craze went so far that it became common for literary persons to classicize their names. For example, the astronomer Johann Müller called himself Regiomontanus. The real name of Crotus Rubianus, the German humanist, was Johannes Jaeger (John Hunter). The family name of Philipp Melanchthon, the great Protestant scholar, was Schwarzerd—black earth, or as we would put it, "muck." Melanchthon is the Greek for black earth. The anatomist, Hiero Fabrizio, became Hieronymus Fabricus da Aquapendente.

VII. ADVANCES IN NATURAL SCIENCE FROM REGIOMONTANUS TO COPERNICUS

The scientific developments of this age were very impressive. But they were not the result of the humanistic impulse, the effect of which on science was, on the whole, disastrous. To the astrology, alchemy, magic, Neoplatonism and the macrocosm-microcosm fantasy of the Middle Ages the humanists added enthusiasm for the weird superstitions of the cabala and the Pythagorean mysticism about numbers. The chief systematizers and purveyors of this pseudo science were Ficinus, Pico, and the German, Reuchlin. The latter was especially erudite in Pythagorean lore.

Humanist "science," in fact, offers a wonderful mine for scholars like Professor Lynn Thorndike who are interested in assembling data about magic and superstitions. It collected almost everything previously known about the occult, and is therefore a disheartening body of material to the historian of natural science. Even the mathematical foundations of Platonism were bent to the service of the occult. The really important science of this era was a natural and unbroken continuation of the later medieval science which we described in an earlier chapter.

Humanism's greatest service to science, perhaps, was its elucidation of Aristotle's treatises on physics and biology, an achievement credited chiefly to Alexandrist Aristotelians like Pomponazzi, Conrad Gesner, and Pierre Belon. It might have been supposed that the humanists' gusto for Greek literature would have unearthed Hellenistic treatises on science. But they were far more interested in Plotinus than in Archimedes or Ptolemy. Hellenistic science filtered into Europe largely by way of the Muslims and their Christian translators, not noticeably by means of the humanists. Artists and architects of this age actually furnished a greater impetus to natural science than the humanists. Painters and sculptors closely observed nature and the human body; architects carefully investigated mathematics and mechanics. The recovery of Vitruvius' treatise on architecture also had momentous consequences.

In mathematics, we may note that the new arithmetic, based upon Arabic notation, was finally adopted by commerce and industry. Together with double-entry bookkeeping it revolutionized commercial computations and methods. The abacus was finally discarded in the West, and commercial arithmetics began to appear in print by the close of the fifteenth century. But on the whole, theoretical arithmetic lagged behind in this era. In algebra, on the contrary, much theoretical progress was made. In this age Europeans advanced the subject definitely beyond the stage it had reached among the Hindus and Muslims. Niccolò Tartaglia (1500-1557) first solved the cubic equation, and also extended our knowledge of coefficients. Girolamo Cardan (1501-1576), genius and charlatan combined, pirated from Tartaglia the solution of the cubic equation, but his *Ars magna* comprised the best algebraic synthesis down to his day. Cardan's pupil, Lucca Ferrari (1522-1565), solved the equations of the fourth degree (quartic equations). More important than these achievements was that of François Viète (1540-1603), usually known as Vieta, who devised modern algebraic symbols, improved later by Descartes. Viète also elaborated the theory of equations. Albert Girard (1595-1632) introduced the concept of imaginary and negative roots. Newton's later discovery of the binomial theorem illustrated the steady progress of algebra. Thomas Harriot (1560-1621) made a competent synthesis of algebraic progress. The *Clavis mathematicae* of William Oughtred (1575-1660) incorporated all existing algebraic knowledge into a textbook.

Francisco Maurolycus (1494-1575) made important investigations in conic sections and projective geometry. Johann Kepler (1571-1630) suggested the concept of infinitesimals and formulated the principle of the continuity of conic sections; Bonaventura Cavalieri (1598-1647) created the idea of indivisibles; Girard Desargues (1593-1662) was also a pioneer in projective geometry and systematized modern geometry. All these advances formed the basis of infinitesimal calculus. The most spectacular geometrical achievement, however, was the construction by René Descartes (1596-1650) of a practicable system of analytical geometry, based on the work of Pappus of Alexandria, Nicolas Oresme and others in the use of coördinates, on the more advanced algebraic notation, and on the developments in trigonometry. Further mastery of analytical geometry was achieved by John Wallis (1616-1703).

The advances in trigonometry consisted of the applications of algebra by Viète, the computation of better tables and the suggestion of new formulae by Georg Joachim (1514-1576), better known as Rheticus, and the invention of logarithms, which considerably simplified computations, by Michael Stifel (1544), John Napier (1614), Joost Burgi (1620), Henry Briggs (1624), and Adrian Vlacq (1628). The formulation of a theory of numbers by Descartes, Pierre de Fermat (1601-1665), and Pascal was the remaining important contribution of this period to mathematics.

The application of the new mathematics to astronomy alone made possible its remarkable advances after Kepler. In the sixteenth century the long-agitated calendar reform was finally achieved. In 1582, by authority of Pope Gregory XIII, the ten days from October 5th to 15th were dropped and centennial years were regarded as leap years only when divisible by 400. Since this was a Roman Catholic reform, Protestant and Greek Catholic states long delayed the adoption of the

Gregorian calendar: England until 1752 and Greek Catholic Russia until the revolution of 1917.

The Copernican revolution, of course, overshadowed all the other astronomical discoveries of the era. Nicholas Copernicus (1473-1543) was a Pole by birth, who studied in the best Italian universities, and finally became a physician at Frauenberg in Poland. In Bologna he had heard his teacher, Maria de Novara, criticize the Ptolemaic system, partly on mathematical grounds, and partly on the basis of the Neoplatonic objection that it was too complicated to satisfy the mystical principle of mathematical harmony.

In his *Revolutions of the Heavenly Bodies,* which, incidentally, appeared as he lay on his deathbed in 1543, Copernicus interchanged the position of the sun and the earth in the Ptolemaic world-scheme. He thus became the first western European to introduce the heliocentric theory which had been partially suggested by the ancient Pythagoreans, embodied in the astronomical doctrine of Aristarchus, and adumbrated in the observations of several late medieval scientists. What Copernicus did was to place the theory on the substantial foundation of closely reasoned argument and adequate mathematical proof.

Copernicus did not abandon the general framework of the Ptolemaic system, with its fixed starry spheres and its theory of epicycles to explain planetary motion. He accepted the ancient theory that each star was attached to a crystalline sphere at a constant distance from the earth, and retained the Ptolemaic epicycles, but reduced them from seventy-nine to thirty-four. Although he did not entirely overthrow the Ptolemaic system, this achievement was epoch-making. "As the proof-sheets of the *De revolutionibus orbium caelestium* fell fluttering to the ground from the dying hand of Copernicus," says Dr. Charles Singer, "something more than his great spirit had gone from the world: the whole system of medieval science was no more." [16]

In physics, Tartaglia's *Nuova scienza* (1537) anticipated Galileo in its mathematical discussions of falling bodies, the range of projectiles and the like. The encyclopedic writer on natural science, Giovanni della Porta (1543-1615), was the leading student of optics, which he treated in his works on *Natural Magic* and *Refraction.* In the former, he discussed lenses and spectacles and gave the first description by a Christian writer of the camera obscura. In his work on refraction he offered a valuable criticism of Euclid and incidentally made one of the first suggestions of a telescope. Another leading student of optics was Francisco Maurolycus whom we mentioned above in connection with his researches in conic sections. He also promoted the study of mechanics. More precise work on refraction may be credited to the Dutch mathematician, Willebrord Snell (1591-1626).

The most original achievement in sixteenth-century physics was contained in the first book ever written on electricity—including the first use of the term— *On the Magnet, on Magnetic Bodies, and on the Earth as a Great Magnet* by Queen Elizabeth's physician, William Gilbert (1540-1603). Gilbert based his volume on many actual experiments. He accepted the Copernican theory and attributed the rotation of the earth to its magnetic character. Gilbert is also supposed

[16] Hearnshaw, *Medieval Contributions to Modern Civilization,* p. 148.

to have been an important chemist, but his chemical manuscripts have been lost.

The most striking researches in physics since Archimedes were made by Simon Stevin (1548-1620), usually known as Stevinus. He extended the knowledge of pulleys, discovered the law of the parallelogram of forces, and did pioneer work on the pressure of liquids. The most phenomenal achievement in physics in that age, of course, was the foundation of modern dynamics by Galileo's law of falling bodies, a description of which we shall reserve for a later chapter. The progress of mathematics and physics was, it may be noticed, interlinked.

Chemistry gradually broke away from alchemy in this period. Perhaps the chief figure in this movement was the erratic Swiss physician, Paracelsus (1493-1541), a revolutionary experimentalist and at the same time an irresponsible and arrogant quack. His significance lies primarily in the fact that he made reckless experiments in treating patients with various chemicals and drugs—experiments in the so-called iatrochemistry. While mainly an alchemist, he tried to free the subject from mysticism and superstition, and concentrated on practical problems instead of attempting to transmute baser metals into gold and to find the elixir of life. More careful chemical research was conducted by the great botanist and physician, Valerius Cordus (1515-1544), whose account of the preparation of ether from sulphuric acid and alcohol ranks him as the first true chemist. The best of early iatrochemists was Andreas Libavius (1540-1616) whose *Alchemia* (1597) became the first real chemical textbook.

In biology, we may note the revival of true Aristotelian biology and the methods of observation it involved. The voluminous *History of Animals* of the first encyclopedic naturalist, the German-Swiss, Conrad Gesner (1516-1565), was based upon Aristotle and much independent study. Gesner was called the German Pliny and many regard his work as the starting point of modern zoölogy. True naturalists began to appear in this age—men who ceased the mere compilation of authorities and began to study nature.

Early modern botany made its appearance in the works of Otto Brunfels (1489-1534), Jerome Bock (1498-1554), and Leonard Fuchs (1501-1566), all German scientists. Brunfels produced the first book on plants embodying accurate drawings of plants based on direct observation. But he showed the effect of tradition by trying to identify German plants with those studied by Dioscorides under the greatly different climatic conditions of the eastern Mediterranean. Bock's drawings were not so good as those of Brunfels, but his descriptions of the nature and habitat of plants were the best performance since the days of the Greek botanists. His work was less marred by the effort to identify north European plants with those of the Hellenic world. Fuchs produced the best collection of woodcuts illustrating plant life, with remarkable indications of minute details in plant structure, and including the first important modern glossary of botanical terms.

William Turner (1510-1568), in England, wrote the first modern work on ornithology, and also inaugurated the study of botany in his native land. Valerius Cordus turned from the commentaries on Dioscorides with disgust, and prepared his *History of Plants,* an unparalleled description of about five hundred species, including the first scientific study of the structure of flowers. Descriptive botany reached its highest level in this period in the careful works of Clausius of Antwerp (1525-1609) and Kaspar Bauhin (1560-1624). Pierre Belon (1517-1564), an Aristotelian, wrote important descriptive treatises on birds and fish and made one of the earliest systematizations of botany. Guillaume de Rondolet (1507-1566) produced the best accounts of marine life in this era, summarizing his extensive observations. The most important efforts in botanical classification were those of Bauhin and of Andreas Cesalpinus (1519-1603) in his work *On Plants*. It is also worthy of mention that in the sixteenth century we first hear of attempts to set up good botanical and zoölogical museums.

Perhaps the most impressive biological achievements of the century were those in anatomy. The leading personage in this branch of science was Andreas Vesalius (1514-1564), whose fame has not been dimmed by the discovery that two centuries of anatomical progress served as the basis of his anatomical work. Charles Singer accounts for Vesalius' success on three grounds: his native genius for dissection, his remarkably complete education in the best anatomical methods of the time, and his realistic attitude towards the study of the human body which the plastic art of his age encouraged. Vesalius placed anatomy on a solid scientific foundation. "By 1543," remarks Singer, "it was as difficult for an anatomist to trace in the lineaments of the viscera the impress of the heavenly bodies as it was for the astronomer to believe that the heavens were foreshadowed in the anatomy of the body of man." Vesalius' great work on *The Structure of the Human Body* was published in 1543 when he was only twenty-nine years old. Vesalius combined better than any other anatomist, except Leonardo da Vinci, the artist and dissector. Vesalius' lecture-demonstrations at the University of Padua were remarkably successful and noted for their clarity and vividness. As a theorist he was far less courageous and brilliant. In spite of his vast knowledge of the body, he advanced little beyond the physiological theories of Hippocrates and Galen.

Vesalius' successors overcame some of his weaknesses. Bartolomeo Eustachi (1520-1574) made important studies of the ear and throat, the tube connecting the throat and middle ear being named after him. He also made careful observations of the vocal cords. Gabriello Fallopio (1523-1562), a pupil of Vesalius, discovered the human oviducts, the Fallopian tubes, which still bear his name. Michael Servetus (1511-1553), burned at the stake in Geneva because of a slight difference of opinion with John Calvin regarding the nature of the Trinity, discovered the lesser circulation of the blood—that between the heart and lungs. Fabricus da Aquapendente (1537-1619), one of the leading dissectors and teachers at the University of Padua, discovered the valves in the veins. William Harvey, who completed the demonstration of the circulation of the blood, was one of Fabricus' students.

In connection with sixteenth-century physiology, mention should be made of *On the Soul and Life* by Ludovicus Vives (1494-1549), a disciple of Erasmus, resident in the Spanish Netherlands. It was the first treatise on psychology to place the subject on a physiological and empirical basis. Although marred by supernatural theories of the soul, it was a remarkable book for the time, its treatment of the emotions being outstanding.

In geography, considerable progress was made by mastering oceanic navigation, sailing around the globe, and adding to descriptive data, matters which we shall later take into full consideration. The problems of map-making growing out of the spherical character of the earth were finally solved by Gerhard Kramer (1512-1594), better known as Mercator. Using the principles of projective geometry, he showed how material taken from a globe could be drawn on a flat sheet by projecting the spherical surface of the earth on a cylinder tangent to the earth. Abraham Ortel (1527-1598), known as Ortelius, was the first map collector of importance, and issued the first atlases. The outstanding work in the related field of geology was the first scientific treatise on mineralogy, the *De re metallica* of Georg Bauer (1490-1555), better known by his Latinized name of Agricola. The translation of this book by Herbert Hoover enhanced his reputation as an engineer.

In medicine, notable achievements were made in anatomy and physiology, as just described. The rash use of chemicals and drugs in medical practice by Paracelsus and his followers led eventually to fruitful results. Paracelsus may also be credited for his diatribes against Galenic and Hippocratic medicine, even if he had nothing better to substitute. The exploitation of discoveries in natural science for the benefit of medicine and surgery occurred mainly in the seventeenth and eighteenth centuries. The outstanding genius in medicine was Girolamo Fracastoro (1484-1553) who invented the name syphilis and whose book, *De Contagione* (1546), forecast the theory of infection by microörganisms and the idea of contagious diseases. In the sixteenth century, also, there lived one of the most famous surgeons in history, Ambrose Paré (1510-1590), notable mainly for his novel and extensive treatment of gunshot wounds. Many of the surgical innovations attributed to him had, however, been in use for centuries.

We come now to the most encyclopedic scientist of the age, the amazing Leonardo da Vinci (1452-1519), perhaps the most versatile genius of whom we have any record—compared with whom Aristotle seems almost a "single-track mind." A great painter, architect, musician, and art critic, he was also an incredibly versatile scientist. As a mathematician he had few peers among contemporaries. In astronomy he anticipated Copernicus and Galileo by his views of the motion of the earth. His investigations of mechanics, hydrostatics, and the expansion of steam and gases were revolutionary. He helped to create the science of chemistry, and came close to the discovery of the chemical composition of water. He devised the best botanical classification before Linnaeus, he was an erudite geographer and geologist, questioned the deluge and fully understood the general nature and implications of fossils, was easily the greatest anatomist before Vesalius, and made the best anatomical drawings of their kind, unsurpassed to this very day. Leonardo's suggested inventions were astonishingly varied and numerous, and included rifled cannon, machine guns, mortars, bombs and shrapnel, submarines, flying machines, the steamboat, a marble saw, and a ropemaking machine. As an engineer he made phenomenal plans for the construction of tunnels, fortifications, water works, and the like. Although Leonardo's scientific works were not published, their nature was known to his contemporaries, and they exerted considerable influence on natural science and engineering. It remained, however, for a French historian of our day, Pierre Duhem, to make a thorough study of Leonardo's scientific activities and to reveal his full stature as a scientist.

Next to Leonardo in versatility we may rank Giovanni della Porta (1543-1615), a famous investigator of optics. He had none of Leonardo's original genius, but earned posterity's gratitude by making a compilation of the leading scientific discoveries of his age.

And thus, even this brief summary may show how erroneous is the familiar contention that science between Galileo and Newton made a sudden and unique spurt. Indeed, the scientific achievements of the seventeenth century would have been impossible without those of the fifteenth and sixteenth centuries. As a result of the scientific achievements between 1450 and 1600, says Dr. Singer:

> We have . . . left utterly behind the Middle Ages and all their works and ways. The old hypothesis of the macrocosm and microcosm was no longer possible to those who had studied and understood the works of Copernicus and Vesalius. Men no longer studied macrocosm and microcosm as such, but they became physicists or physiologists, taking each of them a separate portion of the universe for special study. This disposition to base opinion on observation, involving separation of nature into departments, characterizes the modern method and distinguishes it from the mediaeval. The early morning twilight is over, the dawn is upon us and it was the risen sun that Harvey and Galileo saluted, and in the light of which Francis Bacon and Descartes did their prophesying.[17]

Better scientific instruments helped on the advances in science. Especially notable in this period were the provision of an accurate balance scale for scientifically determining weight, an invention of the alchemists, and the improvement of the suspension of the compass needle. The needle had been originally fastened to a card and then floated on water. In the fourteenth century, Flavio Gioja had mounted the needle on a pivot, but in this era the brilliant mathematical charlatan, Cardan, greatly improved on earlier methods of suspending the compass needle. That invaluable timesaver for mathematical computations, the slide rule, was invented in rudimentary form by William Oughtred. This age was also on the very eve of the most momentous inventions which have aided science: the telescope, microscope, pendulum clock, the barometer, and the thermometer. Indeed, some of them had been provided in crude form before the opening of the seventeenth century. We shall describe their inventions in a later chapter. In the meantime, we may turn to one of the greatest of all inventions in modern history—that of printing by movable type.

VIII. PRINTING BECOMES A PRACTICAL ART

The recovery and editing of many Latin texts, the desire for greater permanence and uniformity in both Greek and Latin, and the growing volume of contemporary literature all made imperative a more facile mode of putting words on paper than the laborious copying which existed from Oriental times to the close of the Middle Ages. Various devices and innovations already in existence were collected.

---

17 Charles Singer, *From Magic to Science,* Dover Publications, Inc., 1958, p. 110.

Together with a new invention, namely, movable type, they made possible the modern printing art.

It is a common practice to refer to the "invention of printing" in the fifteenth century, but no more unhistorical phrase was ever coined. The elements which entered into the achievements of Coster and Gutenberg rested upon a complex of inventions running back over thousands of years.

First, let us take the history of type. The Egyptians suggested an alphabet before there was anything to write upon except stone and clay bricks. The Syrian Semites, the Phoenicians, and the Greeks perfected the Egyptian alphabet, and the Romans invented the particular form of letters now in use. But in classical times formal literature was written entirely in capitals, smaller or lowercase letters being employed only in commercial and epistolary documents. Small letters were first commonly used by Alcuin and his monks in the days of Charlemagne. Their particular script was called Carolingian minuscule.

The first writing material was stone. Then came the clay bricks of Mesopotamia. The Egyptians used papyrus, brittle fabric made from the fiber of a reed. The later Mesopotamians used parchment, chiefly sheepskin, and papyrus. The Greeks and the Romans employed both, but relied mainly on papyrus, which gradually went out of use in the early medieval period. It has been humorously asserted that the prolific church fathers exhausted the supply, but the Muslim occupation of Egypt had something to do with the disappearance of papyrus in the West. Further, the codex, or first paged book, then became popular, and papyrus was not so well adapted for this as for the scroll book—papyrus or other material rolled on a rod. Hence, parchment became the most common writing material from the sixth century to the thirteenth. We have already described the migration of paper from China to Egypt and Spain, and have shown that it was widely used in the West by the thirteenth and fourteenth centuries.

The first modern type of book—the codex—is found in the later Roman Empire. It was a volume cut up like our books into rectangular pages, but much larger than our books. Because of their form we refer to early texts of the Bible, around the fourth century A.D., as the Codex Vaticanus, the Codex Alexandrinus, and the like. While there were many beautiful small books in the medieval period, most had a larger format than is common today.

Bookmaking in the early medieval period was chiefly in the hands of monks, and the closest analogue to our publishing house was the monastic scriptorium, where manuscripts were copied for secular as well as ecclesiastical purposes. With the rise of universities a moderately flourishing book trade developed. University authorities controlled the trade and supervised the copying of textbooks. Lay scribes now entered the profession, although the monks still dominated it. It may be asked how the copyists could meet the demand for books, but it must be remembered that there was no such market as there is today. Few people could read and fewer could write. Of the literate minority only a small fraction needed books. Indeed, many an American artisan today possesses more books than were known even to the greatest scholars of the thirteenth century. Even the schools and universities employed only a few textbooks and these sometimes remained unchanged for centuries. There was none of our present high-pressure book sales-manship which leads to frequent changes of texts. Aristotle's *Logic* was the same basic text in the seventeenth century as in the thirteenth. Until the Protestant revolt the Bible was an ecclesiastical monopoly. Few lay communicants owned it or read it. A flourishing secondhand trade existed and students frequently rented books. All this obviously lessened the need for new books.

In the late fourteenth century and the early fifteenth the practice of printing from letters carved on wooden blocks entered western Europe, a device which had been known in China many centuries before. A slow and expensive process, it was limited to pages on which there was more pictorial matter than print, or to fragments of books in great demand, like Donatus' Latin grammar. These block books were not widely produced and did not materially affect the common practice of hand-copying. However, the increasing intellectual ferment of the later Middle Ages, reports of travelers, the rise of universities, the development of science, and, above all, the humanists' recovery of ancient texts, were a combina-tion of forces which led to the printing of books on paper by means of movable type.

What is customarily described as the invention of printing in western Europe was the origin of printing by means of separate or alphabetical types. Each word was assembled and placed in a printer's stick letter by letter. When a particular page, article, or book had been printed, the type was removed from the form and distributed (sorted), to be reassembled again in the formation of new words and the printing of another work. This alphabetical type was no longer carved out of wood but cast from metal. Once the die or pattern for a letter had been made by the use of a steel punch, millions of letters could be cast from the same pattern. This process of making letters for printing is known as type founding. In. the early days, letters were cast individually, and then assembled by type tweezers as word after word was "set" from manuscript copy. Since the invention of the modern typesetting machine in the latter part of the nineteenth century, the letters and words of each line of print are cast in one process. The early printer, says Professor Preserved Smith:

> . . . first had a letter cut in hard metal, this was called the punch; with it he stamped a mould known as the matrix in which he was able to found a large number of exactly identical types of metal, usually of lead. These, set side by side in a case, for the first time made it possible satisfactorily to print at reasonable cost a large number of copies of the same text, and, when that was done, the types could be taken apart and used for another work.[18]

Type forms (styles) were at first an imitation of the medieval script which had been used in the handwritten manuscripts of the Middle Ages. Only slowly did type take on the forms which we now associate with printed books and journals.

Half a century of careful research by scholars has failed to establish with abso-lute certainty who actually invented printing by movable type. It is known, how-ever, that the invention took place in the middle of the fifteenth century. The

[18] Smith, *The Age of the Reformation*, pp. 8-9.

two men for whom primacy is usually claimed are Lourens Coster of Haarlem in Holland and Johann Gutenberg of Mainz in Germany. Coster died in 1440, and our only authority for his alleged invention of printing is the statement of an individual who lived a century later. Whether or not Gutenberg actually "invented" printing, he was certainly the first to convert it into a practical art and a productive industry. Yet, curiously enough, "nothing printed during his life time bears his name as printer or gives any information about him in that capacity." He was born in Strassburg in 1398 and died in Mainz in 1468. Some authorities believe that he was engaged in printing as early as 1438, but the first work definitely attributable to him is an indulgence printed in 1454. It is also believed that he printed Donatus' Latin grammar and made a particularly beautiful edition of the Bible with forty-two lines to a page. Whoever may have been the inventor of printing, it is certain that by 1455 the practical and revolutionary character of the art had been thoroughly demonstrated, and that it was no longer in the experimental stage.

After the middle of the fifteenth century the printing industry developed rapidly. In 1455 Johann Fust, a former partner of Gutenberg, and Peter Schoeffer formed the first great printing company. Schoeffer introduced many innovations. He originated the use of lead spacing between the lines, also printing in colors, and improved the art of type founding. Strassburg, Augsburg, Cologne, and Nuremberg followed Mainz as important German printing centers. The most famous German printer of the early sixteenth century was Antony Koberger of Nuremberg, who made printing an international industry by sending his agents throughout Europe to find manuscripts suitable for publication.

The craft spread to other parts of Europe. It reached Italy by 1465, Paris by 1470, England by 1480, Sweden by 1482, Portugal by 1490, and Spain by 1499. The recovery of classical manuscripts stimulated the printing trade in Italy, especially in Venice. The freedom of the press in Holland encouraged the printing industry there. It is estimated that by 1500 there were in existence between eight and nine million printed books of various kinds and sizes.

The invention of printing had incalculable consequences in the cultural history of mankind. As Professor Waugh asserts:

> It may be an exaggeration to say that it is the most momentous invention in the history of the world, but it is certainly the most momentous since that of writing, and of more fundamental consequence than any of the countless inventions of the last two centuries, however much they may have transformed the conditions of life.[19]

Or as Professor Smith declares:

> The importance of printing cannot be overestimated. There are few events like it in the history of the world. The whole gigantic swing of modern democracy and of the scientific spirit was released by it. The veil of the temple of religion and of knowledge was rent in twain, and the arcana of the priest and clerk exposed to the gaze of people. The reading public became the supreme court be-

[19] Waugh, op. cit., p. 517.

fore whom, from this time, all cases must be argued. The conflict of opinion and parties, of privilege and freedom, of science and obscurantism, was transferred from the secret chamber of a small, privileged, professional, and sacerdotal coterie to the arena of the reading public.[20]

While Germany gave birth to the printing industry and has taken a prominent place in it to this very day, the presses of the tolerant Netherlands, especially Plantin's and Elzevir's, early became prominent. Christophe Plantin was a Frenchman who set up a press at Antwerp in 1555 and later at Leyden and Paris. He printed the famous Polyglot Bible. Lodovic Elzevir established a press at Leyden in 1580. His more famous son, Bonaventura Elzevir, had an international reputation as a typographer and as a printer in Greek, Latin, and other languages. His type fonts were imitated by many European printers.

Many inventions improved the simple printing devices of the fifteenth and sixteenth centuries. The earliest books were produced with a crude stamping press, using type set by hand. The London *Times* introduced the rotary press at the opening of the nineteenth century but it was not widely used in newspaper printing until the middle of that century. After the Civil War a German-American, Ottmar Mergenthaler, invented the typesetting (linotype) machine which enables compositors (typesetters) to keep up with pressmen. Otherwise a rapid printing press would be of little value.

Printing with movable type means economical large-scale production, but it is still cheaper to copy a book by hand or by typewriter if we wish but one copy. In other words, printing introduced cheap books, democratized literature, and made it available to the masses.

However, no flood of radical or scientific works immediately sprang from the presses. Most of the books printed in the first century after Gutenberg were not scientific and critical works but pious tracts, textbooks, and conventional encyclopedias. Usually they were reproductions of manuscripts which circulated for centuries before the invention of printing. The philosophy, literature, and science of the new age did not reach print in considerable numbers, except in Holland, until the late sixteenth and early seventeenth centuries—in some countries, not until the eighteenth century.

The dominatingly conservative tenor of the first period of printing and its hesitancy to encourage new and subversive ideas are well described by Professor Waugh:

Typography undoubtedly facilitated the spread of the so-called "New Learning" and later of Protestant opinion; but it was equally at the service of conservative propaganda. Printers were no more inclined towards heterodoxy than other men, and there was no ecclesiastical animosity against their craft. The early products of the presses were for the most part either religious books or famous works of the "Old Learning." We have seen that Gutenberg's best-known productions were religious. The first book printed by Fust and Schoeffer was a Psalter, the first by Schoeffer alone was the *Summa* of Thomas Aquinas. The earliest product of the printing-press in Italy was the time-honored Latin grammar ascribed to

[20] Smith, *op. cit.*, p. 10.

Donatus. Caxton's first work as a printer was done on an edition of Bartholomew the Englishman's *De proprietatibus rerum*, a well-known encyclopaedia of the thirteenth century. Mentelin, one of the earliest and greatest printers of Strasbourg, limited himself almost exclusively to theological works, on the ground that they paid best. One of his undertakings was the *Speculum*, the huge encyclopaedia of Vincent of Beauvais, which he published in eight folio volumes. The productions of the great Koberger were mostly works of conservative theology. Missals and other books of devotion appeared in great numbers; and new editions of the Canon Law were likewise common. Besides Donatus, the most familiar school-books and university textbooks, on which the youth of the Middle Ages had been nourished for centuries, were freely printed. Along with these, especially in Italy, there appeared numerous editions of the classics. The fact is that in the controversies of the fifteenth century, and the still more bitter ones of the sixteenth, the part of the new invention was strictly neutral. At the same time, it is true that the quick dissemination and the easy exchange of ideas facilitate the introduction of novel opinions and render it harder for conservative forces to check the flow of subversive thought. Thus the greatest medieval gift to human civilization was destined to hasten the downfall of medieval culture.[21]

IX. POLITICAL THEORY UNDER THE SPELL OF HUMANISM

Since humanism was permeated with Greek and Roman ideals, the political philosophy of this age reflected classical political thought. There was a tendency to emphasize the power of the state and to minimize the pretensions of the church. The theory of secular absolutism common in Greece and Rome, particularly in Rome, was vigorously expounded.

The most conspicuous representative of humanist political theory was Niccolò Machiavelli (1469-1527). He went far beyond Pierre Dubois and Marsiglio of Padua in rejecting the claims of the church to temporal power. The assumption that the church could rival the state, to say nothing of subordinating it, seemed palpably absurd to Machiavelli. He expressed vigorous contempt for the doctrine of the temporal power of the pope because he thought it stood in the way of Italian unity, which he advocated.

Machiavelli not only adopted the thesis of secular absolutism, in which he was chiefly influenced by the Greek historian, Polybius, but he rejected the medieval idea that the state exists primarily to repress sin or promote salvation. To him, the state is an end in itself. Civic considerations override all others: "When the entire safety of our country is at stake, no consideration of what is just or unjust, merciful or cruel, praiseworthy or shameful, must intervene. On the contrary, every other consideration being set aside, that course must be taken which preserves the existence of the country and maintains its liberty." In this way, Machiavelli categorically severed ethics from political theory—the ethics of classical moralists as well as of churchly apologists.

Machiavelli proceeded to make one of the most acute examinations of human nature in the history of modern social philosophy. A perfect child of the "con-

21 Waugh, *op. cit.*, pp. 523-24.

spiral society" which formed his political environment,[22] he frankly based his analysis upon the assumed impulses of self-interest, intrigue, and the insatiability of human desire. He also maintained that personal prestige and material prosperity alone will suffice to take care of human desires, insofar as they can be satisfied. As he cynically observed, a man will forget the loss of his father far more quickly than he will forget the loss of his patrimony. There was no place for sentimentality in Machiavelli's psychological and political theory.

In his *Prince* and his *Discourses* [23]—the latter is the less well known, but by far the more profound work—he logically deduced from these realistic views of human nature methods which a successful monarch and a ruler of a republic, respectively, should follow.

The *Prince* was the keenest sociological study of leadership and the most realistic discussion of political pragmatism which had yet been made. Machiavelli took the position that the end—success—justifies the means and that whatever works well is right. As we have noted, he thus effectively separated political theory from the ethical elements which had colored it for centuries.

In the *Discourses* he outlined with equal candor policies which should be followed by the rulers of an aggressive and expanding republic, and also dealt thoroughly with the problems of social relationships and political processes.

Further, in Machiavelli's criticism of the ideal of social stability, as expressed by Plato and Aristotle, there was the beginning of a theory of social dynamics. He believed candidly that a state must either expand and develop or decay. Finally, Machiavelli took social philosophy out of the realm of abstract speculation and put it on the firm foundation of observation and historical analysis.

In spite of these contributions, Machiavelli's treatment of society was not organic or well balanced. His works resembled manuals for self-seeking despots or imperialistic republics more than systematic sociological and political treatises. They enjoyed, however, wide popularity and exerted considerable direct influence upon rulers and practical politicians.

The economic misery of the age suggested to the English humanist, Sir Thomas More (1478-1535), his brilliant essay in imaginative social reconstruction, *Utopia*. More wrote during the early Tudor period, when English society, particularly the lower classes, was upset by the breakdown of the manorial system and the rise of large-scale sheep-farming. Destruction of English monasteries by Henry VIII added to social malaise. In the opening section of his book More drew a vivid picture of the disorder and suffering of the time.

As a remedy for these sorry conditions, More portrayed the ideal commonwealth of Amaurote, where wealth was equally divided and society was organized on coöperative principles. Everybody engaged in agriculture and, in addition, learned some trade. The government was aristocratic, but judiciously held in tow by the force of public opinion. More thought that the new social order would end most of those evil desires which require legislative restraint.

---

[22] Cf. F. H. Giddings, ed., *Readings in Historical and Descriptive Sociology*, Macmillan, 1904, pp. 13, 52-54.

[23] *Three Books of Discourses on the First Ten Books of Livy*, commonly known as the *Deca*.

The decay of feudalism and the growth of monarchies precipitated theoretical justifications of secular absolutism, as in the works of Pierre Dubois and Marsiglio of Padua, already discussed, and in the *Six Books Concerning the Commonwealth,* by the French publicist, Jean Bodin (1530-1596). Society, according to Bodin, begins with the family, but larger groups appear because of man's social instinct. The state, however, is formed by war and conquest, and possesses absolute, sovereign power, "unrestrained by law." The state is politically supreme, and above any human law. This theory of sovereignty was later elaborated to serve as a prop for modern centralized national states, the essence of sovereignty consisting of the *legibus soluta* concept, i.e., that the state is above law. This challenged the medieval Christian notion of the relation of the state and the law and reintroduced the Roman doctrine of secular absolutism. Bodin asserted that the sovereign state is absolute in secular matters, but remains subject to divine law, the law of nature and the law of nations. The growing interest in Roman law during the humanist period popularized the concept of secular absolutism echoed in Bodin's theory of sovereignty.

Bodin also became famous for his theory of the influence of climate on man's nature and political views. He believed that climatic conditions produce different political mentalities, and that the wise statesman will take cognizance of such facts. Political success can be achieved only where the form of government is happily adapted to the political psychology of the population. Bodin was less scientific in this respect than his doctrines superficially suggest, for his theory of geographical and climatic determinism was based on astrological assumptions.

That man originally lived in a state of nature, moving on to political society through a social contract, was suggested by the Spanish Jesuit historian and philosopher, Juan de Mariana (1535-1625), in his *De rege et regis institutione* (1605). Mariana assumed that men originally lived like animals, without external authority, guided only by instinct. They were, however, free from the greed, avarice, and unnatural immoralities of civilization. Increasing wants, the long infancy of the human offspring, and the insufficiency of the individual apart from the group all combined to encourage the creation of civil society and orderly government. The natural sociability of man accounted for the origins of group life, but a contract was needed to institute the state and government. In less than a century, this political and social doctrine, anticipated by Aeneas Sylvius, became common among liberal thinkers, and was employed to justify representative government, support the pretensions of the middle class, and defend the legal and ethical validity of bourgeois revolutions.

The Protestant revolt brought in appropriate types of political philosophy. Luther depended upon secular rulers for the success of his revolt. Hence, he was inclined to stress the superiority of secular over ecclesiastical authority and to urge passive obedience to the state. Protestant rulers demanded the power to control the religion of their realms under the famous *cuius regio eius religio* (he who controls the region controls the religion) clause of the Peace of Augsburg (1555). John Calvin revived what was roughly the Catholic notion of the separate and coordinate existence of church and state. While supporting the doctrine of political obedience for the individual subject, he affirmed that the church or any other institution was justified in resisting tyrants. Anti-monarchical Calvinists and other Protestants carried this doctrine to extremes. Its antithesis was the hypothesis of the divine right of kings, generally sponsored by Protestant friends of royalty, but also enunciated by Catholics like Bishop Bossuet.

X. THE PROTESTANT REVOLUTION AS AN INTELLECTUAL MOVEMENT

1. Causes of the Revolt

Resentment and restlessness within the Roman Catholic church during the Middle Ages finally came to a head. Open secession ran its course between 1517 and 1648. This is usually called the Protestant Reformation and is also known as the Protestant revolution. Catholic scholars prefer the term "revolution" because the word "reformation" implies that the Protestants actually reformed or improved the Catholic religious system of the Middle Ages. This, of course, the Catholics are not willing to admit. The fact is that the movement started as a reformation within the church and ended in a revolution and secession, the latter inevitably caused by Luther's fiery and violent tactics and the obstinacy and tactlessness of the Catholic leaders who resisted moderate reform.

Like all great historic movements, the Protestant revolt, which disrupted the Western church and created national churches and a multiplicity of Christian sects, was the product of complex factors.[24] It was in no sense, whether in its causes, in the manner in which it expressed itself, or in its consequences, purely a religious movement. Nor should it be viewed as the result of conditions peculiar to Europe around the turn of the sixteenth century. For the Protestant revolt was, in some aspects at least, simply the culmination of truly medieval forces. Even Luther, who acted as detonator of the movement, recognized "that the Reformation was no accident, depending on his own personal intervention, but was inevitable and in progress when he began to preach."[25] The view that the Reformation cannot be correctly regarded as a religious movement, pure and simple, was well expressed by the American church historian, H. C. Lea:

> In the curious theocracy which dominated the Middle Ages, secular and spiritual interests became so inextricably intermingled that it is impossible wholly to disentangle them; but the motives, both remote and proximate, which led to the Lutheran revolt were largely secular rather than spiritual . . . we may dismiss the religious changes incident to the Reformation with the remark that they were not the object sought but the means for attaining that object.[26]

Viewed in its spiritual aspect, the Protestant revolt meant in general a modification of the older Christian theology and the rejection of the Catholic church as the sole instrument of salvation. In its significant nonspiritual aspects, the movement appears primarily: (1) as the culmination of a long-existing critical attitude

24 For a clear and up-to-date treatment, see A. C. Flick, *The Decline of the Medieval Church*, Burt Franklin, 1959, Vol. II, Pt. IV.
25 Preserved Smith, *The Age of the Reformation*, p. 701.
26 *Cambridge Modern History*, I, 653.

towards the tremendous material wealth of the church, the economic advantages it enjoyed, and the financial burdens it imposed; and (2) as a decisive manifestation of the clash between national powers and the international Catholic state. The importance of the last point cannot be overemphasized, and James Harvey Robinson was fully justified in writing: "The Reformation was . . . essentially a stage in the disengaging of the modern state from that medieval, international ecclesiastical state (that is, the Catholic Church) which had its beginnings in the *ecclesia* of the Acts of the Apostles." [27]

The intellectual or spiritual causes of the secession were chiefly associated with religious mysticism, which rejected the mechanical scheme of salvation and the doctrine of elaborate priestly mediation. There was no skepticism about the supernaturalism underlying mysticism. The mystics were men of outstanding piety, far less urbane and worldly-minded than many of their Catholic contemporaries. At the most, the pious critics of the Catholic church in the early days of the revolt brought into play amiable and mild satire, like that of Erasmus. In short, the Protestant upheaval was engineered by very devout men, so far as its leaders were concerned. Indeed the very piety of the reformers, their rejection of the sacramental system, relic-mongering, and the philosophy of "good works" encouraged the secession.

In addition to the larger magic involved in the sacramental system, the medieval church exploited a lesser magic in the form of relic worship. The greater and lesser magic were, of course, associated through the fact that no mass could be said except over an altar stone, which often contained a relic:

> The relics of Christ and the martyrs [says Kirby Page] were thought to possess divine virtue. Pieces of wood from the Holy Cross were the most highly treasured of all relics. Healing and protective power were supposed to reside in every particle of a saint's body, the hair and teeth being especially efficacious. The relics of St. Gratus were given credit for extinguishing a forest fire in 1542. Valuable relics became a source of great income to a church. For centuries the craze for relics was so great that innumerable frauds were perpetrated. At present there are fifty-six fingers of St. Peter the Dominican in the churches of Europe, twenty-six heads of St. Juliene, thirty bodies of St. George, twelve heads of St. John the Baptist, seventy veils of the Virgin Mary, as well as many tears and footprints of Jesus.[28]

In his authoritative *Age of the Reformation* Preserved Smith writes:

> The passion for the relics of the saints led to an enormous traffic in spurious articles. There appeared to be enough of the wood of the true cross, said Erasmus, to make a ship; there were exhibited five shin-bones of the ass on which Christ rode, whole bottles of the Virgin's milk, and several complete bits of skin saved from the circumcision of Jesus.[29]

The Archbishop of Mainz possessed, among other things, "a fair piece of Moses' left horn, a whole pound of the wind that blew for Elijah in the cave on Mount Horeb and two feathers and an egg of the Holy Ghost." At the shrine of

[27] Article "Reformation," Encyclopaedia Britannica, 11th ed., XXIII, 5.
[28] *Jesus or Christianity?* Doubleday, Doran, 1929, p. 167.
[29] Smith, *op. cit.,* p. 29.

Trèves the shirt of Christ was on exhibition. At Loreto in Italy might be seen the sacred house in which the Virgin is supposed to have lived, said to have come from Palestine to Italy in three leaps. The body of St. James, located in Santiago de Compostela in Spain, was said to have proceeded across the sea from Judea in a stone sarcophagus under its own power.

All this sort of thing was extremely repugnant to the pietistic and mystical Catholics of pre-Protestant days. Reformers who promised to abolish these abuses were bound to get their support.

Among economic causes of the revolt may be counted the growing impatience of the capitalist class with the economic ideals and legislation of the Catholic church, the groaning of the peasantry, bourgeoisie, and aristocracy alike under heavy ecclesiastical taxation, and special resentment over the revived sale of indulgences and of sinecures. The economic views of the church were far higher, ethically, than those of the capitalist class, hence the latter's desire to shake off ecclesiastical restrictions in order to be permitted to accumulate larger profits through freer competition.

The political causes of the revolt were related to the economic. The escape from ecclesiastical taxation could be made permanent and assured only by casting off the authority of the ecclesiastical state. Moreover, sovereigns wished greater control over the religion of their subjects. There was a real desire to create national churches.

The German scene at the opening of the sixteenth century, according to Thomas M. Lindsay, was one of "seething discontent and full of bitter class hatreds. . . . It was into this mass of seething discontent that the spark of religious protest fell—the one thing needed to fire the train and kindle the social conflagration. This was the society to which Luther spoke, and its discontent was the sounding-board which made his words reverberate." [30]

2. Humanism and Protestantism

It has been assumed by many that humanism produced the Protestant revolt. But it seems that this is true only in the sense of a somewhat ironical remark once made by Professor Robinson that the mythical Renaissance which exists in the minds of old-fashioned historians may have caused the mythical Reformation which they also envisage.

Between actual humanism and literal Protestantism there was little real intellectual affinity or genetic relationship. They were the product of entirely different strains in medieval civilization. Humanism was the outcome of the growing interest in pagan civilization and of the rise of town life and material prosperity. Protestantism, as a mental attitude, was the outgrowth of increasing otherworldliness and mystical piety. Perhaps we might see in both a revolt against scholasticism; but one was a scholarly secession, the other a religious opposition.

Humanism meant, in its intellectual aspects, a secular cultivation of pagan learning. The Protestant revolt promoted theological controversies over Christian doctrine. The most discernible relationship between the two resided in the fact

[30] T. M. Lindsay, *History of the Reformation*, 2 vols. Scribner, 1928, I, 112-13.

that the scholarly training obtained by some Protestant humanists in their classical studies later aided them in their activity as religious controversialists. Perhaps the most plausible of the indirect influences of humanism on the Protestant revolt was the stimulus which humanism gave to the spirit of individualism. But individuality expressed itself quite differently in humanism and in art from the manner in which it asserted itself in Protestantism. Moreover, the cult of humanity and beauty promoted by humanistic individualism was smothered by supernaturalism under the reign of Protestantism. The quality most evident in both humanism and early Protestantism was mysticism. But even this mystical trend had different antecedents among humanists and Protestants. Humanistic mysticism was based on Neoplatonism and the Jewish cabala. Protestant mysticism was founded upon the ultrapious Christian mysticism of the later Middle Ages.

If any of the Protestant reformers derived theological inspiration from the humanists, it emanated from their incidental piety and Christianity and not from their humanism. If Luther was impelled to ecclesiastical and doctrinal reform by his study of Erasmus' writings, it was because of the ideas of Erasmus the Christian and not of Erasmus the humanist. Erasmus' enthusiasm for the writings and doctrines of Cicero could never have been the starting point for the theological views and intellectual attitudes of Luther, Calvin, Knox, or Jonathan Edwards. Cicero's beautiful motto: "We who search for hypotheses are prepared both to refute without prejudice and to be refuted without resentment" could hardly have inspired Calvin's canons of urbanity, as exemplified in his burning of Servetus at the stake after their verbal tilt over the nature of the Trinity.

The important point is that, strictly speaking, humanism on the one hand, and Lutheranism and Calvinism on the other, were fundamentally opposed. Humanism was, at least incidentally, a moderate revolt against the supernaturalism and otherworldliness of patristic and scholastic Christianity. The Protestant revolt brought in its train an all-pervading revival of the grosser forms of supernaturalism, diabolism, miracle-mongering, witchcraft, and other manifestations of this cultural complex. It is true, of course, that many humanists were critics of ecclesiastical abuses, but they were loyal Catholics, with few exceptions, and merely wished for reform within the church. Humanism may have promoted criticism of the church, but it certainly did not intentionally promote the spirit of Protestantism or secession.

In short, the humanistic movement and the Protestant revolt were highly unlike each other in general cultural interests and intellectual outlook. We may agree with Erasmus' observation that if Luther hatched the egg that he (Erasmus) had laid, the result was quite a different bird from what Erasmus intended it to be.

3. Protestantism and the Catholic System

We may now briefly survey the actual changes introduced by the Protestants into Christian doctrines and practices. In the first place, they stamped out what they regarded as the leading aspects of ecclesiastical corruption and suppressed completely the sale of indulgences. They strove for a simpler and more direct form of worship. They particularly attacked those phases of Catholic worship and ritual which were based on the doctrine of salvation by good works.[31] They abolished the veneration of relics, the adoration of images, and the practice of making pilgrimages to holy places. They profoundly modified the central Catholic doctrine of transubstantiation in the sacrament of the Mass. They denied the miraculous transformation of the bread and wine into the actual body and blood of Jesus, although the Lutherans accepted "consubstantiation" or the "corporeal presence." The Bible, rather than the dogmas of the church fathers and Catholic theologians, became the guide of the Protestant Christian in his religious devotions. The Protestants denied the necessity of a mediating priesthood to bring the believer into contact with God. They contended that a Christian could secure God's attention directly through personal worship and prayer. This caused them to put special emphasis on the importance of the individual conscience in matters religious.

Of course, the degree to which Protestantism differed, even in matters religious, from the parent Catholic church greatly depended upon the particular Protestant sect. With the early Lutherans and Anglicans the divergence from Catholicism in worship was relatively slight—in spite of doctrinal differences. On the other hand, the more radical religious groups, such as the Anabaptists and the later evangelical sects, almost completely abandoned the old Catholic rites and practices.

Nevertheless, as the able German theological writer, Ernst Troeltsch, has made very clear, the fundamental religious differences between Catholics and even the radical Protestants were relatively slight. This fact was commonly overlooked in the fierce partisanship which characterized the controversies between Catholics and Protestants. Both Catholics and orthodox Protestants fully accepted the whole Christian epic as outlined in the Old and New Testaments. To both of them the Bible was the central sacred book of their religion. Catholics and Protestants alike were primarily concerned with making a proper adjustment to the supernatural world and with securing the salvation of the individual soul in the world to come. The medieval doctrines of heaven and hell were adopted with no marked change by all Protestants. To Luther, in particular, the devil and his hosts were real and fearful beings. Evangelical divines of the eighteenth and nineteenth centuries tended to lay far more stress upon the horrors of hell and the dangers of damnation than Catholic theologians of pre-Reformation days. Moreover, the Protestants were just as alert and severe as Catholics in their denunciation of skeptics and freethinkers.

It is no exaggeration to say that upon at least ninety-five per cent of all matters of strictly religious import Catholics and Protestants were in agreement and that they were about equally antagonistic to the inroads of theological liberalism and secular skepticism.

Protestants have taken great pride in their elimination of many alleged idolatrous Catholic practices—an elimination effected by the Protestant revolt. But their exultation rests on dubious foundations. By these changes they enormously weakened the emotional power of the church and deprived it of one of its most

---

[31] The Protestants, while not deploring certain good works, insisted that salvation could be gained by faith alone.

potent appeals; its visual and auricular imagery. The rich emotion-bearing ritual and liturgy of the Catholic church were far better calculated to attract and hold the mass of faithful believers than the metaphysical dogmatism of Calvin or the vocal emotionalism of other Protestant cults. This is even more apparent today than it was in the sixteenth century. Intellectual classes, who were once attracted by Calvinistic metaphysics and doctrinal sermons, have now generally discarded all types of orthodoxy.

4. Intellectual Aspects of Protestantism

Intellectually speaking, the Protestant revolt was most decidedly retrogressive when compared to humanistic Catholicism. Theologically it went back admittedly to the apostolic age. Luther denounced the universities and any form of education not primarily designed to promote the faith; he regarded reason as the devil's most seductive harlot, whose neck faith could easily wring; and he was very credulous with respect to the devil and miracles. Luther not only halted and frustrated German humanism, but was the first important European openly to condemn the Copernican theory. His ground for opposing it was its alleged pre-posterousness in the light of the fact that "in the day when Jehovah delivered up the Amorites before the children of Israel, Joshua said in the sight of Israel, 'Sun, stand thou still upon Gibeon,' and the sun stood still and the moon stayed until the nation avenged themselves of their enemies." Religious bias prevented many Protestant countries from accepting the improved Gregorian calendar—the product of a papal court—for many years. Philipp Melanchthon, perhaps the ablest of German Protestant scholars, said that the burning of Servetus by Calvin because of a slight difference of opinion over the nature of the Trinity was "a pious and memorable example for all posterity."

Calvinistic anthropology, with its morbid conception of human treason before God, and its predestinarian theology, was intellectually depressing, and discouraged human effort. And no person could have been less sympathetic to science and the critical philosophy than an earnest fanatic like John Knox. Further, Protestant emphasis on the infallible nature of the Bible was in some ways more dangerous and obstructive to liberal thought and scientific progress than the Catholic dogma of an infallible church which might, in theory at least, periodically reinterpret its tenets. The Protestants revived the popularity of an interest in the Old Testament, with all its primitive beliefs. This served admirably as a basis for the sabbatarian excesses of the Puritans. The Protestants paid little or no attention, at first, to the noble social passion of Amos and other great Jewish prophets. They were more concerned with primitive passages justifying austere practices and brutal punishments for sin.

Probably no one more sagaciously observed how necessary it is to qualify exuberance regarding the progressive intellectual tone of Protestantism than did James Harvey Robinson:

> The defection of the Protestants from the Roman Catholic Church is not connected with any decisive intellectual revision. Such ardent emphasis has been

constantly placed upon the differences between Protestantism and Catholicism by representatives of both parties that the close intellectual resemblance of the two systems, indeed their identity in nine parts out of ten, has tended to escape us. The early Protestants, of course, accepted, as did the Catholics, the whole patristic outlook on the world; their historical perspective was similar, their notions of the origin of man, of the Bible, with its types, prophecies, and miracles, of heaven and hell, of demons and angels, are all identical. To the early Protestants, as to Catholics, he who would be saved must accept the doctrine of the triune God and must be ever on his guard against the whisperings of reason and the innovations suggested by scientific advance. Luther and Melanchthon denounced Copernicus in the name of the Bible. Melanchthon re-edited, with enthusiastic approval, Ptolemy's astrology. Luther made repeated and bitter attacks on reason; in whose eyes he freely confessed the presuppositions of Christianity to be absurd. Calvin gloried in man's initial and inherent moral impotency; and the doctrine of predestination seemed calculated to paralyze all-human effort.

The Protestants did not know any more about nature than their Catholic enemies; they were just as completely victimized by the demonology of Witchcraft. The Protestant Revolt was not begotten of added scientific knowledge nor did it owe its success to any considerable confidence in criticism. As Gibbon pointed out, the loss of one conspicuous mystery—that of transubstantiation—"was amply compensated by the stupendous doctrines of original sin, redemption, faith, grace, and predestination" which the Protestants strained from the epistles of St. Paul. Early Protestantism is, from an intellectual standpoint, essentially a phase of medieval religious history.[32]

By all odds the outstanding contribution to intellectual progress that can be ascribed to Protestantism was an indirect one, namely, its aid in increasing the difficulty of carrying out ecclesiastical repression of intellectual freedom. This was foreseen and deplored by the great Catholic writer, Bishop Bossuet. As he clearly pointed out in his *History of the Differences among Protestant Churches,* once the unity of Christendom had been broken by the Protestants, there was no reason why the process should not go on indefinitely and lead to an infinite multiplication of sects. Bossuet's prediction was borne out by the historical development of Protestantism.

In thus rendering ecclesiastical interference with thought less unified and effective, Protestantism aided, though quite unintentionally, in advancing intellectual progress. As the famous historian Edward Gibbon observed: "The chain of authority was broken, which restrains the bigot from thinking as he pleases and the slave from speaking as he thinks; the popes, fathers, and councils were no longer the supreme and infallible judges of the world; and each Christian was taught to acknowledge no law but the scripture, no interpreter but his own conscience. This freedom, however, was the consequence rather than the design of the Reformation." Radical religious sects like the Anabaptists both preached and practiced toleration, and the very multiplicity of Protestant sects was a powerful factor in producing eventual tolerance, no matter how intolerant each sect might be within itself.

[32] J. H. Robinson, *The New History,* Macmillan, 1912, pp. 117-18.

If art be considered as a phase of intellectual expression, as it fittingly may, then the Protestant revolt exerted another negative influence. Its attitude towards art was certainly far less favorable and stimulating than that of humanistic Catholicism. This was true not only of plastic and chromatic art, but also of literature and the theater. Protestant obsession with theology and religious controversy diverted intellectual and literary effort from books written primarily for aesthetic pleasure. Puritan opposition to the theater has continued down to our own day. For some centuries in early modern times it acted as a potent obstacle to the writing and performance of plays.

The intellectual reaction of the Protestant revolt upon Catholicism was even more disastrous than its effect upon the followers of Luther, Calvin, Zwingli, and Knox. The cultural decline which accompanied the Catholic Counter Reformation can best be gauged by the intellectual contrast between a typical early "Reformation" Catholic like Erasmus and the most characteristic figure in the Counter Reformation, Ignatius Loyola. While no movement founded by an Erasmus could have produced a Voltaire, as the most cursory comparison of the former's *Adages* with the latter's *Philosophical Dictionary* will readily demonstrate, neither would it have led logically to the creation of the Jesuit order, with its zealous intolerance.

The church had been growing more tolerant and more appreciative of secular learning when it was put on the defensive by Protestant assaults. It then felt it necessary to recover, refurbish, and defend vigorously many archaic dogmas that had been partly allowed to lapse. It was forced to uphold as extreme a supernaturalism as was propounded by any Protestant fanatic. When the Protestants subjected Catholicism to bitter criticism, it was only natural that the Catholics should react in a manner appropriate to the attacks made upon them. Fierce theological intolerance once more became a leading intellectual virtue in the Catholic church. The Inquisition redoubled its efforts and its ferocity. The urbanity of humanist Catholicism disappeared from the European intellectual scene. Never again did there appear at Rome a mental atmosphere comparable to that which existed under "Renaissance" popes, such as Pius II, Nicholas V, Leo X, and the like.

5. New Economic Ideals: The Growth of Materialism

One of the most notable intellectual changes wrought by Protestantism was the attitude it introduced towards work and wealth, and towards the means of obtaining the latter. No intellectual or moral transformation in modern times possessed greater consequences for humanity.

The medieval church emphasized the penitential nature of work, looked askance on the profit system, and tried to eliminate from trade those things which would today be regarded as the very essence of shrewd business—selling at a profit with no economic service, cornering the market, creating a monopoly, and taking interest as a normal procedure. Christians involved in medieval trade may have engaged to some degree in all these prohibited practices, but the church never formally gave its approval to such conduct.

Gradually but certainly, Protestants broke down the medieval Catholic economic doctrines which stressed social considerations and limited the acquisition and use of wealth. Protestantism, especially Calvinism, decisively encouraged individualism in economics as well as in religion. It promoted the spirit of thrift and economic ambition, the acquisition of wealth through shrewd dealings, and sanctioned freedom in all forms of economic operations. The modern theory and practice of "business enterprise" found powerful early support in Protestant morality and economic philosophy. This was accentuated by the rise of the new bourgeoisie or middle class.

Looking at the matter in the broad perspective of the history of civilization, the most important contribution of the Protestant revolt to the modern economic perspective was the sanction and respectability it gave to the profit motive. Not since the period of Oriental antiquity had the acquisitive instinct been so frankly blessed. The Protestant revolt fully removed the stigma from personal enrichment through commercial pursuits, glorified trade and monetary profits, and laid the foundations for our present adulation of the successful business man. The prevailing individualism and the lax hand of a divided church also promoted these developments.

Another leading influence exerted by Protestantism upon economic ideas was the impulse it gave to thrift, frugality, and the alleged virtue of hard manual work. This particular impetus came especially from Calvin and his followers. They lifted from work the taint of servility which clung to it in classical times, and removed the penitential coloring attached to it in medieval Catholicism. Calvin vigorously condemned idleness: "For nothing is more unseemly than a man that is idle and good for nothing—who profits neither himself nor others, and seems born to eat and drink. . . . It is certain that idleness and indolence are accursed of God." He held up to contempt "idle bellies that chirp sweetly in the shade." The general import of the Calvinistic attitude was well expressed in Sebastian Franck's summary of the Calvinistic spirit: "You think you have escaped from the monastery, but everyone must now be a monk throughout his life."

Calvin himself apparently approved of work as a safeguard against sin and corporeal indulgence quite as much as a means to economic enrichment. But the economic assets of labor were stressed by many of his disciples. Hence, it is chiefly from Calvinistic sources that there arose that persistent tradition of the moral and economic blessings of industry which pervades modern thinking. When the bourgeoisie became wealthy, they conveniently found that the virtue of industry belongs chiefly to the employee class, while invidious, conspicuous and honorific leisure should be sought by employers—a development traced with sardonic delight in our day by Thorstein Veblen.

In this way orthodox Protestantism became the strongest bulwark of materialistic philosophy in modern times. Atheists and radicals have been denounced in season and out by Christian ministers for their "materialism." But, for the most part, both atheists and radicals have been singularly impecunious and idealistic persons who repudiate any hope of earthly riches in order to serve what they believe to be a noble cause. If there is a nonmaterialistic type of person, it is the average radical agitator. On the other hand, the great majority of plutocratic bankers, industrialists, transportation magnates, utility kings, and the like have been noted for their public piety. As churches became larger and more magnificent, and church activities more costly, it became necessary to lean more heavily upon benefactions from the very rich. Clergymen have therefore been loath to denounce "malefactors of great wealth." Rather, the latter were showered with honors and their calling extolled in the sight of the Lord. The rise of capitalism and Protestantism, then, transformed a large section of Christian opinion from an idealistic critique of worldly riches and the profit system into a major buttress of materialism, in any sensible and practical use of that term. There have been plenty of incidental rebellions against this attitude within the Protestant church, but they met with no general success.

The Catholic church, whatever its formal allegiance to its medieval economic doctrines, also gradually accommodated itself to the rising capitalistic spirit and practices. While still frequently proclaiming its adherence to principles of social justice, its spokesmen are today extremely alert in branding as "Reds" those who seek to put social justice into practice.

The capitalistic leanings of Protestantism also help to explain the peculiar biases of Protestant morality, especially its perpetuation of the medieval Catholic obsession with the evils of sex. Modern capitalism found the existing Catholic impurity-complex highly useful for its purposes. It therefore did everything possible to encourage a Protestant view of morality that identified the good life with ostensible sexual purity, whatever degree of secret indulgence material wealth may procure and hide from the public gaze. This attitude was very valuable to capitalism because, whatever a man's lack of honesty, integrity, or humanity in business or financial dealings, his morals can scarcely be attacked so long as he is not openly detected in a breach of chastity or conjugal fidelity. Immanuel Kant's classic effort to free ethics from supernaturalism [33] played right into the hands of these bourgeois "purists," a development which Kant himself probably would have deplored. Another capitalistic rationalization which supported the same ethical position was that sexual indulgence by the working classes depleted their energies and made them less vigorous and productive workmen.

XI. THE WITCHCRAFT EPIDEMIC

One of the most deplorable intellectual results of the Protestant revolt and the Catholic Counter Reformation was the witchcraft mania of the sixteenth and seventeenth centuries. This epidemic constitutes one of the most horrible episodes in the history of human superstition and organized cruelty. While belief in witches existed throughout the Middle Ages, the bigotry and emotional fervor provoked by the religious controversies of the sixteenth century prepared the ground for the growth of a veritable epidemic of superstition and persecution. The belief in witchcraft depends for its existence upon a widespread concern with the devil and his works. Never was the Catholic interest in diabolism so

[33] See below, pp. 812, 845-7, 1009.

vigorous and extensive as in the fifteenth century. And Luther matched any Catholic in his devil-mongering. So the late fifteenth and the sixteenth centuries provided an unusually favorable atmosphere for the development of an unprecedented European witch-hunt.

A witch was a person who deliberately sold herself or himself into the service of the devil. A witch served the devil as devoutly as the Christian served God. Witches were supposed to engage in elaborate ceremonies in their devotion to the devil, foremost of which was the fanciful "witches' Sabbath." Here the witches gathered to perform, before his satanic majesty, certain blasphemous and obscene rites, in part a sacrilegious parody on the holy sacraments of the Catholic church.

Most of the ill luck, suffering, and disasters that came to people were attributed to the malevolent intervention of the devil. Hence the fierceness with which men turned upon their human brethren whom they believed to be secretly in the pay of the devil. Moreover, witches were supposed to have carnal intercourse with demons, and hence the purist sentiments of the age encouraged the desire to crush out this particularly odious form of sexual immorality. An Italian Catholic student of demonology, Ludovico Sinistrari, attributed the birth of Plato, Alexander the Great, Merlin and Luther to intercourse between devils and witches. Witches were charged with bringing every kind of misfortune to man—disease and epidemics; droughts; infertility of soil, animals, and human beings; fits and spasms; infidelity; plottings, disloyalty, rebellion, and the like.

One of the first steps in furthering the witchcraft mania was taken in December, 1484, when Pope Innocent VIII launched against the devil and his human servants the famous bull *Summis desiderantes*. In the more than two centuries that separated the papal bull of 1484 from Cotton Mather and the Salem trials in the American colonies, it is estimated by Withington that a quarter of a million persons were put to death for witchcraft—that is, they died under torture or were executed after confession.[34] The bishop of Wurzburg burned 900 witches in a single year. In addition to the hundreds of thousands brutally executed, many millions lived in continuous mortal fear lest they be accused and hideously tortured.

One reason for the amazing spread of the mania was that once a person was accused of witchcraft there was little chance of escape. If one confessed under torture, he was then put to death. Otherwise, he died under torture. Very few survived torture to convince their judges that they were innocent. The tortures were sufficiently ingenious and terrible to make one almost ashamed of belonging to the human race. Any lower form of primate would have bolted in terror from a scene in a torture chamber.

It is often thought that only the lesser, meaner, and more credulous minds of this age took any stock in the witchcraft hypothesis. Such, unfortunately, was not the case. Some of the most learned men of the period defended the witchcraft thesis with a zeal approaching ferocity. This was true of even some who were inclined towards skepticism on general philosophical questions. Jean Bodin was

---

[34] Professor Preserved Smith believes that this estimate of the number put to death is too high; other authorities, however, put the number at a million or more.

one of the outstanding French scholars of the sixteenth century, a leading political scientist, a religious skeptic, and a broad-minded historian. Yet his *Demonology* (1581) was a thorough defense of the superstition and a vicious attack on John Weyer's able exposure of the delusion. An eminent Jesuit scholar, Martin Delrio, produced the most erudite of all apologies for the belief in witchcraft in his *Disquisitions on Magic* (1599). Joseph Glanvill was one of the fathers of English skepticism and free thought,[35] but his *Sadducismus Triumphatus* (1681) was, in the words of Lecky, "probably the ablest book ever written in defense of the superstition." It was a thorough and comprehensive justification of witchcraft. Sir Thomas Browne, the distinguished English savant and physician, and Henry More, the able Cambridge philosopher, both upheld witchcraft and denounced as atheists and blasphemers those who presumed to doubt the delusion. Equally positive on this point was the work of the eminent Protestant divines, William Perkins and Richard Baxter. Baxter's *The Certainty of the World of Spirits* (1691) was one of the most influential and popular works defending the witchcraft superstition. It was widely read in the English colonies, where an eloquent local defense of witchcraft appeared about the same time in Increase Mather's *Wonders of the Invisible World*. John Wesley made a vigorous but unsuccessful attempt to revive the witchcraft illusion, and even in our own day some scholars have mildly supported it. A very learned Anglo-Catholic divine, Montague Summers, wrote two large books on the subject in the 1920's and seemed to credit the reality of witches and witchcraft.

Numerous factors ended the witchcraft epidemic with the approach of the eighteenth century, among them the following: (1) it tended to exhaust itself by its very fury; (2) science undermined its premises; (3) critical writers ridiculed its beliefs and practices; (4) the commercial revolution and other secular influences diverted attention from this crude manifestation of primordial superstition.

Aiding the general trends of the times in discrediting witchcraft were able writings that revealed the absurdities of the delusion. The first of these was John Weyer's *The Deceptions of Demons* (1563). This attacked the witchcraft hypothesis, especially puncturing the idea of the evil potency of old women. But Weyer conceded that professional magicians might work evil spells. One of the most brilliant of the attacks on witchcraft was Reginald Scot's *The Discovery of Witchcraft* (1584), which attempted with much skill and astute reasoning to undermine both witchcraft and magic. In order to obtain toleration for his book in Protestant countries, Scot adroitly tended to blame the mania on Catholics. Less thorough but no less effective was Montaigne's withering *Essay on Witchcraft* (1588). With calm and detached irony he showed how utterly nonsensical the witch persecutions really were. A scholarly and courageous Jesuit, Friedrich Spee, effectively refuted all the arguments of the defenders of witchcraft in his admirable *Cautio criminalis* (*A Note of Caution on Criminal Procedure against Witches*) (1631).

A novel and indirect line of attack, attempting to explode the whole orthodox idea of the devil, was embodied in a work which we have mentioned earlier, that of the enlightened Dutch clergyman, Balthazar Bekker, whose *The Enchanted*

[35] See below, pp. 761-2, 828.

World appeared in 1691. By showing the discrepancies between the views of the devil in scripture and the contradictory ideas of the devil held in post-biblical days, he sought to discredit the whole philosophy of diabolism which underlay the witchcraft delusion. As for witchcraft, he laid it at the door of the pagans and the Catholics. The French skeptic, Pierre Bayle, in his *Reply to the Questions of a Provincial* (1704), denounced witchcraft and praised the skepticism of Holland and Prussia, which he held to be responsible for the disappearance of the delusion in these countries. The most conclusive blow was delivered in Francis Hutcheson's *Historical Essay Concerning Witchcraft* (1718), written when the mania had about run its course. In calm and measured tones, Hutcheson exposed the absurdities of the whole witchcraft complex, and left the strong implication that one who believed it was a subject for contemptuous pity. The journalist and satirist, Daniel Defoe, followed this up with a satire on witchcraft in pamphlets on *The Devil, The Black Art,* and *Apparitions* (1726-27). He held that the acts attributed to the devil are beneath his dignity and concern. He does not bother with instigating old women to petty crimes but gives his attention to tempting kings and misleading nations.

Though written many years ago, the most vivid brief portrayal of the horrors of the witchcraft delusion and of the services of rationalism in rescuing mankind from it, is contained in W. E. H. Lecky's classic *History of the Rise and Influence of the Spirit of Rationalism in Europe:*

It is impossible to leave the history of witchcraft without reflecting how vast an amount of suffering has, in at least this respect, been removed by the progress of a rationalistic civilization. I know that when we remember the frightful calamities that have from time to time flowed from theological divisions; when we consider the countless martyrs who have perished in the dungeon or at the stake, the millions who have fallen in the religious wars, the elements of almost undying dissension that have been planted in so many noble nations and have paralyzed so many glorious enterprises, the fate of a few thousand innocent persons who were burnt alive seems to sink into comparative insignificance.

Yet it is probable that no class of victims endured suffering so unalloyed and so intense. Not for them the wild fanaticism that nerves the soul against danger, and almost steels the body against torments. Not for them the assurance of a glorious eternity, that has made the martyr look with exultation on the rising flame as on the Elijah's chariot that is to bear his soul to heaven. Not for them the solace of lamenting friends, or the consciousness that their memories would be cherished and honoured by posterity. They died alone, hated and unpitied. They were deemed by all mankind the worst of criminals. Their very kinsmen shrank from them as tainted and accursed. The superstitions they had imbibed in childhood, blending with the illusions of age, and with the horrors of their position, persuaded them in many cases that they were indeed the bondslaves of Satan, and were about to exchange their torments upon earth for an agony that was as excruciating, and was eternal. And, besides all this, we have to consider the terrors which the belief must have spread through the people at large; we have to picture the anguish of the mother, as she imagined that it was in the power of one whom she had offended to blast in a moment every object of her affection: we have to conceive, above all, the awful shadow that the dread of accusation must have thrown on the enfeebled faculties of age, and the bitterness it must have added to desertion and to solitude. All these sufferings were the result of a single superstition, which the spirit of Rationalism has destroyed.[36]

XII. THE HANGOVER OF MEDIEVAL INTELLECTUAL INTERESTS IN MODERN TIMES

In the last two chapters we presented many intellectual and institutional developments that challenged the medieval scheme of things and helped to usher in a new era of civilization. Yet we must guard ourselves against the notion that the Middle Ages came to an end in any intellectual sense with Petrarch, Luther, Newton, or even Voltaire. As Professors Lynn Thorndike, Carl Becker, and others have done well to emphasize,[37] there was a very definite hangover of many characteristic medieval intellectual interests well down into modern times.

The mass of mankind remained illiterate until 1800 or later. It still retained the medieval belief in a literal and active supernatural world, whether it belonged to the Catholic or Protestant churches. Medieval superstitions persisted among the peasantry everywhere. Methodist preachers like Lorenzo Dow were setting forth as terrifying doctrines about the devil and his works a century ago as Gregory the Great or any medieval monk ever dreamed of. The Catholic church has come right down into our day with much the same theology it possessed in the age of Aquinas, and with a greatly increased membership. There are many more devout Catholics today than in the time of Dante, in spite of the Protestant defection. Further, the Protestants, as we have just seen, rejected nothing vital in the Christian epic which the fathers had elaborated between Paul and Augustine.

Medieval intellectual interests and attitudes possessed enough momentum to carry them over into modern times. In spite of all his fulminations against scholasticism, Francis Bacon took astrology far more seriously than he did Copernicus or Galileo. We pointed out above the enormous popularity of astrology in the United States in our own day. Alchemy was not seriously jolted until the time of Boyle and Stahl, and the fundamental alchemistic goals of prolonging life and of transmuting the baser metals into gold remained vital human impulses down into the twentieth century. Magicians still abound. It has been estimated by an expert that there are no less than 25,000 professional magicians in New York City alone, who collect at least $25,000,000—a sum about equal to the public income of the Roman Empire—from the gullible annually. The populace, especially in rural areas, still treasures many typically medieval magical devices and conceptions. Magic power in medicine still persists. Bernard Gordon in the Middle Ages was a rather exacting medical scientist compared to some of our own quack doctors.

Political discussion retained its medieval patterns for centuries. Protestant as well as Catholic monarchs presumed to rule by divine right. The claim of absolutism by monarchs was often based in part on the typical doctrines of Roman law which the medieval lawyers had revived and elaborated. Even the great early modern attack upon divine right through the social-contract theory was no more

36 Lecky, op. cit., 2 vols., Appleton, 1897 (Braziller, 1955), I, 152-54.

37 See Lynn Thorndike, "The Survival of Medieval Intellectual Interests into Early Modern Times," Speculum, April 1927; and C. L. Becker, The Heavenly City of the Eighteenth-Century Philosophers, Yale University Press, 1959.

than a development of medieval ideas of popular sovereignty and a governmental contract. The tendency to moralize about the state and politics, a basic medieval trait, still persists among even up-to-date political philosophers. The battle between church and state still goes merrily on. Mussolini and Pius XI disputed in terms that would have been familiar to Philip Augustus and Innocent III. Philip the Fair could understand Herr Hitler. Several great Protestant sects in the United States influence legislation almost as powerfully as the Catholic church did in any medieval monarchy or empire. Censorship of intellectual progress and moral activities by religious interests still persists. The pope in Italy can intimidate moving-picture producers in Hollywood, California, and burlesque magnates in New York City. The divine right of kings has been supplanted by the theory of the divine right of constitutions and the sanctity of courts. The attitude of the average American citizen towards the Supreme Court today is not markedly different from that of the Frenchman of the seventeenth century towards Louis XIV.

Education has never shaken off its characteristically medieval qualities and procedure. Even great "godless" universities have their deans, faculties, examinations, degrees, ritual, and toggery, all of which would have been familiar to Robert de Sorbon at the medieval University of Paris. Teaching methods still often manifest medieval traits. The tutorial system directly apes medieval practices. Natural science was very slow in entering reputable education. Not until the nineteenth century was really adequate scientific instruction offered in universities. Latin long remained the language of scholars. Doctoral dissertations in Latin were common in European universities down to the close of the last century. Diplomas are still written in Latin which the university officers who sign them frequently cannot read. Even some radical trends in contemporary education, like plans for student self-government, hark back to the Middle Ages for historical support and vindication. Under the influence of President Robert Maynard Hutchins and Professor Mortimer J. Adler, of the University of Chicago, a strong effort was made to restore the educational ideals of medieval scholasticism to a dominant place in higher education. Indeed, in an address before the National Catholic Association, President Hutchins accused the Catholic educators of too great moderation in their rendition of scholasticism: "My charge is that Catholic education is not Catholic enough. . . . You have a great tradition to uphold. We have, or think we have, none. The best service Catholic education can perform for the nation and all education is to show that the intellectual tradition can again be made the heart of higher education."

Even rationalism never came to terms with a truly modern point of view. While in revolt against the superstitions and bigotry of Catholicism and Protestantism, it conducted its battles over medieval terms and topics—God, the church, religion, and the like—along typically scholastic lines of argument and disputation, a fact to which Carl Becker has quite properly called our attention.[38]

Medieval economic doctrines have been perpetuated by socially minded Catholic reformers like John A. Ryan, as a curb on the "rugged individualism" of a David Ricardo and a Herbert Hoover. Even economic radicals like the guild

---

[38] C. L. Becker, *The Heavenly City of the Eighteenth-Century Philosophers.*

socialists sought inspiration in the workers' corporations of the medieval period. There was, then, no sharp break or clear hiatus between the medieval and the modern period. The great fact of the continuity of history has never been more forcefully exhibited than in the intellectual record of a considerable section of mankind from Erasmus to Irving Babbitt.

SELECTED READINGS

Bainton, R. H., *Here I Stand: A Biography of Martin Luther*, Abingdon, 1950.

——— *The Reformation of the Sixteenth Century*, Beacon Press, 1952.

Beard, Charles, *The Reformation of the Sixteenth Century*, Ann Arbor Books, 1962.

Dunning, *History of Political Theories: Ancient and Medieval*, chap. xi.

———*History of Political Theories from Luther to Montesquieu*, Macmillan, 1905.

Durant, Will, *The Reformation*, Simon and Schuster, 1957.

———*The Renaissance*, Simon and Schuster, 1953.

Ferguson, W. K., *The Renaissance in Historical Thought*, Houghton Mifflin, 1948.

Fife, R. H., *The Revolt of Martin Luther*, Columbia University Press, 1957.

Flick, *The Decline of the Medieval Church*, Vol. II, Part IV.

Gilmore, M. P., *The World of Humanism*, Harper, 1952.

Graves, F. P., *A History of Education during the Middle Ages and Its Transition to Modern Times*, Macmillan, 1925.

Harkness, G. E., *John Calvin: The Man and His Ethics*, Abingdon.

Höffding, Harald, *History of Modern Philosophy*, 2 Vols., Dover, 1955, Vol. I.

Hole, Christina, *Witchcraft in England*, Scribner, 1947.

Hunter, Dard, *Paper-making*, Knopf, 1943.

Hyma, *The Christian Renaissance*.

Janelle, Pierre, *The Catholic Reformation*, Bruce Publishing Co., 1949.

Kittredge, G. L., *Witchcraft in Old and New England*, Russell, 1958.

Lea, H. C., Howland, A. C., and Burr, G. L., *Materials Towards a History of Witchcraft*, 3 Vols., Yoseloff.

Lindsay, T. M., *History of the Reformation*, 2 Vols., Scribner, 1928.

Lipsky, Abram, *God's Angry Man*, Stokes, 1933.

Manschreck, C. L., *Melanchton: The Quiet Reformer*, Abingdon Press, 1958.

McMurtrie, D. C., *The Book*, Oxford University Press, 1943.

McNeill, J. T., *The History and Character of Calvinism*, Oxford University Press, 1954.

Schevill, Ferdinand, *A History of Florence*, Ungar, 1961.

——— *The Medici*, Peter Smith, 1960.

———*Siena*, Scribner, 1909.

Sellery, G. C., *The Renaissance*, University of Wisconsin Press, 1950.

Singer, *The Story of Living Things*, chaps. iii-iv.

Smith, Preserved, *The Age of the Reformation*, Collier Books.

——— *Erasmus*, Dover Publications, Inc., 1962.

——— *A History of Modern Culture*, 2 Vols., Collier Books, Vol. I.

Tawney, R. H., *Religion and the Rise of Capitalism*, New American Library.

Taylor, *Thought and Expression in the Sixteenth Century*.

Thompson, *History of Historical Writing*, Book V.

Thorndike, Lynn, *A History of Magic and Experimental Science: The Sixteenth Century*, 2 Vols., Columbia University Press, 1941.

Tillmans, W. G., *The World and the Men around Luther*, Augsburg Publishing House, 1959.

Troeltsch, Ernst, *Protestantism and Progress*, Beacon.

Weber, Max, *The Protestant Ethic and the Spirit of Capitalism*, Scribner, 1948.

Whitfield, J. H., *Machiavelli*, Blackwell, 1947.

XIV

Literature, Art,
and Music
1450-1600

I. THE RISE OF NATIONAL LITERATURE

1. *Early Prose and Lyric Poetry*

After living thirty-five years on the Continent, William Caxton (1422?-1491) returned to England and established the first English printing press at Westminster in 1476. Between the following year and his death he printed nearly eighty books. The importance to English literature of the introduction of printing can hardly be overestimated, but Caxton's reputation does not rest entirely on his fame as a printer. Many of the books he printed were his own translations from the French, and as a translator he contributed to the formation of fifteenth-century English prose style. No translation of his, however, has so great an influence on literature as a book he printed in 1485, *Le Morte d'Arthur* (*The Death of Arthur*), by Sir Thomas Malory (d. 1471). Malory, Knight of Newbold Revel and a retainer of the Earl of Warwick, had begun his crowded career with service in the French wars. He returned to England, was a member of Parliament, and if the records of his life from then on are to be believed, he seems to have spent almost all the rest of his days under arrest. Larceny and jailbreaking are a few of the crimes of which he was accused. And although the record of his life is too lurid to be entirely credible, it is true that he spent several years in Newgate Prison in not uncomfortable confinement. Across the street from the prison was the library of Grey Friars, and Malory was permitted the use of it. His great work, like some later English books, was written in prison.

The *Morte d'Arthur* is a compilation of medieval romances. In twenty-one books it tells the story of King Arthur and the Round Table, of Lancelot, Tristram, Merlin, and others. Sometimes called the first English novel, it lacks the consistency of plot and character a novel requires. It is a rich store of loosely

connected episodes in which, as we read, the main characters emerge into prominence. Although it is one of the most romantic of books, there is no faintness, no
mistiness or symbolism in it. Its vigorous, quick, decisive, colorful writing is the
best English prose that had yet been written; in fact, there is not much later
English prose that excels Malory in descriptive power:

> As for that, said Sir Launcelot, come not too nigh, for an thou do, wit thou well
> I will slay thee. And when the knight of the pavilion saw that, he started back-
> ward within the pavilion. And then the dwarf armed him lightly; and so the
> knight thought by force and might to take the sword from Sir Launcelot, and so
> he came stepping out; and when Sir Launcelot saw him come so all armed with
> his sword in his hand, then Sir Launcelot flew to him with such a might, and
> hit him upon the helm such a buffet, that the stroke troubled his brains, and
> therewith the sword brake in three. And the knight fell to earth as he had been
> dead, the blood brasting out of his mouth, the nose, and the ears. And then Sir
> Launcelot ran into the pavilion and rushed even into the warm bed; and there
> was a lady in that bed, and she gat her smock, and ran out of the pavilion. And
> when she saw her lord lie at the ground like to be dead, then she cried and wept
> as she had been mad. [Book XII, chapter 1]

It is easy to see why this story of action, at once quaint and vigorous, is still
popular after four and a half centuries.

Written at the end of the Middle Ages, the *Morte d'Arthur* is the final record
of their departing glory, the chivalric ideal. The men for whom the medieval
romances were written resembled their romantic heroes only very little. The
chivalric ideal was only an ideal, perhaps an illusion, but the illusions of an
epoch are an important part of its history. In the next century men aspired to
different things and had other illusions. One of the most potent forces in creating the culture of the next century was the classical studies of the "Oxford Reformers," men like Sir Thomas More and Erasmus, who knew the thought and
languages of the ancient world and through whom the intellectual vigor of
Greece was brought to Tudor England. All of them scholars to whom scholarship was a vital matter, they carried their scholarship into the affairs of the world.

Sir Thomas More (1478-1535) entered Parliament in 1504, succeeded Wolsey
as Lord Chancellor in 1529, and resigned the chancellorship in 1532 because as
a good Catholic he could not agree to the divorce of King Henry VIII and
Catherine of Aragon. He did not love life as well as he loved his church. He
had a saying that a man might "lose his head and have no harm." More's honesty,
in conflict with Henry's determination to separate England from the Church of
Rome, cost him his head. As he was ascending the scaffold he tripped, and
turning to an attendant he said, "I pray you, Master Lieutenant, see me safe up,
and for coming down let me shift for myself." It was characteristic of him to
refuse to sacrifice his principles to save his life, and to jest on the scaffold.

More did not die simply for the church; the forces which led to his execution
were complex. Henry broke with the church because he wanted a divorce, but
he could not have marshaled the powers of England against the pope if England
had not been beginning to feel its power as a nation. The rising tide of national-

ism was with Henry; to it More was opposed. He stood for the Catholic inter-
nationalism of medieval Europe. More's *Utopia* (1515-1516) was not intended as
his picture of an ideal state; it is an imaginary country created to satirize the
vices of European states. In this sense it is a companion to the lands that Gulliver
visited (*Gulliver's Travels*) and Samuel Butler's *Erewhon.* More describes an
island where the inhabitants hate war, where iron is the precious metal "because
it is useful," where men work six hours a day, and enjoy religious toleration.
The law of the island is communistic. This all sounds more modern than it is.
Although in the present world crisis communism and Catholicism are opposed,
they have at least one thing in common—discipline is the essence of each, as it
was of More. In the island of Utopia men are compelled to submit to the law.
More's Utopia is based on the four heathen virtues: Wisdom, Fortitude, Tem-
perance, and Justice. Though dear to More, the Christian virtues of Faith, Hope,
and Charity have no part in the life of the island because More was satirizing
Christian states through the exaltation of heathen virtue. For some of the material used in writing the *Utopia* More is indebted to Plato's *Republic.* The book,
written in Latin, was not translated until 1551.

No one at this time was more keenly aware of the abuses within the church
than Erasmus (1466-1536), an Augustinian monk, and no one more earnestly
attempted to reform them. In one of his satiric dialogues, *Pilgrimage for Religion's
Sake,* he directs his vigorous satire against the misguided veneration of spurious
relics. In all his life and writings, Erasmus, a Dutch humanist and fellow in the
international world of the mind, was the sworn enemy of ignorance and folly.
He made a new Latin version (*Novum Instrumentum*) of the New Testament.
At the suggestion of his friend, Sir Thomas More, he wrote *Encomium Moriae*
(*In Praise of Folly*), a satiric attack on church dignitaries. Always aware of
human vanity, he "still taught the people knowledge." He studied and taught
at Cambridge and Oxford, and throughout Europe. Though opposed to the
abuses of the church, he would not become a Protestant. His was the difficult
position of the liberal: he wanted to keep what he thought good in both the old
and the new.

In France the new learning found its most vigorous expression in the works of
François Rabelais (1490?-1553), the foremost of French satirists. More and
Erasmus live chiefly through their influence as men (More was canonized in
1935), Rabelais through his eminence as a writer. Educated in the church, he
fell into disfavor because of his continued study of Greek, and he forsook his
studies for the priesthood to become a physician at Lyon, near Geneva, which
was the center of Protestantism. In 1536 John Calvin, having completed his *Institutes of the Christian Religion* in the preceding year, settled at Geneva, and
in France the religious reformation's sharpest struggle was at hand. The issues
became clear cut; one had to be a Protestant with Calvin or a Catholic with the
French king. Rabelais found it increasingly difficult to maintain his liberal position. In *Gargantua* (1535) and *Pantagruel* (1533) he had invented a dynasty of
giant kings (Grandgousier, Gargantua, and Pantagruel), and had used them
to satirize systems of education, the law, and the ignorance, vice, and intolerance

of the clergy. He knew what he did not like, but he was not to be satisfied with any system. He loved life in its entirety, the life of the body and the mind, and all its acts; and he had expressed his love of life in his extraordinarily rich vocabulary and with a coarse, healthy, extravagant humor. His exultant animalism was as offensive to the Protestants as his satire to the Catholics. Preferring residence in France and the favor of the Catholic authorities, Rabelais compromised: he expurgated his works.

The modern student to whom Latin or Greek sometimes seems a strange and elaborate exercise designed to train his mind, must remember that the writers of the fifteenth and sixteenth century, dissatisfied with current literature and hungry for something better, turned to the study of the classics because they could give what their own literature could no longer provide: a more exciting intellectual life, models for imitation, a nobler and more inclusive theory of literature. They wanted the acts of men, as recorded in literature, to provide in part the instruction the church had given in the Middle Ages. Brought up in the humanist tradition, Sir Philip Sidney (1554-1586), in his *A Defense of Poesie,* stated his belief in the power of poetry to instruct; the power of the poet in "the winning of the mind from wickedness to virtue." In the same essay he says that "among the Romans a Poet was called a *Vates,* which is as much as a Diviner, Foreseer, or Prophet," and he speaks of poetry as a "light giver to ignorance." This is a departure from the medieval tradition and a return to the thought of the ancient world.

To the humanists learning was not a matter of the cloister or the study; they made it an essential part of all their acts. Expressed in terms of literature it meant the creation of a new literature to compare with the literatures of Greece and Rome. The humanist movement had begun in Italy, and it is in Italian literature that it flowered first. Petrarch's Italian sonnets had delighted the men of his own century and every century since, and although he realized that he wrote better in Italian than in Latin, he still thought Latin the language of greatest permanent interest and worth. With the men of his time he held that poetry intended to endure should be written in Latin. But a change in this way of thinking was at hand, and when, a century after Petrarch's death, Cardinal Bembo (1470-1547) advised Ludovico Ariosto (1474-1533) to write in Latin, Ariosto replied that he would rather be first among Tuscan poets than second among Latinists. By the close of the fifteenth century imitations of Vergil had been done as well as they could be done, and sixteenth-century poets had to try something else. Ariosto wrote his *Orlando Furioso,* the greatest of Italian romantic epics, in Italian.

The new poets, inspired by the rising nationalism and their studies of the classics, wanted to create a vernacular literature which would rival the classics. This new literature came first in Italy, for there it had only the tradition of classical imitation to oppose. Ariosto pointed the way, and criticism followed it. In 1543 Sperone Speroni, in his *Dialogo delle lingue (Dialogue on Language),* defended the use of Italian on the ground that languages are not by nature fit or unfit for use in poetry. They are created by man and can be *made to express* man's conceptions. This theory implied the deliberate creation of a literary language which would convey to the reader the beauty the poet conceived. This idea found its way to France and was taken up by a group of French poets known as the Pléiade, of whom Joachim du Bellay (1522-1560) and Pierre de Ronsard (1524-1585) were the most important.

The civilization which the word "medieval" calls to our mind is the civilization of France and England, northern and western Europe as opposed to Italy and the South. In France the medieval tradition in literature, which had produced such poems as the *Romance of the Rose,* was strongest. Clément Marot (1495-1544), the most important sixteenth-century French poet before Ronsard, was writing largely in the medieval tradition, and to this tradition the poets of the Pléiade were opposed; they preferred to copy the ancients in style and subject matter. In their break with tradition they were encouraged by the success of Italian vernacu- lar poetry. In a treatise entitled *La Deffence et Illustration de la Langue Françoyse (A Defense and Illustration of the French Language)* du Bellay re- peated the arguments for the use of the vernacular advanced by Speroni and added the argument of nationalism; that the creation of a new literature would serve the greater glory of France. It was part of his program to enrich the French language with words both borrowed from other languages and built from French roots. And he put his theory into practice in composing his sonnets.

The poets of the Pléiade differed from their predecessors in many ways, one of the most important being that the Pléiade was a school, a group of men work- ing together to achieve the same ends. Conscious of the dignity of their calling, they disdained the familiar tone of Marot's poetry and the more bitter, vulgar beauty of Villon's. To them poetry was a religion and they were its priests. Like Matthew Arnold in a later age, they did not always understand the difference between seriousness and solemnity. They could write with delicacy and wit, as in du Bellay's matchless epitaph on his dog; but essentially they were grave literary reformers, and like other men of principle they paid for their reforms by a partial sacrifice of spontaneity. To write learned poetry of the sort they admired re- quired training and scholarship. One of the results of their learning was the in- vention of many new poetic forms and the revival of forms not then in use. Their most important technical achievement was the rehabilitation of the alexandrine, the rhymed couplet composed of six-foot iambic lines, which, through their influ- ence, has been the dominant metrical form in French poetry ever since. Another result of their scholarship is their sometimes excessive use of erudition. This is especially true of *La Franciade* (1572), by Ronsard, in which the poet permits his knowledge to stifle his inspiration. But in his shorter pieces Ronsard has no su- perior in all French literature.

In his youth Ronsard was attached to the court as a page of the dauphin's. En- dowed with the graces that a life at court required, he looked forward to a dip- lomatic career, but a physical misfortune forced him to change his plans. He be- came hard of hearing and turned to the serious study of good books. At first he studied alone, then at the college of Paris; and when, later, du Bellay joined him in his studies, they formulated the beginnings of the Pléiade. The enthusiasm which greeted the publication of his *Odes* and *Amours* was universal. He was called, with justice, "the Prince of French Poets." He won the admiration of Europe and the generous favor of three successive kings, Henry II, Charles IX, and Henry III. He is a reflective poet of love and nature, deeply aware of physical beauty, poignantly knowing that beauty fades. Such knowledge is, of course, common to all poets and is the subject matter of poetry everywhere. But Ronsard's treatment is especially characteristic of the poetry of his times.

His favorite contemporary poet was Ariosto, and of all Ariosto's poetry the passage he imitated most often was the description of Alcina from the seventh book of *Orlando Furioso*. The English translation by Sir John Harington (1561-1612) does not do justice to Ariosto's lines:

> A shape whose like in wax 'twere hard to frame,
> Or to express by skill of painters rare,
> Her hair was long, and yellow to the same,
> As might with wires of beaten gold compare:
> Her lovely cheeks with show of modest shame,
> With roses and with lillies painted are,
> Her forehead fair and full of seemly cheer,
> As smooth as polished ivory doth appear.

Note this woman well; she is the sixteenth-century ideal of feminine beauty—golden hair, skin like ivory, cheeks like roses. First made popular through the sonnets of Petrarch, by the sixteenth century she had found her way into almost every love poem written in Italy, France, and England. Of course, there are some striking exceptions, but by and large the women to whom the poets wrote had a close resemblance to Petrarch's Laura and were described in the same terms. In the sonnet of the Petrarchan tradition the lover is ardent, the lady is fair and chaste. He protests passion; she affects disdain. She has little in common with the heroines of the love poems of Rome or of seventeenth-century Europe, and is not so much a woman as the poet's ideal of womanhood; but real or not, she is the typical heroine of the sixteenth-century sonnet. At that time almost everyone of any literary pretensions whatever wrote sonnets, and since most of these writers might better have been doing other things, there were hundreds of sonnets written over this formula which are as dead as a sonnet can be. But because many bad poets wrote sonnets, we must not conclude that all sonnets are, as many books say, "conventional," or that the sonneteers never meant what they said.

Its fixed length, fourteen lines, makes it impossible for the sonnet to achieve what longer poems achieve, but is just great enough to make it the perfect form for the expression of one idea, the creation of a single mood, or the elaboration of an image. Its fixed form and rhyme scheme demand great technical skill. There must be concentration without waste. In short, there is a double restriction on the use of the sonnet: First, not every poetic idea can be adequately expressed in the sonnet form; and, second, a poet without considerable technical skill had better not attempt the sonnet. Yet within these limitations the sonnet is a perfect medium, which no one was ever better fitted to use than Ronsard. Through his study of foreign literatures and his experience in using intricate forms he had acquired a technical mastery, and his seriousness and dignity was perfectly adapted to the sonnet form. The sonnet beginning "Quand vous serez bien vieille, au soir, à la chandelle" (When you are very old, at evening, by the candle light) defies translation. No English version of it can give the reader an adequate impression of Ronsard's genius. Addressed to the woman he loves, it describes the time in years to come when he will be dead, and she, very old, sitting in the candle light, will regret that she refused the love she might have now. This is in the Petrarchan tradition, and although the tradition produced hundreds of extremely bad poems, a single poem like this one can justify its existence.

Ronsard's sonnets were published in three volumes: *Amours à Cassandre* (1552), *Amours à Marie* (1557), and *Amours à Hélène* (1574). In their joy in life's brief pleasures and their mood of tender regret for the passing of youth and beauty, their sobriety and quiet dignity, and their idealization of love, they stand in sharp contrast to the poems of Villon, who wrote in the tradition of the Middle Ages.

When, in the second half of the sixteenth century, the movement for the creation of a new vernacular poetry reached England, the English profited by the experience of Italy and France. The most important figure in this movement in England was Edmund Spenser (1552?-1599). Unlike the Pléiade, however, Spenser did not have to oppose the defenders of a medieval tradition. The greatest English poet before him had been Chaucer, and Spenser imitated him as Ronsard had not imitated earlier French poets. The English poetic tradition is, therefore, more continuous than the French. There is a reason for the wider contemporary acceptance of the new poetry in England: the movement reached England later than France, and there had been time to prepare for it. In the beginning of the century Erasmus and More had brought a vigorous humanism to England, and two poets, Wyatt and Surrey, had introduced the poetry of the Petrarchan tradition.

Sir Thomas Wyatt (1503?-1542) and Henry Howard, Earl of Surrey (1517?-1547), courtiers who had served Henry VIII on the Continent, became interested in the poetry of Petrarch and, on their return to England, wrote imitations of him. Some of their poems, along with those of other writers, were published in an anthology called *Tottel's Miscellany* (1557), which became immediately popular and went through ten editions in the next thirty years. Some of the poems, especially Wyatt's, are translations of Petrarch, and many lean heavily on Latin poets such as Ovid and Horace. Although there is some excellent poetry in the volume, the importance of the *Miscellany* is largely historical. The English language had changed greatly since the time of Chaucer; modern English had come into being, and it had produced no poetry of exceptional merit. It was the glory of the *Miscellany* that it pointed the way to the creation of important poetry in modern English. It established an immediate connection between modern English poetry and the poetry of Italy and ancient Rome, and its success brought about the popularity of many of the verse forms it used, chiefly blank verse and the Shakespearean sonnet. We shall return to these forms later.

The poets of the Pléiade had defended the French language not on the grounds of what had been accomplished in it but on its possibilities. In England Richard Mulcaster (1530?-1611) in *The Elementarie* (1582) advanced the same arguments: "I love *Rome*, but *London* better; I favor *Italy*, but *England* more; I honor the *Latin*, but I worship the *English*." This love of the Englishman for his language is part of the devotion to England and all things English which grew as England developed into a world power in the sixteenth century. The patriotic impulse was a source of power in the creation of a national literature. The humanism which had come at the beginning of the century had been assimilated; it no longer controlled the writers with the tyranny of the new; it could be modified and used. The desire for a new literature had come to England more slowly, and there was, therefore, no new school of writers opposed to the old, as in France. But there was the same work to be done. A literature which would stand beside that of the ancients required learning and a literary language.

For all practical purposes style may be defined as a writer's way of saying things. And any reader of the poetry between Chaucer and Spenser can readily see that its greatest lack is its weakness of style. If a man is to write noble poetry he must state noble concepts in noble terms. Wyatt, for instance, had taken his notion of what a love poem ought to be from Petrarch; he had therefore the ideas for good sonnets, but he lacked the means of expressing them. Now, it was a fundamental precept with the poets of the Pléiade that if a poet lacked a beautiful and fluid means of expression, he could, by hard labor, create that means. This, Spenser set out to do. He trained himself by translations from foreign languages; he created new verse forms; and he introduced new and poetic words into the language. Some of the new words he invented; some he took from foreign languages; and some long-forgotten words he found in older English writers such as Chaucer and Malory. With these he created a new language of poetry. Ben Jonson, who had more austere tastes, said in later years that Spenser "writ no language." It may be that Spenser was a little prodigal in bestowing these new beauties on his poetry, but we must remember that he was a pioneer in an age which has become noted for its extravagance.

With the publication of Spenser's *Shepherd's Calendar* in 1579, the new poetry for which England had been hoping arrived. Webbe, in his *Discourse of English Poetry* (1586), proclaimed Spenser "the rightest English Poet that I ever read"; other critics were less temperate in their praise. The *Calendar,* a series of twelve poems (one for each month) called eclogues, was written in the pastoral tradition which derives from Theocritus, a Syracusan poet of the third century B.C. Into it Spenser has worked the poetic devices of classical and contemporary poets, especially the French, but the *Calendar* is not simply a collection of importations. Suiting the manner to the subject, Spenser has worked into the vocabulary much homespun English idiom, and he has given the characters rustic English names. If the *Calendar* is no longer popular, it is because Spenser himself was later to write much greater poems whose worth overshadowed his earlier work. Of the twelve eclogues which compose the poem, *October* is best known because it is an early indication of the quality of the poetry Spenser was to write later. We shall quote a stanza from it:

> But ah, Mecaenus is *yclad* in claye,
> And great Augustus long *ygoe* is dead:
> And all the worthies *liggen* [lie] wrapt in lead,
> That matter made for Poets on to play:
> For ever, who in *derring doe* were dreade,
> The loftie verse of *hem* was loved aye.

The words in italics are archaic words which Spenser revived for their poetic effect.

Of Spenser's shorter poems, the *Prothalamion* (a betrothal hymn) and the *Epithalamion* (a marriage hymn) are the most excellent and the best known. The latter, probably written by Spenser in 1594 in celebration of his own marriage, was published in 1595 at the end of a series of sonnets called the *Amoretti*. His sonnets are not among his most distinguished works. They were written in the last decade of the sixteenth century when the fashion for writing sonnets was at its height in England. Then, as in Italy, everyone who wrote poetry at all wrote sonnets. And every English gentleman wrote a little poetry; to be able to turn out some verses now and then was one of the marks of being a gentleman. A man did not necessarily write sonnets with any thought of publishing them. He wrote a sonnet and sent it to a friend. It might serve as a verse epistle, and in any case it was evidence of the writer's accomplishments. These poems, especially if they were the work of a distinguished writer, were likely to be copied by friends of the person who received them, and so it happened that in fashionable circles unprinted poems circulated in manuscript. Manuscript copies of Shakespeare's sonnets are known to have been "among his private friends" in 1598. It was not until 1609 that these sonnets came to the hands of a publisher, Thomas Thorpe, who printed them without Shakespeare's permission. Since Shakespeare had nothing whatever to do with the publication of his sonnets, it is very likely that they are not printed in their proper order, and we cannot be sure that the story they tell is the story Shakespeare wanted them to tell, if, indeed, they were intended to tell a story at all. Many scholars have attempted to restore Shakespeare's sonnets to their proper order, but there seems to be no way in which this can be done with certainty. Although this confusion is due to the somewhat irregular business methods of the publisher, we should not censure Thorpe too harshly. If he had not published them illegally, they might never have been printed at all.

One of the best of Elizabethan sonnet sequences, the *Astrophel and Stella* of Sir Philip Sidney, was not printed until 1591, five years after the author's death. In his sonnets Sidney, the author of the *Arcadia* and one of the most famous of Elizabethan courtiers, tells of his love for Penelope Devereux, who, in 1580, had been married against her will to Lord Rich. Sir Philip was the soul of honor, and the idealized love his sonnets tell is a love hopeless of fulfillment. The situation being parallel to the one under which Petrarch wrote his sonnets to Laura, the sequence falls readily into the Petrarchan tradition. Again the lover is ardent, the lady fair and cold:

With how sad steps O moon thou climb'st the skies,
How silently and with how mean a face,
What may it be that even in heavenly place,
That busy archer his sharp arrows tries?
Sure if that long with love acquainted eyes
Can judge of love, thou feelst of lovers case,
I read within thy looks thy languisht grace.
To me that feel the like, my state descries.
Then even of fellowship O moon, tell me,
Is constant love deemed there but want of wit?
Are beauties there, as proud as here they be?
Do they above love to be lov'd, and yet
Those lovers scorn, whom that love doth possess?
Do they call virtue there ungratefulness?

Not all of Sidney's sonnets are of this high order of poetry. Sometimes his protestations of love are empty of passion, and there remains only the poet's posturing and the devices of the fashionable lingo of the day. The second of four sonnets "made when his lady had pain in her face," probably a toothache, was intended for a pretty compliment:

Wo, wo, to me, on me returne the smart:
My burning tongue hath bred my mistresse paine,
For oft in pain to pain my painful heart
With her due praise did of my state complain.
I praised her eyes, whom never chance doth move,
Her breath, which makes a sour answer sweete,
Her milken breasts the nurse of childlike love,
Her lege (O legs) her aye well stepping feet.

There is more of this, but doubtless this is enough. It is such stuff that Shakespeare (1564-1616) had in mind when he wrote his sonnets to the Dark Lady, who is neither fair nor chaste. She is, in fact, everything that the popular heroines of the sonnets are not:

My mistress' eyes are nothing like the sun;
Coral is far more red than her lips' red:
If snow be white, why then her breasts are dun;
If hairs be wires, black wires grow on her head.
I have seen roses damask'd red and white,
But no such roses see I in her cheeks;
And in some perfumes is there more delight
Than in the breath that from my mistress reeks.
I love to hear her speak, yet well I know
That music hath a far more pleasing sound:
I grant I never saw a goddess go;
My mistress, when she walks, treads on the ground:
And yet, by heaven, I think my love as rare
As any she belied by false compare.

It is as though Shakespeare, tired of the fashionable heroines, had resolved to create a heroine of a completely different sort. On the other hand, it may well be that she was a real woman.

Shakespeare's 154 sonnets fall roughly into two groups: the first 126 are addressed to a friend whose identity is unknown, the rest, except the last two, are addressed to the Dark Lady. There is no better poetry anywhere than in some of the sonnets of the first group, and no poem is a finer tribute to true friendship, "the marriage of true minds," than sonnet 116:

> Let me not to the marriage of true minds
> Admit impediments. Love is not love
> Which alters when it alteration finds,
> Or bends with the remover to remove;
> O, no! it is an ever-fixed mark
> That looks on tempests and is never shaken;
> It is the star to every wandering bark,
> Whose worth's unknown, although his height be taken.
> Love's not Time's fool, though rosy lips and cheeks
> Within his bending sickle's compass come;
> Love alters not with his brief hours and weeks,
> But bears it out even to the edge of doom.
> If this be error and upon me prov'd,
> I never writ, nor no man ever loved.

This splendid bit of truth and poetry is also, technically, a perfect example of the Shakespearean sonnet, a form invented by Henry Howard, Earl of Surrey, but named after Shakespeare because he used it best. Surrey, finding the Italian sonnet too difficult to write, simplified his task. Instead of dividing the sonnet into two parts, the octave and the sestet, he divided it into four parts, three quatrains and a couplet. A quatrain is four lines of rhyming verse, a couplet two. In the Shakespearean sonnet each quatrain is devoted to the development of one idea, or of one aspect of the main idea of the poem. The concluding couplet summarizes the idea and gives it definite application.

Shakespeare sometimes seems to have been an impatient writer and not to have done his best. Now and then he begins an idea and does not follow it through, and very often he mars a poem by playing with words. One sonnet, number 104, begins,

> To me, fair friend, you never can be old,
> For as you were when first your eye I eyed. . . .

The miserable puns at the end of the second line mar an otherwise beautiful poem. But these puns were not intended as humor. We may be very certain that when Shakespeare wrote them, he thought to himself, "That's good." As we have said, the Elizabethans loved their native language, and they deliberately created as many beauties with it as they could, ornamenting their poetry and prose with verbal devices. Some of these went out of fashion very quickly, among them the serious, ornamental pun. Shakespeare himself did not play with words as much as some of his contemporaries. For instance, there is nothing in Shakespeare quite as bad as the line quoted from Sidney: "For oft in pain to pain my painful heart." In all truth it must be said that the same enthusiasm for words which brought about the puns also called into being much of the finest poetry of the sixteenth century.

After a time ornate poetry, whether good or bad, fell out of favor, and a simpler, more direct poetic style came into prominence. The leader of this new school of poets, and its most distinguished and influential member, was Ben Jonson (1573-1637), whose best-known lyric has a directness and deceptive simplicity which many people have imitated with only partial success. Notice how closely the words follow their normal prose order.

> Drink to me only with thine eyes,
> And I will pledge with mine;
> Or leave a kiss but in the cup,
> And I'll not ask for wine.
> The thirst that from the soul doth rise
> Doth ask a drink divine;
> But might I of Jove's nectar sup,
> I would not change for thine.
>
> I sent thee late a rosy wreath,
> Not so much honoring thee,
> As giving it a hope that there
> It could not honored be,
> But thou thereon didst only breathe,
> And send'st it back to me,
> Since when it grows and smells, I swear,
> Not of itself, but thee.

Here Jonson displays complete mastery of his medium. The poem has every formal excellence which the early sixteenth-century poets, like Wyatt, lacked. It shows the care and precision on the part of the writer that we often look for in vain when reading Shakespeare. Perfect as the poem is, it moves the reader by its beauty rather than its passion. The poem is typical of the seventeenth- rather than the sixteenth-century English lyric.

A poet, scholar, critic, dramatist, an eminent man, Jonson exercised a powerful influence over the younger writers of his day. He had little in common with the writers of the Petrarchan tradition, his tastes leading him to the poets of Greece and Rome, on whose work he modeled his own. In his time the type of poetry introduced by Spenser was superseded in the public favor by his own writing and that of his imitators. He established a literary tradition which persisted for almost two centuries. Of his immediate successors, Robert Herrick (1591-1674) is the most distinguished and the one to follow his example most closely. After a time the interest in Spenser revived, and both Spenser and Jonson continue to influence English poetry to the present day.

2. Romantic Epic

Although literature has nothing finer than some of the lyrics of the sixteenth century, the poets of that era did not think their function could be fulfilled by the composition of short poems. "What poet ever lived," asks the contemporary American poet Archibald MacLeish, "who was really satisfied with writing the thin little books to lie on the front parlor tables?" Greece had her Homer, Rome her Vergil, and if the new poetry was to rival the ancients, it had to have epics to place beside the *Iliad* and the *Aeneid*. An epic poem must have an epic hero and sing of heroic deeds. The poets found their heroes in the legends of the age of chivalry and in historic characters of their own time. The Portuguese poet Camoens (Luis de Camoens, 1525-1580) wrote *Os Lusiadas* (the *Lusiad,* 1572) about the descendants of the legendary hero of Portugal, Lusus, and Vasco da Gama (1469-1524), the Portuguese navigator who was the first to sail around the Cape of Good Hope to India. This was the age of adventure, both physical and intellectual. The humanists had rediscovered the world of the ancients; the navigators had brought the news that the world was twice as large as anyone had imagined, that it had another side filled with strange lands and peoples and inestimable riches. To a writer of epics a voyager to this new world was a perfect hero. The writers of Italian epics, Ludovico Ariosto (1474-1533) and Torquato Tasso (1544-1595), found the matter for their poems in the legends of the crusades. In *Orlando Furioso* (published in its final form in 1532), Ariosto tells of Orlando, chief of the Paladins, whose madness, although it gives the poem its name, is not its chief action. In *Gerusalemme Liberata* (*Jerusalem Delivered,* 1581, revised 1593) Tasso recounts the heroic deeds of Godefroi de Bouillon, the leader of the Christian forces besieging Jerusalem. In England, where the nationalistic spirit was stronger than in Italy, Spenser dedicated *The Faery Queen* to the greater glory of his monarch, Elizabeth, "to live with the eternity of her fame."

The Faery Queen is a collection of stories from many sources rather loosely connected with a central story of King Arthur and Gloriana, an allegorical representation of Queen Elizabeth. Spenser planned a poem in twelve books, but he lived to complete only six. Books one to three were published in 1589, four to six in 1596. All of Spenser's earlier poems were preparation for this great work. The supreme English literary artist of his day was not content with writing poetry which excelled only as poetry. He did not think of literature as a "superior amusement." To him, as to Sidney, it was also a source of instruction. He wanted to write of heroes whose actions would stand as models for imitation and through whom he could help to "fashion a gentleman or noble person in virtuous and gentle discipline." This is the primary moral purpose of the poem. Milton thought that through his poems Spenser was one of the best teachers the world has produced, better, even, than St. Thomas Aquinas.

The changes instituted in England by the political, religious, and economic reforms of the reign of Henry VIII began to show their full effect during the reign of Elizabeth. Some of these effects were the rise to prominence of a number of newly rich families and their consequent struggle for prestige and position at court. Never was there more need for a "book of manners" to teach gentlemen what they should be. Caught up in this world of intrigue, Spenser, himself a seeker for preferment which never came, longed for the more honest days of the past. In *The Faery Queen* he re-created these days of heroic battle and antique glory, and he takes us to a land of knights and ladies, jousts and tourneys. A land which never was, it serves all the better to show how men might be.

The reader must not suppose that because it is a moral book *The Faery Queen* approaches even in a small way the austerity of other moral books such as *Pilgrim's Progress*. Spenser was an Elizabethan, and the Elizabethans loved splendor and the delights of the senses. When he closes the book, the reader of *The Faery Queen* remembers chiefly its beauty, the simpler beauty of Spenser's images of nature, or the more gorgeous sensuousness of the following stanza from Spenser's retelling of the Venus and Adonis story:

> And whilst he slept, she over him would spread
> Her mantle, color'd like the starry skies,
> And her soft arm lay underneath his head,
> And with ambrosial kisses bathe his eyes;
> And whilst he bath'd, with her two crafty spies,
> She secretly would search each dainty limb,
> And throw into the well sweet rosemarys,
> And fragrant violets, and pansies trim,
> And ever with sweet nectar did she sprinkle him.

The verse form which Spenser uses in this poem is his own invention, the Spenserian stanza, consisting of nine iambic lines rhymed a-b-a-b-b-c-b-c-c. The first eight lines are pentameter, the last, one foot longer, is hexameter. Two of the poets Spenser read and from whom he took some of the material he used in *The Faery Queen* are Ariosto and Tasso.

Ariosto was not a man of Spenser's moral earnestness. Like Spenser he tells a story of the age of chivalry, of the deeds of Agramante, Orlando, and the loves of Ruggiero and Bradamante, of knights, festivals, jousts, and battles. But unlike Spenser he has no intention of celebrating his heroes as heroes or providing instruction through precept or example. To him his heroes are the characters about whom the world of chivalric fantasy is built, a world which exists for its own sake. It is a dream world undisturbed by the moral considerations which troubled Spenser. And Ariosto writes about it with the skill and simplicity of the finished artist. He chose his subject in order to write about it in that way. The world of chivalry never had existed in Italy; it was the creation of northern Europe. When Spenser wrote about King Arthur, he was, however much he was idealizing, writing about a legendary hero of his own land. Ariosto viewed the world of chivalry from a greater distance. As a young man he had read and imitated Horace, writing odes to peasant girls to whom he gave Horatian names. Uninterested in the world about him, he found in poetry an escape to a world of his own creation, and, ambitious as a poet, he looked about for a subject on which he might try his poetic powers and in which he could lose himself. He found the subject in the unfinished *Orlando Innamorato* of Matteo Maria Boiardo (1434-1494), a poem built on the legends of Arthur and Charlemagne. And he continued the story, apparently not caring what the story was as long as it was one on which he could write well. He began work on his poem in 1505 and devoted all his energies to it for the next ten years. He revised it until the year before his death, publishing it in its final form in 1532.

Tasso intended to produce a poem very different from Ariosto's. An earnest student and a "prodigy of learning at eighteen," he approached the writing of poetry with a well formulated critical theory. His poem was to be written according to the precepts of Aristotle as he understood them; it was to be regular and serious. There was to be nothing of the comic, the grotesque, or the vulgar. He wanted to treat his subject without violence to historical truth and to sing the praises of his Christian hero. His poem begins,

> The sacred armies, and the godly knight,
> Who the great sepulchre of Christ did free,
> I sing; much wrought his valor and foresight,
> And in that glorious war much suffer'd he:
> In vain 'gainst him did Hell oppose her might,
> In vain the Turks and Morians armed be:
> His soldiers wild, to brawls and mut'nies prest,
> Reduced he to peace, so Heav'n him blest.
>
> O heav'nly Muse, that not with fading Bays
> Deckest thy brow by th'Heliconian Spring,
> But fittest crown'd with stars immortal rays
> In Heav'n, where legions of bright angels sing,
> Inspire life in my wit, my thoughts up-raise,
> My verse ennoble, and forgive the thing,
> If fictions light I mix with truth divine,
> And fill these lines with other praise than thine.
>
> [Translated by Edward Fairfax, 1600]

But the poem remains more like Ariosto's than he intended. To be sure it is better built, and the action proceeds more coherently from episode to episode; but the poem is not, as he wished it to be, deeply religious. Religion seems to be a part of the work, not the spirit of it, as in Milton. A comparison of the stanzas quoted above with the invocation to *Paradise Lost* will indicate the difference in mood of the poems. Tasso lacked Milton's passionate assurance and belief, and his poem remains idyllic and elegiac in mood. Great as the romantic epics of the sixteenth century are, none measures up to the epics of the ancients. The world did not produce an epic poet to compare with Vergil until Milton published *Paradise Lost* in the second half of the following century. The greatest literary expression of the sixteenth century was its drama.

3. *Drama*

The modern European drama is the product of the theater's slow evolution through many centuries, reaching its height in different countries at different times. In Spain and England the golden age of the drama came in the sixteenth century. The rise of the English Puritans to power and the closing of the theaters at the time of the Puritan Revolution in 1642 brought the period of the theater's greatest prosperity to a close in England, but in Spain, where there was no organized opposition to the theater, it continued until the death of Calderón. Although Calderón (Pedro Calderón de la Barca, 1600-1681) belongs chronologically with the seventeenth century, he may, as a writer, be discussed in the same chapter with Lope de Vega (1562-1635).

As we have described in an earlier chapter, the drama began with bits of dialogue inserted in ritual of the medieval church at Eastertime and progressed through the miracle and mystery plays, moralities, and interludes. In England the development culminated in the work of William Shakespeare. Although the first three-quarters of the sixteenth century produced one or two plays of merit, by far the greater number of them are interesting only as museum pieces. The most notable of them are those which illustrate the influence of the classics on the native dramatic tradition. *Gorbuduc, or Ferrex and Porrex* (acted 1561), by Thomas Sackville and Thomas Norton, is often called the first English tragedy in blank verse. The play is unhappy enough, but it is not tragedy; and while the verse is "blank" inasmuch as it is not rhymed, it is verse only in the sense that it is not prose. Dreary as it is, the play is an attempt to achieve dignity and orderly composition through the imitation of the Latin plays of Seneca. *Ralph Roister Doister* (c. 1553), by Nicholas Udall, shows the influence of Terence in its plot and characters. The swaggering comic hero is a type common to Latin comedy, while his servant, Merygreeke, is a literary descendant of the Vice of the old morality plays. The action of the English mystery plays had been continuous. The play opened with the introduction of the main character, and everything that happened in the play happened on the stage. In the Latin plays much of the action took place off-stage, the audience learning about it through the report of a messenger to other characters in the play. Seneca, an inexpert dramatist in spite of his reputation, often makes very undramatic use of the messenger. Still, in the hands of a competent dramatist, Seneca's method of presenting his material can make for greater concentration than the method of the native English plays. How to arrange the story for its greatest dramatic effect was one of the lessons the English were to learn from the classics.

The best play of the mid-sixteenth century was *Gammer Gurton's Needle* (c. 1565), by Mr. S[tevenson]. Its hearty, comic story tells how Gammer Gurton loses her needle, of the complications which follow when she suspects Dame Chat of having taken it, and how Hodge, her man, finds the needle in the seat of his breeches. The second act of the play opens with one of the best drinking songs in the language:

Back and side go bare, go bare,
Both foot and hand go cold,
But belly, God send thee good ale enough,
Whether it be new or old . . . etc.

Toward the end of the century a group of young men known as the "University Wits" came to London and began writing plays. By this time Spenser had published *The Shepherd's Calendar,* and the new poetry was coming into its own. Trained (all but one of them) at the universities in the literature of the ancients, they were enthusiastic about the new poetry and wanted to use it and their learning in making better plays. The most influential of these men were John Lyly (1554?-1606), Robert Greene (1560?-1592), Thomas Kyd (1557-1595?), and Christopher Marlowe (1564-1593). What Spenser did for poetry, they did for the theater. Lyly, better known today as a writer of prose, was also a poet of delicate charm and studied artistry, qualities which he brought to the production of such plays as *Endimion* and *Sapho and Phao.* He was the first to write "high comedy" in prose. *The Spanish Tragedy,* by Thomas Kyd, is a gory, thundering melodrama of murder and revenge. Designed to thrill the audience with its horrors, it has thousands of descendants in the theater and movies of today. It popularized the "revenge tragedies," of which Shakespeare's *Hamlet* is the supreme example. Christopher Marlowe was unquestionably the most distinguished member of the University Wits. The blank verse (unrhymed iambic pentameter) in which Elizabethan plays were written was his creation. In the prologue to his first play, *Tamburlaine* (published 1590), he states his determination to reform the versification of English plays, to discard the "jigging" rhymes of earlier dramatists for his own "high astounding terms." This was not an idle boast. No blank verse written before Marlowe's time compares with his. He succeeded so well that almost every educated, English-speaking person has some of his lines by heart:

Was this the face that launched a thousand ships?
And burnt the topless towers of Ilium?

In the season of 1936-1937, *Doctor Faustus,* the play from which these lines were taken, was a hit on the New York stage. When Shakespeare came to London, the paths which the Elizabethan drama was to take had been clearly laid out by the University Wits. As we consider Shakespeare in the light of his present reputation, we are likely to forget how much he owes to the dramatists who preceded him and how eminent some of his associates, Ben Jonson, for instance, were. However, the contemporary dramatist nearest him in greatness was a Spaniard, Lope de Vega.

Shakespeare and Lope de Vega had much in common. Each wrote for a popular theater; that is, a theater attended by all classes of people whose applause the dramatists had to win. Each wrote in a native dramatic tradition which had been strongly modified by the influence of the classics. The drama in each country had sprung from the ritual of the church and had developed along parallel lines. Of the two, Lope was the more varied in his literary projects: he wrote, beside plays and lyrics, novels and an epic poem, *Andromeda.* The most prolific dramatist who ever lived, Lope wrote plays as fast as the American college student can read them. There is no reason to doubt him when he says that he wrote some of his plays within twenty-four hours. In 1609 he listed 483 plays of his own composition, and in the year after his death his biographer, Montalbán, credited him with 2,200. This is doubtless an exaggeration. Nevertheless, nearly 500 of his plays survive today, and since he took no pains to preserve what he had written, the chances are that 500 more have been lost. It seems unnecessary to say that all his work shows signs of haste, that he repeats situations and jokes. It is more important to remember that he never wrote a worthless play, that he wrote in verse, using a variety of metrical forms, and that each play has a complicated plot.

In 1609 he published *El Arte nuevo de hacer comedias en este tiempo* (*The New Art of Writing Comedies*), a long poem written to be recited before a literary academy. In it he said that he looked upon his plays as hack work, that he wrote for money and that the common people who pay him do not understand art, and that he mixed comedy and tragedy because the audiences like variety and action. It is not likely that anyone who worked as hard as Lope would be entirely serious in condemning his own work so thoroughly. He said that the rules of the critics do not apply to the composition of plays, yet he has critical ideals of his own: It is necessary to observe the unity of action and to fit the language to the character; that is, a king must not speak like a beggar nor a beggar like a king. It is necessary to have a complicated intrigue, to hold the audience in suspense, and to have effective "curtains." Whether serious or not, Lope was describing the type of play on which his fame and Shakespeare's rests. It was not the inconsiderable thing he said it was.

He had an unerring eye for dramatic material, and his eye glanced everywhere —at the life around him, at ancient and modern history, the Bible, mythology, lives of the saints, Italian fiction, the stories of his own country, and the literature of the ancients. With equal ease he wrote comedies, tragedies, history plays, "cloak and sword" plays, as they were called, and plays on religious and mythological subjects; but he was not interested in writing plays which could be neatly placed in categories such as these. He mixed comedy and tragedy, varying the type as he wished, and in the process wrote some plays which resemble types of drama common in more recent times. *Fuente ovejuna* (*The Sheep Well*) in its sympathy with the oppressed peasantry resembles later social plays. It had extraordinary power. The cloak and sword comedies (*comedias de capa y espada*) were plays which combine the qualities of what we now call "comedy of manners" with a complicated plot of surprise and intrigue. Some of the best of them are *The Girl with the Water-Jar, Her Gallant's Slave, The Miracles of Disdain,* and his last play, *The Eccentricities of Belisa.*

Tirso de Molina (pen name for Gabriel Tellez, 1570?-1648) was another prolific dramatist. Only eighty of his plays survive. Like Lope, Tirso wrote for the people, his dramatic theories in general agreeing with those of his more famous contemporary. His masterpiece, *El Burlador de Sevilla* (*The Deceiver of Seville*), is a dramatization of the story of Don Juan Tenorio, better known in world literature as Don Juan. Where Tirso got the story is not known; it probably derives from folk tales and ballads. In any case, since Tirso wrote his play Don Juan has been the second most popular character of Spanish literature. His story is re-told in Byron's *Don Juan* (1819-1824) and he is the hero of Mozart's great opera, *Don Giovanni* (1787). In Tirso, Juan is a character of greater magnitude than in any of the later Juan stories. He is not a hypocrite as in Molière, nor is he the unregenerate rake of the popular imagination. He is a hero of indomitable will who brings about his doom through his superhuman bravery.

Although the plays of Lope de Vega and Calderón, Spain's greatest dramatists, have much in common, they are the work of men essentially different in back-ground, training, and point of view. Educated at the University of Salamanca after earlier training by the Jesuits, Calderón delighted in subtleties and took end-less pains to write as carefully as he could. His plays, models of construction, were planned to the last detail before he began writing. Their poetry is the work of a fine literary craftsman, some of it worthy of Milton. But his love of fine dis-tinctions sometimes leads him to describe human actions that many people find improbable. Improbability in itself is not necessarily a blot on a play. Important parts of many of Shakespeare's finest plays describe events inconsistent with our impressions of reality, but the intense humanity of his characters usually makes their actions *seem* probable. It is the interest in men as men, which Lope and Shakespeare had so abundantly, that Calderón lacks. Uninterested in the world of ordinary men, Calderón is essentially an intellectual and a courtier. In him we find little of the contemporary world. The last great dramatist of the golden age, he found the things he liked most in the age which had passed. When he died, the great age of Spain's drama died with him. After he became a priest in 1651, he wrote only court plays and *autos,* a type of allegorical religious drama popular in Spain. His best-known works are *La Vida es sueño* (*Life Is a Dream*) and his *autos,* such as *La Cena del rey Baltasar* (*The Supper of King Balthasar*).

In the plays of William Shakespeare (1564-1616) the virtues which distinguish the works of Lope and Calderón are combined. A greater genius than either Spaniard, Shakespeare did not write with the care of Calderón or the carelessness of Lope. Although Ben Jonson, who knew him well, wished that he had revised his work more closely, he could build a play as well as anyone, and if he some-times let inconsistencies stand in them, it was usually because he knew they would not be noticed. Most of the defects which scholars observe in the study pass unnoticed in the public theater. Textbooks are fond of pointing out the "double time" in *Othello,* the anachronisms in *Julius Caesar,* and other things which, had they been pointed out to Shakespeare, he would have laughed at. What real dif-ference do most of them make? In the excitement of watching *Othello* you do not "count the clock." What is more important in Shakespeare is his depth and range. He can, like Calderón, pack his lines with meaning. He sometimes puts as much into a line or two as other writers get into a chapter:

> Here, take this purse, thou whom the heaven's plagues
> Have humbled to all strokes. . . .
> So distribution should undo excess,
> And each man have enough.   [*King Lear*, IV, l. 65]

But he is not an intellectual; his own ability to think does not lead him to dislike thoughtless people. With equal skill he gives us Hamlet and the garrulous, scatter-brained Nurse in *Romeo and Juliet.* If he were alive today and collecting the same royalties from his plays that living dramatists get from theirs, the income from his productions during the current New York theatrical season would be more than $100,000. No dramatist has succeeded like Shakespeare, and in a large measure his success is due to his having something for everybody. He could take a popular thriller of the type of *The Spanish Tragedy* and turn it into *Hamlet,* which has the reputation of being a play about a thinker for people who like to think. This does *Hamlet* some injustice. To be sure, it is a reflective play; its hero is a thoughtful young prince; the play is full of wise and sententious passages; it portrays profound emotions and human situations; some of the speeches are part of the world's best poetry, Hamlet's dying speech to Horatio among them:

> If thou did'st ever hold me in thy heart,
> Absent thee from felicity a while,
> And in this harsh world draw thy breath in pain,
> To tell my story.

These are all things which cultivated men enjoy, but they are only part of the play. For people who take their cultivation less seriously there is grotesque and vulgar comedy; and, for the good people who like stories in which "something happens," a ghost walks, an army marches, there is suicide and murder, death by drowning, stabbing, poisoning. There is music to please the ear and pageantry for the eye, and when the play is over, everyone has something to remember. Shakespeare owes his public favor to his ability to bring greatness to a popular drama without destroying the qualities of it which had made it popular.

A man cannot do anything superlatively well and remain unaware of his excellence. Shakespeare knew his own worth; in one of his sonnets he writes:

> Not marble nor the gilded monuments
> Of princes shall outlive this powerful rime.

It is a just estimate of its worth. But in spite of his gift of poetry he never lost his sturdy common sense. He was a poet, a playwright, an actor, and a theater manager. If he ever thought of himself as both a business man and an artist, he did not think the combination strange. He wrote his plays to be acted in a theater of which he was a manager by an acting company of which he was a member. If we do not remember this theater and his relation to it, we are likely to misunderstand him. His stage was not the realistic stage of the modern theater; on the other hand, it was not the bare stage it is sometimes said to have been. It did use stage properties, but the properties were used for dramatic effect; there was no intention of representing the locality of the action. The audience accepted the stage as Verona at one moment and as Padua the next. This was a dramatic convention and no more strain upon the audience than many conventions of the modern stage, on which, for instance, night falls in ten seconds. We accept this because it is better to have night fall quickly than to sit in the audience for an hour while night comes on as in nature. A convention is an improbability which the audience agrees to disregard. Writing for the Elizabethan audience, Shakespeare did not divide his plays into acts and scenes. (That was not done until after his death.) He wrote his plays for continuous performance, one scene following another, as in the movies.

For this theater Shakespeare wrote farces, comedies, history plays, and tragedies, although, like Lope de Vega, he was not much interested in classifications. He put his thoughts into their most effective dramatic form; that was his job. And he knew so well the art of moving an audience that he unerringly takes us with him as he passes from rowdy comedy to highest tragedy. His versatility, his wide range of human understanding, his skill as a dramatic craftsman, his genius as a poet, enabled Shakespeare to give us the best comedy, the best history play, the best tragedy of the modern world. When, at about the age of forty-five, he retired to his native Stratford to spend the rest of his days in ease, he left to Ben Jonson (1573-1637) the impossible task of filling his place in the English theater.

In his plays as in his poems, Ben Jonson was the apostle of conscious art. We do not mean to suggest that Shakespeare's art, like the song of Shelley's skylark, was "unpremeditated." We do mean that Jonson, a critic and a scholar, built his plays according to preconceived critical theories and sometimes in conscious imitation of the classics. His two Roman tragedies, *Sejanus* and *Cataline,* sacrifice their vitality to his scholarship. It is on his comedies that his reputation rests. The same devotion to literal truth which made him keep the tragedies faithful to historic fact led him to set his comedies in contemporary London. *Bartholomew Fair* (1614) teems with realistic portraits of common types: ballad-singers, cut-purses, stall-keepers, Zeal-of-the-land Busy, a Puritan, and Justice Overdo. We can see more of London in a play or two of Jonson's than in all Shakespeare. And no other English comedies have had so strong an influence on later writers. He is the father of the "comedy of humors." We will recall the medieval belief that a man's temperament was determined by the proportion of the four "humors" or fluids within him: blood, phlegm, bile, and black bile. If there is a preponderance of blood, he is sanguine; of phlegm, phlegmatic; of black bile (melancholé), melancholy; or of bile (cholé), choleric. Thus, "humor" comes to stand for a dominant characteristic. Jonson's humor characters are men with a ruling passion, their humor being indicated by their names. In *The Alchemist,* the cheating alchemist is named Subtle; in *The Silent Woman,* Morose is "A Gent. that loves no noyse," and Epicene is "A yong Gent., suppos'd the Silent Woman." Every reader of Restoration comedy, or of Sterne, Thackeray, or Dickens, knows how much Jonson has influenced characterization in later English literature.

4. Prose

In the present age so many people read novels that it is sometimes a little difficult to imagine a time when the novel did not exist, but the English novel is none the less a rather new thing, having come into existence about two hundred years ago. In the sixteenth century the young Englishman ambitious to be a writer tried his hand at poetry or drama, the dominant art forms. To be sure, storytelling is as old as the world, and stories have been printed in prose since the time of printing; but not every piece of prose fiction is a novel. There were no novels in Elizabethan England. The novel as a literary form is too earthbound to have won the admiration of the men who created Elizabethan literature. They admired grandeur (and the grandiose), the ideal, the poetic, the elegant. Intent upon creating a style appropriate to their elevated concepts, the serious prose writers of the day created a manner of writing totally unsuited to the composition of novels. The most influential writers of prose toward the end of the century were Sir Philip Sidney [1] and John Lyly (1554?-1606). In Lyly's *Euphues* [2] the plot is slight, the main body of the book is devoted to a display of manners and learning imported for the use of newly rich gentlemen who needed such instruction very badly. Euphues, a young Athenian, visits Italy and England, conversing as the young Englishman of the day would have liked to converse. Immediately popular, the book established a manner of speaking and writing called euphuism, an elegant and elaborate use of alliteration and learned allusions, balance and antithesis. The fashion of euphuism was short-lived, but it left its mark on Elizabethan prose, and, what is more important, it illustrates the current notion of what literary prose should be like. Euphuism has its uses, but the novel is not one of them.

The books of Thomas Deloney (1543?-1600) are the nearest approach to the modern novel. Deloney was a weaver and a peddler, a writer of ballads and pamphlets who was almost completely untouched by the new learning of the day. He was, therefore, beyond the notice of literary men. In a fine example of his studied manner, Robert Greene called Deloney's books "trivial trinkets of threadbare trash." Yet *Thomas of Reading* and *Jack of Newbury* have the earthy vigor we associate with novels:

> Then, said Cuthbert, Fair Mistress, I have often mused that you, being a proper [that is, handsome] woman, could find in your heart for to match with such a greazie carle as this, an evil mannered mate, a foul lump of kitchen stuff, and such a one as is indeed a scorn of men. How can you like him that all women mislikes? or love such a loathsome creature? . . .
>
> Indeed sir, quoth she, I had but hard fortune in this respect, but my friends would have it so, and truly my liking and my love toward him are alike: he never had the one, nor never shall get the other. Yet I may say to you before I married him there were divers proper young men who were suitors unto me, who loved me as their lives, and glad was he that could get my company. Those were my golden days. . . .
>
> [From *Thomas of Reading*]

In spite of his sturdy virtues, Deloney is not a novelist. He escaped the excesses that came with the new learning and literature, but he also escaped its advantages: he never learned how to build a story. Both his plots and his characters lack unity.

There was no prose fiction in sixteenth-century Europe to compare with the Spanish. Spain, too, had had its rebirth of learning, and her poets had also learned to imitate Petrarch; but Spanish literature did not break with the Middle Ages as

---

[1] Sidney's *Arcadia* is discussed in our section on the eighteenth-century novel.
[2] The term *Euphues* is used to refer both to Lyly's *Euphues, the Anatomy of Wit* (1579) and his *Euphues and His England* (1580).

completely as other European literatures. When Henry VIII was establishing the prestige of England as a nation, Charles V of Spain (1516-1556) was governing one of the world's greatest empires. For a century Spain had been a unified and powerful nation. Unlike the English, the Spanish did not associate the new literature with their national glory. And the Spanish Inquisition effectively prevented the religious struggles which in other nations helped sever their connections with the past. Such aspects of the literature of the Middle Ages as are represented in England by the hearty honesty of Chaucer and in France by the more brutal honesty of Villon continue uninterrupted in Spain and find expression in Spain's two greatest prose works, the *Celestina* and *Don Quijote* (*Don Quixote*).

The *Celestina,* or *The Tragicomedy of Calisto and Melibea,* is in dialogue form, although it is not in any sense a play. The first extant edition (1499) is in sixteen acts, the edition of 1526 in twenty-two acts. It was a story of great influence and popularity, going through sixty-three editions in the sixteenth century. Acts two to sixteen are by Fernando de Rojas (fl. 1525); the author of the other sections is unknown. The *Celestina,* made up of incidents from many writers, relates the tragic story of two lovers, Calisto and Melibea, who are brought together by Celestina, a professional go-between. The characters are of more interest than the plot, and of the characters the more vulgar ones are best. Celestina dominates the work. A heartless hag, she is completely devoted to evil. Carrying on her profession with no thought of its possible cruel consequences, she is the ultimate cause of her own death and that of the lovers. Nevertheless, she is not a despicable character. The story, grimly truthful, has wit and eloquence, and its continued favor testifies to its universality. James Mabbe translated it into English in 1631, entitling it *The Spanish Bawd.*

Something of Celestina's spirit pervades a type of Spanish fiction called *picaresque,* taking its name from the Spanish word for rogue, *picaro*. A popular genre, the picaresque novel has been widely imitated in many lands, the numerous and diverse examples of it making the term hard to define. Any description of it must be inclusive. Loosely constructed, it is biographical in form. The adventures of its hero are presented in chronological order, and when the story is finished there is usually the possibility of a sequel. The hero is a rogue who lies and steals and has in general a somewhat cynical and merry unawareness of the ten commandments. Born in poverty and pitted against a hostile world, he cannot afford the moral scruples which sometimes dominate the actions of more fortunate men. He wants to live, and if society disregards him, why, then he will disregard society! The picaro cheats because he wants to eat, and this is his distinguishing characteristic. In *Till Eulenspiegel* (1483), a German counterpart of the picaresque story, Till plays his tricks because of a love of roguery.

Lazarillo de Tormes (earliest extant edition, 1554), the first important picaresque novel, is of unknown date and authorship. We are first introduced to Lazarillo's criminal family, and then follow his adventures as an apprentice to a dishonest blind man, as a servant to an avaricious priest, and so on. One of the seven sections of the story tells how he acted as servant to a proud and poverty-stricken member of the lower nobility who, although he lived on what his servant stole, maintained his pride in his aristocracy. Satire is an essential element of the picaresque.

In *Don Quijote* (*El ingenioso hidalgo don Quijote de la Mancha*, first part, 1605; second part, 1615), Cervantes does not adhere to the picaresque tradition; he was too great a genius to be bound by a type. But he had an intense interest in the stuff of which picaresque fiction is made, and his story conforms to the tradition in many respects. Its chief point of difference is the human sympathy he felt for his absurd hero. A burlesque on the old romances, *Don Quijote* tells of a poor and amiable gentleman who, sane in other respects, imagines himself called upon to wander about the world in search of adventure. Mounted on an old nag and accompanied by his squire, Sancho Panza, he treats the most ordinary people as though they were characters from an Arthurian romance. Cervantes is entirely incapable of the cynicism of *Lazarillo,* and Don Quijote, like his English descendants, Uncle Toby in *Tristram Shandy,* and Parson Adams in *Joseph Andrews,* is as lovable as he is foolish. While he sees things as they are not, Sancho sees them as they are, and the comedy which they provide between them has won Cervantes the title of the world's foremost humorist.

Although his reputation outside Spain rests on *Don Quijote,* Cervantes wrote many other things. Between the years 1583 and 1587 he wrote twenty plays, but finding that he could not compete in the theater with Lope de Vega, he turned to other forms. The publication of *Don Quijote* brought him fame which he did not long enjoy. He died in 1616, believing to the end that he would be remembered for *Galatea,* an ornate romance he had written in 1585.

Other prose was written during this period: the *Heptameron* (published 1558) by Marguerite de Navarre, a collection of stories somewhat like the *Decameron* but much inferior to it; critical treatises such as the *Poetique* of Scaliger (1540-1609), and those of Speroni and du Bellay, discussed earlier in this chapter; treatises on education and politics, such as *The Boke Named the Governour* (1531), by Sir Thomas Elyot. The age of the rise of nationalism inevitably saw the production of many histories with national bias, of which the realistic and cynical *Memoirs* of Philippe de Commines (1445-1509) on late fifteenth-century France were far and away the ablest and most important. The enthusiasm for learning brought about translations of the classics: Golding's *Ovid* and North's version of Plutarch's *Lives* (a translation of a French rendering by Jacques Amyot); and, most important of all, translations of the Bible. Martin Luther's version of the Bible (completed 1534) not only marked the triumph of Protestantism in Germany, but was a monument of German prose and an inestimable force in the formation of modern German. The King James translation, which has made the Bible the most influential book in English literature, was not completed until 1611.

Of the serious prose works, none played a greater part in the creation of sixteenth-century culture than *The Prince* (1513) and *The Courtier* (1528). In the former, Niccolò Machiavelli (1469-1527), a statesman of the Florentine Republic and a practical man of affairs, presents a minute analysis of the qualities of character necessary to a ruler of a unified and powerful state. Machiavelli also won fame as an historian by his *History of Florence,* but this was far surpassed by the

History of Florence of Francesco Guicciardini (1483-1540), through which modern historical writing once again attained the level of the best Greek historical prose. Baldassare Castiglione's (1478-1529) *Il Cortegiano* (*Courtier*) is a dialogue discussing the ethical, social, military, and athletic qualifications of the ideal gentleman, an ideal the courtiers of the century universally imitated and sometimes achieved. He was to be a connoisseur of painting, an accomplished musician and writer, a wit and gallant, a soldier and statesman, and, superficially at least, a scholar. He brought all these qualities to the services of his prince. In England the imitation of these ideal figures helped create statesmen like Cecil and Burleigh and courtiers like Sir Walter Raleigh. The ideal is inevitably reflected in literature; Shakespeare's Hamlet was a prince, a writer of verses, a soldier, courtier, and scholar.

Influential as these works were, and great as is the literary value of some of them, they were not primarily intended as literature. Of the more purely literary compositions, the essay is still to be discussed. Any written explanation may be called an essay, but the term "familiar essay" may be applied to relatively few compositions. The familiar essay permits the writer to do anything he wishes; it requires only that he do it well. He may write at any length on any subject, or he may change his subject if he chooses; and making no claim to completeness, he need not be systematic. He writes with only one obligation, to entertain. A good essayist is a born essayist. The originator of the essay, Michel de Montaigne (1533-1592), is its best explanation. In 1571, having freed himself from the vexations of public life, he retired to his château near Bergerac to enjoy the rest of his years in peace. Here, in the tower that served as his library, he made the notes on his reading, which, through repeated additions and revisions, grew into books. He called the new writings "essays"; that is, attempts. He wrote about books, cruelty, constancy, thumbs, glory, Vergil, names, odors, and prayers, about anything that caught his interest. The whole human comedy fascinated him, and he, delighting in the fascination, kept an amiable skepticism toward everything. Above all things he loved independence, to know the affairs of men but not be of them. His skepticism maintained his independence, and his freedom was his integrity. His integrity is the soul of the essays. They belong to that small group of books which Bacon says "are to be read wholly, and with diligence and attention." Like all good essays they are self-portraiture; whether he is writing of coaches or vanity, he is always there. And our reward for reading him is a conviction that we have been associating for a time with Michel de Montaigne, wise, learned, gracious, somewhat aloof perhaps, but no matter. The essay demands a full mind, an expert and honest pen, self-knowledge, and an eye for the minutiae of daily life in which human hope and folly find unintended expression. Writers of lesser or more pretentious qualifications may try the essay if they will.

The sixteenth, the century of enthusiasm and adventure, had begun in the midst of the humanist movement. It had brought to the old world a stimulating knowledge of the new. It had seen the rise of Protestantism and individualism, not so much a systematic individualism as exultant self-assertion. It had seen the rise of nationalism and the creation of a new literature to describe and dignify all these things. It had looked around at its brave new world and found it good. In an earlier century a man would not have thought it worth his while to record, like Montaigne, the details of everyday existence, but this century had lent human actions a new dignity. Earlier, in the more spacious days of the century, men wrote about more ambitious things; but now the end of the century, grown a little weary, produced Montaigne's essays, his delight in the external world, and his realization that, for all the world's pageantry, he could face it only with stoicism and doubt. His conclusion is, "Que sais-je?" (What do I know?)

Had Francis Bacon (1561-1626) been born in a later and more discriminating century, he could not have taken all knowledge to be his province, and we would not have his minor works, the essays, the by-products of his mind's encyclopedic activity. He devoted the years after his enforced retirement in 1621 and the intervals of his earlier life to a projected synthesis of all knowledge, of which his *Advancement of Learning* and his *Novum Organum* are only a part. He thought of his essays as trifles, "dispersed meditations," useful observations on life and character. A man of his time, his studies were only a part of his work, he was a statesman and a politician, and he rose by slow stages to be Lord Chancellor of England. As a practical man of affairs he knew the stratagems and compromises which public life imposes, and, unlike Montaigne, he did not try to escape them. He places the ideal and the practicable side by side and measures their advantages. His essays, packed with worldly wisdom and salty observation, are studies in antithesis:

> The joys of parents are secret; and so are their griefs and fears. They cannot utter the one; nor they will not utter the other. Children sweeten labors; but they make misfortunes more bitter. They increase the cares of life; but they mitigate the remembrance of death. The perpetuity by generation is common to beasts; but memory, merit, and noble works are proper to men.
>
> [From *Of Parents and Children*]

In *Of Marriage,* he weighs the merits of marriage and single life, and his conclusion is that "a man may have a quarrel to marry when he will. But yet he was reputed one of the wise men, that made answer to the question, when a man should marry,—'A young man not yet, an elder man not at all.'" We may compare his essay on friendship with Shakespeare's sonnet on the "marriage of true minds." To Bacon the "two noble fruits of friendship" are "peace in the affections, and support of the judgment." Belonging to that group of people whom Shakespeare describes as "the lords and owners of their faces," he measures things in terms of himself. His essays were first published in 1597. Urbane, witty, learned, and, within his limitations, wise, he brings the century to a close.

II. THE IDEALISTIC ART OF THE SIXTEENTH CENTURY

1. *Painting*

No other period in the history of the Western World has contributed so much creative genius to the plastic arts as the epoch between 1475-1600. Not even the golden age of Pericles can compare with it in the variety and number of master-pieces. The new period completed the secularization of culture begun in the 1300-1475 transition. Significant art production was not confined to Italy and Flanders primarily but extended into Germany, Holland, Spain, and France as well, although Italy was still the leader. The other countries of Europe were brought into contact with Italian art through travel, war, and the general dif-fusion of culture. The development of printing, of engraving, and of woodcuts helped to spread abroad the influence of Italian style and compositions. Artists from all countries came to Italy to study the great masterpieces as later, in the nineteenth century, they would go to Paris. With this accumulation of inspira-tion and ideas they helped found schools of art in their own countries.

The art of the early fifteenth century (discussed in Chapter XII) set the stage for the accomplishments of the second half of that same epoch and for further developments in the next century. With the technical and scientific equip-ment gathered by such artists as Masaccio, Castagno, Uccello, Piero della Fran-cesca, Brunelleschi, Ghiberti, Donatello, and Luca della Robbia, the new gen-eration could climb to the supreme efforts of Botticelli, Leonardo, Ghirlandajo, Pollaiuolo, Michelangelo, Raphael, Titian, Giorgione, Dürer, Holbein, and others. At the beginning of this period the Florentines were still leaders in painting, but instead of the relatively experimental character of the earlier period (1300-1475), the new epoch of the so-called Renaissance reached a full-blown flowering indica-tive of complete maturity and assurance.

Before discussing the greatest masters of the period, it would be well to carry to an end the two main streams we followed in the first half of the century. Among the scientific painters who solved the anatomical problems begun by Masaccio and Castagno, we find Antonio Pollaiuolo (1429-1498), a sculptor and goldsmith, whose painting reflects the sculptural viewpoint. In such paintings as *Hercules and the Hydra* he shows not only the interest in musculature and its dilation but a serious advance over previous anatomically concerned artists in his preoccupation with the nude in motion. His famous engraving, the *Battle of the Nude Men,* is a clear example. In both works we find the typical tight linear drawing of the Florentine school.

Andrea del Verrocchio (1435-1488), a man of many talents, was an interest-ing proof of the strong interrelationship between sculpture and painting in this period. Not only was Verrocchio a successful painter (and teacher of Leonardo da Vinci) but the sculptor of the magnificent equestrian statue, *Colleoni.* A care-ful workman, he transmitted his meticulousness to his celebrated pupil with whom he collaborated in the *Baptism of Christ,* a painting typical of his ener-getic realism and earnestness of mood.

The three main masters of the end of the fifteenth century in Florence were Botticelli, Filippino Lippi, and Ghirlandajo. Sandro Botticelli (1446-1510) was one of the chief exponents of the lyrical type of painting represented by Fra Lippo Lippi, whose pupil he was. Botticelli's introspective quality, however, is bound up with a certain nostalgia that may be associated with the end of an important historical epoch, the kind of feeling we call today *fin de siècle.* Although he was a remarkable colorist and draughtsman, he can hardly be called a realist, for the curious golden blond tonality which he favored was as much a stylization as his draughtsmanship was unusually tight. The incisive quality of his drawing and the hard, metallic surfaces of his figures were the result of his asociation with Pollaiuolo the goldsmith. In fact, Botticelli himself was a goldsmith for a time. A protégé of the Medici family, he came into close contact with the humanist scholars whom they patronized as well as their other intellectual friends, many of whom were interested in the study of Dante. Botticelli's own illustrations for the *Divine Comedy,* intensely spiritual in quality, are an interesting evidence of the current attempt to reconcile the ideals of paganism and Christianity. As examples of sensitive and lyrical draughtsmanship, these drawings have seldom if ever been equaled; and the only modern illustrations to compare with them are the famous interpretations by William Blake.

Botticelli was particularly interested in pagan subject matter, and in such paintings as his *Allegory of Spring, Birth of Venus, Calumny of Apelles,* he gives ample testimony not only of his interest but of his deep classical learning. Botticelli's women are introspective like those of Fra Lippo Lippi, but even more intensely so, sometimes verging on the psychopathic, as may be seen in some of the figures in the *Allegory of Spring.* In this picture as in his other work whether allegorical, religious, or illustrative, realism was tempered by a passion for expressive line. This revealed itself in a "lyrical" flatness of design and "a musical quality" of linear composition. Individual lines, when analyzed, have a peculiar writhing quality which helps build up a feeling of nervous elegance and emotional instability. His men and women are unusually tall and commensurately slender, which adds to the undulating quality of their figures.

Just as his teacher Fra Lippo Lippi had brought madonnas down to earth, Botticelli invested religious subjects with the same characteristics observed in his classical allegories. The famous *Madonna of the Magnificat* in its circular frame, is derived, as a composition, from the earlier efforts of Fra Lippo Lippi, but here the madonna has become a full blooded, even sensuous type to whom the word pagan would hardly do justice. Toward the end of his career, however, Botticelli came under the influence of the mystic reformer Savonarola. His art turned toward a more intense expression as seen in his *Pietà* at Munich whose exalted emotion symbolizes the period of reform initiated by the monk.

A contemporary and pupil of Botticelli was Filippino Lippi (1457-1504), son of Fra Lippo Lippi, whose intense emotional quality and sharp drawing are reminiscent of the work of his friend. In such a painting as the *Madonna Appearing to St. Bernard* there is a nervous delicacy in the expression of the faces and an elongation of the figures, with charming landscape and an interesting handling of light.

Last in the late fifteenth-century Florentine group was Domenico Ghirlandajo (1449-1494), whose work was primarily important in perfecting the narrative style in painting. He is a typical example of the solid middle-class spirit of fifteenth-century Florence, and it is to this class that much of his work is dedicated. Although influenced in his love of detail by contemporary Flemish painting, his larger compositions (the frescoes) are based in their arrangement upon the earlier work of Giotto. His most famous paintings are the frescoes in the choir of Santa Maria Novella in Florence. These are important not only for the fine portrait heads of members of the Medici circle and the Tornabuoni family (for whom the paintings were produced) but for the fact that never before in Italian painting had the donors of a picture obtruded themselves so much into a group of religious scenes. Sometimes this becomes so exaggerated as to negate the religious narrative itself. Although Ghirlandajo is an important link between the tradition of Giotto and Masaccio and the great narrative art of Raphael, we must admit that his style is frequently dry and prosy, and that he never reaches the emotional heights of his contemporary Botticelli.

The second half of the fifteenth century brings forth a number of other schools in Italy. To the Umbro-Florentine group belong such artists as Piero della Francesca, Melozzo da Forli, and Luca Signorelli who, although born outside of Florence, are artistically related to it. Piero della Francesca we have already discussed in connection with out-of-doors lighting. Melozzo da Forli (1438-1494) was a master of perspective and illusionist space composition particularly as applied to difficult wall decorations on ceilings, apses, etc. His fresco of *The Ascension of Christ* in the half-dome of the Church of the Holy Apostles in Rome is a famous example of his power to create an overhead illusion.

The third important member of the Umbro-Florentine group is Luca Signorelli (1441-1532), a master of the nude in action. His elaborate and skillful compositions in the Cathedral of Orvieto representing the events of the *Last Judgment* (executed between 1499-1505) are the mightiest emotional manifestation in Italian art up to that time. It is true that his anatomy, like Pollaiuolo's, was exaggerated, and that he rendered too vividly sinews, bones, and muscles; but it is perhaps for this very reason that they convey to us the essential mortality of humankind. Pathetic and fearful figures crawl painfully from their holes in the ground, some mere skeletons, others partly decayed, and all testifying to the frailness of humanity. As a predecessor of Michelangelo in the latter's treatment of the same subject, the *Last Judgment* of Signorelli has more than casual importance.

The Umbrians proper are significant for having expressed a gentle religiosity, often sentimental to a degree that makes us uncomfortable but it was eminently suited to the provincial taste of the small Umbrian towns for which most of the work was done. Characterized by softness of expression and delicacy of forms, the Umbrian tradition became one of the important influences in the evolution of the style of Raphael, who was the pupil of its most celebrated master, Perugino. Pietro Perugino (1446-1524) combined the native warmth of this territory with the scientific leanings of the Florentines and, to a certain extent, the bright color of the Venetians. In his later life, the success he enjoyed with sentimental religious subject matter led him to repeat his most popular formulas so that for us today, he is more than a bit tiresome. Nevertheless Perugino's great contribution was the development of space composition to a point where the spectator was no longer aware of the two-dimensionality of the canvas, so convincingly did the artist add the third dimension.

Andrea Mantegna (1431-1506) of the school of Padua was a follower of the great Florentine sculptor Donatello. He inherited from Donatello a bronze-like sculptural realism and derived from the famous architect Alberti his interest in perspective. In his *Legend of St. James* these are combined with his interest in classical antiquity, shown in the costume, architectural details, etc. Sociologically, perhaps, Mantegna's most interesting productions are the marvelous frescoes in the ducal palace at Mantua, done for the Gonzaga family in 1474—unquestionably the high point of naturalistic fresco art in Italy (or anywhere else) during the fifteenth century. In a pair of frescoes for the marriage chamber in this palace, Mantegna has shown on one wall the meeting between the Marquis Ludovico Gonzaga and his son Cardinal Francesco and on the other the *Reception of an Ambassador*. This representation of a typical fifteenth-century court, the adults and the children with retainers and shrewd advisers, is one of the masterpieces of the figure art of the time. No other picture gives us such an immediate insight into one aspect of Italian life. The characterizations are bold, fearless, and realistic. The last thing to be noted, but by no means the least, is the important influence Mantegna exerted upon the development of the Venetian school of painting at this period.

The three great Florentine masters of the sixteenth century are Leonardo da Vinci, Michelangelo, and Raphael. With Leonardo (1452-1519) we bridge two centuries, for he represents a complete synthesis of all the scientific accomplishments of the fifteenth century absorbed into the mature, highly developed production of the period frequently referred to as "High Renaissance" art. Although here we are primarily interested in Leonardo the painter, we must not lose sight of his other accomplishments—engineer, mathematician, naturalist, physicist, musician, philosopher, architect, sculptor. In this "myriad-minded" man we see one of the best examples of the culturally developed and versatile individual produced by this great period. Almost every important artist of the fifteenth and sixteenth centuries could do more than one thing well. We know, in fact, that a client could come into an artist's studio of that time and have executed almost anything from a brooch to a building. Leonardo's attitude toward painting is typical of his entire thought. As author of a *Treatise on Painting,* he had many concrete ideas as to how a picture should be planned and executed. The best time to paint, he thought, was the late afternoon when the shadows were soft and the harsh outlines of the figure became more indistinct. His was a twilight mood—there was no more poetic artist in the entire period than Leonardo da Vinci. It would be reasonable to think of him as the perfect mean, a combination of the sentiment descended from Fra Lippo Lippi and Botticelli and the scientific acumen of the other branch of the Florentine school.

A typical example of the unfortunately few extant paintings of Leonardo is the *Madonna of the Rocks* where he used his characteristically geometric composition. The figures are arranged triangular fashion against a minutely but romantically conceived landscape showing the darkling crags of Lombardy where it was painted. The mood of the subjects is of that soft smiling gentleness we have come to associate with the work of Leonardo. The landscape itself is carefully represented and in great detail, with accurate observations of the formation of rocks and plants, betraying a keen interest in the natural world. As individual studies, they may be found in any of the innumerable notebooks he has left us. We may find plants, stones, and insects carefully analyzed and described with the accuracy of a modern geologist or botanist, yet drawn with such tenderness that they become surpassing examples of the draughtsman's art. Leonardo felt that the universe was a well-ordered place and that there was a system in nature which could be felt in every organism he studied. His religion was order and science and he worshiped with such devotion that he frequently forgot he was a painter and lost himself in contemplation of the infinite variety of nature. The scientific studies which he made in preparation for his paintings frequently absorbed him to such a point that the painting itself was forgotten; it is probably for this reason that so few of them were ever finished. The finished works of Leonardo can be counted on the fingers of both hands, yet his contribution to the progress of civilization is immeasurable.

His procedure in painting is as interesting as the other elements in his work. More often than not he would invent some new base upon which to use his oils or his fresco and in most cases these experiments have been unfortunate, resulting in either the blackening or molding of the pigment. His great contribution to the technique of oil painting is his use of an intricate process of light and shade known as *sfumato* which differs from the ordinary method of gradual transition from dark to light (*chiaroscuro*) in that Leonardo's technique consists of darks that are themselves shot through with little spots of light, and vice versa. The result is a gentle haze (sfumato) about the faces and forms of his figures which gives them their soft and tender look. We find this in the celebrated *Mona Lisa.*

Most of his paintings were the result of careful thought and planning. He was never satisfied; always changing, always modifying. His habit of standing before his work for hours in contemplation has been remarked upon by all biographers. It is an interesting index to the meticulous approach to art which he must have inherited from his master, Verrocchio. He was able to work upon a number of things simultaneously, to turn his attention from one to the other without any appreciable loss of momentum.

If we recognize in other artists a similarity of types used throughout their work, it is usually the result of the use of the same model (as in Lippo Lippi) or the success of a particular formula (as in Perugino). In Leonardo the evident resemblance between such diverse types as the *Madonna of the Rocks,* the *Mona Lisa, Bacchus* and *St. John the Baptist* is due to his development of a new conception of humanity, gracious in aspect. Observing nature, Leonardo painted man not as he saw him but as he *thought* him. Michelangelo, Raphael and others of this period concurred in this approach and this abstraction from nature is what removes the art of the so-called "High Renaissance" from the more specific art of the early fifteenth century. This is, in essence, the keynote of this period, and it was first sounded by Leonardo da Vinci.

A great deal of capital has been made of the fact that the artists of this epoch were, because of the humanistic and classical tendencies, not as religious as their predecessors, and Leonardo has been cited as an example. This is far from true, however, for in the *Last Supper* Leonardo has given us as moving a representation as the history of art affords of the moment when Christ says, "Verily, verily, I say unto ye, that one of ye shall betray me." Biographers point, further, to the curious resemblance between the *Bacchus* and the *St. John the Baptist* with the implication that their mocking smiles are proof of the irreverence of the artist and of the fact that he had his tongue in his cheek when he painted them. The evident analogy between pagan and Christian subject matter has been noted in Botticelli. There we attributed the likeness to the literary and philosophical attitude of the artist who was attempting, in a typical Neoplatonic fashion, to reconcile the pagan and Christian views. For Leonardo the mystery of the universe was his primary interest and since in nature all things were carefully ordered and responded to the same rules, for him Christianity and paganism were merely different ways of saying the same thing, variations on the worship of nature.

Michelangelo (1475-1564), the greatest genius to be brought forth in this period of the history of art, was one of its most tumultuous figures. Like Leonardo, he unswervingly strove toward a high ideal; a vague yearning and dissatisfaction led him to produce some of the greatest sculpture of all time and one of the mightiest efforts in painting the world has ever seen. As a typical Florentine artist he was more interested in line than in color, and as a man who thought himself a sculptor, primarily, his paintings convey a stronger impression of three-dimensionality than any others of the time. With him the humanistic idea—man as the measure of all things—reaches its logical climax. Even landscape is completely subordinated to his purpose of creating a mighty human race. Michelangelo's vehicle is the nude, male or female, with emphasis upon mighty muscular articulations and a general impression of the gigantesque. This effect he can convey even in a small space, for size and monumentality have nothing to do with each other.

There is only one complete panel painting by this artist, *The Holy Family*. His foremost creation, and the most overwhelming single pictorial creation of this age, is the decoration of the ceiling in the Sistine Chapel of the Vatican. Here, upon a curved surface, interrupted by several window spaces, he has outlined the Creation and Fall of Mankind in a series of over-life-size frescoes which are the despair of every artist who views them. Coming to this task with no experience whatever in the fresco medium and very little practice generally in painting, he succeeded in outlining for all time the story of the early chapters of Genesis and in creating a new Michelangelesque race of human beings. Although it is exceedingly difficult to single out individual figures in a vast project of this kind, we may call attention to the *Creation of Adam* panel which shows the recumbent giant with his arm lazily outstretched waiting for the finger of the Creator to touch him into life. How effective is the contrast between the dynamic figure of God flying through space and the implicit though still unexpressed power of the gigantic Adam. One is struck by the resemblance between the Adam and the figure of Theseus from the pediment of the Parthenon in ancient Greece, a circumstance that derives more from a similar psychological aim than from any borrowing, since Michelangelo could never have seen the Greek figure. The men and women painted and carved by this artist are of the same Olympian character as the heroes of Greece, and are not only over life-size in proportions, but conceived on such a monumental scale that they defy all ordinary, merely human categories and become impressive symbols of power and the great mind of their creator.

There is no longer any question of ordinary realism in the work of Michelangelo, and although his method and its effectiveness depend upon a highly developed knowledge of anatomy, the various scientific elements have been completely digested and absorbed to produce these mighty and beautiful mathematical equations. This does not necessarily mean that the work of the great Florentine is devoid of emotional significance, for the sorrowing *Jeremiah* of the Sistine Chapel ceiling disproves that immediately, but rather that his emotions are extraordinary, akin in their universal quality to Greek tragedy. Strength such as his invariably creates a high emotional response in the mind and heart of the spectator but in trying to compare him with other artists we are at a loss, for few if any have ever risen to these expressive and cosmic heights. Perhaps Beethoven in his *Ninth Symphony* or Wagner in his *Götterdämmerung* can give us an analogous experience.

Much later than the work on the Sistine Chapel ceiling, Michelangelo decorated the far wall of this same room with his *Last Judgment* (1535-1541). Using the age-old formula of the avenging God and the division of humanity into two groups, the saved and the damned, Michelangelo has rendered a perhaps too energetic and athletic conception of this scene. Losing a good deal of the classical force with restraint that had marked his ceiling frescoes, he proceeded here to let himself go in an overwrought and physically exaggerated work which no longer belongs to the serene classicism of the previous work. The *Last Judgment* anticipates some of the emotional and exaggerated elements of the next century.

The third of the trio of great Florentine painters is Raphael (1483-1520), a pupil of Perugino (the great representative of the sentimental Umbrian tradition). Raphael's painting is indelibly stamped with a gentleness and sweetness which make him the most appealing of religious painters. Unquestionably what he has to say is not as intellectually stirring as the paintings of Leonardo nor as emotionally powerful as Michelangelo's, but no other artist has maintained his popularity through the ages with the steadfastness of this charming young painter from Urbino.

Raphael's association with Perugino developed in him the preference for charm rather than power; however, the fifteenth-century style of his teacher was soon supplanted by the modeling and strength of such Florentines as Donatello, Leonardo, and others. He was called to Rome to work in the Vatican in the papal apartments adjoining the Sistine Chapel where Michelangelo was decorating the ceiling.

The series of frescoes which he painted in these chambers (some with the aid of assistants after the orders began coming in too rapidly to be handled by one man) are some of the finest produced during this period, and ample testimony of the eclectic character of Raphael's art. The early ones (*The Disputa*) still show some of the sentimental traces of his master, Perugino, but in the most famous example, *The School of Athens,* he reaches the full flower of his precocious genius. Here, in a vast architectural background he has set out the great philosophers, poets, scientists of the golden age of Greece in such a manner as to give for the first time a concrete idea of what that age must have been. Although the architecture is that of the early sixteenth century, there is an impression of vast space and a conciseness in the setting out of the figures on the steps and back through the arcades which shows us how Perugino's space composition has reached its highest perfection in his pupil.

As an example of illusionistic wall treatment no fresco of the so-called Renaissance approaches Raphael's *School of Athens* and as a model of serene power and strength it shows how much the young artist had managed to absorb from the style of his older colleague, Michelangelo, who was working next door. Many of the other frescoes in the papal apartments cannot be credited entirely to Raphael but were done with a great deal of apprentice help and suffer considerably therefor. Like most work of this type produced in the early sixteenth century, these paintings were dedicated not to the church (even though they were executed in the Vatican) but rather to the pope who employed the artist.

Other fields covered by Raphael in the course of his thirty-seven years include the portrait, small religious painting, and classical allegory. Of his portraits, one of the most famous is that of *Baldassare Castiglione.* The average mood of these portraits is gentle and refined, not pompous, nor overbearing. It is in the small religious painting, particularly the madonnas, that Raphael reaches his greatest popularity. The most famous example of this group is his *Madonna of the Chair,* where his harmonious attitude and universal appeal brings him closest to the restrained and refined temperament of classical antiquity. From a simple peasant theme (the madonna wears a brightly colored scarf about her head) he worked out one of the most ingenious and smooth compositions that any painter of this time achieved. Although the layman probably will not appreciate the intricate rhythmical flow of his linear arrangements nor the casually studied manner in which he has fitted the forms in this picture into the circular frame, everyone will be charmed by its warmth and human appeal. It is significant that for a great many pious Catholics the madonnas of Raphael are *the Madonna.*

Raphael's great appeal for his contemporaries apparently lay in the fact that he was able to take old themes and refresh them through the joyousness of his own personality. In spite of the fact that he used everyday models for some of his madonnas, the result is a Raphael that everyone was able to recognize. Like Leonardo and Michelangelo, he created his own world of men and women. He was more popular than others (and still is today) because he was not bothered with the intellectual and emotional problems which beset such artists as Leonardo and Michelangelo, but was more concerned with the creation of an *ideal* type of beauty which would be attractive and appealing. How much of this was the result of his practical nature and his love of success is problematical—but in the worldly atmosphere in which he moved, the friend of prince and pope, he managed not only to change the entire status of the artist in society but to bring art once and for all into the ken of every person.

With Andrea del Sarto (1486-1531), commonly known as "the faultless painter," we reach the last great name in the history of the Florentine school. Although he painted religious pictures almost exclusively, his attitude was worldly in the extreme, a fact manifested not only in the beautiful and joyous types he preferred to paint, but in the wonderfully glowing quality of his color. He is probably the only Florentine who used color in this happy manner, both in his panel paintings and in his large frescoes whose execution bring the history of the monumental wall painting in Florence to a close. Del Sarto, however, was not of the stature of the three great masters just studied, although he was more consistent in his quality than Raphael. All of the works of del Sarto are on the same high level of *technical* excellence in draughtsmanship, composition, and color, and yet there is a certain something lacking, perhaps the emotional and intellectual spark that set the other three ablaze, which leaves the creation of Andrea del Sarto in a high position but in the second rank.

In such a painting as the *Madonna of the Harpies* Andrea del Sarto's most characteristic qualities may be seen. The severe architectonic arrangement of the figures, with the madonna placed in an artificial position as she holds the rather heavy but beautiful child, is an indication of the combination of artificiality and warm human beauty so frequently seen in him. Of his frescoes, the famous *Madonna of the Sack* exemplifies his warm and glowing color of which he is an even greater master in this medium. We must remember that the fresco (a quickly drying technique) does not readily lend itself to subtle modulations of color and light, and yet Andrea, the great technician, was able to create these effects better than any other Florentine artist of the sixteenth century.

Before the middle of the sixteenth century, following the invasion of Rome by foreign powers in 1527 and the threat of the Reformation, many Italian artists had come to feel spiritually and economically threatened. Some were taking courtly posts in other parts of Europe. Others turned to alchemy, or sought a profounder religious experience than that which they considered had been afforded them during the High Renaissance. Actually the immense prestige of Rome as the city in which the Renaissance had culminated was short-lived, and men of lesser status than that of a Bramante or a Michelangelo or a Raphael were disquieted in the 1530's. In addition to the more immediate instabilities caused by the dislocation of religious and economic foundations, a growing dissatisfaction with the normative classicism of the earlier sixteenth century was beginning to be felt. The art of Michelangelo himself reveals after 1530 certain tensions traceable at least in part to these changing values.

The resulting expression in painting, sculpture, and architecture which appears in Italy, France, Spain, the Netherlands, and elsewhere has been called the "Anticlassical Style" or Mannerism. Among the first of twentieth-century scholars to isolate Mannerism as a special phenomenon were Max Dvorak and Walter Friedlaender; but later sixteenth-century artist-critics were also well aware of its existence.

The specific traits of Mannerism vary somewhat from one country to the next, but the salient elements of this style are recognizable everywhere: extreme elegance in portraiture, arbitrary and sometimes sharp lighting, posturing rather than posing of the figure, attenuation of forms generally, and a crowding of the composition in larger figure groups. Also, a majority of Mannerist painters made new and sometimes exciting interpretations of picture space; in one part of the canvas, space would be treated as extremely deep; in another, shallow or quite flat. There are intentional inequalities in treatment of detail within the same plane. Linear perspective is given bizarre application. As often as not a certain melancholy appears in Mannerist works.

Among the outstanding Italian Mannerists are Jacopo Pontormo (1494-1556), Parmigianino (1503-1540), Bronzino (1503-1572), Il Rosso (1494-1540), and Beccafumi (1486-1551). Another, Primaticcio (1504-1570), was a resident artist at the court of Francis I in France.

While most religious paintings of the Mannerists followed Renaissance themes, traditional others, such as Parmigianino's *Madonna of the Long Neck*, afford enigmatic reinterpretations. Both Pontormo and Bronzino excelled at the strangely elegant portraiture which we associate with this style. There is about the finest of Italian Mannerist painting an intensity and moodiness which has almost certainly influenced twentieth-century Surrealists.

Mannerism in Italy developed at least partly as a result of an anticlassical attitude among painters of the 1530's. The founding of an art academy in Bologna by the Carracci family in 1583 was in turn an anti-Mannerist procedure. Students at this prototype of most subsequent art schools were required to study selected qualities of Renaissance masterpieces and to combine these in a search for the perfect academic style. Unfortunately, though not at all illogically, much of the product of this academy lacks distinction. Of the Carracci family, Annibale (1560-1609) made the greatest individual contribution to painting. Guido Reni (1575-1642) and Domenichino (1581-1641) are among the most accomplished followers of the school.

The painters of Spain during this period are directly related to the Italian tradition. Beginning with the work of El Greco (c. 1548-1614) we find an interest in religious emotionality, expressive light, genre, and other phenomena of realism. El Greco had apparently studied in Venice under the influence of Tintoretto from whom he derived his interest in tall figures and emotional coloring and light. El Greco is more typically Mannerist than any other member of the Spanish school. He conveys his ideas through an aristocratic and nervous refinement. In his art, as in that of the modern "Expressionist" painters, the forms are deliberately warped and the colors changed to arouse a powerful emotional reaction in the mind and a "disturbance" in the eye of the beholder. *The Crucifixion*, with the tortuous elongated figure of the Savior, the tall and aristocratic figures at either side, and the dull grayish-green background, is an interesting example of the emotional possibilities latent in the technique of distorted color and form. Although ordinary problems are not of great importance to El Greco, he remains so typical of the period that his work is the most powerful emotional summation of the Jesuit point of view. The Metropolitan Museum of Art in New York City contains some fine examples of his art: the early *Portrait of Cardinal Guevara* (still related to the Tintoretto tradition); the starkly emotional *Portrait of a Man* in which slight alterations are made in the relative size of ears, eyes, and the like to produce an agitated reaction in the spectator; the flame-like *Adoration of the Child* in which the preternaturally tall figures are set in an undefined space and clothed in unrealistically modeled garments in unearthly colors. Perhaps the most interesting of the El Grecos in this collection is the *View of the City of Toledo* where the artist has shown this Spanish city under a bleak and forbidding sky made up of his typical grays and greens and where human beings occur as small worm-like figures in the foreground. It is in this painting that his relation to the twentieth-century Expressionist artists, particularly the post-war Germans, is clearly seen. When modern artists were moved to distort nature in order to produce a highly emotionalized effect they naturally turned to one of the greatest exponents of the practice, El Greco, for justification.

2. *Sculpture*

Of the sculpture of this period in central Italy, we may treat separately the last part of the fifteenth century and the sixteenth century proper. During the first period, the sculptors constitute two distinct groups: those who work in bronze and those who work in marble primarily. The first of these groups includes the names of Verrocchio (Leonardo's teacher) and Pollaiuolo (also celebrated as a painter). These men are primarily technicians in the fifteenth-century scientific sense and are interested in physical and sometimes violent expression, particularly the last-named. Verrocchio's famous equestrian statue of *Colleoni*, in the tradition of Donatello's great figure, was to serve as a model for the similar work of his pupil, Leonardo.

The marble workers, on the other hand, are distinguished for a fineness of sentiment and an almost lyrical quality in their work which is quite different in its emphasis from the efforts of the bronze sculptors. Much of this sculpture was produced for the elaborate religious and secular buildings of the time.

Among the great masters of the early sixteenth century, those whom we have singled out in painting were also important for sculpture. Although none of Leonardo's sculptures has survived, we know that in his own day no work was as celebrated as the great equestrian monument he was preparing for the Duke of Milan, for which he had completed the clay model. For political and economic reasons this was never cast and was finally destroyed by the invading French armies. Raphael we may be sure also produced some sculpture, but it is impossible to identify any of it today. It is certain that he was very much interested in antique sculpture, since one of the commissions he held from the pope was that of general inspector of excavations for the territory of Rome.

The greatest sculptor of the sixteenth century and probably of all time is Michelangelo. In this field, the monumentality of conception he showed in his painting of the Sistine Chapel is even more striking. Here his individuality and intense subjectivity reach their highest expression, even though in the process of forming his style he absorbed as much as he could from the study of the antique and from nature herself. No artist of the period, with the exception of Leonardo, spent as much time in the study of anatomy, but the total result of his efforts (psychological effects of which are described in the sculptor's sonnets) was the perfection of a style which is a mingling of the abstract and the specific. To paraphrase the words of Michelangelo himself, his work was like no one else's, and bore that stamp of individuality which is the hallmark of the entire period. He played upon the nude human body as though it were an instrument for the expression of his own emotions, in melodies full-bodied and forceful as those of a cathedral organ. A master of the body in motion, he was able to express in the complicated postures he preferred the most violent personal reactions and sentiments.

His sculpture is almost entirely in marble, which he handled in his own unique fashion. So great a technician was he that he did not have to go through the elaborate preparations which usually precede working in marble—marble does not lend itself to corrections—but he attacked the stone directly and literally tore the figure out of the block. His works, like those of the ancient Egyptians, are controlled and confined by the original block, for he himself believed that one of the tests of a piece of sculpture was to be able to roll it downhill without any part breaking from the figure—all of which means that a figure should be carefully composed and integrated, and that diffuseness is not permissible in something which was originally a rectangular block of stone.

One of his most famous works is the great *David,* commonly known as "The Giant" because of its size and overwhelming effect. Here, as in most of his works, the energy of the figure is controlled, but its potential power is radiant in this adolescent shepherd boy with his sling drawn back over his shoulder. At first the *David* seems an idealization and cosmic abstraction, but upon examination it proves to be full of fine, subtle indications of Michelangelo's tremendous knowledge of anatomy. The carefully modeled finger nails, the knobby knuckles, and the large hands and feet all bear the impress of a close familiarity with the specific anatomy of the subject.

Another important work is the *Moses,* one of a group of figures done for the Tomb of Julius II that was never finished (the *Bound Slave* and the *Dying Slave* belong to this group as well). Here, in the flashing expression of the great leader, Michelangelo has best expressed his quality of "terribilità" in a figure that is a combination of Moses, Michelangelo, and Julius II. The gesture with which the prophet grasps at his beard and the knee withdrawn under him express the controlled emotional and physical force lying at the basis of this artist's expression.

The age in which Michelangelo lived was a troubled one, particularly in Florence, and the sense of disillusionment and dissatisfaction is expressed in the well-known *Medici Tombs.* Here he has portrayed a pair of contemporary Medicis in allegorical guise, one representing the active phase of life, and the other, the passive. Below these full-length seated figures on each side of the chapel in which they are set are two pairs of gigantic men and women, one group representing *Dawn* and *Twilight*, the passive aspect of the day, and the other *Day* and *Night*, the active one. In Michelangelo's hands the allegory, ordinarily a mawkish form of expression, becomes something universal, a symbol of power or spent energy as the subject demands. Toward the end of his life, his sculpture, like his painting, tended to become more emotional and overwrought, as the *Pietà*, designed for his own tomb and now in the apse of the Cathedral of Florence. Here the figures are attenuated and seem to shape themselves into curious spiral patterns which shoot off into space much like the later figures of El Greco in Spain. The sculpture of his last period, like the *Last Judgment*, strikes the Baroque note of the seventeenth century in its exaggerated emotional and personal quality.

The rest of the sixteenth century, after Michelangelo, is a period of exaggeration in sculpture. Some artists tend to overemphasize elegance and a certain Hellenistic swing. Others merely imitate the largeness of size found in Michelangelo's work, without achieving any of his real monumentality.

3. *Venice*

The case of Venetian art is most interesting to the student of history and culture, for here we have the extraordinary phenomenon of a city which produced very little literature, philosophy, architecture, or sculpture, yet became preëminent in painting. Venice was, of course, one of the most powerful commercial centers in Europe, standing at the gateway between the West and the East and in closest contact with Byzantium. Venetian gaiety, lavishness, and color were the expression of a highly developed middle-class culture for which the intellectual refinements of the Florentines held little appeal, but where having a good time and embellishing one's own person and house were a prime consideration. Here, more than in other centers of Europe, art was used to glorify both the citizens and the serene republic itself.

The most striking characteristic of Venetian painting is its color, a factor which had played relatively little part in the art of Florence (except for Andrea del Sarto). Florence for the most part displayed its virtuosity in the manipulation of linear forms and composition, predominantly mental processes compared with the sensuousness of the brilliant Venetian color. The difference between the two styles is not all a mattter of intellectual level. Venetian painting began very late in the fifteenth century, and did not have to endure an arduous period of apprenticeship as did the Florentine. During the period of learning, the Florentines had used the very tight tempera technique which emphasized draughtsmanship above all else and subordinated color. When the Venetians came upon the scene, the oil technique was definitely emerging as a substitute for tempera, and this new system which built up its forms primarily by modulations of color could forego the more sober and precise manipulation of line of the Florentines.

Venetian painting may be said to emerge with the work of the Bellini family: Jacopo Bellini, the father, and Gentile and Giovanni, his two sons. Jacopo worked for a time in Padua where he came in contact with Mantegna, to whom he married both his daughter and his art. In Jacopo's surviving work (a few paintings and some marvelous notebooks) the relationship between the two artists is clear.

His son Gentile Bellini (1429-1507) is interesting to us for his meticulous portrayals of Venetian life in the fifteenth century. His three pictures of *The Story of the Holy Cross* show the typical ostentatious Venetian love of parades and processions. The people in these pictures are ordinary tradespeople who have dressed themselves elaborately for the holiday. Gentile Bellini, like most later Venetian artists, stresses a lovely, delicate out-of-door tonality which aids tremendously in the building up of a true local color.

The most important Venetian painter of the fifteenth century was Giovanni Bellini (c. 1430-1516), influenced during his early work by the slightly hard sculptural quality of Mantegna, but later developing into the true founder of the Venetian tradition. In him we find the first full development of the Venetian oil technique which brings about his warm and glowing color. The typical worldliness of Venetian painting is emphasized in Bellini's wise and mature madonnas of which we have many examples, always different enough not to become boring. They are full-bodied matrons of the type which was undoubtedly congenial to Venice, and are far removed from the delicate girls of Fra Lippo Lippi or the slightly nervous types of Botticelli. To call them gross would be a great exaggeration, for they are more refined than the figures of Andrea del Sarto, and yet they are based upon an unquestionably physical conception.

The three great masters of Venetian painting corresponding in period with Leonardo, Michelangelo, and Raphael (end of the fifteenth and beginning of the sixteenth century) are Giorgione, Palma Vecchio, and Titian. Giorgione (1477-c. 1511) was one of the most interesting masters of the entire Italian tradition who, although he died early, wielded a tremendous influence on his contemporaries. No other artist has inspired so many romantic and unauthenticated stories as Giorgione, but it is undoubtedly true that he was a most extraordinary character and a great poetic artist. Of a surpassing imaginative mind, he created artistic types whose influence was destined to last for centuries. The characteristic note in his art is first struck by the *Madonna of Castelfranco* with its sublimely removed madonna and her two saints who stand about utterly unconcerned with one another in complete self-absorption, the entire scene worked out against a subtly modulated landscape.

Although there are very few of his pictures about whose authenticity controversies do not rage, we may be reasonably certain of the *Concert Champêtre* (*Concert in the Fields*) and *The Gypsy and the Soldier*. The latter picture is probably an earlier work in which we find a man leaning upon a lance at the left with a nude woman suckling a child at the right. For background, Giorgione has used a cloudy sky showing an impending storm, conveying a sensation of restlessness and oppressiveness which is psychologically interesting even though we have not the faintest idea of what is taking place in the picture as far as story is concerned. This juxtaposition of apparently unrelated elements is repeated in modern times by Manet, in the nineteenth century. The dictum, it is not so much what one paints as how one paints it, is strikingly shown in *The Gypsy and the Soldier*. In the *Concert Champêtre* the artist has brought together a pair of clothed young aristocrats and a corresponding pair of nude young ladies and infused such an air of thought and suspended animation into the work that the world seems to stand still. Developed against a bucolic background (shepherd and flock in the rear), this painting strikes a gentle Arcadian mood characteristic of the school of Giorgione. This form of romantic escapism can be explained either in terms of Giorgione's own glamorous biography or as the result of a disharmony between the artist and his environment. (This composition is repeated in the famous *Breakfast on the Grass* of Manet in the nineteenth century.) What strikes us as most unusual in the Venetian paintings of this period is that landscape, which does not exist in the city of canals, plays such an important part. We may say that these are really memory pictures of the places from which the artists originally came, for Giorgione, Palma Vecchio, and Titian were all born outside Venice.

The art of Palma Vecchio (c. 1480-1528) is in direct antithesis to Giorgione's, for he is as realistic as the other is fanciful, as calm and untroubled as the other is melancholy. A pupil of Giovanni Bellini, he carried farther the fine full feminine figures of his teacher and gives us the apogee of a refined and placid representation of his epoch. In his portraits he frequently tends to idealize the characters in a fashion reminiscent of the English portraitists of the eighteenth century, Reynolds and Gainsborough. His so-called *Three Sisters* is a fine example, for the figures are posed and drawn in the English manner of well-being and calm contentment which may be regarded as an expression of one aspect of the commercial civilization from which they spring.

The greatest painter of this period in Venice and one of the great names in the history of art is Titian (1477-1576), whose life spans a century and whose art mirrors the finest ideals of Venetian painting. He is her strongest colorist and in his hands the technique of oil painting reached such heights that he may be regarded as the predecessor of Velasquez and Rubens of the seventeenth century. With his great technical endowment he was able to express an emotional quality in religious painting which, though frequently worldly, is still of a high order indeed. His subject matter covers all fields, although he was most distinguished for his portraits, of which he did a considerable number for most of the princes and crowned heads of Europe. As a painter of the female nude, he is the most important of the Venetians and, in a sense, a purveyor of a not too refined sensuousness.

His early painting is related to that of Giovanni Bellini (his teacher) and his fellow student, Giorgione, in such a work as the so-called *Sacred and Profane Love* where a nude and a clothed woman are placed at opposite ends of a classical sarcophagus used as a fountain. The careful outlining of the forms, the smooth handling of color, the self-absorbed attitude of the figures, all betray the Bellini influence. The fully formed Titian is revealed to us in the *Madonna of the Pesaro Family* in which the splendid matronly figure of the madonna is worshiped by St. Francis and by the beautifully portrayed members of the Pesaro family. This is one of the most impressive examples of the worldliness of religious painting in the first half of the sixteenth century.

To this same period of Titian's career belongs the famous portrait of *Charles V on Horseback*. It is characteristic of Titian's talent for idealizing a person to a point where native ugliness or stupidity gives way before a material splendor and color which take up all of our attention. The armor of the king and the beauty of his horse's trappings are, in every sense, a deviation from the realistic portraiture practiced in the fifteenth century in Flanders. Not only does this painting furnish the prototype for the aristocratic portrait of the seventeenth century (Velasquez, Rubens, Van Dyck, etc.) but it founds a tradition which will endure in the academic schools of Europe down to our own day. There is little question that Titian was the greatest portraitist of the time, but he had the perhaps unfortunate quality of desiring the favor of his patrons to such an extent that he was willing to stretch a point.

Tintoretto (1518-1594), the last of the sixteenth-century Venetian masters, attempted to combine the color of Titian with the drawing of Michelangelo. While he planned his compositions in a careful, almost academic fashion (he is said to have suspended little models on strings within a cardboard box to see their actual positions and to control the light), he is important for a highly emotionalized interpretation of his subject matter. In this sense, he anticipated the arbitrary lighting, diagonal compositions, and exaggerated sentiments of the seventeenth century. His light is not as subtle as Titian's, but consists of dark colors out of which brilliant lights emerge. We find examples of his broad, warm sympathy in the *Crucifixion* and the *Presentation of Mary in the Temple*. For the most part he is a greater emotional artist than Titian, and more concerned with humanity than with splendor in the material sense.

The worship of Venice is the preoccupation of Paolo Veronese (1528-1588) who raises Venetian painting to its greatest lavishness in the richness of his costumes, his color, and interior accessories. Frequently working on a huge scale, he is the culmination of the Venetian love of splendor, shown in his famous *Wedding at Cana*.

4. *The Spread of the Italian Idea*

During the sixteenth century Italian influence reached the other countries of Europe to produce the first Spanish, French and, to a lesser degree, German schools of painting. In Spain and France the borrowings stand out in sharp relief. Spain had invaded Italy frequently during this period and had taken for her own what she chose to use. The court painters of this time in Spain follow the tradition of Venetian art. We should remember that Titian had painted portraits of Charles V and his son Philip II, some of which were, naturally, in Spain. Spanish religious art, although partially the result of its own fifteenth-century tradition (which leaned very heavily on Flanders), also showed distinct traces of Italian influence. Such a painter as Morales, known as the "divine one," betrays derivations from Leonardo and others.

In France the connection was based, first, upon direct invasion (occupation of Milan and the destruction of Leonardo's horse) and, secondly, upon the fact that Francis I had imported a great many Italian artists into France with the intention of founding there a school of art. Leonardo, for example, died in France, and Francis was a valuable patron of Benvenuto Cellini, the goldsmith. Other artists, some less important, were brought in and the French schools of painting and sculpture were started. The most important French painters of this period were the Clouet family, primarily court portraitists and fine draughtsmen. Their crayon portraits founded a tradition which was to survive until the time of Degas in the nineteenth century. These works are analogous to the contemporary efforts of Holbein in Germany. French sculpture of this period was dominated by Jean Goujon whose greatest work is the series of bas-reliefs on the *Fountain of the Innocents,* in Paris, with their complicated postures and beautiful drapery. The Clouets as well as Goujon belong to the Mannerist phase of sixteenth-century French art.

The German school of painting was the most important outside of Italy in this period. Here upon the characteristic emotionality of Germanic art was overlaid the form and color derived from the Italians. Germany's outstanding artist in the early sixteenth century was undoubtedly Albrecht Dürer (1471-1528). He is celebrated for his fine engravings and woodcuts as well as for his paintings and drawings. Of the former, the well-known engraving of *The Knight, Death, and the Devil* is one of those curious combinations of the past and the present for which Dürer is famous; and in this sense he becomes the transition out of the Gothic into modern times. The dark and mysterious background of this work, the macabre skeleton, and the insistence upon small details of Gothic realism are combined with a majestic horse and rider which derive from such models as Donatello or Verrocchio. The relationship between Dürer's art and Venetian art is evident in the two large panels showing *Four Apostles,* for here the monumentality of the later style of Giovanni Bellini as well as his clear and bright colors come through very clearly.

The second of the great German sixteenth-century artists, Hans Holbein (1497-1543), now classified generally as a Mannerist, was even more Italianate than Dürer in such a work as his *Madonna of Burgomaster Meyer.* The use of the elaborate conch-shell motif behind the head of the madonna, the lovely children, and the bright coloring are all reminiscent. Holbein is particularly famous for his portraits, especially those of the court of Henry VIII of England, *Jane Seymour, Anne of Cleves,* etc. They represent the usual sixteenth-century German combination of Gothic detail and meticulousness plus the breadth and sweep of Italian art. We esteem Dürer and Holbein primarily for their draughtsmanship rather than their color, since they turned out so many fine drawings either as preparation for other works or for their own sake. In their hands the drawing itself became an autonomous work of art. The Germans are particularly distinguished for engravings and woodcuts. They turned out innumerable illustrated books and individual plates. In this field they were far beyond the Italians at a corresponding period of evolution. Dürer's woodcuts, for example, were being pirated in the north of Italy, and he was forced to make two trips to Venice to defend his rights in court.

The essence of German art in this period was a combination of what we may call native elements plus those ideas which Dürer and others imported from Italy. The strength of Germanic art lies in its tremendous vitality and like fifteenth-century Flemish painting it has more religious sincerity and passionate feeling than the art of Italy.

We must not neglect the powerful painter, Pieter Brueghel (c. 1525-1569), associated with the Flemish school. Opposed to the horde of Italianate painters who appeared in the Low Countries at the beginning of the sixteenth century (Jan van Mabuse and Lucas van Leyden), this robust character proceeded to formulate one of the most powerful and realistic arts the world has ever seen. In his own day he was known as "Peasant Brueghel" because of his avowed preference for earthy material which he handled in a direct and sympathetic manner. He was unquestionably one of the most socially conscious artists in the sixteenth century. Of an essentially moral outlook, he occupied himself with the weaknesses and foibles of humanity. Such titles as the *Faithless Shepherd* or *The Blind Leading the Blind* are evidence. The foremost realist of his day, it is only natural that Brueghel, descended from the fifteenth-century painters of Flanders, was an outstanding landscape artist whose cunning is shown in the *Summer* and the *Huntsmen in the Snow*. Brueghel is the great link between the art of the end of the sixteenth century in the Low Countries and the succeeding epoch of Dutch landscapists, religious artists, and genre painters of the seventeenth century.

III. "THE GOLDEN AGE" OF MUSIC

1. *Late Fifteenth Century*

The period 1450-1600 witnessed the supreme exaltation of polyphonic art. In fact, the sixteenth century in particular has been characterized by more than one writer as the "golden age" of music.

The formulation of the polyphonic technique of the music of the period was accomplished by a group of Flemish masters who flourished in the latter half of the fifteenth century, the so-called "second Flemish school." The segregation of Flemish composers into "first," "second," and "third" schools, while convenient, is misleading if not incorrect. What is usually called the "first" Flemish school we have treated before (Chapter XII) as the Burgundian school.

The Flemish School.—The prominent names in this group of composers were Jean Ockeghem (c. 1430-1495) and Jacob Obrecht (c. 1430-1505). Ockeghem, who served as *maître de chapelle* to two kings of France, Charles VII and Louis XI, made the more significant technical contributions, and his music, while not lacking in expressiveness, often appeals more to the eye than to the ear. Obrecht, *maître de chapelle* at the Cathedral of Antwerp and at one time Erasmus' music teacher, wrote works in which technical facility and melodic inventiveness are so well combined that the music almost seems a spontaneous creation. Ockeghem's compositions are full and sonorous and possess broad melodic lines. Obrecht's, on the other hand, are in a more popular vein. His melodies are more sharply defined, and are occasionally pictorial or descriptive. His rhythms are always vital and pulsing, and his works show a clear feeling for what may be called "vocal orchestration."

The great contribution of the school was the principle of "imitation." Imitation as an artistic device we have already observed in the Italian *caccia* with its accompanied canon; it had been frequently utilized by Dufay and his school. Now, however, the resources of imitation were carried far beyond the level of so strict a form as the canon. Imitation as found in the works of Ockeghem and his contemporaries was produced by having the individual voices of a polyphonic work commence not simultaneously, but one after another; each individual voice repeated the words of the text to at least the initial musical motive of the preceding voice. This procedure offered a repetitive device of great elasticity and singular effectiveness. Imitation has remained one of the standard devices of music ever since.

Composers of this period apparently took great delight in the creation of intricate polyphonic patterns. Ockeghem, for example, wrote a motet in no less than thirty-six parts, consisting of four nine-part canons. One of his most celebrated works is a *Missa cujusvis toni* ("Mass in whatever mode you wish"), a clefless composition which can be performed in any of the four principal modes. The writing of "puzzle canons" was also one of the scholarly diversions of the Flemish composers. These canons were written out ostensibly as one melody; but by following the directions hinted at by an enigmatical motto at the beginning, the melody might be sung in canon. These inscriptions when deciphered implied that one voice might begin at the end and proceed backwards, sing backwards with all the intervals inverted, imitate in different time values, and so forth.

Undue emphasis seems to have been placed on the technical accomplishments of the Flemish composers. Great as their technical dexterity was, however, it never got out of hand. There is hardly a composer possessing the necessary ability who has not at some time or other set himself a technical problem for the sole purpose of experiencing the creative joy of artistic solution. And the same general phenomenon is encountered in the other arts as well.

Another trend which became distinctly noticeable at this time was the gradual elimination of instruments from vocal music, and the growth of a pure *a cappella* (unaccompanied) style. Hand in hand with this went a development of the musical resources of massed voices and the "color" potentialities of the chorus. Simultaneously the various parts of a polyphonic work came to possess more and more equality as melodies, this tendency manifesting itself more prominently in sacred than in secular music. Melodic individuality of the parts was to Ockeghem and his school the paramount consideration in the composition of a work. Harmonic and formal values were secondary and were frequently neglected. Thus the emphasis fell on the texture of a work and not on its form.

During the fifteenth and the greater part of the sixteenth centuries the Low Countries were the focal point of European music. Flemish musicians were in demand everywhere. Flemish singers and composers found employment in the papal chapel at Rome, in the Cathedral of St. Mark in Venice, at the courts of the Medici family in Florence, the Sforza family in Milan, the Hapsburg family in Austria and Spain, and the Wittelsbach family in Bavaria. The influence of Flemish composers made itself felt over almost all Europe.

Musical styles were continually being exported and imported. The French *ars nova* was fostered in Italy, transmitted to the Low Countries by Dunstable and Dufay, taken up and developed to a high degree of perfection by Flemish composers, and reëxported to Italy as a Flemish product.

The diverse trends—technical virtuosity on one hand and expressiveness on the other—represented by the works of Ockeghem and Obrecht were united in the compositions of the greatest master of the early sixteenth century, Josquin des Prés (c. 1450-1521). Josquin's fame was so great, the influence of his music and of his pupils so extensive that he was called "The Prince of Music." His career bears a curious resemblance to that of Dufay, for he, too, was born in Hainault, spent much time in Italy, and was in charge of the music at Cambrai. It is also worthy of note that Josquin was a pupil of Ockeghem.

Music historians are almost unanimous in declaring Josquin to be the first modern composer. This evaluation of his attainments is, to be sure, somewhat unfair to the efforts of individuals such as Dunstable and Obrecht. What is meant is that Josquin's music, more than that of any other composer before him, contained those stylistic features which we have come to demand from all music.

From no matter what angle we approach Josquin's art, we are struck by its consummate mastery. Josquin was a worthy successor to Ockeghem and could write with great ease in a thoroughly complex polyphonic manner. But his ingenuity was merely accessory to a higher purpose—expression, and this was the aim of all his work.

Unlike the music of his predecessors, the works of Josquin impress us at once by their formal balance. His compositions abound in artfully combined contrasts and pleasing symmetries. His phrases are clear and well-defined, his cadences powerful. (As a musical term, the word *cadence* designates the end of some element of the musical·structure.) Josquin was one of the first polyphonic composers to realize that music could be used to heighten the expressiveness of a text, and he always laid great stress on meaningful accentuation, both melodic and harmonic.

The most important of the several advances in musical expressiveness attributed to Josquin is his revelation of the potentialities of harmony, which now frequently appeared as an end in itself and not as a casual by-product of polyphony. He continually and systematically exploited the ability of a well-placed dissonance to throw a word into high relief.

Important Flemish contemporaries of Josquin were Pierre de la Rue (d. 1518), for some time in the service of the court of Burgundy, and Heinrich Isaac (c. 1480-1517), in the employ of the Hapsburg emperors.

Music Printing.—The invention of the printing press had important repercussions in the field of music. While the first printing of music occurred late in the fifteenth century, the first individual successfully to reproduce music from movable type was a Venetian craftsman, Ottaviano dei Petrucci (1466-1539). His most famous product was the *Odhecaton* (*One Hundred Songs*) issued in 1501. Petrucci's printings contained many works by Flemish composers, notably Obrecht and Josquin, and served further to enlarge their sphere of influence. Petrucci had a host of followers and music publishing soon became a lively industry.

2. The Sixteenth Century

Music reached a high state of development in many countries in the sixteenth century and the number of great composers active at the time was large indeed. A discussion of the period may therefore be advantageously conducted in terms of geographical groupings. But we must not forget that the musicians of the period traveled extensively and that music was a decidedly international art. The various schools which we shall investigate possessed, therefore, only a limited measure of individuality. The *a cappella* polyphonic style formulated by the Flemings predominated; but the period was primarily one of final formulation and not of enterprising pioneering.

The two outstanding sacred forms were the *Mass* and the *motet*. The latter had nothing in common with the thirteenth- and fourteenth-century French form of the same name. Since about 1450, composers have used the term "motet" as a designation for an *a cappella* polyphonic setting of some biblical extract, usually, but not invariably, in Latin.

Secular music, both instrumental and vocal, was now the compeer of sacred music and almost all the great composers were fluent in both types. Popular Italian vocal forms were the *frottola,* an instrumentally accompanied song of simple construction, the *villanella,* a dancelike setting of a rustic text and, most important of all, the *madrigal.* Like the later motet, the later madrigal should not be confused with the type fostered by fourteenth-century composers. The sixteenth-century madrigal, in many respects the secular counterpart of the motet, consisted of a comparatively simple polyphonic setting of a poem, often aristocratic in style. The polyphonic *chanson* was widely cultivated in France, especial fame being achieved by Josquin's pupil Clement Jannequin (c. 1485-1550) with a series of descriptive works bearing titles such as *La Bataille de Marignan* (*The Battle of Marignan*), a musical account of an important encounter at Marignan in 1515, *Le Cacquet des femmes* (*The Gossip of the Women*), *Le Chant des oiseaux* (*The Song of the Birds*), and so forth.

Our modern instrumental music dates from about this time. While instruments had been freely used in conjunction with voices in past epochs, not until the sixteenth century did intrinsically instrumental music arise and well-defined instrumental forms come into being. Most of the new forms were dance forms, of which the archetypes were the stately *pavane* in duple rhythm, and the livelier *galliarde* in triple. The more learned forms were the *ricercare* and the *canzone.* While the lute figured as the musical instrument par excellence, it shared honors with the now prominent viol family of stringed instruments as well as keyboard instruments like the harpischord and clavichord. With the mechanical improvement of the organ, a number of characteristic musical forms were evolved, among them brilliant display types such as the *prelude* and *toccata,* as well as elaborative treatments of sacred melodies.

Italy.—The two important musical centers in Italy were located at Rome and Venice. The Roman school was essentially conservative, content to sum up the traditions of the past and crystallize them for all time. The Venetian group, however, was actively engaged in devising new methods.

Musical activity in Rome befitted the ecclesiastical eminence of the city. The papal choir, easily the most celebrated musical organization of the time, occupied an important position not only in Rome but in the entire Western musical world. The fundamental temper of Roman music was one of high seriousness, of absolute devotion to the church and its precepts.

The greatest Roman master, Giovanni Pierluigi da Palestrina (c. 1525-1594), probably the best known of all sixteenth-century composers, spent over forty years in the service of various Roman churches, eventually becoming the composer to the papal choir. Palestrina's style represents the quintessence of the Flemish contrapuntal technique. All secular elements had now been removed, together with all musical practices not in keeping with the exalted texts of the church. The works of Palestrina constitute the musical embodiment of the Counter Reformation. But in no sense are they typical of the prevailing spirit of their age.

The style of Palestrina, although using every technical device known to the Flemings, is a remarkably simple one. His melodies conform rigorously to the modes, they are purely vocal in their style, and usually scalewise in their flow, changes in the direction of the melodic line being very circumspectly handled. So fitting was Palestrina's idiom for the service of the church that the Council of Trent (1545-1563) commended it to all composers as an official model. His celebrated *Improperia* (*Reproaches*) have been sung in the Sistine Chapel on every Good Friday since 1560. His best-known and probably greatest composition is the *Missa Papae Marcelli* (*Pope Marcellus Mass*). The thirty-three volume complete edition of his works includes ninety-four masses, three hundred and fifty motets, and one hundred and forty madrigals.

The Spaniard Tomás Louis de Victoria (c. 1540-1611) has been rightly called the "Spanish Palestrina," for he was allied with Palestrina both personally and artistically. Victoria's art has often been compared with that of his contemporary El Greco (c. 1548-1614), for it had the same visionary quality and the same fervor of expression. His style, particularly in its harmonic aspects, is not as reserved as that of Palestrina. Victoria restricted himself entirely to sacred music and his productivity as compared to that of contemporary masters was small. A motet for Christmas, *O Magnum Mysterium,* is one of his best-known works.

The music heard in the wealthy cosmopolitan seaport of Venice contrasted strongly with the monastic product of Rome, for brilliancy in choral writing and colorful use of instruments were among the aims of the Venetian composers. Here again the influence of the Flemings made itself felt, and the art of Josquin found a lively continuation. An unusual feature of the Church of St. Mark constituted an equally important molding force in Venetian music: in 1490 a second organ had been placed in the church, and contrasts between alternating bodies of instruments or performers soon became a familiar procedure.

The Fleming Adrian Willaert (c. 1480-1562) became *maestro di cappella* at St. Mark's in 1527, and it is from this date that the ascendancy of the Venetian school is reckoned. Willaert's emphasis on compositions for double-chorus, in which two vocal bodies were continually being juxtaposed, laid the foundations for the Venetian style. Willaert's works also displayed bold departures from conventional practices in their use of chromaticism (semitonal progressions).

The greatest composer of the Venetian school was Giovanni Gabrieli (1557-1612), and his works best typify the brilliance and the effective use of two choirs so characteristic of the group. Gabrieli was the first master of the *concerto* style, a method based on a contrast of groups of instrumentalists or vocalists differing in location, color and strength. He was one of the first composers writing for voices and instruments to assign an independent part to the latter group. All of Gabrieli's music clearly anticipated the style of the seventeenth century. Unlike Palestrina he was an individual of enormous influence, notably on many German composers, among them Jacob Handl (1550-1591), Hans Leo Hassler (1564-1612), and Heinrich Schütz (1585-1612).

The madrigal was the outstanding secular form of the cultured classes in Italy. Strictly speaking the madrigal was not a form, but rather a style of secular vocal composition which came into prominence in Italy about 1530. As before, the initial impetus was supplied by the Flemish musicians. Texts of madrigals were usually subjective in character and seldom lacked an amatory note. The musical texture, while polyphonic, was unusually free harmonically, chromaticism being a common feature. Realism of portrayal was also emphasized, the term "madrigalesque" eventually being applied to any music with a marked use of pictorial figures.

Of the numerous composers of Italian madrigals the more important were the aforementioned Flemings Adrian Willaert, Jacob Arcadelt (c. 1514-1557), Willaert's pupil Cyprian de Rore (1516-1565); and the Italians Constanza Festa (d. 1545), Luca Marènzio (1550-1599) who was the greatest of them all, Gesualdo da Venosa (1560-1613) who was both prince and assassin and a friend of Torquato Tasso, and Claudio Monteverdi (1567-1643). All of these and a host of minor composers helped supply what was an indispensable part of courtly entertainment.

Germany.—The Lutheran Reformation diverted the musical development of Germany into two broad channels. Austria and Bavaria, remaining under Catholic influence, exhibited musical trends similar to those found in Rome. Saxony, on the other hand, as a Lutheran stronghold, was the cradle of important new developments.

A Flemish musician, Orlandus de Lassus (c. 1532-1594), in the service of Duke Albert V of Bavaria, was preëminent in sixteenth-century German Catholic music. His life and that of Palestrina were contemporaneous, although very dissimilar. Divergent as their styles were, de Lassus and Palestrina are counted as the two musical giants of the sixteenth century.

The expressiveness, the universality, the robustness, the fervor, the humor, and the imaginativeness of de Lassus' compositions stamp him as one of the most typical artists of the late sixteenth century. Universally admired, he traveled extensively and was feted by royalty. The Emperor Maximilian conferred a patent of nobility upon him in 1570. It is doubtful that any composer has ever approached de Lassus for diversity of output. The list of his over two thousand compositions, comprising no less than sixty volumes, includes almost every sacred and secular form—masses, motets, magnificats, madrigals, villanellas, French *chansons,* German part songs, and so forth. De Lassus' essential cosmopolitanism is reflected in the fact that his texts were written in many languages—Latin, French, Italian, and German. Among his numerous admirers was the French diplomat-poet Pierre de Ronsard (1524-1585), for several of whose poems he made musical settings. The celebrated cobbler-poet Hans Sachs (1494-1576) also furnished de Lassus with verses, and like many other madrigal composers de Lassus also used sonnets of Petrarch (1304-1374).

De Lassus reached his greatest heights of inspiration in the sphere of the motet. The rigid text of the Mass apparently held his imagination in check, for his masses are not his best works. His motets are happy fusions of the Flemish polyphonic style and the pictorial tendencies of the Italian madrigal. Madrigalesque features continually appear in his works. De Lassus seemingly had an inexhaustible liking for musical illustration, and there is hardly a work by him which does not possess some strikingly effective bit of tonal symbolism. Like his great forebear, Josquin des Prés, de Lassus made full use of the expressive resources of harmony, and to an extent which makes him a much more modern composer than Palestrina. His polyphonic skill was equivalent to that of any contemporary, yet his music is not marred by any traces of effort.

A great emphasis on expression pervaded almost all of de Lassus' music no matter what the subject in hand may have been. An outstanding master of the light touch, de Lassus ranks as one of the first of the world's musical humorists. Such profound and moving works as his settings of the *Penitential Psalms,* however, are equally typical of his talents.

Two other important Catholic composers of the period were the Swiss Ludwig Senfl (c. 1492-1555)—the predecessor of de Lassus at Munich and, although a Catholic, the preferred composer of Martin Luther—and Philippe de Monte (1521-1603). While de Monte's artistic attainments closely rivaled those of Palestrina and de Lassus, he has not yet been accorded the recognition he merits.

The *chorale,* the congregational hymn which serves as the core of the Lutheran church service, stands out as the Reformation's significant contribution to the art of music. Just as Luther's teachings were based not on entirely new foundations but on a transformation of the old, so in music he did not create a new musical liturgy, but refashioned that of the Catholic church into a form more in keeping with the spirit of Protestantism.

For Luther the importance of music lay not in itself, but in its power to move the human heart. Concerned with its moral effect rather than its aesthetic value, he regarded music as a gift of God, not of man. Hence it was capable of "driving out the devil, making sad ones happy and happy ones sad, the disheartened hopeful, the haughty meek." Through music, Luther believed, man was purged of anger, sin, and arrogance, and his soul was thus made ready to receive the words of God. In his estimation music was second in importance only to theology.

With music regarded as such a potent factor in influencing the religious receptivity of man, the important rôle it played in the Evangelical church service is readily understandable. Singing was no longer the exclusive province of the choir and the priesthood as in the Catholic service, but a form of direct communication with God for every man, woman, and child of the congregation. The awesomeness and mystery of the Latin Mass were replaced by hymn texts in the German language, written in clear, simple style. For Luther had the rare gift of being able to express the most profound thoughts and feelings in language which spoke directly to everyday people and which in turn acted as a vehicle for the utterance of their faith. This actual participation of the congregation in the singing of the service made music a vital part of the people's daily life.

Luther went to three sources for his hymn material. He did not scorn the large body of German folk songs as profane and worldly, but realizing the appeal these old familiar tunes had for the German people, he merely substituted "sacred" and "good" texts for the secular verses of the original. Thus many folk-melodies were transformed into chorales. For many of his chorales Luther borrowed from the Catholic church's store of Gregorian chant or from popular hymns of the pre-Reformation period, translating their texts and adapting their melodies to conform with the Protestant spirit.

But while Luther was adept at molding the creations of others to suit his own purposes, he was also a composer in his own right. About eight original hymns are attributed to him. Of these the most famous is probably "Ein feste Burg ist unser Gott" (A Mighty Fortress Is Our God).

A colorful aspect of sixteenth-century Germany has been re-created by Richard Wagner in his opera *Die Meistersinger von Nürnberg* (*The Mastersingers of Nuremberg*) (1867). The Meistersinger guilds were descended from the earlier Minnesinger, the first Meistersinger school having been established by Heinrich von Meissen at Mainz early in the fourteenth century. Schools were later founded at Strassburg, Zurich, Frankfurt, Prague, and Nuremberg. The last-named school, thanks to the association with it of Hans Sachs (1494-1576), became the most famous and eventually numbered about two hundred and fifty members.

The Meistersinger were artisans and tradesmen who cultivated music as a hobby. Their concept of art was somewhat naïve, for they believed that art works could be created by diligent adherence to a long and complicated set of rules. Full membership in their guilds could be attained only by learning all the rules and by composing a new song in accordance with them. The Meistersinger took themselves and their art very seriously. The majority of their poems were biblical in origin, and their musical settings somewhat pedantic.

The actual contributions to the art of music made by the Meistersinger were practically negligible. Nevertheless their activity was of great importance, for it bespoke the growing interest in music on the part of the middle class. With such trends as the amateur composing of the Meistersinger and the participation of the congregation in the singing of the Lutheran church service, we witness the first manifestations of that great love of music which became so firmly rooted in the populace of Germany.

France.—Thirty-eight years after the printing of the Lutheran hymn book (1524), the first completed edition of the French Psalter (*Les Pseaumes mis en rime françoise par Clément Marot et Théodore de Bèze*) was issued in 1562 with the approval of the Huguenot Calvin. One of the first of the popular song books of the Reformation, the French Psalter has survived relatively unaltered to the present day. The text of the French Psalter is composed of one hundred and fifty-odd versified renditions of the Psalms made for the most part by the celebrated poet Marot, and completed after his death by de Bèze. Ten years before they were taken up by Calvin, however, many of Marot's Psalm versifications sung to ballad tunes had won popularity at the French courts.

The variety of subject matter and lyrical pattern displayed in these versifications of the Psalms reflects itself in the music to which they were set. As with the Lutheran hymns, the melodies of the French Psalter trace their sources not only to older ecclesiastical music, but also to folk song, in the case of the French, to the secular *chansons* which were freely adapted to fit the meaning of each individual Psalm text. The resulting tunes, simple but expressive, show much beauty, being in turn majestic or plaintive as the verses demand. The importance of the early French Psalter may readily be seen, when one takes into account the fact that it was not only used by French Protestants, but was also translated into over twenty different languages including English and German. Of the several Huguenot composers the finest was Claude Goudimel (1505-1572), who issued several books of Psalm settings.

England.—English music, like English drama and literature, did not come to full flower until late in the sixteenth century. But although late in maturing, the English school gave forth a luster which outshone all others. It is doubtful that English music will ever again reach the heights which it attained during the reign of Queen Elizabeth (1558-1603).

Elizabeth's father, Henry VIII (1491-1547), had set the English fashion in things musical. The many-sided monarch numbered among his accomplishments not only athletic and linguistic skills, but also the ability to play various instruments, sing well, and compose music. Henry gathered many musicians about him and elaborate performances of music were frequent occasions at his court. His compositions are on the whole undistinguished, although many of his works have been reprinted and some are performed today. His interest in music, however, set the standard for English society, and a great zest for music remained a characteristic feature of English life during the brilliant reign of Elizabeth, herself a tolerably good performer on the keyboard instrument known as the virginal.

The young gallant of the Elizabethan age found it incumbent upon himself to be a master of many arts—fencing, courting, equestrianism, verse making, and the singing or playing of music. The amateur aspect of Elizabethan music cannot be too strongly emphasized. A visitor to a cultured household was considered ill-bred indeed if he could not join the company in an after-dinner madrigal session, or play one of the viols in a "consort." This abundance of performance stimulated the composition of an enormous amount of music.

Although fine sacred music was composed during the Elizabethan era, notably by one of England's greatest composers, William Byrd (1543-1623), the prevailing spirit of the age, in music as well as in literature, was a secular one. The English cultivation of the madrigal constituted, to be sure, a fruitful continuation of an Italian form; but the great original contribution of the Elizabethan era lay in the sphere of instrumental music.

Although Italian madrigals had been sung in England as early as 1564, English interest in the madrigal as a form received its first important stimulus from the publication in London in 1588 of the *Musica Transalpina,* a collection of madrigals by outstanding Italian masters. English enthusiasm for the madrigal both grew and declined with amazing rapidity. Over forty collections appeared, of which the greater part came into existence between 1588 and 1613, a period of only twenty-five years. Some of the more prominent composers of madrigals were the versatile William Byrd, his pupil Thomas Morley (1558-1603), Thomas Weelkes (c. 1575-1623), John Wilbye (1574-1638), who is held to be the greatest of them all, and Orlando Gibbons (1583-1625).

Like their Italian forebears, the English madrigal composers were fond of giving musically illustrative settings to descriptive words. The English, however, excelled in the use of dissonant chords as expressive devices, frequently employing them to impart realistic underscoring to some important word. While the greater part of the collection of madrigals is predominantly gay in mood, it includes sad and pensive works as well. The use of series of *fa-las* ("fa la la la," etc.) as a refrain is typical only of a dancelike type of madrigal, the *ballet.*

The earliest keyboard music which is regularly performed today was written in England in the Elizabethan era. The popular instrument, the virginals, was a rectangular affair with a range about five-ninths of the compass of the modern piano. Its wire strings were sounded by a plucking mechanism, and the tone produced by them was bright and sparkling, although incapable of dynamic alteration and consequently somewhat limited in variety and in the power to accent.

The music written for the virginals constitutes one of the most imaginative products of the Elizabethan age. Here we observe the growth of a purely instrumental idiom, for the greater part of the music written for the virginals is effective only if played on a keyboard instrument. Composers reveled in the newly found style, and their works abounded in the showy passages and elaborate figuration so easily produced by the virginals.

The new technique brought with it the age-old problem of form. Instrumental music, lacking the synthesizing power of a text, must create its own forms if it is to possess any unity. Since the days of the Elizabethans, the world's story of instrumental forms has been immeasurably enriched. Since all of them, however, are attempts to secure the twin objectives of unity and variety, any musical form may be discussed purely in terms of its identities and diversities.

The Elizabethan virginal composers, like all contemporary composers of instrumental music, were partial to two dance forms, the *pavane* and the *galliarde*. A signal advance above the methods of the day, however, was achieved with their preference for the variation form, an earlier type which has already been observed in the case of the *cantus firmus* Mass. Variations for the virginals usually consisted of a series of diverse treatments of a well-known secular song, or an original theme, or were built on a recurring bass figure called a *ground bass,* or *ground*. Pieces of a descriptive nature were common, for example William Byrd's *The Bells* and Benjamin Cosyn's *The King's Hunt* (attributed to John Bull).

The household effects of a typical Elizabethan gentleman included not only several sets of part-books of madrigals and a pair of virginals, but also a "chest of viols," a set of six stringed instruments, a forerunner of the string quartet. The viol, a precursor of the violin, was comparatively easy to play, giving forth a tone pure and distinct, if not so powerful as that of the violin.

In addition to *pavanes* and other forms, polyphonic works called *fancies* or *fantasias* were written for the viols. The style of the fancy is best described in the words of Thomas Morley, who in his *Plain and Easy Introduction to Practicall Musicke* (1597) wrote: "A musician taketh a point [a theme] at his pleasure, and wresteth and turneth it as he list, making either much or little of it according as shall seeme best in his own conceit. In this way more art be showne than in any other musicke, because the composer is tide to nothing else that he may adde, diminish and alter at his pleasure."

The preëminence of English music for the viols was recognized everywhere in Europe, and works for them by English composers are to be found in most of the continental libraries.

In conclusion we cannot too strongly emphasize that all Elizabethan secular music was chamber music, and that it was performed by amateurs. The first public concert to be held in England did not take place until 1672; and it was not until early in the nineteenth century that the public performance of music became preponderantly the concern of professionals.

SELECTED READINGS

Beyd, M., *Elizabethan Music and Musical Criticism*, Norton, 1940.
Bode, Wilhelm von, *Florentine Sculptors of the Renaissance*, Scribner, 1909.
Chambers, E. K., *William Shakespeare*, 2 vols., Clarendon Press, 1930.
Chiesa, A.O.D., *Botticelli and His Contemporaries*, Crown, 1960.
Craven, Thomas, *Men of Art*, Simon and Schuster, 1931.
De Tolnay, C., *Michelangelo*, 5 vols., Princeton University Press, 1945-1960.
Dickinson, H. A. S., *German Masters of Art*, Stokes, 1914.
Einstein, Alfred, *The Italian Madrigal*, 3 Vols., Princeton University Press, 1949.
Fischel, Oskar, *Raphael*, 2 vols., Routledge, 1948.

Fry, R. E., *Characteristics of French Art*, Coward-McCann, 1932.

Goldscheider, Ludwig, ed., *Michelangelo: Paintings, Sculptures, Architecture*, Phaidon, 1953.

Greenberg, N., Auden, W. H., and Kallman, C., *An Elizabethan Song Book*, Anchor, 1955.

Hagen, O. F. L., *Art Epochs and Their Leaders*, Scribner, 1927.

Hamlin, Talbot, *Architecture Through the Ages*, Putnam, 1953.

Hauser, *The Social History of Art*.

Lowinsky, Edward, *Secret Chromatic Art in the Netherlands Motet*, Columbia University Press, 1946.

Madariaga, Salvador de, *The Genius of Spain*, Clarendon Press, 1923.

Mather, F. J., Jr., *A History of Italian Painting*, Holt, 1923.

Meiss, *Painting in Florence and Siena after the Black Death*.

Mérimée and Morley, *History of Spanish Literature*, Holt, 1930.

Myers, *Art and Civilization*.

Parrott, T. M., *William Shakespeare, a Handbook*, Scribner, 1955.

Phillips, M. M., *Erasmus and the Northern Renaissance*, Macmillan, 1950.

Reese, Gustave, *Music in the Renaissance*, Norton, 1959.

Sanctis, Francesco de, *History of Italian Literature*, Basic Books, 1960.

Schevill, Ferdinand, *The First Century of Italian Humanism*, Crofts, 1928.

Schmeckebier, Laurence, *A Handbook of Italian Painting*, Holt, 1938.

Scott, Geoffrey, *The Architecture of Humanism*, Doubleday Anchor Book, 1954.

Stites, R. S., *The Arts and the Man*, McGraw-Hill, 1940.

Strachey, G. L., *Landmarks in French Literature*, Oxford University Press, 1912.

Symonds, J. A., *The Renaissance in Italy*, Modern Library, 1936.

Taylor, *Thought and Expression in the Sixteenth Century*.

Taylor, R. A., *Leonardo the Florentine*, Harper, 1927.

Thomas, Calvin, *History of German Literature*, Appleton, 1909, chaps. viii-ix.

Thompson, Herbert, *Wagner and Wagenseil*, Oxford University Press, 1927.

Tilley, Arthur, *The Literature of the French Renaissance*, Hafner, 1959.

Valentiner, W. R., *Studies of Italian Renaissance Sculpture*, Oxford, 1950.

Venturi, Lionello, and Skira-Venturi, Rosabianca, *Italian Painting: The Creators of the Renaissance*, Skira, 1950.

Walker, Ernest, *History of Music in England*, Oxford University Press, 1952.

Ward and Waller, *Cambridge History of English Literature*, Vols. II-III.

Whitcomb, Merrick, *Literary Source-Book of the Renaissance*, University of Pennsylvania Press, 1904.

Wittkower, Rudolf, *Architectural Principles in the Age of Humanism*, Transatlantic.

Woodfill, W. L., *Musicians in English Society*, Princeton University Press, 1953.

Wooldridge, H. E., *Oxford History of Music*, Oxford University Press, 1932, Vol. II.

Part Four

THE ORIGINS OF THE MODERN AGE

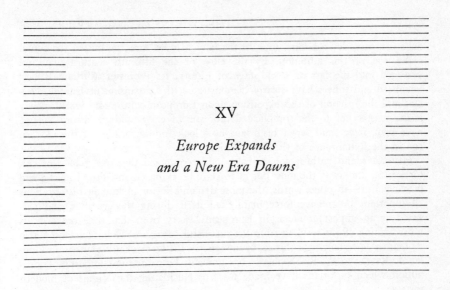

XV

Europe Expands
and a New Era Dawns

I. FROM RIVER TO OCEAN

We have seen that the geographic setting of Oriental civilization started with a fluvial basis and gradually emerged into a thalassic or Mediterranean stage. Similarly, the history of western Europe started with a Mediterranean orientation and ultimately evolved into a world outlook and an oceanic scope of activities. From the decline of the Roman Empire until the discovery of America, civilization moved slowly but steadily toward the west and north.

In laying the foundation for this westward movement of European society the Roman occupation of Gaul, following the invasions of Julius Caesar, was of the greatest significance. The superiority of the Orient in material culture always exerted a strong magnetic force drawing the center of the Roman Empire eastward. This influence became so powerful that, early in the fourth century A.D., Constantine moved his capital to the shores of the Black Sea. The conquest of Gaul, and its subsequent development under Roman control, acted as a counterbalance to this eastward attraction. Otherwise the West would, perhaps, gradually have abandoned civilization and reverted to a barbarism from which it might not even yet have emerged. Gaul not only helped to draw the balance of culture towards the west, but also furnished the Germanic tribes with much of the institutional basis of medieval life. It was in Gaul more than in Italy that classical culture merged with Teutonic barbarism to furnish the institutional groundwork of medieval civilization.

With the gradual return of prosperity in western Europe in the later Middle Ages, due to the revival of trade with the East, the seaboard states became jealous of the Italian monopoly of Oriental trade, and sought direct contact through oversea discoveries with the sources of Oriental commodities. The mariner's compass, devised some time in the later Middle Ages, permitted the actual realization of this ambition. By the close of the fifteenth century mankind emerged into the last or world-stage of history. As Professor William Robert Shepherd and others have clearly demonstrated, the expansion of Europe overseas and the reaction of this expansion upon European culture and world society is the master key to the complicated processes of early modern history. As we have seen, fewer and fewer historians now look for the origins of the modern age in the Renaissance or the Reformation.

Historians and anthropologists have long recognized that the contact of cultures is far and away the most potent force in breaking down cultural inertia and provincialism—in other words, the most dynamic factor in human history. This all-important progressive force manifested itself during the crusades, and persisted as an important factor in European history from that time onward. Its most striking effects resulted from the successful voyages of Columbus and Vasco da Gama. The analysis of this set of influences—the work of historians from Guillaume Raynal to W. R. Shepherd—has probably been the most important contribution which historians have made towards elucidating the origins of modern society.

One of the leading aspects of European civilization during the Dark Ages was its provincialism and its ignorance of foreign cultures and learning. Intellectually speaking, it was an inbred age, and this accounted in part for its relative stagnation. There was some intercontinental commerce and travel, but it was comparatively slight. Each nation, each community even, was sufficient unto itself.

The crusades provided the first important impulse to expansion and growth. They brought the relatively backward peoples of western Europe into contact with the higher civilization of the Eastern or Byzantine Empire and with the amazing culture of the Muslims. Curiosity was aroused and many phases of Muslim civilization were brought back to Europe, as we indicated in an earlier chapter. The curtain was rolled back and western Europe was never again permitted to slumber contentedly in its own ignorance and routine. Merchants who transported soldiers to the Levant used their spare time to develop trading relations with Eastern races. Commerce revived on a large scale, medieval towns sprang up, and a new dynamic element appeared in European civilization which powerfully stimulated that remarkable development of thought and culture following the middle of the twelfth century which we have already surveyed.

The rich and varied products brought from the East—spices, precious metals, perfume, fine woods, tapestry, and the like—together with legendary accounts of the fabulous wealth of these distant lands, drew brave and adventurous men towards them. Distances were great and modes of travel slow and risky, but some intrepid spirits, beginning with Rabbi Benjamin of Tudela in the twelfth century, reached the far Orient, and returned with accounts of incredible riches and strange customs.

In the century following 1250 a number of men penetrated to the centers of Oriental splendor. Some were sent as missionaries. Others were dispatched as political emissaries. Others traveled out of sheer curiosity or adventure. John of

Piano Carpini, an Italian monk, was sent to the Mongols by Pope Innocent IV in 1243. William of Rubruquis, a Franciscan, was sent to Tartary by Louis IX of France in 1253. John of Monte Corvino (1247-1328), a Franciscan, attained the honor of becoming Archbishop of Peking. Jordanus, a French missionary, journeyed to India in 1329 and greatly extended our knowledge of that area. Oderic of Pordenone, a friar, traveled widely in China and India. The most extensive traveler of them all was a Muslim, Ibn Battuta (1304-1378), who covered about 75,000 miles in Africa and Asia and left fairly accurate accounts of his experiences. The most famous of travelers was Marco Polo (1254-1324), who, between 1271 and 1292, explored China, India, and Persia. Thrown into prison after he returned, he had time to dictate to a fellow prisoner of marked literary talents an elaborate account of his varied and thrilling experiences. This work—the classic *Travels of Marco Polo*—has made him deservedly immortal. Professors Yule and Beazley thus briefly and graphically describe the significance of his achievements:

> Polo was the first traveler to trace a route across the whole longitude of Asia, naming and describing kingdom after kingdom which he had seen; the first to speak of the new and brilliant court which had been established at Peking, the first to reveal China in all its wealth and vastness, and to tell of the nations on its borders; the first to tell more of Tibet than its name, to speak of Burma, of Laos, of Siam, of Cochin-China, of Japan, of Java, of Sumatra and other islands of the Archipelago, of Nicobar and the Andaman Islands, of Ceylon and its sacred peak, of India as a country seen and partially explored; the first in medieval times to give any distinct account of the secluded Christian Empire of Abyssinia, and of the semi-Christian island of Sokotra, and to speak, however dimly, of Zanzibar, and of the vast and distant Madagascar; while he carries us also to the remotely opposite region of Siberia and the Arctic shores, to speak of dog sledges, white bears, and reindeer-riding Tunguses.[1]

Knowledge of, and interest in, the Orient were enormously increased by a fictitious but thrilling romantic tale entitled *The Travels of Sir John Mandeville*. Mandeville was a pseudonym. The author based his story on the accounts of medieval encyclopedists and earlier travelers, especially Oderic of Pordenone and William of Boldensele, although it is possible he himself had visited parts of the Near East. The book first appeared in French between 1357 and 1371 and was later translated into Latin and English. It had a great vogue and did much to direct the attention of Europeans to the wealth, splendor, and novelty of the Orient.

While these travelers were arousing the curiosity of the reading classes of Europe regarding the wonders of the East, the Italian city-states were carrying on a large and profitable trade with the Orient. Merchants in western and northern Europe were unable to get into satisfactory direct contact with the East because the Italians had a monopoly of Mediterranean commerce. To the former fell only the small profits from the retail trade in commodities brought from the East by Italians. Some direct commerce with the East was maintained by way of Russia.

[1] Article "Marco Polo," Encyclopaedia Britannica, 11th edition.

The Italian monopoly stimulated merchants of northern and western Europe to think of new routes to the Far East. The best geographical students had long believed that the earth is round. This suggested the possibility of reaching the Orient by sailing west. There was no knowledge of the great American continent which blocked the way. Moreover, the geographers of that day computed the circumference of the earth at somewhat less than half the reality. Therefore, Japan was located by them at about the actual position of Yucatan. Others believed that the Orient could be reached by sailing around the Cape of Good Hope and turning northeast to India. In the middle of the fifteenth century sailors began to skirt the west coast of Africa. Diaz rounded the Cape of Good Hope in 1486, and in May, 1498, Vasco da Gama reached Calicut on the coast of India. In the meantime Columbus had attempted the direct westward journey and touched San Salvador in the Bahamas in October, 1492. Finally, in the first quarter of the next century, Magellan circumnavigated the globe and proved the accuracy of the belief that the Orient could be found by sailing westward.

The Turkish capture of Constantinople in 1453 did not, as was so long believed, have anything directly to do with these explorations. The desire for an oversea route had arisen before 1453. Moreover, the Red Sea route was not closed by the Turks until a generation after Columbus. Further, Professor A. H. Lybyer has shown that there is no evidence from trade statistics that the Turks seriously interfered with overland European trade from the Orient which passed through their territories. Therefore, there appears to be no basis for the old belief that the Turks closed the land routes to the Far East after 1453 and thus forced Europe to seek an ocean passage to the Indies.

Inventions in navigation and improvements in shipbuilding which we mentioned in earlier chapters represent the chief technical advances of the age that were related directly to exploration, industry, and commerce. The expansion of Europe and the commercial revolution depended as much upon these inventions as the industrial revolution depended upon textile machinery, steam power, and metallurgical improvements. The mariner's compass is first referred to in the late medieval period, and was progressively improved before it came into extensive use in the fifteenth century. The quadrant, sextant, telescope, chronometer, and other nautical instruments, devised between the fifteenth and the eighteenth centuries, enabled mariners to find their way at sea with far greater safety and certainty and made extensive ocean travel possible. To these basic instruments should be added the provision of maps, charts, and astronomical tables, indispensable to the sailor. Important also was the discovery of the distillation of water at sea to make ocean water drinkable. Larger and more seaworthy vessels were also constructed. These could withstand the shock of oceanic storms and facilitated the transportation of large cargoes over long distances. The remarkable expansion of commerce brought about by new modes of navigation enormously increased the demand for manufactured commodities. Hence, they greatly hastened the introduction of mechanical methods of manufacturing, and, ultimately, produced the industrial revolution.

II. ECONOMIC CHANGES RESULTING FROM THE EXPANSION OF EUROPE

Overseas explorations enormously widened European markets. There was an increased demand for European commodities by natives and colonists in the New World, particularly for cotton cloth, and, to a lesser extent, for woolen and worsted cloth. There also developed a considerable trade in various types of hardware and weapons used by the colonists, as well as in liquor and trinkets used for trade with the natives. The marked extension of commerce likewise stimulated the shipbuilding industry to a remarkable degree. The fishing industry also considerably expanded, particularly through the sale of salt fish to colonists and natives in tropical areas.

Commercial transformations were more profound and varied than industrial changes. Indeed, this age is now known to economic historians as that of the "commercial revolution." Trade increased notably not only in net volume, but also in geographical scope. Commerce ceased to be thalassic (coastwise) and became oceanic. The center of commercial activity, which had been located in the Mediterranean Sea for nearly five thousand years, shifted to the vast ocean front of northwestern Europe.

The greatly increased extent and variety of trade necessitated new forms of commercial organization. The new commerce presented greater dangers and involved greater expenditures. Hence, we encounter many new regulated companies, which developed very quickly, and some joint-stock organizations, which became prominent after 1500. Among the more important of these new commercial companies were: the Muscovy company, established in 1555; the Turkey-Levant company, 1581; the Morocco company, 1585; the Guinea company, 1588; the English East India company, 1600; the Dutch East India company, 1602; the Company of New France, 1628. Such organizations represented a more extensive coöperative business activity than had hitherto existed in any field of economic life in man's history. They furnished the training, precedents, and embryonic forms of organization for the extensive development of commercial and industrial combinations which followed the industrial revolution.

With the greater demand for capital and the development of more extensive investments there arose a need for better means of providing credit. The medieval limitations on interest-taking rapidly disappeared. Banks as large institutions for assembling capital and providing credit became more numerous and powerful with the progress of the commercial revolution. Stock exchanges arose. At first they chiefly promoted the exchange of commodities, but in due time they began to execute their modern function of facilitating the transfer of securities. Expanding investments and the multiplication of dangers involved in the new commerce stimulated underwriting and insurance. An enormous increase of precious metals, largely imported from the untapped sources of the New World, produced a marked dislocation of prices and stimulated an era of speculation and bubbles.

In many parts of Europe, most notably the Netherlands and England, the guild system was gradually supplanted by the so-called "domestic" or "putting-out" system. In this type of industrial control manufacturing left the establishment of the guild master and was reëstablished once more in the private homes of the workmen. The controlling individual was the merchant-capitalist. His representatives distributed the raw material among the workers scattered about in their homes, and then went around picking up the finished products to be brought back to the central warehouse for ultimate sale and distribution. While this system was better adapted to emergent capitalism than the guild system, its many wasteful weaknesses led to its disappearance with the rise of the factory system.

New commercial theories and policies arose to guide and control trading enterprises. These theories passed through two main stages. The first, mercantilism, was associated with the earlier phases of commercial expansion and with the rise of national states. It represented the expression of arrogant nationalism in commercial activities, and was based upon the theory that the economic interests of a particular state can be advanced only at the expense of its neighbors and its own colonies. Mercantilism advocated complete state control of national and colonial trade, in order to bring about a surplus of exports over imports and thus provide a steady addition to the supply of precious metals stored up within a particular state.

At first, the merchant class enthusiastically supported absolute monarchs in their policy of stringent commercial regulation, but in due time they found that it imposed serious restrictions upon their commercial activities. Consequently, they turned to the new scientific philosophy, based upon the conception of a natural order in the universe, to justify a new commercial policy. They contended that since God rules the heavens by his immutable laws he must also rule the earth and human society. Hence man should not interfere with this divinely controlled process through restrictive legislation. The middle class demanded the repeal of repressive mercantile laws and absolute freedom in business activities. This policy of *laissez-faire* and free trade, while enunciated by the physiocrats in the eighteenth century, made no very significant headway until the first half of the nineteenth century, when it was taken over by Ricardo and the classical economists. The defense of unmitigated competition was buttressed in the nineteenth century by Spencerian dogmas of cosmic evolution, and it has remained the chief obstacle to social justice and constructive social legislation down to the present day.

III. SOCIAL TRANSFORMATIONS

There were many important social changes in the period of European expansion during the commercial revolution between 1500 and 1800. The omnipotence of the landowners, which had persisted during the thousand years following the decline of the Roman Empire, was now gradually challenged by the growing middle class of merchants and manufacturers. The bourgeoisie did not triumph over the landowners until after the industrial revolution had wrought its effects. Yet they were able to hold their own in the conflict, and to induce governments to adopt and forward many of their cherished policies. This rise of the middle class in numbers, power, and prestige, was the oustanding social transformation of early modern history. Furthermore, the middle class became diversified. New aspects of commerce and industry introduced specialization and division of labor. The materialistic philosophy of Protestantism, as we have seen, provided a religious and ethical sanction for the practices and prestige of the bourgeoisie.

The lower classes also profited to some degree by the social and economic changes of this age. Slavery among the white population entirely disappeared, and serfdom was gradually extinguished, although in certain areas in central and eastern Europe the serfs were not emancipated until the middle of the nineteenth century. Serfdom had disappeared in England before the close of the sixteenth century, and was markedly reduced in France before the eve of the French revolution. The status and well-being of the peasantry in western Europe considerably improved, although in England it suffered a decided setback with the rise of capitalistic farming after the middle of the eighteenth century. Many peasants thus driven out of their homes were only too glad to find work at low wages in the new factory towns during the initial stages of the industrial revolution.

The remarkable increase in the power and prestige of the middle class, carrying with it a challenge to the landed aristocracy, and a slight improvement in the condition of the peasantry, constituted the most notable social changes of this period. There were others, however, both significant and interesting.

The mobility of the population increased. The explorations, discoveries, and growing prosperity stimulated travel and enormously extended European knowledge about foreign regions. Further, at this time began the first real movement of people from the Old to the New World—a movement which has become one of the outstanding social phenomena in modern history. Manners and customs altered remarkably, owing to the introduction of ideas and products from overseas. The result was a great increase in comfort, luxury, and ostentatious display among the upper and middle classes. The new products from overseas also brought about interesting and novel social customs and practices. For instance, the importation of coffee and tobacco from the New World was associated with such institutions as coffee-houses and smoking-taverns.

For the first time in European history the population began to increase steadily. In 1600, the population of Europe was about 100,000,000. By 1800 it had reached about 187,000,000.

IV. NEW POLITICAL DEVELOPMENTS

Political changes associated with early modern times were far-reaching and fundamental. That intermediate or transitional stage of political evolution, known as feudalism, dominated the Middle Ages. Early modern times witnessed the termination of feudalism in the advanced states of western Europe, and the subsequent rise of national states characteristic of the modern era.

While some centralization had been accomplished in the later Middle Ages, the extinction of feudalism necessarily awaited the acquisition of adequate resources by sovereigns to enable them to hire their own armies and pay their own officials. In the feudal order money and soldiers had been provided, for the most part, by the barons. It was scarcely to be expected that the latter would liberally or enthusiastically contribute to a cause which meant their own extinction. When the royal income notably increased through various forms of revenue derived from the discoveries, commerce, and colonization of the New World, the kings gradually acquired a standing army and administrative bureaucracy of their own. They were then able to continue with zest the struggle of centuries to destroy the local and decentralized feudal order and to establish centralized national states.

Protestantism gave a strong religious and psychological stimulus to the new movement. The Protestant revolt was, as we have seen, to a large extent a political secession from that great international state, the Roman Catholic church. In some countries, as in England during the Wars of the Roses, the termination of feudalism and the establishment of the national state were forwarded by decimating civil wars among the feudal nobility.

In general, the middle class at first joined with the kings in attempting to overthrow the feudal lords, because of the age-long hatred which the merchant class bore towards the latter, owing in large degree to the oppression and extortion to which the merchant or town class had been subjected by the nobility during the medieval period.

While the establishment of national states was the outstanding political achievement of early modern times, their evolution passed through at least two stages.

In the first they were dynastic and absolute. The alliance of merchants and kings weakened the opposition to royal absolutism. The national dynastic state was established in England in 1485, in Spain by 1556, in France by 1589, in Russia by 1698, and in Prussia by 1713. In the last two the transition was achieved primarily through imitation of the western European states rather than because of direct participation in the new commerce and colonial expansion.

In due time, however, the rising middle class found that absolute monarchs were as repressive and irritating as the feudal nobility. When protests and petitions to kings proved unavailing, the middle class organized forceful resistance. The results were the well-known English revolutions of 1645-1649 and 1688-1689, the American Revolution of 1775-1783, the French Revolution of 1789-1795, the revolts of 1820, 1830, and 1848 in continental Europe, and the Russian Revolution of 1905.

Because of these revolutions, the dynastic national state was replaced by representative and parliamentary government, which was an indispensable requisite to the subsequent growth of democracy and majority rule. Without this supremacy of the elective or legislative branch of the government, the later enfranchisement of the lower classes would have meant little or nothing in actual practice. The triumph of representative institutions and parliamentary government carried with it by both fact and implication a marked transition in the class basis of political power. The landed aristocracy had, for the most part, controlled political institutions since the dawn of written history. Their power was now effectively undermined, and the middle class gradually usurped political ascendancy.

Changes in political theory paralleled these transformations in political practice. Nationalism underlay both the dynastic and the representative phases of early modern political evolution. The assertion of secular absolutism, or the supremacy of the state, was common to both the absolutist and the revolutionary political theory of this period. The monarchs of early modern times, some as a direct defense of their presumptions, and others as a Protestant defense against papal pretensions, vindicated their absolutism on the ground of the alleged "divine right of kings," set forth in such works as those by Sir Robert Filmer, Bishop Bossuet and Claudius Salamasius.

The merchants, in their attack upon royal power, revived and elaborated the social contract theory. According to this doctrine, the state was originally created through a deliberate act for the purpose of securing protection from anarchy. Those who were then chosen to rule over their fellow men contracted to govern according to law and the principles of justice. If they did not do so, the purposes for which government had been established would be undermined. It was not only the right but the duty of the citizens to rise up and drive out such arbitrary rulers and choose a new set who would in their turn promise to rule according to the original contract. The chief spokesmen for this type of political theory were Samuel Pufendorf, Baruch Spinoza, John Locke and Jean Jacques Rousseau. This doctrine of the political right and the moral obligation of revolution constituted the theoretical foundations and justification of the English, French, and American revolutions. This new middle-class state claimed, however, the same supreme powers arrogated by the absolute monarchs. The difference was that secular absolutism rested, in theory, on the consent of the people.

V. NOVEL LEGAL TENDENCIES

Legal changes in this era accompanied social and political evolution. Feudal law was gradually replaced by national codes, comprehensive in scope and savage in nature. Under divine-right rulers, these penalized with special severity any acts which challenged royal supremacy. When the middle class acquired political power, they were particularly interested in protecting property and business enterprise from arbitrary royal interference and confiscation. Hence, the chief influence of the bourgeoisie upon jurisprudence was to emphasize the duty of the state to protect private property, and to stress the desirability of noninterference in business activities. John Locke, perhaps the most influential writer of the age, openly contended that the chief purpose of the state and law was the protection of property.

The doctrine of natural rights was invoked and elaborated to support these basic dogmas of the sanctity of property and the freedom of business. It was maintained that the chief purpose of the state and legislation is to respect and preserve the natural rights of man to life, liberty, and property, with special emphasis on property. Law, which was henceforth mainly devoted to protecting property, became secular and absolute, freed from the earlier theological restraints and ethical norms which had prevailed in the Middle Ages. Here, then, originated that type of juristic thought and practice which has served as the bulwark of business and finance against social regulation, and has found its finest flower in the "due process" clause of the fourteenth amendment to the American constitution.

At the close of the eighteenth century and throughout the nineteenth there developed a widespread movement for constitutions, designed to give property not only the immunities enjoyed under statutory law, but also the more profound and impregnable security of constitutional law.

VI. RELIGIOUS READJUSTMENTS

There were many highly significant changes in religion in early modern times. The unity of Christendom was broken by the Protestant revolt. The so-called Reformation did not, however, embody any very definite break with the Christian epic or orthodox Catholic traditions.

Much more significant in its ultimate effect was the rise of a decisive criticism of orthodoxy, both Catholic and Protestant. The contact of Europe with other continents promoted the study of comparative religion. This was necessarily highly destructive to the theory of a single, unique, revealed religion. Comparative religion, combined with an understanding of the religious implications of the new astronomy and natural science, encouraged the deists and rationalists to repudiate orthodox Christianity, as based upon revealed Scripture. In its stead they proposed the so-called "natural religion," the identification of God with nature, and of natural law with divine law. They held that the teachings of Jesus could easily be harmonized with this more enlightened and humane type of natural religion, but they rejected both orthodox Protestantism and Catholicism.

Not only did the newly discovered facts about the nature of the earth and the universe seem to challenge the authenticity of the Scriptures; the critical and historical investigation of the authorship of the Bible, begun at this time, also weakened scriptural authority.

Religion readjusted itself to new economic and social developments. There was a close relationship, as we noted above, between Protestantism and capitalism. The Protestants regarded business as a divine calling, and Calvin particularly stressed the divine approval of persistent industry and thrift. While considerable doubt was raised as to divine sanction of reckless expenditures of money, there was complete certainty regarding the pleasure which the Almighty derives from witnessing the steady accumulation of pecuniary profits. The rigorous code of private ethics developed by the Puritans was in large part an over-compensation for their absorption in the processes of material gain—for privateering, the slave trade, rum trade and the like.

Thus was reëstablished that intimate association between religion and business enterprise which characterized the civilization of ancient Mesopotamia, and produces in our own day such assertions as those of an American industrial magnate, Mr. G. F. Baer, that modern business leaders are unquestionably "those Christian men to whom God in His infinite wisdom has given the control of the property interests of the country."

VII. INTELLECTUAL EFFECTS OF THE EXPANSION OF EUROPE

First and foremost among the intellectual influences growing out of the expansion of Europe must be placed the stimulation of intellectual curiosity. Nothing is more conducive to stagnation and self-complacency than provincialism and a localized perspective. So long as we know only of our own culture, habits, customs, and institutions, we can be gloriously satisfied with them and have no incentive to criticize and alter them. Once we learn about new and different methods of doing things, we are prone to contrast our ways with those of others and to consider whether we can make significant improvements in our ideas and modes of life. Mental curiosity and social progress are more powerfully promoted by the contact and contrast of cultures than by any other factor in civilization.

The expansion of Europe brought about the most extensive and diversified contact of cultures thus far experienced by man. Europe was brought in touch with an incomparably larger portion of the globe than ever before. Europeans became acquainted with what were then the higher and richer civilizations of China and India, and with all types of primitive peoples. From Oriental sage to savage headhunter, Europe at last faced the whole panorama of human culture. The stagnation, provincialism, and complacency of the medieval European community could not persist after such a psychic shock.

Another result of European expansion was the creation of a spirit of tolerance. The medieval mind was basically a single-track mind. Conditions of life were primitive and restricted in both medieval town and manor. Customs changed but little from century to century. Novelty and variety were taboo in both life and business. The Christian religion was very specific in its moral guidance. There was but one true religion, one permissible attitude towards sex and marriage, one commendable ethical code, and so on.

When educated and thinking Europeans were confronted with the enormous diversity of customs, beliefs, and institutions revealed by travelers and explorers, they could no longer remain so narrow-minded and intolerant. Right conduct seemed to them a relative matter. They noted that where monogamy existed it was regarded as correct, but where polygyny prevailed it was just as decisively approved. Some races favored extensive consumption of alcoholic beverages. Others were completely abstemious. In one territory a certain act might be a crime, in another a virtue. Clothes, habitations, manners, and the like varied widely over the face of the globe.

All this helped philosophic Europeans, like Montaigne, Hume, Voltaire, and Montesquieu, to develop a tolerant outlook and to adopt a relativistic and comparative view of manners, morals, and institutions. It became much more difficult to enforce intolerance, bigotry, and like-mindedness.

In its specific contributions to science the expansion of Europe was by no means unimportant or negligible. Most directly influenced was navigation, with its accessory sciences, mathematics, engineering, and optics. Explorations not only enormously increased geographic information of every kind, but stimulated scientific cartography which could now be based on precisely determined latitude and longitude. Astronomy was enriched by the discovery and observation of constellations visible in the southern hemisphere, and by the scrutiny of known heavenly bodies from new positions on the earth's surface. The discovery of many important minerals, animals, and plants in oversea areas advanced the sciences of mineralogy, botany, pharmacy, and zoölogy. And European contact with a large number of new racial types in widely varying stages of cultural development strongly stimulated what ultimately became the science of man, or anthropology. Hitherto, man had been approached primarily from the theological standpoint. Interest was centered in his soul. There was little concern about his body or his customs and institutions, except as the latter were related to salvation in the world to come.

Oversea discoveries brought to the attention of Europeans all manner of men—red, white, black, and yellow in color; giants and pygmies; civilized, barbarous, and savage. They also confronted Western philosophers with a vast variety of strange customs, folkways, institutions, and social practices. These at first caused astonishment, then curiosity, and finally reflective study. When scholars began to seek an explanation of the physical diversities of races, and the causes of sharply contrasting customs and institutions, the science of anthropology was started on its way to the splendid heights of development it reached in the works of Tylor, Sumner, Boas, Wissler, Rivers, Marett, and Lippert. No subject is more helpful in developing an intelligent and tolerant view of man and his behavior.

Closely related to anthropology is the science of comparative religion, for which there was little possibility before the age of expansion. The contrast had been sharply drawn between the one true religion, Christianity, and an unspeakable paganism, compounded of many varieties. Hence it was difficult to approach religion objectively, and calmly inquire into its origins, its many forms of expression, and its powerful hold on the mind of man. Religion meant worship according to Christian concepts, and hatred of all pagan rituals and doctrines.

Explorers and travelers told of the infinite variety of religious beliefs and practices. Some races worshiped one God, others many. Religious rites also varied greatly in different parts of the world. Furthermore, some religions seemed to propagate a lofty moral code; others encouraged cruel and savage practices.

Most Europeans who heard or read of these strange religions continued to regard them as merely paganistic and, therefore, horrible. Nevertheless, some reflective minds actually began to wonder why religion existed at all, what constituted the vital differences between sects, and what similar elements might be detected in the psychological content of religions which externally seemed quite divergent. In other words, religion was regarded as something to be studied and thought about as well as blindly believed and devoutly worshiped.

The development of comparative religion struck a blow at religious intolerance in Europe. The contrasts between Catholicism and Protestantism seemed slight as compared with the differences between either of them and many aboriginal cults. Further, the comparative point of view is fundamentally opposed to the single-track mind which begets intolerance and intellectual arrogance.

Oversea expansion also promoted the scientific study of language. The philological perspective was extended beyond Latin, Greek, Hebrew, and the vernacular languages of Europe. A veritable new linguistic Babel was uncovered. Attention was directed to such basic problems as the origins of language, the affinities of languages, the relation between language and culture, and the like. Language came to be regarded as an important aspect of racial culture. Indeed, by Fichte and many romanticist philosophers, language was viewed as the most distinctive element in the culture of any people.

European expansion markedly influenced political philosophy. Ever since the Greek period there was a common belief in a state of nature which preceded orderly political society. But this remained purely hypothetical. Few since classical days had actually seen men in this condition. But explorations provided convincing confirmation of this hypothesis. Savages appeared to be men actually living in a state of nature. This view strongly stimulated the revolutionary political philosophy which, as we have seen, asserted that men originally lived in a state of nature and later established political institutions to escape from the inconveniences and dangers of a brutal and disorganized life.

Another effect on political philosophy was the extension of the comparative point of view. Down to this time European writers usually regarded some particular form of government as perfect in an absolute sense. But the observation of many types of government the world over challenged this dogma.

Writers like Montesquieu came to believe that a government is good or bad in proportion to its adaptability to the needs of a given group. For some, an absolute monarchy is best; for others, a constitutional monarchy; and for still others, a republic. Political analysis from the comparative and relative point of view was no longer looked upon as akin to treason. The same reasoning was applied to law. Legal codes were regarded as sound and desirable in the degree to which they harmonized with the civilization of a particular group. Comparative jurisprudence was thus created.

In one special and interesting way the discovery of primitive races exerted a profound influence upon European thought, particularly in France. Some philosophers, especially Rousseau, contrasted the supposedly care-free life of savages with the duties, responsibilities, and repressions of modern civilization. They held that savagery is preferable to civilization, and contended that man lost much through the development of the arts, sciences, government, and the like. Rousseau declared that the most perfect state is that state which is intermediate between savagery and civilization, namely, the patriarchal stage in which Abraham, Isaac, and Jacob lived. But he distinctly preferred even primitive conditions to modern culture. This worship of a glorified and largely imaginary savage—*primitivism*—lingered for many years in the Paris salons and other intellectual centers of western Europe, and has been revived in our day in literary and artistic circles.

It was also inevitable that the new scientific discoveries and the philosophy of nature should react profoundly upon the philosophy of history. The idea of orderly development and continuity in social as well as natural processes was comprehended by Vico, Hume, and Turgot. The older view of social change as a gradual decline or retrogression from a primordial "golden age" was replaced in the writings of Fontenelle, Perrault, Vico, St. Pierre, Turgot, Kant, Godwin, and Condorcet by the concept of progress from lower to higher stages of civilization. The need for miracles to justify history and the other sciences dealing with human activities was challenged by the deist doctrine that man is inherently "decent," a notion widely at variance with the views of the church fathers and Calvin, who maintained that man is hopelessly depraved.

The new discoveries and the secularization of natural and social philosophy also extended the historian's interests beyond politics and religion. In the writings of Oviedo y Valdes, Gómara, Acosta, Peter Martyr, Herrera y Tordesillas, de Laet, Esquemelin, Touron, de Ulloa, de Charlevoix, Raynal, Campbell, Robertson, Montesquieu, Voltaire, Heeren and others, it became apparent that a broader and sounder view of history was being adopted. The historians of the

discoveries and colonization abandoned dry annals, political and military episodes, and religious controversies. They gave attention to geographical settings,
racial traits, cultural contrasts, commercial developments and colonial activities.
With Voltaire and his associates, social history and the history of civilization
made their first appearance. Rationalism, which was in large part an outgrowth
of the intellectual impulses of the expansion of Europe, gave us not only Voltaire's important histories but such works as Hume's *History of England,* William
Robertson's *History of the Reign of the Emperor Charles V,* and, above all, Edward Gibbon's immortal *Decline and Fall of the Roman Empire,* a book still
useful after nearly two hundred years. Professor J. B. Black says of this advance
in historical writing:

> The eighteenth century historians, whatever their other shortcomings may be,
> undoubtedly accomplished their assessment of the past with commendable vigour.
> There is no doubt left in the mind of the reader what Voltaire or Hume, for
> example, think of the matters they describe. The important events of history are
> set in a wide framework, their bearings are indicated to the great moral back-
> ground against which the drama of the race is enacted, and they are judged with
> respect to standards which the writers, rightly or wrongly, regard as ultimate.
> Hence it comes about that to all who look to history for more than factual instruc-
> tion, who believe that a historical fact is not appreciated until it is placed in its
> philosophical as well as its purely causal relationships, the historians of the Age
> of Reason will never quite lose their charm; on the contrary, they will remain as
> perhaps the most brilliant examples of how human culture may be brought into
> fruitful contact with what would otherwise be a dead and, for the vast majority,
> a valueless past.[2]

After the period of exploration and discoveries, painting began to portray maritime life as well as the peoples who had been discovered overseas. The sailor, the
adventurer, the idealized Indian maiden, to some degree displaced the priest, the
martyr, and the Virgin as pictorial subjects. John White in England and Cornelius Kettell in the Netherlands, for instance, achieved reputations for their portrayal of American Indian life. Many painters became interested in ships and
the sea. Dutch art of the seventeenth century exhibited some rather novel and
significant tendencies through its realism and its concern with the commonplace
things of the everyday secular life of this commercial people. It should also be
noted that accurate and artistic portrait painting first appeared in a prominent
way in this period. Successful merchants became leading patrons of the new art.

Even more marked was the influence of overseas expansion in introducing
Oriental decorations and customs. Porcelain ware was introduced from China and
Japan. Screens and lacquered work became popular. The art of interior decoration in Europe practically dates from this period. From the Orient came such
things as wallpaper, wainscoting, upholstered furniture, rich tapestries, and the
like. Oriental patterns and motives revolutionized decorative design. Likewise,
landscape gardening was almost completely guided by Oriental ideas, while
rococo art and decoration were chiefly Oriental importations.

The effect of overseas expansion on literature was incalculable. The manners,

[2] J. B. Black, *The Art of History,* Crofts, 1926, p. 7.

customs, and ideas of non-European races permeated the literature of the sixteenth, seventeenth, and eighteenth centuries. The setting of many romances was placed in America, Africa, or Asia. We need only to refer to the poetry of Camoëns, Spenser, Milton, and Dryden; to the drama of Shakespeare, Dryden, and Molière; to the novels of Cervantes, Defoe, Swift, Bernardin de Saint Pierre, and Samuel Johnson; and to the essays of Montaigne and Bacon, to recall the strong influence exerted upon literature by the contact of Europe with new continents. *The Lusiad, Paul and Virginia, Robinson Crusoe,* and *Gulliver's Travels,* to mention only a few characteristic works of this period dealing entirely with new worlds, have become immortal classics in the history of literature.

If the overseas expansion did not produce an immediate revolution in education and pedagogy, it ultimately exerted a very great influence. The new knowledge of the world, which finally made its way into the colleges and universities, helped to create contemporary education. His study of the life of primitive man impelled Rousseau to assault the artificial and repressive pedagogy of his day. He thus prepared the way for the pedagogical revolution of the next century which demanded a more natural and spontaneous type of education. This was led by men whose names loom large in the history of education—Basedow, Pestalozzi, and Herbart.

SELECTED READINGS

Abbott, W. C., *The Expansion of Europe,* 2 vols., Crofts, 1938.
Barnes, H. E., *An Economic History of the Western World,* chaps. vii-ix.
——— *World Politics in Modern Civilization,* Knopf, 1930.
Botsford, J. B., *English Society in the Eighteenth Century,* Macmillan, 1924.
Day, Clive, *A History of Commerce,* Longmans, 1922, Part III.
Dunning, W. A., *History of Political Theories from Luther to Montesquieu,* 1905.
Gillespie, J. E., *The Influence of Oversea Expansion on England to 1700.*
——— *History of Geographical Discovery, 1400-1800,* Holt, 1933.
Gretton, R. H., *The English Middle Class,* London, 1917.
Hobson, J. A., *The Evolution of Modern Capitalism,* Scribner, 1926.
Lefebvre, Georges, *The French Revolution,* Col. Univ. Press, 1962.
Lewis, Roy, and Maude, Angus, *The English Middle Classes,* Knopf, 1950.
Newton, A. P., ed., *Travel and Travellers of the Middle Ages,* Knopf, 1926.
Packard, L. B., *The Commercial Revolution,* Holt, 1927.
Palm, F. C., *The Middle Class: Then and Now,* Macmillan, 1936.
Perry, J. H., *The Age of Reconnaissance,* World, 1963.
Priestley, H. I., *France Overseas through the Old Régime,* Univ. Cal. Press, 1939.
Reichwein, Adolf, *China and Europe,* Knopf, 1925.
Sanceau, Elaine, *Henry the Navigator,* Norton, 1947.
Sée, Henri, *Economic and Social Conditions in France during the Eighteenth Century,* Knopf, 1927.
——— *Modern Capitalism,* Adelphia Press, 1928.
Sykes, Sir Percy, *A History of Exploration,* Harper Torchbooks, 1961.
Tawney, R. H., *Religion and the Rise of Capitalism,* New American Library.
Wright, J. K., *The Geographical Basis of European History.*

XVI

*Natural Science
in the Seventeenth
and Eighteenth Centuries*

I. PROGRESSIVE INTELLECTUAL PATTERNS IN EARLY MODERN TIMES

We now come to the point where we shall describe one of the most remarkable periods in the intellectual development of Western civilization since the innovations that made possible the Periclean civilization of ancient Greece. The Hellenic thinkers brought free inquiry into the world, questioned the supernaturalism of Oriental antiquity, raised reason to a position of supremacy, directed philosophy towards a solution of human problems, and created a scientific habit of thought. The scientists, philosophers, and critical thinkers of the period from 1600 to 1800, carrying on the work of progressive medieval scholars, performed much the same function in freeing western Europe from the protective blanket of orthodox medievalism. They, too, challenged the older supernaturalism, elevated reason, defended free thinking, brought philosophy down to earth, and achieved important scientific discoveries.

It is not easy to summarize concisely the dominating psychology of early modern times, but the promising undercurrent was the growing secularism of the age. However, the supernaturalism of the Catholic church persisted without any serious break, and was actually intensified by the necessity of defending itself against the assaults of Protestantism. In some ways, the Protestants believed in a more crass and direct supernaturalism than the Catholics. The religious wars and controversies gave this revival of supernaturalism intense and dangerous practical manifestations.

There was, nevertheless, a steady if slow progress towards various types of secularism and rationalism. Protestantism was very closely related to the rise of capitalism. While the Protestants were still absorbed in the problems of the hereafter, they believed that one method of assuring spiritual, as well as earthly, salvation lay in industry, thrift, and the accumulation of pecuniary profits.

This attitude stood in direct opposition to the Catholic position during the Middle Ages. The church had, in theory, repudiated worldly prosperity and had closely restrained business enterprise in the interest of social justice and human welfare, even though the later schoolmen revealed symptoms of realistic economic adjustment to the newer commercial and financial methods. The Protestant bourgeois, asserting themselves in a greater degree of town life, commercialism, and industry, helped to promote secularism in northern Europe, in the same manner that such tendencies in the later Middle Ages had stimulated urbanity and secularism in the Italian cities.

A political basis for secularism was found in the revived prestige and influence of Roman law and in the development of the theory of a social contract. The former emphasized secular absolutism and the latter the mundane and human origins of political institutions. The age of discoveries generated a spirit of adventure and novelty, stimulated economic and social changes, and further aroused secular interests.

In addition to these more diffused forms of assault upon the dominant supernaturalism, there existed a number of direct and immediate modes of attack. The humanists, especially outside of Italy, were for the most part relatively pious Christians. Nevertheless, in their literary and philosophical activities they stressed the excellence of Greek and Latin literature, with its secular cast. The more radical fringe, represented by Crotus Rubianus and Ulrich von Hutten in the *Letters of Obscure Men,* employed the weapon of satire against ecclesiastical abuses. The rationalists, while firmly believing in a sort of benign cosmic God, vigorously attacked orthodox Christianity and the prevailing supernatural beliefs. The rationalists and the deists anticipated our contemporary modernists by contrasting the teachings of Jesus with orthodox Christianity. But they found a great deal in common between the doctrines of Jesus and their own rationalistic natural religion.

The rise of modern astronomy from Copernicus to Newton proved that the sun, rather than the earth, is the center of our system, and also gave some preliminary hint of the vast extent of the universe. Both of these concepts were a direct challenge to the orthodox theory of creation and cosmology. Francis Bacon, the great rhetorical herald of the new scientific age, called attention to the serious inadequacies of the deductive method of orthodox scholastic theology as a tool for scientific research. He demanded a greater reliance upon inductive reasoning from a mass of observed facts. Science, he believed, would be able to revolutionize the world and greatly increase human happiness. He repudiated the scholastic dialectic as a technique for acquiring information on the ground that "nature is more subtle than any argument." The humanists, and particularly the rationalists, resisted the intolerance of Catholics and Protestants alike, and warmly defended not only toleration but complete freedom of thought.

While the seventeenth century itself was one of the most intolerant of centuries, because of the revived religious controversies and the religious wars, yet the tacit but portentous undercurrents associated with the critical philosophy, skepticism, and scientific research, laid the basis for intellectual attitudes which were to prove the undoing of vulgar superstition, crude supernaturalism, religious violence, and dogmatic intolerance.

So far as the mental climate of early modern times marked a break with that of the Middle Ages, it may thus be said to have been characterized chiefly by a growing secularism, tolerance, and freedom, and by an increasing reliance upon the scientific method. Further, a theory of human progress slowly replaced the Christian epic, which had been obsessed with the fall of man and the day of judgment.

II. INTELLECTUAL AND CULTURAL TRENDS ENCOURAGING AND ACCOMPANYING THE PROGRESS IN SCIENTIFIC RESEARCH

Scientific discoveries from Copernicus to Lavoisier were probably more remarkable and numerous than those which took place during the entire history of man from the Stone Age to the middle of the sixteenth century. The causes of this scientific activity are numerous and complex.

In the first place, we have to recognize more thoroughly than most historians of science have been wont to do the important work of hitherto obscure scientists of the late medieval period. We have already made this clear in detail in preceding chapters. We are coming to see that in respect to science and critical thought the Middle Ages moved gradually into modern times—a development comparable to what we have already shown to be the case with respect to the transition of medievalism into humanism.

These considerations do much to end the prolonged discussion of the real genesis of modern science. Scholars have either discovered many fictitious causes for its origins after 1550 or have offered explanations why it advanced in the face of adverse conditions. The truth is that natural science continued steadily along the road on which it had begun to set its feet in the twelfth century. It needed no special impetus around 1550 to support or propel it. And its momentum was sufficient to overcome the hostile atmosphere of religious controversy and prolonged warfare. Yet, we should not go to the other extreme and become indifferent to intellectual and social tendencies which encouraged science in the seventeenth century and made its developments more natural and inevitable.

Humanism produced a secular outlook more concerned with things of this world than with salvation in the next. To be sure, the humanists were usually Christians and only incidentally lovers of pagan culture, but their secular interests looked in a direction which might tolerate or promote scientific curiosity. Although the Protestant revolt in its religious aspects was probably more intensely otherworldly than "Renaissance" Catholicism, it seriously challenged Catholic authority, and lessened the prestige of scholastic philosophy, even though Melanchthon tried to create a Protestant scholasticism. Further, Protestantism encouraged that individuality and personal expression which was closely related to the early stages of scientific progress.

The political and economic tendencies of the time also aided the progress of science. Science cannot flourish under conditions of physical disorder, violence, confusion, and general poverty. The growth of national states and centralized administration which succeeded feudalism helped to create order and justice in the social system. A degree of political stability superseded the disorder of the past. Rising capitalism produced a large wealthy class that had leisure for scientific pursuits or was able to subsidize scientists and their societies, academies, and journals. As the middle class accumulated more of the things of this world they came to think more extensively about its problems—which constitute the data of science.

Paradoxically enough, even the extreme religious intolerance of the sixteenth and seventeenth centuries indirectly aided science. Religious persecutions, religious wars, and the witchcraft mania turned many of the best minds of Europe away from religion towards a compensatory interest in the investigation of scientific problems. This was, however, but a temporary and indirect factor. In the end, political stability and intellectual urbanity had a far more salutary and lasting influence on the growth of scientific activity.

There were also certain very specific aids to scientific endeavor at this time. Mathematics, so essential to most scientific formulations, had been notably developed since western Europe came into contact with Arabic numerals and algebraic notation among the Muslims during the crusades and after. The science of optics had also been absorbed from the Greeks by the Muslims. Al-Hazen and other Muslim scientists had made additional contributions to optics, which were adopted and improved by Witelo, Roger Bacon, and others. In due time progress in pure and applied optics made possible the telescope, microscope, prism, and other invaluable aids to science. Alchemy, cultivated by the Muslims, also gradually lost its mystical aspects and developed into practical chemistry.

The new science was, as has been suggested, intimately related to the expansion of Europe. Also the contact of cultures, which had been greatly extended by the crusades and subsequent developments, was the most potent influence in introducing Muslim and Hellenistic science into Europe and in stimulating that curiosity which is essential to any persistent development of scientific activity. Cultural contrasts and the comparative way of looking at things, which these contacts engendered, also helped to develop toleration and freethinking, both of great assistance to scientific progress.

Even more direct relationship between oversea expansion and the new science is to be discerned in the extensive information brought into Europe as a result of the process of expansion. We have treated this matter in the chapter on the expansion of Europe.

III. THE RISE OF SCIENTIFIC SOCIETIES

The remarkable developments in the natural sciences in the seventeenth century were not wholly the result of isolated work by individual scientists. There was also much coöperative activity. In this period we find the origins of the modern scientific societies, comparable roughly to Aristotle's Lyceum and the workers at

the Alexandrian library and museum. Early modern scientific activity was conducted mainly outside the universities, for the universities scarcely encouraged
natural science and the experimental method. While some of the leading scientists
of the period who joined these societies were university professors, many were
gifted and enthusiastic amateurs. Professor Wolf well summarizes the character
and intellectual environment of these important new organizations created to
stimulate scientific discussion and experimentation:

> The Universities might have been expected to lead, or at least to share, in this
> movement for intellectual emancipation. But they did nothing of the kind. For
> they were controlled by the Church. Philosophy was only tolerated as the hand-
> maid of Theology, and the University as the Cinderella of the Church. It was,
> indeed, highly significant of the times, that the vast majority of the pioneers of
> modern thought were either entirely detached from the Universities, or were but
> loosely associated with them. New organizations, and indeed essentially secular
> organizations, were necessary to foster the new spirit, and to enable it to express
> itself. Francis Bacon dreamed of such institutions in his *New Atlantis*. His suc-
> cessors, partly under the stimulus of his visions, saw his dreams come true. The
> scientific academies came into being in response to the new needs of the new age.
> It was in these societies that modern science found the opportunities and the en-
> couragement which were denied to it at the Universities, not only in the seven-
> teenth century, but for a long time afterwards.[1]

The first important scientific academy was founded in Florence in 1657—the
Academy of Experiments (Accademia del Cimento)—which grew out of earlier
societies formed for philosophical and scientific discussions. The dominant figures
in the creation of this organization were two of Galileo's students, Viviani and
Torricelli. Financial support came mainly from the Medici brothers. Other members were prominent scientists whom we shall have occasion to mention later—
Redi, Borelli, Cassini, and Steno. Their scientific work was mainly limited to
physics and physico-chemistry. Important researches in barometric pressure, thermal changes, and optics were conducted. Out of Torricelli's experiments in barometric pressure came his invention of the barometer. The academy's experiments
were so carefully executed that they constituted the best example of purely experimental work in the whole history of science down to that time. The Academy of
Experiments was disbanded in 1667, but it published in that year the content of
its researches, *Essays of Natural Experiments Made in the Academy of Experiments,* a landmark in the literature of science.

The next scientific academy in point of time was the Royal Society of England.
Since it was organized by followers of Francis Bacon, it was natural that its
founders should take as their model the House of Solomon in Bacon's utopia,
the *New Atlantis*. Meetings were held as early as 1645. The leading spirits included the mathematician, John Wallis; the astronomer and inventor, John
Wilkins; a German savant, Theodore Haak, who suggested weekly meetings;
and a number of scientifically inclined physicians. The group split in a few years,

1 A. Wolf, *A History of Science, Technology, and Philosophy in the Sixteenth and Seventeenth Centuries,*
Macmillan, 1935 (2 vols., Harper Torchbooks, 1959), pp. 54-55.

some of its members going to Oxford. This latter branch wound up its work in 1690.

The London society continued to meet in Gresham College. It was granted a royal charter by Charles II in 1662, and the formal history of the Royal Society begins with that date. The zeal and activity of the Royal Society in its early days were in part the work of its first curator, Robert Hooke (1635-1703), next to Leibnitz the most versatile scientist of the century. He presented several of his own ingenious experiments at each meeting; others were permitted to discuss experiments of their own. It was customary to assign definite experiments to members.

The activities of the society fell into three main channels: physico-chemical, biological, and technological. In the first most of the work was confined to dynamics, measurement of gas pressure, and barometric studies. The law of falling bodies was studied, Boyle's law was tested, and important work was done on the air pump. Scientific expeditions were dispatched to test new theories. The presence of doctors in the society stimulated biological studies—and Hooke was the first to discover the cellular composition of organic bodies. Considerable work was done to blast the mystical and magical biology which had been inherited from the Middle Ages. Biological museums were established. Many important technological investigations were undertaken. The publications of the society began in 1665. Its wide range of activities prevented the organization from turning out much intensive experimental work. But it would be difficult to exaggerate the stimulus and encouragement which the Royal Society gave to English science at the time. Its *Philosophical Transactions* began to appear in 1666.

The French Academy of Sciences grew out of informal meetings of mathematicians and philosophers about the middle of the seventeenth century. Among the leading original members were Descartes, Pascal, Gassendi, and Fermat. Foreign scholars like Huygens, Hobbes, and Steno met with them occasionally. The formal establishment of the Academy of Sciences resulted from a suggestion made to Louis XIV by Charles Perrault, whom we shall meet later in our discussions of the rise of the theory of progress. The academy held its first official meeting at the close of the year 1666.

The researches of the academy covered most branches of science. There was a real interest in Cartesian mathematics. In physics attention focused on barometric studies, thermal measurements, and optics. Huygens wrote his important work on light while a member of the academy. Biological investigations, including anatomical dissections, were carried on. Important scientific expeditions were sent out, including one to French Guiana. Like the Royal Society, the academy also displayed considerable interest in technology and invention. Perrault, Picard, and Auzout, in particular, made valuable improvements in astronomical instruments. Important publications issued from the academy in the *Journal des savants*.

Coöperative scientific societies seem to have originated in Germany early in the seventeenth century. But they appear to have had little permanence or influence until Leibnitz appeared on the scene. Devoting many years of his life to advocating the foundation of a German academy of sciences, he was finally successful in inducing the Elector of Brandenburg-Prussia to establish such an organization. The Berlin Academy was, accordingly, granted a charter in 1700. The activities of the society were devoted chiefly to mathematics, physics, and linguistics. Its publications began to appear in 1710. The Berlin Academy was also important in encouraging Peter the Great to establish the St. Petersburg Academy in 1724. Other scientific societies, of lesser reputation than those described above, came into being. The Dublin Philosophical Society modeled itself after the Royal Society, and several scientific associations were formed in the Netherlands.

More and more, natural science became a coöperative affair, a collection of the results of investigators in all countries of the globe. Not since Hellenistic times had there been so much enthusiasm for coöperative scientific activity as that shown by the scientific societies of the seventeenth century.

As we have just noted, journals devoted to the work of these societies and to other scientific and philosophical matters sprang up. The *Journal des savants* appeared in 1666, followed in the same year by the *Philosophical Transactions* of the British Royal Society. The Italian *Giornale de litterati* began publication in 1668. The first German publication, the *Acta eruditorum,* appeared at Leipzig in 1682.

IV. NEW SCIENTIFIC INSTRUMENTS

We have suggested that one of the main reasons for the failure of Greek science to proceed beyond Archimedes, Ptolemy, and others was that the Hellenistic scientists possessed few instruments of precision. One of the explanations for the outdistancing of Hellenistic science in early modern times was the invention of indispensable instruments for conducting scientific experiments.

The science of optics, as developed by the Hellenistic Greeks, the Muslims, and the late medieval scientists, lay at the basis of some of the most important inventions of this period, especially the microscope and the telescope. The Greeks, the Muslims, and the medieval students of optics were all equipped with magnifying glasses. The Netherlands was the leader in practical work in optics, including lens-grinding, and a flourishing industry in the manufacture of spectacles. It was natural, therefore, that the invention of the microscope and telescope should take place in the Netherlands. It seems clear that the compound microscope was invented by Zacharias Jansen, a spectaclemaker of Middelburg, Holland, in 1590. Galileo appears to have been the first to use such an instrument for scientific purposes. Hooke was the earliest to popularize its scientific uses and he improved upon its details. His *Micrographia* (1665) was the first important treatise to deal with the technique and results of microscopic investigation.

The telescope, likewise, seems to have been invented by Dutch spectaclemakers. Though some claim it to have been the invention of Leonard Digges, an Oxford mathematician who died in 1571, there is no conclusive proof of this contention. The direct evidence is in favor of the invention of the telescope by Hans Lippershey, also a Dutch spectaclemaker of Middelburg. He applied for a patent on his telescope in 1608. Galileo was the first to use the telescope for astronomical observation. He seems to have constructed his own instrument after getting news of Lippershey's invention. Galileo's superior knowledge of optics enabled him to improve the Dutch instrument, and to devise a telescope which would magnify by thirty diameters. A great advance in the telescope for astronomical uses was suggested by Kepler but the construction of such an instrument was the achievement of a Jesuit by the name of Scheiner, about 1617. It provided, among other improvements, for a larger field of vision and for protection against the light of the sun. These telescopes were all of the refractor type. The first reflector telescope was suggested by James Gregory in 1663 and constructed by Newton in 1668. A few years later Newton built a much larger model and presented it to the Royal Society. Hooke made a number of improvements and popularized its use, as earlier he had popularized the microscope. The micrometer invented by Gascoigne, Auzout, Picard, and Huygens, between 1640 and 1666, greatly facilitated precise work with the telescope.

The growing interest in heat and thermal problems stimulated the invention of the thermometer. Hero of Alexandria had constructed a thermoscope, or air thermometer. Improvements on this instrument were worked out in modern times by Galileo, Amontons, and Otto von Guericke. The first proposal of a liquid thermometer is attributed to a French doctor, Jean Rey, in 1632. But the first liquid thermometer was constructed by Grand Duke Ferdinand of Tuscany, one of the members of the Italian Academy of Experiments. He used colored alcohol. Newton worked out a thermal scale. But the thermometer, as we know it, was the invention of D. G. Fahrenheit (1686-1736), a native of Danzig who lived in Amsterdam. His thermometer (1714) used mercury for filling the sealed tube. He laid out certain basic points: zero, or the temperature of ice, pure water, and salt; freezing, or the temperature of a mixture of ice and pure water; the temperature of the human body which he estimated at 96°; and the boiling point at 212°.

The study of air pressure provided a number of important instruments. The barometer was invented by Torricelli and Pascal about 1647-1648. Boyle, von Guericke, Amontons, and Hooke made subsequent improvements. These barometers used a fluid column, ultimately mercury. The aneroid barometer, which eliminates the use of a fluid column, was first suggested by Leibnitz in 1700. Von Guericke invented the air pump about 1654. Later improvements in it were made by Boyle, Hooke, and Huygens. The famous Magdeburg hemispheres were also invented by von Guericke. Invented about the same time as the air pump, they effectively demonstrated the intensity of atmospheric pressure.

One of the most momentous inventions of the time was the pendulum clock which permitted more precise and extended work in dynamics. We have already referred to the invention of improved mechanical clocks by the de Dondis and others in the fourteenth century, and the provision of dials with hours, minutes, and seconds in the fourteenth and fifteenth centuries. But these clocks had serious limitations and could never be adapted to watch construction. The honor of inventing the pendulum and escapement clock must be assigned to Huygens, who patented his clock in 1657 and described it in detail in his *Horologius oscillatorium* (1673). Hugyens later invented a practicable marine clock. Hooke invented the balance wheel in the watch and thus enabled the escapement principle to be transferred to a more compact and convenient timepiece.

These instruments helped to effect the remarkable advances in astronomy, physics, and biology which we shall presently describe. Better and more varied instruments were provided in the eighteenth and nineteenth centuries and natural science moved far ahead of anything imagined by the Greeks. The invention of instruments was both a cause and an effect of scientific progress. The new instruments made possible scientific discoveries and the latter, in turn, suggested better instruments.

V. THE REVOLUTION IN CELESTIAL MECHANICS

One historian, with a flair for the dramatic, has observed that the coming of modern times bore out the scriptural prophecy that the old earth and the old heaven would pass away and be replaced by a new earth and a new heaven. We have described in the preceding chapter how a revolutionary extension of information about the earth sprang up with the expansion of Europe. We may now deal with the exploration of the solar system.[2]

The ancient conception of the heavens that was accepted by the Hebrews is perhaps not familiar to all of us. The earth was represented as a minute slab of earth and water supported in a void and lighted by heavenly bodies of varying intensity which studded the canopy of the heavens—an inverted blue bowl—at no great distance from the earth.

The Hebrew astronomy was not adopted by the Greek and Roman philosophers. They worked out their own conception of the physical universe. Most of them held that the earth was located at the center of a number of transparent spheres. On the latter were fixed planets and stars. Some of these turned clockwise, some counter-clockwise; some moved rapidly and some slowly. This diversity of direction and unequal motion were held to account for the variations in the position of the planets relative to the earth and the fixed stars at different seasons of the year. Later it was seen that the theory of the revolution of the spheres was too simple to explain the shifting position of the planets. Hence, Apollonius, Hipparchus, and Ptolemy resorted to the doctrine of epicycles, namely, the theory that the planets moved in smaller circles on the surface of their spheres.

This pagan notion of crystalline spheres was adopted by the Christian philosophers of the Middle Ages. God, the angels, the saints, and the saved were believed to hold forth in the empyrean paradise out beyond the last crystalline sphere. Dante made one important addition, namely, he portrayed the spaces between the spheres as separate heavens reserved as reception rooms for different grades of the blessed, who normally dwelt with God in the empyrean. This introduced a theological element into the astronomical picture. The Christians, thus, took over and sanctified the Hellenic rather than the Hebrew version of celestial mechanics.

Medieval conceptions of the size of the universe were far short of the reality. Roger Bacon's estimate placed the outside limit of the universe at 130 million

[2] The best introduction to the history of theories of the universe is Woodbridge Riley, *From Myth to Reason*, Appleton, 1926, Books I, III.

miles from the earth. This was then regarded as a very generous figure. Yet Mars is some 140 million miles from the sun, so Bacon's whole universe could be put inside the orbit of Mars. Neptune, the most distant of the major planets in our solar system, is 2,795 million miles from our sun. The galaxy of which our solar system is a part is estimated to be 160,000 light-years in diameter. This distance means 160,000 multiplied by 6,000,000,000,000 miles (the distance light travels in a year). But our galaxy is only one of many millions already accounted for. This will indicate the inadequacy of Bacon's conception of the heavens; yet his was, perhaps, the most expansive estimate of a medieval scientist.

In addition to the scientific problems involved in upsetting the medieval view of the cosmos, there were many theological obstacles to be faced. The heavens were believed to be made of more perfect material than the earth—namely, the mysterious fifth element. Their circular motion was thought to be endless and therefore eternal and godlike. The paradise of the saved souls was linked up with the system of spheres. Moreover, the whole logic of Christianity rested essentially on a geocentric (earth-centered) view of the universe. The earth had to be important enough to hold God's chosen people and serve as the temporary abode of his only begotten son.

Therefore, a new astronomy which proclaimed the heavens to be made of the same material as the earth, which supplanted circles by ellipses and parabolas, which wiped out the fixed starry spheres, which proved our solar system heliocentric (sun-centered), and demonstrated the plurality of universes, was bound to encounter serious theological opposition. It is not surprising, therefore, that the Catholic church listed the works of Bruno, Copernicus, Kepler, and Galileo in the *Index expurgatorius,*[8] where they remained until 1835. Indeed, Dean Inge has suggested that the Christian church has never taken full cognizance of the implications of the Copernican theory of the universe.

We shall now briefly summarize the progress of astronomical knowledge from Copernicus to Newton. As has been pointed out in recent years, Copernicus was influenced by scientists of the fourteenth and fifteenth centuries who had anticipated his views of the rotation of the earth and its revolution around the sun. He was also familiar with Hellenistic astronomy.

Copernicus, as we have seen, did little to modify Hellenic celestial mechanics which had been accepted by Christendom. He simply exchanged the position of the sun and the earth in the scheme of fixed crystalline spheres, thus transforming it from a geocentric to a heliocentric system. Yet this mere interchange of the positions of the sun and earth in the celestial scheme aroused the bitter opposition of the church. The Copernican theory was officially pronounced by the Vatican to be "false and altogether opposed to holy scripture." It was not until 1822 that, in the words of Professor Dampier-Whetham, "The sun received the formal sanction of the papacy to become the center of the planetary system." As late as 1839 not a single Catholic priest could be found to officiate at an unveiling of a statue of Copernicus in Warsaw, in his native Poland.

Giordano Bruno clearly perceived the implications of the shift from a geocen-

[8] See below, pp. 754-60.

tric to a heliocentric universe and set them forth clearly and comprehensively. Among his hypotheses damaging the cosmology of the Christian epic were such things as: (1) The infinite size of the universe; (2) the lack of finite limitations or a fixed center in the universe; (3) the fallacy of the doctrine of rigid crystalline spheres; (4) the conception of the free motion of heavenly bodies in space; (5) the relativity of space, time, and motion; (6) the ever-changing positions and relations of the heavenly bodies; (7) the similarity or identity of constituent materials in the heavenly and earthly bodies; and, above all, (8) the disconcerting notion of a plurality of universes.

When Bruno tried to popularize such doctrines, it is possible to understand why the Catholic church of the Counter Reformation intervened and burned him at the stake, in spite of his pious and mystical theology. Most of his views at the time were pure guesswork, but all have been amply confirmed by subsequent development of astrophysics and celestial chemistry.

The succession of personages who laid the substantial basis for the celestial mechanics that upset the medieval view of the heavens consists of Tycho Brahe, Kepler, Galileo, and Newton.

Tycho Brahe (1546-1601) was the first great modern descriptive astronomer. He added little or nothing to theoretical astronomy and did not directly promote the astronomical revolution. Indeed, he only halfheartedly accepted the Copernican theory. But he was unrivaled in his day for an accurate study of the heavens. He thus gathered the factual material which better theorists, like his assistant, Kepler, could use.

A Danish scholar, Tycho lived on an island between Denmark and Sweden. Here he constructed the best astronomical observatory of his time and called it Uraniborg (the Castle of Heaven). Its windows were arranged so as to provide unique visibility of the heavens. Tycho devised better instruments than his predecessors had used. In particular, he constructed a large mural quadrant, and another large quadrant, with a graduated metal arc, which could be rotated. He also invented an iron armillary sphere which located the major celestial phenomena.

With these instruments he prepared the most comprehensive and accurate star chart down to his day. It superseded the *Almagest* of Ptolemy. Tycho definitely located hundreds of fixed stars. Of even greater importance was his careful study of planetary motion. Tycho was not so accurate in his estimate of heavenly distances. For example, he put Saturn at 48 million miles from the earth instead of the actual distance of 887 million miles. But his data enabled later astronomers to extend those theoretical studies which ultimately produced the Newtonian system.

The first great theoretical advance after Copernicus was achieved by Tycho's brilliant assistant, Johann Kepler (1571-1630). Kepler, a German by birth, had received a good mathematical training at the University of Tübingen. Unlike Tycho, he was an ardent Copernican, but it was his destiny to destroy a part of the Copernican scheme, namely, the fixed crystalline spheres which were supposed to control the motions of the heavenly bodies. As Tycho's assistant, Kepler was fully conversant with the vast body of descriptive material which the former had accumulated. His great theoretical talent, combined with his mastery of mathematics, enabled him to effect one of the major revolutions in astronomical history. Kepler's writings and theories were summarized in his *Epitome of the Copernican Astronomy* (1621). His famous third law of planetary motion appeared in a slightly earlier work, *The Harmonies of the World* (1619).

In addition to his epoch-making laws of planetary motion, Kepler added considerable descriptive material as well as an invaluable mathematical analysis of astral positions and relationships. Kepler denied that the planets move in circles enclosed by crystalline spheres. He believed that they travel freely in space around elliptical orbits. Kepler's new cosmic system was expressed in his famous three laws of planetary motion:

1. The planet describes an ellipse about the sun in one focus.

2. The radius vector drawn from the sun to the planet describes equal areas in equal times (that is, the planet moves fastest when nearest the sun).

3. The squares of the periodic times (i.e. their times of revolution) of the several planets are proportional to the cubes of their respective mean distances from the sun.

The next momentous figure in the astronomical revolution was the Italian mathematician and physicist, Galileo Galilei (1564-1642). At first Galileo accepted the medieval cosmology. He was persuaded by Kepler and others to accept the Copernican view which he then defended with great vigor in his famous *Dialogue on the Two Principal Systems of the Universe* (1629). For this he was haled before the Inquisition at Rome and compelled to recant. But there is no evidence that he recanted in his own mind.

Through the use of his improved telescope Galileo added much to our knowledge of descriptive astronomy. He discovered that the spots on the moon are mountains and valleys. He was thus able to destroy such medieval superstitions as the idea of Adelard of Bath that the spots on the moon are the symbolic stains of Adam's first trangression and a perpetual reminder of the fall of man. Galileo saw that the milky way is a great collection of stars and star clusters. He discovered the satellites of Jupiter and saw the rings of Saturn, though he misunderstood the nature of the latter.[4] Galileo was able to discern sunspots (his researches with an unprotected telescope injured his eyesight). He also gained some inkling of the immense distances of the fixed stars. Much of this new information he published in his *The Sidereal Messenger* (1610), though he did not discover sunspots until a year after its publication.

More important than all of these things for the future of astronomy was Galileo's contribution to dynamic mechanics, his famous law of falling bodies. He tested the old theory of Greek physicists that bodies fall at a speed proportional to their weight and proved that it was wrong. He demonstrated instead that the space covered in the fall increases as the square of the time involved. His famous proof of this hypothesis, in which he employed the inclined plane, was such a classic of experimental method that the contemporary French philosopher, Henri

---

[4] Huygens was the first to recognize the true nature of the rings of Saturn.

Bergson, once remarked in colorful language that modern science came down from heaven along Galileo's inclined plane.

Isaac Newton (1642-1727), about half a century after Galileo, combined Kepler's third law with Galileo's law of falling bodies in his famous law of inverse squares or universal gravitation. According to this theory, the planets sweep through space around the sun in conformity to Galileo's law of falling bodies. They are kept in their elliptical courses by the sun's attraction, which varies directly with the mass of the object and inversely with the square of the distance from the sun.

This Newtonian synthesis, embodied in the famous *Principia* (1687), was not only the crowning achievement of seventeenth-century science, but also the inspiration for much of the liberal philosophy and theology of the eighteenth century. The old heavens, not merely of Genesis and the astrologers, but of Aristotle and Ptolemy, had been destroyed and a new cosmos of infinite expanse and complexity had been substituted.

A pseudoscientific rival to the Newtonian world system became very popular with "reconcilers" who wished to harmonize astronomy with Scripture. This was what is known as Descartes' theory of vortices, set forth in his book on *The World*. He contended that there are great whirlpools or vortices of matter which revolve about the sun with each planet, having smaller vortices which revolve with the satellites. This doctrine enabled Descartes to get around the churchly objection to Galileo's theory that the earth moves. Descartes held that the earth *is moved* by its vortex of encircling matter. He made this revision in his book after he heard of Galileo's condemnation. In spite of the popularity of this notion, it simply retarded the progress of scientific astrophysics.

The rise of astronomy slowly but surely undermined astrology, that strange pseudo-science which had exerted so strong an influence over the minds of men for many thousands of years. Its overthrow by the rise of scientific astronomy has been well described by Franz Cumont:

> The power of astrology broke down when, with Copernicus, Kepler, and Galileo, the progress of astronomy overthrew the false hypothesis upon which its entire structure rested, namely, the geocentric system of the universe. The fact that the earth revolves in space intervened to upset the complicated play of planetary influences, and the silent stars . . . no longer made their prophetic voices audible to mankind. Celestial mechanics and spectrum analysis finally robbed them of their mysterious prestige. Thenceforth, in that learned system of divination, which professed to discover from the stars the secret of our destiny, men saw nothing but the most monstrous of all the chimeras begotten of superstition.[5]

Yet it can scarcely be said that astrology died with the age of Copernicus. Natural astrology, or the literal study of the heavens, passed into astronomy. Judicial astrology, which upheld an occult relation between man and the stars, was soon driven out of scientific circles, though Tycho Brahe, Kepler, Francis Bacon, and other scientists and philosophers continued to believe in it. But, as we have

---

5 F. V. M. Cumont, *Astrology and Religion among the Greeks and Romans*, Dover, 1960, Introduction, p. xi.

noted above, astrology has retained a powerful hold on ignorant and fanciful minds down to our day. There are a hundredfold more readers of astrological lore today than there were in the age of Roger Bacon. The difference is that astrology is no longer believed by informed scientists, as it was in Bacon's era. In short, astrology has lost its authority among intellectuals but not its popularity with the masses.

The new astronomy influenced many other phases of thought. In theology it gave a new conception of the immensity of the physical universe and thus produced the need for a God majestic enough to be the creator and ruler of such a universe. It also emphasized the fact that such a God must be a God of law and order rather than the medieval "God of arbitrariness."

The influence of the new astronomy spread to the social sciences as well. Liberal theologians like the deists, contended that the physical universe is subject to immutable divine laws. They suggested, too, that man and society, as a part of God's creation, are also governed by the laws of the divine order of the universe. Therefore, man should make as few laws as possible so that he may expose himself so far as can be done to control by the divine natural order. Such was the basis of the political philosophy of the French physiocrats and the English classical economists—the first great exponents of *laissez-faire* and free competition.

VI. SOME IMPORTANT ADVANCES IN NATURAL SCIENCE IN THE SEVENTEENTH CENTURY

Partly because of the remarkable achievements in natural science in the fifteenth and sixteenth centuries and partly because of the new scientific instruments, as well as the stimulus from the scientific societies, scientific studies received a new impetus in the seventeenth century and produced striking and momentous results. We may now consider some of the more significant scientific advances of the century. Let us first turn to mathematics.

In a previous chapter we carried the story of mathematics down through Descartes' invention of analytical geometry, though this achievement really falls in the seventeenth century. We did so in order to give continuity to the preceding discussion. Mathematical achievements at the turn of the seventeenth century included work on the theory of numbers, indivisibles, infinitesmals, and the like, some of which were important for analytical geometry and others for the future invention of differential calculus. The invention of logarithms took place in the late sixteenth and early seventeenth centuries.

The next innovation in mathematics was the work on the calculus of probabilities by Pascal, Fermat, and especially Christian Huygens (1629-1695). Huygens also made practical applications of the notion, being the first to apply it to the calculation of the life expectancy of persons at different ages. This forms the basis of the actuarial tables used by life insurance companies at the present time. The astronomer, Edmund Halley, worked out the first mortality tables in 1693.

But the outstanding mathematical discovery of the century—one of the most fundamental in modern mathematics and by far the most useful—was the development of infinitesimal calculus independently by Newton and Gottfried Wilhelm Leibnitz (1646-1716). Calculus involves the mathematical analysis of continuously varying quantities and is, hence, indispensable for computations in dynamic mechanics and engineering. Its invention would have been quite impossible without the preceding innovations in mathematics, particularly analytical geometry and the theory of infinitesmals.

Newton arrived at the fundamentals of calculus as early as 1665, but did not publish his theories and solutions until many years later. He probably borrowed some suggestions, especially for this theory of fluxions, from his teacher Isaac Barrow (1630-1677). The idea of fluxions—a constant flow or change produced by motion—was the basis of Newton's theory of calculus. His version is known as fluxional calculus. Leibnitz took his point of departure from the analytical mathematical theories of Descartes, Fermat, Pascal, and Huygens. He produced his version of calculus in 1673 or 1674. It is known as differential calculus.

The independence of Newton and Leibnitz in this work has been conclusively demonstrated in our day by students of the history of mathematics. But for a long time the followers of Newton and Leibnitz charged one another with plagiarism. Newton's notation was the more profound, but Leibnitz's was clearer and simpler and has been more generally employed since the seventeenth century. It was given popularity by Marquis de l'Hospital and Peter Varignon. No single factor has more influenced the later developments of physical science and technology than calculus. Newton made other important contributions to mathematics, including the solution of the binomial theorem, while Leibnitz introduced determinants into algebra.

We have already described the major achievement in seventeenth-century astronomy in connection with the work of Kepler, Galileo, and Newton on astrophysics, which culminated in the famous Newtonian synthesis. This work not only vindicated the heliocentric hypothesis, but also gave it a proper mathematical and physical setting.

The invention of the telescope and micrometer, which we have also discussed, was vital to the progress of seventeenth-century astronomy. Better observatories were also indispensable. The most famous observatories, after Tycho Brahe's at Uraniborg had fallen into disuse, were set up at Paris and at Greenwich. The leading atronomers at the Paris Observatory, opened in 1672, were Jean Picard (1620-1682), Adrien Auzout (d. 1691), and Giovanni Cassini (1625-1712). They made precise observation with the telescope easier by introducing the micrometer and the pendulum clock. Cassini investigated the rings of Saturn and for the first time studied the parallax of the sun scientifically. The leading early astronomer at the Greenwich Observatory, built in 1676, was John Flamsteed (b. 1646). After many years of careful observation he produced the best star catalogue of the age.

A number of other astronomers of the time should be mentioned. Huygens first explained the nature of the rings of Saturn. His work in optics, particularly his wave theory of light, also proved of great importance for later astronomical progress. Olaus Römer (1644-1710), a Dane, used a transit telescope and obtained more accurate star measurements than had hitherto been possible. Another Scandinavian, Johann Hevel (1611-1687), known as Hevelius, was a master of descriptive astronomy and of star measurement. But the most active and versatile of astronomers was Edmund Halley (1656-1742). He went to the island of St. Helena to take observations in the southern hemisphere. He brought together a remarkably complete star chart which he used in his highly original studies of planetary motion. With relative accuracy he measured the distance of the sun from the earth, and a total eclipse of the sun enabled him to observe the sun's corona. But Halley is best known in astronomy for putting the study of comets on a scientific basis. One of them bears his name. Halley also demonstrated that the so-called fixed stars are not really fixed but are in motion.

If Newton was the greatest physicist at the close of the century, certainly Galileo was preëminent at the beginning. He was truly "the father of modern physics." Not only did he launch modern dynamics; he did notable work in hydrostatics, pneumatics, acoustics, and optics as well. As for the physicists of the whole century, Galileo, Huygens, and Newton tower among many distinguished names.

We noted that a new interest in mechanics was stimulated by the versatile Stevinus, with his work on pulleys, his discovery of the law of the parallelogram of forces, his investigation of the center of gravity, and his work on hydrostatics. Further investigations in hydrostatics were carried on in the seventeenth century by Evangelista Torricelli (1608-1647), particularly with reference to the flow of water from holes at different positions in the side of a barrel. Pascal investigated the equilibrium of liquids. The oscillations of the pendulum were studied by Galileo and Huygens, and the latter applied his results to the invention of the pendulum clock, which facilitated experiments in dynamic mechanics, though Galileo had made his classic discovery of the law of falling bodies before the pendulum clock was devised. Torricelli made many applications of the theory of falling bodies. Huygens was the first to study impact scientifically.

We have already mentioned important beginnings in the study of air pressure in connection with our discussion of the invention of the barometer, air pump, Magdeburg hemispheres, and the like. The leading pneumaticians were Otto von Guericke (1602-1686) and Robert Boyle (1627-1691). Von Guericke experimented with the vacuum and demonstrated the hitherto unsuspected enormity of atmospheric pressure. Boyle attempted to weigh air, studied various forms of behavior in a vacuum, showed that air is a gas, and formulated his famous law that the pressure exerted by a given quantity of gas is directly proportional to its density. The claim of Edmé Mariotte (1620-1684) to the discovery of this law seems unfounded, but he helped to promote an appreciation of its significance on the continent of Europe.

The leading branches of physics in the nineteenth century—sound, heat, light, and electricity—received extensive attention as early as the seventeenth century. Galileo was the first important student of sound in modern times. He suggested the undulatory or wave theory of sound, and made preliminary studies in harmonics, pitch, and acoustics. Marin Mersenne (c. 1635) investigated the vibration of strings and the production of overtones. Brook Taylor (1685-1731) developed the theory of transverse vibrations of strings. Pierre Gassendi (1592-1655) studied the velocity of sound and disproved the Aristotelian theory that high notes are transmitted more rapidly than low notes. But he wrongly supposed that the direction of the wind has no influence on the velocity of sound. This error was corrected by William Derham (1657-1735). The latter and von Guericke investigated the transmission of sound. They found that not only air but other gases, liquids, and even solids can transmit sound.

Since there was no satisfactory thermometer until Fahrenheit's in 1714, the studies of heat in the seventeenth century could not be very precise. Yet there were some positive results. Boyle suggested that heat results from the rapid agitation of the parts of a substance. It is interesting to note that he cited as proof heat generated by the boring out of a cannon, the same example used by Count Rumford in the nineteenth century to demonstrate what we now accept as the scientific theory of heat. Hooke took the same view, asserting that heat is "nothing else but a very brisk and vehement agitation of the parts of a body." The study of the radiation of heat and cold was begun by members of the Academy of Experiments, who also faintly suggested the idea of latent heat. Mariotte showed the differences in radiation of heat from the sun and from a fire. Hooke confirmed this discovery. Newton conceded that heat might be radiated through vibrations in a medium "more subtle" than air. One important result of the study of heat was gradual dispersion of the ancient and medieval confusion of heat, fire, and flame.

Next to the achievements in dynamic mechanics the most striking advances in physics in the seventeenth century were probably those associated with optics and the investigations of light and colors. The first important student of optics after Maurolycus and Porta was Kepler, who showed that the eye is a camera obscura, greatly extended our knowledge of lenses and lens systems, and studied the angles of refraction. But he failed to master the general law of the refraction of light.

The latter was discovered by the Dutch mathematician, Willebrord Snell (1591-1626), and Descartes, and was confirmed and ingeniously applied by Fermat. Descartes formulated the emission theory of light, namely, that light consists of particles running along in straight lines from the point of emission. While erroneous, this doctrine permitted the first mathematical treatment of the propagation of light. Mariotte discovered the blind spot in the eye. He also studied closely atmospheric refraction and color problems revealed by the corona of the sun. The astronomer Römer was the first to demonstrate that light travels at a constant and definite speed. Hitherto, it had been believed that light is disseminated instantaneously. Römer made his discovery in connection with his study of the eclipses of the satellites of Jupiter. He estimated that it takes light eight minutes to reach the earth from Jupiter, traveling 120,000 miles per second. This was not a bad approximation of the actual speed of light: 186,000 miles per second.

An important phase of progress in the study of light was the enunciation of the wave theory, an advance over the older emission theory, by Francesco Grimaldi (1618-1663), Hooke, and Huygens, especially by the latter. While Grimaldi and Hooke offered important evidence for the wave theory, Huygens placed it on a well-reasoned foundation in his *Treatise on Light*. He declared that light, like sound, is transmitted by waves—that is, is periodic in its transmission. This was accepted until the twentieth century, when it was supplanted by the corpuscular theory of light.

Newton's study of the physics of light was almost as important as his investigations in dynamics. He first discovered the spectrum and put spectrum analysis on a scientific basis. This made possible a scientific understanding of color. He also helped to place optics on a solid mathematical foundation. But he still clung to the erroneous emission theory of light. Leibnitz developed the theory that ether, circulating about the earth, is the medium through which light is transmitted. To the list of discoveries in refraction should be added the important studies on reflection by Ehrenfried von Tschirnhaus (1651-1708), whose wealth enabled him to construct larger and more expensive mirrors than had hitherto been available.

While the real origins of electrical physics had to wait until the eighteenth century, there were important developments between the time of Gilbert and the time of Benjamin Franklin. Most attention was devoted to magnetism. A German Jesuit, Athanasius Kircher (1601-1680), popularized magnetic phenomena by collecting a large number of interesting alleged facts. He even attributed the flight of migratory birds to magnetic attraction, interpreted love in terms of magnetism, and regarded God as "the supreme magnet." Niccolo Cabeo (c. 1625) dealt more accurately with the magnetization of iron. Descartes associated magnetism with mechanics, and his work was continued by his student, Jacques Rohault (c. 1675).

The problem of compass variations in any given locality was first scientifically investigated by Henry Gellibrand (1597-1636). Descartes, Henry Bond (c. 1675), and the astronomer, Halley, overthrew Gilbert's theory that the geographical poles and the magnetic poles of the earth are identical. The generation of electrical charges was the subject of experiments by the Academy of Experiments, but the most important electrical discovery of the century was that of electrical repulsion, suggested by Cabeo and definitely established by von Guericke. The most voluminous speculations concerning electricity were offered by Robert Boyle.

It was not until the time of Lavoisier, who was beheaded in the French Revolution, that chemistry reached the stage at which physics had arrived with Galileo in the first third of the seventeenth century.

We have already referred to the so-called iatrochemistry originated by Paracelsus and his disciples, and first put on a scientific basis by Libavius and François Dubois (1614-1672), sometimes known as Franciscus Sylvius. Dubois is the first chemist known to have possessed a laboratory. Paracelsus and his group advocated a more sensible attitude towards alchemy but their experiments with drugs were reckless. They also invented a rival to the fantastic Aristotelian theory of the elements. They declared that there are three basic elements—salt, mercury, and sulphur—the so-called spagyric theory. Dubois first clearly distinguished between acids and alkalis.

Most chemical investigations and literature down to 1650 were the work of physicians. Johann Glauber (1604-1668) did very competent work in metallurgy, extended our knowledge of distillation, and anticipated the modern concepts of chemical affinity, decomposition, and the theory of reagents. Jean Rey (c. 1630) was the first important student of calcination, in which he faintly anticipated Lavoisier's creation of quantitative chemistry and the discovery of the conservation of mass. The best known of medical chemists was the Belgian doctor, Jean Baptiste van Helmont (1577-1644). Although a superstitious pedant, we owe to him the origin of the word "gas," and also important observations regarding the qualities and behavior of certain gases. His most valuable discovery was carbon dioxide, a contribution overlooked for generations.

Boyle was the greatest chemist of the seventeenth century. He destroyed both the Aristotelian theory of the four elements and the spagyric theory of Paracelsus in his *Skeptical Chymist* (1661), one of the landmarks in chemical history. It is impossible to overestimate the importance of having cleared away this venerable and influential rubbish. Boyle was not productive as an experimental chemist, but he adopted the atomic theory, aided in the recognition of the nature of phosphorus, and barely missed discovering oxygen. His atomic theory, however, resembled Democritus more than it anticipated Dalton.

The problems of combustion and respiration attracted considerable attention in the latter half of the seventeenth century. Boyle's researches in combustion, during which he almost discovered oxygen, were extended by Hooke, Richard Lower (1631-1691), and John Mayow (1643-1679). Mayow made the best synthesis of existing knowledge on combustion and respiration. He clearly recognized the existence of oxygen in the air and its function in respiration and combustion, but he did not isolate and discover it.

No sooner had the vagaries of Aristotle and Paracelsus been destroyed by Boyle, than the fantastic phlogiston theory, evolved by a German, Georg Ernst Stahl (1660-1743), arose to plague the science of chemistry. Phlogiston was considered a quality, or even a substance, transferable from one body to another, and accounting for the phenomena of combustion and calcination—it was the active principle of fire. A hundred years were required to explode this myth.

A fairly good synthesis of existing chemical knowledge, as well as of the elements of organic chemistry, appeared in the *Elements of Chemistry* by Hermann Boerhaave (1668-1735), a distinguished physician. Newton, though he devoted more of his time to chemistry than to mathematics or physics, made no momentous contributions to the science.

In contrast to the lagging chemistry, there was striking progress in biology in the seventeenth century. This was in part the result of the important heritage of achievement from the sixteenth century—the anatomical work of Vesalius and his students, physiological discoveries, including the lesser circulation of the blood, the progress of botanical description and classification—and in part the result of the increasing impact of oversea discoveries in the recognition and introduction of new animals and plants. Previous researches provided the impetus for the discovery of the circulation of the blood and for revolutionary studies in microscopic anatomy. European explorations aided zoölogical and botanical description and classification, which culminated in the books of John Ray (1628-1705).

In general, zoölogists concentrated on description, classification, and systematization. This type of work reached its highest point in Ray's *Methodical Synopsis of Quadrupeds and Serpents* (1693), which not only helped to dispel medieval illusions about fabulous monsters and animal habits, but systematically described the true nature and habits of animals. In establishing systematic zoölogy Ray was considerably assisted by his pupil and friend, Francis Willughby (1635-1672).

The science of entomology, or study of insect life, was originated by Jan Swammerdam (1637-1680), a Dutch microscopist. He carefully described the life history of insects from the caterpillar stage to maturity. He also classified the insect world, and conducted microscopic investigations of insect anatomy. The results were published in his *General History of Insects*.

The great physiological discovery of the century was the demonstration of the circulation of the blood by William Harvey (1578-1657). His views were promulgated in his *Anatomical Dissertation upon the Movement of the Heart* (1628), one of the epochal treatises in the history of physiology. Harvey also wrote *The Generation of Animals*, a study of genetics and embryology, which, though excellent in description, is pathetic in theory. The philosopher, Descartes, helped Harvey's theory of the circulation of the blood to gain general acceptance among scientists. Richard Lower sought to reduce the circulatory system to the laws of physics. Jean Pecquet (1651) and Olaus Rudbeck (1653) explored the thoracic duct and the lymphatic system, thus adding much to knowledge about the physiology of nutrition.

Anatomy made spectacular progress in the seventeenth century. Victor Robinson says that

> . . . if seventeenth century surgery did not advance further than Paré, workers in anatomy and physiology poured far beyond the broad gate that the scalpel of Vesalius had opened: half the structures in the human body are named after seventeenth century men—Graafian follicles, Haversian canals, Glaserian fissure, Pacchionian bodies, Bellini's tubes, antrum of Highmore, Malpighian layer, circle of Willis, valves of Kerkring, Schneiderian membrane, Glisson's capsule, Casserio's artery, Peyer's patches, Lower's tubercle, Pecquet's cistern, Poupart's ligament, Wormian bones, Ruysch's tunica, Spigelian lobe, Ridley's sinus, Riolan's muscle, Tulpius' valve, Vieussens' ganglion, Nuck's canal, Wirsung's duct, Wharton's duct, Stensen's duct, Rivini's duct, Bartholin's glands, Brunner's glands, Cowper's glands, Meibomian glands.[6]

The microscope now for the first time permitted minute anatomical research, as contrasted with the preceding so-called gross anatomy. We have already mentioned that Hooke first recognized the cellular nature of organic tissue. One of the leading seventeenth-century microscopists was Antony von Leeuwenhoek (1632-1723). To him we are indebted for the discovery of the minute animalcula —protozoa and bacteria. He also discovered the red corpuscles, investigated the vascular circulation, and revealed the multitude of spermatozoa. Marcello Malpighi (1628-1694) pioneered in the microscopic study of genetics and embryology. His description of the development of the chick in the egg remains a classic. Malpighi did far more extensive work than any other microscopist of the century

6 Victor Robinson, *The Story of Medicine*, Boni, 1931, p. 319.

in anatomy and histology. He discovered the capillaries in the circulatory system. He studied the kidneys, liver, and spleen. Incidentally, he disposed of the old Hippocratic myth about yellow and black bile. The microscopic anatomy of the brain was first carefully studied by Thomas Willis (1621-1675).

A very important theoretical discovery grew out of the use of the microscope at this time, namely, disproof of spontaneous generation, by Francesco Redi (1626-1679). In his *Generation of Insects* he showed that no maggots breed in meat from which flies have been excluded. Leeuwenhoek and Swammerdam supported this theory, which was of vast significance for pathology.

One of the most ingenious of biological and anatomical developments was the application by Giovanni Borelli (1608-1679) of the mechanical principles of Galileo and others to the interpretation of muscular activity. He explained the movements of the body according to the principles of the lever, pulley, and the like. But he understood that other than mechanical principles were at work. For example, he attributed the contraction and swelling of muscles to neural stimulation. Francis Glisson (1597-1677) discovered muscular irritability and showed that a muscle in contracting changes in form but not in bulk, thus disposing of one of Galen's dogmas.

The microscopic study of plant anatomy at this time was as notable as that of animal and human anatomy. Hooke established plant anatomy. In his investigations of plant tissue he, first among human beings, saw the cell. Malpighi investigated plant fibers, proved that plants breathe through their leaves, described the rise and distribution of sap, and seems to have recognized the sexuality of plants, a theory denied since Aristotle's day. Nehemiah Grew (1641-1712) made protracted microscopic studies in plant anatomy and described his observations with exceeding care and skill. Like Malpighi, he noted the sexuality of plants and their respiration through the leaves. A detailed investigation and exposition of the sexuality of plants and its botanical significance was the contribution of Rudolf Camerarius (1665-1721) and Sebastian Vaillant (1669-1722). A comprehensive view of plant life was enunciated by Joseph de Tournefort (1656-1708) in his *Institutes of Botany*. But the masterly synthesis and classification of all botanical knowledge was contained in Ray's three-volume *History of Plants* (1686-1704), a work comparable to Newton's *Principia* in physical science. Many important botanical gardens were opened.

In a previous chapter we noted that Ludovicus Vives originated the scientific study of psychology, which progressed to some extent in the seventeenth century, although, with the exception of Hobbes and Locke, psychological theories were still swaddled in mysticism and theology.

Very popular in this age was the dualistic psychology which insisted upon a sharp distinction between body and mind. The founder of this school was Jacob Boehme (1575-1624). Descartes believed that body and mind are separate and distinct. They cannot act directly upon each other, and must even be studied by different methods. The method of studying the mind is introspective. The method of studying the body is mathematical. The brain does not enter into pure thought at all.

The test of mental reality is rational consciousness—"I think, therefore, I am," was Descartes' formula. The soul, which is the source of thought, is merely imprisoned in the body—in the pineal gland, to be specific. The basic ideas, sometimes called innate, are not the products of experience. They exist in the mind as latent potentialities, and experience, at the most, only evokes them. Some fundamental ideas are the concept of God, the conscious self, mathematical axioms, and basic categories like space, time, and motion.

Pure thought is entirely a function of the soul. The passions are the "feelings and emotions of the soul" which arise from the influence of "animal spirits"— the highest and most active substance in the blood. The actions of the body are purely automatic and may be explained by the principles of mechanics—a fact later demonstrated in detail by Borelli. The lower animals are pure *automata*— automatic machines devoid of the power of thought.

Spinoza provided a more logical exposition and unification of the dualistic psychology. He believed as firmly as Descartes in the fundamental difference between body and mind and their basic independence of each other. But both mind and body are equally dependent upon God, the ultimate substance. Both are attributes of God. Hence, what takes place in one must affect the other, not because body acts on mind, or vice versa, but because God acts on both: "Whatever takes place in one of the attributes, say a thought in the attribute mind, or a movement in the attribute body, must have a corresponding place in each of the other attributes, since it is a modification of the one substance, God." In a manner reminiscent of the Neoplatonists, Spinoza divided thinking into three grades: sense perceptions, reason, and intuition. The driving mental force is the will to self-preservation, successful efforts being pleasurable, and failures painful.

The role of God in human thinking was further emphasized by the so-called Occasionalists, of whom Nicolas Malebranche (1638-1715) was the leader. They distinguished between the real cause of thought and action, which lies in God, and the mere occasion of the thought or action, which may be produced by an external stimulus or by the action of the mind and will. "Both sensation, which seems to be caused by the external object, and movement, which seems to be caused by the mind, are in reality caused by God." Malebranche even denied that the soul can know things as they really are: "The soul cannot know things themselves: things are only the occasion of the rise of ideas in the mind. The true cause of all ideas is God, in whose presence and action the world is perceived." All this was reminiscent of Plato and a harbinger of the later German idealistic psychology and philosophy.

The most extreme version of the doctrine of innate ideas and of the immunity of thought to external influence was set forth in the psychology of Leibnitz. He believed that reality exists in irreducible monads or spiritual force centers, which exist in three stages: unconscious, conscious, and self-conscious. Mental life is wholly and exclusively an unfolding of the monads from within. Ideas are, therefore, entirely innate. They do not arise from external stimulation. Leibnitz's conception of unconscious monads helped to install the idea of unconscious mental activity in psychological thinking—his only scientific contribution to the subject, and even this was unscientific in Leibnitz's interpretation. Few men have entertained psychological views further removed from scientific facts. That Leibnitz, whose mentality was rivaled only by that of Newton in this period, could hold such absurd views shows how far psychology was from the status of a true science.

A closer approach to scientific psychology was made by Thomas Hobbes (1588-1679) and John Locke (1632-1704), the creators of what is known as empirical psychology—the theory that mental life is derived from physical experiences operating upon the brain and nervous system. It repudiated the psychology of dualism and innate ideas. Hobbes believed that cognition—knowing—is the result of stimuli applied by external objects to the sense organs. Sensations, images, and concepts arise in this way. They are interpreted through symbols, made possible by the use of language. Hobbes was, perhaps, the first to realize fully the importance of language in human thought and culture, although Francis Bacon had given some attention to the subject. The will, said Hobbes, arises from the reaction of the cognitive processes upon the brain, expressing themselves from the brain outward through the heart.

Locke was the most effective assailant of innate ideas. He repudiated the contention that there could be any mental life without experience—external stimulation. There is no such thing as innate ideas—even latent categories. The mind is a blank tablet at birth—a *tabula rasa*—as Locke called it. Upon it experience, arising from external stimuli and sense impressions, writes what we call ideas. In this way, the mind, knowledge, and the thinking processes are developed. Simple ideas result directly from responses to sense impressions. Complex ideas are a rational elaboration of simple ideas, but the content of complex ideas in any individual mind must always be limited and determined by the nature of its basic simple ideas. With Hobbes and Locke, psychology became something of a science. But there were many later regressions into a mysticism as murky and farfetched as that of Malebranche or Leibnitz.

There were notable advances in medical science in the seventeenth century, and an intimate relation was formed between natural science and medicine. A majority of the leading scientists whom we have mentioned in the preceding pages were also physicians.[7] Medicine and surgery in this age were able to exploit previous progress in anatomy and physiology, as well as the experiments of Paracelsus and his followers with drugs.

While the authority of Hippocrates, Galen, and Muslim physicians like Avicenna was still formidable, a determination existed to base medicine exclusively on observation. In Paracelsus' revolution the remedy was as bad as the disease, but in the work of Thomas Sydenham (1624-1689) the protest against medieval medical follies was sane and constructive. Sydenham rejected the claims of all schools to final authority, although he respected Hippocrates more than others, and insisted on careful clinical observation of each case. He contended that a careful study of each type of disease and of each example of such disease is imperative. If in doubt about a remedy, the physician should give none. Sydenham is the greatest name in seventeenth-century medicine, and it is not going too far

[7] Cf. Wolf, *op. cit.*, p. 445.

to say that he is the father of modern clinical medicine. The other leading physician of the century was Boerhaave, in the next generation, who transferred European medical supremacy from Padua to Leyden.

Some progress was achieved in the study of contagious diseases, especially syphilis and the bubonic plague. Athanasius Kircher asserted that the plague was caused by bacteria, which he claimed to have seen through a microscope. In this he was mistaken. Specialists began to appear who made detailed studies of particular diseases. For example, Mercato studied intermittent fever; Real, diphtheria; van Helmont, diseases of digestion; Hafenreffer, skin diseases; Glisson, rickets; Wepfer, apoplexy; Lower, diseases of the heart; Willis, diabetes; Sydenham, gout; and so on. New medical instruments were developed, among them the clinical thermometer, introduced by Sanctorius (1561-1636), the clock, and the ear speculum. The thermometer and clock enabled physicians to obtain more exact temperatures and pulse-beats. New remedies were introduced. Mercury began to be applied to syphilitics. Cathartics competed for popularity. Glauber prepared sodium sulphate in 1648 and the result has been known since as Glauber's salts, and today forms the basis of a popular present-day commercial laxative. Nehemiah Grew derived Epsom salts from the springs of Epsom in Surrey. Pierre Seignette, an apothecary at Rochelle, made Rochelle salts out of sodium and potassium tartrate. Since the three were of German, English, and French origin, respectively, there was a sort of patriotic rivalry involved. Ipecac, cinchona, and quinine (Peruvian bark) came from the New World. Quinine became vital in combating malaria, a deadly malady before quinine was introduced.

In contrast to the late medieval period, surgery made less progress than medicine, in fact advanced little beyond the technique of Ambrose Paré. For instance, Richard Wiseman, the greatest English surgeon of the century, was a reactionary compared to Paré. Richard Lower performed the first successful blood transfusion on animals, and Jean Baptiste Denys of Paris first successfully repeated the operation on human beings in 1666. Hospital service remained poor, characterized by overcrowding, failure to isolate contagious diseases, and an almost total lack of knowledge of antisepsis.

In the seventeenth century the science of geology made its appearance, veritably passing slowly from "myth to science." Various hypotheses were offered about the origins and nature of the earth. Descartes believed that the earth was originally an incandescent globe like the sun, but had gradually cooled, while a burning mass remained in the center, causing earthquakes and volcanic eruptions. Kircher and Leibnitz accepted this hypothesis. The latter believed that crystalline rocks like granite and gneiss might be products of the cooling process. Newton suggested that the sun and planets might have coagulated as a result of the operation of the principle of gravitation. These credible hypotheses were accompanied by a number of silly ones, such as that of John Woodward (1665-1728), who believed that the earth was originally full of water which burst forth at the time of the flood.

In structural geology the most striking progress was accomplished by a Danish scientist, Niels Steensen (1631-1686), better known as Nicolaus Steno, who went to Tuscany, Italy, to study its rock-formations. His discussion of stratification was remarkably intelligent and comprehensive for his day, and completely superseded earlier analyses of the formation of sedimentary rocks. Hooke offered the most sensible explanation of earthquakes, attributing them to the contraction of the earth in the cooling process and to internal terrestrial readjustments. Leibnitz distinguished between igneous and aqueous rocks. Pierre Perrault (1608-1680) suggested original hypotheses about subterranean waters and the sources of springs and rivers. He believed that surface waters were sufficient to account for them. Woodward offered sane observations on stratigraphical phenomena. Martin Lister (1638-1712) first emphasized the desirability of accurate and comprehensive geological maps.

In this period there was some understanding of the nature of fossils. Steno quite frankly stated that fossils were skeletal remains of objects which had lived in the stratum in which they were found. But he did not fully realize that fossils attested to the vast age of even the external features of the earth's surface. He was inclined to believe that the deluge accounted for all paleontological problems. Woodward was another diluvialist, but he gathered the best collection of fossils in existence, even though he did not grasp their implications. The diluvialist theory was devastatingly attacked by Hooke, who pointed out that the deluge did not last long enough to account for stratification, nor for the distribution of fossils. He declared that a long period of time must be predicated in order to make the conception of fossils intelligible. He came the nearest of any seventeenth-century geologist to a true geological perspective. The study of crystallography was put on a scientific basis by Hooke, Steno, and Boyle.

In our treatment of sixteenth-century science we emphasized the revolution in geographical knowledge created by oversea discoveries. Exploration in the seventeenth century extended geographical information, which publications like Richard Hakluyt's *Voyages* (1589) and Jean Chardin's *Travels* (1686) helped to popularize. We have already referred to the scientific modern maps of Mercator and Ortelius, the latter's being the forerunner of the atlas. One of the earliest attempts to reduce the new data to generalized form was Philip Cluverius' *Introduction to Universal Geography* (1624). The first comprehensive treatise on geography fully incorporating the new knowledge was the *Geographia generalis* of Bernard Varen (1622-1650), better known as Varenius. It contained a broad treatment of descriptive geography, combined with a lucid discussion of the mathematical and astronomical foundations of geographical science.

This brief review of seventeenth-century science will make clear the relative volume of achievement and will explain why historians of science, not too well acquainted with the period between 1300 and 1600, might regard the age of Newton, Boyle, Hooke and Leibnitz as a renaissance, sudden, unique, and wonderful.

Seventeenth-century science culminated in Newton's *Principia* which assumed a position comparable to that enjoyed by Aristotle's works among medieval theologians. The astronomer, Joseph Lagrange, said that Newton was the greatest genius in the history of the world: "There is but one universe, and it can happen to but one man in the world's history to be the interpreter of its laws." Professor Smith thus characterizes the nature and influence of Newton's *Principia*:

A brief and jejune outline can give no idea of the enormous richness of the work. Every page is crowded with a mass of new mathematics, physics, and astronomy such as has never been compressed into one volume before or since; and the cosmological picture is surrounded by a massive and luminous frame of philosophical comment on scientific method. The Latin style, while lucid and powerful, lacks all adornment to recommend it to the amateur of language. No meretricious epithet, no emotional overtone, no sounding rhythm, no clever phrase for a moment either relieves or distracts the mind of the reader from the main thought.

Judged historically, the *Principia* must still pass as the most momentous work of science ever produced. The accuracy of Newton's theory proved amazing. For more than two centuries every fancied discrepancy was resolved. For at least a century a large number of brilliant minds found their life-work in elaborating the Newtonian system. Many a great feat of science was performed by following his casual hints. Only in the twentieth century have physicists tried to supersede Newton on account of minute discrepancies supposed to be found between his theory and the observed facts.[8]

While paying tribute to Newton, one should not overlook his great rival, Leibnitz, whose reputation and influence in the seventeenth and eighteenth centuries was smaller, but who was even more learned than Newton. As Professor Smith observes, Leibnitz was the last scientist who took all knowledge for his province. Hence he has been called the "Aristotle of the seventeenth century." From his day onward, specialization became necessary. Moreover, Leibnitz's fundamental conceptions have proven more accurate and enduring than Newton's. To the latter, space and time were absolute. Leibnitz believed that they were relative, a view which has been fully demonstrated by Planck and Einstein and the astrophysicists of the twentieth century.

The evolution of science in the seventeenth century profoundly influenced the philosophy of the period by focusing attention on the hitherto unsuspected extent of the universe, the relative insignificance of the earth in the cosmos, the apparent reign of law in the development and processes of the universe, the conception of God as a lawmaking and law-abiding entity instead of a lawless, arbitrary being, and, finally, the recognition of the antiquity of the earth. Remarkable scientific discoveries also stimulated speculation about the scientific method and the place of science in human thought, with which we shall deal in the next chapter describing the impact of the new scientific order upon philosophy.

Scientific progress also influenced the growth of tolerance. It is often asserted that increasing tolerance and rationalism made scientific activity possible. In reality, it is more true that the scientific activity helped to create a spirit of tolerance. The seventeenth century, when the scientific movement leaped into full swing, was characterized by vicious religious wars, persecutions, and witchcraft delusions. The scientific advances of the seventeenth century chiefly made possible

8 Preserved Smith, *A History of Modern Culture*, Holt, 1934 (2 vols., Collier Books), II, 34-35, 37.

the tolerance and enlightenment of the eighteenth. Some exponents of tolerance, however, such as Montaigne, Milton, Locke, and Bayle, were scarcely affected by science, and were motivated by their own intellectual insight or class aspirations.

VII. LEADING ASPECTS OF SCIENTIFIC DEVELOPMENT IN THE EIGHTEENTH CENTURY

Natural science in the eightenth century was to some extent restrained by the brilliant achievements of the seventeenth. It almost seems as though science had to pause to get its bearings. Further, the scientific progress of the seventeenth century had brought to light many strange phenomena and ideas. Scholars stopped to speculate upon their meaning and relation to human endeavor and social life. Indeed, speculation about Newton's *Principia* alone, together with researches which tested or supplemented it, occupied the attention of a whole generation of scientists and philosophers. Moreover, oversea explorations brought back still more new plants, animals, and minerals, which required study and classification. These factors, along with some others, strongly conditioned scientific activity during the first two-thirds of the eighteenth century.

The deists and the rationalists tried to discover the meaning of the new science with respect to the laws of the universe, the nature of God, and the duties of man. Others endeavored to deduce the supposed lessons of science and theology for social philosophy and the reform of humanity. The Physiocrats and the Encyclopedists took the lead here.

Natural history, originated by John Ray, was continued and expanded by the French scientists Buffon and Cuvier. The profusion of botanical and zoölogical data necessitated a system of classification if confusion was not to reign. The Swedish naturalist, Carolus Linnaeus, in his *System of Nature,* produced perhaps the first complete classification of natural phenomena since the days of Aristotle. The summation, codification, and interpretation of the scientific discoveries of the previous century occupied the attention of many scholars, in particular Diderot and his associates who compiled the *Grand Encyclopedia.*

In the latter part of the eighteenth century, however, the zeal for experimentation and rigorous scientific exploration returned, and these paved the way for the sweeping scientific revolution of the nineteenth century.

Although by no means as many important scientific instruments were invented in the eighteenth century as in the seventeenth, there were some worthy of mention. The chronometer was devised in 1734 and perfected by John Harrison in 1761. The sextant was invented independently by John Hadley of the British navy and Thomas Godfrey of Philadelphia in 1731. These made navigation more exact and safe, and astronomical measurements more accurate. A Swedish scholar, Andreas Celsius (1701-1744), invented the centigrade thermometer. The Royal Society invented the anemometer to measure the force of the wind. Most important of all, good instrument makers arose—thus relieving scientists of the necessity of manufacturing their own apparatus—among the more famous being Muschenbroek in Holland and Leupold in Leipzig.

Eighteenth-century mathematics consisted mainly in perfecting calculus and investigating higher equations. Colin MacLaurin (1698-1746) devoted himself to elucidating Newtonian calculus in his extended work on fluxions. The greatest mathematical dynasty of the century were the five Bernoullis of Basel in Switzerland—two brothers, two sons, and a nephew. The eldest of the group, Jakob Bernoulli (1654-1705), worked on the theory of numbers and the laws of chance, all of signal importance in the future of statistical science. Johann Bernoulli (1667-1748) wrote an excellent treatise on differential calculus and first systematized integral calculus. The other Bernoullis devoted themselves chiefly to the application of mathematics to mechanics and social statistics.

Leonhard Euler (1707-1773) was one of the most productive and brilliant mathematicians who ever lived. He studied mathematical series, higher differential equations, and the perfection of calculus. More than anybody else in the century he helped to simplify mathematical analysis. He put the various branches of higher mathematics in approximately the form in which they have been taught in university textbooks to our day. Abraham de Moivre (1667-1754) applied higher mathematics to statistical problems and formulated what is known as the normal curve and the curve of error, subjects that received fuller attention later from Christian Gauss. Joseph Louis Lagrange (1736-1813) invented the calculus of variations and systematized the study of differential equations. But his most remarkable achievement was the application of higher mathematics to dynamic mechanics. Jean le Rond d'Alembert (1717-1783), one of the most precocious of mathematicians, produced a very lucid treatise on integral calculus at the age of twenty-two. His chief work consisted of the application of his mathematical researches to the field of mechanics. Girolamo Saccheri (b. 1667) first anticipated the principles of non-Euclidean geometry in his *Euclid Vindicated* (1733).

The chief astronomical activity of the eighteenth century was the buttressing of Newtonian celestial mechanics by mathematics. Newton had applied all the mathematics he knew to the support of his synthesis, but further mathematical knowledge soon became available, in large part as an elaboration of Newton's own contributions to the subject. Representative mathematical restatements of the Newtonian synthesis were supplied by Jean Bernoulli, Euler, Alexis Clairaut (1731-1765), and d'Alembert. The latter produced the first definitive mathematical treatment of the precession of the equinoxes, a phenomenon first discovered by Hipparchus. But the outstanding application of mathematics to celestial mechanics was the classic work of Pierre Simon Laplace (1749-1827), *Celestial Mechanics*. Laplace restated the Newtonian system in terms of a better knowledge of calculus and differential equations, thus rounding it out. His work was in some ways a better statement of the new theory of the universe than Newton's *Principia,* but it could lay no such claim to originality. Laplace showed that planetary motion is stable and that the universe will not be deranged in time by its own motion, as Newton had feared. In his *System of the World,* Laplace reviewed the history of astronomy and suggested the famous nebular hypothesis, namely, that the solar system evolved from scattered whirling masses of incandescent gas or nebulae.

Two important astronomical discoveries were made by James Bradley (1693-

1762), director of the Greenwich observatory. He demonstrated the aberration of light, namely, the fact that light does not travel straight from its source but is deflected by the motions of the universe. He also proved the inclination (nodding) of the earth's axis. Both discoveries were of great importance for astronomical calculation. Bradley also prepared an admirable star catalogue.

The next outstanding English astronomer, Sir William Herschel (1739-1822), discovered the planet Uranus in 1781, and studied extensively double stars and nebulae. He also studied the satellites of Saturn, and proved that the rings of Saturn revolve. Nicolas de Lacaille (1713-1762) published the first relatively complete catalogue of stars visible in the southern hemisphere. Many private and public expeditions were sent to make astronomical observations.

One of the leading aspects of eighteenth-century physics was the application of higher mathematics to the solution of various problems in mechanics, especially dynamic mechanics. Johann Bernoulli discovered the principle of virtual velocity and realized some implications of the theory of the conservation of energy. Daniel Bernoulli put hydrodynamics on a mathematical basis and discovered the kinetic theory of gases. Leibnitz and Pierre Maupertuis (1698-1759) enunciated the principle of least action in dynamics. But the crowning achievement in eighteenth-century physics was Lagrange's *Analytical Mechanics,* a mathematical synthesis of the whole field of mechanics, based upon the newly discovered principles of virtual velocity, least action, and the persistence of energy.

With the help of mathematics the laws of optics were restated, but the outstanding optical achievement of the century was Chester Moore Hall's discovery of achromatic lenses and their importance for telescopes about 1750. John Dollond (1706-1761) continued the research relative to achromatic lenses and constructed an achromatic telescope. The theoretical basis for such study had been provided by Daniel Bernoulli's investigation of the dispersion of light.

Joseph Black (1728-1799) discovered the principle of latent heat by observing the change of ice into water and water into steam. He found that during these changes a large amount of heat is absorbed without producing any change in temperature. Investigating the amount of heat necessary to effect the same changes of temperature in different substances, he established the theory of specific heat. His discoveries had a direct relation to James Watt's invention of the steam engine.

The most important contribution to the physics of sound in this period was the acoustical investigations of Ernst Friedrich Chladni (1756-1827). By covering plates of glass with fine sand, and causing them to vibrate, he discovered the fundamental principle of acoustics, namely, that the vibrations of material bodies are subject to constant mathematical laws. He was the author of several systematic works on acoustics, and also conducted research in overtones or harmonics.

Probably the most momentous advance in physics in the eighteenth century was the creation of the science of electricity. Francis Hauksbee (1650-1713) discovered electrical glow and electrical induction. Charles Dufay (1698-1739) learned that there are two kinds of electricity, positive and negative. Stephen Gray (d. 1736) demonstrated the existence of conductors and nonconductors. He also made preliminary investigations into the problems of electric induction. Jean Théophile Desaguliers (1683-1744) continued Gray's researches in conductivity. Luigi Galvani (1737-1798), by experimenting on frog's legs, discovered what was formerly known as "animal magnetism," but has since been designated galvanism. Alessandro Volta (1745-1827) continued Galvani's researches, constructed the first important electric battery, overthrew the notion of animal magnetism, and established the identity of galvanism and electricity. Henry Cavendish (1731-1810) and Charles Coulomb (1736-1806) demonstrated that Newton's law of inverse squares, that is, universal gravitation, applies to the attraction and repulsion of electrical charges. Benjamin Franklin (1706-1790) proved (1752) that lightning is only a gigantic electrical spark. Professor Hansen of Leipzig showed that there are three kinds of electrical discharges—spark, brush, and glow. The accumulation of a high charge of electricity for experimentation was made possible by the invention of the Leyden jar by Nicholas Cunaeus, Peter von Musschenbroek, and Ewald von Kleist.

The great mechanical genius of the century, an eighteenth-century Hero, was Denis Papin (1647-1712), professor of mathematics at Marburg. He developed innumerable pneumatic and steam devices, being the father of the modern steam engine. He was also the first to invent a submarine.

If the more phenomenal scientific discoveries of the seventeenth century were astronomical and physical, those of the eighteenth occurred in chemistry, a science which had been notoriously backward until then. These revolutionary discoveries in chemistry were, for the most part, delayed until the last part of the century. Étienne Geoffroy prepared the first important table of chemical affinities in 1720. While van Helmont had discovered carbon-dioxide gas (carbonic acid) a century earlier, his work had been forgotten and it was rediscovered by Joseph Black, who called it "fixed air." Torbern Orlof Bergmann (1735-1784) in Sweden experimented with "fixed air" and discovered that it was an acid. Joseph Priestley (1733-1804) prepared oxygen (1774) and showed it to be indispensable to the respiration of man and animals. Karl Wilhelm Scheele (1742-1786) found that water consists of two fundamental gaseous components, one of which is "fire air," or oxygen. Cavendish further demonstrated the compound nature of water and showed that it could not be a unified and integral element, as Empedocles and Aristotle had contended. Although he discovered hydrogen, he did not name it such. By implication, Priestley, Scheele, and Cavendish upset the phlogiston theory, but they still clung to its fanciful nomenclature. For example, Priestley called oxygen "dephlogisticated air."

The phlogiston dogma was finally destroyed by the "Newton of chemistry," Antoine Lavoisier (1743-1794), a man who became a tragic sacrifice to the Reign of Terror. Lavoisier proved that phlogiston was neither demonstrable nor necessary to explain combustion and calcination. He showed that the two constituents of water are gases which behave like other gases, and he named them oxygen and hydrogen. He proved that combustion and respiration are identical in principle, both are forms of oxidation—combustion, rapid oxidation and respiration, slow oxidation. Lavoisier clearly revealed that life is a chemical process and expatiated upon the chemical cycle of life. He also advocated the adoption of a clearer and more adequate chemical nomenclature. He created quantitative chemistry through his discovery of the law of the conservation of mass. He showed that "although matter may alter its state in a series of chemical actions, it does not change in amount, the quantity of matter is the same at the end as at the beginning of every operation, and can be traced by its weight."

The exposition of atomic and molecular weights, and the enunciation of the fundamental principles of qualitative chemistry, soon appeared in the work of Proust, Berthollet, Dalton, Gay-Lussac, and Avogadro. The reign of Aristotle, alchemy, mysticism, and magic in chemistry, challenged by Boyle and Stahl, was now brought to an end. Stahl's phlogiston theory also received its death-blow. The path was clear for the tremendous strides made by chemistry in the nineteenth century.

The custom of writing elaborate natural histories which aimed to describe all the known plants and animals, begun with John Ray at the turn of the eighteenth century, culminated in the vast and eloquent *Natural History* of George Louis Leclerc, Count de Buffon (1707-1788), in forty-four volumes. Although sometimes fanciful, it comprised the greatest repository of descriptive zoölogy before our times. The best section was the history of quadrupeds.

Another outgrowth of the vast accumulation of new data was the trend towards classification which had begun earlier in the writings of Cesalpinus on botany and Gesner on zoölogy as well as in the work of Ray. The first comprehensive classifications of all natural science was embodied in the *System of Nature, System of Plants,* and *Botanical Philosophy* of Carolus Linnaeus (1707-1778). He divided natural objects into three kingdoms: stone, vegetable, and animal. Each kingdom was subdivided into classes, orders, genera, and species. Structural similarity and dissimilarity were the main bases of Linnaeus' system. Man was at last linked to the rest of the animal kingdom. He appeared in Linnaeus' classification as *Homo sapiens linnaeus,* of the class of quadrupeds, of the order of *anthropomorpha* (primates), of the genus *homo,* and divided into four species, white, yellow, red, and black. Linnaeus, however, held to the orthodox theological distinction between man and the other animals, so far as man's soul was concerned.

Linnaeus' system was convenient rather than profound, but it was greatly respected. It was observed that "God created and Linnaeus arranged." His nomenclature has persisted to the present day with some modifications. Buffon criticized Linnaeus' scheme, but his proposed substitute was even more completely subjugated to convenience and would have meant chaos. A better classification was applied to animals by the famous naturalist and morphologist, Georges Cuvier (1769-1832). In his *Animal Kingdom,* he divided the animal world into vertebrata, mollusca, articulata, and radiata. Improved classifications were later suggested by De Candolle in botany and Lamarck in zoölogy.

The outstanding entomologist of the eighteenth century was Réne Réaumur (1683-1757), whose *Memoirs on a History of Insects* (1734-1742) comprised the first systematic work in the field. He was a well-trained physical and natural scientist, conducted his research with great patience and precision, and had a real talent for describing what he saw. Incidentally, by observing wasps making their nests, he discovered the principles which were later exploited in making paper out of wood pulp.

Insect anatomy was carried far beyond Swammerdam by Pierre Lyonet (1707-1789), who studied the willow moth in great detail. The reproduction of insects was investigated by Maria Merian (1647-1717) and Charles Bonnet (1720-1793). The former was a brilliant expositor and produced the best illustrated descriptions of insect life and insect reproduction. Bonnet discovered the phenomenon of parthenogenesis in plant lice, and made ingenious contributions to a general theory of genetics. By reviving and extending Aristotle's theory of an ascending scheme of nature, he became a protoevolutionist. Caspar Friedrich Wolff (1733-1794), in his *Theory of Generation,* made important contributions to physiology, genetics, and embryology, in both the plant and animal world. But scientific embryology had to wait for the work of von Baer in spite of Wolff's careful observations.

In the progress of anatomy the name of John Hunter (1728-1793) is worthy to rank with Vesalius. As the latter put the study of human anatomy on a thoroughly scientific basis, so Hunter created comparative anatomy. He was one of the greatest surgeons of the century and used his income unselfishly to promote his studies. He established the best anatomical museum of the age, admirably and systematically arranged. Fortunately, it was purchased by the British government and handed over to the Royal College of Surgeons in London. Comparative anatomy was further promoted by Cuvier who, while not an anatomist or dissector, was an able comparative morphologist.

Eighteenth-century physiology was deeply influenced by the mechanistic theories of Descartes. Greatly impressed by Harvey's theory of the circulation of the blood, he had conceived of the body as a pumping plant with the heart as the pumping station. The mechanistic hypothesis was valiantly expounded by Friedrich Hoffman (1660-1742), a medical professor at Halle, but the classic exposition of the doctrine was given by Julien de la Mettrie (1709-1751) in his *L'Homme machine* (1748), which was not only an important contribution to physiological theory but exerted a powerful influence on the materialistic philosophy of the age that culminated in the work of Baron d'Holbach.[9] The chemist, Stahl, espoused the religious or vitalistic hypothesis which opposed the mechanistic.

Less partisan and more strictly scientific was the greatest physiological work of the century, *The Elements of Physiology,* by Albrecht von Haller (1708-1777), a systematic statement of existing physiological knowledge about all parts of the body. Haller himself made notable investigations of the mechanics of respiration, muscular irritability, neurology, and embryology. A synthetic view of physiology was presented by François Bichat (1771-1802) who studied body tissues (he invented the term) and declared that the life of the whole organism depends upon the lives of the constituent tissues. He was the father of modern histology. Stephen Hales (1677-1761), a physician, botanist and chemist, discovered blood pressure by experiments on a horse. Reflex action was revealed by Robert Whytt (1714-1766)

---

[9] On La Mettrie and mechanistic theories see especially Riley, *From Myth to Reason,* pp. 206 ff.

of Edinburgh. Réamur and the Abbé Spallanzani (1729-1799) investigated the chemistry of digestion, proving that food is dissolved by the action of gastric juice and not, as hitherto supposed, by muscular churning—the stomach being regarded as a mechanical churning-mill. Borelli had stressed the latter idea.

Pathology, which had been originated by Redi, was extended by Spallanzani, who confirmed Redi's contentions. His implicit argument for antisepsis was that no forms of life can develop in materials boiled vigorously and kept from the air. Human pathology was established by Giovanni Morgagni (1682-1772), professor of anatomy at Padua and an indefatigable dissector of corpses. He gave attention to the pathology of the organs involved in the cases of persons who had died of particular organic diseases. His five volumes of letters on *The Sites and Causes of Diseases* mark the real foundation of human pathology in medical practice.

The recognition that man is an animal and therefore an object of legitimate anatomical study and classification created the science known as physical anthropology. Buffon and Cuvier made important contributions, but the leading pioneer in physical anthropology was Johann Friedrich Blumenbach (1752-1840), who applied the methods of comparative anatomy to human races.

The outstanding descriptive botanist of the eighteenth century was Linnaeus, who, besides his essays in classification and description, made valuable contributions to our knowledge of plant reproduction and ecology. Stephen Hales's *Vegetable Statics* discussed intelligently the water consumption of plants, and described the upward flow of sap, explaining it by the hypothesis of transpiration, capillarity, and root pressure. Hales also investigated the breathing of plants and their reaction to light. The best studies of plant nutrition were conducted by Nicholas de Saussure (1765-1845), who embodied his results in an important work, *Researches on the Chemistry of Vegetation*.

Perhaps the most striking botanical contribution of the century was the exposition of what is known as the theory of the "balance of life" by Jan Ingenhousz (1730-1799), a Dutch engineer and botanist, and a man of great originality. He showed that, when exposed to light, plants absorb carbon dioxide from the air. As Charles Singer observes: "This discovery is the foundation of our whole conception of the economy of the world of living things. Animal life is ultimately dependent on plant life. Plants build up their substance from the carbon-dioxide of the atmosphere together with the products of decomposition of dead animals and plants. Thus a balance is kept between the animal and the plant world." [10]

Psychology in the eighteenth century reflected very clearly the scientific trends of the age. The leading school attempted to apply the data of physical science to mental phenomena. This provoked an extreme reaction. We noted above that Hobbes and Locke tried to establish an empirical or scientific psychology by tracing the origin of simple ideas to sense impressions.

David Hume (1711-1776) carried Locke's views even closer to pure naturalism. He abandoned Locke's distinction between sensation and reflection, and between sense and reason. He believed knowledge is derived from sense impressions and that we learn through the association of ideas. Hence, his school of psychology

[10] Charles Singer, *The Science of Living Things*, Harper, 1931, p. 371.

became known as the sensationalists. Hume believed that there are three main types of association of ideas: those based on resemblance, on contiguity, and on an assumed cause and effect relationship. Hume also stressed the psychological importance of habit and the tendency to regard things as true and necessary simply because they are habitual.

The sensationalist psychology was espoused in France by Étienne de Condillac (1715-1780), who carried it to the logical extreme: "Sensations alone, accompanied by feeling, reproduced as ideas, and dominated by association, account for the entire mental life." Reason is simply the grouping of sensations, achieved by means of the association of ideas.

It was only a step from the extreme sensationalism of Condillac to an overt physiological psychology, and this step was taken by David Hartley (1704-1757) and Joseph Priestley in England, and by La Mettrie in France. These psychologists stood at the opposite pole from Descartes, who had argued that there is no direct relationship between the brain and the mind. According to these early physiological psychologists, just mentioned, the brain and the mind were considered identical. An impression in the mind has its direct cause in the brain. The organization of mental states is a direct reflection of the organization of the brain centers.

These extreme developments of empiricism and naturalism were opposed by the intellectualists or idealists, of whom the chief exponents were Bishop George Berkeley (1685-1753) and Immanuel Kant (1724-1804). Berkeley's psychological theories were set forth in his *New Theory of Vision* (1709), and his *Treatise Concerning the Principles of Human Knowledge* (1710). He rejected Locke's idea of a distinction between primary qualities like figure, motion, and extension, and secondary qualities like color, sound, and taste. Locke had held that our ideas of primary qualities reveal to us an actual reality, though secondary qualities are only subjective inferences. Berkeley held that the mind does not reveal to us any form of reality—either primary or secondary qualities. Going further, he contended that the notion of a material reality, existing independent of the mind, is an illusion. An active spirit, namely, God, the author of nature, is the source of all our ideas. Kant believed that there can be no real science of psychology, since the scientific method and experimental observation are not applicable to the mind. He admitted that sense impressions may accurately reveal the world of nature as it appears to the senses. But beyond this phenomenal world is the real world, the "noumenal" world, which cannot be penetrated by sense impressions, can only be hypothetically pictured by the reason, and can never be known by man in its entirety. By sharply distinguishing between sense, intelligence, and reason, Kant helped to establish the unfortunate and artificial "faculty psychology." As the mechanistic doctrine of La Mettrie, Hartley, and Priestley was the extreme development of Hume's naturalism, so the return to simple faith as the path to knowledge in the psychology of Friedrich Jacobi (1743-1819) constituted the extreme reaction against it.

The eighteenth century was a period both of remarkable medical progress and of immense popularity of grotesque nostrums. For instance, Joanna Stephens in

England received a Parliamentary grant of $25,000 for a remedy composed of barnyard rubbish, praised by a reputable doctor, Stephen Hales, and taken in large doses by Robert Walpole, the prime minister. The Dark Ages produced no greater medical travesty than this.

Of real importance to medical science were the achievements of Haller in physiology, Hunter in anatomy, and Bichat in histology, to which we have already referred. Leopold Auenbrugger's (1722-1809) discovery of the value of percussion of the thorax (tapping the chest with the finger tips) was the beginning of accurate physical diagnosis.

The enunciation of the theory of immunity, which received its first application in the form of inoculation against smallpox, revolutionized preventive medicine. Lady Montagu, wife of the British ambassador to Turkey, described in 1717 the method of direct inoculation with smallpox virus, long in use by Muslims. This method was first applied systematically in the Western World by Zabdiel Boylston (1679-1766), a Boston physician, to check an epidemic of smallpox in 1721. The practice became rather general later in the century. The method of producing immunity to smallpox through the milder method of vaccination—inoculation with cowpox—was first applied by Edward Jenner in May, 1796, forming a milestone in medical progress.

Samuel Hahnemann (1755-1843) introduced at this time homeopathic therapy, based on the theory that like cures like, and that very small doses of drugs are most efficacious. While the idea lacked substantial medical foundation, it is a curious fact that some of the most successful physicians have followed this technique to our own day, probably a testimonial to the power of mental suggestion in medical therapy.

Psychiatry, or medical psychology, faintly emerged in the eighteenth century. Franz Anton Mesmer (b. 1734) introduced mesmerism, a kind of mystical and rudimentary hypnotism, which became a craze after the middle of the century. Hypnotism, in the hands of Charcot and Bernheim in the nineteenth century, served as a basis for psychiatric therapy. Philippe Pinel (1745-1826) was the first to remove the chains from the insane and to treat them humanely.

Hoffmann, the mechanist, and Stahl, the vitalist, were among those who tried to systematize medicine at the beginning of the century, but the great name in the first half of the century was that of Boerhaave, an immensely popular teacher who made the medical school at Leyden supreme in Europe. His *Institutes of Medicine* (1708) were to the eighteenth century what Galen was to the Middle Ages. One of his great services was the rejection of ancient authority and reliance upon clinical observation. Students of Boerhaave founded the famous Vienna school of medicine, of which Auenbrugger was a member, and Gerhard van Swieten (1700-1772) its leader. The outstanding Italian physician was Antonio Scarpa (1747-1832), an expert clinician and surgeon and a specialist in diseases of the eye. Benjamin Rush (1745-1813) put medical science on a sound basis in the United States.

Eighteenth-century surgery was best represented by the Paris school of surgeons, founded by François de Lapeyronie (1678-1747). A Royal Academy of Surgery was established in Paris in 1731. Nowhere else was competent surgical instruction available until it was introduced in England a half century later by John and William Hunter. Victor Robinson provides a good summary of the work of the Paris surgeons at this time:

> The French surgeons, finally freed from this same blight, made definite progress through Jean-Louis Petit's screw tourniquet, and his pioneer work in mastoiditis; Dominique Anel's treatment of traumatic aneurysm by ligation of the brachial artery, and his operation for lacrimal fistula, with the probe and syringe which carry his name; Hugues Ravaton's double-flap amputation; Pierre-Joseph Desault's teaching of surgical anatomy; François Chopart's mediotarsal amputation; Jacques Daviel's extraction of the lens in cataract, and his spoon; and Jean-Pierre David's dissertation on the effects of movement and repose in surgical diseases.[11]

Veterinary medicine was elevated to a science by Johann Gottlieb Wolstein (1738-1820), a well-trained doctor, one of the first to understand that fever is a result of nature's battle against disease. The most important addition to the materia medica was the utilization of digitalis (foxglove) for heart ailments, first adequately described by William Withering in 1785.

Geology moved closer to a science in the eighteenth century. We have already discussed Laplace's nebular hypothesis of the origin of the earth, which was undisputed for a century. Although greatly ridiculed at first, Buffon's theory of the earth's origin is now accepted, with proper astronomical modifications. He suggested that the planets came into existence as a result of a collision between the sun and a comet or another astral body. Buffon also suggested a plausible conception of the ages or periods of earth history since its origin. He believed that the earth is much older than theologians would admit. He offered what was for the time a liberal estimate of 75,000 years.

The major contribution to structural geology in the eighteenth century was the destruction of the catastrophic theory (catastrophism), which Professor Judd describes as follows:

> At a number of successive epochs—of which the age of Noah was the latest—great revolutions had taken place on the earth's surface; during each of these cataclysms all living things were destroyed; and, after an interval, the world was restocked with fresh assemblages of plants and animals, to be destroyed in turn and entombed in the strata of the next revolution.

Close observance of structural geology undermined this fanciful doctrine. John Mitchell (1724-1793) made the best study of earthquakes in this period, showed that certain areas, especially near volcanoes, are most subject to them, and suggested that they might be caused by contact between subterranean fire and water. He had a sane view of the sequence of geographical strata and of the subsequent disturbances to which they had been subjected. Further development of structural geology we owe to Abraham Werner (1749-1817), the most influential teacher of the subject in the eighteenth century. He systematized the classification of geo-

---

[11] Robinson, *op. cit.*, p. 340.

graphical strata, and believed that most rocks are of aqueous origin. Hence his school was known as Neptunists. Werner was also a brilliant mineralogist.

James Hutton (1726-1797), in his *Theory of the Earth* (1785), an important landmark in the history of geology, overthrew the catastrophic theory. Hutton believed that the geological processes now observable have been at work in the past, and are quite sufficient to account for the earth's history, given enough time for their operation. Hutton also contended that it is not the province of geology to enter into theological and philosophical discussions as to the origins of the earth or its final destiny. It is enough for geology to describe earth processes as they can be observed at work. The position taken by Hutton came to be known as "uniformitarianism"—geological processes are always the same—in contrast to the catastrophic doctrine. In essence, this means that we must explain the geological present by the geological past. With the publication of Lyell's great work on geology, which we shall describe later, the uniformitarian hypothesis gained general acceptance among geologists. Hutton stressed the importance of igneous rocks, and his school of interpreters, in this sense, were called the Vulcanists. There was considerable debate between Neptunists and Vulcanists.

The study of structural geology and a saner conception of the earth's age were both aided by a more intelligent study of fossils. We have already noted that the best collection of fossils was gathered by John Woodward at the close of the seventeenth century and presented to the University of Cambridge. Woodward was a diluvialist and regarded his fossils with piety, but more open-minded students were able to make intelligent use of them. Antonio Lazzaro Moro (1687-1764), probably the most competent paleontologist of the eighteenth century, contended that the rocks must have been in a process of formation when the fossils were laid down in them. The earth is evidently constructed of strata superimposed on one another. Hence, the lower the stratum the older the fossils. Further, the character of the fossils reveals the conditions of the earth when the rocks were formed—whether in fresh or salt water, and the like. The anthropologist, Blumenbach, first recognized that the fossil mammoth was related to extant forms of elephant life. Both Werner and Hutton intelligently interpreted fossils in their general geological studies.

Geology in the eighteenth century was thus laying the foundations for Lyell's classic work in the next century and providing important data to support the hypothesis of terrestrial and organic evolution, which was already beginning to be propounded in the closing years of the eighteenth century.

Geography also moved ahead in this century. Important geographical explorations were undertaken for the express purpose of adding to geographical and allied knowledge. Samuel Wallis circumnavigated the world in 1766 and discovered Tahiti. His tales about it encouraged the eighteenth-century tendency to extol the alleged idyllic life of savages. Further information about Tahiti and the South Seas was reported by the French explorer, Louis de Bougainville. But the foremost explorer of the century, and one of the greatest of all time, was Captain James Cook (1728-1779), who proved a martyr to his quest for geographical and ethnographic information. He covered the oceans from the Arctic to the Antarctic.

He explored Australasia and discovered many islands of the Pacific. The Russian expansion eastward through Siberia added greatly to existing knowledge of northern Asia. The most important theoretical addition to geographical knowledge during the period was the demonstration by Bouguer, Maupertuis, and others, between 1735 and 1740, that the earth is flat at the poles.

Improvements in printing, as well as the greater volume of precise geographical information, made possible more accurate, more complete, and more beautiful maps, thus vastly improving the science and art of cartography. Among the best eighteenth-century cartographers were Alexis Jaillot, the Cassinis, and Jean d'Anville in Paris, J. B. Homann in Nuremberg, and Herman Moll in London. D'Anville made the first passably accurate map of Africa. J. F. W. Desbarres in London first applied to cartography the geographical knowledge brought to light by Captain Cook.

The best synthesis of scientific knowledge, as it stood at the close of the eighteenth century, was contained in the great *Encyclopedia* prepared by Diderot and his associates, about which we shall have more to say in a later chapter.[12]

Finally, the scientific method, albeit of a crude type, began to be applied to social science. With the work of Halley, Montesquieu, Ferguson, Gall, the physiocrats, Adam Smith, the cameralists, Bentham, and others, the old and inclusive political philosophy tended to differentiate into sociology, economics, political science, jurisprudence, and ethics.

Another aspect of scientific progress in this period was the gradual entry of natural science into the university curriculum. Scientific research became less a matter of individual initiative and the collaboration of enthusiastic laymen. It slowly formed a part of the organized system of academic activities, competing successfully with logic, metaphysics, theology, and the classical languages. Not until the twentieth century did the natural sciences gradually drift away in part from universities to commercial laboratories and highly endowed private foundations, the latter roughly comparable to the academies of the seventeenth and eighteenth centuries. Even this recent movement has been limited chiefly to the United States.

These scientific advances of the seventeenth and eighteenth centuries, which we have now surveyed briefly, may seem obscure and hardly related to contemporary problems. But they really lie at the base of twentieth-century civilization. Science enables us to live in quite a different manner from Miles Standish or George Washington, whose physical surroundings more closely resembled those of an Egyptian farmer of 3000 B.C. than ours. For the enormous gains in material culture which we enjoy we must thank scientific progress since Copernicus, however much the science of his age built on earlier foundations. The science and technology of the twentieth century would have been unthinkable without the science of the seventeenth and eighteenth centuries. Therefore, the achievements which we have just chronicled are of immense immediate practical significance for those of us who are living today.

12 Cf. Lynn Thorndike, "L'Encyclopédie and the History of Science," in *Isis*, 1924, VI, 361-86.

SELECTED READINGS

Adams, F. D., *Birth and Development of the Geological Sciences,* Dover, 1954.
Baumgardt, Carola, *Johannes Kepler,* Philosophical Library, 1951.
Bell, E. T., *Men of Mathematics,* Simon and Schuster, 1937.
Brett, G. S., *History of Psychology,* Macmillan, 1953.
Brodetsky, Selig, *Sir Isaac Newton,* Methuen, 1927.
Butterfield, Herbert, *The Origins of Modern Science, 1300-1800,* Collier Books.
Crew, Henry, *The Rise of Modern Physics,* Williams and Wilkins, 1926.
Dingle, Herbert, *The Scientific Adventure,* Philosophical Library, 1953.
Garrison, F. H., *Introduction to the History of Medicine,* Saunders, 1929, chaps. vi-x.
Ginzburg, Benjamin, *The Adventure of Science,* Simon and Schuster, 1930, chaps. iv-viii.
Guerlac, Henry, *Lavoisier: The Crucial Year,* Cornell University Press, 1962.
Hall, A. R., *The Scientific Revolution, 1500-1800,* Beacon Press, 1956.
Hart, I. B., *The World of Leonardo da Vinci,* Viking, 1962.
Hogben, Lancelot, *Mathematics for the Million,* Norton, 1951.
Johnson, F. R., *Astronomical Thought in Renaissance England,* John Hopkins University Press, 1937.
Keltie, J. S., and Howarth, O. J. R., *History of Geography,* Putnam, 1913, chaps. vi-x.
Kuhn, T. S., *The Copernican Revolution,* Vintage Books.
Lenard, Philipp, *Great Men of Science,* Macmillan, 1933, pp. 12-170.
Leonard, J. L., *Crusaders of Chemistry,* Doubleday, 1930, chaps. iv-x.
Locy, W. A., *The Growth of Biology,* Holt, 1925, chaps. x-xvii.
Nordenskiöld, Erik, *The History of Biology,* Tudor, 1960, Part II.
Ornstein, Martha, *The Role of Scientific Societies in the Seventeenth Century.* 1913.
Riley, Woodbridge, *From Myth to Reason,* Appleton, 1926, Books III-IV.
Robinson, Victor, *The Story of Medicine,* Boni, 1931, chaps. ix-x.
Shipley, A. E., *The Revival of Science in the Seventeenth Century,* Princeton University Press, 1914.
Smith, Preserved, *A History of Modern Culture,* 2 vols., Collier Books, Vol. I, Part I; Vol. II, chaps. i-iv.
Stimson, Dorothy, *The Gradual Acceptance of the Copernican Theory of the Universe,* Baker and Taylor, 1917.
——*Science and Amateurs: a History of the Royal Society,* Abelard-Schuman, 1948.
Thorndike, Lynn, *A History of Magic and Experimental Science,* 8 vols., Columbia University Press, 1923-1956. Vols. V-VI.
Thorpe, Edward, *History of Chemistry,* 2 vols, Putnam, 1909, Vol. I.
Wolf, A., *A History of Science, Technology and Philosophy in the Sixteenth and Seventeenth Centuries,* 2 vols., Harper Torchbooks, 1959.
——*A History of Science, Technology and Philosophy in the Eighteenth Century,* 2 vols., Harper Torchbooks, 1961.

XVII

*The Impact
of the New Intellectual
Order on Philosophy
and Education*

I. INTRODUCTORY

Philosophy mirrors the age in which it is conceived. Philosophers speculate on the character of the universe, nature, God, man, morals, happiness, and the like. Their cogitations are colored by their method of approaching problems, by their premises, by their world outlook, and by their habitat.

In the Middle Ages the Ptolemaic theory of the universe, modified by Jewish and Christian accretions, prevailed. God was the highly personal anthropomorphic deity of the Jewish and Christian Bible. Theology was the "queen of the sciences," and the chief interest of philosophers was the way of salvation in the world to come. Nature was viewed as the immediate handiwork of God, created and ordered according to the account in holy writ. Man was regarded chiefly as the repository of an immortal soul. His physical characteristics were not seriously considered, except insofar as they related to the soul and salvation. The moral problem was evaluated in terms of righteous and sinful conduct, the former being obedience to God's revealed will and the latter its violation. Happiness was projected mainly into the world to come. This earth was the vale of tears. True beatitude was to be hoped for only in the blessed state of immortal salvation. The outlook was predominantly otherworldly. Even learned men knew little about the earth, with the exception of the Mediterranean world and western Europe. Few had any close knowledge of other than a local area. Provincialism and localism were the dominant traits of social life. Subtle logic was considered the surest road to truth.

Developments between Roger Bacon and Francis Bacon shattered this whole cultural complex. The Copernican theory of the universe gradually made headway. As science revealed more of the extent and workings of the physical universe, the tribal deity of the Jews who had been adopted by the Christians became less compatible with the new picture of the cosmos and the laws of nature. Inductive science slowly ousted deductive logic from its supremacy.

Sociology, in fact if not in name, gradually began to crowd out theology as the science of sciences. The kingdom of man challenged the kingdom of God. Nature, while not divorced from God in the early modern era, came to be regarded as an impressive and complicated affair. The simple biblical explanations no longer satisfied the best minds. Natural causes were sought to explain the workings of phenomena. God was portrayed as a law-giving and law-abiding being.

Man was still believed to possess an immortal soul, but a new interest arose in the physiological process within his complex make-up. The natural philosophers and physiologists were no longer willing to let man pass merely as the image of God. Among advanced thinkers, morality was gradually divorced from the supernatural conception of sin and related to behavior on this earth and its effect upon the individual and society. Some even dared to defend happiness, viewed as a state of satisfaction and adjustment here and now. This attitude was greatly stimulated by the secular trends in humanism.

A growing optimism regarding the future of man came into being and flowered into a crop of new theories of progress. The explorations overseas brought to Europe new information, revealed new and divers ways of living, stimulated curiosity, and developed the comparative attitude towards customs and institutions. A world point of view slowly superseded medieval provincialism.

It was inevitable that so profound and extensive a series of intellectual and cultural changes would produce a revolutionary effect upon philosophic speculation. In this chapter we shall briefly point out the most conspicuous novelties in philosophy, in no way even aiming to sketch systematically the history of philosophy during this period.

Giordano Bruno glimpsed something of the significance of the new universe revealed by the Copernican system. Montaigne was led by humanism and the discoveries overseas to defend urbanity, tolerance, and diversity. Bacon assailed scholasticism, became the great herald of the scientific method, and speculated upon the possibility of applying science to human betterment here on earth. Descartes and Hobbes attempted to go further and make mathematical science the basis of a new theory of knowledge, a new scheme of nature, and a novel mode of social control. Spinoza indicated the bearing of the new scientific discoveries upon the reconstruction of the conception of God. Leibnitz attempted to blend scholasticism and the new physics and to restate Aristotle's metaphysics and Augustinian mysticism in terms of calculus. Locke attempted to make experience rather than revelation the basis of knowledge. Hume carried empiricism to its logical extreme and upset the older theories of causation.

II. GIORDANO BRUNO AND THE NEW UNIVERSE

We have seen above that Copernicus overthrew, in part, the Ptolemaic theory of the universe by proving it to be heliocentric rather than geocentric. He interchanged the position of the earth and the sun in the system of fixed crystalline spheres, making the sun the center of the universe. But he kept the essentials of the old astronomy by retaining the system of spheres and epicycles. He possessed no inkling of astrophysical relativity, of the plurality of worlds and universes, or of the free motion of the heavenly bodies in space. It remained, as we have earlier noted, for a disciple of Cusanus and Copernicus, the Italian philosopher, Giordano Bruno (1548-1600), to make the first thoroughgoing assault on the Ptolemaic astrophysics and the philosophical complex associated therewith.

Bruno was born in southern Italy and died at the stake in Rome, but he spent most of his adult life north of the Alps. He traveled widely, partly from compulsion. He was in rebellion against the more reactionary aspects of Catholicism, while his Catholic antecedents made many Protestants suspicious of him. Hence, he was not entirely welcome in either camp during this period of heated religious controversy. But he was honored by scholars, and he taught in many important centers of learning, among them Toulouse, Paris, Oxford, and Wittenberg. He made the mistake of returning to Italy, was betrayed by his pupil, Giovanni Mocenigo, and turned over to the Inquisition. He was condemned to the stake and executed in February, 1600, the first conspicuous martyr to the new world-scheme.

Some have regarded Bruno as a hardheaded realist and naturalist because of his brilliant intuitions respecting the new universe and have envisaged in his philosophy a sort of foreshadowing of the mechanistic empiricism and determinism of Hobbes and Hume. Nothing could be further from the truth. His philosophical assumptions were thoroughly antique and primarily mystical. They were derived from the pre-Aristotelian hylozoism—the conception that all nature is alive—and from the mystical Neoplatonic appreciation of the beauty and harmony of the universe. His philosophy was thus a composite and mystical pantheism. A similar attitude had been formulated by Cusanus, and the latter directly influenced Bruno, who was, then, a poetical mystic and a devout Christian in his philosophical attitudes. He had no intention of upsetting supernaturalism or the Christion epic. Yet Bruno was not without some scientific equipment. He had mastered the existing body of mathematics and thoroughly comprehended the Copernican system. He thus had some technical preparation for carrying out his astrophysical revolution, but it was all conceived within a devout and pious mental climate.

In the old astronomy the earth had been regarded as the fixed center of the universe. In the Copernican scheme the sun had taken the place of the earth as the center of the system. Bruno rightly argued that there can be no such limitation of the physical universe as was implied in the system of crystalline spheres. There is neither limit nor center to the universe. All depends upon the place of observation. Each observer on the earth may regard his point of observation as the center, but it would not so appear to an observer on the sun or on one of the other planets or the fixed stars.

Everything, then, is relative to the point of observation. Position is relative. Up and down are terms that have precise meaning only when used with regard to a particular spot in the universe. The same applies to motion; it is likewise relative, depending upon the point from which it is observed and calculated. There is no absolute direction. Time, also, is relative. With us it is calculated on the basis of the motions of heavenly bodies with respect to the earth. But from other planets and from stars those astral movements which give us terrestrial time would be calculated in quite a different manner.

Bruno's notion of relativity not only upset the old astronomical conceptions; it also challenged a basic notion in Aristotle's physics. Aristotle had contended that light and heavy are absolute phenomena. Heavy matter seeks the center of the universe. This is the earth, and the earth is the heaviest element. Bruno insisted that this is an error, due to assigning a false importance and pivotal significance to the earth. Light and heavy are relationships that apply with exactness only to a specific planet, sun, or star.

Even more revolutionary was Bruno's hypothesis of a plurality of worlds and universes. Not only may there be other earths like ours; other universes may also exist, with central suns, and planets revolving about them. Further, Bruno repudiated the notion that the materials in the heavens are of a higher order than the supposed four sublunar elements, namely, earth, air, fire, and water. It had been a basic dogma of the old astronomy that the heavenly bodies are composed of a mysterious fifth element. Bruno believed that other heavenly bodies are presumably made up of the same materials as the earth, a guess which required the spectroscope of the nineteenth century to prove scientifically valid.

Finally, Bruno broke away entirely from the notion of fixed starry spheres and epicycles. He declared that the heavenly bodies move freely in space, though it required the subsequent work of Galileo, Kepler, and Newton to elucidate the problems associated with their movements and orbits. These epoch-making generalizations Bruno embodied chiefly in three works, *On Cause, Principle and Unity; On the Infinite Universe and the Worlds;* and *On the Immeasurable and Countless Worlds.*

When one recalls that the medieval synthesis had revolved about the Christianized Ptolemaic system, as embodied in such works as Dante's *Divine Comedy,* it is not difficult to see why the faithful looked with horror on Bruno's challenge of the geocentric cosmos, his refutation of the dogma of the perfection of the heavens as exemplified by their material composition and their circular motion, and his suggestion that there might be a vast number of other universes and worlds.

The last hypothesis was particularly disconcerting. Though Bruno had no such purpose in mind, it directly opposed the creation tale in Genesis, and constituted a grave logical challenge to the divinity of Jesus and his vicarious sacrifice for the sins of a small group of persons living on one little planet. Hence, Bruno's heresy in the eyes of the church is understandable, particularly when he put it in clear and popular language. There was grave danger that he might stir up widespread skepticism of the Christian world-scheme. Yet Bruno, himself, never remotely verged on agnosticism or a mechanistic outlook. He regarded God as at work in a creative and directive capacity in every portion of the vast universe of universes which he imagined. In his theology and his views of God and nature, Bruno was, as we emphasized above, a pious mystic and ardent Christian.

III. MONTAIGNE INCARNATES URBANITY AND SERENITY

One of the most complete repudiations of the typically medieval views of man and society is to be found in the charming essays of Michel Eyquem, generally known as Montaigne (1533-1592). Montaigne is important in the intellectual history of Europe because his general viewpoint was so different from that of the orthodox Christian, whether Catholic or Protestant. He was the foremost apostle of urbanity and detachment after Plato, Cicero and Plutarch. Erasmus went to no such lengths as Montaigne.

Yet Montaigne clearly illustrates how the modern era failed to break sharply with the medieval. A critic of scholasticism, he was at the same time a moderate follower of the most dogmatic and intolerant of Christian theologians, Augustine. Like many French thinkers of his and later times, he adopted the Augustinian attitude of highly personal introspection, mystical skepticism of positive empirical knowledge, and self-conscious analysis of nature and human problems. But this did not prevent Montaigne from emerging with intellectual attitudes and moral doctrines at exactly the opposite pole from those held by the author of *The City of God*.

In part, Montaigne's education and training explain his remarkable divergence from the orthodox patterns of thought. His religious background was highly diversified, his father being a devout Catholic and his mother a Jewess converted to Protestantism. This made it difficult for him to take seriously the pretensions of any one sect to a monopoly of divine revelation. Then, in his studies and reading, Montaigne was admirably prepared for intellectual·detachment and moderation. The typical Christian of Montaigne's day devoted himself to the Scriptures and theology, which were of necessity intolerant in nature and implication, and he knew little of the diverse customs of the world outside of his limited observations.

Montaigne, on the other hand, was given a thorough classical education. He was remarkably well-read in Latin and Greek literature and found his favorite authors among the great pagan expositors of tolerance and secularism: Plato, Plutarch, Cicero, the Skeptics and the Epicureans. The pagan slogan that those who seek the truth must both refute without prejudice and accept criticism without resentment was reincarnated in Montaigne. Moreover, there was in Montaigne much of the same effort to acquire an attitude of mental serenity that we noted in connection with the post-Aristotelian Greek philosophers. The old world-system—medievalism—was dissolving in his day as the Attic world did after Aristotle. Philosophical calm had to be created from within rather than secured by external assurances and institutions.

Further, Montaigne was born in the early stages of the era of oversea discoveries and was greatly impressed by them. He was exceedingly interested in the diversity of customs and beliefs entertained by mankind in various parts of the earth.[1] Such interests and knowledge made it difficult for him to take seriously the Christian contention that there was but one safe and proper moral code. From his early training and from his reading, then, Montaigne was admirably fitted to become the apostle of tolerance and moderation. Furthermore, he was thoroughly convinced of the diversity of human values and behavior.

In his attitude towards the purpose of philosophy, conceived in its broadest possible form as the sum total of human learning and reflection, Montaigne completely repudiated the orthodox Christian position. The Christians contended that the chief purpose of intellectual effort is to secure salvation in the world to come; in other words, philosophy's chief function, as the handmaiden of theology, is the preparation of man for a safe death. Theology was inevitably regarded as the "queen of the sciences." Montaigne contended, on the contrary, that knowledge should teach man how to live more adequately and happily here on this earth. To him, the leading forms of knowledge were what we would today call social psychology, ethnology, and aesthetics. Montaigne thus reversed the whole objective of life and study, as it had been accepted by both great camps of Christians, and directly anticipated Francis Bacon's suggestion that the kingdom of man should be substituted for the kingdom of God as the chief object of human interest and intellectual endeavor. Immortality is uncertain, but of life on earth there is no doubt. Hence we should do all possible to make the latter worth while.

The starting point of Montaigne's philosophy was true intellectual humility. It was not the Christian religious debasement, founded upon the assumption of sin, the fall of man, and the spiritual unworthiness of human beings. Montaigne had little use for this attitude. Rather, he understood well the paucity of information which any one individual could obtain and assimilate, and was equally convinced of the intellectual limitations of the race as a whole. Consequently, he believed that it is necessary ever to bear in mind the severe limitations of our assumed erudition, and to subject ourselves frequently to the most searching intellectual self-examination, in order to impress upon ourselves how little we really know. This was a marked contrast to the intellectual arrogance of the scholastic theologian, who believed that, armed with the Scriptures and the masters of theology, he possessed the sum total of saving knowledge.

Next, whereas the Christians had emphasized the unity of all true wisdom and the uniformity of conduct essential to salvation, Montaigne was wont to stress the opposite, namely, that diversity and pluralism seem to be the rule of nature, and hence of God. He arrived at this view of matters (1) as a result of his consciousness of the varying moods of the human individual from day to day and from year to year, and (2) as an outgrowth of his observation of the enormous variety of human customs and beliefs, reported by ancient observers and by contemporary explorers. Montaigne was one of the first writers to understand thoroughly how variable each individual is, and how one's moods change from day to day, because of external conditions and internal stimuli. Hence, he once profoundly observed that we differ more from ourselves than we do from one another. In his ideas on education Montaigne stressed the civilizing and educational value

[1] Cf. *The Essays of Michel de Montaigne*, ed. by W. C. Hazlitt, Burt, 1930, II, 387 ff.

of travel and the contact of cultures: "I would have travel the book my young gentleman should study with most attention: for so many humors, so many sects, so many judgments, opinions, laws and customs, teach us to judge aright of our own, and inform our understanding to discover its imperfection and natural infirmity." Miss Irene Cooper Willis has effectively expressed these foundations of Montaigne's defense of cosmic and social diversity:

> The diversity of human nature, the inconstancy of our actions, the uncertainty of our judgments, the curious, inexplicable, essentially unreasonable foundations of our opinions, these are Montaigne's favorite themes. . . . "Whosoever look-eth into this narrowly, hardly ever finds himself twice in the same state. . . . If I speak diversely of myself, it is because I see myself diversely. All contrarieties are found in me at some moment and in some fashion. Bashful, insolent; chaste, lustful; talkative, taciturn; laborious, delicate; witty, dull; melancholy, gay; lying, truthful; learned, ignorant; both liberal and avaricious and prodigal. All these things I perceive in myself in some degree according as I turn myself about. . . ."
>
> His cogitations led him over a wide field, the field of his reading (wide for those days, his library consisted of a thousand books and he was an indefatigable though impatient reader), of his experience and observation as courtier, politician, and country gentleman, of the illimitable and, as he grew older and more and more absorbed in his *Essays,* the increasingly fascinating field of his self. The then recent discovery of the New World, upsetting all traditional views of the size and geography of the universe—those marvellous, rich cities of the Indies, were no more alluring to the curiosity and imaginations of the Old World than were the unexplored regions of the soul to Montaigne. . . .
>
> Like a Mohammedan fearful of destroying any scrap of paper lest perchance the name of Allah should be written on it, Montaigne dared not ignore a jot of evidence concerning the waywardness of man. All that he could read and collect of human customs, habits, and opinions he reported: he travelled, not as many people do, "to find Gascons in Sicily," but to seek "Greeks and Persians" there. He was insatiable in pursuit of the diversity of other men's lives; he was fascinated by the unending list of human vagaries and foibles.[2]

The combination in Montaigne of intellectual humility with a full comprehension of the inconstancy of man and the diversity of conduct to be observed in the world, served to develop in him a remarkable degree of tolerance and intellectual detachment.

Another factor making for this tolerance and urbanity was his repudiation of the otherworldliness of Christian theology, with its logical insistence upon the importance of religious truths and the all-absorbing significance of ultimate salvation. The Christian could not be tolerant or detached, for he could not well remain indifferent to something which inevitably meant the loss of his soul and perdition for countless thousands of others. If he were a true and consistent believer he found it necessary to be absorbed in the task of salvation and become intolerant of dissent.

Through his secular outlook and his doubts about immortality, Montaigne

---

[2] I. C. Willis, *Montaigne,* Knopf, 1927, pp. 10 ff. This little work is much the most useful and intelligent treatise on Montaigne for the beginning student in intellectual history.

freed himself from the medieval hell-neurosis. He could take for granted full safety in contemplating the human scene. If philosophy is to teach us how to live rather than how to die, we must gather the largest possible amount of information as to the ways in which men live and then analyze this mass of material in calm and judicious fashion. Insofar as we allow our emotions and prejudices to enter into the process of assimilating and evaluating such material, to that degree do we fail to derive wisdom from the exercise. If nature reveals diversity to be the rule, then the theological effort to teach and enforce uniformity in thought and action must be fundamentally stupid and wrongheaded.

It was inevitable that in his discussion of morality Montaigne should depart widely from the Christian identification of morality with religious dogmas, and from the Christian tendency to regard morality as chiefly a matter of chastity in sexual relations. Montaigne may rightly be regarded as the father of the contemporary civilized approach to ethics. Because of his secularism, Montaigne was able to attack the problem of ethics in a detached fashion. He perceived that man has devised a great variety of ways of meeting the chief problems of existence. Hence, he could not subscribe in any sense to the Christian view that the only defensible solution of moral problems consisted of the narrow standards of conduct insisted upon by orthodox Christianity. To him God and nature seemed to approve of diversity rather than uniformity. His theory of ethics was empirical rather than revealed. As Miss Willis states the matter:

> True morality was that way to which reason, acting upon our experience of life, and our knowledge of ourselves, pointed. He believed that the origin of all moral codes, though the codes had since become stereotyped and insensitive to realities, lay in reason, and that mankind's notions of good and evil were not, as Socrates thought, deposited in our minds by a God who created us, but were reasonably derived from men's contact with life and with themselves. This explained why the customs and moralities of different peoples and races were so different.[3]

Starting from this line of thought, Montaigne gravely challenged many of the leading tenets of Christian ethics. He repudiated entirely the Christian tendency to separate the body from the mind or soul, to regard the soul and its pleasures as good and the body and its enjoyments as base, and to represent bodily pleasures as separate from, but disastrous to, the operations of the mind. He held that both body and soul are given to us by nature and God, that bodily pleasures are as natural and defensible as the experiences of the soul, and that in reasonable indulgence in corporeal delights the mind may actually be freshened and stimulated. He thus broke down the untenable theological dichotomy of the world of the spirit and the realm of the flesh—the dualism of body and mind—and insisted upon viewing the human organism as a unity. As Montaigne phrased this aspect of his doctrines:

> The body hath a great part in our being. . . . Those who would sunder our two principal parts and disunite the one from the other are to blame. We ought to

[3] Willis, *op. cit.*, p. 82.

recouple and rejoin them. We must bid the soul not to withdraw and entertain herself apart, not to despise and abandon the body (which she cannot well do without except by some counterfeit apish trick), but to combine with it, embrace, cherish, assist, and control it, to counsel and correct it and bring it back when it goes astray; in short, espouse and act towards it as a husband. . . . Xerxes was a ninnyhammer, who, given to all human voluptuousness, offered a reward to him that should discover new pleasures for him. But not much less of a simpleton is he that abridges those which nature has devised for him. . . . There are some (as Aristotle saith) who with a savage stupidity find bodily pleasure distasteful. Why renounce they not also breathing? Why live they not on what is theirs alone and refuse the light? . . . Will they not seek the quadrature of the circle, even when they lie with their wives? . . . Nature hath, like a kind mother, seen to this, that such actions as she for our necessities hath enjoined unto us should also be pleasurable unto us, and doth invite us to them not only by reason, but also by appetite. It is not right to break her rules. When I behold both Caesar and Alexander at the thickest of their great labors enjoying so fully human and corporeal pleasures I say not that they thereby relaxed their minds; I say that they strengthened them, by vigour of spirits submitting their violent occupations and laborious thoughts to the usage of ordinary life. . . . There is nothing so goodly and so lawful as to play the man well and duly; nor any science so difficult as to know how to live this life well; and of our infirmities the most savage is to despise our being. . . . It is an absolute perfection and, as it were, divine for a man to know how to enjoy his existence loyally. We seek for other conditions because we understand not the use of our own and we go outside of ourselves because we know not what is happening there. Thus it is in vain that we mount upon stilts, for, be we upon them, yet we must go with our own legs; and sit we upon the highest throne in the world, yet we do but sit upon our own behind.[4]

From such considerations it is apparent that Montaigne in no sense shared the orthodox Christian view that morality is almost entirely a matter of sexual prudery and chastity. He held that sex relations in themselves are not evil. They only need to be controlled by a sense of moderation and honor. Montaigne was thus preeminently a man of honor rather than a moral man, to adopt Mr. H. L. Mencken's very useful distinction. But, more fundamentally, he held that morality is something far broader than sex. It must also be deeply concerned with decency and justice. While not going as far as the third Earl of Shaftesbury in this regard, Montaigne exhibited a similar tendency to formulate an aesthetic approach to morality, identifying it with good taste and moderation. Then, he viewed tolerance and justice as more important than sexual matters in the ideal moral code. An aggressive war, the torturing of witches, or the oppression of the weak, he regarded as more reprehensible than sexual indulgence. In general, however, he advocated outward respect for, and conformity to, the prevailing customs and conventions as a matter of convenience and economy of effort. But he warned against taking these so seriously as to produce intellectual hypocrisy or lack of poise and insight.

4 Cited in Willis, *op. cit.*, pp. 84-87.

Indeed, in his social and political philosophy Montaigne was a traditionalist, if not a downright reactionary. He thought that all security must be mental, created from within by a personal philosophy. Therefore, he could not see how human betterment would result from institutional changes. He believed it wiser to retain traditional institutions and laws and permit the philosopher to disregard them as best he could in his inner life. There is no dodging the fact that this was a somewhat cowardly and unintelligent attitude. An intelligent personal philosophy is always dangerous in an unintelligent world. Even the philosopher can only succeed in maintaining intelligent attitudes by dissimulation, "pussy-footing," and hypocrisy. The French perfectionists, and social reformers, like Helvétius, were far more logical and consistent in this regard than Montaigne.

The conception of God entertained by men has tended to conform to their own general world outlook and personal philosophy. Montaigne thus conceived of God as a sort of magnified Montaigne, detached, tolerant, and complacent in the face of the varied follies of fallible men. It is usually held that Shaftesbury was the first to make the discovery that God may be a gentleman, but it would seem that to Montaigne rightly belongs this honor, though he did not develop this conception as conspicuously as Shaftesbury. Such a view marked a wide break with the orthodox Jewish and Christian theory of a jealous, arbitrary, and petty God, confessedly guilty of most of the offenses for which he had cruelly punished the human race. Montaigne enlarged God as decisively from the moral and aesthetic point of view as the astrophysicists of the next century magnified our conception of his power and his rule over the universe.

Yet Montaigne's conception of God was characteristically free from dogmatism. He fully recognized that it is all a matter of conjecture, for he frankly asserted that man cannot hope to know what God is actually like. To know God literally is quite beyond the power of the human mind. If we must guess about God, then we should at least hazard an opinion which does justice to God.

If we were to select one dominant feature of Montaigne's philosophy it would probably have to be his praise and practice of urbanity and serenity. As Miss Willis expresses it: "His so-called 'skepticism' or 'indifference' was to a great extent good manners; good manners, that is to say, in the intellectual sense." After all, it is probable that these two qualities of urbanity and serenity are the most valid criteria of true civilization, and our failure as yet to realize them to any great degree may well be one of the best proofs of our actual cultural and philosophic barbarism in the midst of a new era of machines and material conveniences.

The progress of knowledge since Montaigne's time has permitted men to become more learned than he, but it is doubtful if there has been a more truly civilized intellect than the great French essayist of the late sixteenth century. Striking indeed was the advance he marked over Erasmus in intellectual freedom. The latter was indeed tolerant and urbane, but he applied these qualities almost exclusively to supernatural and religious problems. With him, philosophy still remained entirely the handmaiden of theology. With Montaigne, it was already becoming an introduction to sociology and aesthetics.

IV. FRANCIS BACON ASSAULTS SCHOLASTICISM

A man of a different intellectual complexion was Francis Bacon (1561-1626), whose *Essays* are known to most readers of English prose, but whose position in the development of the modern mind is variously evaluated. He is celebrated by many as the earliest thinker to grasp the implications of the scientific method, while others, like the late J. W. Draper, have sought to discredit him by pointing to the fact that he rejected the most celebrated scientific discoveries of his own time. The truth is somewhere between the two points of view.[5] It may truly be said that Bacon was the first important philosopher to draw up an eloquent and itemized bill of indictment against the deductive method of scholasticism, to outline a method of inductive science, and to apprehend imaginatively the great social changes made possible through scientific discovery, a prospect which he pictured in striking and convincing rhetoric, especially in his *Novum Organon,* his *Advancement of Learning,* and his *New Atlantis.*

Bacon's career was spectacular. Born with every prospect of high success, he was carefully educated, only to be brought to the bottom of the ladder by the early death of his father, a high government official under Queen Elizabeth. As a younger son deprived of his father's patronage he was obliged to carve out a career for himself. He turned to the law and showed himself willing to accept the current morality. He believed that any means justified the achievement of his great end: leisure to extol science and to devote himself to the literary labors incident to that interest. In spite of his adaptability he did not succeed under Elizabeth, even though he turned on his closest friend in an effort to advance himself. He had to wait until the reign of James I for his chance.

Under James he went forward rapidly by the common device of concealing his true political opinions, which were sensible and progressive and for which more admirable characters sacrificed their posts. By dint of playing the sedulous courtier he advanced to the high position of Lord Chancellor and was given the titles Lord Bacon of Verulam and Viscount of St. Albans. To fortify his position he shared in the freely circulating graft and favored the King's friends whenever he could. When one particularly atrocious case of favoritism came to light, Parliament directed its fire against King James, who "passed the buck" to Bacon, who was prosecuted and convicted. His fall was rapid and complete, but his punishment was almost entirely remitted, since he had merely been so unfortunate as to be caught in a common political swindle. According to the "King's pleasure" he spent but a few days in jail, and he was never called upon to pay his fine. This occurred in 1621. He died five years later in retirement.

Certain moralists, more striking for the aberrancy of their judgments than for their insight into human character, have attempted to use Bacon's political disaster to discredit his philosophy, arguing that he was immoral because he thought as he did. With such exercises in metaphysical ethics we have no interest in this

[5] The best brief analysis of Bacon's place in science and philosophy is Wolf, *History of Science, Technology and Philosophy in the 16th and 17th Centuries,* pp. 632-40.

place. It is more pertinent to set forth the striking phases of Bacon's thought.

In spite of the fact that no modern scientist would undertake to work according to the Baconian rules of procedure, it may be conceded that he was the herald of modern science. He picturesquely repudiated the scholastic method of arriving at truth through deductive logic,[6] and attempted to turn men's minds from the kingdom of God to the kingdom of man. Bacon protected himself from religious attack by eliminating God and final causes from the scope and realm of scientific analysis. In Bacon's utopia, *The New Atlantis,* the laboratory, not the cathedral, is the center of interest. Naturally, he repudiated authority, which he opposed with experimentation and the inductive method. If his program were followed, he felt that men would be able to grasp the tremendous power inherent in the scientific method, and profit from the alleviation or improvement of their earthly condition which must inevitably result.

While he was robustly optimistic about the possibilities of science, he was far from blind to the forces opposing the acceptance of the new knowledge. He designated the four principal obstacles to clear thinking as the Idols of the Tribe, the Cave (Den), the Marketplace, and the Theater.

His conceptions may be briefly explained. By the Idols of the Tribe he meant the persistence of traditional attitudes and erroneous ideas common to all mankind and accepted on that ground alone. Their very universality stands in the way of any critical examination of them. Today we talk of such ideas as the product of cultural lag and herd instinct or as examples of anthropomorphism, illusion, and dream logic.

The Idols of the Cave are those convictions or prejudices ("conditioned responses") which afflict a given individual and stand in the way of his acceptance of other and contrary ideas. They are derived from our social experiences and personal contacts. Such notions may be the product of emotional predispositions in favor of an idea or opinion derived at our mother's knee. In short, idols of the tribe are generalized prejudices, while the idols of the cave are individual prejudices. When the fixation upon a prejudice of a personal sort becomes too obvious we now regard the individual as suffering from "complexes." But the disease afflicts us all, and the modern individual is superior to the ancient only in the existence of techniques for discovering his complexes.

The Idols of the Marketplace refer to such things as the hazy thinking engendered by rhetorical language. The inevitable result of worshiping this idol is a weakness for substituting well-said for well-thought, for encumbering the mind through concentration on verbal problems, and for imagining that words always correspond to things. Words are very imperfect vehicles for the expression of ideas, even in the case of persons with the widest vocabulary and the most acute sense of verbal fitness and precision. And even if one is well informed and exact in his own expression of ideas, it is difficult to transmit the same meaning with precision to others. Again, people are so entranced by the music or cadence of

---

[6] Bacon was not, of course, a thoroughgoing opponent of Aristotelian logic. While he attacked the excessive scholastic emphasis on deductive logic, he advocated a greater use of Aristotle's inductive logic.

their words that they become relatively indifferent to the thought content. Stuart Chase has described this in our day as "the tyranny of words."

The Idols of the Theater are closely related to the Idols of the Cave, for they refer to the habit of paying allegiance to conventional systems of thought, or bodies of congealed belief, to the extent that all disinterested and original thinking becomes virtually impossible. This fourth idol produces all the evils of intellectual discipleship, loyalty to creeds, cults, and systems of thought, and devotion to panaceas. In short, it creates the single-track mind which has led even great men like Woodrow Wilson into disaster.

Bacon's notion of the idols which stand in the way of intellectual progress is so important as to warrant a reproduction of his summary characterization of them:

> Four species of idols beset the human mind, to which (for distinction's sake) we have assigned names, calling the first Idols of the Tribe, the second Idols of the Den, the third Idols of the Market, the fourth Idols of the Theatre.
>
> The formation of notions and axioms on the foundation of true induction is the only fitting remedy by which we can ward off and expel these idols. It is, however, of great service to point them out; for the doctrine of idols bears the same relation to the interpretation of nature as that of the confutation of sophisms does to common logic.
>
> The idols of the tribe are inherent in human nature and the very tribe or race of man; for man's sense is falsely asserted to be the standard of things; on the contrary, all the perceptions both of the senses and the mind bear reference to man and not to the universe, and the human mind resembles those uneven mirrors which impart their own properties to different objects, from which rays are emitted and distort and disfigure them.
>
> The idols of the den are those of each individual; for everybody (in addition to the errors common to the race of man) has his own individual den or cavern, which intercepts and corrupts the light of nature, either from his own peculiar and singular disposition, or from his education and intercourse with others, or from his reading, and the authority acquired by those whom he reverences and admires, or from the different impressions produced on the mind, as it happens to be preoccupied and predisposed, or equable and tranquil, and the like; so that the spirit of man (according to its several dispositions) is variable, confused, and, as it were, actuated by chance; and Heraclitus said well that men search for knowledge in lesser worlds, and not in the greater or common world.
>
> There are also idols formed by the reciprocal intercourse and society of man with man, which we call idols of the market, from the commerce and association of men with each other; for men converse by means of language, but words are formed at the will of the generality, and there arises from a bad and unapt formation of words a wonderful obstruction to the mind. Nor can the definitions and explanations with which learned men are wont to guard and protect themselves in some instances afford a complete remedy—words still manifestly force the understanding, throw everything into confusion, and lead mankind into vain and innumerable controversies and fallacies.
>
> Lastly, there are the idols which have crept into men's minds from the various dogmas of peculiar systems of philosophy, and also from the perverted rules of demonstration, and these we denominate idols of the theatre: for we regard all

the systems of philosophy hitherto received or imagined, as so many plays brought out and performed, creating fictitious and theatrical worlds. Nor do we speak only of the present systems, or the philosophy and sects of the ancients, since numerous other plays of a similar nature can be still composed and made to agree with each other, the causes of the most opposite errors being generally the same. Nor, again, do we allude merely to general systems, but also to many elements and axioms of sciences which have become inveterate by tradition, implicit credence, and neglect.[7]

This analysis of the various obstacles in the way of scientific thinking is probably one of Bacon's soundest contributions to human thought.

Bacon was perhaps the first to conceive of intellectual history and its potential services in combating tradition, conservatism and error.[8] He believed that the most illuminating type of history is the history of ideas. Indeed, without giving proper attention to the succession of dominating ideas, history is blind. A thorough understanding of the genesis of accepted opinions will help us to perceive the errors residing therein. Bacon was thus the true precursor of James Harvey Robinson's views of intellectual history and of the pragmatic use of history, in the best and only defensible application of this conception.

If Bacon aided the intellectual revolution by exposing the obstacles to thinking and suggesting ways of overcoming them, he inflamed men's imaginations in other ways as well. He elaborated the theory formulated by certain late medieval thinkers that "we are the ancients," pointing out that the latest generation is culturally older and intellectually more mature than the preceding, and has more known experience at its command. Presumably, all other factors being equal, our best-informed contemporaries can render more cogent and substantial judgments on difficult problems than our predecessors.

This is a decided reversal of the more familiar attitude which asks us to believe that the "ancients," from the standpoint of accumulated wisdom, are those who lived in times far removed from us and that, as we retrace our steps to the dawn of history, we thereby approach the fountainhead of true wisdom. The seats of wisdom for the Western World have for many centuries been located in Greece and Palestine, but other peoples have their intellectual homelands. The invocation of an ancient to demolish a modern is a familiar device in all intellectual argumentation, and the Baconian reversal of the device has, unfortunately, been put to comparatively little avowed use. Many men who today assume the Baconian position do so without realizing that the argument to sustain their position was developed three centuries ago. A widespread revival of it would bring acute discomfort to the traditionalists of any age. The "dead hand" from the past is the most formidable obstacle to human betterment today, as it was in Bacon's time, and the Baconian attitude is as necessary and useful as ever.

But if "we are the ancients," Bacon was far from advising us to rest on our laurels, and he was particularly eager to shake his own generation of "ancients" out of their lethargy. He was fond of representing mankind as more viciously assailed by traditional ideas and systems of thought than by the overt temptations

7 *The Novum Organon*, Book I, 39-44.   8 See Robinson, *The New History*, p. 101.

of a personal devil. He thus suggested that the real devil who menaces mankind is the whole complex of archaic ideas—i.e., tradition and the dead hand.

Bacon pointed out that the potentialities of the scientific method far outran its actual achievements. He sought, therefore, to turn men's imagination to science, and wrote a prospectus of the inductive method which today is chiefly remarkable for its opposition to the scholastic method. He directed men's thoughts to the study of particulars, and incited them to the accumulation of numerous facts so that they might by comparison and exclusion build up, slowly and carefully, valid generalizations. By shifting the emphasis from arguments to facts he genuinely assisted his cause. Nature, he thought, is more subtle than any argument. Ironically enough, it proved more subtle than his own argument. Like most pioneers of a rhetorical turn of mind, he was inadequately prepared to evaluate actual scientific theories. He rejected most of the advances of his time, treating Copernicus with particular severity. He thus came dangerously close to being a victim of his own idols of the cave and the theater.

All in all, Bacon stands out as an enthusiastic and eloquent propagandist for science. His name has come down to us with that connotation attached to it. Even to this day those who hope that by the general utilization of the scientific method mankind will be led out of the difficulties in which it currently wallows are called Baconians. If they have, in late years, lost some of the all-embracing optimism of their spiritual father, they have not given up belief in the method which fired his imagination.

Bacon not only astutely and persistently attacked scholasticism and wrote more beautifully and persuasively in behalf of the inductive method than any other scholar except Thomas Henry Huxley; he also let his imagination run to the creation of a scientific utopia. In his *New Atlantis* the central establishment was the so-called House of Solomon, the laboratory of the coöperating scientists. These were honored above all other men—usurping the place of the priests in medieval society—and the rest of mankind was continually incited to learn and apply immediately their discoveries of science. As we have already indicated, this House of Solomon was taken as the model for the creation of the Royal Society in London. Other than in this instance, Bacon had far less influence on actual scientific research than on the general scientific impulse.

Though Bacon laid much stress upon the originality and merits of his own particular program of scientific research, it had, and could have, no serious influence on the actual scientific activities of his day. Despite his attack on the scholastics for their adherence to Aristotle, Bacon's own scientific conceptions were almost purely Aristotelian—based on Aristotelian categories and his notions of causes. Bacon underestimated the importance of originality and innate sagacity in scientific discovery, and hoped that he could lay down a plan so that any well-meaning and industrious person could make important scientific discoveries. Especially farfetched was his notion of having one group of scientists formulate hypotheses and another group test them out. It is little wonder that scientists gave scant attention to his much vaunted scheme for research procedure.

In spite of Bacon's enthusiasm for science, the part he played, as we have suggested, was that of an enthusiastic publicist rather than a scientist in his own right. No man has ever surpassed him as a propagandist. At the same time, very few men formally devoted to science have ever been less capable of appreciating existing scientific activity. While writing enthusiastically in support of the scientific method, Bacon, as we have noted, either ignored or attacked most of the actual scientific work carried on in his day. He held up to ridicule the Copernican system. He scoffed at the work of Gilbert, who founded the scientific study of electricity and magnetism, and he depreciated the significance of mathematics for natural science. Incredible as it may seem, he also believed in astrology and witchcraft.

These facts have led to severe attacks upon Bacon's standing as a scientist. They began when Harvey, discoverer of the circulation of the blood, implied that Bacon was a rhetorician rather than a scientist. He said that Bacon wrote science more like a lord chancellor than like a scientist. Since the days of Liebig, a century ago, scientists have assailed Bacon's incomplete grasp of scientific method. Aspersions have even been cast upon Bacon's intelligence and integrity by some historians, most conspicuously John W. Draper. The flavor of Draper's criticism may be discerned from the following:

> Few scientific pretenders have made more mistakes than Lord Bacon. He rejected the Copernican system, and spoke insolently of its great author; he undertook to criticise adversely Gilbert's treatise "De Magnete"; he was occupied in the condemnation of any investigation of final causes, while Harvey was deducing the circulation of the blood from Aquapendente's discovery of the valves in the veins; he was doubtful whether instruments were of any advantage, while Galileo was investigating the heavens with the telescope. Ignorant himself of every branch of mathematics, he presumed they were useless in science, but a few years before Newton achieved by their aid his immortal discoveries. It is time the sacred name of philosophy should be severed from its long connexion with that of one who was a pretender in science, a time-serving politician, an insidious lawyer, a corrupt judge, a treacherous friend, a bad man.[9]

When all is said and done, however, Bacon wrote most effectively in behalf of the experimental attitude and made himself one of the leaders in that intellectual movement which lays special emphasis upon the importance of science in human affairs. In short, he was one of those rare humanists who praised instead of despised natural science.

V. DESCARTES AND THE MECHANISTIC UNIVERSE

A firmer grasp of the direct significance of the new scientific knowledge is exhibited in the work of the French philosopher, René Descartes (1596-1650). Unlike Bacon, he was less interested in prophecy and exhortation than in creating a system of investigation with the materials at hand.

Descartes was born of a noble family and was educated by the Jesuits. His early

[9] J. W. Draper, *History of the Intellectual Development of Europe*, rev. ed., 2 vols., Harper, 1904, II, 60.

life was a mixture of action and study. He was a courtier and soldier and saw action in various military campaigns. He retired from the army in order to devote himself completely to intellectual endeavor. He first settled upon the family estates in France which he inherited, but soon moved to Holland. Late in life he was called to Sweden to become tutor to Queen Christina, and while there he contracted pneumonia as the result of rising to teach his royal student mathematics at four in the morning.

Descartes had one great failing, namely, a lack of courage in fighting opposition. He desired to live in peace and quiet, even at the expense of intellectual honesty. He was even capable of withdrawing his own works when they were regarded as heretical in the eyes of the church, and nothing disturbed him so much as to know that his ideas were the cause of exasperating contention in the Dutch universities. One of his favorite mottoes was a phrase from Ovid—*bene vixit qui bene latuit*—which may be freely translated as "he lives most happily who hides his opinions most effectively."

Descartes' philosophic approach was purely mathematical. In that discipline he thought he had found the key to the secrets of the universe. As he once expressed it: "I am convinced that it [mathematics] is a more powerful instrument of knowledge than any other which has been beqeathed to us by human agency, as being the source of all others." His greatest practical contribution was the creation of analytical geometry. Yet Descartes was no mathematical mystic. He had little use for pure mathematics. What interested him was the mathematical method and its application.

To secure support for his mathematical physics, Descartes turned from the Aristotelian position, which had an opposing physics of its own, to the Augustinian doctrine, in which God was identified with the "mathematical order of nature." While he went back to Anselm's ontological proof of God to substantiate his theism, his views of God were quite different from Anselm's. In his correspondence, Descartes once said: "You can substitute 'the mathematical order of nature' for 'God' whenever I use the latter term"—a view not so far from that of Jeans, Eddington, and Millikan in recent years. In this sense, Descartes' proofs of God were not the result of "preconceived notions," as is often charged, but of the need for such a concept in order to hold his thought together—combined, of course, with the strategic desire to get the support of the most influential party of French theologians for his revolution in physics—in which aspiration he was eminently successful.

Descartes is important in the history of thought mainly because of his contributions to philosophical and scientific method. In his *Discourse on Method* (1637) he set forth an admirable body of principles. He asserted that the first step is to wipe away all earlier and accepted authority and to start with a clear and unbiased mind. The philosopher must never accept as true anything that cannot be proven so. Everything must be stated at the outset in the clearest and simplest form, gradually and logically advancing to more complex and involved formulations. Each specific problem must be divided into as many parts as may be necessary to solve it. Thoughts and propositions must be arranged in an orderly sequence of ideas. In the end, there must be a complete analysis and a sufficiently comprehensive review of the whole problem to omit nothing. The *Discourse on Method* was written in lucid French for the intelligent layman, and hence had a very wide influence on the history of philosophical thought and scientific method.

The basis of Descartes' thinking was the omnipotence of rational consciousness, summed up in the famous maxim, "I think, therefore I am." He thought that he could discover truth by deductive thinking in mathematical terms. In doing so he created, with the help of mathematics and logic, a completely mechanistic world. As Randall admirably summarizes Descartes' epistemology: "To Descartes space or extension became the fundamental reality in the world, motion the source of all change, and mathematics the only relation between its parts." [10] As Descartes once observed, "Give me extension and motion and I will construct the world."

From the mechanistic explanation he exempted but two things, God and the soul of man. Man is the only being in nature who possesses a soul, and the latter is the only part of man which escapes mechanistic necessity. The lower animals he regarded as pure automatons—mere machines. Man, thanks to his soul, is a conscious, reflective, and directive machine. Descartes, as we have seen, retained the strict medieval dualism of body and soul in his psychology. The probability is that the mechanistic view of the universe was suggested to him by Kepler's researches and that his mechanistic physiology was derived from Harvey's discovery of the circulation of the blood, the human body being conceived as a pumping plant. His mystical conceptions of the soul and his strict dualism were derived in part from Augustine, who had, in turn, taken them from the Neoplatonists.

Descartes' conviction that his explanation was true was confirmed by the fact that he conceived of God, the Absolute Substance, as infinite goodness, as a perfect being, who can have no reason for deceiving us. "The trustworthiness of human perception follows from God's veracity." With Descartes, God thus became the basis of a sound epistemology, just as Kant later made God the source of practical ethics.

It is perfectly clear that Descartes, by exempting the soul and God from his mechanistic universe, opened the way for a return of many medieval conceptions about man and destiny. Give the supernaturalists an inch and they will take a mile. This proved to be the case with Descartes. If the modern Catholic controversialists tend to condemn Descartes for the encouragement he gave to scientific thinkers, in the past his way of thinking has been of considerable use to compromisers.

Descartes' idea of God, of course, had no relation to the finite, personal, anthropomorphic deity of the Jews and Christians. As Höffding puts it: "The idea of God is for him the idea of a continuous, all-embracing unity of existence, in which everything that possesses reality must be able to find a place." God, to Descartes, was Absolute Substance, not a petty tribal deity intimidating puny man, or wrestling with Jacob. Descartes was careful to state that neither the method of reason nor mathematical measurement can be applied to the study of God and the supernatural.

10 J. H. Randall, Jr., *The Making of the Modern Mind*, Houghton Mifflin, 1926 (rev. ed., 1940), p. 241.

Like Bacon, Descartes is chiefly important today because he assisted in breaking down the pretensions of authority. If he underestimated the more obscure storehouses of tradition, like the subconscious, and was inconsistent in both disclaiming and accepting authority, he managed to destroy some of the more obvious hindrances to clear thinking.

In formal histories of philosophy Descartes is usually considered the founder of the so-called Rationalist school, in which the other leading thinkers were Spinoza and Leibnitz. This label is based on Descartes' emphasis on the crucial importance of consciousness and man's rational nature, the adequacy of faith in scientific activity, and the power of the mind, when equipped with the mathematical technique, to solve scientific problems. So far as science is concerned, these men may have been rationalists, but the term is misleading because it identifies or confuses them with the later thoroughgoing rationalists like Hume, Voltaire, Holbach, and the like. In philosophy and in religion, Descartes, Spinoza, and Leibnitz were flagrant rationalizers rather than true rationalists. Though stressing the rational power of the mind, they all viewed mind in an extremely mystical fashion and their interpretations of the operations of the mind were equally enveloped in mystical notions. Their philosophy and theology were really an effort to rationalize Augustinian mysticism (in the case of Spinoza, a comparable Neoplatonic and Jewish mysticism) in terms of the new mathematical and physical science. They had confidence in reason in matters scientific, but they took their religion on faith, whatever their pretensions to the contrary. Despite their formal tribute to the powers of human reason, the thought of Descartes, Spinoza, and Leibnitz ended up in a mystical fog and colossal rationalizations.

VI. HOBBES FOUNDS SCIENTIFIC MATERIALISM AND ETHICAL HEDONISM

By involving himself in supernaturalistic ideas Descartes introduced hopeless contradictions into his system. A more thoroughgoing naturalistic thinker who also attempted to utilize the new knowledge was the Englishman, Thomas Hobbes (1588-1679). According to Höffding, Hobbes "instituted the best thought-out attempt of modern times to make our knowledge of natural science the foundation of all our knowledge of existence. The system which he constructed is the most profound materialistic system of modern times." [11]

Hobbes was educated at Oxford and became a tutor in the Cavendish family which protected him all his long life. For a while he was secretary to Francis Bacon, assisting the latter in getting his works into acceptable Latin. Long before he published philosophical works of his own he had written solicited objections to Descartes' *Meditations*. One day he came upon Euclid's *Elements of Geometry* and from then on he was deeply influenced by the possibility of unfolding a valid philosophy on deductive lines, once the fundamental propositions had been laid down in accordance with scientific truth. Hobbes, like Descartes, looked upon philosophy as primarily an exercise in logical deduction, as the reasoned knowledge of effects from causes and of causes from effects. Once fundamental proposi-

11 Harald Höffding, *History of Modern Philosophy*, Dover, 1955, I, 264.

tions are laid down, all else follows deductively in clear and inevitable fashion. Hobbes's chief philosophical works were his *Elements of Philosophy, Human Nature,* and *Leviathan,* the latter the best statement of his social and political philosophy.

Hobbes abandoned the obscurantism and dualism of Descartes and the so-called rationalists and applied the new mathematical and mechanical principles to mind as well as matter. He thus destroyed the contradictory and confusing dualism in Cartesianism and established mechanical empiricism. He believed that all materials of positive knowledge are the direct result of the impact of bodily particles on sense organs. Whereas Descartes regarded the basic physical fact as extension, Hobbes viewed it as motion. He held that "all that exists is body (matter); all that occurs is motion."

Motion being the underlying physical fact, we should be able to build a complete and coherent philosophy on this foundation, proceeding from matter to man and from man to the state. All changes in matter are due to motion. Even consciousness is the product of motion—of the impact of particles on brain substance. The life of man and social institutions are the result of a higher complexity of motion.

Hobbes believed that there are two kinds of bodies ruled by the fundamental principle of motion: the natural bodies of the physical and organic world; and artificial bodies, or social groups, culminating in the state. Man is a representative of both. As an organism he is a natural body; as a member of the state he lives in an artificial body. Mind is the link which connects the natural and artificial bodies. Three branches of philosophy are needed to study all of these— physics which studies natural bodies; psychology which investigates man as an individual; and politics which deals with artificial bodies. By the rigorousness of his logic Hobbes succeeded in working out a purely naturalistic philosophy which had great influence.

Hobbes imposed impressive limitations on philosophical knowledge. It can never enable us to know the external world. The latter may be real, but if so we cannot detect or prove its reality. All we can know about it is the result of stimuli coming from the motions of the external world and acting upon our brain-substance. The resulting sense perceptions are all that we can be conscious of, and they reveal only our reactions to external stimuli—not the external world as it really is. This point of view was adopted by the later English empiricists.

Like Bacon and Descartes, Hobbes eliminated the supernatural from his scheme of physical analysis. Physics deals with bodies in motion. In the supernatural world there are no bodies in motion. Hence, we cannot extend physical analysis or mathematical deductions to the supernatural world. Matter and mind may be identical, but spirit stands apart from both matter and mind. It is super-material, a theory which it remained for Hume to destroy.

In Hobbes's interpretation, man is by original nature self-seeking and egoistic— driven on by self-interest and the quest of power. In a state of nature, warfare predominated. In such a state, human life was "poor, nasty, brutish, and short." In an effort to bring some sort of order out of anarchy, men contracted to live together in peace, governments were created, and the king established absolute power. Consequently, it follows that ethics and morality are creations of the state. Even religion is legitimately under the control of the state. In fact, the fundamental thing about the power of the state is its absoluteness. It is not based upon any contractual relation between the king and the people. If any agreement— social contract—exists, it was entered into by the naturally hostile groups who desired that some third power arise to keep order. The king, therefore, is not responsible to the people. He was not king when the social contract was made; hence, he was not a party to it.

Now the curious thing is that while Hobbes was consistently naturalistic in his philosophy, he did not establish his moral and social principles on the same foundations as his view of the physical world. The latter was grounded on the laws of mechanical motion. The former were based on direct psychological experience and derived from the principle of self-preservation. As a moralist and social philosopher, Hobbes thus stands as a pioneer in the great English psychological tradition of naturalism and hedonism. But no contradiction is involved in this divergence of method. While he recognized that he might have deduced his morals and sociology from physics, he could with equal precision and consistency arrive at them from psychological data. Since he wrote his discussions of man and society before he went deeply into natural philosophy, he no doubt found the psychological method more inviting. However Hobbes approached a problem, he produced a naturalistic answer which was in harmony with the new knowledge as he understood it.

Hobbes's insistence on basing social psychology and ethics on the premises of egotism and self-preservation in human conduct was one of the most realistic aspects of his philosophy. Machiavelli had assumed a similar premise in his political philosophy, and indicated that man is wont to shed more tears over the loss of a patrimony than over the death of a dear relative. But to Machiavelli this was an opinion incidental to his political speculations. Hobbes was systematic and relentless in basing his interpretation of man and society on the assumption of an all-pervading egotism and calculating self-interest. He even traced the benevolent sentiments of compassion, sympathy, and love to secondary manifestations of self-preservation and the sense of power. He believed that conduct is strictly determined and refused to turn any logical somersaults to defend freedom of the will.

We may leave it to others to decide whether Hobbes presented a more or a less valid conception of human nature than that which rests upon the exhortation to love our neighbors as ourselves and to turn the other cheek. At least, Hobbes was resolute and consistent in his ethical deductions. Hobbes's materialism was assailed by the traditionalists, especially the mystical Cambridge Platonist, Henry More (1614-1687).

VII. SPINOZA AND THE ALL-EMBRACING NATURALISTIC GOD

Another impressive attempt to work out a mechanico-naturalistic philosophy of the universe was made by the Portuguese Jew, Baruch Spinoza (1632-1677). His personal life differed markedly from the lives of the other thinkers we have been considering. His parents came to Holland as refugees from the Inquisition. He was educated to be a rabbi, but early developed heretical notions and was excommunicated in 1656. Thereafter he lived in semiseclusion, refusing such proffers of official positions as came his way, and earning his living as a lens grinder, a practical optician. His philosophical writing culminated in his *Ethics Geometrically Demonstrated,* completed in 1675, which he did not publish, but showed to intimate friends in manuscript. He died at forty-four of tuberculosis, a disposition to which he had inherited from his mother.

In Spinoza's work several strands of thought are brought together and welded into a whole, a circumstance which has led some historians of philosophy to call him "the central thinker of the seventeenth century." In particular, he showed how to combine mysticism and naturalism in an all-embracing system. Spinoza drew upon such various traditions as the scholastic philosophy of the Catholic church, Talmudic and medieval Jewish philosophy, the mysticism of Neoplatonism and the cabala, and the work of both Descartes and Hobbes. He assimilated these various elements, rather than borrowed uncritically from them. From Hobbes, for instance, he obtained psychological and political ideas, but did not adopt his system as a whole. Descartes and Hobbes had exempted the soul and God from mechanistic principles, but Spinoza included both in his naturalistic analysis of the universe. Extension and thought are but attributes of God.

Spinoza never was, nor will be, a popular philosopher. His thought is too abstruse. He is a philosopher's philosopher. Nevertheless, the general import of what he taught is not difficult to grasp. He was deeply impressed by the "universal laws" of nature and by the universality of God. His aspiration is subsumed under the desire to reduce everything to an expression of universal law. He felt that ". . . there should be one and the same method of understanding the nature of all things whatsoever, namely, through nature's universal laws and rules." [12]

Such an all-embracing vision was the highest flight of the mechanistic philosophy of the time. By including God and man within the same system, Spinoza brought the general outlook and method of the period to a climax. He drew the natural and supernatural together by repudiating the old notions of the supernatural and then deifying the natural.

It is interesting to observe what became of the God-concept under his handling. Spinoza definitely ruled out the practice of conceiving God in anthropomorphic terms, and was particularly severe on the current habit of attributing human qualities to God. Instead, Spinoza insisted that God exists distributively in all the various manifestations of mind and matter. In other words, Spinoza was a pantheist. God is regarded as the supreme and only real substance in the universe. Accordingly, God is the only object of true knowledge. The love of God, Spinoza always asserted, motivated his philosophical writings. This fact reveals the basically mystical character of his philosophy in spite of all rationalistic labels.

Since God thus exists as the all-encompassing substance, he is not a "moral" being, and to attribute moral judgments to him for ratification is nonsense. In

[12] Cited by Randall, *Making of the Modern Mind,* p. 247.

fact, attributions of worth, good, bad, order, and the like, have no cosmic reality. Similarly, Spinoza banished all teleological notions from his universe and insisted that "nature has no particular goal in view and that final causes are mere human figments." There is nothing save mathematical and mechanical necessity. Hence, it is apparent that Cardinal Spellman could obtain little legitimate satisfaction from Einstein's assurance that he found Spinoza's conception of God acceptable. To Spinoza, God is the supreme and most abstract universal.

And what of man? Man is also brought within the scope of universal laws. The essence of life is, as in Hobbes's world, self-preservation, action, and passion. Men are kept in bondage by ignorance. They strive for knowledge. Freedom is attained by disciplining the emotions (or passions) and gaining a position beyond them in a sure knowledge of good, that is, of the conditions of self-preservation. In striving for this realization of freedom man will discover other persons similarly engaged, and the sense of a common struggle will lead to coöperation. The individual thus moves upward in stages. First, he gains scientific knowledge. Second, he disciplines his emotions for the coöperative struggle for good. And third, having achieved this last position, it becomes apparent that man is simply one of the many forms in which God demonstrates his nature. A realization of this brings inner peace, which is characterized by a sense of union with the eternal and infinite being which is God.

Spinoza resorted to the same general rationalization as the Stoics did in resolving the problem of human freedom in a mechanistically determined universe. By understanding that what happens must happen, that all is a result of universal law and destiny—or of God—we are delivered from intellectual bondage. In other words, a knowledge that we are not free makes us free. As Mr. Webb puts Spinoza's position: "In proportion as a man sees in all he is and does and suffers, a consequence of the eternal and unchangeable nature of the universe, or, as Spinoza would say, of God, he is delivered from the bondage in which he remains, at the mercy of vain hopes and fears, so long as he thinks of himself as having interests and possibilities of his own apart from the whole of which he forms a part."

Spinoza's vision, then, embraced all the various experiences for which man yearns. It aimed to satisfy his desire for knowledge, for union with his fellows in the struggle for self-preservation and for union with God. It was both mechanistic and mystical; both scientific and religious. In all probability, it is one of the most ingenious philosophic systems based upon a combination of devout mysticism and scientific information that has ever sprung from the mind of man.

VIII. LEIBNITZ FORMULATES A NEW SCHOLASTICISM IN TERMS OF MATHEMATICAL PHYSICS

We have already called attention to the scientific work of Leibnitz in the seventeenth century. Leibnitz was a brilliant mathematician, physicist, geologist, philologist, historian, and editor, and the last human being to undertake the mastery of all existing knowledge. Leibnitz was an important personage in public affairs, as well as a scientist and philosopher. He undertook many diplomatic missions, was devoted to a plan for the union of western Europe, and gave much time to preparing a history of the house of Brunswick.

We pointed out that he showed a more profound grasp of the implications of the new astrophysics than Newton himself, since he definitely forecast the principle of relativity, a contribution which, in due time, will probably be regarded as far more important than his curious philosophy. But to the latter we must now turn our attention. Leibnitz, a master of ancient and medieval thought, made the most intrepid effort to restate the Augustinian philosophy in terms of mathematics and physics, thus creating a new scientific scholasticism. His philosophy found expression mainly in his *Monadology* and his *Theodicy*.

Leibnitz believed that Descartes' assertion that the ultimate reality is extension and that Hobbes's declaration that it is motion, are both inadequate and incorrect. To Leibnitz, the ultimate physical principle is force. But force must be "super-spatial and immaterial—a dynamic metaphysical substance." His elaboration of this concept formed the heart of his philosophy.

Leibnitz started with the atomism of Democritus as interpreted by the French philosopher, Pierre Gassendi (1592-1655), and the English thinker, Robert Cudworth (1617-1688). He agreed that matter consists of atoms, but he contended that these atoms are not, in the last analysis, physical at all. Beyond and beneath the divisible physical atoms are the indivisible metaphysical atoms or spiritual force-centers which Leibnitz called *monads*. Since the ultimate fact of nature is the monad, a vital spiritual entity, all nature is basically alive. Each monad is really a microcosm—a miniature reflection of the cosmos as a whole. There are three main grades or types of monads: (1) the lowest which constitute what is known as matter; (2) those which possess an animated perception and may be called animal souls; and (3) the self-conscious and rational minds of men, also known as spirits.

Any organic being is a combination or colony of monads with a central ruling and directing monad. The directing monad may be regarded as the soul of the organism and the rest of the monads as constituting the body. The monads are independent of each other but they are brought into a rational organization through a predetermined harmony arranged by the mind of God. As each group of monads is ruled by a soul-monad, so the totality of all groups of monads are ruled by God, who stands at the apex of the monadal pyramid. Hegel used to state that Leibnitz held God to be the "monad of monads" or the supreme monad, but this interpretation is inaccurate. To Leibnitz, God stood outside the whole system of monads and superimposed his mind and will upon them. To substantiate his belief in God, Leibnitz borrowed all the best scholastic proofs of the existence of God.

Leibnitz faced the same problem that confronted the Stoics in reconciling the freedom of the human personality with a doctrine of deterministic causation. Since the nature of each monad is fixed from the beginning and the course of its development is likewise predetermined, it must follow a strictly predetermined plan. How can man—an aggregate of such predetermined monads—be free?

Leibnitz gave the same answer as the Stoics and Spinoza did. Man's knowledge of his predetermined nature sets him free. He knows that his life is determined by the laws of his own nature and not by external circumstances. This was as obvious a rationalization as that of the Stoics and Spinoza.

Leibnitz's view of God and his works led him to a robust theistic optimism. God is a free and rational being. He could have created any type of world that he desired. Naturally, as God, he must have created the best of all possible worlds, a universe inhabited by free agents in which conduct is rewarded and punished according to our deserts. God is not responsible for evil; the latter is a result of human freedom. This optimism was devastatingly ridiculed by Voltaire in his novel, *Candide*.

Leibnitz, in spite of his rationalized physical philosophy, thus emerges with essentially the same results as Augustine did. The following passage from his *Monadology* will make this clear:

> It is easy to conclude that the totality of all spirits must compose the City of God, that is to say, the most perfect state that is possible, under the most perfect of monarchs. The City of God, this truly universal monarchy, is a moral world in the natural world, and is the most exalted and the most divine among the works of God; and it is in it that the glory of God really consists, for he would have no glory were not his greatness and his goodness known and admired by spirits. It is also in relation to the divine city that God specially has goodness, while his wisdom and his power are manifested everywhere.[18]

It is hardly necessary to emphasize the fact that this is Augustinianism, pure and undefiled, simply translated into seventeenth-century terms. What a fifth-century theologian had drawn from religious texts and historical excursions the most learned savant of the seventeenth century brought forth from the impressive mathematical and scientific discoveries of his century. It was veritably old wine in new bottles. Some have hailed Leibnitz as a revolutionary philosopher because he bridged the gulf between mind and matter, but if he did so he accomplished the feat wholly in the realm of his own exotic imagination. His system is chiefly interesting as illustrating the colossal rationalizations of which even a supremely well-informed mind may be capable. It also exemplified admirably the point we made in an earlier chapter concerning the survival of medieval intellectual vestiges in modern times.

Leibnitz is usually regarded as one of the leading rationalist philosophers, who, as we have seen, were really pseudo-rationalists and rationalizers. He insisted that all true and definitive knowledge consists of truths which can be rationally demonstrated and are eternally valid. They do not depend upon mathematical or physical proofs. They are capable of logical demonstration according to the elementary logical laws of identity and contradiction. Their opposites are inconceivable. Not even God could make them different from what they are. Thought is prior to experience and can make experience conform to its decisions and dictates. Yet, Leibnitz's whole system, as we have shown, was a gigantic rationalization of ancient philosophies and religious mysticism, and not in any true sense a system of rationalistic philosophy. Leibnitz's practical application of his thinking was as antirationalistic as the content of his philosophy. He was a fervent advocate of the most extreme censorship of the press and of the suppression of freethinking. He desired to muzzle the true rationalists—even so mild a group as the deistic religious thinkers.

However fanciful Leibnitz's philosophy may seem to us today it had, nevertheless, a very great influence. It was the inspiration of the philosophy of the German enlightenment, as the philosophy of Locke and his followers constituted the guiding principles of the English and French enlightenment.

IX. JOHN LOCKE MAKES EXPERIENCE THE BASIS OF REALITY

The men with whom we have just been dealing—Descartes, Hobbes, Spinoza, and Leibnitz—were all interested in erecting complete systems of philosophy by utilizing the new scientific knowledge. In the case of John Locke (1632-1704) the subjects treated were still diverse, but Locke concentrated mainly on the faculty of knowledge, or the problem of how we come to know.

Locke was the son of an attorney. He was educated at Oxford during a period of unusual toleration, but learned little to his taste or profit. On his own initiative he studied Descartes, who awakened his interest in philosophy, and Hobbes, who had a great deal to do with forming his ideas. He planned to be a clergyman, but his views were too broad to allow of that, so he studied chemistry and medicine. This brought him into contact with the scientist, Robert Boyle, and the physician, Thomas Sydenham. Locke did not find his life work in either of these pursuits, although he practiced medicine. He met the Earl of Shaftesbury and served his family as secretary, doctor, and tutor. Under Shaftesbury's patronage he held political office, and when the Whigs went into eclipse he followed them into exile in Holland. He returned to England with William and Mary in 1689, and wrote his chief political treatise as an apology for their regime.

While in exile he composed his *Essay concerning Human Understanding,* published in 1690, a work which was sufficiently vital and enduring to figure prominently in William James's *Principles of Psychology* two hundred years later. Locke began by clearing away what he regarded as antique rubbish. He asserted that philosophy should pretend to deal only with problems and conceptions that the human mind is capable of encompassing. Admitting definite limitations to the human mind, he excluded from consideration many issues which earlier philosophers and theologians had attempted to meddle with.

Locke directed heavy fire against the doctrine of innate ideas, that is, against the dogma that ideas are inherent at birth in the human mind and that they are not to be tampered with except on pain of upsetting the natural constitution of society. This doctrine had originated with Plato. In attempting to combat this notion, he used the figure of the *tabula rasa* ("blank tablet") to signify the condition of the mind at birth.

Contemporary critics and subsequent scientific investigation have destroyed the validity of this figure by demonstrating the existence of instincts and other deep-seated trends at birth. Nevertheless, they have not come to the rescue of innate ideas, a dogma that Locke utterly shattered. It should be noted, however, that few, if any, modern philosophers ever put the doctrine of innate ideas as baldly and in so extreme a fashion as Locke contended that they had. To a certain degree, he was demolishing a straw man. But his attack was justified because many reactionaries in Locke's day tried to justify their prejudices as innate ideas, in the same way that many conservatives of our day employ human nature as an argument against reform.

Locke then turned to the problem of how we come to possess the ideas with which the mature human mind is stocked. He contended that these are the product of experience and of reflection on experience—i.e., reason. He thus expressed his famous theory in the *Essay concerning Human Understanding:*

> Let us then suppose the mind to be . . . white paper, void of all characters, without any ideas; how comes it to be furnished? Whence comes it by that vast store which the busy and boundless fancy of man has painted on it with an almost endless variety? Whence has it all the materials of reason and knowledge? To this I answer, in one word, from experience; in that all our knowledge is founded, and from that it ultimately derives itself. Our observation employed either about external sensible objects, or about the internal operations of our minds, perceived and reflected on by ourselves, is that which supplies our understandings with all the materials of thinking. These two are the fountains of knowledge, from whence all the ideas we have, or can naturally have, do spring.[14]

Höffding clarifies Locke's fundamental conceptions and the dynamics of his theory of knowledge as follows:

> All ideas—by which he understands the whole content of consciousness—spring from experience, partly from outer experience (sensation), and partly from inner experience (reflection). Outer experience arises when a stimulus or motion of any part of the body excites a perception in the soul. Inner experience arises because the soul also receives the impression of the activity which (e.g., in memory and comparison) is unfolded in the elaboration of the ideas given in outer experience. By means of "reflection," then, we perceive our own states and activities, and by means of "sensation" the effects of other things. In all such immediate conception or perception of other things, consciousness is, for the most part, entirely passive. Still, it is only the simplest ideas which arise by means of such immediate and passive perception.[15]

By the rational elaboration of simple ideas we arrive at complex ideas. The processes involved are the uniting of simple ideas, synthesizing activity, and abstracting activity. Simple ideas are valid when they agree with observed reality. Complex ideas, naturally, cannot resemble things, but they correspond to things. By employing derived ideas in thinking we can reflectively test the validity of our concepts and discover whether the combination of qualities implied is to be found in experience.

[14] Book II, chap. i, ¶ 2.
[15] Höffding, *History of Modern Philosophy,* I, 383.

While Locke believed that there were two major types of experience, sensations or direct impressions, and reflections of the mind "on its own operations within itself," he seemed to be more interested in the second. This led him away from his more direct and mechanistic conceptions and into labyrinths of generalized reasoning and reflective analysis. Later empiricists found it necessary to criticize Locke drastically on this point.

Some commentators have pictured Locke as rather more modern in his thinking than he actually was. They have imagined him as a definite forerunner of Charles Peirce, William James, John Dewey and the pragmatic philosophy which these writers represent. According to pragmatism, those things are true and useful which prove such in actual experience. Locke had no idea of testing reality and truth in such a fashion. To him, the test of truth is the possibility of logical deduction from first principles. The idea of testing truth by conformity to experience was a post-Kantian development.

Locke believed that man is free in the matter of developing his ideas, but is conditioned or circumscribed by a dualistic world. As Cushman expresses it: "He belongs to the world of an unexplained spiritual substance on the one hand, and he is surrounded by a world of an unknown material substance on the other." [16] It remained for Berkeley and Hume to clear away this dualistic world. Berkeley destroyed the concept of material substance, and Hume that of spiritual substance.

In his ethical doctrines Locke also exhibited elements of both the old and the new order. He believed that human happiness rather than the salvation of the soul must be regarded as the supreme good, but he sought the origins and nature of moral law in the will and law of God. In political theory, Locke was easily the leader of the new liberalism that justified revolution against tyranny on the basis of the social contract doctrine.

Among the numerous and important personalities who created the enlightenment of the eighteenth century, John Locke was rivaled only by Bayle and surpassed only by Voltaire. He was the most popular philosopher of his generation and, hence, the most influential. He created a new and progressive type of psychology, led the fight against intolerance, defended reason against faith in a period when this was more dangerous than a century later, started the revolt in education against pedantry and classicism, and was the most important figure of the age in systematizing the type of political and legal theory that dominated the enlightenment. If he did not go so far as Voltaire, the path of the latter was made easier because of Locke's work. If his manner was timid and his style heavy when compared to Bayle, his thought was more profound and his influence greater.

X. HUME ENTHRONES SKEPTICISM

The increasing subtlety of the English philosophers in dealing with the psychological bases of knowledge is excellently illustrated in David Hume (1711-1776). His earliest ambitions were literary, and his dearest wish was to live in retirement and devote himself to intellectual pursuits. His first literary efforts

16 H. E. Cushman, *A Beginner's History of Philosophy*, 2 vols., Houghton Mifflin, 1918-1920, II, 170.

failed to arouse popular interest, and therefore he abandoned what has subsequently been regarded as his greatest work, a *Treatise of Human Nature* (1739-1740). In later days he hesitated to acknowledge that he had written it, chiefly to avoid controversies with ecclesiastical pundits. He turned instead to the reformulation of his ideas in more popular and condensed form and won for himself an audience which was increased by his *History of England* and his discussions of religion. Hume's later philosophical treatises, the *Enquiry concerning Human Understanding* and the *Enquiry concerning Principles of Morals,* were merely elaborations of his first great and more truly original work. Most of Hume's life was spent in public service of one sort or another, such as secretary to the ambassador to France, librarian, and under-secretary of state for Scotland. From his last position he retired to die of a lingering illness. Hume was remarkable for his mild temperament and for the acuteness of his reasoning in fields rarely before exploited.

In philosophy Hume is famous for his relentless skepticism, naturalism and determinism, in the development of which he annihilated prevailing conceptions of matter and causation. He carried the suggestions of Hobbes and Locke to their logical extreme, thus creating a truly naturalistic empiricism and a complete skepticism.

We have seen that Locke believed that man and his ideas are encompassed on one side by spiritual substance and on the other by material substance. The obliteration of the reality of physical substance was the work of Bishop George Berkeley (1685-1753), who accepted Locke's idea that all human knowledge is derived from sense impressions. As an inveterate idealist, Berkeley was determined to get rid of the concept of material substance—physical matter. His attack was twofold: psychological and logical. Psychologically speaking, Berkeley believed that we learn only through experience, but experience comes to us through sense impressions or sensations. Therefore, all we can know are sensations, and matter is thus reduced to a complex of sensations. If the problem is approached logically, matter is just as easily disposed of, thought Berkeley. His theory of psychology indicated that abstract ideas have no reality. The idea of matter—material substance—is an abstract idea and, hence, it has no real existence. But Berkeley clung doggedly to the notion of the reality of spiritual substance, which, culminating in God, he believed to be responsible for all our ideas. The latter cannot be caused by the impact of matter on the senses, since matter does not exist. This skeptical idealism Berkeley expressed in his *Theory of Vision* and his *Principles of Human Knowledge.*

Hume carried this skeptical analysis farther and did not spare even Berkeley's sanctified ideas or spiritual substance. He had the most penetrating mind of any philosopher of the period of enlightenment. He blasted away the pseudo-rationalism of Descartes and his followers. Hume contended that the only realities are ideas, and then proceeded to call upon his psychological theories to show that all ideas are derived from sense impressions. There is no more place for spiritual substance in Hume's system than for material substance. Both are wiped out.

For the dynamic impulse of spiritual substance, which Berkeley invoked, Hume substituted the theory that our whole mental life is no more than an association of ideas, a matter which we discussed when treating Hume's psychology in the previous chapter. Therefore, Hume concluded that the only discernible reality is the complex of impressions—the bundle of perceptions—which we can detect through our senses by the process of association.

Hume is famous in philosophy for his searching treatment of the problem of causation. He was the first important philosopher since Aristotle to handle the subject profoundly. And he pretty well disposed of the Aristotelian and all other traditional theories of causation.

Hume's attitude towards causation differed according to whether he was using the term as a common-sense scientist and critic of religion or whether he was searchingly examining the concept as a metaphysician. As a scientist and critic, Hume did not question the validity of a notion of causation founded on observation. He constantly used the concept of causation—cause and effect—in criticizing miracles and other theological concepts.

What Hume objected to was the conventional doctrine which implied that "a necessary connection" or logical necessity must be an integral part of any sound theory of causation. Further, the traditionalists held that there must be a cause for whatever is observed, even though that cause is unobservable—thus making inferences beyond the scope of observation. Hume attacked these older views of causation with great gusto and devastating results.

Hume derived his workable or common-sense theory of causation from his psychological doctrines. One of the modes of the association of ideas is the law of contiguity in time and space. When we see things happen in what appears to be a temporal and logical sequence, we associate them as a cause and effect.[17] We take it for granted that what follows is a result of what has preceded. Hence the whole concept of causation is merely a mental picture—a form of association of ideas—arising out of "the constant conjunction of impressions." The belief is engendered that what has been observed as joined together in an apparently causal sequence will always be thus constantly conjoined. This is all there is to the notion of causal relationships and cause and effect phenomena, so far as the human mind can resolve the problem.

Such a conclusion was quite different from the conventional dogma that "there is in nature and history a causal law so binding that every event is a necessary result of what has gone before and a necessary cause of what will come." It was Hume's critical analysis of causation which inspired Immanuel Kant to elaborate his monumental system of skeptical philosophy. We shall treat Hume's important contributions to ethical and religious problems in another chapter.

[17] In the previous century an English freethinker, Joseph Glanvill (1636-1680), had warned against identifying a sequence with a causal relationship.

XI. MAIN TRENDS IN EDUCATION

Our last discussion of education left that subject as it existed in the sixteenth and early seventeenth centuries under the full impact of humanistic ideals. We noted that the universities, for the most part, held firm to the scholastic program of education in Catholic countries, though even here some concessions were made to the classics. In the Protestant universities, the classics made greater headway and in due time all but conquered the curriculum. In the secondary schools, especially in the Protestant schools, the classics completely dominated. The older emphasis on the humanizing value of the classics was abandoned in favor of the barren study of language and grammar and the utilization of the classics as a means of promoting mental discipline. In the Jesuit schools a balance was struck between the classical pedantry and the humanizing perspective of Vittorino da Feltre and the schools maintained by the Brethren of the Common Life.

The classical obsession in the schools was accompanied by an appropriate system of intellectual and physical discipline. The revival of the classics did not actually bring with it any of the naturalness and sophistication that had characterized Hellenic education. Rather, Greek and Latin became mainly a severe mental discipline linked up with stern Christian tenets. Nothing in human experience has been less in accord with the spirit of Hellenism than the study of the classics in western European and American education. The classics themselves were looked upon more as a means of imposing punitive mental discipline than as an avenue to the true appreciation of a pagan civilization. In spite of their pagan origins, the classics in European education were inculcated in a strongly Christian atmosphere which rejected the whole pagan theory of life.

Accompanying this went the general acceptance of the doctrine that rigorous physical punishment is essential to strengthen the will and toughen the pupil against fear. Professor Preserved Smith recounts the instance of a Württemberg schoolmaster who estimated that in fifty years of teaching he had given 911,527 strokes with a stick, 124,000 lashes with a whip, 136,715 slaps with the hand, and 1,115,800 boxes on the ear. There was a feeling that a carefree and joyous attitude on the part of the pupil was akin to sin. Nothing that a student really enjoyed could be a legitimate or useful element of instruction.

During the seventeenth and eighteenth centuries education and pedagogy, in one way or another, felt the impact of the leading intellectual and institutional developments of the age—the Protestant revolt, nationalism, the progress of natural science, rationalism, and romanticism.

The Protestant revolution led the Protestants to recommend that the state control education as well as religion, while the Counter-Reformation Catholics renewed their conviction that the church should dominate education. In addition to the Jesuits, new Catholic teaching orders, notably the Christian Brothers, sprang up. Nationalism gave added force to the Protestant support of public education. Though free public education of a compulsory sort did not appear on any considerable scale until the nineteenth century, the eighteenth century was the era in which western European society very widely accommodated itself to the idea that the state should assume extensive responsibility for education.

Rationalism endeavored to free education from clerical influence and to end the fears arising from religious superstitions. It aimed to produce a sophisticated and urbane outlook on life. The study of manners and customs among native peoples overseas led to a eulogy of the noble savage, tended to raise doubts about the harsh disciplinary methods then in vogue in European schools, and aroused enthusiasm for naturalness and spontaneity in pedagogy. This emphasis on cultivating the innate qualities of the individual and allowing full and free expression to the human personality was further stimulated by Rousseau and romanticism, though in the latter case it was often somewhat modified and restrained by pietistic strains and religious qualms.

We may now examine a little more in detail some of the main phases of the revolt against the obsession with scholasticism and the classics in the universities and with the classics and punitive discipline in the schools; the revolt, too, against the idea that education should remain the privilege of the favored few.

The Protestant revolt brought a number of new notions into the European educational tradition. It encouraged the education of the masses, stressed the importance of elementary education, and upheld the notion that the state should assume responsibility for popular education. These Protestant notions had more influence upon Germanic states than they had in England at the time. In the latter country, the chief educational progress came in the nonconformist schools of the seventeenth century. While they were mainly devoted to training preachers, they rebelled against the classical mania in the respectable Anglican schools and gave much more attention to mathematics, natural science, and the vernacular language and literature.

Even in the Catholic schools there were progressive trends, especially associated with the establishment of the Christian Brothers' schools by Jean Baptiste de la Salle (1651-1719). He created a more flexible system of instruction than that of the Jesuits, greatly improved teaching methods, trained efficient teachers for the elementary schools, gave more attention to history and the sciences, and even made provision for manual training. The movement did much to give a realistic cast to elementary education in Catholic schools.

Another impetus to the study of science and the modern languages came from the *Ritterakademien* (schools for young nobles) which sprang up in Germany in the seventeenth century. While they did not reach the masses, they did help to make more realistic and practical education respectable in the European educational tradition.

The philosopher Montaigne had characteristically novel and sensible views on education. Though he was himself steeped in the classics, this fact did not blind him to the need for wider training. While he believed that a mastery of the classics is desirable for the cultivated gentleman, he held that the first necessity is to study the languages of one's own country and the languages of neighboring states. He also stressed the importance of physical education. In harmony with his urbanity and tolerance, he emphasized the great educational value of travel.

The chief educational theorist of the seventeenth century was a Moravian schoolmaster, John Amos Comenius (1592-1670), author of *The Great Didactic* (1657). He proclaimed that the increase of "knowledge, morality and piety" should be the aim of education. He fought against the dominion of both the medieval arts curriculum and the classical monopoly established by humanism, and he also opposed the harsh disciplinary system of the schools of the era. He enthusiastically urged universal education for both boys and girls. He recommended more practical and realistic subject matter, arranged according to types and to stages in mental growth, and the adaptation of instruction to the age of pupils. He anticipated Rousseau in his emphasis upon the value of following the easy and gradual method of nature in developing the mind of children and in inculcating information.

Comenius was so far in advance of his age that he had more influence upon nineteenth-century education than he did on the educational theories and practices of the seventeenth century. Some of his notions were, however, put into application by August Hermann Francke (1663-1727) of Halle, foremost educator among the German pietists. While chiefly interested in religious education, Francke did a good deal to stress education for the poorer masses, to improve elementary instruction, and to give much more attention than usual to the sciences and to the vernacular languages and literatures. The methods and ideals of Francke were transferred to Berlin in 1747 by Johann Hecker, who opened his *Realschule* there in 1747. He proposed to prepare children for actual life, and to teach them relevant subject matter from realistic models or directly from nature. His method gave added impetus to the revolt against sterile classicism in the elementary and secondary schools.

With the coming of rationalism and the period of the enlightenment there was a marked revolt against religious severity and disciplinary rigor. Rationalism manifested a desire to wipe out the fears and worries that earlier religious superstitions had instilled into the minds of pupils. Tolerance, urbanity, and serenity were the great intellectual virtues that rationalism wished to inculcate. The sophisticated gentleman was its most cherished product. An admirable example of this rationalistic ideal appeared in the code of conduct drawn up by Lord Chesterfield for his son.

The chief educational theorist of rationalism was John Locke, who applied his empirical psychology and philosophy to educational doctrine. Holding that our minds are a blank at birth and that our knowledge and behavior are a result of experience, he logically argued that every opportunity should be given for such experiences as would produce the ideal personality and provide the most useful body of information. Much stress was laid on a rational guidance and on discipline in training. But Locke was frank enough to admit that his theory was applicable only to the children of the well-to-do. He suggested manual training for the children of the poor. Generally similar views were held by the German philosopher Leibnitz, who laid special stress upon practical subjects, especially natural science. This emphasis on natural science was later warmly seconded by Diderot.

Voltaire's contribution to education, like his contribution to European thought in general, was chiefly critical. He assailed the servile pedantry of the classical schools and the inculcation of religious superstitions in the Catholic schools and in the pietistic Protestant institutions. He advocated the cultivation of reason, the achievement of mental emancipation, and liberal instruction in natural science. But his educational theory had the same aristocratic cast that had characterized Locke's doctrines. He had little hope of elevating the masses through education and intellectual emancipation.

The democratization of rationalist educational theory was the contribution of Helvétius and of Rousseau. Helvétius rejected the snobbish views of Locke and Voltaire with respect to the alleged mental inferiority of the masses. He believed that they were just as capable mentally as the upper classes. They simply lacked opportunity. He believed that apparent differences in ability were mainly due to differences in opportunity. Education would remove these handicaps and elevate all groups in the population. He expressed this idea in the following words:

> This fact being well weighed, who can be certain that a difference in educa-
> tion does not produce the difference observable in minds? Who can assert, that
> men are not like those trees of the same species, whose seed, being absolutely
> the same, but never sown exactly in the same earth, nor exposed entirely to the
> same winds, the same sun, or the same rain, must in unfolding themselves nec-
> essarily produce an infinity of different forms? I may then conclude, that the in-
> equality observable in the minds of men may be indifferently considered, either
> as the effect of nature or of education. . . .[18]

Helvétius, accordingly, was a strong supporter of the campaign for educational opportunities for all classes, thus anticipating the ideals of Horace Mann.

Even more revolutionary were the educational ideas of Jean Jacques Rousseau, set forth in his famous *Émile* (1762). In this he argued for giving greater play to naturalness in education and for democratizing the educational process by opening its opportunities to all—at least to all boys. The learning process was to be chiefly that of a rational direction of natural curiosity. By the "natural" Rousseau did not mean the qualities of savage man so much as the inherent traits of the human personality. He bespoke an adjustment of educational practice to the actual character of human beings.

Rousseau did, however, overwork his valid criticism of the old educational order. He minimized the value of utilizing the accumulated wisdom of the ages and the more useful techniques for inculcating information. Much time would be wasted if we depended as fully upon spontaneous forms of self-expression as he recommended. Rousseau's emphasis on the social elements in education made him the father of the sociological movement in education.

The pedagogical revolution launched by Rousseau was developed by Johann Bernard Basedow (1723-1790). Basedow was converted from the views of a conventional pedagogue by his reading of *Émile*. He devoted the rest of his life to promoting a modified version of Rousseau's educational and psychological ideals.

[18] Teggart, *The Idea of Progress*, p. 135.

He set down Rousseau's ideas in formal manuals on educational theory and wrote textbooks for children embodying these notions. A model school, called the "Philanthropium," was established under his influence. This gave prestige to the new methods and trained many teachers to put it into application. More than anybody else of his time, Basedow popularized Rousseau's ideas in German education.

An interesting anticipation of modern genetic psychology, associated especially with the work of G. Stanley Hall in our own day, is to be observed in the voluminous *Course of Studies* by the freethinker, Étienne de Condillac. Condillac held that in his educational experience the child should recapitulate the cultural evolution of the race, and in the same order of development—that is, he should proceed from myth to natural science.

The education of women was defended by Fénelon in a treatise on this subject (1687), but he was no seventeenth-century feminist. Women were to be educated solely for family responsibilities and housekeeping.

Condorcet (1743-1794) was more advanced in his views on the education of women. He was fully convinced of the equality of the sexes and of the necessity of equal educational opportunities for women. He wrote that "one cannot see why one of the sexes reserves for itself certain subjects of knowledge, why matters that are generally useful to both sexes should not be taught equally to both sexes." Even if "woman's place is in the home," Condorcet maintained that no woman could make a good wife for an educated man unless she was equally well educated. Nor is an ignorant woman fit to bring up children. As to educational procedure, Condorcet warmly recommended coeducation as the natural and sensible method, valuable for moral as well as formal education.

Romanticism brought with it an even more decided revolt against the older order of artificial disciplinary repression than rationalism had incited. Viewing, as it did, the feelings and emotions as the most important item in the human make-up, romanticism naturally rebelled against compressing them within the strait jacket of conventional school discipline. It recommended an adaptation of the curriculum and discipline to our instincts and to the spontaneous expression of the individual human personality. It labored heartily to set up the freedom of the human spirit as a pedagogical ideal and practice. It was especially hospitable to the educational theories of Rousseau and his pedagogical disciples.

In spite of all this talk and writing about education for the masses, there were few regular schools set up to offer free education for the children of the poor. For the most part, the latter had to rely upon fragmentary instruction in charitable and religious schools. They fared a little better in Germany than elsewhere, but even in Germany free public instruction was, in the main, an achievement of the nineteenth century. The charity schools and Sunday-school movement were characteristically an English development. The Society for the Promotion of Christian Knowledge was founded by the Rev. Thomas Bray in 1698 and, under Anglican auspices, it gave a great impetus to charitable instruction among the poor. Its influence was extended to the colonies in America, though the dissenters often opposed it because of its Anglican bias. The Sunday-school movement was set up in England in the latter part of the eighteenth century, and was especially supported by Wesley and the Methodists. It was at first designed to provide secular as well as religious instruction. As public education developed in the nineteenth century, the Sunday schools tended to give up their work in secular education and to restrict their instruction to religious matters.

There is less progress to report in the universities. The religious wars of the sixteenth and seventeenth centuries were for the time being a blight on higher education and helped to perpetuate intellectual stagnation in the universities. A number of important new universities were, however, established, such as Louvain in Belgium, Leyden in Holland, and Leipzig, Halle, and Göttingen in Germany. The Catholic universities remained loyal to the scholastic curriculum, though they made a place for the classics. In the Protestant universities the classics held sway, though in the German universities we may observe some beginnings in scientific instruction. As in the previous period, the main attention given to science in the universities was bestowed on medicine. Here Leyden, the Italian universities, and Vienna took the lead.

While the university curriculum before 1800 remained in most places incredibly archaic and sterile, there were evidences of discontent and certain harbingers of progress. The English philosopher, Joseph Glanvill, shortly after the middle of the seventeenth century, assailed the classical education in the English universities and proclaimed it to be all but worthless. Even more notable was the revolt against pedantry, humanism, and irrelevance led by Christian Thomasius (1655-1728), a professor at Leipzig. He had the audacity to lecture in German [19] and to treat of manners, customs, and other problems of daily life. For this breach of good taste and "sound" pedagogical principles, he was expelled from Leipzig but found a position at Halle. There was little progress in university instruction outside Germany during this period, though a few slight rumblings against pedantry and sterility were to be detected in the English universities as a result of the influence of the German Hanoverian dynasty, which came to England with George I. It hardly needs to be pointed out that the social sciences were accorded no place in university instruction, save as they might be involved in the formal instruction given in moral and political philosophy. Technical schools first put in their appearance in the eighteenth century. The first was the School of Mines at Brunswick, Germany, opened in 1745, and the second the Freiberg School of Mines, opened in 1765.

In short, one may say that in the seventeenth and eighteenth centuries the basis was laid for a great educational revolution in the nineteenth century, but much less was achieved in practice than in theory. The elementary and secondary instruction, in which notable progress was made, was limited mainly to the children of the well-to-do, and in the universities very little relative advance was made either in subject matter or instruction. In the nineteenth century, free public instruction was realized in all civilized countries, and the natural and social sciences were installed in leading universities.

[19] Classical Latin was everywhere the respectable language of university instruction.

SELECTED READINGS

Aaron, R. I., *John Locke,* Oxford University Press, 1955.

Anderson, F. H., *Francis Bacon,* University Publishers, 1962.

Boronowski, J., and Mazlish, Bruce, *The Western Intellectual Tradition from Leonardo to Hegel,* Harper, 1960.

Boulting, William, *Giordano Bruno,* Dutton, 1917.

Bowen, C. D., *Francis Bacon,* Little, Brown, 1963.

Brett, *History of Psychology,* Vol. II.

Browne, Lewis, *Blessed Spinoza,* Macmillan, 1932.

Bryson, Gladys, *Man and Society,* Princeton University Press, 1945.

Burnham, W. H., *The Great Teachers and Mental Health,* chaps. vii-viii.

Catlin, G. E. G., *Thomas Hobbes,* Blackwell, 1922.

Compayré, Gabriel, *Montaigne,* Crowell, 1908.

Davidson, T., *Giordano Bruno and Free Thought.*

Dowden, E., *Michel de Montaigne,* Lippincott, 1905.

Eby, Frederick, and Arrowood, C. F., *The Development of Modern Education,* Prentice-Hall, 1952, chaps. ii-xiv.

Farrington, Benjamin, *Francis Bacon: Philosopher of Industrial Science,* Collier.

Gibson, James, *Locke's Theory of Knowledge,* Cambridge University Press, 1931.

Gooch, G. P., *Political Thought in England From Bacon to Halifax,* Oxford, 1946.

Hazard, Paul, *The European Mind: The Critical Years (1680-1715),* Yale Press, 1953.

———— *European Thought in the Eighteenth Century,* Yale University Press, 1954.

Hendel, C. W., *Studies in the Philosophy of David Hume,* Bobbs-Merrill, 1962.

Höffding, Harald, *The History of Modern Philosophy,* 2 vols., Dover, 1955, Vol. I.

Jones, M. G., *The Charity School Movement,* Macmillan, 1938.

Keeling, S. V., *Descartes,* Smith, 1934.

Laing, B. M., *David Hume,* Smith, 1932.

Lowndes, M. E., *Michel de Montaigne,* Cambridge University Press, 1898.

Monroe, Paul, *A Textbook in the History of Education,* Macmillan, 1912, chaps. vii-x.

Morris, C. R., *Locke, Berkeley and Hume,* Oxford University Press, 1931.

Pollock, Frederick, *Spinoza, His Life and Philosophy,* Duckworth, 1935.

Randall, J. H., Jr., *The Making of the Modern Mind,* chaps. xi-xii.

———— *The Career of Philosophy from the Middle Ages to the Enlightenment,* Columbia University Press, 1962.

Ratner, J., *Spinoza on God,* Holt, 1930.

Riley, *From Myth to Reason,* Books III-IV.

Rogers, A. K., *A Student's History of Philosophy,* Macmillan, 1932, pp. 208-361.

Savelle, Max, *The Genesis of the American Mind,* Knopf, 1948.

Shearer, E. A., *Hume's Place in Ethics,* Bryn Mawr Press, 1915.

Sichel, E. H., *Michel de Montaigne,* Dutton, 1911.

Smith, Preserved, *History of Modern Culture,* Vol. I, chap. vii; Vol. II, chap. v.

Stephen, Leslie, *Hobbes,* Ann Arbor, 1961.

Taylor, A. E., *David Hume and the Miraculous,* Macmillan, 1907.

Vartanian, Aram, *Diderot and Descartes,* Princeton University Press, 1953.

Williams, Charles, *Bacon,* Harper, 1934.

Willis, I. C., *Montaigne,* Knopf, 1927.

Wilson, A. M., *Diderot: The Testing Years,* Oxford University Press, 1957.

XVIII

The Growth of Tolerance
and Freedom of Thought

I. SOME MAJOR CAUSES OF INTOLERANCE

The human race has been extremely intolerant of dissent and novelty. Countless thousands, since the dawn of history, have come to an untimely end or have endured excruciating tortures because they have dared to think or act in opposition to the majority. A heavy penalty has been placed upon nonconformity. The way of the doubter and the heretic has been far harder than that of the proverbial transgressor.

Among the chief causes of intolerance are fear and laziness. Primitive man believes that all his institutions and social habits are revealed and established by the gods. There is a deep-seated fear of any departure from routine habits and any deviation by an individual from the safe customary ways of life is highly dangerous, for it will arouse the anger of the spiritual powers and bring disaster to the group. Consequently, taboos are set up specifying what cannot be done if group customs and divine pleasure are to be maintained unimpaired. Fierce punishment is visited upon him who dares to violate a taboo and who thereby places in jeopardy the safety and prosperity of the group. The whole primitive scheme of life depends upon a strict observance of wont and custom. While this fear of innovation and change is far greater in primitive society, much of it has been perpetuated in modern society. As causes of intolerance, Hendrik Van Loon rightly concedes a large rôle to primitive ignorance and imagined self-interest, traits which are often the underlying causes of the fear complex.

The dominating factor in the genesis and enforcement of conformity is the so-called instinct of the herd. Man is relatively helpless by himself. Group life and coöperative endeavor have always been essential to human safety and progress. For this reason group discipline must be enforced in order to unify the com-

munity and make it more efficient. Rules of conduct and thought must be prescribed and their violator made to suffer. However, group discipline, so essential
to human survival, has exacted a high price in the way of ruthlessly stamping
out the innovator and the rebel. The history of civilization is, in a sense, a record of the extension of the area or degree of dissent that society will tolerate.
John H. Dietrich thus describes the eternal association of the fear-ridden herd
instinct and intolerance:

> After all, intolerance is merely the manifestation of the protective instinct of
> the herd. The life of the individuals is so dependent upon the life of the group,
> that the group, and the various individuals in the group, are afraid to let any
> individual say or do anything that might endanger the protective power of the
> group.
>
> Thus a pack of wolves is intolerant of the wolf that is different and invariably
> gets rid of this offending individual. A tribe of cannibals is intolerant of the in-
> dividual who threatens to provoke the wrath of the gods and bring disaster upon
> the whole community, and so drives him into the wilderness. The Greek com-
> monwealth cannot afford to harbor within its sacred walls one who dares to
> question the very basis of its organization, and so in an outburst of intolerance
> condemns the offender to drink the poison. The Roman cannot hope to survive
> if a small group of zealots play fast and loose with laws held indispensable since
> the days of Romulus, and so is driven into deeds of intolerance. The Church de-
> pended in early days for her continued existence upon the absolute obedience of
> even the humblest of her subjects and is driven to such extremes of suppression
> and cruelty that many prefer the ruthlessness of the Turk to the charity of the
> Christian. And in a period of hysterical fear, even we Americans are assured that
> our government cannot withstand criticism, and so we throw into prison or de-
> port from our shores those who dare offer it.
>
> And so it goes throughout the ages until life, which might be a glorious ad-
> venture, is turned into a horrible experience, and all this happens because human
> existence so far has been entirely dominated by fear.[1]

Laziness is another cause of intolerance. The habitual and the traditional are
not only safe, they are also easy. Our muscular reflexes and our mental patterns
are adapted to doing things in the way we have been taught to do them. It is
easiest to think and act in the old grooves to which we have become accustomed
since childhood. Habit, as William James pointed out, is the great flywheel of
society. We need to give but little conscious attention to habitual modes of
thought and behavior. Years of adjustment have made them seem natural to us
and have made us largely unconscious of their operation. New ways and thoughts,
on the other hand, are troublesome and painful. This pain is not only psychological, it is mildly physiological, as the new science of endocrinology has made
clear.[2] Any innovation upsets our whole established scheme of things, cuts across
our habitual reactions, and forces readjustments that our timid and lazy nature
resents and resists.

[1] J. H. Dietrich, *The Road to Tolerance,* privately published, Minneapolis, 1929.
[2] Particularly in the study of the psychology of the emotions. Cf. W. B. Cannon, "What Strong
Emotions Do to Us," *Harper's Magazine,* July, 1922.

Fear and laziness, then, beget intolerance of change and novelty and lead us to hate the innovator. Fear doubtless produces a far more vigorous expression of intolerance than does laziness, but the latter adds its quota to the total social resentment against the person who suggests a new way of regarding morals, religion, politics, economics, law, education, and art.

Conscious self-interest, as well as fear and laziness, creates and guides intolerance. A class, group, or organization may endeavor to stamp out movements or individuals that threaten rivalry or more serious dangers. The feudal lords were intolerant of the rising merchant class. The new middle class, or bourgeoisie, became intolerant of the workers, and the conservative proletariat became, in turn, intolerant of radical workers. The Catholic church was intolerant of Lutherans and of Calvinists who threatened the integrity of the church, and, in turn, these original Protestant sects became intolerant of new ones which were formed. Catholics and Protestants, alike, tend to be intolerant of freethinkers and atheists. Plutocratic employers are intolerant of conservative unions, who are intolerant of socialists, who are intolerant of communists.

II. THE INTOLERANCE OF THE CATHOLIC CHURCH

We have already referred to the sharp intolerance of primitive society and to the even more thoroughly organized repression of innovation in the military-religious culture of the ancient Orient. In classical society a considerable freedom of opinion and action existed for the educated and favored classes. With the rise of Christianity something approaching the intolerance of Oriental antiquity once more reappeared. Christianity added a new source of fear and intolerance. Before this time, there had been little concern with the future life. The violator of a taboo might bring temporal disaster to his social group, but he was not so often regarded as placing immortal souls in jeopardy. With the Christians the future life came to be all-important. Earthly disaster was of slight significance compared to eternal damnation. For two reasons, therefore, Christian opinion during the Middle Ages was resentful of innovation. It might bring immediate earthly disaster and it might also cause the immeasurable tragedy of damnation in the life to come.

The intolerance of the medieval Catholic church rested on two grounds, political and religious.[3] The church, in an administrative sense, was modeled after the Roman imperial system. It was veritably a new and greater Rome. It became the most impressive international state the world had ever known, or was to know down to the British Empire of the nineteenth century. Any challenge to its authority in the form of heresy was thus not only a doctrinal menace but politico-ecclesiastical treason. This, more than any sympathy for the damned, was the basic cause of the ferocious treatment of medieval heretics.

On the religious side, of course, there was ample reason for the church to be

---

[3] See J. H. Robinson, *Introduction to the History of Western Europe*, rev. ed., 2 vols., Ginn, 1924, I, 243-47, and *Mind in the Making*, Harper, 1921, pp. 132 ff. A good summary of up-to-date opinion, correcting Lecky's views on heresy, intolerance and persecution, is that by E. W. Nelson, in *Persecution and Liberty*, Century, 1931, pp. 3-20.

impatient with those who departed from the letter of Christian doctrine. Salvation was the reward only for those who followed the literal teachings of the church. The heretic was doomed to damnation and the more he persisted in his false teachings, the greater his punishment in hell. Moreover, the longer he was permitted to teach and convert, the more souls he dragged to hell after him. Hence, there was every logical reason why the church should stamp out heretics expeditiously and savagely.

The attitude of the Catholic church towards those who held views at variance with Catholic doctrine has differed according to the epoch and to the class of the persons involved. Down to the Counter Reformation, when the repressive activities of the church were revived and extended, there was by no means such ferocity towards heterodox opinions as certain Protestant and skeptical historians have asserted. Abelard's persecution was as much a result of his own irascible nature and the savage personal hatred of Bernard as it was of the church's general policy. The mistreatment of Roger Bacon by the church now appears to have been exaggerated in many older historical accounts. While by no means encouraging intellectual independence, the church was prone to overlook heterodox views expressed within the cloistered walls of colleges and universities.[4]

With heretics—people who attempted to start a popular doctrinal rebellion—the reaction of the church was quite different. It moved swiftly and forcibly against all heretics. Even repentant heretics were frequently put to death. The crusades were in a way a manifestation, on a vast scale, of Christian intolerance, but the most notorious example of medieval Christian intolerance was, perhaps, the brutal extermination of the admirable Albigensian cult and Provençal culture in the thirteenth century. In Spain especially, the Jews and the Moors were treated with great brutality, and many thousands put to death after the most barbarous tortures. With the establishment of Protestantism a new enemy arose for the church to cope with, and many Catholic countries lost no time in repressing the Protestants with extreme cruelty. The most striking examples were the Catholic retaliations in the Thirty Years' War, the massacre of St. Bartholomew's Day in France in 1572, and the slaughter which followed the revocation of the Edict of Nantes in 1685.

The chief Catholic instrument for enforcing intolerance was the Inquisition —an agency for the investigation and punishment of heresy and infidelity. While active in the later Middle Ages, it became especially energetic after the Counter Reformation. The most savage and notorious of these inquisitorial bodies was the Spanish Inquisition. Founded in the latter part of the fifteenth century to curb Jews and Moors, it was subsequently used with terrifying force against Christian heretics, real and suspect. The church did not execute its victims. It sentenced them, tortured them, and turned them over to the state for killing. These butcheries (autos-da-fé), carried on in the name of the Lord, were often made festive days for the countryfolk and city dwellers.

---

[4] For notable exceptions, see G. G. Coulton, in Hammerton, *Universal History of the World,* V, 3016-18.

The disastrous intellectual effects of the Inquisition have been well stated by Professor George Gordon Coulton in his little work on *The Inquisitor:*

> The Inquisition must be held responsible not only for the lives that it took, but for the processes which it arrested. The barrenness of medieval thought in certain important directions cannot easily be accounted for on any other theory. We must not merely count the number of saints the Inquisition burned. . . . The million little tyrannies which a Reign of Terror exercises over a million little people weigh more heavily, when the ledger of history is accurately balanced, than one startling injustice done to one extraordinary person.

We may now examine a little more in detail the practice of intolerance by the Catholic church in modern times, especially following the Protestant revolt. The latter, quite naturally, stimulated the Catholic church to unprecedented vigor in its intolerance and repression. Never before had there been such a threat to the power and integrity of the church. Hitherto the church had dealt only with scattered and helpless individual traitors (heretics) or with inoffensive and unaggressive heretical groups like the Albigenses, Waldenses, and Lollards. Now it was forced to cope with a movement which was militant and defiant, which challenged many of the most crucial dogmas and practices of the Catholic church, and which was backed by some of the strongest monarchs in Europe. It was inevitable that Catholicism should combat Protestantism with zeal and ferocity.

A systematic defense of the theory and ethics of persecution was elucidated by the eminent ecclesiastical lawyer and political philosopher, Cardinal Robert Bellarmine (1542-1621), who proved by both sacred and secular law that the church had not only the right but the duty to persecute and slay heretics. It was even good for the heretics themselves, since the longer they lived in heresy the worse would be their later punishment in hell.

The Society of Jesus (Jesuits), founded by Ignatius Loyola (1491-1556) during the Catholic Counter Reformation, was the most militant of the Catholic forces directed against Protestantism and heresy. It provided the shock troops in the Catholic war against Protestantism, new heresies, and new scientific and philosophical conceptions. But the Inquisition still remained chiefly in the hands of the Dominicans.

Machinery for swift extinction of heretics was immediately reinforced by the Catholic church to contend with the new and alarming menace of Protestantism. The Roman Inquisition, established by Pope Paul IV in 1542, operated throughout Italy and made intellectual freedom even more of a rarity than it is in present-day Fascist Italy. Indeed, the murder of one prominent anti-Fascist, Matteotti, all but wrecked Mussolini's regime, whereas the Roman Inquisition murdered thousands of innocent and inoffensive persons, including the pious and mystical Giordano Bruno. In Naples in 1561 no less than 87 Waldenses were massacred in one day by the Inquisition. Seven of them were burned alive at the stake. A veritable reign of terror encompassed Italy. It was not necessary to be the author of a spectacular heresy or to be a Protestant in order to feel the iron heel of the church. Professor Preserved Smith quotes an eminent English traveler of the time to the effect "that the least idle word against the pope, the church or religion, will draw a man into the Inquisition, where he will lie a long time close prisoner."

We have already referred to the origins of the notorious Spanish Inquisition, designed at first to deal with Jews and Moors. After wholesale tortures and executions the Jews were expelled in 1492, and the Moors in 1609. It is one of the strange travesties of history that the descendants of these Moors were shipped back from Africa by Spanish rebels in 1936 to serve as the battering ram of the military forces which sought to reëstablish the hold of the Catholic church on Spain. The tortures and festive massacres of the Spanish Inquisition were later applied to Protestants and heretics, numerous in the Spanish Netherlands. In the words of Professor Smith, "A steady stream of blood flowed through the whole sixteenth and seventeenth centuries." In the long history of human depravity, few incidents have matched the systematic and fiendish cruelty and the blood-lust of the Spanish Inquisition.

In France, the presence of a large number of French Protestants, called Huguenots, offered a special incitement to Catholic frenzy and religious butchery. For a half century after the beginning of the Protestant revolt the Huguenots were persecuted only sporadically in France because the party known as *politiques* was more interested in civic peace than in religious unity.

The first great slaughter of French Protestants—one of the darkest pages in the scandalous history of religious fanaticism—was the notorious massacre of St. Bartholomew's Day on August 24, 1572. It had a peculiarly cowardly origin. To distract attention from her plot to assassinate Coligny, the leader of the French Protestants, the queen mother, Catherine de Medici, faked a story of a great Huguenot conspiracy. A horde of Huguenots had come to Paris to witness a court wedding. At the signal agreed upon, the Catholic butchers began their work and within twenty-four hours over two thousand Huguenots were wantonly murdered in Paris. From the capital the slaughter spread far and wide and 10,000 or more Huguenots were murdered in other parts of France. The pope sent his hearty congratulations on this singularly forceful application of Christian grace.

When a former Huguenot, Henry of Navarre, ascended the French throne, he issued the famous Edict of Nantes in 1598, granting equal civil rights to the Huguenots and giving them restricted freedom of worship. As the French Catholics grew stronger, however, they determined to crush the Huguenots. After ingenious and diversified persecutions, they resorted in 1680 to the notorious and terrible "dragonnades." Squadrons of dragoons were sent to the homes of Huguenots and given permission to maltreat them in any way necessary to bring about their conversion to Catholicism. Property was destroyed, people were tortured and mutilated, women raped. In fact, all of the atrocities falsely imputed by the French to the German soldiers in Belgium during the World War were freely perpetrated against French Protestants at this time. Finally, in 1685, Louis XIV was persuaded to revoke the Edict of Nantes. Laws were passed which deprived Huguenots of all civil rights and practically declared open season on them. Wholesale brutal repression ensued. Catholic leaders praised Louis' Christian charity in letting loose the Catholic mobs. The famous Bishop Bossuet, intellectual leader of Catholic France, wrote:

> Let us publish abroad this miracle of our days; let us pour forth our hearts on the piety of Louis; let us push our acclamations to the sky, and let us say to this new Constantine, this new Theodosius, this new Marcian, this new Charlemagne, "this is an act worthy of your reign, and its true glory; through you heresy has ceased to exist; God alone had done this miracle." [5]

Cruel and bloody persecution followed the revocation of the Edict of Nantes. The dragonnades were revived. Louis XV continued the policy of persecution, enacting a particularly savage law in 1732. But the writings of Voltaire and other French exponents of decency and tolerance fostered enlightenment in France to such a degree that it was difficult to enforce the organized brutalities after 1750.

In Germany, Catholic intolerance prevailed in Bavaria and other Catholic states but could not be carried to Protestant strongholds. The struggle between the two religious camps brought on the horrible and devastating Thirty Years' War (1618-1648). The following description by Professor David Ogg of the capture of Magdeburg by the Catholic forces offers a good example of the Catholic fury: "On the 20th day of May the Imperialists took the city by assault, and their entry was followed by a massacre which horrified even contemporaries. An orgy of rape, murder and robbery was ended only when the city was in flames and more than twenty thousand persons perished." Some degree of religious toleration was introduced by the treaty of Westphalia which closed the war. Pope Innocent X, however, denounced the articles of toleration in the treaty as "null, void, invalid, wicked, unjust, damned, and reprobate." Catholics joined Protestants in savage persecution of the Anabaptists. In Poland, the Jesuits began a fierce campaign against the Protestants under King Sigismund II (1587-1632). A brutal persecution of Protestants in Bohemia was carried on in the first half of the eighteenth century. In Austria the Jews were banished in 1742, and in 1752 Maria Theresa made conversion to Protestantism a capital crime in Austria.

The chief Catholic butcheries in England occurred during the brief Catholic restoration under Mary (1553-1558), when 290 Protestants were martyred as against 221 Catholics during the forty-five year reign of Mary's Protestant sister, Elizabeth.

The Catholic machinery of persecution was extended to the New World, beginning with the setting up of the Spanish Inquisition in Peru in 1570. It was not applied, however, to the Indians. It was reserved for the white settlers. In 1574 some thirty-six English Protestants were sent to the stake or the galleys by the Mexican Inquisition.

While the Catholic church never abated its theoretical and doctrinal intolerance, it encountered more and more difficulty after the eighteenth century in using strong measures against heretics and Protestants.

[5] Smith, *History of Modern Culture*, I, 468.

III. PROTESTANT INTOLERANCE

We made it clear in dealing with the Protestant revolt as an intellectual movement that the early Protestants were no more interested than Catholics in free thought or tolerance. Luther was as intolerant as Bellarmine. Calvin burned at the stake the gentle scientist, Michael Servetus, because the latter did not accept unconditionally Calvin's view of the Trinity. Philipp Melanchthon, the most scholarly Protestant of his generation, pronounced Calvin's act memorable and glorious for all posterity. And in the latter part of the eighteenth century, the learned Anglican, Dr. Samuel Johnson, talked as Tomás de Torquemada, chief inquisitor of the Spanish Inquisition, had talked at the close of the fifteenth. Johnson declared that: "The only method by which religious truth can be established is by martyrdom. . . . False doctrine should be checked on its first appearance; the civil power should unite with the church in punishing those who dare to attack the established religion." [6]

Yet Protestant intolerance never matched the Catholic savageries, and for a number of reasons. There were fewer Protestant states of importance. There was no such long tradition of intolerance. There could be no comparably centralized direction of brutal repression. There was no relatively powerful or widely distributed machinery for the suppression of dissent. Further, intelligent Protestants more quickly succumbed to doctrines of enlightenment and tolerance. It was primarily, indeed, almost exclusively from among Protestants that the great leaders of the movement for tolerance were drawn.

There could be no Protestant intolerance in Catholic countries like Italy, Spain, France, Poland, and the like. Even in Germany, there were as many Catholic states as Protestant. And the strongest of these Protestant states, Brandenburg-Prussia, quickly adopted a policy of tolerance—for political and economic as well as religious reasons. Frederick the Great set up the most tolerant regime known at the time in any important European state. In the Netherlands tolerance reigned.

The Peace of Augsburg (1555) was designed to end the religious wars and to introduce religious freedom for both parties in Germany. The freedom was, however, chiefly for the princes and not for their subjects. Catholic princes persecuted Protestant subjects and Protestant princes made life miserable for Catholic subjects. In the Thirty Years' War the Protestants were no slackers in taking care of their share of the religious butchery. After the treaty of Westphalia, a more tolerant policy was introduced in Prussia by Frederick William, the Great Elector.

Protestant intolerance was most completely and continuously applied in England and Scotland, though it never approached the Catholic ferocity in Spain, France, and Italy. Under Henry VIII and Edward VI there was sporadic but at times bloody and brutal persecution of Catholics. The suppression of the monasteries was probably the most serious blow struck by Henry against the Catholics. His daughter, Elizabeth, was at first reasonably tolerant of Catholics,

---

[6] Smith, *op. cit.,* II, 550.

but attacks against her by Catholics, at home and abroad, led to retaliation. In 1585 the Jesuits were expelled under threat of the death penalty. In 1591 an act was passed confining Catholics to movements within five miles of their homes. Yet the fact that there were only 221 victims of persecution in Elizabeth's long reign—far less than the number executed in Italy or Spain in many single years—attests to the relative moderation of Anglican intolerance.

The Gunpowder Plot of 1605, engineered by Robert Catesby and Guy Fawkes, revealed a Catholic plan to overthrow the Protestant government. Parliament passed further restrictive laws against Catholics by way of retaliation in 1606, but, because of James I's conciliatory policy and his desire to be on good terms with Catholic Spain, these laws were laxly enforced. From the time of the Stuarts onward, English religious intolerance directed its repressive measures against Protestant dissenters as well as against Catholics. But in 1678, as a result of the alleged Catholic plot of Titus Oates, further disabilities and tests were imposed specifically on Catholics.

English intolerance of Catholics in its most ferocious form was directed against Catholic Ireland, especially in Oliver Cromwell's brutal and crushing conquest of the island in 1649-1650. Tens of thousands of Irish Catholics went to their death by the sword, plague, and famine. This was the only example of Protestant intolerance that matched in extent and savagery Catholic intolerance in Italy, Spain, France, Catholic Germany, and Poland. And Cromwell's arrogant attitude equaled that of Bossuet. He declared that his wholesale butcheries were "a righteous judgment of God upon these barbarous wretches." The only thing that can be urged in extenuation is that they were wartime atrocities and not peacetime massacres like those in Spain and France. Yet, even Cromwell was relatively tolerant for his time. As Lord Protector, he shielded English Catholics and Unitarians so far as his position would permit.

Protestant Scotland laid a heavy hand on Catholics, though few were put to death. In 1567 Parliament declared the Protestant confession of faith to be infallible. In the same year, the celebration of the Catholic Mass was penalized by banishment for the second offense and death for the third. In 1587, the Jesuits were banished and Catholic property was confiscated. It was declared to be treason to consort with Jesuits or Catholic priests generally. Innkeepers were forbidden to lodge Catholics. In 1589 all citizens were ordered, under heavy penalties, to embrace Protestantism.

Protestant intolerance in England was, as we noted above, extended to dissenters, especially after the Anglican victory in the restoration of the Stuarts in 1660. In the period of the rebellion and the Commonwealth the non-Anglican elements temporarily got the upper hand. During the Long Parliament and the Commonwealth stringent laws were passed not only against Catholics but also against Episcopalians and extreme Protestant sects. The Anglican severity under the Restoration was a natural retaliation.

A new Act of Uniformity (1662) imposed the revised Anglican prayerbook and the Anglican articles of faith on all churches and schools in the land. Thousands of clergymen resigned in protest and many undertook common labor to support their families. Charles II tried to stem the tide of Anglican intolerance, but his ministers and Parliament successfully opposed his broad-minded attempt. Charles declared that he was "in nature an enemy to all severity for religion and conscience." Instead of abating the brutalities, Parliament answered by imposing more onerous severities in the Conventicle Act of 1664 and the Five-Mile Act of 1665, which outlawed nonconformist religious services and still further persecuted nonconformist preachers and teachers. In 1673, the civil rights of Catholics and dissenters were impaired by the Test Act which excluded them from civil and military offices. This act was not fully repealed for a century and a half (1828-1829).

Protestant intolerance was also carried to the English colonies in America. Virginia imposed characteristic Anglican disabilities on dissenters and ultimately banished them. In New England, the Congregationalists created what amounted to a state church and suppressed those who did not accept their religious program. Its two outstanding banishments were those of Anne Hutchinson and Roger Williams. Quakers and radical dissenters were given quarter in few colonies, save Rhode Island and Pennsylvania. Catholics were fairly treated only in the colonies of Maryland, Rhode Island, and Pennsylvania. The common idea that the new America was a haven for the persecuted in colonial times is far from true.

IV. THE RISE OF CENSORSHIP OF THE PRESS

The invention of printing raised new and more serious problems with respect to keeping seemingly dangerous ideas from literate persons. In the days before printing, the manufacture and sale of books were chiefly in the hands of monks, although many secular persons engaged in the business in the later Middle Ages. At any rate, it was fairly easy for the medieval church to enforce literary censorship. Further, relatively few copies of any dangerous book could be made by hand and circulated. When printing came into existence, then a whole new set of problems arose, since thousands of copies of subversive books and pamphlets could be quickly struck off and distributed.

The answer to this challenge to pious obscurantism was the licensing of presses, the preparation of indices of prohibited and expurgated books, and the exaction of heavy penalties from those who printed books without a license, who sold forbidden books, or who had in their possession tabooed printed material.

The first recorded licensing of the press appeared in an edict of the Archbishop of Mainz in 1485. The Council of Trent, in 1546, prohibited the unlicensed printing of anonymous books and of any works on religious subjects.

At an even earlier period the Spanish Inquisition had assumed the right to license presses, but in 1554 Charles V limited the licensing authority to the government, which was, however, completely under the control of reactionary Catholic elements. It quickly passed a savage law in 1558, destroying at a stroke the freedom of the press in Spain. In France, the government also retained control of the licensing of the press, and it likewise passed drastic laws against unlicensed printing. The death penalty was commonly prescribed for continued violation. The French laws became especially severe in the eighteenth century for the purpose of suppressing Jansenism. In Protestant Germany, the eminent scholar, Leibnitz, incredible as it may seem, proposed the most stringent of all schemes for licensing the press. For a time, he was able to get this authority conferred on the Berlin Academy of Sciences. But Frederick the Great revoked all restrictions and established a freedom of the press unknown elsewhere in Europe save in the Protestant Netherlands. Denmark introduced compulsory licensing of the press in 1713.

In England an ingenious device was hit upon by incorporating the Stationers' Company in 1557 and conferring upon it a temporary printing monopoly. Elizabeth imposed stringent penalties upon unlicensed printing and hanged, drew, and quartered one printer who violated the law. The court of the Star Chamber, in 1586 and 1637, issued two comprehensive and rigorous ordinances for compulsory licensing of the press. In 1643, the anti-Anglican Long Parliament showed an equal intolerance by ordering the strictest licensing of the press. The Anglican Restoration government quickly revived the licensing order in a law passed in 1662, repassed with additions in 1685, and upheld as late as 1693. Scotland imposed a rigorous licensing law in 1599.

Censorship of printing was extended to the English colonies in America. In Virginia all presses were for a time excluded, and in 1662 laws directing the licensing of printing were passed in Massachusetts. The first newspaper in America, the Boston *Publick Occurrences,* was suppressed within twenty-four hours after its first edition in 1690.

The licensing of the press gave reactionary political and ecclesiastical powers complete authority over printed matter. If a man disobeyed the licensing laws, he took his life in his hands. And if he obtained a license and then printed forbidden or dangerous books he would lose his license, go out of business and be punished in the bargain.

In Catholic circles, however, the licensing laws were not enough. Indices of forbidden books or of books needing expurgation were prepared. Dire punishments were prescribed for those who sold or owned such tabooed works. Pope Alexander VI, a notorious profligate, extended papal censorship throughout Europe in 1501. The first list of forbidden books was issued by Cardinal Wolsey in England in 1526. In 1546 a much longer list issued from the University of Louvain by authority of the Holy Roman emperor.

In 1557, the Roman Inquisition listed many books to be burned—beginning a long series of prohibitions issued by the Catholic church down to our own day. The Council of Trent authorized an index of books forbidden to Catholics. Pope Paul IV published the first formal Catholic *Index of Prohibited Books* in 1559.[7] Pius IV issued a much more complete index in 1562 and threatened excommunication against Catholics who read any of these banned books.

The fear engendered by censorship is admirably illustrated by Osiander's famous introduction to the great work of Copernicus. Osiander was a leading printer of Nuremberg. Fearful lest the church revoke his printing license for

---

[7] Far and away the best brief history and explanation of this famous Index is Joseph McCabe, *The History and Meaning of the Catholic Index of Forbidden Books,* Haldeman-Julius, 1931. It is, incidentally, important for its illuminating criticism of George Haven Putnam's *Censorship of the Church of Rome,* 2 vols., Putnam, 1906.

issuing so revolutionary a book, Osiander, of his own volition, inserted an introduction stating that Copernicus had not been too serious about his theories—that, at the most, he merely intended them to be regarded as interesting hypotheses. This statement did great violence to Copernicus' intentions and created considerable misunderstanding of his real beliefs.

In 1571, Pius V created in the papal curia a special department known as the Congregation of the Index, headed by four (later seven) cardinals. To date, the Congregation has issued more than forty indices of prohibited books, the most complete being those of 1758 and 1900.[7a]

Another duty of the Congregation of the Index was to prepare a list of passages for deletion before books could be lawfully read by Catholics. The expurgations were often ruthless and stupid. As Milton observed: "The expurgating indexes rake through the entrails of many an old, good author, with a violation worse than any that could be offered to his tomb."

The list of banned works is quite enlightening.[8] Not only were skeptics like Bruno, Montaigne, Bacon, Hobbes, and Milton placed on the *Index,* but also prominent Catholic authors, like the great historian, Cardinal Baronius, the pious Catholic scientist and philosopher, Blaise Pascal, and the ultra-theistic psychologist, Malebranche, who believed God to be the direct source of human thought. The selection of books for the *Index* has always been very curious. While Pascal was banned, the atomist and Epicurean, Pierre Gassendi, was not. Defoe's *Robinson Crusoe* was put on the *Index,* but not Tom Paine's *Age of Reason,* the culmination of rationalistic religious thought in early modern times. Erasmus Darwin's writings were placed on the *Index,* but not those of his grandson, Charles. John Stuart Mill is on the *Index* but not Ernst Haeckel, Robert G. Ingersoll, or Andrew D. White.

The reactionary French Bourbon government suppressed books indiscriminately as well as all save semiofficial newspapers. The Protestant countries also banned many books and publications, but there was never any system of censorship and suppression to vie with the Catholic *Index.* Until the close of the seventeenth century the situation was bad enough, however, in all Protestant countries save the Dutch Netherlands. Alexander Leighton and William Prynne were brutally mutilated and imprisoned in England for their publishing activities. John Lilburne, the noble leader of the Levelers, was whipped, pilloried, and imprisoned for his writings. Charles Ripley Gillett has prepared two sizable volumes dealing solely with books suppressed and burned in England in the sixteenth and seventeenth centuries.[9]

Not satisfied with licensing the press and banning books, governments imposed severe penalties on those who sold banned books or operated unlicensed presses. In Catholic countries—in Spain and the Spanish Netherlands, in particular—punishment was meted out to those who merely possessed forbidden books.

The general effect of this sweeping and stupid censorship in Catholic and Protestant countries was greatly to curtail the spread of information and the

7a For a discussion of more recent developments in Catholicism, see Chapter XXVI.
8 See Smith, *op. cit.,* I, 514.
9 C. R. Gillett, *Burned Books,* 2 vols.. Columbia University Press, 1932.

progress of enlightenment. Protestant countries repudiated censorship most rapidly and, hence, the disastrous influences of censorship there were not so serious or prolonged as in Catholic states. Commenting on the Catholic *Index* and censorship, Professor Preserved Smith makes the very restrained statement that:

> It is not too much to say that most of the important works of modern science, philosophy and learning, and not a few of the chief products of Catholic piety, have been forbidden by the church as dangerous to the faith of her children; and that, in addition, many of the ornaments of fair letters have been tampered with in order to protect the sensitive pride of ecclesiastics or the squeamish prudery of priests. . . . That servile faith, bigotry, and obscurantism have been fostered, and that science, philosophy, and liberty were long sorely hampered in Catholic lands, is due to the *Index* even more than to the Inquisition.[10]

V. THE GROWTH OF TOLERANCE

The growth of tolerance, urbanity, and free thought constitutes the most convincing evidence of the progress of civilization. The case for tolerance may rest on one of two grounds. The first is the purely emotional protest of the minority that is being trampled on. Examples of this were the early Christians in the Roman Empire, the repressed nationalities in Europe before 1914, or the Russian communists before 1917. In such cases, there is rarely any general intellectual comprehension of the broad merits and implications of intellectual freedom. It is merely the distressed howl of the underdog, who is all too willing to use similar methods of repression once he obtains control of the state. Witness, for example, the speedy and sweeping Christian proscription of paganism after Constantine, the brutal repression of the present Yugoslav government in dealing with Croats and Macedonians, the severe intolerance of dissent from orthodox Marxism in Bolshevik Russia, and the fury of the Fascists after they have attained power.

The second or intellectual justification of tolerance is something quite different. It has no relation to the possession of dominant physical or political power.

In the first place, the intellectual justification of tolerance requires a good historical sense, enabling a person to recognize how harmless are most of the ideas, opinions and policies concerning which man has been intolerant in the past. History also reveals the lack of success which attended most efforts to establish a doctrine or policy by sheer physical force.

In the second place, tolerance is dictated by intellectual humility, for such humility arises from a knowledge of the relative weakness of the best human intellects, and the highly incomplete character of human knowledge on any topic whatsoever. We have no such absolute certainty on any point as to justify its forcible inculcation.

In the third place, an understanding of the really adroit technique of conversion makes it clear that convincing argumentation is far better than coercion.

[10] Smith, *op. cit.*, I, 513-14.

Moreover, if we have real faith in the ultimate victory of truth and justice, we can afford to let them triumph gradually and moderately, rather than jeopardize their success by unwise ardor and precipitance.

Finally, the spirit of urbanity and a sense of humor are admirable safeguards against intolerance, particularly when they are joined to the cosmic perspective which is possible today.

The Catholic church has been consistently and logically intolerant in its official policy. In actual practice, it has often been far more tolerant at certain times and in certain quarters than the Protestants. But its formal attitude is one of unyielding intolerance of what the church regards as heterodox. From Augustine and Cardinal Bellamine to Bishop Sheen and Father Gillis in our own day, the intolerance of Catholicism has been defended on the ground that the church possesses the key to divine truth. As Bossuet put it: "I have the right to persecute you because I am right and you are wrong; but you have no right to persecute me for the same reason." Granting the premises of the church, which loyal churchmen must accept, there would seem to be no logical objection to this view. It simply happens that these premises are becoming progressively more susceptible of effective criticism.

While there are plenty of Protestants who, even in our day, are as intolerant as Cardinal Bellamine was in the sixteenth century, it is, nevertheless, true that most of the arguments favoring tolerance and freedom of thought have come from liberal-minded Protestants and freethinkers. We shall now survey briefly some of the leading efforts to defend tolerance, and some of the victories over intolerance.

The skeptical Montaigne was, as we have already noted, heartily opposed to dogmatism and intolerance. An intolerant attitude, he thought, implied vulgar conceit and insufferable egotism. As he satirically remarked, "It is overvaluing one's own conjectures to cause a man to be put to death because of them." His whole philosophy was a subtle but devastating annihilation of the case for intolerance. Francis Bacon, regarding the massacre of St. Bartholomew's Day and the Gunpowder Plot, suggested that if Lucretius could only have been alive to view such things he would certainly have formulated a much more bitter indictment of the evils of religion than he did on the basis of classical practice. Bacon recommended tolerance for all save radical sects like the Anabaptists and atheists. Sir Thomas Browne (1605-1682), whom Professor Smith calls a sort of English Montaigne, indirectly revealed the absurdity of intolerance in his work, *Religio Medici*. He showed, on the basis of doubts and inconsistencies among creeds, sects, and biblical passages that no sane and thoughtful man could very well accept wholeheartedly any single religious point of view. He must pick and choose, and select that which seems best to him. Such an attitude is the very essence of tolerance.

Closely related to Browne's views was the attitude of an Anglican divine, William Chillingworth (1602-1644). In his *Religion of the Protestants a Safe Way to Salvation* (1637) he was, perhaps, the first Englishman to develop systematically the argument for religious tolerance. The essence of his reasoning was that a

Protestant could be saved even though he did not believe every word in a given creed. What is necessary for salvation is a firm belief in the few real essentials of religion. Chillingworth denounced unreasoning faith and declared that firmness of belief should correspond to the relative credibility of the doctrine offered. As for that which must be accepted if one is to secure salvation, Chillingworth stated the case in a noble passage: "I am fully assured that God does not, and that therefore men ought not to require any more of any man than this, to believe the Scripture to be God's word, to endeavor to find the true sense of it, and to live according to it."

Chillingworth's judicious and broad-minded book was so distasteful to fanatics that a Calvinist preacher, Francis Cheynell, gave it a formal burial with the words: "Get thee gone, thou cursed booke, which hath seduced so many precious soules; get thee gone, thou corrupt, rotten booke, earth to earth, dust to dust; get thee gone into the place of rottennesse, that thou maiest rot with thy author, and see corruption." [11]

A similar point of view was embodied in a very powerful, but not too sincere, statement by another Anglican divine, Jeremy Taylor (1613-1667). He wrote his *Discourse on the Liberty of Prophesying* (1647) at a time when the Anglicans were being hard-pressed by the anti-Anglican forces. Therefore, he was in a mood to ask for tolerance, and he presented a telling argument in its behalf. But when the Anglicans returned to power with the Restoration Taylor denounced his previous broad-mindedness. Taylor pointed out the uncertainty and inadequacy of theological tradition, the difficulty of expounding the scriptures with precision, and the fallibility of any available arbiter on disputed points. He concluded that it is absurd and wicked to persecute others for mere differences of opinion. He agreed with Chillingworth that unity on essentials is all that is necessary for salvation and religious harmony. The essentials of Christianity Taylor found in the Apostles' creed. Arthur Bury, in his *Naked Gospel* (1690), urged that all that is necessary to salvation is faith in Christ and a willingness to trust him as a practical guide in life.

An important blast against intolerance was embodied in the "Agreement of the People of England," drawn up in 1647 under the influence of the Levelers and their leader, John Lilburne. This held: "That matters of religion and the ways of God's worship are not at all entrusted by us to any human power because therein we cannot remit or exceed a tittle of what our consciences dictate to be the mind of God without wilful sin; nevertheless, the public way of instructing the nation (so it will not be compulsion) is referred to their discretion."

John Milton (1608-1674) anticipated Locke by holding, in his *Treatise on Civil Power in Ecclesiastical Cases,* that it is not permissible for government to enforce religious belief or to demand conformity to any one creed. Yet Milton would not grant tolerance towards Catholics. His argument was more logical on this point than many, however, for he rightly pointed out that the Catholic church is as much a state as a religious system.

More thoroughgoing in his views of toleration was Roger Williams (c1603-1683),

[11] Gillett, *op. cit.,* I, 10.

the founder of complete religious tolerance in America and the modern world. In his *Bloudy Tenent of Persecution* and other works, he argued that the state has no right or authority to determine or enforce religious beliefs. Williams went the whole way in his views of tolerance. Even Catholics, atheists, Jews, and Turks, he said, should be completely tolerated. The other important apostle of religious tolerance in America, William Penn (1644-1718), declared, in his *Great Cause of Liberty of Conscience,* that government has no right to determine or force the conscience of believers and that persecution is contrary to the principle and end of government.

The philosopher, Spinoza, in his *Theologico-Political Treatise,* ironically but sadly called attention to the impropriety of bitter hatreds among Christian sects, all of whom pretended to follow the gospel of brotherly love. He further remarked upon the great diversity of religious beliefs among those who regard their own cult as infallible. He concluded that religious persecution does irreparable damage to religion and the state alike.

Of all the arguments for tolerance in this age probably the most influential was that of the broad-minded Anglican philosopher, John Locke, embodied in his *Letters on Toleration.* The first of these is the most interesting and cogent. He agreed with Spinoza that love is the basic tenet of Christianity and that those who persecute each other are violating this first principle of their religion. He also accepted the view of Milton and the Quakers that the state should not presume to deal with matters of conscience and religious belief. Further, it would be dangerous to allow the state to enforce belief in any one religion. In some states the effort would inevitably be made to enforce a false religion and thus send many to damnation by a political fiat. The best procedure is to permit religious freedom, and then the true religion will triumph through its very superiority. Locke even doubted the propriety of missionary enterprise. But, with all his breadth of mind, Locke stopped short of tolerating Catholics and atheists. The former owe allegiance to the pope, who is a foreign prince, and moreover they break their faith with heretics. Atheists cannot be bound by oaths and, hence, not by civil obligations. Moreover, they have no religion to tolerate.

An English deist, Matthew Tindal (c1656-1733), effectively defended liberty of conscience in his *Essay on the Power of the Magistrate* (1697); and the next year in his *Liberty of the Press* he argued eloquently for freedom in religious discussion and witheringly attacked the proposal to license the press. But even Tindal would not tolerate atheists. A satirical contribution to the cause of tolerance came from the pen of Daniel Defoe in a little tract called *The Shortest Way with the Dissenters* (1702). He deliberately assumed the point of view of a very intolerant English high churchman and argued for the utmost severity in repressing dissent. His work was really a *reductio ad absurdum* of Anglican intolerance. For a moment his intent was misunderstood and the book was hailed by the reactionaries as a masterpiece in defense of intolerance. Soon afterwards the hoax was discovered and Defoe was put into the pillory.

Encouragement of tolerance was echoed by latitudinarian bishops, such as Bishop Benjamin Hoadley of Bangor (1676-1761) and Bishop William Warburton (1698-1779). The former went even beyond Chillingworth and Taylor and claimed that religious sincerity is all that can be demanded of a Christian. Warburton espoused Locke's argument that the state has no rightful authority to interfere in religious matters.

In France, tolerance was supported by Turgot (1727-1781), Rousseau (1712-1778), and by Diderot and the Encyclopedists. Turgot insisted that the state keep out of religious matters: "No religion has the right to demand any other protection but liberty; and it loses this right to liberty when its doctrines or worship are repugnant to the interests of the state." Rousseau declared that persecution is worse than atheism and advocated the tolerance of all who accepted moderate deism. In their articles the Encyclopedists included arguments for tolerance.

Germany and Holland also contributed polemics in favor of tolerance. The eminent German publicist and historian, Samuel Pufendorf (1632-1694), in his *Relation of Religious Liberty to Civil Life,* invoked the doctrine of natural law, as well as political expediency, in behalf of tolerance. The courageous scholar, Christian Thomasius (1655-1728), advanced almost identical arguments based on natural law and political propriety, asserting that rulers should keep the peace and not try to save souls. His pupil, Justin Böhmer (1674-1749), emphasized the same point of view and added that heresy is a sin, not a crime, and must be punished by individual conscience and not by the state. Geraert Noodt (1647-1725), of the University of Leyden, took Browne's and Taylor's line of argument by stressing the variety and lack of certainty among sects. He believed that every man has a natural right to choose his own religion.

Since the lesser and more radical sects tended to suffer most from persecution it was natural that they should present strong arguments against state support of religious persecution. The Socinians, so called because of their founders, Laelius and Faustus Socinus, favored the union of the dominant church with the state, but added that there should be full toleration of all other sects and cults. We have already mentioned the Quaker attitude. The Anabaptists, whose chief stronghold was at Münster in Westphalia, went even further. They advocated complete separation of church and state.

Such were the arguments for tolerance. Some will, doubtless, wonder why there has been no mention of men like Glanvill, Bayle, Collins, and Voltaire, famous for their battles in behalf of religious freedom. They are reserved for separate mention, because they represent a step beyond those who advocated mere tolerance; they fought for free thought, which is something rather different from tolerance, although the two are frequently identified.

VI. THE CASE FOR FREE THOUGHT

While tolerance represents a vast step in advance over intolerance, there is a certain element of intellectual arrogance in the attitude of tolerance, which usually assumes that there is an absolutely correct belief or opinion, a true religion, and the like. Being sure of our own position, we can afford to tolerate the "brethren who sit in darkness." Tolerance thus frequently involves patronizing indulgence. We pity those who live in error, but we will let them continue their erroneous and unfortunate lives without molestation.

Rather more advanced and admirable is the attitude known as free thought. Persons who take this position do not assume that there is absolute truth, that any single point of view is completely correct. The limitations of the human intellect are recognized and it is conceded that the most perfect wisdom is only an approximation to truth. Intellectual humility is the desirable keynote. Under the most favorable circumstances, human thought will be weak and fallible enough. It should not be further handicapped by arbitrary repression at the hands of relatively stupid functionaries. The wider the freedom of thought, the greater the probability of approximating truth. But nobody is sufficiently wise or omniscient to take a patronizing or pitying attitude towards another's beliefs.

Such are some of the leading characteristics of free thought as contrasted with the less advanced position of tolerance.

The first true exponent of free thought was an English thinker whom we have already met, strangely enough, as one of those who believed in witchcraft. There has rarely been anything more incongruous in the history of human thought than the fact that this great skeptic should also have been an apologist for the most vulgar and disastrous illusion of his century. Such a man was Joseph Glanvill (1636-1680), whose *Vanity of Dogmatizing or Confidence of Opinions* (1661) constitutes the earliest modern defense of complete open-mindedness and intellectual humility. In some ways Glanvill excelled Bacon in describing the dangers of error in human thinking, since he laid particular emphasis on the menace of prejudice and bigotry. He called attention to what he termed "the changing climates of opinion," namely, the fact that what is most dogmatically regarded as truth in one generation may be completely ridiculed and discredited in another. Glanvill agreed with Descartes that we must put aside all received and accepted opinion before we can safely tackle any intellectual or scientific enterprise. Not only must we free ourselves in this way from conventional prejudices; we must also be rigorously on our guard against the fancies of our imagination, which betray us into error, and therefore must be disciplined and kept under control. The most powerful human intellect is relatively weak when faced with the multiplicity and difficulty of life's problems. Human ignorance is almost unbounded when contrasted with the slight amount of positive knowledge that man possesses. Hence, intellectual modesty is not only the most appropriate but also the most useful of all attitudes. The more confident we are about any belief, the greater our probable fallibility. In the final chapter of his work Glanvill summarized his arguments against dogmatizing:

> Opinionative confidence is the effect of ignorance. . . . He is the greatest ignorant that knows not that he is so. . . . The exercised understanding is conscious of its disability. . . . Confidence in opinions evermore dwells with untamed passions, and is maintained upon the depraved obstinacy of an ungoverned spirit. . . . Dogmatizing is the greatest disturber both of ourselves and the world with-

out us: for while we wed an opinion, we resolvedly engage against every one that opposeth it. . . . To be confident in opinions is ill manners and immodesty; and while we are peremptory in our persuasions, we accuse them all of ignorance and error that subscribe not to our assertions. . . . Obstinacy in opinions holds the dogmatist in the chains of error, without hope of emancipation. When we are confident of all things, we are fatally deceived in most. . . . It betrays a poverty and narrowness of spirit in the dogmatic asserters. . . . There are a set of pedants that are born to slavery. But the generous soul preserves the liberty of his judgment and will not pen it up in an opinionative dungeon; with an equal respect he examines all things, and judgeth as impartially as Rhadamanth: when as the pedant can hear nothing but in favour of the conceits he is amorous of; and cannot see but one of the grates of his prison. The determinations of the nobler spirit are but temporary, and he holds them but till better evidence repeal his former apprehensions. He wont defile his assent by prostituting it to every conjecture, or stuff his belief with the luggage of uncertainties. The modesty of his expression renders him infallible; and while he only saith he thinks so, he cannot be deceived or ever assert a falsehood.

Glanvill applied his philosophy to a searching reconstruction of theological thinking. Lecky has well described his profound and revolutionary approach to the problem:

While his contemporaries seem to have expected as the extreme consequences of his philosophy, on the one hand a period of passing disturbance, arising from the discovery of apparent discrepancies between science and the Bible, and on the other hand increased evidence of the faith, arising from the solution of those difficulties and from the increased perception of superintending wisdom exhibited in "the wheelwork of creation," Glanvil perceived very clearly that a far deeper and more general modification was at hand. He saw that the theological system existing in a nation is intimately connected with the prevailing modes of thought or intellectual condition; that the new philosophy was about to change that condition; and that the Church must either adapt herself to the altered tone, or lose her influence over the English mind. He saw that a theology which rested ultimately on authority, which branded doubt as criminal, and which discouraged in the strongest manner every impartial investigation, could not long co-exist with a philosophy that encouraged the opposite habits of thought as the very beginning of wisdom. He saw that while men maintained every strange phenomenon to be miraculous as long as it was unexplained, each advance of physical science must necessarily be hostile to theology; and that the passionate adoration of Aristotle, the blind pedantic reverence which accounted the simplest assertions of dead men decisive authorities, the retrospective habits of thought the universities steadily laboured to encourage, were all incompatible with the new tendencies which Bacon represented.[12]

With regard to theology, Glanvill took much the same latitudinarian view as Chillingworth and Taylor, asserting that the religious doctrines which can be defended with assurance are few and simple.

The next important figure in the history of free thought was the brilliant and extremely influential skeptic, Pierre Bayle (1647-1706), a fugitive French Huguenot

[12] Lecky, *op. cit.*, I, 131-32.

whose unfettered intellect was evident in all his works. His arguments for freethinking and religious toleration were best summarized in his famous *Philosophical Commentary on the Words of Jesus Christ, "Compel Them to Come In,"* published in 1686.

Like Montaigne and Glanvill, Bayle stressed the great diversity of opinions which may be held regarding any subject, and pointed out that the partisans of each opinion believe it to be absolute truth. He said that while we may consider our neighbors as foolish heretics, they probably entertain the same idea of us. He added that no one can be so sure of possessing absolute truth as to justify forcing his views upon another person. Moreover, coercion is a poor method of converting anyone to our point of view. We may club a man into admitting that he agrees with us, but in his own mind he is likely to be more than ever set against us. Urbane argumentation is the only wise method for trying to convince another. If this fails we may as well relegate the task to someone else. Of all his arguments for freedom of thought, Bayle seemed to lay most stress upon our inability to judge the minds of others and to know what is best for them. Professor Howard Robinson thus summarizes Bayle's basic conviction:

> One of the most important reasons for tolerance, in Bayle's opinion, is our limited knowledge of other people's minds. The convertist cannot be a searcher of hearts. "None but God alone can judge of the measure of our understanding, and the degrees of light which are sufficient to each, its proportion varying infinitely." (i, 271) Just as the quantity of food sufficient for one man is not suitable for another, so the amount of light needed for convincing persons must vary. And this led him to write of religion and of its varying attractions much as he would of taste or the power of artistic appreciation. *De Gustibus non est disputandum* is thus applied to religion. People look at a picture by Raphael and make a thousand different judgments. "You may think Canary wine the best, but men with as good a taste as you cannot abide it." It is the saddest of mistakes to make a judgment of other men's perceptions by your own.[13]

Bayle had no fear that the introduction of freethinking would lead to universal and devastating skepticism. By nature and social conventions, the mass of men are sufficiently protected against the inroads of skepticism. As he remarked ironically:

> Only a small number of men are capable of being deceived by the arguments of the sceptics. The grace which God bestows upon the faithful, the force of education, the power of ignorance, if I may say so, and the natural inclination of men to have positive opinions, are impenetrable shields against the darts of the Pyrrhonists (sceptics), though that sect now fancies it is more formidable than it was formerly.[14]

Bayle's arguments against intolerance were cogent and forceful.[15] The violence of religious persecution discredits religion in the minds of thinking people and really breeds freethinking and irreligion. Coercion is an utterly mistaken way

[13] Robinson, *Bayle the Sceptic*, Columbia University Press, 1931, pp. 80-81.
[14] *Ibid.*, p. 202.
[15] *Ibid.*, pp. 71 ff.

of establishing religious conviction. Bayle quoted Athanasius to substantiate this point of view: "For it is not with the sword and spear, nor with soldiers and armed force that truth is to be propagated, but by counsel and sweet persuasion." The very gospel of Jesus Christ condemns coercion as a method of religious conversion. Likewise, by his own example, Christ repudiated force: "He did not arm legions of angels which were always, as it were, in his pay, nor send them in pursuit of the deserters to round them up by force." Coercion simply breeds hypocrisy. A man under torture may say he accepts a religion, but in his heart he will hate it worse than ever.

If one were to accept the validity of the doctrine of compulsion it could be used against Christianity as well as for it. An infidel sovereign could exclude all Christians from his realms or persecute those who remained. The record of Christians in using force leaves little ground for legitimate criticism of infidels. Kings have no right to issue edicts concerning religion and conscience. Hence, it is futile to say that heretics are punished for disobeying the law and not for their religion. The existence of many sects is a blessing rather than a curse. Their competition produces a higher grade of religious thought and moral outlook. Uniformity of belief stultifies religion.

Like Roger Williams, Bayle went the whole length in his attack on intolerance. He would tolerate Catholics, Jews, Turks, and atheists. His toleration of Catholics was a certain proof of his sincerity, for he and his family had suffered severely from Catholic persecution in France. Bayle leveled his satire against halfway tolerationists (demi-tolerationists). He concluded his arguments against intolerance by maintaining the right of every person to believe what he would, even though his conscience might be in error. We have a right to our own errors of belief.

A half-century after Glanvill the case for freethinking was forcefully restated in England by Anthony Collins (1676-1729) in his *Discourse of Free Thinking* (1713). Neither as profound nor as philosophical as Glanvill's work, it went farther than the latter, for Collins was more emancipated in his religious views than Glanvill. Collins drew heavily on Bayle's *Historical and Critical Dictionary* for his materials and arguments. He was primarily interested in gathering arguments to support freethinking in religious matters. He called attention to the dissensions among orthodox believers who led in the movement for intolerance of other believers. Catholics and Protestants, Anglicans, Presbyterians, and Congregationalists all appeal to authority, but they are unable to agree as to what it is that authority dictates or where the ultimate authority in religion resides. The fact that the orthodox cannot agree on religious truth is sufficient to demonstrate that it is so uncertain and elusive as to make intolerance absurd.

Collins then proceeded to develop a strong case for "free inquiry" in religion. He made a powerful plea for the right, duty and utility of freethinking wherever it may lead. Truth is "elicited by the fullest and freest discussion." Those unwilling to agree to this proposition automatically convict themselves of fear lest their position will not stand up under the light of reason. Hence, the burden of doubt and suspicion falls on those who oppose freethinking. If the latter protest against any such conclusion, they have only to withdraw their opposition to the freedom of thought and prove that they have no fear of a discussion of their beliefs. If they refuse to do so, they cannot complain if freethinking comes to be identified with infidelity, since only infidels permit it.

The individual reason, free from any external restraint, must be the supreme guide for all men. Everyone should be encouraged to follow clear and logical reasoning to whatever extreme it may lead. Whatever conflicts with reason and logic may legitimately be suspected. Complete freedom must be accorded to both religious and irreligious thought. All sound religious conclusions must rest upon free inquiry. The latter helps to undermine superstition and to vindicate the true religion. This is proved by the disappearance of witchcraft and diabolism in tolerant Holland. The example of antiquity affords ample proof that political disorder does not result from according full freedom in religious thinking. Collins, like Bayle, stressed the usually virtuous life of unbelievers and atheists. Being unpopular, atheists have to be especially careful of their conduct. Furthermore, they are absorbed in intellectual pursuits and so have no time for wicked indulgence. Collins was savagely attacked by orthodox pedants, but, as Stephen and Benn point out, his critics were careful to confine themselves to irrelevant details and to avoid meeting his main arguments.

The outstanding French exponent of freethinking after Bayle was Voltaire (1694-1778). As Professor Smith declares:

> While Rousseau still lingered at the half-way house of the many who, in his generation, would enlarge the bounds of toleration without consistently demanding it for all, Voltaire urged complete liberty of conscience with a brilliance and a courage that made his efforts in this cause the most glorious and heroic part of his great services to mankind. I have not been able to find the expression often quoted and attributed to a letter from Voltaire to Helvétius: "I wholly disapprove of your opinions and will fight to the death for your right to express them"—but if the passage be not authentic it exactly expresses the spirit of the sage who demanded freedom of conscience for all and who risked much to procure it to the obscure and persecuted.[16]

That Voltaire was deeply influenced by the English deists and freethinkers has been generally recognized. But it is not so well known that he owed as much or more to Bayle.[17] As Professor Robinson expresses it: "It has been well said that freethought and tolerance took the offensive with Bayle, who had his soldiers in the eighteenth century 'under the generalship of Voltaire.'"

The defense of freethinking runs through all of Voltaire's writings, but it appears most explicitly in his *Henriade,* his *Treatise on Tolerance,* his *Philosophical Dictionary,* his *Letters,* and his *Candide.* The flavor of his thought can be gleaned from the following passages taken out of the *Philosophical Dictionary:*

> What is tolerance? it is the consequence of humanity. We are all formed of frailty and error; let us pardon reciprocally each other's folly—that is the first law of nature.

16 Smith, *op. cit.,* II, 559. 17 Robinson, *op. cit.,* pp. 285 ff.

It is clear that the individual who persecutes a man, his brother, because he is not of the same opinion, is a monster. That admits of no difficulty. . . .

Of all religions, the Christian is without doubt the one which should inspire tolerance most, although up to now the Christians have been the most intolerant of all men. . . .

This horrible discord, which has lasted for so many centuries, is a very striking lesson that we should pardon each other's errors; discord is the great ill of mankind; and tolerance is the only remedy for it.

There is nobody who is not in agreement with this truth, whether he meditates soberly in his study, or peaceably examines the truth with his friends. Why then do the same men who admit in private indulgence, kindness, justice, rise in public with so much fury against these virtues? Why? it is that their own interest is their god, and that they sacrifice everything to this monster that they worship. . . .

If it were permitted to reason consistently in religious matters, it is clear that we all ought to become Jews, because Jesus Christ our Savior was born a Jew, lived a Jew, died a Jew, and that he said expressly that he was accomplishing, that he was fulfilling the Jewish religion. But it is clearer still that we ought to be tolerant of one another, because we are all weak, inconsistent, liable to fickleness and error. Shall a reed laid low in the mud by the wind say to a fellow reed fallen in the opposite direction: "Crawl as I crawl, wretch, or I shall petition that you be torn up by the roots and burned"? [18]

Voltaire was not content with working for freedom of thought in the abstract only. At grave personal risk, he plunged into the actual battle against brutal intolerance in France, especially in three famous cases of religious persecution— those of Jean Calas, Paul Sirven, and the Chevalier de la Barré. He not only defeated the forces of organized and official intolerance but also made these cases internationally famous. He made intolerance henceforth more difficult in France and helped to discredit it all over Europe. Egon Friedell, in his *Cultural History of the Modern Age,* has stated in characteristically colorful fashion Voltaire's devotion to intellectual freedom and the historic results thereof:

> The root passion of his life was, indeed, a flaming desire for justice, a burning, consuming, almost drunken hatred of every kind of public despotism, stupidity, malice, or partisanship. And if our world of today consists of no more than two-fifths villains and three-eighths idiots, we have largely Voltaire to thank for it.

VII. THE ATTACK ON THE CENSORSHIP OF THE PRESS

For a time even scholars and publicists acquiesced in the censorship of the press by church and state. They regarded it as necessary to protect the public against the dissemination of dangerous errors. Even if these errors might not harm the wise man, who knew how to defend himself against them, they might do infinite damage to the unlettered masses. The argument rested chiefly on the "I am my brother's keeper" line of reasoning. It was deemed better to hang the millstone of censorship around the necks of philosophers and scientists than to give offense to "one of the least of these, my brethren."

[18] *Op. cit.,* Woolf ed., pp. 302-4.

But the drastic censorship imposed by the Long Parliament in 1643 was too much for an intelligent Puritan to endure. It provoked the most eloquent plea for the freedom of the press which has ever been published, John Milton's *Areopagitica: a Speech for the Liberty of Unlicensed Printing* (1644). Milton argued that it is useless, even dangerous, to shelter persons from erroneous doctrines. Truth can triumph only when given free sway. The best way to overcome error is to battle with it publicly:

> I can not praise (he wrote) a fugitive and cloistered virtue, unexercised and unbreathed, that never seeks out and sees her adversary, but shrinks out of the race, where that immortal garland is to be run for, not without dust and heat. . . . That virtue which knows not the utmost that vice promises to her followers, and rejects it, is but a blank virtue, not a pure. . . .
> Let the truth and falsehood grapple. Who ever knew truth put to the worse in a free and open encounter? . . . Her confuting is the surest suppressing. . . . She needs no policies, nor stratagems, nor licensings to make her victorious. These are the shifts and defenses that error uses against her power. . . .[19]

Among Puritans themselves Milton's arguments fell on deaf ears, and increasingly severe censorship was imposed during the Long Parliament and the Commonwealth era. Indeed, Milton himself fell into a rôle dangerously near to that of acting as a censor for the Cromwellian regime. But his words became immortal and were a perpetual inspiration to those who fought against stupid censorship.

A more effective, if not so original attack on censorship was made by Charles Blount (1654-1693), a religious liberal, who used most of Milton's arguments in his *Just Vindication of the Liberty of the Press* and his *Reasons for the Liberty of Unlicensed Printing*. He cleverly appealed to Protestant partisanship by arguing that a free press would deal a fatal blow to English Catholicism, which, he alleged, thrived on the ignorance of believers. In a pamphlet Blount then attempted a piece of strategy later used by Defoe against religious bigots. He pretended to defend the censor, Edmund Bohun, but reduced Bohun's arguments to absurdity. Bohun took Blount's statements seriously, and forthwith licensed his pamphlet. Notwithstanding this, however, Parliament proceeded to censor it. The excitement which followed this absurdity helped to do away with licensed printing in England.

Matthew Tindal aided in the campaign for a free press in England by publishing, shortly after Blount's works appeared, a book on the *Liberty of the Press* (1698). He launched a devastating attack on the whole conception of a licensed press, and argued in particular for complete freedom in discussing religious matters in print.

The French *Philosophes* joined in the fray. Montesquieu assailed censorship as an act of sheer tyranny. Voltaire declared that of all essential civil liberties the freedom of the press is the most indispensable and valuable. He summed up the situation thus: "I know many boring books, but not one that is really harm-

[19] Quoted by Smith, *op. cit.,* I, 520-21.

ful." The reformer and idealist, Claude Adrien Helvétius (1715-1771), argued forcefully for freedom of the press as essential to public education. He observed that: "Most governments urge their citizens to search for truth; but almost all governments punish them for finding it." The argument for the supreme importance of a free press was vigorously supported in America by Thomas Jefferson, among others. Jefferson even went so far as to declare that if he had to choose between a government and no newspapers, and no government and a free press, he would unhesitatingly select the latter.

Some famous "free press" battles helped in the crusade against censorship. One of the first, the noted Zenger case, occurred in America. John Peter Zenger had founded the New York *Weekly Journal* in 1733 and proceeded to attack the royal governor. For this he was thrown in prison. Zenger thereupon demanded trial by a jury, received it, and was set free.

The John Wilkes case in England, just before the Revolutionary War, was a less clear-cut case of freedom of the press, but it served to educate the public on that issue. Wilkes was a brilliant but erratic and indiscreet young member of the House of Commons. Failing to gain a higher government post, he established a paper called the *North Briton Review* and briskly attacked the government of Lord Bute in 1763. Wilkes was arrested and thrown into the Tower. Because of his parliamentary privilege he was freed by the Lord Chief Justice. Hence the case was not tried on the issue of the freedom of the press.

Wilkes got into further trouble by printing for private circulation a racy *Essay on Woman*. One of his friends in the House of Lords, Lord Sandwich, betrayed his confidence and circulated it in the Upper House. Wilkes fled to France and was outlawed. About a decade later, however, he returned to England, was re-elected to the House of Commons and died in good repute. Legally, the Wilkes case settled nothing concerning freedom of the press, but the vast excitement it created brought the question forcibly before England, Europe, and America.

After the Napoleonic wars there was a new wave of intolerance and censorship. The outstanding advocate of free speech in those days—the forerunner of men like Clarence Darrow, Arthur Garfield Hays, and Roger Baldwin—was William Godwin (1756-1836), the courageous philosopher, publicist, and lawyer. He was one of the leading Rationalists of his age, and is often regarded as the founder of philosophical anarchism.

Intelligent and educated persons have long since come to understand the futility of censorship. Most ideas we desire to keep from the people are not actually harmful. Even if they are, censorship usually results in a greater dissemination of the very ideas we want to suppress. Moreover, all censorship is likely to be unenlightened, for ignorance and stupidity are usually implicit in the consent of persons to act as censors. Perhaps no one has put the case against censorship more concisely than James Harvey Robinson did in an interview published in the *Literary Digest* of June 23, 1923:

> I am opposed to all censorship, partly because we already have Draconian laws, and police willing to interfere on slight pretense in cases in which the public

sense of propriety seems likely to be shocked; partly because, as Milton long ago pointed out, censors are pretty sure to be fools, for otherwise they would not consent to act. Then I am a strong believer in the fundamental value of so-phistication. I would have boys and girls learn early about certain so-called "evils" —and rightly so-called—so that they begin to reckon with them in time. I have no confidence in the suppression of every-day facts. We are much too skittish of honesty. When we declare that this or that will prove demoralizing, we rarely ask ourselves, demoralizing to whom and how? We have a sufficiently delicate ma-chinery already to prevent the circulation of one of Thorstein Veblen's philosophic treatises and Mr. Cabell's highly esoteric romance. For further particulars see the late John Milton's "Areopagitica" *passim*. To judge by the conduct of some of our college heads the influence of this work is confined to a recognition of its noble phraseology, with little realization of the perennial value of the sentiments it contains.

VIII. THE TRIUMPH OF TOLERANCE AND FREEDOM OF THE PRESS

We may now undertake the relatively pleasant task of chronicling the victories won in behalf of tolerance and freedom of the press, victories which were enor-mously aided by those vigorous and courageous attacks upon intolerance and censorship we have just summarized. General historical developments in the seventeenth and eighteenth centuries also spurred the movement towards free-dom and civilized decency. Such were the rise of science and the growing im-portance of the scientific frame of mind; the increase of skepticism among the learned; the growth of commerce and capitalism and the evolution of a more worldly point of view; the trend towards representative government and the curbing of absolutism; and the contact of Europe with the diversity of thought and culture overseas.

Tolerance first triumphed in Holland, or the Dutch Netherlands. For this there were a number of reasons. For one thing Protestants and Catholics were so equally balanced in numbers that it was hard for either to gain unquestioned supremacy. It also proved economically advantageous to be tolerant. Skilled laborers, like the French Huguenots, sought refuge there and helped to develop Dutch industries. Freedom of the press made the Dutch cities, especially Amster-dam and Leyden, leading centers of the printing trade. Open-mindedness also brought intellectual prestige, since many a distinguished fugitive scholar, as, for instance, Spinoza, came to Holland and lent luster to the land. From the close of the sixteenth century Holland was an oasis of civilized freedom in a Euro-pean desert of obscurantism and bigotry.

In England enlightened legislation began with the Toleration Act of 1689 which gave freedom of worship to all save Catholics and Unitarians. But the old civil disabilities of Catholics and dissenters under the Test Act continued. From 1727 to 1828 Protestant dissenters were able to get around these by a series of annual indemnity acts freeing them from the obligation of receiving the sacraments of the Anglican church. In 1779, a law was passed making it no longer necessary for dissenters to subscribe to the thirty-nine articles of Anglicanism in order to hold office. The Test Act was abolished in 1828, insofar as it applied to Protestant dissenters. In 1829, the civil disabilities of Catholics were also erased from the statute books. In 1858 and 1866, steps were taken which admitted Jews to public offices. Finally, in 1888, the civil disabilities of atheists were removed.

In the American colonies, complete tolerance existed only in Rhode Island. Pennsylvania granted freedom of worship to all Christians, as did Maryland, although the latter kept the death penalty for atheists and Socinians. After the Toleration Act of 1689 was adopted in England there was a rather general tendency to extend its operation to the colonies. Massachusetts enacted a similar law in 1691.

There was a considerable growth of tolerance in Sweden after the death of Charles XII in 1718. Frederick the Great of Prussia was a freethinker and the friend of Voltaire. Under his rule, Prussia became the most tolerant country in Europe. When Frederick came to the throne he stated that: "All religions must be tolerated, and the magistrate must notice them only to prevent any religion disturbing another; for in this country every man must go to heaven his own way." Frederick was motivated as much by civic and economic considerations as by his own skepticism, for he knew that religious persecutions were politically disturbing and economically costly. He especially wished tolerance for the industrious Huguenots who had come to Prussia.

While savage laws still remained on the books in France, so powerful and effective were the *Philosophes* in their battle for tolerance that the Huguenots had the courage to call a national synod in 1744. The French Revolution turned the tables by favoring free thought and imposing strict limitations on the Catholics. The civil constitution of the clergy was a sharp blow at the former Catholic autocracy. While there was a tendency to attack the Protestants and freethinkers at the time of the restoration of the Bourbons in 1815, relatively little savagery resulted. Since 1830 there has been a fair degree of religious tolerance in France, and in 1905-1907 the church was definitely separated from the state.

In Spain, ferocity continued until the period when the country was brought under Napoleonic influence; savagery was resumed after the Bourbons were restored. No complete relief was achieved until the revolution of 1931, although there had been some improvement after the reconstruction necessitated by the disgraceful defeat of Spain in the Spanish-American War of 1898. In Italy, the unified government, reflecting the love of Cavour for British institutions and liberties, ended papal domination in 1870 and extended the basic civil and religious liberties to the Italian people. These lapsed after 1922 under the Fascist regime, for Mussolini declared liberty to be too great a luxury for the Italians to enjoy. Austria-Hungary gradually gained civil and religious liberties after the failure of the revolution of 1848. Intolerance lay like a heavy blight in Russia until the revolution of 1917, after which the erstwhile oppressed turned savagely on their erstwhile oppressors.

Freedom from censorship, like religious freedom, was first known in Holland, where authors issued books they did not dare to publish in their own homeland. Holland developed a notable printing industry and a flourishing book trade. Some freedom was gained in the many weak and divided German states, and the profits from the great Frankfort book fair encouraged the authorities of that free city to take a very lenient attitude towards the press. Frederick the Great permitted unheard-of freedom in printing skeptical books and even laughed at libels directed against himself, but he allowed no criticisms of his fiscal and military policies. Thus Frederick was one of the first to reveal an attitude which has come to be rather common today, namely, indifference to religious radicalism but great sensitivity to political and economic dissent. England allowed the law providing for the licensing of the press to lapse in 1695. Sweden abolished all censorship in 1766. Freedom of the press was slowly realized in continental Europe, outside Spain and Russia, during the nineteenth century.

While there never has been complete tolerance and freedom of the press, it is probable that the greatest degree of freedom existed in the United States around 1850 and in the Third French Republic since 1880. About 1850 there were as yet no obscenity laws on the books in the United States, the old religious and property disabilities had been abolished, and the right of debate and petition was freely recognized. Many of the most distinguished American literati were followers of Fourier and other European radical idealists. The New York *Tribune,* under Horace Greeley, was a radical and reformist sheet. A little later, Greeley employed Karl Marx as his European correspondent. At this time Abraham Lincoln was declaring that the international bond of the workingman is more sacred and binding than any other save the family bond, and William Henry Seward was talking about a "higher law than the Constitution." But Negro slavery was a blot on the record. After the Civil War, the growth of plutocracy lessened the scope of human freedom. Economic dissent was discouraged and refused when possible. In France under the Third Republic, anticlericalism became dominant, and Zola in his realistic portraits of life made moral candor more facile and reputable. On the other hand, such episodes as the Dreyfus case showed that French liberty was by no means complete.

IX. THE STRUGGLE FOR CIVIL LIBERTIES

We may here appropriately describe in some detail the way in which man has established his right to certain liberties and privileges highly prized in modern democratic countries. We have just dealt with two of the most precious of those liberties, freedom of worship and freedom of the press. But there are many other personal liberties that have come to be regarded as indispensable under democracy. Such liberties are the right to life, trial by jury, free assemblage, and many others. As convenient a list of civil liberties as is likely to be gathered is offered by Professor Leon Whipple:

I. THE RIGHTS—PERSONAL LIBERTY

1. The Right to Security—life, limb, health.
2. The Right to Liberty—freedom of the body, and freedom of movement, with the privilege of emigration or immigration.

3. The Right to Equality—protection against slavery, involuntary servitude, and imprisonment for debt; against discriminations on account of color or sex, and (in general) race; and against special or hereditary privileges. These are the Civil Rights, or rights of the citizen.
4. The Right to Reputation.
5. The Right to Bear Arms and to Organize the Militia.
6. The Right to Law:

   a. Before Trial:

      Justice shall be free;
      The accused shall have the right to the common law;
      No unreasonable search or seizure;
      The right to the writ of habeas corpus shall not be denied;
      The accused shall hear the accusation;
      Bail shall not be excessive;
      Trial shall be on indictment after investigation by a grand jury;
      Witnesses shall be protected in their rights;
      The accused shall be protected against "lynch law."

   b. During Trial:

      The accused shall have "due process of law, law of the land, and judgment by his peers";
      He shall have a trial by a jury of the vicinage; defined as to size, and the need for unanimity;
      He shall have counsel;
      He may summon witnesses;
      No inquisitorial methods shall be used;
      He shall not be put twice in jeopardy for one offense;
      The crime of treason shall be defined;
      There shall be no attainder.

   c. After Trial:

      No excessive fines, or cruel or unusual punishments;
      No *ex post facto* law shall be passed;
      Provision for pardoning is usually made;
      There shall be no corruption of blood.

II. THE FREEDOMS—SOCIAL LIBERTY

1. Freedom of Conscience—especially religious liberty, including no state support, or enforced individual support of an established church; and no religious tests for participation in the government.
2. Freedom of Speech and Assemblage, including petition.
3. Freedom of the Press—with legal provisions against tyrannical coercion by libel proceedings or for contempt of court.[20]

Most of these rights and liberties first played their rôle in discussion and controversy in the sixteenth and seventeenth centuries under the guise of the "natural rights of man," rights which were regarded not as man-made, or a product of human institutions, but as inherent in the cosmic scheme—a part of the

---

[20] Leon Whipple, *Our Ancient Liberties,* Wilson, 1927, pp. 13-14.

natural order. Man had enjoyed them when he lived in the hypothetical state of nature prior to formal social control.[21] When man emerged from the state of nature into society and placed himself voluntarily under a government—according to this theory—he did not give up any of his natural rights. The state guaranteed their continuation.

This whole doctrine is, of course, absurd when taken in any literal historical sense, however valuable a purpose it may have served as propaganda for a truly noble cause. There is no such thing as a natural right to anything—even to such an elementary matter as life itself. So far as nature is concerned, we have no more rights than a wild animal—which is the right of the strong or the crafty to get all they can or wish. All the rights which man has ever enjoyed in even the most sophisticated democracies are wholly and solely the product of social relationships and historical experiences.

In the course of time, classes and individuals have wrested from society as a whole—the herd—certain rights and privileges. These remained valid so long as the said classes and individuals, or their descendants, could defend them. There is no certainty that these rights have always been wise demands or concessions. The point we are making is that persons or groups which wanted them and were powerful enough to get them succeeded in establishing certain rights and immunities. In other words, human prerogatives were always secured in the give-and-take process between society, classes, and individuals. They are not natural rights. They are conferred by society, willingly or not. No man has any natural right even to keep his jugular vein intact, to retain his pocketbook, or to have a trial before being thrown into jail.

We may now briefly review the development of human liberties down to the sixteenth century. In primitive society, there were no formal guaranties of individual prerogatives. Custom and usage, however, created certain personal rights which were well observed within the group. Life within the kinship group was respected, certain property and religious privileges were recognized, and so on.

In the ancient Orient a much more authoritarian order arose. While certain rights of property, contract, and the like were protected, there was little personal freedom. The philosopher of history, Hegel, is said once to have remarked that in this Oriental era only two were free—God in heaven and the king on earth. Certainly, there was no freedom of religion, conscience, the press, speech, assemblage, and the like. Even semidivine kings found it impossible radically to alter the religious system.

Among the Attic Greeks and the Romans a large degree of personal liberty was enjoyed by the aristocracy. The right of criticism and free thought arose among the Greeks and continued to exist in Rome until the establishment of an Oriental despotism. It had its limitations in practice, to be sure, but its legitimate place in a social system was well established. The Greeks originated the custom of trial by jury. The Romans scrupulously preserved the legal rights of citizens. In Roman law, the individual emerged as an entity. According to

21 See above, p. 661.

law he had certain rights, which the government was bound to respect. This was the origin of the legalistic aspect of our civil liberties, for in the eyes of the law these rights are our civil liberties. The state, acting through the constitution, announces that there are certain rights and immunities which the individual may enjoy and which the government cannot take away. Only the action of the state through a change in the constitution can deprive the individual of these rights and immunities.

In the Middle Ages there was a marked reversion to a cruder type of civilization, politically controlled by semibarbarous kings and dominated by a church absolute in its power over faith and morals—and even over life. This was not a healthy atmosphere for the growth of human liberties. Extensive freedom during the medieval period existed only in the towns. But town liberty was corporate rather than personal. A man possessed rights as a member of a class or a group like the guilds. And in matters of religion and conscience the church ruled about as absolutely in the town as in the country.

The age of humanism promoted, as we have seen, the sense of individuality, of the worth of man as man, providing an important moral foundation for the later struggle for the legal rights of individuals. Humanism made individual rights seem worth battling for. The Protestant revolution carried the emancipation further by proclaiming the individual nature of worship and religious conscience. To be sure, individual conscience had to identify itself with the beliefs of the majority in any Protestant sect and with the approved doctrines of the religion supported by the state. But the theory was promulgated in the Protestant revolution that the individual could go directly to God according to the dictates of his own conscience.

The circumstances which gave rise to our historical civil liberties were, however, primarily associated with the commercial revolution, the rise of capitalism, the growth of the bourgeoisie, and the latter's desire to protect private property and business rights.

During the Middle Ages, the feudal lords were ruthless enemies of the merchants, robbing them and exploiting them shamefully. Hence, when the kings turned against the barons in early modern times, they found willing allies in the merchant class, who eagerly availed themselves of the opportunity to even the score with their ancient enemies. It was not long, however, before the merchant class discovered that the kings were as arbitrary and avaricious as the barons had been; that they levied excessive and arbitrary taxes, threw men into prison without trial, confiscated property, and quartered soldiers on them.

Therefore, the bourgeoisie clearly recognized that they must overthrow arbitrary royal rule. They outlined a set of goals necessary for their well-being and prosperity. They had to have the right to carry on a campaign of propaganda in order to promote their cause and gain followers. This made them ardent supporters of free speech, a free press, and the right to assemblage. The sanctity of property rights naturally appealed to a commercial class, and this idea furnished an argument against the practice of royal confiscation. Trial by jury would help to avert arbitrary imprisonment, and the right of habeas corpus would save them from rotting in jail at the pleasure of some autocrat. Freedom from the quartering of soldiers in homes would remove one particularly obnoxious manifestation of royal arrogance and oppression. Along with these specific goals went the more generalized ambition to create representative government, so that arbitrary royal rule could be ended and the sovereignty of the people made supreme.

Our civil liberties, then, were created on the basis of a set of class interests and aspirations. Between the age of Elizabeth and the reign of William and Mary—approximately a century—those fundamental civil liberties which we still treasure were won in England. From England they passed to the British colonies in America, were embodied in colonial charters and the Declaration of Independence, and finally made permanent in the first ten amendments to our Federal Constitution. From England and America, jointly, these civil liberties were absorbed by the French revolutionists of 1789. In the nineteenth century, the heritage of civil liberties was claimed by most European countries. Russia was a particular exception.

As we have just suggested, the middle class first triumphed in England. They embodied their precious civil liberties in the Bill of Rights of 1689, but the foundations of this bill rested upon a number of famous English charters. First in point of time was the Magna Carta of 1215, a reactionary feudal document which has rarely been fully understood.[22] Misinterpreted in the seventeenth century by the opponents of Stuart absolutism, it was elevated to the position of a major shibboleth in the campaign for English civil liberties.

More literally in harmony with later democracy was the Model Parliament (1295) of Edward I which confirmed the rights of Parliament and made that body representative of the nobility, clergy, and burghers. Henceforth, Parliament had a real right to voice the wishes of the realm.

A landmark in the struggle for civil liberties was the Petition of Right, exacted from Charles I in 1628. It secured the promise that there would be no further arbitrary taxation or confiscation of property, that no freeman would be imprisoned without show of cause, that soldiers would not be billeted in private homes, and that martial law would not be used in time of peace. The famous Bushel case of 1670 and the Fox libel act of 1792 strengthened and safeguarded trial by jury. The Habeas Corpus Act passed in 1679 directed speedy trial and made it impossible to hold a prisoner for more than twenty days without trial or bail. After the "Glorious Revolution" of 1688, most of the contents of earlier charters of English liberties were, as we noted, embodied in the famous Bill of Rights of 1689. This Bill, condemning the conduct and offenses of James II, included the following important articles:

1. That the pretended power of suspending laws, or of execution of laws, by regal authority without consent of parliament, is illegal.
2. That the pretended power of dispensing with laws, or the execution of laws, by regal authority, as it hath been assumed and exercised of late, is illegal.

22 See W. S. McKechnie, *Magna Carta*, Macmillan, 1914.

3. That the commission for erecting the late court of commissioners for ecclesiastical causes, and all other commissions and courts of like nature, are illegal and pernicious.

4. That levying money for or to the use of the crown by pretense of prerogative, without grant of parliament, for longer time or in other manner than the same is or shall be granted, is illegal.

5. That it is the right of the subjects to petition the king, and all commitments and prosecutions for such petitioning are illegal.

6. That the raising or keeping a standing army within the kingdom in time of peace, unless it be with consent of parliament, is against law.

7. That the subjects which are Protestants may have arms for their defense suitable to their conditions, and as allowed by law.

8. That election of members of parliament ought to be free.

9. That the freedom of speech, and debates or proceedings in parliament, ought not to be impeached or questioned in any court or place out of parliament.

10. That excessive bail ought not to be required, nor excessive fines imposed, nor cruel and unusual punishments inflicted.

11. That jurors ought to be duly impaneled and returned, and jurors which pass upon men in trials for high treason ought to be freeholders.

12. That all grants and promises of fines and forfeitures of particular persons before conviction are illegal and void.

13. And that for redress of all grievances, and for the amending, strengthening, and preserving of the laws, parliament ought to be held frequently.

The Bill of Rights was supplemented by the Toleration Act of 1689 which, as we noted above, extended civil and religious liberties to all save Catholics and Unitarians; and by the Mutiny Act of the same year which provided for parliamentary control over the army, made annual meetings of Parliament essential, and, incidentally, promoted parliamentary power over the finances of the realm. Finally, in 1701, the Act of Settlement gave Parliament power to dispose of the crown and to determine the line of succession.

The essentials of the English Bill of Rights were embodied in the state constitutions of American commonwealths after the adoption of the Declaration of Independence in 1776. Eleven of the thirteen states adopted such constitutions. Then, at the insistence of the Jeffersonian liberals, the same general list of liberties was incorporated in our Federal Constitution in the form of the first ten amendments.

France adopted the English and American liberties in the Declaration of the Rights of Man of 1789, and in the revolutionary charters and constitutions which followed. In the next century most western European states wrote many of these liberties into their constitutions.

In this manner were won those rights which hypothetically deliver citizens of democratic countries from arbitrary imprisonment, censorship, and religious discrimination, and guarantee free speech, press, and assemblage. These rights were chiefly, though by no means exclusively, the result of the crusade by the new mercantile classes, in an effort to secure freedom for their economic activities and to insure safety for their property against the dangers of arbitrary taxation and confiscation. Most of those rights which did not directly concern business and property were deemed valuable because they were essential to the political defense of business and property. That is, the bourgeoisie, to safeguard their cause, would have been fatally hampered without a free press, free petition, and the right to assemble in groups. And they would have been seriously handicapped if they could have been thrown into prison without fair trial and kept there indefinitely without show of cause.

In due time the proletariat invoked the same civil liberties in order to protect itself from the mercantile and industrial classes. Since, however, the latter usually controlled the governments of industrialized nations, the proletariat has met with much difficulty in attaining equality with the bourgeoisie in the enjoyment of the conventional civil liberties. As Professor Arthur W. Calhoun has observed, the Supreme Court would not intervene to save Sacco and Vanzetti but it would eagerly have intervened to protect a utility company in a small Massachusetts town from what it regarded as an excessive degree of municipal rate regulation. Indeed, the bourgeois civil liberties have frequently been utilized as a powerful defense against legislation designed to give the workers liberty and security. It is a strange irony of history that the constitutional liberties established by seventeenth-century merchants and lawyers in England were invoked in twentieth-century America to outlaw such things as child labor laws, minimum wage legislation, and the right of labor to organize. When labor became strong enough to assert itself in politics it was soon evident that it would not be too sensitive about civil liberties in the struggle against the capitalistic employers. A good example was the Wagner National Labor Relations Act of 1935 in the United States. While the provocation was admittedly great, this law placed limitations upon employers which constituted a startling violation of the freedom of speech and the press.

The fact that the conventional civil liberties were a bourgeois product, designed primarily to protect private property and capitalistic enterprise, helps to explain the attitude of Soviet Russia toward them. Americans frequently wonder how Russians can submit to the extinction of these liberties. The fact is that the Russians never enjoyed them and hardly know what they mean. Under the tsars, the Russians enjoyed few civil liberties. Despite the revolution of 1905 the bourgeois movement in Russia was not strong enough and did not endure long enough to promote civil liberties. When the Marxian Bolsheviks came into power in 1917 they had no interest in establishing typically bourgeois legal devices and safeguards. Russia thus skipped almost entirely the bourgeois stage of civilization in its precipitate progress from quasi-feudalism to collectivized industry. There is as little likelihood that the Soviet rulers will ultimately establish the bourgeois civil liberties of the seventeenth and eighteenth centuries as that they will introduce other basic elements of bourgeois culture.

The rise of civil liberties was closely associated with the establishment of constitutional government, a process which extended from the seventeenth century in England to the early twentieth century in Russia. The mercantile classes were not content merely to have civil rights and guarantees of liberty enacted into statute law; they also wished to have them written into constitutional law, since it is far more difficult for a government to modify a constitution than to alter ordinary laws. This explains the inordinate enthusiasm of the bourgeoisie in the seventeenth, eighteenth, and nineteenth centuries for written constitutions. The latter were not the product of mass clamor for freedom and democracy, but the result of bourgeois demands for an extreme protection of the civil liberties which would put their property rights and business practices beyond the reach of the government.

Most of the early European constitutions were designed to protect liberty and property from arbitrary action by kings and nobles. The Federal Constitution of the United States was the first to be chiefly concerned with protecting property rights against possible inroads from the lower classes—the embattled farmers and urban workers. A defensive psychology—known technically as "constitutionalism"—was also developed by the bourgeoisie to supplement the legal protections offered by constitutional law. These constitutions, which embodied bourgeois safeguards, were enveloped in myth and fantasy and were endowed with something of the sanctity once bestowed upon kings. This has made it very difficult to change constitutions which legally protect bourgeois property and policies. In time, the proletariat learned the same strategy. Hence, in the first proletarian constitution, that of Soviet Russia, we find the tables turned. The Russian constitution, which outlaws capitalist ideals and practices, is surrounded by the same halo of sanctity that has buttressed capitalistic constitutions in other countries prior to the Russian revolution.

X. LATER FORMS OF INTOLERANCE

We have now traced some impressive early victories against intolerance and oppression. But the battle was not won. Old forms of intolerance have been pretty much suppressed, although bitter persecution of Jews continued into the twentieth century. There has been mainly a shift in the forms of intolerance, as was the case in the passage from the Roman Empire to medieval Christianity. In the Roman Empire, intolerance had been mainly political and economic. From the beginning of the Middle Ages until the eighteenth century it was chiefly religious. After the eighteenth century intolerance again became primarily political and economic—particularly the latter.

The economic and social changes which are best envisaged under the general concept of the rise of capitalism provided a broad framework for intolerance, namely, an economic basis. Private property and material wealth assumed a new importance. The vested economic interests became as jealous of their material possessions as the medieval church had been of its theological pretensions and responsibilities. It gradually became almost as hazardous to challenge the institution of property and the profit motive as it had been to question the accepted theory of the Trinity. As already shown, Christian institutions came to the defense of capitalism, and the two combined to create the most powerful forms of modern intolerance.

Therefore, when it seemed as though freedom had been won from the incubus of supernaturalism, new intimidations arose in the shape of capitalistic dogmas and controls. Martyrs among economic radicals have died or been imprisoned in large numbers since 1700: Babeuf, matching Servetus; the Chicago anarchists of 1886 being comparable to the Huguenots of St. Bartholomew's Day; Tom Mooney to Roger Williams; and Vanzetti to Giordano Bruno. And if great scholars had concurred in the martyrdom of original minds at the hands of the Inquisition, so two distinguished university presidents personally sanctioned the martyrdom of Sacco and Vanzetti. Wholesale deportation and frequent imprisonment of economic dissenters became common in the United States, while in Fascist and Nazi countries their treatment recalled the intolerance of medieval and early modern times.

The elimination of capitalism would not, however, for a time at least, relieve us of economic intolerance. The Russian Communists are as intolerant of the very concept of private property and free enterprise in the production of goods as the capitalists are of attacks upon property and freedom. And Stalinists have been very intolerant of Trotskyites, and vice versa. Stalin's purges in 1935-1937 were probably the most brutal and bloody in the whole history of political and economic persecutions—indeed, in the history of any and all kinds of persecution.

As hinted above, Fascism and Nazism in the twentieth century were as obstructive of civil liberties as the autocratic church or monarchs of the sixteenth and seventeenth centuries. Mussolini cryptically remarked that liberty is a wasteful luxury that efficient government cannot afford. Hitler made it an even more dangerous luxury in Germany. But Americans should not be too contemptuous of Fascism. The military state capitalism that developed as a result of the Cold War has all too many similarities to this European system.

Nazism in Germany and Fascism in Italy were destroyed by the second World War, although dictatorship of a Fascist type remained in power in Spain. But the Communists, who suppress civil liberty as ruthlessly as the Fascists or Nazis, extended their power over territory and peoples far greater than the combined area and population of Germany and Italy. Conditions in some of the liberated non-communist countries were even worse for a time. Most notorious was the situation in France. Here, over 100,000 alleged collaborators were killed during the confusion which began with the liberation in 1944 and enabled the Communists and other radicals to incite violence far more bloody than the Reign of Terror of 1793-1794 or the Communard uprising of 1870-1871. Upwards of 50,000 Fascists and their families were killed in Italy after the end of hostilities. Trials of war criminals upset many of the main traditions and practices of accepted jurisprudence.

The second World War and the Cold War which followed from 1947 onward greatly curbed civil liberties. The Smith Act of 1940 in the United States made it a crime to teach or advocate the overthrow of the government of the United States by force—a right to which every prominent "father" of the American constitutional system had subscribed with vigor. Communist leaders were sentenced to long terms in prison. The Cold War greatly increased both international and internal tensions, a state of so-called emergency became chronic, and it appeared to justify extreme measures to preserve national security. Repressive policies and actions, hitherto unknown in peacetime, became common. They were encouraged by the violent and largely unfounded accusations of Senator Joseph R. McCarthy. The situation has been especially drastic in regard to Federal employees, where anonymous and unchecked information often sufficed to bring about the dismissal of persons with a previous good record.

A false sense of protection from further inroads on civil liberties was provided by the discrediting of McCarthyism, which aroused enough publicity to encourage the public to resist. What may prove far more disastrous is quietly slipping through new legislation and rules of which the public knows little or nothing. This began even in the Eisenhower administration, which had opposed McCarthy, and increased in frequency and scope under the Kennedy administration thus proving that a liberal administration is no guarantee against curtailing our liberties, even when simultaneously getting publicity for seeking to extend civil rights. This current threat was well summarized by Congressman John V. Lindsay in an article in *Harper's Magazine*, September, 1963. The danger in all this was well summarized by a leading American lawyer and president of the American Bar Association, Mr. Frank E. Holman:

> Our country has endured much through government by crisis in recent years. Public officials have too easily fallen into the habit of asserting that some crisis exists which justifies extraordinary and extra-legal procedures. Almost always these "temporary" expedients tend to become permanent. We often permit our rights and liberties to be whittled away in this manner.

If this was the situation in the leading country among the so-called Free Nations, it was far worse behind the Iron Curtain. While the intolerance and curtailing of liberty had a different cultural background, basis, and impact, there is little doubt that the repression of intellectual freedom was almost as great in the middle of the twentieth century as it had been in the days of the Inquisition, witchcraft, and the religious wars. Evidence to support this assertion is available in the annual reports of the American Civil Liberties Union. It is significant and instructive that it proved necessary to establish this private and self-supporting organization to help prevent American citizens from depriving themselves of the very liberties which our Revolutionary forefathers had fought to establish.

XI. CULTURAL LAG AND CIVIL LIBERTIES

The failure to establish and preserve more successfully the traditional civil liberties which had been worked out in an agrarian age during the seventeenth and eighteenth centuries admittedly constitutes a serious problem. But full success in this would not have sufficed to deal with the questions and perplexities concerning human rights and liberties in our present urban and industrial age. Most of the situations which face citizens today were either unknown or little developed in the days of the Bill of Rights of 1689. A new Bill of Rights is needed to meet the requirements and responsibilities of all classes of citizens in the highly complex urbanized and industrialized life of the twentieth century. Such a list of up-to-date and adequate rights was formulated by the National Resources Planning Board in 1942:

1. The right to work usefully and creatively during the productive years.
2. The right to fair pay, adequate to command the necessities and amenities of

life in exchange for work, ideas, thrift, and other socially valuable services.
3. The right to adequate food, clothing, shelter, and medical care.
4. The right to security, with freedom from fear of old age, want, dependency, sickness, unemployment, and accident.
5. The right to live in a system of free enterprise, free from compulsory labor, irresponsible private power, arbitrary public authority, and unregulated monopolies.
6. The right to come and go, to speak or be silent, free from the spyings of a secret political police.
7. The right to equality before the law with equal access to justice in fact.
8. The right to education for work, for citizenship, and for personal growth and happiness.
9. The right to rest, recreation, and adventure, and the right to enjoy life and take part in an advancing civilization.

Admirable as such a formulation may be, little was being done to bring about the implementation and realization of these rights in the middle of the twentieth century, despite adequate technological equipment. Attention throughout the world was centered upon military technology and armed might which appeared to look forward more to the extermination of humanity and civilization than to the promotion of a more abundant life and greater human liberties.

SELECTED READINGS

Anschen, R. N., ed., *Freedom: Its Meaning,* Harcourt, Brace, 1940.

Bates, E. S., *This Land of Liberty,* Harper, 1930.

Benn, A. W., *History of English Rationalism in the Nineteenth Century,* 2 vols., Longmans, 1926, Vol. I.

Biddle, Francis, *The Fear of Freedom,* Doubleday, 1951.

Bury, J. B., *History of the Freedom of Thought,* Oxford University Press, 1952, chaps. iii-vi.

Carr, R. K., *Federal Protection of Civil Liberties,* Cornell University Press, 1949.

Cassirer, Ernst, *The Philosophy of the Enlightenment,* Beacon, 1955.

Cheyney, E. P., *Law in History,* Knopf, 1927, chap. ii.

Cobban, Alfred, *In Search of Humanity: The Role of the Enlightenment in Modern History,* Braziller, 1960.

Coulton, G. G., *Inquisition and Liberty,* Beacon, 1959.

Ernst, M. L., and Lindey, Alexander, *The Censor Marches On,* Doubleday, 1939.

Garrison, W. E., *Intolerance,* Round Table Press, 1934.

Gillett, C. R., *Burned Books: Neglected Chapters in British Literature and History,* 2 vols., Columbia University Press, 1932.

Hallgren, M. A., *Landscape of Freedom,* Howell, Soskin, 1941.

Haynes, E. S. P., *Religious Persecution,* London, 1904.

Hibschman, Harry, *What Price Tolerance?* Haldeman-Julius, 1931.

Huddleston, Sisley, *France: The Tragic Years, 1939-1947,* Devin-Adair, 1955.

Huttman, M. A., *The Establishment of Christianity and the Proscription of Paganism,* Columbia University Press, 1914.

Joad, C. E. M., *Liberty Today,* Dutton, 1935.

Johnson, Donald, *The Challenge to American Freedoms: World War I and the Rise of the American Civil Liberties Union,* University of Kentucky Press, 1963.

Jordan, W. K., *The Development of Religious Toleration in England*, 4 vols., Harvard University Press, 1932-1941.

Kallen, H. M., ed., *Freedom in the Modern World*, Coward-McCann, 1928.

Klein, A. J., *Intolerance in the Reign of Elizabeth*, Houghton Mifflin, 1925.

Lecky, W. E. H., *Rise and Influence of Rationalism in Europe*, Braziller, 1955.

Manuel, F. E., *The Age of Reason*, Cornell University Press, 1951.

Martin, E. D., *Liberty*, Norton, 1930.

Mecklin, J. M., *The Story of American Dissent*, Harcourt, Brace, 1934.

Muzzey, D. S., "Toleration," in *Essays in Intellectual History Dedicated to James Harvey Robinson*, Harper, 1929, chap. i.

Nelson, E. W., *et al.*, *Persecution and Liberty: Essays in Honor of George Lincoln Burr*, Century, 1931, pp. 3-20, 171-226.

Nussbaum, F. L., *The Triumph of Science and Reason: 1660-1685*, Harper, 1953.

Oppenheim, F. E., *The Dimensions of Freedom: An Analysis*, St. Martins Press, 1962.

Palmer, Frederic, *Heretics, Saints and Martyrs*, Harvard University Press, 1925 chap. i.

Perry, R. L., ed., *Sources of Our Liberties*, New York University Press, 1959.

Robertson, J. M., *Short History of Free Thought*, Russell.

Rogge, O. J., *Our Vanishing Civil Liberties*, Gaer, 1949.

Rolland, Romain, *et al.*, *French Thought in the Eighteenth Century*, David McKay, 1953.

Rovere, Richard, *Senator Joe McCarthy*, Harcourt, Brace, 1959.

Ruffini, Francesco, *Religious Liberty*, London, 1912.

St. George, M. J., and Dennis, Lawrence, *A Trial on Trial*, National Civil Rights Committee, 1946.

Seaton, A. A., *The Theory of Tolerance under the Later Stuarts*, Putnam, 1911.

Siebert, F. S., *Freedom of the Press in England, 1476–1776*, University of Illinois Press, 1952.

Smith, Frank, *Thomas Paine: Liberator*, Stokes, 1938.

Smith, Preserved, *History of Modern Culture*, Vol. I, chaps. xiv-xvi; Vol. II, chaps. xv-xvi.

Smith, T. V., *Creative Sceptics*, Willet, Clark, 1934.

Soule, George, *The Future of Liberty*, Macmillan, 1936.

Spink, J. S., *French Free Thought from Gassendi to Voltaire*, Oxford University Press, 1960.

Stark, W., *America: Ideal and Reality*, Humanities Press, 1947.

Stephen, Leslie, *History of English Thought in the Eighteenth Century*, 2 vols., Peter Smith.

Utley, Freda, *The High Cost of Vengeance*, Regnery, 1949.

Van Loon, Hendrik, *Tolerance*, Boni and Liveright, 1940.

Verrill, A. H., *The Inquisition*, Appleton, 1931.

Villari, Luigi, *The Liberation of Italy, 1943-1947*, Nelson, 1959.

Walsh, W. T., *Characters of the Inquisition*, Kenedy, 1940.

Watkins, Frederick, *The Political Tradition of the West*, Harvard University Press, 1948.

Whipple, Leon, *Our Ancient Liberties*, Wilson, 1927.

—— *The Story of Civil Liberty in the United States*, Vanguard, 1927.

White, A. D., *A History of the Warfare of Science with Theology*, 2 vols., Dover Publications, Inc., 1960.

Wilcox, Clair, *Civil Liberties under Attack*, University of Pennsylvania Press, 1951.

Wish, Harvey, *Society and Thought in America*, 2 vols., McKay, 1950-1962.

XIX

*The Revolution in Religious
and Ethical Thought*

I. RATIONALISTIC SUPERNATURALISM

We left our story of religious development with the Protestant revolt and the Counter Reformation. Both of these promoted a revival of religious fanaticism, extreme dogmatism, doctrinal wrangling, and, ultimately, overt and bloody physical warfare. Neither camp could reflect calmly and tolerantly about religious issues. Emotion and controversy reigned supreme. Reason was held in contempt or actually feared. The conception of a God of arbitrariness still prevailed. The science of the late sixteenth and seventeenth centuries had not yet intervened to impress upon those who did any independent thinking the orderly workings of nature and the physical universe.

By the latter part of the seventeenth century a number of new developments had encouraged a more sane and considered discussion of religious issues among thoughtful theologians and philosophers. Of course, the majority of the clergymen retained their bigoted self-assurance and creedal narrowness, and were ferocious in their emotional denunciation of any evidence of enlightenment and tolerance.[1] But some outstanding religious leaders, both devout and skeptical, were impressed with the need of foregoing emotion and applying some intellectual effort to religious analysis.

Striking scientific discoveries impressed some minds with the orderly workings of nature and suggested that God may be a lawmaking and law-abiding entity. Others were influenced by the emphasis currently laid upon reason and by the attempt to arrive at truth through a rational analysis of problems. Some were driven into philosophical reasoning as a reaction against the prevailing fanaticism and violence.

---

[1] They bitterly attacked even the mild and pious deists.

For one cause or another, then, reason was reinstated in religious discussion for the first time since classical times. There had been considerable talk about reason in the medieval period, especially in the age of scholasticism. But reason, as employed by the scholastics, was a narrow and technical interpretation of the term. Scholasticism was marked by little that was broadly rationalistic. Reason, as the scholastics interpreted it, meant the application of technical logic to theological issues. It did not imply at all a broad or fresh philosophical examination of religious problems. It was merely an attempt to fortify accepted dogmas by dialectical methods.

In the seventeenth and eighteenth centuries, reason was applied to religion in a more fundamental and comprehensive manner. Attempts were made to show that Christianity is a strictly reasonable body of faith, and to defend it upon that ground. Other philosophers were more interested in laying down the principles of a rational religion, letting Christianity qualify if it could. Still others tried to show that reason, relentlessly applied, would undermine Christianity and every other form of supernaturalism.

We shall now proceed to trace the more interesting developments which grew out of the application of reason to religious discussion. We shall first treat what is known as rationalistic supernaturalism. Then we shall discuss the character of deism. Finally, we shall describe the growth of more thoroughgoing skepticism and its evolution, in some cases, into rather evident atheism.

Rationalistic supernaturalism represented an enlightened form of Christianity that gained powerful adherents, especially in England, during the seventeenth century. Its supporters agreed that religion must conform to reason, but they believed that Christianity did so conform. They also maintained that, in order to have a well-rounded and completely defensible religion, its reasonable character should be supplemented by convincing evidence of divine revelation. They insisted, however, that even the evidence from revelation must accord with reason.

Perhaps the first example of such an attitude on the part of an important thinker was expressed in the *Anti-Fanatical Religion and Free Philosophy* of Joseph Glanvill. This book was Glanvill's answer to his own call for a theology suitable to the new age. In marked contrast to the views of Luther, it rebuked the current controversial dogmatism and stressed the fact that faith and reason must not be regarded as diametrically opposed. Rather, faith should be represented as one of the chief manifestations of reason.[2]

But the theologian who is most often associated with the origins of rationalistic supernaturalism in England was the archbishop of Canterbury, John Tillotson (1630-1694). His religious thought was embodied mainly in a series of powerful doctrinal sermons. His whole attitude was a rebuke to mysticism. He would have none of the yearning intuition of the Cambridge Platonists, led by Henry More. Religion must be established and vindicated by rational analysis in a broad philosophical sense. It must be treated as a series of rational propositions, to be tested and demonstrated by logical evidence. Tillotson declared that religion is not to be regarded as an end in itself, nor is it to be valued for itself alone. It

[2] See above, p. 762.

is socially significant and worth-while because it provides supernatural sanctions for moral conduct. But these divine sanctions must conform to the rational scheme of the whole body of religion.

Tillotson laid some stress on prophecy, and on Christ's being the logical fulfillment of the Old Testament prophecies regarding his coming and his mission. But he emphasized primarily the rôle of miracles in demonstrating the divine origins and nature of Christianity. To Tillotson, a miracle must clearly be an act quite obviously beyond human power to perform, and it must convey to our senses a definite conviction of its miraculous character. Further, valid miracles must be compatible in their nature and implications with a conception of God founded upon reason. Christianity, said Tillotson, is proved to be a divine religion, not only by its agreement in principle with the religion of reason, but also because of many evident miracles performed by Christ, their complete reasonableness and their logical compatibility with the religious conceptions of Old Testament prophecy and with the theology of the New Testament.

Tillotson's religious views were placed on a more formal philosophical basis by John Locke in his *Essay concerning Human Understanding,* his *Reasonableness of Christianity* (1695), and his *Discourse on Miracles* (1706). In a manner consistent with his general philosophy, Locke contended that there is no such thing as an innate idea of God. But the existence of God can be proved by the processes of rational demonstration.

Locke's general system of reasonable religion rested on certain basic principles: (1) there is one God who is the ruler of the universe; (2) he demands that man shall lead a virtuous life in conformity with divine will; and (3) there is a future life in which evil deeds will be punished and good conduct rewarded. In a word, it means that we should have faith in Christ and lead the righteous life which is possible only on the basis of a prior repentance. All this is implicit in a pure religion of reason, but revelation must be introduced in order to make the system complete and effective. Locke believed that this supernatural element is necessary in order to lead men back to God, to freshen their sense of moral duties, to clarify and simplify worship, and to incite them to virtue by reminding them of the scheme of future rewards and punishments.

Locke contended that however essential supernatural revelation may be, it must not conflict with elementary rational considerations. It may be above reason, but it cannot be contrary to reason. Yet Locke, himself, actually accepted all the irrational elements in the Christian epic. As evidence of supernatural revelation, Locke, like Tillotson, relied chiefly upon the validity of the miraculous. A miracle is something beyond the comprehension of the observer and so contrary to the normal operations of nature as to impress him with its unquestionably divine character. It must not, however, run counter to logical consistency with the religious system. Locke concluded that Christianity is a satisfactory religion because it is amply documented with impressive miracles and because its principles are wholly consistent with the strictest rationality.

A similar attitude was taken by Samuel Clarke (1675-1729), who became, after Locke's death, the outstanding English philosopher of his day. His views were

expressed in his Boyle lecture of 1705, entitled *A Discourse concerning the Unchangeable Obligations of Natural Religion, and the Truth and Certainty of the
Christian Revelation.* Clarke contended that the foundation of religion rests on
reason. This natural religion of reason brings us directly to all the fundamentals
of Christianity, namely, the ability to distinguish good from evil, the realization
that our moral obligations express the will of God, the notion that good must
be rewarded and evil punished, and the conviction that a future life must exist
in order that rewards and punishments may be distributed more widely and
more justly than they are on this earth.

But natural religion, however close it may drive us to the Christian religion,
must be supplemented by revelation. Christianity supplies both of these essential
elements of reasonableness and supernaturalism. It is a wholly rational religion,
Christ's character was unique, he was obviously the fulfillment of prophecy, he
wrought many impressive miracles, and the apostles freely testified to his divine
nature. The essentials of this position are admirably summarized by Professor
McGiffert: "Thus, in the opinion of Clarke, as well as of Tillotson and Locke,
natural religion is good and true so far as it goes, but it does not go far enough,
and hence needs to be supplemented by revelation which must not in any way
contradict it, but must be consistent with it in all its parts." [3]

This was the chief line of demarcation between the rational supernaturalists
and the deists. The latter held that a religion of reason is enough. Anything beyond this is likely to be pure superstition or priestly imposture created by self-
interest. The deistic position in this regard was best set forth in William Wollaston's *The Religion of Nature Delineated* (1722). Wollaston contended that
a religion of reason is completely adequate in all respects to the needs of man
and society. How far the conventional divines of England were from even Tillotson and Locke is to be seen in the fact that they greeted Locke's work as "a
coarse occasion for atheism."

The transition to deism was illustrated by the work of John Toland (1670-
1722), *Christianity not Mysterious* (1696). Toland was an enthusiastic disciple
of Locke, but he undermined an important element in the religious thinking of
his master. He held that revelation could not convey anything above reason, in
the sense of being mysterious and incomprehensible. Revelation may extend our
knowledge of reasonable matters, but it cannot transcend our rational powers.
If God has anything to reveal to us he is capable of revealing it clearly, thus
avoiding any possibility of our misunderstanding his meaning. Hence, true revelation must be in accord with reason. All pretended revelations which conflict
with reason are to be rejected as fictitious. In other words, whereas Locke had
said that faith must rest on reason, Toland held that faith must agree with reason. Toland found that some rather important miracles, including the virgin
birth of Christ, should be rejected on the ground of incompatibility with reason.
Toland was bitterly attacked, but he rendered an important service to clear thinking and intellectual emancipation by exploding the super-rational category which

3 A. C. McGiffert, *Protestant Thought before Kant*, Scribner, 1915 (reprint, Harper Torchbooks), p. 209.

had been the refuge of innumerable superstitions and mystical illusions since the days of the Pythagoreans, Plato, the Neoplatonists, and the Christian mystics.

II. THE COURSE OF DEISM

The deists, as they were called, represent a group of moderate religious liberals whose writings extended over about a century and a half, from Lord Herbert of Cherbury (1583-1648) to Thomas Jefferson (1743-1826). Deistic thought came into being in England for obvious reasons, and then spread to the Continent and to the United States, where such writings were popular later than in England. The term "deist" was coined by Pierre Viret (1511-1571) of Geneva to describe men who believed in God but not in Christ. As the term came to be used later, it would be more accurate to describe a deist as one who believed in God but not in orthodox Christianity, since most of the deists distinguished between the teachings of Christ and Christianity, accepting the first and rejecting the latter.

The background of deistic thought is to be found in three leading historical achievements of the age: (1) Newtonian astrophysics; (2) oversea discoveries; and (3) the rationalism of Locke and his school.

From the first of these achievements, the deists derived their notion of a mechanistic universe operating under divine direction. God became the source of universal law. He was no longer the God of arbitrariness, but the maker of those laws which Newton had discovered. Having made these laws, he is logical and consistent enough to abide by them. To assume that God's laws are not worthy of him, nor observed by him, is to accuse God of either levity or inconsistency.

From the oversea discoveries the deists obtained information about the religious views of both advanced and primitive peoples which served to vindicate deistic religious dogmas. They believed that a Chinese sage, an illiterate African Negro and an American Indian held many common and basic religious beliefs. This seemed to the deists to prove that certain elemental and indispensable religious convictions are common to all men at all times. Hence, travel tales buttressed deductions drawn from both rational analysis and the new conception of the universe.

Of course, the travelers and explorers often brought back fanciful stories of oversea beliefs. And the deists were not infrequently farfetched in their interpretations of even authentic primitive customs. But such matters are not relevant to the present discussion. All that need concern us is to note that the deists believed that a natural religion of reason was vindicated by the similarity of widespread religious beliefs as well as by the implications of the Newtonian system. The direct relation of deistic thought to the rationalistic supernaturalism of Locke will be obvious as we proceed.[4]

Whatever the variations of emphasis by particular writers, the fundamental contentions of deism were the following: (1) that a natural religion of reason is entirely adequate without any supernatural buttressing, and (2) that prophecy

---

[4] Cf. S. G. Hefelbower, *The Relation of John Locke to English Deism*, University of Chicago Press, 1918.

and miracles afford no valid proof of the reality of the supernatural—indeed, that there have been no authentic prophecies or miracles.

We may first look at the deistic conception of a natural religion. It was, first of all, a religion based on reason. It had no recourse to supernatural vindication. It rested its case solely upon its appeal to the minds of reasonable men. Secondly, it was a religion common to all men at all times. In other words, it was not only a reasonable religion; it was also a universal one.

While certain earlier suggestions had been made by Bodin, Campanella, and others, the first systematic statement of deistic doctrine was embodied in the works of the sophisticated English aristocrat, Lord Herbert of Cherbury (1583-1648), *On Truth* and *The Religion of the Gentiles*. In the former he argued that truth—including religious truth—is to be found in the innate common sense of mankind. In the second he maintained that all religions have much in common; the good elements are owing to the universality of the innate sense of God's existence and of human virtue, and the bad to the selfish inventions of the priestcraft. The latter idea became a common and effective deist blast against the conventional cults of their day. It was common custom for deists to attribute the evil elements in religion to priestly avarice, diabolism, and ingenuity. While these traits should have been imputed to primitive ignorance and cultural inertia, to blame them on the priesthood was a retort courteous to the bitter attacks which the conventional clergy made on deism.

Lord Herbert accepted many things in the Bible as valid, but to him their validity depended on their reasonableness and not on their presence in the Bible. He rejected the cornerstone of Christianity by saying that it is as absurd to believe that God assumed the form of a man as it would be to believe that the circle assumed the form of a square.

Lord Herbert was also the first to state systematically the fundamental doctrines of the universal religion of reason. As he saw it, there were five of these doctrines: (1) belief in the existence of God; (2) the encouragement of the worship of God; (3) the belief that the chief end of worship is to promote better living; (4) the contention that better living must be preceded by the repentance of sins; and (5) the belief in a future life, in which man will be dealt with justly, according to his conduct here on earth.

It will be plain from this that there was little, if any, difference between the basic tenets of deism and the religion of Locke, Tillotson, and others of their school. The former simply left out the necessity of supernatural sanctions. It will be equally clear that this deistic religion was very similar to that of conservative modernists in religion today.

The first effective popularization of deism was the achievement of Charles Blount (1654-1693), who gave the most complete and systematic statement of the tenets of deistic religion in his *Oracles of Reason*.[5] Blount expressed with special force the deistic contention that the extensive superstitions and the elaborate machinery of worship in conventional religion were invented by the priesthood to further their political and economic ambitions. Such was the burden of

---

[5] For Blount's summary, see McGiffert, *op. cit.*, p. 213.

his *Anima mundi* and his *Great Is Diana of the Ephesians*. In his life of *Apollonius of Tyana* he drew satirical comparisons between pagan wonder-workers and the early Christians who wrought miracles. In all his writings, Blount tended to represent the miraculous elements in Christianity as fabrications of the Apostles, fathers, and priests. If this argument were accepted it meant that the supernatural sanctions of religion insisted upon by Tillotson, Locke, and their school were flagrant human impostures.

Since the rationalistic supernaturalists had based on prophecies and miracles their claims to supernatural sanctions for a reasonable religion, it was only natural that the deists should scrutinize the validity of these alleged prophecies and miracles.[5a] In 1722, William Whiston (1667-1752), who had succeeded Newton as professor of mathematics at Cambridge and had been ousted from his chair for liberal religious views, published *An Essay towards Restoring the True Text of the New Testament*. He contended that the only impressive claim of Jesus to messiahship rested upon the proof that his coming was the literal fulfillment of the prophecies of the Old Testament. Whiston thought that he found evidence of such fulfillment in the case of some prophecies, but pointed to notable discrepancies in a number of other instances.

This line of argument was carried much further by one of the ablest of all deist writers, Anthony Collins. His *Discourse on the Grounds and Reasons of the Christian Religion* was published in 1724. He agreed with Whiston that prophecies constitute the foundation, if there is any, of the dogma of the divine origin of the Christian religion. And the only relevant prophecies are those which relate to the messiahship of Jesus. Whereas Whiston had found only a few inconsistencies and discrepancies, Collins maintained that in no case of an alleged Old Testament prophecy of the coming of Jesus was there any literal and historical fulfillment. These prophecies of the messiahship of Jesus can, at best, be accepted only in an allegorical sense. Since, by Collins' time, the allegorical method had lost much of its original repute in intellectual circles, this conclusion was a serious charge against Christian supernaturalism. In his *Scheme of Literal Prophecy Considered* (1727), Collins went considerably further, admitted that allegorical interpretations of prophecy have no real validity, and contended that Christianity cannot base any claim to supernatural sanctions on the fulfillment of scriptural prophecies. Hence, according to his original assumption, it can make no valid pretense to a supernatural foundation.

Collins' view of the futility of the argument from prophecy was supported by a fellow deist, Thomas Woolston (1669-1731). Indeed, Woolston, in his *Old Apology for the Truth of the Christian Religion against the Jews and Gentiles Revived* (1705), had emphasized the allegorical attitude nearly twenty years before Collins' first book was published. Woolston's *The Moderator between an Infidel and an Apostate* (1725) was a sparkling satire which purported to denounce Collins as an enemy of the true faith but actually and cogently supported Collins' attack upon the argument from prophecy.

[5a] For the work of the deists on these matters, see F. C. Conybeare, *A History of New Testament Criticism*, Putnam, 1910, chap. iii.

Equally devastating was the deist attack on that other alleged supernatural sanction of Christianity, namely, miracles. Here the most important critic was Woolston, whose withering analysis of miracles was embodied in his six *Discourses on the Miracles of Our Saviour* (1727-1730). He argued that many alleged accounts of miracles were probably false anyhow. Even if true, they must be taken allegorically if they are to possess any real spiritual lesson. Many miracles, if taken literally, either savor of mere sorcery or are downright silly. Woolston gave many illustrations, of which we may select the blasting of the fig tree:

> What if a yeoman of Kent should go to look for pippins in his orchard at Easter (the supposed time that Jesus sought for these figs) and because of a disappointment cut down his trees? What then would his neighbors make of him? Nothing less than a laughing-stock; and if the story got into our *Publik News*, he would be the jest and ridicule of mankind.

Woolston went on to show that if this miracle were regarded as an allegorical portrayal of the curse placed upon Jerusalem for failing to bear spiritual fruit, it would be elevated from a joke to a profound and noble religious lesson. Finally, Woolston suggested that Christ's demonstrable power to work miracles would be no proof of his divinity. The most devout Christian writers have admitted the power of the devil and his worshipers to work many and sundry miracles.

Woolston was the one outstanding deist martyr. He paid the penalty for his boldness, was prosecuted for blasphemy and profanity, fined £25, and sentenced to a year in jail. Being unable to raise the security of £4,000 demanded as a condition of his release, he eventually died in jail. His fate, and that of Peter Annet, who was sent to the pillory and to prison, illustrate the fact, which must not be forgotten, that all of these men risked severe penalties for their ventures into religious criticism. They were hampered by blasphemy laws and by all sorts of social and legal penalties. If the conditions in England were more favorable than those in many continental states, they were not yet ideal for the dissenter.

One of the most effective of all deist attacks on miracles was made by a very moderate individual, whom some do not regard as a deist at all, Conyers Middleton (1683-1750). A clergyman, Middleton explicitly accepted the miracles described in the Bible. But he rejected the miracles attributed to the saints in post-apostolic days. His most important writings were his *Introductory Discourse* and his *Free Inquiry into the Miraculous Powers Which Are Supposed to Have Subsisted in the Christian Church* (1747-49). Since these post-apostolic miracles are attested to in great detail by leading church fathers, Middleton went to some lengths to point out that the fathers were utterly unreliable chroniclers. However lofty their underlying moral motives, he showed that they lived in a credulous era, given to forgery, allegory, and miraclemongering. Holy fiction and pious fancy were in the very air.

This argument might have sufficed to accomplish what Middleton set out to do, namely, discredit post-apostolic miracles. But he did not stop there. He went on to compare these miracles with pagan wonder-workings, analyzed the absurdities in the testimony concerning many miracles, and showed that one must accept all such miracles or none.

Middleton thus overshot his mark and tended by implication to discredit the biblical miracles which he approved and conceded. His arguments against patristic and later miracles were just as valid when directed against biblical miracles. Moreover, his contention that the miracle complex stands or falls as a whole made it illogical to accept one group of miracles and not another. Skeptics were encouraged to ask just how and why the original power to work miracles was lost—the church being as much an instrument of God in later times as in the apostolic age.

Some of the more radical deists dealt harshly with the most sacred of Christian miracles. Peter Annet, in his *Resurrection of Jesus Considered* (1744), branded as a fabrication the apostolic accounts of the miraculous character of the resurrection of Christ. He went on to declare that other New Testament miracles were a product of the impostures of the apostles, who thereby profitably duped a group of followers. More restrained and amiable, but equally powerful, was the argument of Matthew Tindal (c.1656-1733), who contended that even a valid miracle could not prove the divine character of a doctrine, which must be judged by its content. If it accords with reason and promotes goodness and virtue, that is sufficient proof of its divinity. No miracle is needed.

Defending their own belief in a religion of unblemished reason, the deists delighted in exposing what they regarded as the unreasonable character of historical Christianity, or at least of those elements in the Christian faith which they believed could not be harmonized with the deistic conception of a natural religion.

Blount took special pleasure in calling attention to what he looked upon as the extraneous and unreasonable elements in Christianity. He especially denounced the absurd and unreasonable character of the doctrine of original sin. As we noted, Blount attributed all these unreasonable items to self-interested fabrications and inventions of the priesthood. He particularly accused the latter of inventing the notion of heaven and hell in order to increase their hold over the terror-stricken and ignorant masses. Annet, as we have seen, even accused the apostles of having devised all the irrational impostures in early Christianity. Tindal held that only those elements in Christianity which are concerned with the promotion of virtue and goodness have any rationality or validity. All else is priestly invention and ignorant superstition. He examined in detail the irrational elements in the Old and New Testaments:

> As in the Old Testament there are several things, either commanded or approved, which would be criminal in us to observe, because we can't reconcile our doing this with the reason of things, so in the New Testament its precepts are for the most part delivered, either so hyperbolically that they would lead men astray were they governed by the usual meaning of the words; or else expressed in so loose, general, and undetermined a manner that men are as much left to be governed by the reason of things as if there were no such precepts: And the Scripture not distinguishing between those precepts which are occasional and those which are not, we have no way to distinguish them but from the nature of things, which

will point out to us those rules which eternally oblige, whether delivered in Scripture or not.[6]

Middleton, with his animus against early Catholic Christianity, showed in his *Letter from Rome* how many superstitious and unreasonable ideas were carried over from paganism into early Christianity. He was one of the first to have an appreciation of what we now call the syncretic or composite character of Christianity. The great liberal moralist of the day, Anthony Ashley Cooper (1671-1713), the third Earl of Shaftesbury, described Christianity as a cross between superstition and fanaticism, and said that the more he studied Christian beliefs the less Christian his ideas became.

If the deists rejected historical Christianity, with all its dogmas and elaborate machinery of worship, they had a good word to say for pure and original Christianity—"the true Christianity"—which they found in the teachings of Jesus. They were the earliest group to distinguish clearly between the doctrines of Jesus and the whole body of historical Christianity which had developed since Christ's time. They accepted the teachings of Jesus as a demonstrable religion of reason which is compatible with deism, but they rejected historical Christianity.

One of the most forceful statements of this view was embodied in Tindal's *Christianity as Old as the Creation* (1730). He endeavored to prove that true Christianity, mainly the teachings of Jesus, is identical with the deistic natural religion of reason and, hence, thoroughly valid:

> And therefore, I shall attempt to show you, That Men, if they sincerely endeavour to discover the will of God, will perceive, that there's a law of nature or reason; which is so called as being a Law, which is common, or natural, to all rational Creatures; and that this Law, like its Author, is absolutely perfect, eternal, and unchangeable; and that the design of the Gospel was not to add to, or take from this Law; but to free Men from that load of Superstition, which had been mixed with it: so that True Christianity is not a religion of yesterday, but what God, at the beginning, dictated, and still continues to dictate to Christians, as well as others. If I am so happy as to succeed in this attempt, I hope, not only fully to satisfy your doubts, but greatly to advance the honour of external Revelation; by showing the perfect agreement between that and internal Revelation; and by so doing, destroy one of the most successful attempts that has been made on Religion, by setting the Laws of God at variance.[7]

Indeed, Tindal took special pride "in proving that true Christianity is so far from being indefensible, that it carries its own evidences with it; or in other words, all its doctrines plainly speak themselves to be the will of an infinitely wise, and good God; as being most friendly to society, most helpful to government, and most beneficial to every individual; or, in one word, free from all priestcraft."

Equally enthusiastic was Dr. Thomas Morgan, who called himself a "Christian deist." In his *Moral Philosopher* (1737) he maintained that Christianity is the most perfect exemplification of the rational religion of nature. He held that Christianity was

---

[6] Cited in McGiffert, *op. cit.*, p. 224.   [7] Cited in *Ibid.*, p. 225.

a revival of the religion of nature; in which the several duties and obligations of moral truth and righteousness are more clearly stated and explained, enforced by stronger motives, and encouraged with the promises of more effectual aids and assistances by Jesus Christ, the great Christian prophet, than ever has been done before by any other prophet, moralist, or law-giver in religion.[8]

Morgan made an important contribution to the history and psychology of religion by attributing the origins of myths and superstitions to the ignorance and imagination of early peoples rather than to deliberate fraud on the part of priests, many of whom were as much the victims of these same illusions as were the masses.

Thomas Chubb (1679-1747), himself an artisan, endeavored to state the deistic doctrines in such a manner as would appeal to the literate masses. In his *Discourse concerning Reason* (1731), Chubb clearly and eloquently expounded the nature and adequacy of a religion of reason. In his more important book, *The True Gospel of Jesus Christ Asserted* (1738), he abstracted what he regarded as the very essence of the Christian religion and showed that it fully conformed to the religion of reason. The essentials of Christianity comprise, according to Chubb, the practice of rational conduct, the recognition that God resents any violation of the rule of moral reason, repentance of our sins, and a belief in a future life where we shall be treated in accordance with our earthly lives. All this seemed to Chubb quite in harmony with the fundamentals of the religion of reason. Christianity could thus handsomely qualify for admission into this lofty category of religious types.

A similar, though less earnest and pious view, was advocated in the *Essays Philosophical and Theological* of Henry St. John Bolingbroke (1678-1751), the eminent English publicist and statesman. He praised highly the actual gospel of Jesus, which, he thought, is founded upon the principle of universal benevolence. Hence, it fully accords with a natural religion of reason. But he rejected historical Christianity with equal decisiveness. He held that the rational gospel of Jesus had been corrupted and covered over by the inventions and impostures of a "motley crowd of Jews and heathen." Bolingbroke took special delight in discrediting the various conflicting Christian creeds.

Though the deists were regarded by the orthodox and intolerant clergy as atheists, they were really devout and earnest believers in God. They produced the most notable transformation in the conception of God since the days of the major Hebrew prophets of the eighth and seventh centuries B.C. The nobler conceptions of God prevalent in the eighteenth and nineteenth centuries of our era may be attributed largely to the deists.

Alexander Pope (1688-1744) in his *Universal Prayer* (1737), and other writers of kindred spirit, endeavored to express a theory of the physical universe and of God compatible with the new astronomy and natural science. The tribal God of the early Hebrews was manifestly inadequate to serve as the ruler of the new universe revealed by astronomers from Copernicus to Newton. It was necessary, therefore, greatly to magnify God in order to create a supernatural being

---

[8] *Ibid.*, p. 228.

logically suitable to the requirements of the Newtonian cosmic perspective. Further, the Christian God was one of divine arbitrariness. To orthodox Christians, God functions vividly only when he is apparently leading nature to deviate from her natural and normal course in such manifestations as earthquakes, volcanic eruptions, tidal waves, comets, and the like.

Pope and his school, on the contrary, were impressed with the new laws and processes revealed by natural science, and came to regard God as a lawmaking and law-abiding deity. He was especially manifest in the unending repetitions and orderly behavior of nature. Natural law was identified with divine law, God being regarded as the source of all natural manifestations. God was not only enlarged and his acts made harmonious with orderly nature, but his character was reinterpreted and ennobled. This was especially the work of the third Earl of Shaftesbury. He replaced the orthodox idea of a harsh, cruel, and arbitrary deity by one whose kindliness, urbanity, and tolerance resembled a typical cultivated English gentleman of the eighteenth century. Shaftesbury and Montaigne are said by historians to divide the honor of having been the first to discover that God may be a gentleman. Tindal stressed benevolence as the supreme attribute of God.

The deists rounded out their religious system by vigorously emphasizing the complete adequacy of their natural religion of reason and by a determined defense of the idea that the promotion of virtue and goodness is the sole purpose of religion. The most important propagators of these views were Thomas Wollaston (1659-1724), Tindal, Morgan, Pope, and Shaftesbury.

In his above-mentioned work, *The Religion of Nature Delineated*, Wollaston held that sin is nothing else than unreason—the result of irrationality and faulty logic in matters religious. Likewise, sound reasoning is the essence of religion, which he defined as "the pursuit of happiness by the practice of reason and truth." If reason is not always perfectly rewarded on this earth, it will be in the life to come.

Tindal contended that the natural religion of reason has always existed in a state of perfection and, hence, it cannot be improved by revelation, even if the latter were possible and demonstrable. Any additions to this fundamental religion of reason are not only unnecessary but false. Tindal defended with zest the proposition that the only purpose of religion is to promote good living. It "consists in a constant disposition of mind to do all the good we can, and thereby render ourselves acceptable to God in answering the end of our creation." Man's supreme obligation is to live so as to promote the public good. Benevolence is the highest virtue. This reasoning was an important contribution to the religious thinking of the age. As Professor McGiffert says: "Tindal's book constituted a very telling argument against the common Christian assertion of the day, that God demands something more from man than the practice of virtue, and that true religion involves and salvation depends upon the performance of duties in themselves morally indifferent." [9]

Tindal's assertion that religion consists of the promotion of virtue and that

[9] McGiffert, *op. cit.*, p. 215.

other matters are irrelevant was echoed by Morgan. In his *Essay on Man* (1733), Pope urged and, aided by Bolingbroke, defended the idea that the main purpose of religion is to encourage virtue, which, in turn, makes for human happiness—not merely the happiness of an individual but of all mankind. Pope was not, however, a militant deist, for in spite of his contributions to the deist cause, he regarded himself as orthodox in his religious beliefs. Shaftesbury departed from the usual deist position by holding that religion is not necessary for the encouragement of virtue among intelligent men. Morality does, however, depend upon an innate sense of reason which enables us to discern right from wrong and to wish to do right. For the illiterate mob, Shaftesbury conceded that religion and the fear of future punishments may be essential.

The various threads of English deistic arguments were brought together and synthesized by Thomas Paine (1737-1809), one of the most interesting figures of the late eighteenth century. Paine was not only a propagandist for enlightenment but an important practical figure in two great revolutions, the American and the French. It was in France that he wrote his famous work, *The Age of Reason*.

Paine has suffered under the accusation, hurled at him by, among others, Theodore Roosevelt, of being a "filthy little atheist," [10] but it is perfectly obvious to any reader of *The Age of Reason* (1796) that his only crime was to sum up the whole deistic framework of ideas in a manner designed for successful dissemination among the middle class and literate artisans. Paine was, as we shall see, in no sense an atheist. Civil authorities in England had reached the point where they tolerated religious heterodoxy in the "better classes," but they feared the unsettling effect of deistic propaganda among the "lower orders." Paine's book, therefore, came under the ban, his publisher was sent to prison, and Paine was compelled to flee from England. The work, however, has for many years been the "bible" of the "village atheist," usually, in reality, the village agnostic or modernist. The following passages from *The Age of Reason* perfectly illustrate Paine's line of argumentation:

> Everything we behold carries in itself the internal evidence that it did not make itself. Every man is an evidence to himself that he did not make himself; neither could his father make himself, nor his grandfather, nor any of his race; neither could any tree, plant, or animal make itself; and it is the conviction arising from this evidence, that carries us on, as it were, by necessity, to the belief of a first cause eternally existing, of a nature totally different to any material existence we know of, and by the power of which all things exist, and this first cause man calls God.
>
> The true Deist has but one Deity; and his religion consists in contemplating the power, wisdom, and benignity of the Deity in his works, and in endeavoring to imitate him in everything moral, scientifical, and mechanical.
>
> The God in whom we believe is a God of moral truth. . . .
>
> Mankind have conceived to themselves certain laws, by which what they call nature is supposed to act, and that a miracle is something contrary to the operation

10 See J. P. Bland, *President Roosevelt and Paine's Defamers*, Boston Investigator Co., 1903.

and effect of those laws; but unless we know the whole extent of those laws, and of what are commonly called the powers of nature, we are not able to judge whether anything that may appear to us wonderful or miraculous, be within, or be beyond, or be contrary to, her natural power of acting.

It is a duty incumbent on every true Deist, that he vindicate the moral justice of God against the calumnies of the Bible. . . .

The character of Moses, as stated in the Bible, is the most horrid that can be imagined. If those accounts be true, he was the wretch that first began and carried on wars on the score or the pretence of religion, and under that mask, or that infatuation, committed the most unexampled atrocities that are to be found in the history of any nation.

Anyone who has read the account of deistic opinions given above will recognize these passages from Paine's book as being common to most deistic literature. Nevertheless, *The Age of Reason* is one of the few notable books in the history of religious controversy and intellectual emancipation. It sums up the whole deistic case brilliantly, clearly, and with impressive force.

Paine had not read much of the earlier deistic literature. Hence, many ideas and facts which he believed he had discovered for the first time were already commonplaces of deistic thought. While this sometimes gives Paine's writings the impression of being naïve, it also gives them a freshness and vividness which is lacking in the more scholarly deistic compilations. Moreover, Paine possessed much native shrewdness and wrote with a great deal of force. All this made *The Age of Reason* an especially striking statement of the more critical deistic attitude and conclusions.

While Paine possessed little technical knowledge in the field of biblical criticism, few writers before or since his day have been more successful in analyzing the Bible from the standpoint of common sense and sound logic. Paine stated in devastating fashion all the logical reasons against the thesis that Moses had written the Pentateuch. He noted clearly the inconsistencies in the accounts of the Creation, remarking that he (Paine) could write a book without forgetting on one page what he had written on another. He held that we should expect "God Almighty to do as well." Paine was a firm believer in the God of a rational religion—the supreme ruler of the universe—but was relentless in his exposure of the weaknesses and limitations of the Jehovah of the Bible. Paine said that he desired, above all else, to clear the true God of the libels on his character which had resulted from identifying him with the biblical Jehovah. Paine denied vigorously "that the God before whom reasonable creatures should bow in awful reverence could be the supernatural tyrant of priestly imagination, who was responsible for the Jewish massacres, who favored a petty clan at the expense of his other creatures, who punished the innocent for the guilty, who lighted the fires of everlasting torment for the mass of mankind, and who gave a monopoly of his favors to priests or a few favored enthusiasts." [11]

One thing, in particular, that should impress itself upon readers of deistic

11 Leslie Stephen, *History of English Thought in the Eighteenth Century*, 2 vols., Putnam, 1902 (reprint, Peter Smith), I, 463.

literature is the relatively moderate character of their doctrines when judged by contemporary attitudes. Scandalous and blasphemous as such ideas may have seemed even to the learnedly devout in the seventeenth and eighteenth centuries, they have today become the commonplace dogmas of literate Protestant Christians and are accepted tacitly by not a few professing Catholics. The all too common conception of these men as bellicose and crusading atheists is preposterous and completely unhistorical.

The example of the deists fully illustrates how little the conventional clergy and scholars of the eighteenth century were interested in a religion which would promote virtuous conduct. On the one hand, Professor McGiffert tells us that "The tremendous interest of most Deists in the public good, and their hostility to selfishness and self-seeking, are very noticeable." On the other hand, Professor Smith points out, with equal accuracy, that "A perfect torrent of ridicule, abuse, and slander poured down upon their every publication. Men of strong religious feelings hated them as infidels; men of the world feared them as disturbers of the peace. Addison disliked them as much as he could dislike anything; Swift hated them venomously; the novelists represented them as futile coxcombs; the divines could find no grounds for their opinions except vicious passions; and even Pope, whose *Essay on Man* was founded on the writings of a Deist patrician, had nothing but sneers for the plebeians of that persuasion." [12]

The outstanding French deist was Voltaire, the most influential and engaging intellectual figure of the eighteenth century. When he appeared religious rationalism comprised no more than the solemn observations of retiring and often fugitive savants in England, or the detached and subtle satire of Montaigne and Bayle in his own country. He left it a powerful and popular intellectual force throughout the Western World.

By native talents and personal experience Voltaire was perfectly suited to such a rôle. He lacked all paralyzing reverence for any human thought or institution. Nor was he hampered by a debilitating conception of conventional good taste. He had infinite courage. His versatility in philosophy, science and letters has rarely been equaled. He ranged from Newtonian physics to drama, and from anthropology to the novel. He could thus reach a remarkable variety and number of readers. He was immensely witty and entertaining, thereby escaping the obscurity of the erudite but solemn pedant. When thoroughly aroused in propagandist activity, he possessed an energy and capacity for work that were almost miraculous and were regarded by his enemies as veritably diabolic. Finally, he received lucky "breaks," attracted the attention of famous and influential persons, and was invested with a prestige which made him an international figure and gave his writings vast repute.

Voltaire absorbed English deistic arguments.[13] He was also deeply impressed by the work of John Locke. It should be noted here that Voltaire was simply typical of the time in being a bit of an Anglomaniac, for England had temporarily assumed the leadership of the intellectual world. From its shores most

---

12 Smith, *History of Modern Culture*, II, 481.
13 Cf. N. L. Torrey, *Voltaire and the English Deists*, Yale University Press, 1930.

of the dissident doctrines were exported. Will Durant admirably summarizes Voltaire's admiration for the English as expressed in his suppressed *Letters on the English:*

> What surprised him was the freedom with which Bolingbroke, Pope, Addison, and Swift wrote whatever they pleased; here was a people that had opinions of its own; a people that had remade its religion, hanged its king, imported another, and built a parliament stronger than any ruler in Europe. There was no Bastille here, and no *lettres de cachet* by which titled pensioners or royal idlers could send their untitled foes to jail without cause and without trial. Here were thirty religions and not one priest. Here was the boldest sect of all, the Quakers, who astonished all Christendom by behaving like Christians. Voltaire never to the end of his life ceased to wonder at them.[14]

Voltaire thus admired the English, and his development was based in large measure on intellectual capital he borrowed from them. One should not, of course, suppose that France in Voltaire's youth was entirely barren of ideas. For many of his disconcerting ideas recent scholarship has uncovered plenty of precedent in the writings of Frenchmen who preceded him by a generation or so. Indeed, Voltaire's seeming intellectual indebtedness to English deism was in part an outgrowth of his propagandistic strategy. Owing to the current Anglomania in France, arguments drawn from English writers had more prestige than similar ideas borrowed from earlier French rationalists. Voltaire actually drew heavily upon his French predecessors, especially Bayle, but he sometimes failed to acknowledge this debt.

Voltaire was a man of astounding intellectual fertility. Almost no form of writing adapted to propaganda escaped his exploitation. He poured forth a stream of histories, essays, dramas, poems, novels, and short stories, most of them designed to destroy smugness and intolerance. While he was liberal in politics, he was not revolutionary. He approved nothing more advanced than a liberal monarchy. But even to be a liberal in those days was dangerous. Furthermore, Voltaire was not a lover of the common people, and he aimed to convert only the cultivated classes. He was especially opposed to spreading religious emancipation and skepticism among the masses. It would have suited him to perfection if he could have eradicated Catholicism and substituted the liberal deistic religion he had found in England.

What marks Voltaire out for special admiration is certainly his courage and energy. French liberals were confronted with a hostile church and a hostile state. They were in a situation infinitely more desperate than the English, and it required a proportionately greater amount of courage to defy the powers that ruled. By his wit, nimbleness, and persistence Voltaire carried on a "one-man revolution." His zeal against every form of religious bigotry made him seem to be really more than one person; it made him a veritable intellectual movement. His famous biographer Lord Morley said of him:

[14] W. J. Durant, *The Story of Philosophy,* Simon and Schuster, 1926, pp. 226-27. See also J. H. Robinson and C. A. Beard, *Readings in Modern European History,* 2 vols., Ginn, 1908, I, 146 ff., 161 ff., 179 ff.

When the right sense of historical proportion is more fully developed in men's minds, the name of Voltaire will stand out like the names of the great decisive movements in the European advance, like the Revival of Learning, or the Reformation. The existence, character, and career of this extraordinary person constitute in themselves a new and prodigious Era.[15]

Will Durant has put it even more forcefully:

Italy had a Renaissance and Germany had a Reformation, but France had Voltaire; he was for his country both Renaissance and Reformation, and half the Revolution. He carried on the antiseptic scepticism of Montaigne, and the healthy earthly humor of Rabelais; he fought superstition and corruption more savagely and effectively than Luther or Erasmus, Calvin or Knox or Melanchthon; he helped to make the powder with which Mirabeau and Marat, Danton and Robespierre blew up the Old Régime.[16]

Voltaire's consummate controversial skill gave him a reputation far beyond the boundaries of France. Not since Erasmus had there been a personality in the intellectual history of Europe with so wide a reputation, and Voltaire was a far more vigorous, dramatic, and spectacular figure than the essentially devout and mildly ironic Erasmus. The student who desires to gain a direct insight into Voltaire's mind, methods, and learning should read the famous *Philosophical Dictionary*, perhaps the best anthology of Voltaire's erudition, satire, courage, and critical observations.[17]

While Voltaire evinced deistic leanings from the time of his visit to England as a young man, his vigorous crusade against Christianity came late in life. Up to that time he had been moderate and diffuse in his skepticism. But the Calas affair stirred him profoundly and he determined to make short work of the religious system which encouraged such bigotry and savagery. He said that whereas it had taken twelve men to launch the Christian religion, it would take only one to destroy it. While he used many English deistic writings as ammunition in his battle, he drew particularly upon Bolingbroke and Annet, and from Bayle's devastating *Historical and Critical Dictionary*.

Voltaire drew no such distinction between historical Christianity and the teachings of Jesus as Tindal, Chubb, Morgan, and Bolingbroke had done. His desire was to wipe out both organized Christianity and the gospel of Jesus. He even had little use for Jesus, whom he called a combination of an amiable publicity-seeker, a priest-hater, an ignorant peasant, and a religious fanatic. He derided the alleged Christian miracles as impostures contrary to the laws of nature. He was even more sweeping in his condemnation of the Old Testament, its peoples and its religion. He declared that, compared to the "Chosen People," the American Indians were a humane and civilized race. He ridiculed the idea that the Bible is a sacred book and held up the Old Testament God to bitter scorn.

---

[15] John Morley, *Voltaire*, Macmillan, 1871, p. 1.
[16] Durant, *op. cit.*, p. 220.
[17] For a good selected abridgment, see the edition by H. I. Woolf of Voltaire's *Philosophical Dictionary*, Knopf, 1924. Students of the intellectual history of the eighteenth century have long since recognized that this work is very "Baylian" in content.

All this has led many to denounce Voltaire as a blatant atheist. But such was far from the truth. While he said that no god at all is to be preferred to the Jewish and Christian God, yet he made the famous observation that if there were no God we would have to invent one. He, himself, believed wholeheartedly in a benevolent deist God, to whom he built a chapel on his estate. Voltaire was especially convinced that religion is essential to keep the masses disciplined, and he even had some qualms lest he might promote anarchy through his assaults on Christianity. The following passage admirably expresses Voltaire's religious conceptions and interests:

> Every man of sense, every good man, ought to hold the Christian sect in horror. The great name of theist, which is not sufficiently revered, is the only name one ought to take. The only Gospel one ought to read is the great book of nature, written by the hand of God and sealed with his seal. The only religion that ought to be professed is the religion of worshipping God and being a good man. It is as impossible that this pure and eternal religion should produce evil, as it is that the Christian fanaticism should not produce it.[18]

A far more moderate deist was Jean Jacques Rousseau (1712-1778). Voltaire rejected both Christianity and the gospel of Jesus. The English deists accepted the gospel of Jesus and rejected Christianity. Rousseau accepted both Jesus' teachings and Christianity, thus standing in this respect at the opposite pole from Voltaire. The most poetic statement of Rousseau's deistic faith is contained in the confession of the Savoyard vicar in *Émile*. Its flavor is fully revealed by the following passage:

> My son, keep your spirit always in such a state as to desire that there be a God, and you will never doubt it. And then, whichever side you may take, believe that the true duties of religion are independent of the institutions of men; that a just heart is the true temple of divinity; that in every country and every sect to love God above all else, and one's neighbor as one's self is the sum of the law; that there is no religion which dispenses one from the duties of morality; that there are no essentials but these; that the worship of the heart is the first of these duties, and that without faith there is no true virtue.[19]

In his *Social Contract,* Rousseau proposed to establish deism as the civil religion. He thus summarized his conception of its basic dogmas: "The dogmas of civil religion should be simple, few in number, announced with precision, without explanation or commentary. The existence of a powerful, intelligent, benevolent, prescient, and provident divinity, the life to come, the happiness of the just, the punishment of the wicked, the sacredness of the social contract and the law— these are the positive dogmas." In sharp contrast to Voltaire's slashing attacks on the inconsistencies and superstitions of the New Testament was Rousseau's attitude of reverent humility toward them. He recommended that one should remain ever "modest and circumspect: (to) regard in silence what cannot be either

---

18 Cited in McGiffert, *op. cit.,* p. 244.
19 Cited in *Ibid.,* pp. 245-46.

disproved or comprehended, to humble (one's self) before the Supreme Being, who alone knows the truth." [20]

A return to the vigorous critical deism of Voltaire was contained in the book, *Ruins: or the Survey of the Revolution of Empires,* by Count Constantin François de Volney (1757-1820). While the work was concerned primarily with the causes of the fall of the empires of antiquity, it paid much attention to religion. Volney, like Voltaire, rejected both historical Christianity and the teachings of Jesus. He was particularly caustic about priests. He held that they "had universally found the secret of living in tranquillity amidst the anarchy they occasioned; secure under the despotism they sanctioned; in indolence amidst the industry they recommended; and in abundance in the very bosom of scarcity; and all this, by selling words and gestures to the credulous." [21] Volney predicted that ultimately all sects would unite on the basis of the natural religion of reason which underlies most of them.

The first important German deist was Hermann Samuel Reimarus (1694-1768), whose ideas were embodied in his *Principal Truths of Natural Religion* and his *Apology or Defense of the Rational Worshippers of God,* edited and published in part by Lessing after Reimarus' death. He was led towards skepticism by his studies in linguistics and textual criticism. He was a rather advanced deist who rejected all revealed religion, including any claim to revelation by the teachings of Jesus. He rendered a service, however, to those deists who were insistent upon retaining the teachings of Jesus, for he was the first to make a searching attempt to disentangle the historical Jesus from the husk of dubious prophecies, uncertain miracles and extraneous theological dogmas. Gotthold Lessing (1729-1781), Reimarus' editor, inclined to the position of Tindal, Chubb, and others, who conceded the teachings of Jesus high rank as a natural religion of reason. He contended that true Christianity is a simple and beautiful religion of love, its sole tenet being to love our neighbors. Lessing thought that the history of religion is merely the revelation of "steps in a progressive education of the human race in the knowledge of God."

Johann Christian Edelmann (1698-1767), a follower of Spinoza and the English deists, assailed revelation in his *Innocent Truths,* and defended deism in his *Divinity of Reason.* He sharply questioned the dogma of the inspiration of the Bible and pointed out the contrasts between the gospel of Jesus and existing Christianity. Johann Salamo Semler (1725-1791), in his *Liberal Interpretation of the New Testament* (1767), supplemented the work of Reimarus by tracing a progressive evolution of religious doctrine in the New Testament and opening the way for an appreciation of the rôle of Paul in Christian thought.

Immanuel Kant is usually associated with the origins of the religious emotionalism which formed a part of the German romantic movement. But his *Religion within the Bounds of Mere Reason* (1793) was a clear defense of religion unsupported by revelation. He agreed with Lessing that true Christianity is a

---

20 Cited in H. M. Morais, *Deism in Eighteenth Century America,* Columbia University Press, 1934 (Russell, 1943), p. 52.
21 Cited in *Ibid.,* p. 127.

perfect natural religion because it inculcates the doctrine of loving God and our neighbors. The personal example of Jesus himself gives it further force and sanction. But Kant relentlessly rejected the supernatural and mechanical aspects of existing Christianity. McGiffert thus summarizes his notions:

> It needs no other support, neither prophecy nor miracle; it is rational and self-vindicating. As a revealed religion Christianity contains positive precepts, which are legitimate only in so far as they make the duties of natural religion clearer, or enforce them more strongly. As an end in themselves they are wholly evil. The notion that we can do anything to please God, except to live rightly, is superstition. And to suppose that we can distinguish works of grace from works of nature is a delusion. All such supernaturalism lies beyond our ken. There are three common forms of superstition—the belief in miracles, in mysteries, and in means of grace. The genuine rationalism of all this is evident. It is simply a clear and forceful statement of a mild and lofty type of eighteenth-century Deism.[22]

We may now glance at the transfer of deistic doctrines to America.[23] It is well established that Jefferson, John Adams, Franklin, and perhaps George Washington and James Madison, were deists, although some of them occasionally tempered their opinions because of political exigencies.

Franklin was an out-and-out deist. He once formulated his religious ideas in response to a request from the President of Yale university. He said: "I believe in one God, the Creator of the universe. That he governs it by his providence. That he ought to be worshiped. That the most acceptable service we render him is doing good to his other children. That the soul of man is immortal, and will be treated with justice in another life respecting its conduct in this." It would be difficult to imagine a more concise summary of the fundamental postulates of deism.

Washington was also cordial to deistic doctrines. Though he frequently attended the formal Episcopal services, he never received communion. John Adams was an advanced Unitarian—a type of belief that a leading historian of American religion of this period has called "respectable deism." Jefferson was an aggressive deist. He extolled reason and declared that we should follow wherever it leads, even if we must as a result deny the existence of God. He vigorously attacked the priesthood and the Calvinistic clergy. In the campaign of 1800 he was bitterly assailed as an atheist, but the charge was not well founded. Strange as it may seem, none of the first seven presidents of the United States was a professing Christian. As DeWitt has sagely observed, the private beliefs of the fathers were, however, more advanced than their public utterances:

> In different degrees, Jefferson, Franklin, Gouverneur Morris, John Adams, were free-thinkers, but without intolerance or display, without ostentatious irony, quietly, almost privily; for the masses remained believers. Not to offend them, it was necessary to speak with respect of sacred things; to produce a deep impression upon them, it was requisite to appeal to their religious feelings; and prayers and public

[22] McGiffert, op. cit., pp. 249-50.
[23] See especially G. A. Koch, Republican Religion, Holt, 1933; and Morais, op. cit.

fasts continued to be instruments resorted to whenever it was found desirable, whether by agitators or the State, to act powerfully on the minds of the people.[24]

Religious liberalism was, naturally, not limited to our early presidents. That doughty Green Mountaineer, Ethan Allen, was an active foe of orthodoxy and evangelical religion. He composed several large books on the subject, the most notable of which was *Reason: The Only Oracle of Man* (1784). The chief organizer of militant deism was Elihu Palmer, who also wrote many pamphlets, representative of which was *Thoughts on the Christian Religion* (1794). He vigorously assailed orthodoxy and was especially outspoken in his denunciation of the dogma that the Bible is the revealed word of God. Allen and Palmer were more advanced in their religious ideas than were mild deists like Franklin. They followed Europeans like Collins, Annet, and Voltaire—"militant deists," as Professor Morais designates them. Thomas Paine spent his last years in the United States and lent the weight of his influence to American skepticism. Deism even affected the American pulpit, as illustrated by the defense of the deistic notions of God by the Rev. Charles Chauncey of Boston in *The Benevolence of the Deity* (1784).

Deism was, however, soon smothered in the United States under the rising tide of evangelicalism and the powerful Christian apologetics of President Timothy Dwight of Yale College. By the middle of the nineteenth century it is doubtful if any candidate holding Jefferson's religious views could have been elected President of the United States, or even have been nominated for the office. Robert G. Ingersoll's views on religion in the eighties did not differ widely from those of Jefferson, and though the Republican party sadly needed a man of his luster, oratorical powers, and personal integrity, he was not regarded by party leaders as "available" on account of his agnostic opinions.

Both the traditionalism and the novelty in deism have been overestimated, as Carl Becker has done well to point out in his *Heavenly City of the Eighteenth Century Philosophers*. The deists were still chiefly interested in the heavenly city. What they did was to build a new one with different materials. Whereas Augustine had based his *City of God* on the New Testament, the church fathers and Neoplatonism, and the Scholastics had erected theirs on Augustine and Aristotle, the deists constructed their heavenly city out of the Newtonian world-machine, Locke's rationalism and the growth of comparative religion drawn from oversea discoveries. As Professor Morais accurately summarizes the situation, deism as an active religious movement declined because it fell between two stools. It went too far to suit the devout and was too timid and hesitant to satisfy the skeptical: "In the last analysis, deism proved too conservative and compromising for the atheist and yet, in its destructive phase, too radical and unyielding for the Christian: thus it eventually passed into the limbo of unfortunate causes attempting to steer a middle course."[25]

Nevertheless, deism introduced one of the greatest intellectual revolutions in the history of mankind. If it did not satisfy more advanced skeptics, it at least

24 C. H. DeWitt, *Jefferson and the American Democracy*, London, 1862, p. 17.
25 Morais, *op. cit.*, p. 28.

made them possible. Preserved Smith sagaciously observes that while deism as a movement evaporated, deistic thought became "the common thought of the nineteenth century and the prevailing thought of the twentieth."

III. THE RISE OF SKEPTICISM

We shall now consider a number of writers on religion who found dogmatic deism too restrained and timid, and yet would not openly go the whole way toward atheism as Holbach and his followers did. Unwilling to acknowledge as absolutely certain the existence of God or the truth of any dogmatic religion, they would not grant special consideration to "true Christianity" as a religion of absolute certitude.

The first important skeptic was the English philosopher, Thomas Hobbes. Hobbes adopted this useful strategy: he loudly proclaimed his orthodoxy and then proceeded to offer the most devastating criticism of religion set forth by anybody in his age.[26] In the first place, Hobbes expounded a natural history of religion, in which he ascribed religious origins and development to the operation of natural and historical causes without calling upon supernatural explanations. This view was entirely in accord with his philosophical and psychological principles which maintained that we can know only through sensations and these sensations give us no real knowledge of the external world. Hobbes attributed the origin of religion to "belief in ghosts, devotion to objects of fear, ignorance of secondary causes which led to the assumption of a First Cause, and augury, or the practice of prognosticating the future." With a few qualifications and elaborations, this belief would accord fairly well with present-day anthropological and historical accounts of religious origins. It was thoroughly in agreement with the anthropological explanations of religious origins in the nineteenth century.

Hobbes offered the devastating suggestion that religion is simply accepted superstition: "Fear of power invisible feigned by the mind or imagined from tales, publicly allowed, is religion; not allowed, superstition." Religions decay when the body of ideas they represent becomes palpably absurd to thinking persons, or when the insincerity of priests in thought or action becomes apparent to believers. He swept aside as preposterous such things as miracles and derided the system of future rewards and punishments. He heaped contempt on the vast collection of religious and theological writings "which fill our libraries and the world with their noise and uproar, but wherefrom the last thing we may expect is conviction." Professor Smith believes, with plenty of evidence, that Hobbes was "in his heart an atheist." [27]

The outstanding skeptic of the period was David Hume, whose critique of religion was in complete accord with his sweepingly agnostic philosophy. As Professor Smith puts it: "After assimilating all that science, philosophy, and history could tell of this subject, his acute mind perceived, better than any other had done, the inconsistency of the apologists, the psychological causes of belief, the material factors governing religious revolution, the sophistry of the credulous,

[26] Smith, *op. cit.,* I, 201 ff., 233 ff., 408.   [27] *Ibid.,* p. 408.

and the repugnance of faith to reason." [28] Hume's writings on religion, a subject to which he also often referred in his general philosophical works, were embodied in the following treatises: *Of Superstition and Enthusiasm* (1742), *Essay on Miracles* (1747), *Essay on Providence and a Future State* (1748), *Natural History of Religion* (1757), and *Dialogues concerning Natural Religion* (1779). Hume's critical analysis of religion gained immense force because of the calm and urbane way in which he approached the problem. Guilty of none of the heated excesses of Voltaire, he was far less useful as a crusader against bigotry and persecution, but it is true that his temperate arguments against religion won greater respect and acceptance among the thoughtful.

Hume was remarkable for being the first to study religion scientifically as a mode of human behavior. He believed that there is nothing unique about religious experience. Hence, it should be approached in the same secular fashion as any other form of human behavior. History and psychology, rather than deductive theology, offer the master keys to an understanding of man's religious experiences and conduct. Though Hume set forth these views nearly two centuries ago, it is still considered daring to reaffirm them seriously, and despite the striking work of experts in the history and psychology of religion, little has been done to popularize these views. Hume contended that there is nothing in the human mind which necessitates a belief in a divine being. Such a belief, together with other religious concepts, emerged gradually in early civilizations, and is now customarily handed down and inculcated in childhood. If not so inculcated, it would develop through the course of one's life as a result of the operation of the emotions of fear, uncertainty and hope.

In treating the history of religion, Hume believed that it first arose in the form of polytheism as a result of man's experiences of good and evil. The good things which happened to man were attributed to benevolent gods, while unhappy events were assigned to malevolent gods. In either case, the gods were interpreted as manlike—anthropomorphic. Monotheism grew out of the observation of nature. Man interpreted strange occurrences, prodigies, impressive natural phenomena, and the like, as the actions of a powerful and arbitrary God. As between the two types, polytheism has been the more tolerant.

In his *Dialogues* on religion, Hume anticipated Kant by completely demolishing all previous proofs of the existence of God—the ontological, cosmological and teleological. He exposed the absurdity of any dogmatic anthropomorphic conception of God: "Assuming that the universe had an author, he may have been a bungler, or a god since dead, or a male or female god, or a multiplicity of gods. He may have been perfectly good, or perfectly evil, or a mixture of good and evil, or morally quite indifferent—the last hypothesis being the more probable." [29] Finally, Hume drove home the mutually destructive character of dogmatic religious controversy. Each side makes the other seem ridiculous and paves the way for the skeptic who can thus see the untenable character of all cults and creeds.

Hume's treatment of miracles was so thorough and logical as to leave little

---

[28] Smith, *op. cit.*, II, 522.   [29] McGiffert, *op. cit.*, p. 242.

to be said on the subject thereafter; at least, so far as it related to apologetic arguments for revealed religion. As Professor McGiffert states: "It did destroy the apologetic value which had been ascribed to miracles. Against the apologetic position of the day Hume's argument was really final. Miracles had been regarded, not simply as a proof, but the supreme proof of Christianity. This they could no longer be where his essay was understood." [30]

Hume insisted that we must assume that a miracle is an event opposed to nature in all of its observed manifestations. We cannot be expected to accept testimony regarding the occurrence of a miracle unless a lie or mistake on the part of the witnesses would be more marvelous than the miracle itself. Hume proceeded to point out that there was no miracle on record which had witnesses so numerous and unimpeachable that their word would stand up against the logical assumption of nature's uniformities. Further, if the event cannot be denied, it is hard for us to be sure that a miracle has really taken place. It may be nothing more than a natural phenomenon which we are as yet unable to explain on scientific grounds. And, finally, even if a miracle is assuredly "proved," it may not be a sign from God, but simply a miracle of the devil. The last qualification was suggested by Woolston, who had called attention to the fact that the ability of the devil to work the most impressive miracles was a basic Christian dogma. Hume, thus, did not deny that miracles could take place. But he made it clear that it is almost impossible to obtain evidence sufficient to demonstrate a miracle and that, even if this were possible, it would be no proof of Christian revelation.

Along with miracles, Hume rejected the doctrine of a future life with its compensatory rewards and punishments. He freely admitted that there are plenty of cases in this life where rewards and punishments have not been distributed according to human deserts, but he said that it is utterly silly to hold that God will take cognizance of such a fact and even the scores.

Yet Hume did not dismiss religion altogether. While acutely aware, on the one hand, of the contradictions and inadequacies of all known religious schemes, and, on the other, of the limitations of our faculties for obtaining knowledge, he still protested chiefly against the habit of mind which leads to attributing human qualities to a supreme being. His great concern, thus, was to deanthropomorphize God. In this aspiration he was in harmony with the advanced thinkers of his age. His attempt at a psychological and historical treatment of religion exerted a considerable influence upon Edward Gibbon and his *Decline and Fall of the Roman Empire,* especially Gibbon's famous chapter explaining Christian origins naturalistically. Hume did not, like Kant, undermine his skepticism by subsequent changes of emphasis or viewpoint. He remained resolutely and consistently skeptical in all his writings to the very end.

The first important French skeptic was Montaigne whose urbane philosophy we have examined in an earlier chapter. We may here look briefly at some of its applications to religion. Montaigne anticipated Hobbes in what we may call the strategy of argument. He formally proclaimed the pious wish that his writ-

[30] McGiffert, *op. cit.,* p. 221.

ings might not offend the Catholic church in which he was born and expected to die. Then he proceeded to raise fundamental doubts concerning the whole body of belief upon which the Catholic church rested. But he was not partial to the Protestants. His skepticism was in part engendered by his unfavorable reaction to the multiplicity of Protestant sects, and he asserted that Luther had raised far more doubts than he had settled.

Montaigne maintained that although God may be regarded as urbane and benevolent, his very existence and nature may be guesswork, since we certainly cannot know God in any definite way. Miracles are no proof of revelation, for even when reported by a father of Augustine's reputation, they were, more likely, the product of "ignorance, simplicity, malice, credulity, or imposture" than real miracles. If prophecies were ever valid they have long since ceased to be so. And one can place more reliance on dice than on divination. Montaigne expressed grave doubts about the reality of a future life and, as we have already noted, believed that the purpose of learning is to enable us to live happily and artistically rather than to die safely. Montaigne accepted enough of the Epicurean philosophy to be able to despise death.

Bernard de Fontenelle (1657-1757) contributed in two major ways to the growth of French skepticism. His *Plurality of Worlds* was a clear and far-reaching statement of the implications of Copernican astrophysics for science and religious thought. In his *History of Oracles* he indulged in the customary skeptical exposure of prophecies and miracles. He compared the former to the utterances of antique soothsayers, and the latter to the wonder-working of pagan sorcerers and priests.

The next important figure in French skepticism was Pierre Bayle, whose heroic contributions to freethinking we have already described. In the field of religious thought Bayle's skepticism found its widest range and most enthusiastic exploitation.

Bayle was exceedingly wily in his methods and by a pose of impartiality did a great deal to break down prejudice. One of his earliest works was the critical consideration of the text "Compel them to come in" (Luke 14:23), which we described in the previous chapter. In persecuting Protestants, Catholic authorities in France used this text as a justification. Bayle countered with the argument that one can never be sufficiently certain about the truth of one's position justly to use force in compelling others to agree with it.

In his great work, *A Historical and Critical Dictionary,* he used, as John M. Robertson phrases it, a "Pyrrhonian impartiality." Though he never dropped the pose of orthodoxy, yet he succeeded in advancing free thought on a scale never before equaled.

Bayle was the first writer to treat sacred history with thorough skepticism. His handling of Old Testament characters was one of the most devastating examples of skeptical satire in all literature. In the midst of the most burning ridicule Bayle would interject ostensibly pious comments and protestations of orthodox reverence. In the course of his scorching treatment of David, for example, we find the assertion that "David's piety was so conspicuous in his Psalms and in many of his actions that one cannot sufficiently admire him." The net result of Bayle's satirical analysis of the Old Testament was to break down the long-existing distinction between sacred and profane history. This he did by profaning sacred history. He set forth the crimes of David in great detail and implied that no gentleman would shake hands with such a fellow.[31]

Bayle not only adroitly handled Old Testament characters, but he was equally devastating in his attack on the Christian epic. He was one of the first to understand its dualism and to hold it up to ridicule:

> However detestable the opinion of two principles has constantly appeared to all Christians, they havè, nevertheless, acknowledged a principle of moral evil. Divines teach us that a great number of angels having sinned, made a party in the universe against God. The devil—a brief name for this party—having declared war against God from the moment of his fall, has always continued in his rebellion. . . . He succeeded in his first hostilities with regard to man. In the Garden of Eden he became the master of mankind. But God did not abandon this prey to him, but delivered them out of their bondage by virtue of the satisfaction which the second person of the Trinity (Jesus, the Son) undertook to pay to his justice. This second person engaged to become a man, and to act as a mediator and redeemer. He took upon himself to combat the devil's party, so that he was the head of God's party against the devil.
>
> The design of Jesus Christ, the Mediator and Son of God, was to recover the country which had been conquered. That of the devil was to hold it. The victory of the Mediator consisted in leading men into the paths of truth and virtue, that of the devil in seducing them into the road of error and vice. So that, in order to know whether moral good equals moral evil among men, we need only compare the victories of the devil with those of Jesus Christ. But in history we find very few triumphs of Jesus Christ, and we everywhere meet with the triumphs of the devil.[32]

The satire of Bayle had full rein in dealing with miracles, especially those of the Old Testament. His treatment of Jonah and the whale is a classic. He was equally skeptical about New Testament miracles, although he said relatively little about those attributed directly to Jesus. Bayle derived special satisfaction from comparing pagan wonder-working with Christian miracles. He advanced none of the closely reasoned arguments against miracles which Hume was to muster in the next generation. He employed the method of subtle historical ridicule.

Bayle took particular care to emphasize the moral excellence of all the free-thinkers he had occasion to treat. When it was objected that he was not exactly serving the cause of orthodoxy thereby, he replied that he "would have been delighted to dwell on their vices," but he "knew of none." [33] He once ironically remarked that the conduct of atheists is so generally immaculate and praiseworthy that a special divine grace must have been bestowed upon them. He

[31] Cf. Robinson, *Bayle the Sceptic*, pp. 164-68.
[32] Cited in Robinson, *op. cit.*, p. 209. For further development of this idea, see *ibid.*, pp. 209 ff.
[33] Bury, *History of the Freedom of Thought*, p. 136.

divided honors with Shaftesbury in being one of the first to hold that religion has little to do with morality.

When criticism grew menacing, Bayle put forth an ingenious argument in favor of faith. He said that faith becomes more meritorious in proportion as revealed truth surpasses our capacity to reduce it to rational expression; and that in accepting what our minds simply cannot understand, we show how deep is our submission to God. This was followed by a long catalogue of the objections raised by reason to the doctrines usually supported by faith, with the subtle idea of showing that there is no hope of squaring orthodox religion with reason. The upshot was that by glorifying faith and appealing to its power to save religion, he was really seeking to make faith repugnant to the minds of intelligent men. By such adroit methods, Bayle advanced his cause in a way hitherto unparalleled, although many other writers of the time also took refuge in irony and satire as a foil against persecution.

In his famous *History of the Rise and Influence of the Spirit of Rationalism in Europe,* Lecky gives the following splendid summary of Bayle's qualities as a religious skeptic:

> The intellect of Bayle was very different from those of his predecessors, and was indeed in some respects almost unique. There have been many greater men, but there never perhaps was one who was so admirably fitted by his acquirements and his abilities, and even by the very defects of his character, to be a perfect critic. With the most profound and varied knowledge he combined to an almost un-rivalled extent that rare faculty of assuming the standing-point of the system he was discussing, and of developing its arguments as they would have been developed by its most skilful advocate. But while he possessed to the highest degree that knowledge and that philosophical perception which lay bare the hidden springs of past beliefs, he appeared to be almost absolutely destitute of the creative power, and almost absolutely indifferent to the results of controversy. He denied nothing. He inculcated nothing. He scarcely exhibited any serious preference. It was his delight to bring together the arguments of many discordant teachers, to dissect and analyse them with the most exquisite skill, and then to develop them till they mutually destroyed one another. His genius was never so conspicuous as when lighting up the wrecks of opposing systems, exhuming the shattered monuments of human genius to reveal their nothingness and their vanity. In that vast repertory of obscure learning [the *Historical and Critical Dictionary*] from which Voltaire and every succeeding scholar have drawn their choicest weapons, the most important and the most insignificant facts, the most sublime speculations to which man can soar, and the most trivial anecdotes of literary biography, lie massed together in all the irony of juxtaposition, developed with the same cold but curious interest, and discussed with the same withering sardonic smile. Never perhaps was there a book that evinced more clearly the vanity of human systems or the disintegrating power of an exhaustive enquiry. To such a writer nothing could be more revolting than an exclusive worship of one class of opinions, or a forcible suppression of any of the elements of knowledge. Intellectual liberty was the single subject which kindled his cold nature into something resembling enthusiasm. In all he wrote he was its earnest and unwavering advocate, and he dif-

fused his own passion among the scholars and antiquarians of whom he was the chief.[84]

If Voltaire was a littérateur turned propagandist, Denis Diderot (1713-1784) was essentially a scholarly journalist before the days of journalism, who became interested in the same general task of promoting enlightenment. Diderot is one of the most appealing personalities of the period, for Voltaire, in spite of his brilliance, could be intensely disagreeable, while the other great contemporary French thinker, Rousseau, was often positively hateful and inordinately suspicious and quarrelsome.

Diderot was the son of a cutlerymaker and like many of his contemporaries was educated by Jesuits. Like Voltaire and many other French writers of the day, he could read English and thus absorbed the main current of English ideas. His philosophical and religious viewpoint was compounded of progressive English and French doctrines. In his early life a good deal of his time was taken up with hack work. He wrote many plays that are now considered very dull; some novels that are still readable but not exciting; and some very witty and admirable dialogues and essays. He was one of the earliest of journalistic art critics and wrote reams of ephemeral comments on current exhibitions. He also undertook to execute commissions of a strange sort, like the writing of a series of sermons for a Portuguese missionary who was going to Africa. He was, thus, an early "ghost writer." Harold J. Laski thus summarizes the remarkable scope of Diderot's interests:

> Diderot's versatility is such that any picture of its achievement would end only at the boundaries of knowledge. If his political ideas have no claim to originality, at least they are well expressed and representative of all that is most creative in the liberalism of his time. The writings on education are more important. They show not only his sense that the problem was urgent; there is a modernity of temper about them—especially in his preference for modern languages and science over the scholastic discipline of his day—which is noteworthy. On physiology, on the principles of legislation, on music and mathematics there are vast collections of memoranda, never, indeed, of the first importance, but rarely without point and distinction. All of it is conceived in what may be termed the Baconian spirit; in all of it there is that restless and exciting sense that, to use his own words, "we touch the moment of a great revolution in the sciences." All of it is also is inspired by a large humanism before which it is difficult not to feel humble. They are fragments from a great man's workshop, the outpourings of a mind so full of ideas, so rich in invention, that he can hardly stay to hold the pen which should express the thoughts which crowd one another. And even in their incompleteness, they make one understand why the range of Diderot's inventiveness fertilized so much of what was best in the creation of his age.[85]

Fortunately for Diderot, he was invited by a bookseller to direct the writing of an encyclopedia. It was this enormous task which won for him his reputation as an historian. As originally planned, the encyclopedia was to be a translation and

---

[84] Lecky, *op. cit.*, II, 64-65.
[85] Laski, "Diderot: Homage to a Genius," *Harper's Magazine*, April, 1931.

adaption of an English work, but under Diderot's hand it became an independent work and the great repository of rationalistic thought. Although in the beginning the work had official sanction and although Diderot was secretly aided by the chief of police in Paris even after it was banned, the encyclopedia was produced under the most difficult conditions.[36] As soon as it was discovered that the work was rationalistic in tone, it became the butt of clerical opposition, and eventually gained the added ill-favor of the king. Nevertheless, the popularity of the encyclopedia was immense, and subscribers increased in number almost in proportion to the difficulties of publication.

For his work Diderot drew upon all sorts of writers, but the backbone of his staff consisted of his freethinking friends. His chief associate was d'Alembert, a learned mathematician and physicist. Diderot aimed to publish not only articles on scientific, religious, and philosophical topics, but also detailed accounts of the trades. Many of the latter articles he wrote himself, for his natural good-fellowship enabled him to approach the working people in a friendly manner. Furthermore, he made it a point to have articles on the practical arts written by someone who practiced the particular art. For example, the article on brewing was prepared by an intelligent brewer. He thus anticipated the procedure of the editors of the last edition of the *Encyclopaedia Britannica*.

The total result was that the *Encyclopédie* (1752-1772), as it is known, was a work of genuine utility, and marked an epoch in the history of such monumental surveys of knowledge. It became the first impressive compilation of the knowledge and interests we have been discussing in the preceding chapters of this book. It was also the great intellectual monument of the enlightenment. An illuminating historical exercise would be to compare with it the spirit and the contents of the earlier compilations by Pliny, Isidore of Seville, Rhabanus Maurus, and Vincent of Beauvais.

Diderot thus figures in the history of the time as the leading editorial genius of the rationalist circle. His charming personality enabled him to get along with all the various freethinkers of the day. It is recorded that he quarreled with but two men in all his life, his father and Rousseau. Such a record stamps him as remarkably accommodating. How far it accounts for his success in getting the coöperation of naturally dissident minds is another matter. But he carried his project through and lived to old age at peace with the world.

In his religious thought Diderot qualifies admirably for admission into this section on skepticism, for he wavered between deism and atheism. He wrote a deistic tract on *The Sufficiency of Natural Religion*, but at other times launched out into an atheistic assault on the evils of all religion. In the latter vein he once said that "if God really exists, he will not be devilish enough to punish us for doubting his existence." [37]

Diderot's able associate, d'Alembert, was one of the few skeptics of the age who believed in freethinking for all. Most of them, including Voltaire, had felt that it would be a calamity to enlighten the general populace. D'Alembert forth-

[36] Cf. Robinson and Beard, *Readings in Modern European History*, I, 185 ff.
[37] Smith, *op. cit.*, II, 515.

rightly asserted that we should teach the people the whole truth, since nothing has ever been gained by deception and evasion.

The social idealist and "perfectionist," Helvétius, must be listed among advanced French skeptics. He was a bitter critic of Christianity in all its aspects, particularly Catholic Christianity. He held that Christianity has always been opposed to good laws, sound government, and social morality. Helvétius was one of the first to emphasize the fact now stressed by psychological students of religion, namely, that our religious convictions are primarily a product and hangover of childhood teachings and experiences. He observed that we obtain from our nurse or tutor our religious views, as well as our conviction that our religion is true and others false. In his work, *On Man,* he summarized the essentials of his rationalistic civic religion. It consisted in a belief in God, and the cultivation, through reason, of social and civic duties.

The most distinguished of German skeptics was Frederick the Great, who had a thorough contempt for Christian dogmas, for the quarrels between Christian sects, and for the intolerance of the churches. His personal views seem to have verged rather definitely on atheism. But, good Machiavellian that he was, he made practical use of Christian beliefs in controlling his realm. He was perhaps the first ruler to welcome a multiplicity of religious sects and to regard this situation as good for the state. He anticipated contemporary historians in realizing that the chief contribution which Luther made to intellectual enlightenment consisted of his disruption of the church and the resulting impossibility of unified suppression of intellectual originality and independence.

In one sense the most devastating of German skeptics—in fact, the most sweeping of all the skeptics of the age—was the philosopher, Immanuel Kant. His *Critique of Pure Reason* was the most thorough and carefully reasoned philosophical defense of agnosticism ever written. It was more comprehensive and systematic than the skeptical writings of Hume, who first aroused Kant's inquiring mind. In this book Kant destroyed for all time any conceivable philosophical or theological proof of the existence of God. At the same time, Kant, even if unintentionally, furnished the stimulus for the greatest religious revival in the history of modern Germany, which won him followers in every camp from utterly mystical romanticists to liberal modernists.

This is to be explained by the fact that Kant did not remain at all consistent in his writings on religion. His *Critique of Pure Reason* was the final philosophical defense of agnosticism. But his *Religion within the Bounds of Mere Reason,* to which we have already referred, was an excellent statement of the least advanced of all forms of deism—the Christian deism of Tindal, Chubb, and Morgan. In his *Critique of Practical Reason,* Kant suggested that even if we cannot prove the existence of God it would be of great practical value to assume his existence in order to give greater assurance and logic to moral action. Hence, in the end, perhaps without so intending, Kant undermined his skeptical arguments and became the fountainhead of the most notable European religious revival since Luther and Loyola.

In the United States there were some evidences of rather thoroughgoing skepticism. Franklin, as a young man, was decidedly skeptical, although he lapsed in his mature years into a moderate brand of deism. Ethan Allen and Elihu Palmer, while formally deists, were pretty far out to the left of the movement, and hence well-advanced skeptics. Jefferson was at heart highly skeptical, but his prominent public position made him fairly cautious in expressing himself. It is probable that the most advanced skeptic of importance in America was Gouverneur Morris (1752-1816), whose critical strictures on Christianity were the source of much opposition to his appointment as minister to France.

IV. MECHANISTIC MATERIALISM AND ATHEISTIC DOCTRINES

While the mildest deists like Tindal—indeed, even rational supernaturalists like Locke—were denounced as atheists, there were very few prominent thinkers in this period who actually denied the existence of God. The frequent denunciation of atheists in the eighteenth century admirably illustrates the truth of an observation once made by James Harvey Robinson that, in practice, an atheist is usually one "who has a more sensible idea of God than his neighbors."

The earliest important atheist and the first conspicuous martyr to atheism in modern times was the Italian, Lucilio Vanini (1585-1619), a philosopher and scientist. After traveling and teaching in various European countries he was finally seized in Toulouse, condemned, and sentenced to have his tongue cut out and to be burned at the stake. He went to his death taunting his persecutors with cowardice. About the same time, a French atheist, Jacques de Barreaux, was condemned in Paris (1625) for blasphemy and suffered nothing more serious than banishment. If Hobbes was an atheist, he protected himself by protesting his orthodoxy. And nobody could do anything about Frederick the Great, even if he doubted the existence of God.

The first well-reasoned arguments for atheism appeared in the writings of certain French mechanists of the eighteenth century. Their theological deductions from the Newtonian physical synthesis were exactly the opposite of those made by the rational supernaturalists and the deists.[38] Of these atheistic mechanists Julien de la Mettrie was the earliest of note. We have already referred to his *Man the Machine* in connection with the mechanistic physiological doctrines of the eighteenth century. He offered a completely mechanistic interpretation of the universe and man. Examining all the existing proofs of God, he contended that they are utterly unconvincing. Further, even if God does exist, he has given us no reason for worshiping him. La Mettrie declared that religion is useful only to priests and politicians and in no way improves moral conduct.

La Mettrie was warmly defended by Paul Henri Thiry, Baron d'Holbach (1723-1789), a wealthy German who settled in Paris. Holbach was a chemist by training, but, in harmony with the spirit of the times, engaged in antireligious pamphleteering.

Several of Holbach's works were issued anonymously or pseudonymously, but none of the rest of them was so powerful or memorable as *Le Système de la*

---

[38] Cf. Riley, *From Myth to Reason*, pp. 206-17.

nature (1770). Of this Höffding writes: "It contains no really new thoughts. Its significance lies in the energy and indignation with which every spiritualistic and dualistic view was run to earth on account of its injuriousness both in practice and in theory." [39] This judgment by Höffding is criticized by many students of the history of European thought who contend that *The System of Nature* is one of the most stimulating and provocative of all statements of the uncompromising naturalistic position—much clearer and more satisfactory than most nineteenth-century attempts.

Holbach held that the concepts of God and the supernatural were a result of the ignorance of primitive men who did not understand natural phenomena. Now that we understand nature, there is no longer any need of clinging to these primitive superstitions. He proceeded to refute all the proofs of God given by such theistic scientists as Newton and Descartes. Like Bayle and Shaftesbury, he contended that morality does not depend upon religious support, and he agreed with d'Alembert that atheism might be taught safely and profitably to the masses. He believed the religion of his day to be the tool of self-seeking priests and politicians.

Holbach argued that it would be necessary to posit God as first cause only if matter were passive. But if there is movement in matter then God serves no other purpose than to push the question of first cause back another step. This gesture not only fails to make the whole problem more intelligible, but actually confuses matters. The assumption of two kinds of being, spiritual and material, leads, Holbach contended, to all sorts of obscurities and evasions. The spiritual principle admits the priests, and a train of oppressions then naturally follows. Above all, the assumption of a spiritual principle is not required in explaining the universe and its operations. The latter can be adequately accounted for on the basis of materialistic determinism, a system in which God has no logical place. Everything from the cosmos to human conduct is a product of causal necessity. There is no room for the notion of arbitrary freewill. Man is simply a complex manifestation of nature. He is neither better nor worse than other natural objects. Indeed, in Holbach's scheme the subjective Christian judgments of good and bad have no application to man. It may be observed that Holbach's fundamental views of nature and causation do not, however, necessarily involve dogmatic atheism. They represent the contemporary scientific conception of nature and man, shared by agnostics and not a few theists.

Holbach's conclusions were the logical outcome of the successive positions taken up by eighteenth-century critics of religion. The progression was natural from (1) Locke's attempt to relate supernaturalism to rationalistic natural religion, to (2) the deists' natural religion without supernatural sanctions, to (3) thorough skepticism of all revealed religion, without denying the existence of God, and to (4) the materialistic atheism of Holbach. The next development analyzed religion on entirely new grounds—a nineteenth-century achievement to which we shall devote attention later.

---

[39] Höffding, *History of Modern Philosophy*, I, 481.

While we ordinarily think of biblical criticism as a modern innovation, the earliest criticism was that of the Jews themselves while they were writing, editing, and constantly reshaping the Old Testament. They were not at all reluctant to criticize, alter, reject and rearrange what came to be regarded by Christians as holy writ.[40] Several of the early church fathers in the later Roman Empire questioned some of the conventional legends about the authorship of the Bible, but no truly critical attack on the problem was made before the Jewish scholar, Aben Ezra (A.D. c. 1150), challenged the tradition of the Mosaic authorship of the Pentateuch.

Concurrent with the development of a new outlook on religious philosophy in early modern times, came a change in the attitude towards the Bible. It was reëxamined by certain critics as though it were a secular document, the authenticity of which they wished to determine.

The earliest critical work on holy writ was devoted to Old Testament problems. The doctrine of the verbal inspiration of the Old Testament was dealt a hard blow by a French Protestant scholar, Louis Cappel (c. 1625), as a result of his linguistic studies. He found that what had been regarded as very ancient Hebrew characters were really Aramaic script of a far later date. This made it clear that texts written in Aramaic could not have been composed at such a time as was assumed by orthodox biblical critics, nor dictated by God to particular scribes, like Moses, who were supposed to have taken down his words.

Thomas Hobbes used the weapons of logic and common sense against orthodox opinions of Old Testament chronology and authorship. He pointed out how strange it was that a writer of an autobiography should discuss his own death and burial. Yet the Pentateuch relates the secret burial of Moses and describes the sorrow of the Jews following his death. Hobbes further showed that the books of Joshua, Judges, Samuel, and Kings were written long after the events they narrated. He held that the Psalms had been put together after the return from exile, but he wrongly conceded that some of the Psalms were written by David and the wisdom literature by Solomon.

A somewhat similar attack was made by Spinoza who added linguistic scholarship to logic. He showed that the Book of Genesis could hardly have been written by a single author and drew upon his knowledge of Jewish literature to discredit the theory of Mosaic authorship. He further proved that the books of Judges, Joshua, Ruth, Samuel, and Kings could not have been written by any of the persons mentioned in these books. They were composed far later than the period which they describe. The Psalms were a postexilic product, and the books of the prophets were not written by these prophets. Spinoza was right in assuming the late authorship of most biblical books.

The next important contribution was made by Richard Simon, a French Catholic scholar, in his *Critical History of the Old Testament* (1678). He made the discovery, all-important for his time, that the Old Testament books did not exist in the form in which they were originally written down. He understood, quite

---

[40] Archibald Duff, *History of Old Testament Criticism*, Putnam, 1912, chaps. i-iii, v.

correctly, that they had been rearranged and mixed up by Hebrew scribes over many centuries. Bossuet had the first edition of the book destroyed, though its printing had been licensed. A new and better edition was printed in Amsterdam in 1685. In 1722, William Whiston called attention to the falsification, in several places, of the Old Testament text and suggested how the original might be restored. Five years later, in his *Literal Scheme of Prophecy Considered,* Anthony Collins proved the late date of the Book of Daniel, thus upsetting the legend of the prophetic powers of the author.

In the middle of the eighteenth century (1753) a learned French physician, Jean Astruc (1684-1766), anticipated what has come to be accepted as the scholarly version of the nature and composition of the Pentateuch. He intuitively established the two basic source documents in these books—that which calls God Elohim, and that which designates him as Jehovah. These came to be known as the "E" and "J" sources. The work of Astruc was rendered somewhat less valuable because of his assumption that Moses had assembled the Pentateuch from various sources, but his identification of the two foundation documents was an epoch-making contribution. At the end of the century (1799) a German savant, Karl David Ilgen, indicated that there were at least seventeen different documents in Genesis, compiled by three groups of writers. This is the substance of the present view of the composition of Genesis.

Much less attention was given to New Testament criticism in this period. Perhaps the first to devote himself to it was the rationalistic supernaturalist, John Toland, in his *Nazarenus, or Jewish, Mahometan, and Gentile Christianity* (1718). He showed the marked divergences between the Jewish and Gentile churches and challenged the canon of the New Testament by comparing it with apocryphal writings. More famous was the work of the German deist, Hermann Reimarus, to which we have already referred. In his effort to reconstruct the historical Jesus he advanced far beyond any previous writer in clarifying the actual nature of the New Testatment, its times and its personages.

During this period much attention was given to biblical and historical chronology, a subject which had long intrigued historians and had been settled tentatively for Christians by Eusebius, Jerome and Bede.

All computations in Christendom were still based upon the biblical statement of creation, and human history was supposed to begin with Adam. The Jewish chronology assumed creation as having taken place in the year 3761 B.C. The Christian chronologers modified this to conform with their symmetrical scheme of history. This was based upon the idea that there would be seven symbolic ages of man—a cosmic week—each enduring a thousand years. Creation was placed at 4000 B.C., and it was believed that the Christian Era would last for 2,000 years more, after which the final millennium would come. Luther sanctified this scheme, placing Noah at 2000 B.C.

The erudite scholar and student of chronology, Joseph Justus Scaliger, estimated that creation took place in 3947 B.C. and that Christ was born in 4 B.C. He believed that Adam was created on April 23d. Johann Kepler, relying on astronomy as well as the Bible, dated creation in 3992 B.C. and the birth of Christ in 5 B.C. Most influential of all these chronological reconstructions was that of Bishop James Usher, who attained great exactness in his *Annals of the Old and New Testament* (1650-1653). He declared that the week of creation began on Sunday, October 23d, 4004 B.C., and that Adam was created on Friday, October 28th, 4004 B.C., while Christ was born in 4 B.C. This was made more precise a little later by the rabbinical scholar, John Lightfoot (1602-1675), who dated creation to the hour by contending that Adam was created on Friday, October 28th, 4004 B.C., at 9 A.M. Newton looked into the problem in his *Chronologies of the Ancient Kingdoms,* but he revised the date of creation in the wrong direction by placing it about 500 years nearer our era than Scaliger and Usher did.

Others were making faint advances towards the expansive computations of our own day. The deists, beginning with Charles Blount, less restrained by orthodox Christian conceptions and more influenced by the new science, were cordial towards more liberal estimates of time than Usher and his followers. Above all, the natural historians and geologists were coming to see that the orthodox date of creation could not be harmonized at all with scientific conceptions of the history and age of our planet and of the life existing upon it. For instance, the great French naturalist, Buffon, estimated that the earth must have an age of 75,000 years. This may seem absurdly brief today, but it was a revolutionary figure for the eighteenth century.

VI. THE SECULARIZATION OF ETHICS

The development of a more liberal attitude towards religion was accompanied by comparable progress in ethical doctrine. With the exception of certain schools of Greek naturalists, ethics, or the science of conduct, was closely linked with religion down to modern times. This connection has no logical necessity, for religion is certainly not always the key to the discovery of right conduct. But the association is easy enough to understand historically.

As Professor William Graham Sumner has shown in *Folkways,*[41] the classic study of the actual evolution of moral codes, it has been believed from earliest times that the codes of conduct which man follows implicitly were revealed by the gods. Since religion consists of that body of thought and action primarily concerned with the supernatural, it was inevitable that it should have dominion over conduct. Christianity accepted the doctrine of supernatural ethics with great enthusiasm and completeness. The Bible and the precepts of the church fathers were regarded as infallible sources of moral guidance. The bearing of a particular form of conduct on earthly happiness and well-being was not given even a passing thought. Questions of right and wrong were determined solely as regards their effect upon salvation in the world beyond life. Nor were problems of right and wrong related to individual differences in need, capacity, taste, or desire. There was, in theory at least, one rigid and undeviating course of moral conduct for king and slave, rich and poor, genius and moron, strong and weak. Some ancient skeptics, most notably the Sophists and Epicureans, questioned

41 W. G. Sumner, *Folkways,* Dover Publications, Inc., 1959.

this absolutist theory of revealed ethics. They had already arrived at something approximating our modern scientific views. They believed that notions of right and wrong had evolved naturally by a sort of trial-and-error method as man was compelled to face life under diverse conditions. While later generations might attribute a supernatural origin to codes of conduct, they were really man-made. Their validity depended upon their utility, namely, their relative capacity to promote human happiness. Aristotle, likewise, rejected supernatural ethics and held that right is to be ascertained by rigorous logical thinking; specifically, it is that happy mean between overindulgence and asceticism. From the triumph of Christianity until the coming of humanism the hold of the church over the minds of men was so firm that classical ethical doctrines were completely suppressed.

From the days of humanism onward, the supernatural ethics of the Christian church were subjected to criticism and substitute theories were suggested. Machiavelli offered a hedonistic approach to morals, holding that man is by nature greedy and self-seeking. He had little regard for supernatural sanctions or objectives in moral conduct, and projected definite doubts as to how far religion exerted a dominating influence on behavior. A deliberate effort to prove that morality does not depend upon religious sanctions was embodied in the work on *The Human Passions* by Giordano Bruno. Bruno also rejected the orthodox Christian glorification of asceticism and chastity. Even earlier, Bernard Telesius (1508-1588), one of the first to suggest a naturalistic philosophy, proposed a strictly utilitarian morality developed out of the instinct of self-preservation. He definitely foreshadowed Hobbes and later hedonism.

We have already described Montaigne's secular view of ethics, his divorce of morality and religion, his inclination towards evaluating conduct according to aesthetic canons, and his theory that the purpose of life is to secure happiness here and now instead of salvation in the world to come. There were Epicurean strains in Montaigne's doctrine of morals. But a more complete Epicureanism was evident in the theories of Pierre Gassendi. Gassendi regarded the pursuit of happiness as the supreme virtue, declared that the pleasures of the mind are more enduring than those of the body, and evinced an indifference to death.

The first important rationalistic and hedonistic system of ethics was set forth by Hobbes. His ethics, like his social psychology, was based on the premise of self-interest. Our passions, as a complex expression of motion, are divided into two main classes—attractive and repellent. The former are represented by pleasure, love, and desire. The latter are constituted of pain, hate, and fear. Calculating self-interest leads man to follow the attractive passions and avoid the repellent. Hobbes not only gave an impetus to hedonistic and utilitarian ethics, but definitely anticipated the famous felicific (pleasure versus pain) calculus of Jeremy Bentham, the leader of the utilitarians.

The orthodox Christian conception of a single-track code of ethics, equally applicable to king and peasant, was challenged in the *Moral Reflections* of Duke François de la Rochefoucauld (1613-1680). Basing his ethical system on self-interest and self-love, he worked out the most elaborate and intriguing code of honor ever put into print. It embodied the strictest obligations between gentlemen, and an arrogant contempt for a gentleman's relations to his inferiors. A gambling debt, for example, must be paid at all costs, but a commercial debt never, if it can be avoided. The Duke remarked with urbane cynicism that the code of honor among gentlemen stood at the opposite pole from the ethical doctrines inculcated by the church.

It was natural that, in this age of religious ferment, a school of ethical theory would arise which would seek to divorce ethics from religion. We have already made it clear that Pomponazzi and the humanist students of Aristotelian ethics, as well as the French skeptic, Pierre Charron, had clearly stated their belief that virtuous conduct need not be founded upon religion. While he was not directly interested in formulating an ethical system, Pierre Bayle made one of the most forceful statements of the era relative to the independence of conduct and religious belief. He maintained that religion has little, if any, effect on conduct. He even took the extreme example of atheists, who reject all religion, and called attention to the higher-than-average conduct of such men. The implication was that a man intelligent enough to cast off religious superstitions would know how to behave himself in such a manner as to be a credit to himself and to the state. A similar view was expressed by Anthony Collins.

The most ambitious effort to establish an ethical system on the theory of an innate sense of human decency and good taste, quite independent of religious sanctions, was undertaken by the third Earl of Shaftesbury, whose complimentary view of God we have touched upon. His ethical theories are contained in his essays on *The Characteristics of Men, Manners, Opinions, Times, etc.* (1711), of which the most relevant for our purposes were *An Inquiry concerning Virtue* and *The Moralists.* The Platonic and Stoic foundations of his general philosophy were best revealed in his *Philosophical Regimen.*

Shaftesbury's ethical theories are remarkable for two major tenets: (1) the idea that true virtue in no way depends upon religion as conventionally understood; and (2) the essentially Greek conviction that virtue is basically identical with good taste and a deep appreciation of the true and the beautiful.

The severing of morality from religion was a bold stroke, but Shaftesbury executed it unhesitatingly. As Emma Peters Smith expresses it: "That lover of virtue for its own sake, the amiable Earl of Shaftesbury, was one of the first to disassociate religion and morality and to pay his fellow-creatures the compliment of believing them able and willing to lead lives of the highest integrity without the assistance or threats of supernatural powers. That by thinking too well of man, he was assumed to think too little of God cast small credit on a theology which appeared to depend on the continued depravity of man and his consequent need of redemption." [42]

Shaftesbury supported by several lines of argument his theory that morality does not depend upon religion. In the first place, we need only compare the lives of those who pretend to an earnest belief in orthodox religious dogmas and of those who profess no religious convictions. We frequently find that those who pretend to be most religious lack even common decency and ordinary humanity.

[42] "The Philosophy of Anthony, Third Earl of Shaftesbury," in *Essays in Intellectual History Dedicated to James Harvey Robinson*, Harper, 1929, pp. 21-22.

They are too often oppressive, intolerant, corrupt, or even degenerate. On the other hand, even many so-called atheists are exceedingly urbane, sympathetic, considerate, and generous. Shaftesbury did not go to the silly extreme of declaring that all pious folk lack virtue, and all nonbelievers possess it, but he drove home effectively the argument that religion per se does not make a man virtuous, nor the lack of it villainous.

Another way of supporting his argument was to show that ideas of right and wrong develop in the mind of the individual before he is mature enough to have intelligent views of the supernatural world. We are able to apprehend the good before we can possess any "settled notions" about divinity. In other words, our ideas of right and wrong are formed before our conceptions of God and of future rewards and punishments arise. Morality is antecedent to religion, not dependent upon it.

Shaftesbury was caustic in discussing the theory that virtue is the product of an essentially magical bargain with the supernatural powers to reward good and punish evil. He had nothing but contempt for those who seek virtue because they imagine that it will confer upon them some personal advantage: "If virtue be not really estimable in itself, I can see nothing estimable in following it for the sake of a bargain."

No philosopher has ever been more thoroughly convinced than Shaftesbury was that virtue is decidedly "estimable in itself." He believed that morality is dependent upon an inherent moral sense. Man just as naturally apprehends what is good and bad as he recognizes different colors: "Virtue is something in itself, not constituted from without and dependent upon custom, fancy or will; not even on the supreme will which can in no way govern it." Virtue is "an affection for and a deliberate choice of the good." Good taste supplements our inherent moral sense, and morality is essentially sound aesthetic appreciation: "There is nothing so divine as beauty. . . . Will it not be found that what is beautiful is harmonious and proportionable; what is harmonious and proportionable is true; and what is at once both beautiful and true is of consequence agreeable and good?" Shaftesbury declared that the main purpose of all his writings was "to assert the reality of a beauty and a charm in moral as well as natural subjects and to demonstrate the reasonableness of a proportionate taste and determinate choice of life and manners." Shaftesbury was influenced by Plato's notion that over and above the beautiful things of nature stands the universal and immutable beauty of the soul. Beauty is virtue and the worship of it the only true religion.

Shaftesbury, in spite of the nobility of his moral teachings, was as wide of the truth in his views of the origins of right and wrong as were those who attributed it to divine revelation. There is no more an innate moral sense of right than there is a divine revelation of right. Conceptions of right and wrong are a reflex of customs, folkways, and mores, based upon the life experience of any particular group.

A sardonic but realistic contribution to ethical analysis was contained in the writings of Bernard Mandeville (1670-1733), a Dutchman resident in London. He exposed with great effect the sham and hypocrisy of the conventional moral theories of the time. While "humility, unselfishness, and abstinence" were exalted by the church and orthodox moralists, as the ideals of conduct, "pride, greed and luxury" actually motivated man and society. Mandeville performed a real service in delineating the abysmal gulf between ethical preaching and practice. He showed that, whether his contemporaries liked it or not, the theories of Hobbes were nearer to the facts of life in the eighteenth century than the idealistic abstractions of the conventional school.

Francis Hutcheson (1694-1747), David Hume, and Adam Smith (1723-1790) developed more thoroughly a psychological theory of morality. They based their doctrines upon the concept of reflective or subjective sympathy. An observer tends to project himself into another's situation and to imagine how he would feel under the same circumstances. Happiness in others creates joy in the observer, while misery in others generates sorrow. We are instinctively driven to consider how we would feel under identical conditions. Hence, we are naturally impelled to do those things which will promote happiness and avert evil. The most complete statement of this theory was contained in Smith's notable *Theory of Moral Sentiments* (1759), a book which exerted a wide and continued influence on psychological and sociological, as well as ethical, theory.

Hume's contributions to ethics were not limited to his observations of the power of sympathy. He put the earlier and cruder hedonism on a sounder empirical basis. Accepting human happiness as the goal of conduct, how shall we work out a practical code on this basis? Hume frankly stated that this must be done in a strictly empirical fashion by studying different forms of action and observing whether they increase or decrease happiness. In other words, conduct is good in proportion to its capacity for producing happiness, that is, in proportion to its utility. Hume's hedonism was heartily shared by the French thinkers, Holbach and Helvétius. The latter broadened the doctrine by emphasizing the fact that social well-being, as well as individual happiness, must be taken into consideration in any complete system of hedonistic ethics. To Helvétius is often attributed the origin of the phrase "the greatest good for the greatest number" as the test of any ethical doctrine or social policy. This became the slogan of the English utilitarians.

Hedonism developed naturally into utilitarianism with Jeremy Bentham (1748-1832), one of the most interesting personalities of the era. According to Bentham's theory of human nature, man is a cold, calculating animal. In his choice of conduct he is governed chiefly by the desire to receive pleasurable sensations and to avoid pain. Projected into society, this desire leads man to wish for the greatest happiness for the largest number of his fellow beings. The test of the moral validity of any practice is the degree to which it contributes to the greatest good of the greatest number of men. This is the core of utilitarian ethics.

An important contribution to ethical theory was made in the famous *Spirit of Laws* by Charles de Secondat, baron de Montesquieu (1689-1755). He may almost be said to have founded the comparative or sociological school of ethics. He maintained that notions of right and wrong and codes of conduct naturally arise to meet varied conditions of life, especially those conditions which are geographical and climatic in origin. For example, polygyny is approved in warm climates, where women mature and fade early, but is frowned upon in temperate and cold climates. Drunkenness is denounced in warm zones because alcohol is not there needed to create additional bodily warmth, whereas it is very common in cold areas. Despotism is the right kind of government for the torrid areas, constitutional monarchy for temperate zones, and republicanism for the colder regions. In short, whatever exists as a result of natural causes in any given area is regarded as right. The details of Montesquieu's theory have proven more vulnerable than his general hypothesis about the origin of moral codes.

SELECTED READINGS

Aldridge, A. O., *Man of Reason: The Life of Tom Paine*, Lippincott, 1958.
Brandes, Georg, *Voltaire*, 2 vols., Boni, 1930.
Broad, C. D., *Five Types of Ethical Theory*, Littlefield, 1959.
Brumfitt, J. H., *Voltaire: Historian*, Oxford University Press, 1958.
Conybeare, F. C., *A History of New Testament Criticism*, Putnam, 1910.
Cragg, G. R., *From Puritanism to the Age of Reason*, Cambridge Press, 1950.
Cushing, M. P., *Baron d'Holbach*, Lemcke and Buechner, 1914.
Duff, Archibald, *History of Old Testament Criticism*, Putnam, 1912.
Foner, P. S., *Life and Major Writings of Thomas Paine*, Citadel, 1961.
Haller, William, *The Rise of Puritanism*, Columbia University Press, 1938.
Höffding, *History of Modern Philosophy*, Vol. I.
Lecky, W. E. H., *History of European Morals*, London, 1869.
Koch, G. A., *Republican Religion*, Holt, 1933.
McGiffert, A. C., *Protestant Thought before Kant*, Harper Torchbooks.
Mack, M. P., *Jeremy Bentham*, Columbia University Press, 1963.
Manuel, F. E., *The Eighteenth Century Confronts the Gods*, Harvard University Press, 1959.
Meyer, Adolph, *Voltaire: Man of Justice*, Howell, Soskin, 1945
Morais, H. M., *Deism in Eighteenth Century America*, Russell, 1943.
Morley, John, *Voltaire*, Macmillan, 1871.
——— *Diderot and the Encyclopaedists*, 2 vols., Macmillan, 1878.
Mossner, E. C., *Bishop Butler and the Age of Reason*, Macmillan, 1936.
Palmer, R. R., *Catholics and Unbelievers in Eighteenth-Century France*.
Randall, *The Making of the Modern Mind*, chaps. xi-xii, xv.
Robinson, *Bayle the Sceptic*.
Rogers, A. K., *Morals in Review*, Macmillan, 1927, chaps. vi-xiii.
Shackleton, Robert, *Montesquieu: A Critical Biography*, Oxford University Press, 1961.
Shearer, E. A., *Hume's Place in Ethics*, Bryn Mawr Press, 1915.
Smith, E. P., in *Essays in Intellectual History Dedicated to Robinson*, chap. ii.
Smith, Preserved, *History of Modern Culture*, Vol. I, chaps. xiii, xviii; Vol. II, chaps. xiv, xvi.
Torrey, N. L., *The Spirit of Voltaire*, Columbia University Press, 1938.
Wilbur, E. M., *A History of Unitarianism*, Harvard University Press, 1952.

XX

*The Kingdom of Man
and the Vision
of Progress*

I. CYCLES AND THE GOLDEN AGE

It is a fact eminently worth noting that such advances in human culture as were actually achieved by man down to the close of the Middle Ages were brought about without the aid of any working theory of human progress. In primitive society there was little place for a doctrine of progress. Institutions were believed to have been revealed by supernatural powers, and hence were perfect and immutable. Custom and taboo marked out the path of conduct. Primitive man could scarcely conceive of altering society and culture for the better. In addition to fear of punishment by gods and men for violating social codes, primitive man was, as Paul Radin has made clear, extremely sensitive to the ridicule which might arise from conduct which was socially disapproved.

In Oriental antiquity much the same attitude prevailed as in primitive times. The supernatural outlook continued unabated, and custom was as much revered as in earlier eras. Indeed, conservatism was more thoroughly organized and more consciously defended than in the primitive period. The arrested civilizations of the Oriental era were the result of rigorously enforced mores and sumptuary legislation characteristic of this "military-religious" stage of civilization.

There were, however, at least two exceptions to the generally static outlook of the ancient Orient. One was the protest near the close of the third millennium B.C. of certain idealistic Egyptian writers who denounced the social injustices of their day and expressed the hope of a better time to come. The other was the messianic hope of the Jews, which was probably derived from this Egyptian aspiration for a happier future.

Among the classical pagans, the prevailing view of the past was either that of a decline from a golden age or a cyclical theory of history. The doctrine of a decline from a golden age, hinted at by Hesiod and Homer, was best formulated by Seneca. The golden age was later identified by the Christians with paradise and man's moral perfection before his fall. The doctrine of cycles represented human development as a series of repetitions always returning to the original starting point.

The cyclical theory of history was most clearly described by Plato, Aristotle, Polybius, and others in connection with their political philosophy. It was held that governments tend to pass from monarchy to tyranny, from tyranny to aristocracy, from aristocracy to oligarchy, from oligarchy to democracy, from democracy to anarchy, and from anarchy back to monarchy, thus commencing the cycle all over again. Other classical philosophers elaborated this hypothesis and represented civilization as repeating itself with great exactness in successive ages. In both the golden age doctrine and the cyclical theory of history, there was little place for the concept of a permanent advance in civilization. Lucretius, alone, with his evolutionary theory, possessed a definite notion of progress.

In their outlook upon secular civilization, the Christians likewise offered little encouragement to the theory of progress. They accepted the Hebrew doctrine of the fall of man from paradise, and they therefore located the most perfect of civilizations in the remote past. Perfection had existed at the outset and could never quite be regained in this world.

To be sure, the Christians held that religious and secular conditions had notably improved with the advent and triumph of Christianity. This attitude was best expressed in Orosius' *Seven Books of History against the Pagans,* which contrasted the horrors and miseries of earlier pagan civilization with the happier conditions which appeared after the coming of Christianity. Yet Christian writers never for a moment felt that any earthly felicity approximating the primordial paradise could again be attained on this planet. Indeed, there was a tendency to discourage interest in secular reforms, for fear that they might distract the faithful from the much more important problem of salvation. Instead of a secular theory of mundane progress, the Christians devised, as we have seen, an elaborate eschatology and looked forward to an imminent day of judgment, after which the earth would pass away and the faithful would be taken to the bosom of God. They projected the New Jerusalem, rather than an earthly utopia, as the goal of man. Further, the belief that the end of man's reign upon earth was likely to come soon, erected an obstacle to a deep interest in material progress.

A secular theory of progress is compatible only with the assumption that civilization will exist on our planet for a long time. In our own day, ultramodernist Christians, who abandon the older belief in eschatology and reject the orthodox heaven and hell, accept with enthusiasm the theory of human progress and work earnestly to make it a reality. But their attitude bears little resemblance to the views held by orthodox Christians, Catholic or Protestant, before the twentieth century.

In early modern times, under the influence of humanism, scholars were inclined to revive the classical theory of cycles of growth and decline. Characteristic of this tendency was Jean Bodin's conception of the natural history of the state or commonwealth, which, like man, passes through stages of growth, maturity, decline and death:

. . . But that these things may the better be perceived, it is to be understood, that all conversions and changes of Commonweales, are either voluntary or necessary, or else mingled of both: and as for necessity, it is also either natural or violent. For albeit that the birth of things be more fair and pleasing than their death, yet for all that so it is, that the source and course of flowing nature ravishing all things, giveth us also to understand, that the one cannot be without the other: so that all things which had beginning, although they have stood many hundred years, yet must at length in time take end and perish also. But, as we deem that death more tolerable which by little and little creepeth on through the weakness of age, or the course of some long lingering disease, and that almost without any sensible feeling thereof: so also may we say the change or fall of a Commonweale, which proceeding as it were of age, and after having endured a long tract of worlds, to be necessary, and yet not violent: for that nothing can well be called violent, which is agreeing unto nature: seeing also that the course of every thing's age is certain, and a certain ripeness unto every age appointed: so that in due time to take end seemeth to be a thing of everything to be wished for. . . .[1]

In other writings, however, Bodin showed a grasp upon the theory of progress. He divided history into three periods: (1) the history of Oriental peoples; (2) Mediterranean peoples; and (3) northern European peoples. He discarded the conception of descent from a golden age, and seemed to regard successive historical periods as marking demonstrable human progress.

II. FRAGMENTARY CONTRIBUTIONS TO THE THEORY OF PROGRESS IN EARLY MODERN TIMES

Among Western writers perhaps the earliest vision of mundane progress may be discovered in a curious letter written by Roger Bacon shortly after the middle of the thirteenth century. While Bacon, as we have seen, was interested in promoting the inductive and experimental method, he was a medievalist at heart, and proposed to make use of the newly acquired information for characteristically medieval ends, such as getting out better editions of the Bible and Aristotle, clearing up problems in scriptural geography and chronology, and locating heaven and hell more exactly. Nevertheless, in his letter on the ultimate effects of applied science he drew a remarkable picture of future technological progress, all of which has subsequently been realized.

The first definite enunciation of a theory of progress came from a Muslim writer, the foremost historian of that culture, Ibn Khaldun (1332-1406). His importance lies in the unique feat, for the time, of having been able to rationalize the subject of history and to reflect upon its methods and purpose. In his *Prolegomena to Universal History,* which contained the systematic presentation of his theoretical views, he drew a sharp distinction between the conventional annalistic and episodical historical writing of his time and history as he conceived of it,

---

[1] F. J. Teggart, *The Idea of Progress,* University of California Press, 1925, p. 58.

namely, as the science of the origin and development of civilization. Anticipating Vico and Turgot, he comprehended the unity and continuity of historical development. In marked contrast with the static or eschatological conceptions of contemporary Christian historiography was his dynamic thesis that the processes of historic growth are subject to constant change, comparable to the life of the individual organism. He made clear the coöperation of psychic and environmental factors in this evolution of civilization. Robert Flint makes the following estimate of the significance of his work: "The first writer to treat history as the proper object of a special science was Mohammed Ibn Khaldun. Whether on this account he is to be regarded or not as the founder of the science of history is a question as to which there may well be difference of opinion; but no candid reader of his 'Prolegomena' can fail to admit that his claim to the honor is more valid than that of any other author previous to Vico."

The earliest theories of progress in Europe arose in the seventeenth and eighteenth centuries. Three new developments seem to have been chiefly responsible for this. One was the growth of natural science and the perception of the possible application of its results to human betterment. This attitude naturally fostered a secular outlook, which reduced to some degree the earlier obsession with spiritual matters and the hope of salvation in a world to come. The growing aspiration to improve mankind by the application of science was probably the chief influence which helped to shift the interest of many European thinkers from the kingdom of God to the kingdom of man. It also impressed upon them the achievements of modern scientists.

Another main stimulus to the propagation of theories of progress was the effect of oversea expansion. By observing mankind in various stages of cultural development, philosophers glimpsed the reality of social evolution from primitive culture to modern times. This gave rise to a dynamic conception of human culture.

Finally, in the eighteenth century the rising humanitarian movement strongly encouraged the theory of progress by leading men to formulate plans to escape from existing abuses through building a better social order here on earth.

Three eminent philosophers all influenced by humanism, the rise of modern science, and the discoveries overseas—Montaigne, Francis Bacon, and Descartes—made incidental contributions to the development of the conception of progress. Montaigne insisted that the purpose of human learning is to teach mankind how to live more successfully here on earth rather than how to die with assurance of salvation in the world to come. This was a complete repudiation of the Christian objectives. Another incidental phase of Montaigne's independence was his capacity, though an enthusiastic humanist, to criticize candidly those classical writers whose ideas or style bored and irritated him. He was not bound down by any notion that every single ancient had been perfect. Montaigne did not, however, conceive of social progress as a reality. He was, as we have seen, conservative in this regard and counseled against changing institutions.

Francis Bacon achieved a definite advance over his famous namesake of the thirteenth century. Francis not only agreed with Roger in accepting the inductive and experimental method as the most promising avenue to the acquisition of knowledge, but went the whole way and rejected the medieval theory that theology should be the prime object of intellectual activity. He not only accepted the scientific method, but proposed to apply its results to nonreligious purposes; namely, to the improvement of the secular estate of mankind. Bacon sharply expressed his disapproval of the methods and limitations of the scholastic philosophers. The futility of the deductive or dialectical method as a means of acquiring knowledge was aptly stated in his famous phrase, "nature is more subtle than any argument."

One of Bacon's most relevant contributions to a theory of progress was his denunciation of the current tendency to look back to the ancients as the source of infallible wisdom. Bacon correctly held that the latest generation are the real "ancients." "These be the ancient times," he said, "when the world is growing old; our own age is more truly antiquity than is the time which is computed backwards, beginning with our age." As a mature man is considered wiser than a child, so we may expect a greater accumulation of knowledge and a progress of civilization in recent rather than in past generations. To worship the past because we think that it can furnish us with wisdom unique in both quantity and quality is one of the chief obstacles to intellectual and cultural progress. Bacon asserted that the kingdom of man, based on science, should displace the kingdom of God, founded on faith and theology, as the center of human interest. As we noted in an earlier chapter, Bacon's utopia or ideal society portrayed in the *New Atlantis,* pictured a society organized around scientific research and its achievements.

The philosopher and scientist, Blaise Pascal, adopted Bacon's theory that the latest generation is the most ancient and created out of it a real theory of progress in which he anticipated Fontenelle and Perrault:

> Those whom we call the ancients were really new to everything; whereas it is in ourselves, who have added to their knowledge the experience of other ages, that we must look for the antiquity which we revere in them.[2]

René Descartes' most important generalization relating to a theory of progress was the declaration, in his *Discourse on Method,* that the scientifically inclined philosopher must resolutely cut himself off from ancient authority and reject preconceived notions. Only by so doing can he expect to arrive at a sound and logical body of knowledge. Of course, it is true that Descartes was not entirely consistent, but his belief that we must free ourselves from the illusions of the past was a valuable contribution. It was heartily reëchoed by the English philosopher, Joseph Glanvill. Descartes was also one of the first to envisage the possibility of exploiting natural science in such a manner as to improve man's earthly condition:

> We shall be able to find an art, by which, knowing the force and action of fire, water, air, stars, the heavens, and all other objects, as clearly as we know the various trades of our artisans, we may be able to employ them in the same way

[2] Smith, *History of Modern Culture,* I, 255.

for their appropriate uses, and make ourselves the masters and possessors of nature. And this will not be solely for the pleasure of enjoying with ease and by ingenious devices all the good things of the world, but principally for the preservation and improvement of human health, which is both the foundation of all the goods and the means of strengthening and quickening the spirit itself.[3]

One of the most interesting of the fragmentary contributions to a theory of progress at the close of the seventeenth century was a by-product of the pedantry of the classicists in England. It is sometimes known as "the battle of the books." [4] The more ecstatic humanists contended that, in all respects, the writers of pagan antiquity surpassed modern authors. The most extreme statement of this view was contained in the *Essay upon Ancient and Modern Learning* (1690) by Sir William Temple. Temple went so far as to deny the validity of the Copernican theory and of Harvey's discovery of the circulation of the blood, and held that Thales, Pythagoras, and Plato far surpassed Galileo, Newton, and Huygens as scientists. In literature and art the ancients even more clearly surpassed the moderns. Jonathan Swift, a protégé of Temple, upheld to a moderate degree the superiority of the ancients in his satire, *The Battle of the Books* (1697). But he conceded high achievements to the moderns, and ridiculed the whole controversy.

William Wotton in his *Reflections upon Ancient and Modern Learning* (1694) replied to Temple and contended that the moderns have infinitely greater knowledge than the ancients. Temple's glaring errors in classical knowledge were exposed by the eminent classical scholar, Richard Bentley (1662-1742). Daniel Defoe, in his *Essay upon Projects* (1702), declared that while his generation might not be happier than the ancients, yet it possessed scientific and industrial knowledge quite unknown to the pagan world. Joseph Glanvill compared the pedantic admirers of the classics to explorers who brought back cargoes of worthless stones, imagining that they must be gold or gems because they came from so far away. So we admire classical writers because of their antiquity, without a realistic examination of their writings. Glanvill denounced as worthless, or almost worthless, humanistic education in the English universities, especially Oxford.

III. THE AGE OF RATIONALISM AND IDEAS OF PROGRESS

A disciple of Descartes, Bernard de Fontenelle (1657-1757), may be said to have formulated the first fairly thorough and consistent theory of progress. In his *Dialogues of the Dead* (1683), chiefly a dialogue between Socrates and Montaigne, Socrates assumed that the moderns had advanced far beyond the civilization of the ancients, while Montaigne denied that this was true. The implied conclusion of the book was that civilization is essentially static. On the whole, while containing many interesting and satirical passages, it is a rather illogical and disappointing performance. Yet it did at least abandon the conception that either the Christian or the pagan past was remarkably superior to the civilization of the seventeenth century.

[3] W. D. Wallis, *Culture and Progress*, McGraw-Hill, 1930, p. 285.
[4] Smith, *op. cit.*, I, 230-32.

Five years later, however, Fontenelle published a brief but much more trenchant and satisfactory work, *A Digression on the Ancients and the Moderns*. He laid down the following fundamental principles: (1) from a biological standpoint the ancients were certainly not superior to the moderns, human nature having remained essentially the same since pagan times; (2) in science and industry, where one achievement depends upon another, progress is cumulative, and here the moderns have advanced far beyond the ancients; (3) this does not mean that the moderns possess greater innate capacity, since they are able to utilize and develop the previous achievements of the ancients; (4) in poetry and oratory, which are spontaneous expressions of human nature, the works of the ancients were distinguished—perhaps perfect—but there is no reason for doubting that the moderns can equal them; and (5) at all events, unreasoning admiration of the ancients is one of the chief obstacles to progress. The general tenor of Fontenelle's argument may be discerned from the following passages:

> However this may be, we have here, I think, the solution of the great problem of the ancients and moderns. The centuries produce no natural difference between men. The climate of Greece or of Italy and that of France are too nearly alike to cause any sensible difference between the Greeks or the Latins and ourselves. Even if they should produce a difference of some sort, it would be very easy to efface, and, finally, it would be no more to their advantage than to ours. We are all, then, perfectly equal, ancients and moderns, Greeks, Latins, and French. . . .
>
> It is true that, in order to add to the first discoveries, greater mental effort is often necessary than was needed to make these discoveries in the first place; but, on the other hand, we experience much greater facility in making this effort. We have benefited intellectually by those same discoveries which we see before us; we have inspirations borrowed from others in addition to those which we have of ourselves; and if we outdo the first inventor, it is he himself who has helped us to outdo him; and so he always has his share in the glory of our work; and were he to withdraw what belongs to him, we should find our own share to be no greater than his. . . .
>
> And so, seeing that we are in a position to benefit by the discoveries of the ancients and by their mistakes even, it is not surprising that we surpass them. To merely equal them would mean necessarily that we were of a nature vastly inferior to theirs; it would almost mean that we were not men as well as they.
>
> However, in order that the moderns may always continue to outdo the ancients, circumstances must be propitious. Eloquence and poetry require only a certain rather limited number of views in comparison with other arts, and they depend largely upon the keenness of the imagination. Now men can in a few centuries have accumulated a small number of such views; and the keenness of the imagination has no need of a long succession of experiences, nor of a great many rules, to reach all the perfection of which it is capable. But natural philosophy, medicine, and mathematics are composed of an infinite number of views, and depend upon accuracy of reasoning, which perfects itself very gradually, and is forever perfecting itself; it is often necessary even that they be helped along by experiences which are purely accidental, and which occur when least expected. It is evident

that all this is an endless process, and that the most recent natural philosophers or mathematicians must naturally be the most skilled. . . .

As for eloquence and poetry, which are the subject of principal dispute between the ancients and moderns, although they are not very important in themselves, I believe that the ancients can have reached perfection, because, as I said, it can be reached in a few centuries, and I don't pretend to know exactly how many it takes.[5]

Views essentially similar to Fontenelle's were set forth in a discursive dialogue by Charles Perrault (1628-1703), *A Comparison of the Ancients and the Moderns,* which appeared between 1688 and 1691.[6] Perrault, too, believed that there had been little or no biological change since ancient times. Animals are as strong and fierce, and men as vigorous and intelligent, as they ever were. On the other hand, human knowledge is cumulative; hence, there has been remarkable progress in human learning since ancient times. Each generation inherits all that its predecessors possess and adds to this inheritance its own achievements. Perrault was pardonably proud of the remarkable advances in science in the late seventeenth century. These were more notable, he said, than all the scientific discoveries of the pagans. This eulogistic interpretation of contemporary intellectual progress tempted Perrault to regard his age as having arrived at perfection. He thought that later generations would have little to learn. The following passages fairly summarize Perrault's conclusions:

I believe that we all agree to this principle, for nothing is more unreasonable, or even more ridiculous, than to suppose that nature is no longer capable of producing men as great as those of former centuries. The lions and the tigers which rove the deserts of Africa to-day are quite as proud and as cruel as those of the time of Alexander or of Augustus, our roses are as deep a crimson as those of the golden age; why should men be excepted from this general rule? And so, when we compare the ancients and moderns, it is not with respect to their purely natural talents, which have been the same and of the same force in the great men of all ages, but solely with respect to the beauty of their works and the knowledge which they possessed of the arts and sciences, in which there may be found a great deal of difference and inequality according to the different centuries.

For, inasmuch as the sciences and arts are nothing more than a mass of reflections, of rules, and of precepts, the author of the poem referred to maintains rightly, and I maintain strongly with him, that this mass, necessarily augmented from day to day, is the greater the farther we advance in time, especially when Heaven gives us some great monarch who loves, protects, and favors these pursuits. . . .

We need only read the French and English journals and glance over the noble achievements of the Academies of these two great kingdoms to be convinced that during the last twenty or thirty years more discoveries have been made in the science of nature than during the whole extent of learned antiquity. . . .

As for myself, I confess I hold myself fortunate to know what happiness we enjoy, and that I take great pleasure in glancing back over all the earlier centuries, where I see the birth and the growth of everything, but where I see nothing which

[5] Teggart, *op. cit.,* pp. 96-99.
[6] Also in a poem, *The Century of Louis the Great.*

has not received new growth and new lustre in the times in which we live. I rejoice to see our century arrived in some sort at the highest perfection. And since for some years now progress has been much slower, and seems almost imperceptible, just as the days seem to discontinue to lengthen as they approach the Solstice, I have the further joy of thinking that very likely we have not many things for which to envy those who will come after us.[7]

The Abbé Charles Castel de St. Pierre (1658-1753) is famous in the history of the development of the idea of progress because he seems to have been the first to suggest clearly that man's future lies in his own hands. He embodied his theory of progress in his *Observations on the Continual Progress of Universal Reason* (1737). His predecessors were interested chiefly in showing that there had been some progress since antiquity. The Abbé was more concerned with the idea that man might plan a better future and work directly to achieve this end. In his *Discourse on the Polysynodie* (1718) he anticipated Turgot, Saint-Simon, and Auguste Comte by declaring that we must depend primarily upon social science and an academy of experts to aid us in planning a happier future. He is also well known for a specific contribution to the betterment of the race, namely, a comprehensive plan for perpetual peace through arbitration, published in three volumes in 1713-1717. He regarded war, along with religious superstition and political despotism, as the main obstacles to progress.

With the Italian philosopher of history, Giovanni Battista Vico (1668-1744), the idea of progress passed beyond the debate concerning the merits of the ancients and moderns. Vico attempted to reconstruct the history of civilization and to formulate the principles which govern the evolution of society. These ideas were embodied in his *Principles of a New Science* (1725).

Vico's philosophy of history was psychological in essence, although he has been called a geographical determinist. His basic thesis was that social evolution is determined by the collective mental outlook of the successive periods of historical development. This anticipated the doctrine of Auguste Comte and Karl Lamprecht, namely, the interpretation of history in terms of changes in the collective psychology.

Vico saw everything in history in terms of a threefold division: "There were three kinds of nature, three types of character, three epochs of religion, three species of language, of writing, of governments, of natural law, of jurisprudence, of legal judgments, etc." While Robert Flint contended that this is a fairly logical and tenable conclusion, it appears more probable that, as Professor W. A. Dunning wrote, "Vico's triposis is at some points rather forced and unreal, yet he presents on the whole a very remarkable interpretation of institutions social and political, in connection with the various phases of human government."[8]

Quite in harmony with the above doctrine was his three-stage theory of historical development. This differed considerably from the famous scheme presented by Comte a century later, although the first stage in both plans are identical. The three stages suggested by Vico are: (1) the divine stage, or the age of

[7] Teggart, *op. cit.*, pp. 110-12.
[8] *Political Theories from Luther to Montesquieu*, Macmillan, 1905, p. 388.

the gods; (2) the heroic stage; and (3) the stage of man. These divisions he borrowed admittedly from Herodotus and Varro. Throughout all stages certain important psychological principles have conditioned social development.

Vico believed that the three stages of cultural development repeat themselves in a sort of cycle. But the repetition is never exact. Each turn of the cycle marks a definite advance. Progress is, then, real. Instead of perfectly recurring cycles we find that mankind progresses in a spiral course. Civilization moves around but it also moves upward. As Flint says: "His whole attitude towards the future seems irreconcilable with the notion that he imagined that it would be a transcript of a page which had been already written. His belief in cycles or 'ricorsi' was, indeed, inconsistent with a belief in continuous progress in a straight line, but not with advance on the whole, not with a gradually ascending spiral movement, and still less did it imply that any cycle was perfectly like another, and that history merely repeated itself." [9]

More penetrating, and less fantastic in detail, was the philosophy of history sketched by the French statesman and publicist, Anne Robert Jacques Turgot (1727-1781). These views were embodied in a "Discourse," entitled *On the Successive Advances of the Human Mind,* delivered at the Sorbonne on December 11, 1750. Conceived when the writer was only twenty-four years of age, it is almost unique in the history of historiography and social science as a combination of precocity and profundity.

Turgot's philosophy of history was based upon a broad conception of cultural evolution. He believed that civilization is the product of geographical, biological, and psychological factors. He thus avoided a narrow historical determinism. Like Fontenelle and Perrault, Turgot asserted the biological fixity of human nature and the physical unity of mankind: "The same senses, the same organs, the spectacle of the same universe have everywhere given to men the same ideas, just as the same needs and the same propensities have everywhere taught them the same arts." [10] In an eloquent passage he expressed his theory of the unity and continuity of history. This may probably be regarded as his most original and enduring contribution to social science and the idea of progress:

Natural phenomena, governed by constant laws, traverse forever certain fixed cycles of change. All things perish, all things revive; and in those successive generations which mark the reproduction of plants and of animals, time merely restores continually the likeness of what it has annihilated.

The succession of mankind, on the contrary, presents from age to age an ever-varied spectacle. Reason, the passions, liberty, continually give rise to new events. All the ages are linked together by a chain of causes and effects which unite the existing state of the world with all that has gone before. The manifold signs of speech and of writing, in giving to men the means of insuring the possession of their ideas and of communicating them to others, have made a common treasure-store of all individual knowledge, which one generation bequeaths to the next, a heritage constantly augmented by the discoveries of each age; and mankind,

[9] Robert Flint, *Vico,* Edinburgh, 1884, p. 228.
[10] Teggart, *op. cit.,* p. 116.

viewed from its origin, appears to the eyes of a philosopher as one vast whole, which itself, like each individual, has its infancy and its growth.[11]

In another essay, Turgot projected what was manifestly a clear anticipation of Auguste Comte's three stages of the intellectual progress of mankind—the theological, metaphysical, and scientific. Turgot wrote that:

> Before knowing the connection of physical facts with one another, nothing was more natural than to suppose that they were produced by beings, intelligent, invisible, and like to ourselves. Everything which happened without man's own intervention had its god, to which fear or hope caused a worship to be paid conformed to the respect accorded to powerful men—the gods being only men more or less powerful and perfect in proportion as the age which originated them was more or less enlightened as to what constitutes the true perfections of humanity.
>
> But when philosophers perceived the absurdity of these fables, without having attained to a real acquaintance with the history of nature, they fancifully accounted for phenomena by abstract expressions, by essences and faculties, which indeed explained nothing, but were reasoned from as if they were real existences.
>
> It was only very late that from observing the mechanical action of bodies on one another, other hypotheses were inferred, which mathematics could develop and experience verify.[12]

Turgot not only asserted that there had been notable progress in the past, he accepted the doctrine of "perfectionism," advocated by Helvétius, Condorcet, and Godwin. The advances of the past are but preliminary to the perfection of the future. Turgot was almost as exuberant about the cultural progress of his time as Perrault had been a half century before, but this did not, as with Perrault, prevent Turgot from looking forward with keen anticipation to the greater achievements of the future.

Doubtless the most elaborate and enthusiastic statement of the theory of progress prior to the nineteenth century was contained in the *Outline of an Historical Picture of the Progress of the Human Mind* by the Marquis de Condorcet (1743-1794), published in 1795. In this work Condorcet made a thorough effort to appraise the progress of the past, was an optimist regarding contemporary achievements, and presented a glowing picture of the more striking advances which he anticipated of the future. In the following sections Condorcet summarizes his firm belief in the reality of progress and in the possibility of creating a more perfect state of civilization:

> Such is the object of the work which I have undertaken, the result of which will be to show, through reasoning and through facts, that nature has assigned no limit to the perfecting of the human faculties, that the perfectibility of man is truly indefinite; that the progress of this perfectibility, henceforth independent of any power that might wish to arrest it, has no other limit than the duration of the globe on which nature has placed us. Doubtless this progress can be more or less rapid; but never will men retrograde, so long, at least, as the earth occupies the

[11] Teggart, *op. cit.*, p. 115.
[12] Robert Flint, *The Philosophy of History in France and Germany*, Scribner, 1874, p. 113.

same place in the system of the universe and the general laws of that system do not effect on the globe either a general destruction or changes which would no longer permit human kind to preserve or to exercise thereon the same faculties, and to avail themselves of the same resources. . . .

Our hopes regarding the future state of humanity can be reduced to these three important points: the destruction of inequality between nations; the progress of equality within one and the same nation; and, finally, the real perfecting of mankind. Shall all nations some day approach the state of civilization attained by the most enlightened, the freest, the most emancipated from prejudices of present-day peoples, such as the French, for example, and the Anglo-Americans? Shall not that vast interval which separates these peoples from the bondage of nations subservient to kings, from the barbarism of the African tribes and the ignorance of savages, gradually disappear? [13]

Condorcet divided the past, from the earliest primitive society to the French Revolution, into nine epochs, offering an estimate of the progress which had occurred in each. The French Revolution he regarded as the dividing line between the past and the glorious future. The political and social achievements of the age of enlightenment which were brought to fruition by the French Revolution, together with the remarkable advances in pure and applied science, would inaugurate a new and happier era. The Canadian scholar, James Bonar, has succinctly described the scope and leading contentions of Condorcet's work:

He divides history into ten great epochs: (1) that of hunters and fishermen; (2) that of shepherds; (3) that of tillers of the soil; (4) that of commerce, science, and philosophy in Greece; (5) that of science and philosophy from the conquests of Alexander to the decline of the Roman Empire; (6) that of the decadence of science till the Crusades; (7) from the latter date till the invention of Printing; (8) from the invention of Printing to the attacks on the Principle of Authority by Luther, Descartes, and Bacon; and (9) from Descartes to the French Republic, when reason, tolerance, and humanity were becoming the watchwords of all. In conclusion, he looks forward to the future [the 10th epoch], and sees not only enlightenment extending, but science more and more completely mastering nature.

The progress of the race, in every respect, is without limit; and it will result in equality of material, comfort, and security of livelihood, as well as moral and intellectual perfection, universal peace, and political liberty. Industry by the aid of the sciences will make the soil capable of yielding support without limit. He pauses to ask, Will not the increase of men be without limit too? and answers, In any case, at a very distant time, and before that time arrives we shall no longer be prevented by "superstition" from limiting our numbers in ways obvious enough, but not now followed.

The equality of the sexes, which progress will certainly bring with it, will make this consummation more easy of fulfillment. Progress in the art of medicine will so prolong life, that death will be the exception rather than the rule. Persecuted philosophers may console themselves by looking away from the present to this glorious future.[14]

[13] Teggart, op. cit., pp. 142, 155.
[14] Bonar, Philosophy and Political Economy, Macmillan, 1893, pp. 204-5.

By dividing the past into nine epochs, based upon definite stages and typical achievements, Condorcet not only assumed progress to exist, but, like Turgot, demonstrated it to be a reality which can be tested.

Far more than any other contemporary believer in progress, Condorcet was confident of the future. In the following radiant and defiant paragraph Condorcet, writing as a fugitive in the shadow of the scaffold, implies that his survey of the past and his prophecy regarding the future, constitute the best consolation of the true philosopher and create a vision of the future which no enemy or persecutor can snatch from him:

Such are the questions examinations of which must end this last epoch. And how admirably calculated is this picture of the human race, freed from all these chains, secure from the dominion of chance, as from that of the enemies of its progress, and advancing with firm and sure steps towards the attainment of truth, virtue, and happiness, to present to the philosopher a spectacle which shall console him for the errors, the crimes, the injustice, with which the earth is still polluted, and whose victim he often is! It is in the contemplation of this picture that he receives the reward of his efforts towards the progress of reason and the defense of liberty. He dares then to link these with the eternal chain of human destiny; and thereby he finds virtue's true recompense, the joy of having performed a lasting service, which no fatality can ever destroy by restoring the evils of prejudice and slavery. This contemplation is for him a place of refuge, whither the memory of his persecutors cannot follow him, where, living in imagination with man restored to his rights and the dignity of his nature, he forgets him whom greed, fear, or envy torment and corrupt; there it is that he exists in truth with his kin, in an elysium which his reason has been able to create for him, and which his love for humanity enhances with the purest enjoyments.[15]

The next writer we may consider is the English rationalist, William Godwin (1756-1836), author of the famous *Enquiry Concerning Political Justice* (1793). Taking seriously the idea which Burke suggested ironically, namely, that government is an evil, he created a sensation by the publication of a book which embodied this view as its central thesis. The French Revolution was then at its height. H. S. Salt, in the introduction to his edition of that part of Godwin's *Political Justice* which deals with property, says:

It is difficult for us, who live in a less speculative and sanguine age to realize the keen interest which attached to the publication, in 1793, of William Godwin's "Political Justice," at a crisis when men's minds were strung to a high pitch of expectant enthusiasm by the thrill of excitement of which the French Revolution was the cause; but the testimony of contemporary writers, whatever their personal sympathies might be, is explicit on this point. "No work of our time," says Hazlitt, "gave such a blow to the philosophical mind of the country as Godwin's celebrated *Enquiry Concerning Political Justice*. Tom Paine was considered for the time as Tom Fool to him; Paley an old woman; Edmund Burke a flashy sophist. Truth, moral truth, it was supposed, had here taken up its abode, and these were the oracles of thought." "Burn your books on chemistry," was Wordsworth's advice to a student, "and read Godwin on Necessity." "Faulty as it is in

15 Teggart, *op. cit.*, pp. 175-76.

many parts," wrote Southey, "there is a mass of truth in it that must make every man think." We are told by De Quincey that Godwin's book "carried one single shock into the bosom of English society, fearful but momentary." "In the quarto," he adds, "that is the original edition of his Political Justice, Mr. Godwin advanced against thrones and denominations, powers and principalities, with the air of some Titan slinger or monomachist from Thebes and Troy, saying, 'Come higher, ye wretches, that I may give your flesh to the fowls of the air.' " [16]

The chief doctrines of this sensational treatise are: (1) man has not made striking progress in the past, and the present is about as deplorable as one could imagine; (2) the evils of society arise from the detrimental effects of coercive and oppressive human institutions; (3) all government, as far as it is coercive, should be abolished; (4) the ideal society is composed of free and equal individuals—free in everything except the moral censure of their associates; (5) no coercive political organization larger than the parish should be permitted to exist; (6) the unequal distribution of property should be rectified; (7) marriage as a coercive institution should be abolished; (8) man is perfectible; (9) man may be improved mainly through the influence of reason which can fully dominate the emotions; (10) reason and truth must ultimately prevail; and (11) the three chief agencies which will produce their triumph are literature, education, and political justice, the latter of which Godwin made the chief topic of his treatise. Education, which is to inculcate the principles of reason, must be given privately, not by public agencies.

As Bonar puts it, "Godwin's theory is the apotheosis of individualism and in a sense of Protestantism; a purified and enlightened individualism is not to him the beginning, but the end of all human progress. He is the father not so truly of philosophical radicalism, as of anarchism." In the following paragraph Godwin expounds his guarded yet confident doctrine of human perfectibility:

By perfectible, it is not meant that he is capable of being brought to perfection. But the word seems sufficiently adapted to express the faculty of being continually made better and receiving perpetual improvement; and in this sense it is here to be understood. The term perfectible, thus explained, not only does not imply the capacity of being brought to perfection, but stands in express opposition to it. If we could arrive at perfection, there would be an end to our improvement. There is, however, one thing of great importance that it does imply: every perfection or excellence that human beings are competent to conceive, human beings, unless in cases that are palpably and unequivocally excluded by the structure of their frame, are competent to attain.[17]

IV. ROMANTIC PHILOSOPHY AND THEORIES OF PROGRESS

The German philosopher of history, Johann Gottfried von Herder (1744-1803), was a founder of romanticism rather than a mature romanticist. He recognized the marked influence upon man of external factors, such as the physical environ-

---

[16] H. S. Salt, *Godwin's Inquiry concerning Political Justice*, Sonnenschein, 1890, pp. 1-2.
[17] *An Enquiry concerning Political Justice*, by William Godwin, ed. and abridged by R. A. Preston, 2 vols., Crofts, 1926, I, xxix.

ment, but he also emphasized the potency of a complex of mysterious psychic forces, which he defined under the rather elusive term, *Geist* (the universal spirit). Indeed, the historical process is chiefly a matter of the gradual education of the race, which has been impelled onward through the joint impetus of *Geist* and geographic factors.

While Herder was essentially pious, he believed that the historical development of man is strictly determined by natural forces and psychological factors. While God originated these forces, he does not interfere arbitrarily to modify or alter their operation. Herder summarizes his views of history in the following five propositions:

I. The end of human nature is humanity; and that they may realize their end, God has put into the hands of men their own fate.

II. All the destructive powers in nature must not only yield in time to the preservative powers, but must ultimately be subservient to the perfection of the whole.

III. The human race is destined to proceed through various degrees of civilization, in various revolutions, but its abiding welfare rests solely and essentially on reason and justice.

IV. From the very nature of the human mind, reason and justice must gain more footing among men in the course of time, and promote the extension of humanity.

V. A wise goodness disposes the fate of mankind, and therefore there is no nobler merit, no purer or more abiding happiness, than to co-operate in its designs.[18]

Much more important than Herder in the history of the idea of progress was the distinguished German metaphysician, Immanuel Kant (1724-1804). Kant's reputation as a philosopher rests chiefly upon his metaphysical demonstration of philosophical agnosticism in his *Critique of Pure Reason,* and upon his rôle as the founder of Protestant modernism and the notion of unconditioned morality in his *Critique of Practical Reason*. His contributions to the idea of progress were, however, embodied in two brief works, *The Idea of a Universal History from a Cosmopolitical Point of View* (1784) and *On the Common Saying* (1793).

We may first consider Kant's philosophy of history as presented in the essay on *Universal History*. In the first place, he says, whether or not the human will be free in theory, its manifestations in action are determined by universal natural laws. Therefore, if the operation of the will is examined from the standpoint of universal history, its movements may be seen to follow a regular path of progressive development.

While this march of progress may seem tangled and unregulated in the case of individuals, the historical record of the human species is a slow and gradual, but continually advancing, development of its "original capacities and endowments." Individuals or even nations, in pursuing their personal ends, little know that they are unwittingly guided by a great cosmic purpose, and are unconsciously working toward an impressive goal. Hence, the task of the philosophical

18 Flint, *The Philosophy of History in France and Germany*, p. 386.

historian is to see whether he cannot discover some universal plan of nature in the complex and paradoxical movements of humanity.[19]

Kant, therefore, set about to seek a clue to the program of nature, as revealed in history. He hoped that his discovery would reveal the historical scheme of things, as Newton had explained the discoveries of Kepler by the law of universal gravitation. Kant put forth his philosophy of history in a series of nine progressive propositions, each followed by a short explanation and elaboration. His most important proposition is the fourth, dealing with the social significance of the principle of antagonism. This contains the essentials of his theory of history and society.

By the term antagonism Kant says that he means the "unsocial sociability of men," that is, the struggle that goes on in each man and in society between collectivism and individualism, between the love of society and our neighbors, on the one hand, and the love of self-achievement and independence, on the other. This antagonism awakens man's latent powers, overcomes his natural indolence, and starts him on the road to progress. Without this struggle mankind might have led a happy and contented life in a rudimentary type of culture, but he could never have produced a higher form of civilization. There would have been nothing to stir men into activity.

Kant contended that the keener the struggle between these conflicting forces of collectivism and individualism, the more rapid is the progress of the race. Consequently, the state which provides the greatest scope for this struggle, yet prevents anarchy or oppression, will do the most to propel society towards its final goal. Therefore, the creation of a civil society that combines the greatest amount of legalized liberty with an ultimately irresistible state is the most indispensable achievement within the range of human inventiveness.

Yet the establishment of this ideal civil society is closely connected with the attainment of world peace. In this phase of his writings Kant was influenced by the Abbé de St. Pierre and Rousseau. It is likely to prove futile, he said, to attempt to regulate relations between men within a single state if the various independent states continue their violent antagonisms. The same sort of evils which afflict individuals, if given unrestricted freedom, operate among nations whose external relations are not subject to legal control and adjustment. But here also, nature is constantly seeking to produce that ultimate harmony which she attempts to secure among the citizens of each separate state. Devastation and exhaustion resulting from war are leading nations towards ultimate federation. Only through the realization of world peace can the rulers of separate states free themselves from the distractions of war and diplomacy. This they must do in order to devote their attention to perfecting domestic institutions, thus regulating the conflicting forces of collectivism and individualism, and thereby achieving progress.

Kant's conception of progress was, then, a moral view of human development. It harmonized the romanticist protest against rationalism with the latter's primary interest in science and technology. In the latter part of his *On the Common Say-*

19 Cf. J. B. Bury, *The Idea of Progress*, Dover Publications, Inc., 1955, pp. 243-44.

ing, Kant admitted that his conception of progress was a moral notion and re-affirmed his belief that definite moral progress can be demonstrated.

In conclusion, it may be held that there is a vision of the social teleology of Lester F. Ward and others in Kant's ninth and final proposition, in which he declared that by formulating tentative principles of progress we may assist, in some degree, in guiding and accelerating the processes of human advancement.

The culmination of the romanticist and idealist tendency in the interpretation of human progress was reached in the philosophy of history set forth by the ponderous and abstruse German metaphysician, Georg Wilhelm Friedrich Hegel (1770-1831). He organized his scheme of historical analysis about the evolution of human liberty. Professor Dunning admirably characterizes Hegel's view of the historic process:

> The final channel through which the state is revealed as perfected free will is, according to Hegel, world history (*Weltgeschichte*). To him the process of events is an unfolding of universal spirit (*Geist*). The culture of every people—its art, religion, political institutions—expresses a particular stage in the activity and reve-lation of the absolute idea. Each successive age in world history since civilization began offers to view some people in whose spirit (*Volkgeist*) is reflected the world-spirit (*Weltgeist*) so far as that has been revealed.
>
> The process of revelation and realization of the idea, according to the principles of the Hegelian dialectic, is a fourfold process. It is not surprising, therefore, that Hegel's survey of general history detects four great world-historic political systems (*Reiche*) in whose successive careers the idea of freedom has progressed to perfect realization. These four systems are the Oriental, the Greek, the Roman, and the German. With benumbing legerdemain the philosopher makes the common-place facts of familiar history fit themselves nicely at the word into the categories and relations of his logic, and shows us mankind through all the ages marching steadily but unconsciously along Hegelian lines toward the Germanic perfection of the nineteenth century. In the modern world, freedom is revealed to be the uni-versal principle of state life. The Orient knew and to the present day knows only that *One* (i.e., the despot) is free; the Greek and Roman World, that *Some* are free; the German World knows that *All* are free!
>
> Such is Hegel's generalization of the world-historical process. It displays the usual tendency of a philosophy of history—to represent the thinker's own time and place as the climax and summation of progress. But with whatever qualifica-tions we judge the speculation and conclusions of Hegel, it is impossible to deny that the scope and coherency of his system of political science and the boldness and vast sweep of his historical inductions reveal a mind of titanic power.[20]

In addition to his general philosophy of history, viewed as the gradual realiza-tion of liberty within the absolute state, Hegel made another important contribu-tion to the idea of progress, namely, his so-called "dialectic of development." He declared that the mode of progress is essentially the following: an affirmation or a movement—the thesis—appears. It is immediately opposed by an opposite con-tention or movement—the antithesis. The conflict between thesis and antithesis results ultimately in a creative achievement, the synthesis of the best in the oppos-

[20] W. A. Dunning, *Political Theories from Rousseau to Spencer*, Macmillan, 1920, pp. 164-65.

ing principles or movements. But this synthesis immediately becomes a new thesis, to be opposed by a new antithesis, and the process starts over again. This doctrine has more than curious interest, since it was adopted by Karl Marx in his theories of history and economics, and by Lester F. Ward in his sociology.

Hegel, in his attitude towards progress, past and future, stood at almost the opposite pole from Godwin. The latter held that the past made but little progress, but hoped for infinite future advancement. Hegel contended that man had progressed a great deal in the past, so much indeed that he had almost attained perfection here and now—especially in the Germanic countries. Therefore, little was to be expected or desired from the future beyond extending Teutonic achievements to other peoples.

Herder, Kant, and Hegel were only the more prominent among romanticist and idealist philosophers who offered suggestions about the nature of human progress, most of them having a strong theological cast. We shall later meet some of these writers, namely, Fichte, Schelling, and Schlegel. Others, such as the French romanticists Cousin, Jouffroy, and Quinet, we shall not have occasion to consider in any detail.[21]

V. EARLY SOCIOLOGY AND THEORIES OF PROGRESS

The idea of progress was probably the leading current in the sociological thought of the nineteenth century. The chief interest of most early sociologists was to discover the nature of progress and the means of realizing it.

The need for a science of sociology was first conclusively expressed by an enthusiastic devotee of the idea of progress, Count Claude Henri de Saint-Simon (1760-1825). His belief in progress is amply attested by the following eloquent paragraph:

> The imagination of poets has placed the golden age in the cradle of the human race. It was the age of iron they should have banished there. The golden age is not behind us, but in front of us. It is the perfection of social order. Our fathers have not seen it; our children will arrive there one day, and it is for us to clear the way for them.

Saint-Simon held that the rapid transformation of social and economic conditions by the scientific and industrial revolutions necessitated a real science of social progress, based upon thoroughly positivistic grounds, which he called *la science politique*. His disciple, Auguste Comte, soon christened it *sociology*. Saint-Simon accepted the law of three stages of intellectual progress which had been anticipated by Turgot and Burdin and was later developed in great detail by Comte.

In his early days, Saint-Simon pinned his hopes of progress on liberal and rational politics. But the reaction after the French Revolution disillusioned him, and he turned to the technology introduced by the industrial revolution as the

---

21 For these romanticist conceptions of progress and the philosophy of history, see H. E. Barnes, *A History of Historical Writing*, Dover Publications, Inc., 1962, chap. viii.

mainstay of his program of social improvement. No other writer of his day was so eloquent a propagandist for industrialization, a trend reminiscent of Francis Bacon's enthusiasm for natural science. At the same time, Saint-Simon was one of the first to understand that permanent industrial advances should be paralleled by comparable institutional readjustments. These essential readjustments could not, he believed, be produced by emotional schemes for social reform, but required the guidance of social science, thoroughly grounded on facts and rigorously positivistic in its attitudes and methods. This is the indispensable service of sociology to social readjustment.

In his *New Christianity,* Saint-Simon advocated the socialization of Christianity to provide a dynamic moral force. In another essay he anticipated the Technocrats by proposing that we place the material destiny of society in the hands of technological experts, namely, industrial engineers who can master and apply the new social science and technology. Professor Dunning thus summarizes Saint-Simon's specific plan for socio-political reconstruction:

> The new social order must rest on the political leadership of the useful class. Capacity rather than possessions must become the qualification for control of the public service. The producers must supplant the mere consumers—the bees the drones—in political authority. For the realization of which end in France Saint-Simon sketched out the reorganized political system. Without requiring the abolition of the monarchy, he called for a government with supreme power in a new species of parliament. This body should include, first, a house of invention, consisting of civil engineers, poets (*ou autres inventeurs en littérature*), painters, sculptors, architects, and musicians; second, a house of examination, consisting of physicists and mathematicians; and third, a house of execution, consisting of captains of industry (*chefs des maisons d'industrie*), unsalaried, and duly apportioned among the various kinds of business. The first house would present projects of law, the second would examine and pass upon them and the third would adopt them.[22]

Auguste Comte (1798-1857) developed Saint-Simon's ideas in great detail. He accepted the argument for the necessity of a science of social reconstruction, described with surprising thoroughness the stages of intellectual and social progress, and created an elaborate positivistic utopia, based upon his sociological doctrines.

In his *Positive Philosophy* Comte asserted that the mental evolution of the race consisted of three stages: the theological, metaphysical, and positive or scientific. Many writers have imagined that this trilogy represented Comte's conception of the stages of civilization, and have criticized him for so narrow an interpretation of history.[23] In Comte's *Positive Polity,* however, one finds a more comprehensive scheme of historical development which takes full cognizance of elements other than psychological ones. Here he divided history into three great epochs: the theological-military, the metaphysical-legalistic, and the scientific-industrial. Each of these stages was elaborately subdivided and minutely analyzed.

In Comte's positivist utopia, social guidance was to be supplied by the sociol-

---

22 Dunning, *op. cit.,* p. 357.
23 Especially F. H. Giddings, whose own theory of historical stages was almost identical with those set forth by Comte in his *Polity.*

ogist-priests, moral stimulus produced by the influence of women, and administrative acumen made available by the captains of industry. Religion was divorced
from supernaturalism and transformed into a socialized emotional force supporting secular reforms and social justice.

In the writings of the eminent English philosopher, Herbert Spencer (1820-
1903), the idea of progress was merged with the theory of cosmic evolution.
Spencer regarded everything in the universe as in a state of evolution, a conception which envisaged both progress and decline. In general, however, Spencer
was a cosmological optimist. When talking about evolution he usually meant
progress, manifesting itself in accordance with his well-known laws of the in-
tegration of matter and the accompanying differentiation of structure and
function. Social evolution passes through three stages, devoted respectively to
war, industry, and ethical attainment of peace.

Spencer did not believe that man can effectively hasten the process of evolution by legislation. He defended *laissez-faire* on the grounds of cosmic evolution,
much as the Physiocrats had defended it on the basis of deductions from Newton's celestial mechanics. Spencer contended that social evolution, like cosmic
and organic evolution, is a purely naturalistic process which man may seriously
retard or distort by legislative interference. The Spencerian position was upheld
by William Graham Sumner and many others, notably Ludwig Gumplowicz
and Jacques Novicow.

The opposite thesis, namely, that social initiative may hasten man's progress, was
defended by Lester F. Ward, Albion W. Small, Ludwig Stein, and Leonard T.
Hobhouse. Ward admitted that social evolution has thus far been, for the most
part, purely naturalistic or genetic. But he contended that, with the growth of
human knowledge and social science, man can gradually control the processes
of social development. He may thus supplant the wasteful method of nature
(*genesis*) by the more rapid and economical method of *telesis* (social guidance
towards a desired goal).

VI. PRESENT-DAY RESERVATIONS RELATIVE TO THE THEORY OF PROGRESS

The latest phase of the theory of progress, as discussed by sociologists and
historians, has been devoted to a critical analysis of the term and its implications and to a consideration of the validity of the concept.

It is widely insisted that conceptions of progress tend to be subjective or one-
sided, with no objective tests or standards. Consequently, it seems to many writers
better for the time being to abandon the term "progress," and to use instead
the word "change," concerning the reality of which there can be no doubt. To
illustrate: although we can demonstrate unprecedented progress in material culture in the past fifty years, we cannot assume that this is a proof of human
progress in general. If material progress ends by creating a civilization so complex that mankind is unable to control it, and it terminates in devastating world
wars, then certainly technological advances since 1750 are not indicative of progress as a whole.

Certain writers, like the late Professor A. A. Tenney, proposed comprehensive and objective tests of progress, so that we may begin to deal with the subject in a scientific and discriminating manner. W. F. Ogburn, in his book on *Social Change,* has emphasized the differential rate of progress between technology and institutions and among social institutions, and has described what we call "cultural lag." Further, it is interesting to note that the ancient and humanist theory of the cyclical nature of history has been revived by Oswald Spengler in his widely read work, *The Decline of the West,* a view criticized by another eminent German philosopher, Ludwig Stein, in his *Evolution and Optimism.*

These uncertainties about progress are a candid reflection of our legitimate doubts. For the first time in human history man stands very close to either utopia or chaos. If science and technology are made to serve man constructively, then utopia is easily within his grasp. If, on the other hand, they are used for destructive purposes through economic exploitation and war, then chaos and reversion to barbarism are all but unavoidable.[24]

SELECTED READINGS

Barker, Ernest, *Political Thought in England: 1848-1914,* Oxford Press, 1947.

Brailsford, H. N., *Shelley, Godwin and Their Circle,* Oxford University Press, 1951.

Burlingame, A. E., *Condorcet, the Torch Bearer of the French Revolution,* Stratford Press, 1930.

Bury, J. B., *The Idea of Progress,* Dover Publications, Inc., 1955.

Crocker, L. G., *An Age of Crisis: Man and World in Eighteenth-Century French Thought,* Johns Hopkins Press, 1959.

Delvaille, Jules, *Essai sur l'histoire de l'idée de progrès,* Paris, 1910.

Dunning, W. A., *History of Political Theories: Rousseau to Spencer,* Macmillan, 1920.

Flint, Robert, *The Philosophy of History in France and Germany,* Scribner, 1874.

———— *Vico,* Edinburgh, 1884.

Frankel, Charles, *The Faith of Reason: The Idea of Progress in the French Enlightenment,* Columbia University Press, 1948.

Ginsberg, Morris, *The Idea of Progress,* Beacon Press, 1953.

Hertzler, J. O., *Social Progress,* Century, 1928.

McCloy, S. T., *The Humanitarian Movement in Eighteenth-Century France,* University of Kentucky Press, 1957.

Muzzey, D. S., ed., *Essays in Intellectual History dedicated to James Harvey Robinson,* Harper, 1930, chaps. iv, x, xiii.

Ogburn, W. F., *Social Change,* Viking, 1950.

Salt, H. S., *Godwin's Inquiry concerning Political Justice,* Sonnenschein, 1890.

Sampson, R. V., *Progress in the Age of Reason,* Harvard University Press, 1957.

Schapiro, J. S., *Condorcet and the Rise of Liberalism in France,* Harcourt, Brace, 1934.

Stephen, Leslie, *The Life and Writings of Turgot.*

Teggart, F. J., ed., *The Idea of Progress,* University of California Press, 1925.

Todd, A. J., *Theories of Social Progress,* Macmillan, 1918.

[24] See below, Chap. XXVIII.

XXI

The Reaction
Against Reason
and the Critical Spirit

I. THE REACTION IN PHILOSOPHY

1. *The Background*

The rationalists of the seventeenth and eighteenth centuries placed their faith in reason. They believed that through his intellectual faculties man can discover the fundamental realities. To the rationalists, the world as revealed through sense perception, gradually extended and sharpened by the new instruments of scientific investigation, was a sufficient reality. They believed that the Newtonian system embodied a definitive synthesis of nature. God manifests himself in the phenomena of nature and in those laws discovered by science which culminated in Newton's scheme.

Progress may be achieved, the rationalists believed, through scientific research and the application of its discoveries to social improvement. From Francis Bacon to Condorcet, this constituted an undercurrent of social optimism. The rationalists did not repudiate the feelings and emotions, but they placed chief reliance upon the intellect in all matters pertaining to truth and enlightenment. Towards the end of the eighteenth century, under the influence of the French Revolution, some rationalists became extremely optimistic concerning the possibility of uprooting human traditions and institutions, and rapidly transforming society through the application of a few "self-evident dictates of pure reason."

The conservative mind inevitably reacted against such doctrines. Traditional and sentimental thinkers not only opposed specific rationalist attacks upon religious beliefs and social institutions, but they also developed a fundamental philosophical defense of their own position. This reaction in philosophy is often summarized under the term "romanticism," although it soon developed into the transcendental idealism of the Germanic philosophers. Whether called romanticism or idealism, it was in any case a depreciation of the intellect, a buttressing of faith, and an emphasis on the primacy of emotion. It is not inaccurate to say that the metaphysics of the new philosophy may be termed idealism, while its social and cultural applications are most appropriately designated as romanticism.

The writers of this school turned to the emotions with the same confidence that the rationalists bestowed upon the intellectual faculties. In the following pages we shall endeavor to summarize the most important aspects of the philosophical revolt against rationalism. We shall in no way pretend to give a technical assessment of idealistic metaphysics, but shall indicate rather the most important points developed by these writers in their attack on "pure reason." The idealist and romanticist philosophers frequently assumed that they were utilizing "pure reason," but after Kant's day what they meant by the term was more literally "pure faith." The philosopher mainly responsible for this confusion and for the false identification of faith with reason was Friedrich H. Jacobi (1743-1819). He agreed with the Neoplatonists and the medieval mystics that intuition and inward vision provide the only road to ultimate knowledge. He called this intuitive faculty Reason (*Vernunft*), giving the name Understanding to what had hitherto been called reason.

The inevitable reaction against an excessive emphasis upon man's intellectual faculties was already in evidence in the theories of Rousseau. But Rousseau was merely one of a large group who, in one way or another, aimed to destroy the eighteenth-century intellectual outlook and replace it by something more appealing to the average sensual man. The mass of human beings cannot live by their minds alone. They must feed their emotions and imagination.

2. *Immanuel Kant, the Great Salvager*

The metaphysical basis for idealism and romanticism was laid, in part unintentionally, by the famed Immanuel Kant (1724-1804). Kant had been chiefly interested in science and had been inclined towards rationalism. But, as he tells us, he was aroused from his "dogmatic slumbers" by David Hume's destruction of the conventional concepts of substance and causation. He then devoted himself to producing the most cogent and comprehensive contribution to critical metaphysics and epistemology in the whole history of philosophy, the *Critique of Pure Reason*, published in 1781.

Kant's philosophy was in many ways a development of Locke's general propositions. We have seen that Locke regarded elementary ideas as the product of sensations, and complex ideas as the result of reasoned analysis. We noted that he believed that religion should be based upon reason but that this does not eliminate supernatural religion or the supernatural basis of ethics. Further, Locke accepted the conventional theories of causality and material substance. To a certain extent, the Kantian philosophy provided a more imposing structure of rationalized support for such theories. It rescued them from Hume's destructive critique.

Kant's purpose was to preserve the validity of Locke's empirical philosophy and Newtonian science and yet save philosophy from Hume's devastating conclusions regarding the illusion of substance and the absence of inevitable cause-and-effect relationships.

In harmony with the empirical psychology, Kant agreed that the material content of our knowledge is derived from sensations. But, he said, the forms or patterns through which this knowledge is organized and interpreted in our minds are a product of reason. Substance and causality may not be capable of absolute demonstration, but they are real as mental concepts and are necessary intellectual categories, for without them we could not interpret experience. Equipped with the concepts of substance and causality, the mind can arrive at assured knowledge of the phenomenal world, which is studied by natural science. The laws of nature are the laws apparent to the mind, and the physical world is only a mental representation (picture).

But this realm of physical nature or the world of experience (the phenomenal world) is all that man can know. He can never penetrate the unknowable world of ultimate reality which lies beyond the range of both sensation and reason. This is the realm of "things-in-themselves"—the *noumenal* world, and must be accepted, if at all, on faith.

Kant thus held that philosophy can make clear to us the world of experience, the content of which is revealed to us by sensations, and the organization and interpretation of which is made possible through the rational powers of the mind. But we must not confuse this world of experience with ultimate reality. Kant created in this manner a classic dualism of experience and reality which his idealist successors sought to resolve. This problem occupied Germanic philosophy from Fichte to Hegel.

While Kant himself remained agnostic, his philosophical speculations enabled those readers who wished to do so to harmonize faith and reason. They could retain Christianity, as a portrayal of the noumenal world, on faith and yet have full regard for natural science and the rationalistic philosophy. Some consider this Kantian synthesis of reason and faith as the outstanding achievement of modern philosophy, while others look upon it as a colossal obfuscation, matched only by the system of Aquinas. Bertrand Russell, certainly a competent authority on philosophy, says: "Kant deluged the philosophic world with muddle and mystery, from which it is only now beginning to emerge. Kant has the reputation of being the greatest of modern philosophers, but to my mind he was a mere misfortune." [1]

If Kant was a philosophical muddler, the state of social science in his age may be blamed. Natural science had made much progress, but psychology and social science as yet were hardly born. Therefore, a whole realm of human experience, such as apparent moral freedom, seemed to him unintelligible from the standpoint of science. Kant rationalized this alleged unintelligibility and created out of it a world of unknowable reality. If he were writing today and showed equal capacity for mastering available knowledge he would hardly have invented his noumenal world of things-in-themselves. The social sciences make

[1] Russell, *An Outline of Philosophy*, London, 1927, p. 83. See also G. T. Whitney and D. F. Bowers, *The Heritage of Kant*, Princeton University Press, 1939, pp. 163 ff.

most of the problems which baffled him much more intelligible. Yet his argument that no knowledge can be absolute and final would still be valid.

There is no denying the truth or logic of the Kantian position about the relativity of knowledge. Man can only know and interpret the universe in terms of his own abilities and powers. How close his observations and conceptions come to absolute actuality we can never know. This attitude furnishes the foundation for recognizing the slight and fragmentary character of human knowledge. It should discourage dogmatic references to absolutes and the ultimate implications of the physical universe.

Unfortunately, the Kantian exposition had exactly the opposite results. It opened the floodgates to a torrent of the most diverse fancies, speculations, and wishful thinking. That which should have sounded the death knell of dogmatism became the bugle call which summoned forth the most illustrious crop of dogmatists which philosophy ever produced except for the scholastics.

Once the omnipotence of the intellect was challenged, an appeal was made on all sides to emotion and wishful thinking. If the feelings are to be our guide, the sky is veritably the limit of philosophical speculation. The products of the intellect can be subjected to some degree of control and criticism, but not so the products of the emotions. One deep sentiment is as real and as good as another. Even Kant did not prove immune. In his *Critique of Practical Reason,* which we shall discuss later, he abandoned his critical humility, evolved a God from wishful thinking, and deduced therefrom a type of ethical doctrine admirably adapted to justifying the primitive, provincial, and emotionally starved experiences of the chaste bachelor philosopher of Königsberg.

3. Romanticists and Idealists

While Kant's views encouraged later romanticist and idealistic philosophers, the latter scarcely remained true to his doctrine. Kant clearly stated that the intellect is potent and valid only when applied to the realm of the knowable—to a description of the sensual world and of human experience. Later idealists tried heroically to secure intellectual assurance about the mysterious realm of the unknowable—the supersensual world of God—which they insisted is really knowable. Hence, they invented all sorts of farfetched hypotheses regarding the mystical and subjective union of man, intelligence, nature, and God. Kant had consistently held that ultimate reality—the realm of things-in-themselves—is unknowable through human experience. The idealists, beginning with Fichte, contended that personal experience, especially the religious experience of union with God and the universe, does reveal to us the ultimate realities. There can be nothing beyond human experience. John Herman Randall admirably describes the manner in which Kant, however unintentionally, prepared the way for this deluge of romantic mysticism:

> Kant's book stimulated Romanticists to a flood of special systems founded on faith. Man, they claimed, is not fundamentally intellectual. Rather human nature is at bottom made up of instincts and feelings; and his instinctive and emotional

life should dominate his career and paint for him both his conception of the world and his conception of human life. In other words, the poet or the saint is a truer and better guide on the pathway of life and thought than the scientist. Religion, morals, art, literature, social and political philosophy, and education should recognize this fundamental fact and build upon it. Religion is not a science to be demonstrated, but a matter of the heart, a life to be lived. Morality is not a science, but essentially the good will and the performance of one's duties. Art is not a matter of form and structure, but of rich sentiment and feeling. Society is not a cold-blooded enterprise founded on self-interest, but a vast organism pressing onward to realize dimly seen ideals, in which all are members one of another. The whole universe is not a machine, but a living body, to be interpreted on the analogy of man's life.[2]

The abandonment of reason for feelings and personal experience was forcefully recommended by Johann Gottfried von Herder (1744-1803), author of *Ideas for a Philosophy of the History of Mankind* (1784-1787), and *Dialogues on God* (1787). He bitterly opposed Kant's critical philosophy, but approved the latter's opening of a path to emotional dominion. More than any other early romanticist, Herder was responsible for elevating the feelings and faith to supremacy over reason. But he had little knowledge of, or talent for, technical metaphysics, really possessing no competent grasp of Kant's doctrines which he attacked. He believed firmly in the unity of the human mind and the absolute, and resented the dualism of experience and reality which Kant implied. He held that the universe is divine and that man and nature are united in God, emphasized the primacy of individual religious experience, and was especially attracted by art, poetry, and language. He greatly encouraged the study of comparative philology, while his most distinguished work was in the philosophy of history. He believed that human culture is a product of the interworking of external environment and *Geist* (the universal spirit or dynamic totality of subjective impulses), for which there is no exact English term. Through his emphasis on the coherence and uniqueness of national culture he became a powerful factor in establishing the philosophy of nationalism in Germany.

The Kantian distinction between human experience and ultimate reality was even more vigorously attacked by Johann Gottlieb Fichte (1762-1814), the father of idealist metaphysics. Fichte's philosophy is best expressed in his lectures on *The Characteristics of the Present Age,* delivered in 1804. He suggested what he regarded as a solution of the Kantian dualism—experience versus reality. Man is a manifestation of God, and nature an expression of the spirit. "Knowledge is not mere knowledge of itself, but of being, and of the one being that truly is, namely, God." As Dr. H. C. Engelbrecht epitomizes Fichte's system of thought: "The world itself, according to Fichte, is the creation of Free Spirit, not the reverse; and Free Spirit set up an external world in order to provide a field for moral endeavor. Or to put it in another way, because man is fundamentally a moral being he has found it necessary to set up an outer world; and this world is merely the stuff of moral action. God is the Moral Order of the Universe." [3]

[2] J. H. Randall, *The Making of the Modern Mind*, pp. 409-10.
[3] H. C. Engelbrecht, *Johann Gottlieb Fichte*, Columbia University Press, 1933, p. 28.

Fichte's metaphysics possessed a dynamic cast. The absolute or thing-in-itself appeared to him to be the ego which creates the phenomenal world and then overcomes it by a free and conscious effort of the will. To Fichte, the dynamic factor in human experience is the will to strive and conquer in the interest of progress. The ultimate factor in life is not what is but what ought to be—not being but duty. Man's goal is a rationally ordered society which will permit the maximum of striving for further perfection. Fichte's great contribution to ethics was the socialization of Kant's conception of duty as the chief human drive. He held that all social relations rest on duty. When there is nothing left to strive for we can attempt to create an adequate concept of God, a task which will never be finished. Fichte's philosophy was, thus, of the crusading type, eulogizing a constant and unending struggle for improvement through the impulse of the will in obedience to the concept of duty.

Fichte was especially interested in language as a mode of personal expression and a precious element in national culture. One of the chief proofs of Prussian superiority, he thought, was the primordial German *Ursprache* (i.e., primitive or stock language). This mystical view of language provided the proper aura for the work of philologists like the brothers Grimm and their successors. Fichte was the high priest of German nationalism after the Prussian defeat by Napoleon at Jena. His *Lectures to the German Nation* during the winter of 1807-1808 were the spiritual rallying point for those who brought about the regeneration of Prussia.

Fichte's effort to unite experience and reality was continued by Friedrich W. J. von Schelling (1775-1854), who is especially noted for his philosophy of aesthetics. In his *System of Transcendental Idealism,* he tried to effect the synthesis which Fichte had forecast. "Nature is visible soul, soul is invisible nature, and both advance incessantly by an uninterrupted succession of stages and gradation of forms. . . . Just as nature exhibits to us the series of dynamic stages by which spirit struggles towards consciousness of itself, so the world of intelligence and practice, the world of mind, exhibits the series of stages through which self-consciousness with its inevitable oppositions and reconciliations develops in its ideal form." Neither nature nor man is static. Professor Edward Caldwell Moore thus summarizes Schelling's basic thought:

> Nature is always in the process of advance from lower, less organized and intelligible forms, to those which are more highly organized, more nearly the counterpart of the active intelligence in man himself. The personality of man had been viewed as standing over against nature, this last being thought of as static and permanent. On the contrary, the personality of man, with all its intelligence and free-will, is but the climax and fulfillment of a long succession of intelligible forms in nature, passing upward from the inorganic to the organic, from the unconscious to the conscious, from the non-moral to the moral, as these are at last seen in man. . . . Philosophy has to treat of the inner life which moves the whole of nature as intelligible productivity, as subject, no longer as object. . . . Schelling has here rounded out the theory of absolute idealism which Fichte had carried through in a one-sided way.[4]

4 E. C. Moore, *Protestant Thought since Kant,* Scribner, 1915 (Allenson, 1947), pp. 61-62.

Schelling thus laid the basis for his profound interest in art: "The supreme ideal is not that ever increasing mastery of nature by man which Fichte contemplated, but their reconciliation as achieved by Art. For just as natural philosophy carried an element of consciousness into the material universe, so aestheticism recognizes a corresponding element of unconscious creation in the supreme works of artistic genius where spirit reaches its highest and best." [5]

The unity and harmony of the inner life of man—the reality-revealing experience—claimed the special attention of Karl W. F. von Schlegel (1772-1829). Robert Flint thus summarizes Schlegel's philosophy of history and his conception of the central problem of philosophy:

> Philosophy is the science of the inward life of man. It makes, he insists, but one presupposition, namely, the existence of the internal life; and its chief or central problem is to determine how unity and harmony may be conferred upon that life, how the image of God, which it has lost, may be restored in it. To point out how this may be effected in the individual consciousness, is the task of pure philosophy—the philosophy of life, distinctively so-called. To point out how the process has been so far actually carried on among the different peoples and in the various ages of the world, is the task of the philosophy of history. [6]

Schlegel devoted himself primarily to the philosophy of history, although he made notable contributions to philology and the history of literature. His survey of history is chiefly a record of man's apostasy from God. He sought evidence from history that man would return to an "unquestioning and unqualified submission to authority," but even Schlegel had to admit that his investigation ended in hope rather than assurance that this blessed end would be realized. Like John Henry Newman, Schlegel himself sought refuge, solace, and infallibility in Catholicism.

The most heroic effort to unite experience and reality, the phenomenal world and God, is found in the work of Friedrich D. E. Schleiermacher (1768-1834). The antithesis between the real and the ideal is only a practical and convenient illusion. "We must assume a real identity of the ideal and the real behind the antithesis which constitutes the world." It is our eternal problem to resolve this apparent conflict between the real and the ideal: "The whole effort and end of human thought and action is the gradual reduction of the realm and power of this antithesis in the individual, the race, and the world." Universal reason (faith) is the unifying principle of nature. The absolute unity behind everything is God, in whom "the real is manifold and the spirit is one." In other words, "the universe is God, God is the universe." Unless one accepts such an attitude, no really constructive work is possible. "No great man ever lived, no great work was ever done, save in an attitude towards the universe which is identical with that of the religious man towards God." It was natural that Schleiermacher should be the romanticist most famous for his philosophy of religion.

These philosophic trends culminated in the work of the famous dialectician, Georg W. F. Hegel (1770-1831). Other romanticists and idealists had sought the

---

[5] A. W. Benn, *Modern Philosophy*, Putnam, 1913, p. 133.
[6] Flint, *The Philosophy of History in France and Germany*, p. 457.

key to reality in religion, in art, in language, or in history, subjectively considered. In the works of Hegel we find philosophy raised to a lofty rôle as the master-guide to reality: "At the basis of all reality, whether material or mental, there is thought. . . . It only appears in consciousness as the crowning development of the mind. Only with philosophy does thought become fully conscious of itself in its origin and development."

Fichte had spoken of the universal process as a synthesis of opposites. With Hegel this notion of "thesis, antithesis, and synthesis" became the "perpetual law of thought." We have already described the Hegelian dialectic of development through the synthesis of the thesis and the antithesis. Hegel gave little attention to the problem of the "unknowable." He was concerned with the processes whereby the knowable, those things which "are observable within experience," develop and manifest themselves. Indeed, Hegel expressly repudiated the Kantian theory that there is an unknowable world. He contended that there is nothing in the universe except the world and man's social experience of it—that there is no reality beyond what man can observe. He took for granted at the outset what his immediate predecessors had sought to demonstrate, namely, the identity of experience and ultimate reality. He stressed the social basis of all thinking.

Hegel looked at the problem of the universe and reality in a dynamic manner. "The universe is a process of the Absolute—in religious language, the manifestation of God. The rhythmic movement of thought is the self-unfolding of the Absolute." It is not surprising, then, that one of Hegel's most notable works was his subjective philosophy of history, devoted to the unfolding of *Geist,* or universal spirit, in the development of mankind. This influential contribution we have briefly described in the preceding chapter.

Hegel revolutionized the social sciences through abandoning the artificial and intellectualistic notions of the Enlightenment and insisting that social institutions, government, religion, and the like, are the natural products of an evolutionary development. The followers of Hegel created the social sciences and the critical study of religious origins. Hegel's influence upon the history of art was also far-reaching.

The outstanding thing about all romantic and idealistic philosophers is that, whatever their intellectual pretensions, their systems were essentially based on faith. Their dogmas were quite incapable of rational demonstration.

The value of the metaphysics of this philosophy must be left to the judgment of more competent persons, but the whole discussion of the relative significance of the intellectual and emotional faculties has no more than a curious interest to anyone acquainted with modern psychology. The notion that the intellect and emotions function independently of each other is an antique fallacy. The most critical of men may be operating under the influence of deep-seated emotional complexes. Our "self-evident dictates of pure reason" may be no more than rationalizations of childhood impressions. As has often been pointed out, we can usually give a good reason for our attitudes, but rarely know the real reason for them. Modern psychology emphasizes the great importance of the emotions, but not as a comprehensive justification for muddled thinking or a reservoir of ignorance and credulity. Man's emotional life is as much subject to scientific probing and investigation as his most objective cogitations. The controversy between rationalists and romanticists is hardly thinkable in terms of modern psychological knowledge.

Another important contrast between rationalists and romanticists is their different emphasis on the importance of the individual. The rationalists were chiefly interested in social maladjustments and in the oppression of mankind as a whole. The conflicts within society arrested their attention. Their popular ethical slogan was "the greatest good for the greatest number," a phrase adopted from the rationalists by Bentham and the utilitarians. The romanticists, with the exception of Fichte and Hegel, were more concerned with the struggle within the individual—with his conflicts and problems. In modern terms, romanticism was introvertive and introspective. Self-expression became a primary motive and encouraged the literary masterpieces of Goethe, Chateaubriand, Wordsworth, Carlyle, and Emerson.

An interesting offshoot of this German idealist philosophy was what is known as transcendentalism, which derived its name from its reliance upon what Kant called the a priori or transcendental elements in human reasoning. In another sense, the transcendentalists might logically have been accorded this title because they transcended the dualism of Kant.

Kant, as we have seen, clearly differentiated the realm of experience, which man can know, from the realm of ultimate reality, which man cannot know. Herder, Fichte, Schelling, and Schleiermacher denied this dualism and sought to bridge the gulf between experience and reality by holding that reality can be experienced. This feat may be achieved by an act of intuitive faith. We have already noted that Friedrich Jacobi called this intuitive faith reason. However absurd it may have been to do so, this terminology was widely followed after Jacobi's day. Transcendentalist philosophy was built up around the rejection of Kant's dualism, the idealist dogma that experience reveals reality, and the confusion between intuitive faith and reason which Jacobi introduced. There was also an infusion of Platonism and Neoplatonism.

This transcendental thought was carried to England by Coleridge and Carlyle and enjoyed much popularity there in the first half of the nineteenth century. It was even more warmly received in the United States by such distinguished persons as William Ellery Channing, Ralph Waldo Emerson, Henry Thoreau, and Margaret Fuller. In the United States the transcendental philosophy took on a liberal trend in relation to various reforms. Its followers gave their support to such things as Unitarian liberalism in religion, utopian socialism, reforms in philanthropy, abolitionism, and feminism.

II. THE RELIGIOUS REVIVAL

1. Kant and Schleiermacher

We have already seen that most rationalists were deeply religious men. They believed in a natural religion conforming with reason. But they generally repudiated dogma, religious tradition, miracles, and other aspects of supernaturalism. Further, they judged moral conduct mainly in relation to the improvement of human well-being here on earth. Their test of morals was essentially secular— those things are moral which help to increase happiness here and now.

These attitudes naturally antagonized conservative and pious thinkers. Immanuel Kant not only let down the bars for the anti-rationalist movement in philosophy, he also paved the way for a definite reaction in religious and moral philosophy. In his *Critique of Pure Reason,* Kant demolished all traditional arguments for the existence of God—the cosmological, ontological, "argument from design," and the like. This work still remains a monument of philosophical agnosticism. Yet when Kant proceeded to build his own system of religion and morals, he shelved his agnosticism.

Kant's religious and ethical thought is best expressed in his *Critique of Practical Reason* (1788). Here, while he did not argue dogmatically that God exists, he asserted that the assumption of God's existence would be highly useful to the religious and ethical thinker. Since we can neither prove nor disprove the existence of God, we are justified in assuming God's existence because of its religious and ethical utility. In other words, while Kant may not himself have believed in God, he held that he had a right to do so. He thought that the belief in God is practically worth while, since it elucidates many facts about human experience which would otherwise remain unintelligible. Randall thus summarizes Kant's pragmatic justification of faith and the belief in God:

> We do and must act from a sense of moral obligation, we do and must feel a religious reverence for something in the world greater than ourselves, we do and must respond to a beauty in things that cannot be scientifically explained. Hence, since we can neither prove nor disprove by the methods of science that we must choose the right rather than the wrong, that we are free so to choose, and that the universe is governed somehow by a moral law, and since we are absolutely compelled, being the creatures we are, to live as though these things were true, we are justified in assuming that they are. Where science can neither prove nor disprove, we are justified in having faith.[7]

Kant's own religious views, as we have noted, were those of a "Christian deist" like Chubb, Tindal, and Morgan. He held that Christianity completely fulfills the requirements of a religion of reason and that the life of Jesus was the most perfect incarnation of rational religious experience. It is doubtful, however, if Kant accepted the biblical God.

Kant's ethics, derived in part from Rousseau, were not in any sense sociological or secular. He denied that morality should be judged by its social effects. Instead, he promulgated the concept of the "categorical imperative," or the theory of unconditioned and obligatory morality. We should not be guided by an expectation of immediate benefits or penalties as a result of our earthly conduct. Rather we must live in such a manner that our lives may seem a model for, or an imitation of, the moral law of the universe. This is a veritable deification of the abstract

[7] Randall, *op. cit.,* pp. 408-9. See also Whitney and Bowers, *op. cit.,* Parts II, IV.

sense of duty. Professor Moore thus describes Kant's conception of the categorical imperative:

> The claims of duty are the higher ones. They are mandatory, absolute. We do our duty whether or not we superficially desire to do it. We do our duty whether or not we foresee advantage in having done it. We should do it if we foresaw with clearness disadvantage. We should find our satisfaction in having done it, even at the cost of all our other satisfactions. There is a must which is over and above all our desires. This is what Kant really means by the categorical imperative.[8]

This is, obviously, a repudiation of the hedonistic trends in rationalism and comes dangerously close to a philosophical justification of the inner compulsion of the Puritans. We now know, of course, that Kant's divinely derived "categorical imperative" is no more than a metaphysical rationalization of the "still, small voice of the herd." His ethical writings appear rather naive in the light of the writings of William Graham Sumner and of Wilfred Trotter on folkways and herd psychology. Here, even more than in his general philosophy, Kant's views were limited and conditioned by the fact that he had no social science to clarify his judgment. The same charge of fanciful unreality can be directed against Fichte's notion that Free Spirit created an outer world for man to battle against.

In religious thought, Kant's mantle passed to Schleiermacher. The latter's religious theories were drawn not only from Kant but also from Herder's conviction that the universe is divine and from Fichte's dynamic ethical optimism. We noted above that Schleiermacher asserted that religion is essential to any truly great achievement. Schleiermacher contended that "religion is a condition of devout feeling, specifically the feeling of dependence upon God." His belief that the universe as a whole is the only proper object of religious feeling is pantheistic. He would have agreed with Einstein that in the last analysis religion is the "cosmic sense."

Schleiermacher laid great stress upon the life and teachings of Jesus, an idea which Kant had emphasized. We may know God chiefly through the character of Jesus. The real task of religion is to reproduce within the believer, as far as possible, "the consciousness, experience, and character of Jesus." A true religious experience will deliver us from the great sin—the dominion of the senses. This is the greatest evil which besets us: "It is the dominance of the lower nature in us, of the sense consciousness. It is the determination of our course of life by the senses. This preponderance of the senses over the consciousness of God is the secret of unhappiness, or the feeling of defeat and misery in men, of the need of salvation." The Christian experience will save us from this materialistic pessimism and will provide full redemption and psychic calm.

Schleiermacher's most distinctive and influential accomplishment was to identify religion with "religious experience" rather than with any form of intellectual belief. Yet he was no mystic—he vigorously denied that religious experience conveys any knowledge at all—and combated the mystical tradition in Christianity. Theology—the intellectual element in religion—can only provide symbols for de-

[8] Moore, op. cit., p. 49.

scribing the great diversity of man's religious experiences, and hence every man must have a private description of his feelings, an individual theology. Although Schleiermacher expressed his pantheism in terms of idealism, nothing in it conflicts with a completely naturalistic view of religion. Consequently, he is the source of all the "religious experience" theories current today, and, in a broad sense, of the whole psychological treatment of religion, as by William James, for example. Schleiermacher also suggested that religion is, in a sense, a branch of aesthetics, promoting, as it does, an appreciation of the beauty of nature and the universe—all works of God.

The religious conceptions of Schleiermacher were discriminatingly revived, on the basis of a much more elaborate scholarship, by Adolph Harnack in the late nineteenth century. They were passed on to America through his students, such as Edward Caldwell Moore and Arthur C. McGiffert.

In France the most enthusiastic disciple of Kant and Schleiermacher was Benjamin Constant (1767-1830). The latter proclaimed that religion "is a universal and beneficent reaching of the human spirit to the power behind Nature." This emotional personal religion he contrasted with Catholic dogmatism and Protestant creeds. He attempted to prove that such a religion is also essential to political freedom. He assailed the English freethinkers, especially Thomas Paine, about whom he knew little at first hand. In England Schleiermacher's ideas were popularized by Frederick Denison Maurice (1805-1872), a noble character and one of the founders of Christian socialism.

2. The Evidences of Christianity

Deism had its birth in England, where rationalism ran its full course, even suggesting to Hume that the belief in God was by no means an inherent faculty of the human mind. Echoes of Holbach's materialistic atheism also reached British shores. The atheists suggested that the universe and man might have come into existence without divine creation. The forces of faith were rallied to repulse such alarming doctrines.

The first important answer to deism was contained in William Law's *The Case of Reason or Natural Religion Fairly and Fully Stated* (1731). He attacked the argument of both the rationalistic supernaturalists and the deists that revelation must accord with reason. Revelation must be impressive enough to convince us that God is its author. That is all that is necessary. Law held that nature is as full of mystery and logical difficulty as Christianity. Hence, it is as easy to believe in a revealed religion as in a natural religion. The skeptics agreed, with a different emphasis, proclaiming that both are equally impossible of belief.

The most famous attack upon deism was *The Analogy of Natural and Revealed Religion,* by Bishop Joseph Butler, published in 1737. Butler tried to meet the deists on their own ground. The deists contended that natural religion was a religion of reason, and that a revealed religion, when valid, was no more than a special announcement of the eternal truths of natural religion. They particularly repudiated historical Christianity. Butler, like Law, tried to show that revealed religion, as well as natural religion, would meet the tests of reason.

Butler started with the common-sense attitude that it is discreet to assume the existence of God and of a future life of punishments and rewards, even if we cannot prove these. If we are wrong in assuming the existence of God it will do no harm, while eternal and irrevocable calamity may result from denying the existence of God.

Butler attempted to show that an appeal to nature would support revealed religion as well as the natural religion of the deists. He was one of the first in this period to argue that nature is so impressive that it must be God's handiwork —the argument from design. But he entered upon very dangerous ground in the course of this argument. In trying to discredit the deistic dogma that nature is a sufficient basis for religion, he fell into the trap into which Law stumbled. He called attention to many mysteries, inconsistencies, imperfections, and injustices in nature, seeking to show thereby that nature will hardly vindicate a rational religion. But he had himself already appealed to nature as a partial justification of revealed religion and had held that nature is the work of God. So, to skeptics and clear thinkers, he seemed, quite unintentionally, to prove that both natural and revealed religion are equally unreasonable and untenable. Butler thus failed in his effort to lend philosophical strength to the Anglican faith. As A. W. Benn observes: "Butler's *Analogy* tended to send its bolder readers to agnosticism, and its more timid readers to Rome."

Indeed, the futility of Law's and Butler's method was satirically revealed by Henry Dodwell in his *Christianity Not Founded on Argument* (1742). Dodwell wished to promote skepticism by showing that the unreasoning faith and infallibility of Catholicism are a safer foundation for religion than either reason or revelation. Dodwell implied, of course, that faith, reason and revelation are all untenable.

A lesser intellect than Butler's but a more indefatigable advocate of revealed religion was William Paley (1743-1805), who became the leading spirit in what is known as the "Christian Evidences" movement. His two chief works were *View of the Evidences of Christianity* (1794) and *Natural Theology, or Evidences of the Existence and Attributes of the Deity Collected from the Appearances of Nature* (1802). Paley's effort to demonstrate the existence of God was based upon the familiar "argument from design," namely, the contention that the wonders, perfections, and delicate adjustments of nature must certainly imply a designing and creative intelligence, or God: "The works of nature want only to be contemplated. . . . Of the vast scale of operation through which our discoveries carry us, at one end we see an intelligent Power arranging planetary systems, fixing, for instance, the trajectory of Saturn, or constructing a ring of two hundred thousand miles to surround his body, and be suspended like a magnificent arch over the heads of his inhabitants; and, at the other, bending a hooked tooth, concerting and providing an appropriate mechanism for the clasping and reclasping of the filaments of the feather of the humming bird."

Paley set the precedent of appealing to the perfection of the human anatomy as a proof of the existence of God. In his *Natural Theology* he wrote: "For my part, I take my stand in human anatomy." He held that it is absolutely necessary to assume "an intelligent designing mind for the contriving and determining of the forms which organized bodies bear." This line of argument was adopted in the *Bridgewater Treatises*. Ironically enough, Paley perished as a result of defects in his own kidneys.

Paley was neither a great scholar nor an original mind, but he was a masterly expositor and controversialist. "Paley's defense," said J. B. Bury, "is the performance of an able legal adviser to the Almighty."

An attack on freethinking in England was also embodied in *A Practical View of the Prevailing Religious System of Professed Christians* (1797), by William Wilberforce (1759-1833), a leader in the English movement for the abolition of the slave trade. Wilberforce's immensely popular polemic called for a return to the true principles of Christianity based on the sacrifice of Christ. The classic orthodox answer to Thomas Paine's *Age of Reason* was Richard Watson's *An Apology for the Bible* (1796). Its result was almost as unsatisfactory as the effect of Butler's book, for it introduced Paine to many who would not otherwise have come in contact with his ideas. It thus served to raise doubts among those capable of doubt, while to those lacking the capacity to doubt it was superfluous.

The culmination of apologetic line of thought was the publication of the so-called *Bridgewater Treatises*. When the Rev. Francis Henry Egerton, eighth earl of Bridgewater, died in 1829, he set aside £8,000 to be awarded to writers of books showing "the power, wisdom, and goodness of God, as manifested in Creation." Davies Gilbert, president of the Royal Society, in whose custody the grant was left, divided the task among eight well-known authors. The most celebrated winners of these awards were Peter M. Roget (of the famous *Thesaurus*), Sir Charles Bell, and William Whewell, philosopher and historian of the scientific method. Their books were entitled, respectively, *Animal and Vegetable Physiology with Reference to Natural Theology; The Hand, Its Mechanism as Evincing Design;* and *Astronomy and General Physics Considered with Reference to Natural Theology.*

Chemistry, meteorology, physiology, geology, and mineralogy were also subordinated to the service of God. The alleged complexity and perfection of the human eye was especially regarded by apologists as proof of the creative ingenuity of God. It was not until many years later that Hermann Helmholtz, the great student of optics, remarked that he would be ashamed to lay claim to so clumsy a mechanism as the human eye. For several generations the Bridgewater frame of mind pervaded the natural sciences. It played a part in the Darwinian controversy, and occasionally crops out even today in the writings of apologetic scientists like Eddington, Millikan, and Pupin.

Courses in "Christian Evidences" soon became an integral unit in higher education in England and America. Butler's *Analogy* and Paley's *Natural Theology* were the favorite texts. Later writers often prepared textbooks chiefly based upon them. These courses were usually taught by the president of the college, who was himself almost invariably a clergyman, thus giving prestige to the subject and greater assurance to students regarding their faith. Such courses kept higher education in accord with orthodoxy. So effective was Mark Hopkins in presenting Christian evidences at Williams College about the time of the American Civil War that Granville Stanley Hall, the famous American educator, then a student at Williams, felt it necessary to hide in a neighboring cow stable and read Darwin's *Origin of Species* by the light of a barn lantern. Special college honors and emoluments were bestowed upon essays on the subject of Christian evidences. The degrees of doctor of divinity and doctor of philosophy were freely given to those who submitted a thesis defending orthodox Christianity. These were, for the most part, rather wooden compilations from Paley and his successors and from the *Bridgewater Treatises.*

The defense of revealed religion also stirred English Protestants to establish various societies devoted to the dissemination of Christian literature, cheap books, appropriate pamphlets, and earnest tracts.[9] It took a century for the rationalists to reply in kind in the publications of the *Rationalistic Press Society* in England and the Haldeman-Julius booklets in the United States. Clergymen paid more attention to their duties, and the institution of family prayers became exceedingly common. Even the popular magazines devoted a great deal of space to religion.

3. *The Oxford Movement*

A religious current destined to be nearly as important in the theological reaction as the exposition of Christian evidences was the famous Oxford movement, so called because most of its leaders were students at Oriel College, Oxford. It has been described as the most important religious development at Oxford since the Protestant revolution, and such a characterization is hardly an exaggeration. From it emerged not only a strong pietistic reaction but also the later High-Church and Anglo-Catholic developments. Some of its members fell into the arms of the Catholic church itself.

The leaders of the Oxford movement were John Keble (1792-1866), Richard Hurrell Froude (1803-1836), John Henry Newman (1801-1890), and Edward Bouverie Pusey (1800-1882). Keble was the guiding spirit at the outset. In 1827 he published a book of mystical poems entitled *The Christian Year.* Froude brought Newman and Keble together. Pusey devoted his well-stored mind to the movement.

These men were not only distressed by the skeptical and critical tendencies of the day but were also dissatisfied with the Anglican church. They resented the idea that the church was in any sense a creature of the state, and asserted that it was of "heavenly origin and divine prerogative." They criticized the purely formal character of much Anglican worship, and condemned the worldly fox-hunting clergy. They desired to make Anglicanism a religion distinguished for piety, faith, devotion, and otherworldliness. To do so they turned to patristic theology for inspiration.

The keynote was struck in Keble's sermon in July, 1833, on "The National

---

[9] The Society for the Promotion of Christian Knowledge was founded by Thomas Bray in 1698, and the Society for the Propagation of the Gospel in Foreign Parts in 1701. The London Missionary Society, the Religious Tract Society, the British and Foreign Bible Society, the Church Missionary Society, and the Baptist Foreign Missionary Society expanded rapidly after their foundation around the opening of the nineteenth century.

Apostasy." In the same year Newman began to publish the *Tracts for the Times,* by members of the University of Oxford (1833-1841), a series of pamphlets setting forth the articles of the new faith. Hence, this religious uprising is sometimes known as the Tractarian movement. Under the influence of patristic dogmas the movement leaned more and more towards Catholicism. Finally Newman's famous *Tract Number 90* attempted to show that nothing in the Thirty-nine Articles of faith of the Anglican church was incompatible with the Roman Catholic creed. He even held that the ritual of the Mass was lawful in Anglican worship. This was too much for the conventional Anglicans, and they bitterly attacked the Oxford movement.

The assault marked the parting of the ways. Some of the members were satisfied to promote High-Church ritual within Anglicanism. Others laid the basis for Anglo-Catholicism which, even at the present day, is the cause of animated discussion in English and American ecclesiastical circles. Still others, like Newman and Manning, went over to Roman Catholicism, bag and baggage. This latter development makes necessary some special mention of Cardinal Newman.

Newman was the son of a London banker and was educated at Oxford. Of a mystical turn of mind, he was also gifted far beyond the average man in eloquence of discourse. He turned phrases beautifully, but unfortunately was deficient in both critical capacity and mental self-reliance. He was bred an Anglican, and had he remained one, he would undoubtedly have become one of the most eminent of its nineteenth-century clergy. But, drawn into the Oxford movement, he was on a road which led logically to the Catholic church.

The Oxford movement, which was chiefly important in its relation to Newman, aimed, as has been indicated, to give the Anglican church a more Catholic orientation and to slough off the later Protestant accretions which were adopted as protective coloration during the popularity of rationalism. In addition, these men wished Anglicanism to capture some of the emotional fervor which was surging up as the result of romanticist and evangelical influences.

Newman at first turned to what is called the High Church. But his yearning for an aesthetically appealing and intellectually sustaining authoritarianism led him by quick stages to Rome. He was by far the most distinguished English convert in his century, and his career epitomized and carried to its logical conclusion the mystical drift of many men of his time. What he actually did, others aspired to do but were estopped by social conventions or intellectual scruples.

Newman longed for infallible support for his Christian convictions, and was not illogical in holding that this infallibility could be found only in the Roman Catholic church. He quickly saw through the frailty of the Protestant claim to an infallible Bible. The essence of Newman's attitude is illustrated by the following sentences from his *Apologia:*

> The Church's infallibility is the provision adopted by the mercy of the Creator to preserve religion in the world. Outside the Catholic Church all things tend to atheism. The Catholic Church is the one face-to-face antagonist, able to withstand and baffle the fierce energy of passion and the all-dissolving skepticism of the mind.

I am a Catholic by virtue of my belief in God. If I should be asked why I believe
in God, I should answer, because I believe in myself. I find it impossible to believe in myself, without believing also in the existence of Him who lives as a personal, all-seeing, all-judging being in my conscience.

Here is Christian piety and credulity incarnate. Newman was accompanied in
his flight into Roman Catholic infallibility by Henry Edward, Cardinal Manning (1807-1892), a calculating ecclesiastic and a man of action rather than of
thought.

4. The Catholic Reaction

The Roman Catholic church had been the target for some of the sharpest shafts
of the rationalists. Deism completely repudiated Catholicism as a valid religion.
Voltaire closed his letters with exhortations to "crush the infamous thing," namely,
the Catholic church, with its intolerance and oppression. This theoretical attack
was given practical embodiment in the distinctly anticlerical decrees of the
French Revolution. The civil constitution of the clergy and the confiscation of
church property struck a heavy blow at French Catholicism. In other countries
as well French ideas challenged the Roman faith.

When Napoleon was driven out of France and the reactionary coalition gained
control of Europe, the signal was given for a revival of Catholic fervor comparable to the political reaction under Metternich. In this Catholic renaissance the
most popular figure was François René de Chateaubriand (1768-1848).

Chateaubriand began life as a mild rationalist—a disciple of Rousseau—and returned to the church, so he tells us, because of a promise given his mother on
her deathbed. His Catholicism was almost devoid of intellectual content and his
appeal was entirely to sentiment and imagination. His most famous book was
called *The Genius of Christianity* (1802), its original title being *Beauties of the
Christian Religion*. Chateaubriand stressed the potential value of Christianity to
art and poetry and its stimulus to human progress and perfectibility. His work
was characterized by beautiful imagery, especially the descriptions of nature.
Chateaubriand had visited the new world and made the most of his observations and even more of his imagination. The influence exerted on his imagination by his travels was illustrated by his romance, *Atala, or the Love of Two
Savages* (1801), which outdid Saint-Pierre's *Paul and Virginia*. His line of approach to Christianity can be gauged by a passage on the value of mystery:

> There is nothing beautiful or sweet or great in life that is not mysterious.
> The most wonderful feelings are those which move and perplex us. Bashfulness,
> chaste love, pure friendship, are full of mystery. . . . Is not innocence, which in
> its essence is nothing but holy ignorance, the most ineffable mystery? Women,
> the more admirable half of the human race, cannot live without mysteries.[10]

Chateaubriand's poetic view of the Christian epic is epitomized in the following sentence: "We do not know what objections could be offered to a means of
grace which evokes such a chain of poetical, moral, historical, and supernatural

---

[10] Cited by Georg Brandes, *Main Currents in Nineteenth Century Literature,* 6 vols., Boni & Liveright, 1923, III, 82.

ideas, a means of grace which, beginning with flowers, youth, and charm, ends with bringing God down to earth to give Himself as spiritual sustenance to man." The inevitable upshot of this flowery mode of thought is apparent in such an unrestrained appraisal of the Catholic contributions to civilization as the following:

> Of all the religions which have ever existed, the Christian religion is the most poetical, the most human, the most favorable to freedom, to art, and to literature —that to it the modern world owes everything from agriculture to the abstract sciences, from asylums for the unfortunate to churches built by Michelangelo and ornamented by Raphael—that there is nothing more divine than its morality, nothing more beautiful and noble than its dogmas and rites—that it favors genius, purifies taste, approves and stimulates virtuous passion, invigorates thought, provides poets and artists with the noblest themes. . . .[11]

The conclusion of this burst of eloquence is that the Christian (Catholic) religion is true and the proper faith of all right-thinking men.

Chateaubriand illustrated the thesis of the *Genius of Christianity* in a work on early Christianity, *The Martyrs* (1809). This book is characterized by pious sentimentality, eulogy of the early Christians, and magnificent descriptions, especially of the forests of ancient Gaul, life in the catacombs, and Roman civilization under the Empire. Chateaubriand's pictorial descriptions and verbal gifts powerfully stimulated a new and more sentimental view of Christian origins. His works, more than any others, for a time discredited the rationalist conception of Catholicism and the Middle Ages.

Chateaubriand's virtues were, however, more literary than scholarly. As Professor Charles Wright says: "Chateaubriand was one of the great poseurs and one of the worst liars and plagiarists in literature, but he had qualities which partly justified him, and he influenced his times as perhaps no other man since Rousseau. He is the father of [French] Romanticism." [12]

Chateaubriand's enthusiasm for Catholicism was echoed in the writings of de Bonald, de Maistre and de Lamennais. Louis de Bonald (1754-1840) devoted more attention to arguments for the restoration of political authority than to religious matters, although he was intensely interested in the latter. His large work, *The Theory of Political and Religious Authority in Civil Society* (1796), contained most of his religious doctrines. He laid even more stress on language than Fichte had done, pointing out its alleged divine origin and deducing therefrom most of his religious ideas. He eloquently supported the infallibility of supernatural religion, spiritual truth, and the authority of the church. He also warmly defended the supernatural sanctions and objectives of morality. The writings of Joseph de Maistre (1754-1821) were still more decisively political, but he stoutly upheld Catholicism and religious authority. His *St. Petersburg Evenings* (1821) was a staunch defense of religious authority and an attack upon Voltaire and the freethinkers. More influential was his book, *On the Pope* (1819),

---

[11] Quoted from Brandes, *op. cit.*, III, 84.
[12] C. H. C. Wright, *A History of French Literature*, Oxford University Press, 1925, p. 619.

which expounded forcefully the theory of papal infallibility as well as the divine sanction of secular monarchy.

Next to Chateaubriand, the strongest popular influence in the Catholic revival was exerted by the early writings of the Abbé Robert de Lamennais (1782-1854). His *Reflections on the State of the Church* (1808) were a slashing criticism of the humiliation of the Catholic church by the French Revolution and a protest against its limited powers under the Concordat of 1801. Much more widely read was his *Essay on Religious Indifference* (1818), which both assailed the doctrines of skepticism and indicated at length the indispensable services rendered by religion to man and society. Lamennais' most notable disciple was Jean Baptiste Lacordaire (1802-1861). Originally a deist, he was converted by his reading of Lamennais' work on indifference, became a priest, and attracted a great deal of attention through his powerful sermons at Notre Dame. He wished to revive the Dominican order in France and to make Catholicism a leading influence in French politics.

The French religious revival was short-lived and not by any means so popular as the pietistic revival in Germany and England. The Bourbon dynasty was thrown out in 1830 and a tolerant bourgeois government installed under the Orleanists. Even French Catholicism became more liberal in writers like Lamartine, Buchez, and Leroux. Indeed, Lamennais himself showed great capacity for intellectual growth and, indignant at the opposition of Catholicism to political liberalism, became the most important liberal antagonist of the church which he had earlier zealously defended. Lacordaire also became disillusioned with the Catholic church because of its opposition to the French Revolution of 1848.

The social philosopher, Saint-Simon, wrote an influential book on *The New Christianity* (1825), in which he denounced religious formalism and ecclesiasticism and emphasized the message of religion as an aid to reform and social justice. His disciple, Auguste Comte, boldly cast aside all supernaturalism, theism, and otherworldliness, and created a frank religion of humanity, called Positivism, which glorified man and worked for his betterment here and now. It relied upon sociology rather than theology for guidance. Before the end of the nineteenth century France had become the most openly skeptical of important modern states —perhaps the only one, after the age of the "fathers" in the United States, in which agnosticism and atheism were highly respectable in the best political, social, and intellectual circles.

5. *Methodism, Evangelical Religion, and the Appeal to Emotion*

The religious reaction against rationalism, deism, and skepticism was not confined to Kantian Lutheranism, Anglican developments, or the Catholic reaction. It found perhaps its most popular and widespread expression in the pietistic and evangelical movements and their revival of a religion of overt faith and emotion. This takes us back to the pietistic movement founded by a German Lutheran pastor, Philipp Jakob Spener (1635-1705). He advocated the true religion of the heart and the pious and ardent daily study of the Bible. He had little interest in erudite theological discussions and declared that "Christianity consisted not in learning but in practice." His teachings were popularized by August Hermann Francke and Gottfried Arnold.

Far more momentous was the foundation of Methodism by John Wesley (1703-1791). He firmly believed that religion must be based on the emotions rather than the intellect—that true religion is "heart religion." Wesley asserted that religion must rest upon faith rather than reason, and agreed with Luther that faith is fully able to "wring the neck of reason." This was a complete repudiation of Tillotson, Locke, and the deists, who held that religion should be a calm expression of the dictates of reason. What was with Tillotson, Locke, and the deists a dignified intellectual enterprise became with Wesley an emotional orgy.

Wesley also denounced the deistic theory of man's natural dignity and worth. For this he substituted the old dogma of the fall of man, his innately sinful nature, total unworthiness, and full dependence upon divine grace for restoration and redemption. This led him particularly to emphasize the doctrine of the atonement and the saving power of Jesus Christ. Man must be brought to righteousness through forceful conviction of sin. Such an attitude involved ardent approval of evangelistic methods and a sheer appeal to brute emotion. A direct consequence was the evangelistic type of preaching which Wesley inaugurated. Professor Preserved Smith thus describes its character:

> This style of preaching, maudlin and ecstatic as it appeared to the cultivated, did fearful execution among the poor and ignorant to whom it was primarily addressed. John Wesley recorded in his diary, with satisfaction, the violent effects of his sermons, effects which he esteemed as signs of God's approving intervention. During the years 1739 to 1743 he reported that his preaching had caused 234 cases of hysteria, manifested in convulsive tearings, trembling, crying, groans, tears, and occasionally much more serious symptoms. Eighty-five of his hearers, he reported, had "dropped as dead"; two had developed psychogenic blindness, fourteen had been made temporarily insane, and nine had been driven into incurable madness.[18]

Wesley was particularly harsh on the man who was able to live a decent life according to his own sense of honor and justice, without dependence upon God. Such a man was far worse than the most dissolute and carnal sinner. For the latter there was some hope, but none at all for the former. The sinner might be converted, but a man of honor could not be convinced of his sins. This was a direct challenge to the ethical theories of Bayle, Shaftesbury, Hume, and the like.

Methodism, with its reliance upon emotion, made a strong appeal to the miserable British workers and peasants during the distressing period of the great enclosures and the industrial revolution which coincided with Wesley's movement. George Whitefield (1714-1770) and Francis Asbury (1745-1816) carried the Gospel to America, where it found fertile soil among those who had to bear the harsh and dangerous life of the frontier. It became the quasi official religion of the frontier. As it developed, it turned from the question of personal righteousness, emotionally experienced and affirmed, to the regulation of social conduct. It be-

18 Smith, *History of Modern Culture*, II, 465-66.

came a powerful force behind prohibition, "moral" crusades, censorship, and similar movements.

Yet frequent indiscriminate abuse of Methodists in our generation is certainly not entirely fair. Even though they are still an ecclesiastical bulwark of the moral inquisition, they likewise furnish a large number of ardent apostles of Christian socialism. If Wayne Wheeler, Clarence True Wilson, and Bishop Cannon were among the Methodists, so were Francis J. McConnell, G. Bromley Oxnam, Harry Ward, and other crusaders for justice and decency.

The evangelical movement in America was not limited to the Methodists. Soon the Baptists joined its ranks. This sect, which started as the Anabaptists in Germany and had been brought to America by Roger Williams and others, was originally a liberal and tolerant religious group. But it soon became evangelical and departed widely from the ideals of Williams. In later years the Baptists contributed Aimee Semple McPherson, the most popular female evangelist of twentieth-century America.

Another evangelical ally appeared in the Disciples of Christ, sometimes shortened to the single word "Christians." This group was founded by Alexander Campbell as a secession of devout and dissatisfied Baptists and Presbyterians who believed that the parent sects had strayed from the essentials of the Apostolic faith. They laid great stress upon the literal word of the Bible, demanded total immersion of all converts, ordered weekly open communion, and believed in complete congregational government. Today the bulk of the Disciples are still relatively reactionary and orthodox, but they have also produced some of the most advanced Christian modernists, men like Edward Scribner Ames, Kirby Page, Burris Jenkins, Herbert Lockwood Willett, A. Eustace Haydon, et al. They have published, under the editorship of Charles Clayton Morrison, one of the most liberal and influential of Christian weeklies, the Christian Century.[13a]

The Presbyterians trace their origins to a meeting held in Zurich, Switzerland, in October, 1523, but they really date from the organization of the Presbyterian church in Scotland by John Knox in the late sixteenth century. The Presbyterians were originally distinguished by their zest for metaphysical theology, but in the nineteenth century they, also, succumbed to the evangelical impulse. Today the Presbyterian church is frankly evangelical. Dignified evangelicalism is well represented by the activities of Robert E. Speer, while, in the person of Rev. Dr. William Ashley (Billy) Sunday, Presbyterianism contributed the most sensational evangelist of the twentieth century.

Evangelical religion meant quite literally a strong reliance on evangelistic methods of conversion. Great evangelistic orators like Lorenzo Dow went before congregations, camp meetings, and other gatherings to terrorize sinners and unbelievers and to bring them to a sharp realization of their unworthiness and the necessity of throwing themselves upon the grace of Christ. These evangelists, who took their preaching methods from Wesley and Whitefield themselves, revived the medieval and early Protestant emphasis upon the stark realities and unspeakable horrors of hell, and sprayed a heavy mist of verbal sulphur and brimstone

13a The twentieth century has seen the merging of many Protestant denominations. For information about this and other recent tendencies of Protestantism, see Chapter XXVI.

over their oratory. Preserved Smith cites a contemporary description by Theophilus Evans of a typical Methodist evangelistic sermon: "The manner of the itinerants' holding forth is generally very boisterous and shocking and adapted, to the best of their skill, to alarm the imagination and to raise a ferment in the passions. . . . The preacher has recourse to frightful representations: that he sees hell-flames flashing in their faces; and that they are now! now! now! dropping into hell! into the bottom of hell! the bottom of hell!" [14]

Professor J. B. McMaster presents plenty of material descriptive of these evangelistic methods in his account of American history in the middle of the last century. Much of this, with additional information, is collected in Dr. Frederick Morgan Davenport's *Primitive Traits in Religious Revivals*.

However emotional, anti-intellectual, and benighted may have been the evangelistic prowess of a Benjamin Abbott, a Lorenzo Dow, a Hezekiah Calvin Wooster, or a Dwight L. Moody, there is no doubt that such men, even if mentally erratic, were fully sincere. They possessed little of that commercialized fervor which is exploited by prominent contemporary evangelists and is forcefully exposed in Sinclair Lewis' *Elmer Gantry*.

III. REACTIONARY POLITICAL THEORY

Rationalism, when applied to political theory, had a pronounced liberal cast. It represented the application of the new bourgeois conceptions to government. Most rationalists contended that government is an artificial creation of man designed for social convenience and the protection of property. Revolution is permissible when rulers violate the original contract between them and their subjects. The later rationalists favored written constitutions as legal guarantees against arbitrary confiscation of property and other forms of interference. Only a few, such as the Abbé Mably, favored real democracy, but Thomas Jefferson believed that we could at least trust the common people to elect the competent few as governmental officials. Finally, the rationalists came to believe that it is possible to reconstruct society easily and rapidly by legislation which embodied the dictates of reason.

These views were vigorously attacked by the exponents of romanticism and conservatism in political theory, among whom the most conspicuous figures were Burke, de Bonald, de Maistre, and von Haller. These men rejected the rationalism of Sieyès and Godwin, as well as the intuition of Rousseau, and reverted to the worship of tradition and authority.

Edmund Burke (1729-1797) attacked with special vehemence the idea that institutions can be arbitrarily changed by means of revolution and legislation. Political institutions, he said, are an organic unity produced by the peculiar genius and the historical experiences of a given people. Institutions may alter with the passage of time, but change is safe only when left to the slow and orderly processes of natural evolution.

Holding this view, Burke was bitterly hostile to the French Revolution. In a

[14] Smith, *op. cit.*, II, 465.

famous essay on the "Vindication of a Natural Society," he reduced to absurdity the idea of a social contract as a literal historical explanation of the origins of the state. His own theory of the social contract was a corporate unity growing out of historical experience—a view appropriate to a romanticist philosopher. He thus expressed his conception: "It is a partnership in all science, a partnership in all art, a partnership in every virtue and in all perfection. As the ends of such a partnership cannot be obtained in many generations, it becomes a partnership not only between those who are living, but between those who are living, those who are dead, and those who are to be born." Burke's *Reflections on the Revolution in France* constituted the most powerful and bitter theoretical attack to which that movement was subjected. He used every resource of oratory, invective, and irony to discredit the Revolution, its aims and achievements. He was effectively answered by Thomas Paine in his *Rights of Man*.

As a constructive political theorist, Burke appears as an almost mystical eulogist of the British monarchy and ruling aristocracy. In Burke's view, these constituted a perfect vindication of the political theory of romanticism. The unwritten British constitution, he said, is the product of centuries of English culture, an extraordinary monument of national genius. Its workings are so perfect and harmonious as to be a very replica of nature herself. The way to secure a perfect political system is by an imitation of English methods, not by the cataclysmic orgy of the French Revolution. Burke thus conveniently overlooked the English revolutions of the seventeenth century, when French writers were saying the same things about the English which Burke said of the French.

The most competent defense of the old French regime appeared in the works of the Marquis Louis de Bonald, entitled *An Essay on the Natural Laws of the Social Order* and *Primitive Legislation*. In these he made a forceful plea for an absolute hereditary monarchy and a privileged nobility. De Bonald claimed that under every form of government a single will always dominates. In a popular government we never know whose will is prevailing. The result is instability and uncertainty. In a monarchy we know exactly whose will is predominant, and thus is created a sense of stability and security. The religious strains of romanticism appear in de Bonald's justification of the absolute power of the monarch. The supreme sovereignty resides in God, the monarch rules through the will of God.

To de Bonald the privileged nobility is no mere social ornament. Its members constitute the real agents of absolute monarchical authority. In a popular government there is no test of personal success save in the acquisition of wealth. Hence, officials in a democracy are bound to use their offices for the sake of pecuniary gain. There is no such temptation to nobles whose superior social status is already assured. They are in a position to give unselfish service to the state. Only through them can we secure competent and disinterested administration—a view which he shared with Burke. De Bonald thus set forth the first comprehensive functional and nonfeudal defense of monarchy and aristocracy.

De Bonald also believed that the source of all valid law and legislation may be discovered in the teachings of the Bible and in the customs and institutions of a particular people. He went even beyond Burke in denouncing precise written constitutions.

Medievalism was mingled with romanticism in the political theory of Joseph de Maistre, a Savoyard publicist. His chief works were *Observations on France; An Essay on the Source of Political Constitutions;* and *On the Pope.* The starting point of his political theory was the typical medieval combination—an infallible pope and an absolute monarch, for which there is no need to seek human justification. God wills that it should be so. Constitutions live in the spirit of a people as a result of their historic experience. They can never be really reduced to writing. A constitution is lifeless and inadequate exactly in proportion to the degree that it is put into writing. People can only know and operate what already exists in their nature. They can never create any new form of political organization. He agreed with Burke that the most perfect modern constitution is the British because it remained unwritten. In de Maistre we find the classic subordination of rationality to authority and custom.

A highly realistic argument for absolutism appears in the voluminous work of the Swiss political scientist, Ludwig von Haller (1768-1854) on *The Restoration of Political Science.* He claimed that the fundamental rule of nature is inequality. Mastery and subjection, then, are perfectly natural and inevitable. Political authority comes from above by nature and the grace of God, not from below by the consent of the people. The dogma of popular sovereignty is a dangerous fiction. Civil society is an issue of fact, not of right. There are no legal limitations on the absolute power of the monarch, although he may find practical moral limitations in the expediency of a just and capable administration. The people may rebel, but that will accomplish nothing, for if the monarch were not the stronger he would not be ruling. Von Haller admits the possibility of a republican government, but he seems to confuse it with what we ordinarily regard as an aristocracy.

The romantic philosophy in jurisprudence received its classic statement in the writings of Friedrich Carl von Savigny (1779-1861). It permeates all his voluminous work, but emerges most clearly in his debate with Thibaut. The latter's proposal for codifying German law horrified Savigny. Law, he said, in his pamphlet, *On the Necessity of a General Code for Germany,* is an ever developing product of national culture. Codification would kill its growth and would be as preposterous as embalming a growing plant. He vigorously opposed the idea of extending the Code Napoléon to Germany, saying: "I regard the law of each country as a member of its body, not as a garment merely which has been made to please the fancy, and can be taken off at pleasure and exchanged for another." [15]

The reactionary political philosophy found its practical champion in Prince Metternich, who was able to hold continental Europe in subjection to absolutism from the defeat of Napoleon down through the revolutions of 1848.

[15] For a good account of the controversy, see A. W. Small, *Origins of Sociology,* University of Chicago Press, 1924, chap. ii.

IV. ROMANTICIST CONCEPTIONS OF THE PAST

One of the most vital contributions of romanticism to European thought and culture was the zest it gave to the study of the past. The rationalists contributed, on the whole, abler historians than the romanticists—Voltaire, Robertson, Gibbon, Montesquieu, and their followers. But these men had little enthusiasm for the past, save for those special epochs which appealed to their fancy. Robertson admired the Protestant revolt, Gibbon and Montesquieu the Roman epoch, Voltaire the Greeks and the Muslims, but for the most part they looked upon the past as a dreary record of superstitions and savagery. They respected only those periods when reason was free and when at least men thought approximately as they did. None of the leading rationalists was enthusiastic about the Middle Ages, which represented the dominion of the Catholic faith.

The romanticists, on the other hand, showed great interest in the past. Their concern with art, folklore, religion, and the like made them enthusiastic medievalists. Particularly important in directing their thoughts towards the medieval era was their theory of the organic continuity of national development. They believed that it was necessary to go back to medieval times in order to find the beginnings of national culture and institutions.

The romanticists, incidentally, introduced many historical misconceptions. They overemphasized the racial factor, especially in their mythical theory of unique Germanic and Anglo-Saxon political genius. They painted far too rosy a picture of the Middle Ages, were uncritical of the age of faith, and devised grotesque philosophies of history. But they had a better idea of historical continuity than the rationalists, and their vivid portrayal of the past first elevated historical writing in modern times to the rank of popular literature. They made the literate population read history and created a popular taste for history, capitalized upon by the more scientific scholars who took it in hand. Most important of all, however, was the fact that they introduced what might be called a historical perspective into European thought.

The basic historical premise of romanticist historiography was the gradual and unconscious nature of cultural evolution. It upheld the unique character of all forms of national culture. There was a decidedly mystic strain in romanticist thinking which maintained that cultural development is subject to the operation of mysterious, unanalyzable psychic forces termed *Volkgeist*. Great emphasis was laid upon the traditions which constitute the spirit of an age and a nation. These romanticist conceptions naturally produced the dogma of political fatalism which represented the individual or the nation as powerless before the mystic complex of creative spiritual forces. Revolution was represented as particularly wicked and futile, and the philosophy of political "quietism" (inactivity) arose which fitted in excellently with the current *laissez-faire* doctrines in economics and politics.

Out of this tendency developed the notorious myth which represented the Germanic and Anglo-Saxon peoples as perfect examples of political quietism, and, hence, of inherent political capacity. An equally erroneous doctrine pictured the French as the typical example of a revolutionary and unstable nation, utterly devoid of political capacity. This fundamental error, more than anything else, marred the accuracy of nineteenth-century political history and philosophy, and has not even yet been fully eradicated.

Again, the idea of an indigenous and spontaneous national culture introduced a less cosmopolitan outlook than the rationalists exhibited, and centered attention on purely national history. Language was believed to be the most vital criterion of nationality. This doctrine took its deepest root in Germany, where language was almost the sole bond of nationality, and inspired the important philological researches of Humboldt, Wolf, the brothers Grimm, and Lachmann. The Middle Ages were regarded as particularly fertile for historical research, a view owing in part to the belief that in this era national cultures were created and fixed, and in part to the mystical affinity of romanticism with medieval attitudes. Yet, romanticist enthusiasm for art and literature also sent historians to Greece and the so-called Renaissance.

Since the romanticists maintained that rational analysis of historical causation is impossible, their philosophy of history represented a hopeless confusion of cause and effect. Without giving a scientific explanation of the development of national spirit, they attributed the peculiarities of institutions, laws, literature, and government to national genius, and then represented national character as the product of the art, literature, laws, and institutions of the people.

In spite of their semiobscurantist tendencies and philosophical crudities, the romanticists must be given credit for correcting the superficial catastrophic theory of history held by the rationalists, for emphasizing the element of unconscious growth in historical development, and for stressing the organic unity of a cultural complex. It was left for Lamprecht, nearly a century later, to adopt what was really valuable in romanticist doctrines of history and work it into his famous theory of transformations within the collective psychology of both the nation and humanity.

Expressions of romanticism in historiography were many and varied. Its doctrines were employed by Karl Friedrich Eichhorn (1781-1854) in his *Political and Legal History of Germany* which was devoted primarily to early German law; and, above all, by Savigny in his *History of Roman Law in the Middle Ages,* the best dogmatic defense of the concept of law as a product of national "genius."

In history, religion, and literature, romanticism received its most notable expressions in Chateaubriand's *Genius of Christianity;* in Madame de Staël's (1766-1817) *Literature in Its Relation to Social Institutions;* in Abel François Villemain's (1790-1870) *Sketch of the Eighteenth Century;* and in the *History of German Poetry* by Georg Gottfried Gervinus (1805-1871). The outstanding impulse to increased interest in the history of art was embodied in *The History of Art in Antiquity* by Johann Joachim Winckelmann (1717-1768). Winckelmann lived before romanticism really got under way, but his work was eagerly used by romanticists when they appeared on the scene. Moreover, Winckelmann's own views anticipated the romanticist reaction against the historical ideals of the rationalists.

Romanticism entered the philosophy of history in the works of Herder,

Schlegel, Schelling, and Hegel, whose views we have already discussed. In France, Cousin, Quinet, and Jouffroy followed suit.

The narrative school of romanticist historians was dominated not only by the general theories enumerated above, but also by the historical novels of Sir Walter Scott, with their great emphasis upon the element of "local color." This tendency was really antihistorical. It destroyed the sense of historical perspective and portrayed episodes or periods in such a manner as to give them the vividness and intimacy of contemporary events. It was a contribution to literature rather than scientific history. Nevertheless the historical novel aroused a wider interest in history than ever before, and inspired many eminent scholars whose contributions to historical knowledge were greater than those of all the narrative and romanticist historians combined. Of this local color variety of romanticist historical writings the most important were the *History of the Conquest of England by the Normans* and the *Narratives of the Merovingian Period* by Augustin Thierry (1795-1856); the *History of the Dukes of Burgundy* by Baron Amable de Barante (1782-1866); and the *History of the Italian States* by Heinrich Leo (1799-1878).

The subjective element in narrative history was greatly intensified in the works of Michelet, Carlyle, and Froude, where an attempt was made not only to bring the reader into immediate touch with the setting of events, but also with the personal impressions of the author. In the *History of France* by Jules Michelet (1798-1874), the most brilliant product of French historical literature, the author was dominated by a passionate attachment to his country, and possessed a marvelous creative imagination and a style notable for its word-painting and its power of symbolic representation. Michelet was the historical apologist for French democracy. The best portions of his work deal with the picturesque figures of the Middle Ages and with the French Revolution.

The least attractive personality of this group of romanticist historians, and perhaps the least accurate, was Thomas Carlyle (1795-1881). In radical contrast to Michelet he possessed a sour contempt for the masses and an equally exaggerated interest in the picturesque figures of history. To him, history is only the collective biography of heroic figures, and, more than any other historian, Carlyle created the conventional disdain for those commonplace things of daily life which have had incomparably greater influence upon social development than picturesque personalities. Carlyle indulged his historical prejudices in his *Letters and Speeches of Cromwell,* his *History of Frederick the Great,* and his *French Revolution.* While possessing only moderate value as sources of information, because of the writer's uncontrolled biases and lack of critical method, they earned him the undisputed position as "the greatest of English portrait painters."

While his name is identified with chronic inaccuracy in historical investigation, Carlyle's disciple, James Anthony Froude (1818-1894), was a greater historian than his master. His inaccuracies were unconscious rather than intentional, since he had a keen appreciation of critical methods, and his work was the first extended English history written on the basis of unpublished materials. His *History of England from the Fall of Woolsey to the Defeat of the Spanish*

Armada was an epic of the English Reformation—the deliverance from the "slavery of Rome"—and his Carlylian interest in great personalities found ample scope for expression in his portraits of Henry VIII and Burleigh. As a writer he was approached only by Lord Macaulay. "No other English historian," says Gooch, "has possessed a style so easy, so flowing, so transparent."

America found its sole distinguished representative of the school of Carlyle and Froude in John Lothrop Motley (1814-1877), who devoted his life to a study of the struggle of the Netherlands against Spain. Surpassing even Edward A. Freeman in his passion for liberty, he found a congenial theme in the successful revolution of the Dutch and the establishment of their republic. For word-painting and dramatic scenes only Carlyle equaled him among historians writing in the English tongue.

While romanticism gained some dominion over greater scholars like Leopold von Ranke, they stimulated interest in history rather than vitiated scholarship. In short, romanticism, with its emphasis on the "genius of a nation" and its deep emotional basis, stimulated the nationalistic enthusiasm which dominated the historical writing of the nineteenth century.

V. CONCLUSION

The total result of the romantic revolt was to reinforce reaction in religion, both Catholic and Protestant, in politics, and in social life. Protestantism retreated from the advanced positions taken up under deism and reverted to literalism and emotionalism. Politics was characterized by the revival of absolutism and reactionary statecraft under Metternich and the League of the Three Emperors. Socially, this movement was stimulated by Napoleon's spectacular career, which also caused many revolutionary romanticists to retreat to conservatism, as, for instance, the English poet Wordsworth, and produced the anti-French outburst in American politics in the early nineteenth century. In morals there was a regression from the fruitful efforts of the deists and Hume to find guidance for human conduct in empirical investigations of man's personality and social life. For this the romanticists substituted purely authoritarian doctrines, based either on an appeal to a "categorical imperative," or merely to traditional Christian practice.

The fact remains, however, that romanticism was in the full flush of its power for only a little over half a century. The reaction was never sufficiently general to frustrate intellectual progress, and when, following 1850, new scientific ideas began to appear, the success of the modernists became more certain. The acerbity of late nineteenth-century controversies may be attributed to the fact that the religious reaction intervened between the triumph of intelligence in the eighteenth century and the rise of the doctrine of evolution in the nineteenth. The religious reaction had strengthened traditionalism, but before the cumulative effect of the new knowledge the reactionaries proved impotent outside of religious circles.

The rising tide of science gave birth to a social optimism which swept the intellectual world and lingered well into the twentieth century. It required a social catastrophe like the two World Wars to create another reaction, that through which we are living at present. In this respect, the intellectual reaction following the World Wars is similar to that which followed the French Revolution. Yet, if we have had our fundamentalist Protestants, our neo-Thomists like the Catholic Jacques Maritain, our High-Church Anglicans like T. S. Eliot, our philosophical authoritarians like Irving Babbitt and Mortimer Adler, and our theologically oriented historians such as Arnold J. Toynbee, we also have had a strong belief in the efficacy of physical and social science in the writings of men like Émile Durkheim, H. G. Wells, Bertrand Russell, Lester F. Ward, John Dewey, William F. Ogburn, George A. Lundberg, and Leonard T. Hobhouse.

In spite of its generally reactionary cast, however, one should not overlook certain contributions to progress in this romanticist movement. Hegel's influence on Marxism and on the development of the social sciences is a case in point. Further, the historical point of view in writers like Herder and Hegel prepared the way for an evolutionary philosophy. Schleiermacher's theory of religion as actual psychological experience was a refreshing emancipation from dead forms and dogmas. The contribution of romanticism to art and literature was very remarkable. Romanticist literature escaped to a marked degree from the reactionary trends of romanticism in general, and was deeply influenced by the French Revolution and the spirit of reform.

SELECTED READINGS

Asbury, Herbert, *A Methodist Saint,* Knopf, 1927.
Atkins, G. G., *Life of Cardinal Newman,* Harper, 1931.
Babbitt, Irving, *Rousseau and Romanticism,* Meridian Books.
Baumer, F. L., *Religion and the Rise of Skepticism,* Harcourt, Brace, 1960.
Benn, *A History of English Rationalism in the Nineteenth Century.*
Brandes, Georg, *Main Currents in Nineteenth Century Literature,* 6 vols., Boni & Liveright, 1923.
Buckley, J. M., *A History of Methodism in the United States,* Harper, 1898.
Canavan, F. P., *The Political Reason of Edmund Burke,* Duke University Press, 1960.
Cell, G. C., *The Rediscovery of John Wesley,* Holt, 1935.
Church, R. W., *The Oxford Movement,* Macmillan, 1892.
Clark, R. T., *Herder: His Life and Thought,* University of California Press, 1955.
Davenport, F. M., *Primitive Traits in Religious Revivals,* Macmillan, 1905.
Dunning, *History of Political Theories: From Rousseau to Spencer.*
Engelbrecht, H. C., *Johann Gottlieb Fichte,* Columbia University Press, 1933.
Ergang, R. R., *Herder and the Foundations of German Nationalism,* Columbia University Press, 1931.
Flint, *The Philosophy of History in France and Germany.*
Gooch, G. P., *History and Historians in the Nineteenth Century,* Beacon, 1959, chaps. xxvi-xxvii.
Green, F. C., *Jean-Jacques Rousseau,* Cambridge University Press, 1955.
Gwynn, D. R., *The Catholic Reaction in France,* Macmillan, 1924.
Heidegger, Martin, *Kant and the Problem of Metaphysics,* University of Indiana Press, 1962.
Höffding, *History of Modern Philosophy,* Vol. II.
Jaspers, Karl, *The Great Philosophers,* Harcourt, Brace, 1962.

Kirk, Russell, *The Conservative Mind,* Regnery, 1960.
—— *A Program for Conservatives,* Regnery, 1954.
Laski, H. J., *Authority in the Modern State,* Yale University Press, 1919.
—— *Political Thought in England from Locke to Bentham,* Oxford University Press.
Lovejoy, A. O., *Essays in the History of Ideas,* Johns Hopkins University Press, 1952.
Lunn, A. H. M., *The Flight from Reason,* Dial Press, 1931.
McCunn, John, *The Political Philosophy of Edmund Burke,* Macmillan, 1913.
McGiffert, A. C., *The Rise of Modern Religious Ideas,* Macmillan, 1915.
Marcuse, Herbert, *Reason and Revolution,* Beacon, 1960.
Moore, E. C., *History of Christian Thought since Kant,* Allenson, 1947.
Morley, John,*Edmund Burke,* Knopf, 1924.
—— *Rousseau,* 2 vols., Macmillan, 1891.
Morris, G. S., *Hegel's Philosophy of the State and of History,* Scott, Foresman, 1892.
Muret, C. T., *French Royalist Doctrines since the Revolution,* Columbia University Press, 1933.
Osborn, A. M., *Rousseau and Burke,* Oxford University Press, 1940.
Osborn, A. R., *Schleiermacher and Religious Education,* Oxford University Press, 1934.
Palmer, *Catholics and Unbelievers in Eighteenth-Century France.*
Rossiter, Clinton, *Conservatism in America,* Knopf, 1955.
Scott, J. W., *Kant on the Moral Life,* Macmillan, 1924.
Stephen, *History of English Thought in the Eighteenth Century.*
Strachey, Lytton, *Eminent Victorians,* Modern Library, chap. i.
Webb, C. C. J., *Kant's Philosophy of Religion,* Oxford University Press, 1926.
Wenley, R. M., *Kant and His Philosophical Revolution,* Scribner, 1911.
Whitney, G. T., and Bowers, D. F., *The Heritage of Kant,* Princeton University Press, 1939.
Winchester, C. T., *Life of John Wesley,* Macmillan, 1906.

XXII

Literature and the Arts in the Seventeenth and Eighteenth Centuries

I. GROWTH AND DECLINE OF THE CLASSIC IDEAL IN LITERATURE

1. *England before the Restoration*

Shakespeare's *Hamlet* was produced in 1602, one year before the end of Queen Elizabeth's reign. It marks symbolically the end of one age and the beginning of another, for Hamlet is a prince of the sixteenth century, delighting, as Henry VIII and Sidney and Spenser did, in all that pleased the age of the humanistic revival: in classical literature, the theater, the fine arts, in all the achievements of man. Before Fate selected him to avenge his father's murder he had felt in this wise about life:

> What a piece of work is a man! How noble in reason! how infinite in faculty! in form and moving, how express and admirable! in action how like an angel! in apprehension how like a god! the beauty of the world! the paragon of animals!
> [*Hamlet*, II, 2, 323-327]

Disillusioned by experience, he found all this delight turned to doubt and disgust, and man became to him "this quintessence of dust."

Most young men of sensibility felt this disillusionment as the new century opened, and it colors most of the literature they wrote or read. The reasons for the fading of the warmth and excitement of the past age are many. Always when a ruler dominates for so long a period—Elizabeth had ruled for nearly fifty years—the outward unity of a peaceful reign conceals divisions widening within. The gulf between the Puritans and the High-Church party—the later Cavaliers—was already opened, though the Civil War was a half-century in the future. The middle and lower orders were in general Puritan; the court circle for the most part was aligned with the established church, so the split was economic as well as religious. The coming struggle already occupied the minds of many writers. Such a bold spirit as Lord Herbert of Cherbury (1583-1648), author and diplomat, talked with a dangerous freedom—some called it atheism—about revealed religion. It became the fashion at the court of James I and Charles I to affect a libertinism—as it was called—in their speech if not in their actual behavior. From France had come the pervasive skepticism of Montaigne whose urbane "Que sais-je?" (What do I really know?) is reflected in many an English writer after 1600. The humanistic revival had all but spent its force.

In the drama this changed spirit is especially plain to see. Shakespeare's plays embraced the experience of all kinds of Englishmen, from high to low, from Richard II to Falstaff and Gobbo. The new drama of such men as John Fletcher (1579-1625), Philip Massinger (1583-1640), and John Ford (fl. 1640) is much narrower in scope and more sophisticated in tone. Their characters are noble or gentle, the plots are complex, the themes involve psychological problems, mostly dealing with sex, which are often hardly universal. The setting is usually a foreign court where political and amorous intrigue is rife. The author aims, above all, to keep emotion stimulated. This special audience favored a new type of drama—tragi-comedy, a hybrid form, in which during four acts the chief characters are driven nearer and nearer to death or loss of honor, only to be rescued in the end by some ingenious trick of the author.

Beaumont and Fletcher's *Philaster* (1608) is the most notable example of tragi-comedy. Philaster's crown has been usurped, but he loves the usurper's daughter, Arethusa. He sends his page Bellario to be a messenger between them. A wicked lady of the court and her lover accuse Arethusa of misconduct with Bellario. Philaster believes the calumny, though, as he later learns, Bellario is not a youth but a girl who has fallen hopelessly in love with him. This hothouse story, for all its triviality, allowed the authors to keep the emotional tension high. We feel resentment at Philaster's fate; disgust for the villains; pity for Arethusa; tenderness towards Bellario; exultation at the final triumph of poetic justice when Philaster is restored and married to Arethusa.

In their search for novel sensations the dramatists abandoned the cruder bloody horrors of the old revenge plays and the patriotic fervors of the chronicle histories and emplored psychological horror. No one excelled John Webster's *Duchess of Malfi* (c. 1616) in this genre. The scene is Italy where, in the English imagination, moral corruption flourished and peculiarly refined methods of torture were practiced. The action is related to the attempts of the Duchess, a widow, to keep the fact of her secret marriage to her steward from her avaricious brothers. They place a spy, Bosola, in her service who finally betrays her. The power of the play lies in the silences, the whisperings, the suggestions of horrible acts performed in darkness. But these dramatists did not stop with extreme if natural horrors of this sort. They attempted equivocal themes such as variations on the incest-motive. Thus Ford in *'Tis Pity She's a Whore* (1633) dramatizes the guilt of a brother and sister which is partly expunged when the brother kills his sister-wife and slays their dupe to whom she had been married.

It is customary to condemn this Jacobean and Caroline drama as licentious and decadent. Viewed from the standards set by the universality of Shakespeare's *Lear* and *Othello* it is such. On the other hand it can be said in its behalf that it explored realms of human passion into which no earlier English writers had ventured and that it is expressed in fine poetry, subtle in thought and superbly adapted to the dramatic uses to which it is put.

In comedy the changes which took place over forty years are not so momentous, though it is significant that Ben Jonson (1573-1637), whose vigorous comedies of London life, like the *Silent Woman* (1609), the *Alchemist* (1610), and *Bartholomew Fair* (1614) were popular in their day, failed to please the court of Charles I when he returned to the stage after a decade's absence. Charles's French queen, Henrietta Maria, tried to influence the court poets to imitate the *preciosité* which she brought with her from across the Channel. Naturally the rough humor of Jonson's gulls, bragging soldiers, cheating quacks and pig-eating Puritans, which had pleased James I, seemed intolerable to her. The fashionable dramatist of the end of Charles's reign was the prolific James Shirley (1596-1666) whose comedies, like *Hyde Park* and *The Lady of Pleasure,* mildly satirize social climbers and young rakes who are converted from their libertinism by the steadfastness of their intended victims. The humors of Falstaff and Dame Quickly and of Jonson's Doll Common and Zeal-of-the-Land Busy are in the forgotten past.

No poet of the new century better reflects the revolt against the Elizabethan literary fashions than John Donne (1573-1631). Born a Roman Catholic when that religion was under surveillance, he nevertheless sought preferment at court. His early poems—the *Songs and Sonnets* (written 1592-1602)—show him to have been a full-blooded highly intellectual young man—"not dissolute but very neat, a great visitor of ladies, a great frequenter of plays, a great writer of conceited verses." He learned at length that the only path to preferment would be through the church. This path he took, after an honest conversion to religion. As he had been earlier the greatest poet of love and the greatest satirist of his day, he became finally a great preacher and religious poet. For the last ten years of his life he was Dean of St. Paul's Cathedral in London and was on the verge of a bishopric at his death. His influence, both as poet and churchman, lasted well into the Restoration period.

Donne's lyric poetry is written out of intense emotion, but there is cast over it a thoughtfulness characteristic of his age. The feeling is no less deep for this, but the subtle thought makes him a difficult poet:

> Dear love, for nothing less than thee
> Would I have broke this happy dream;
>   It was a theme
> For reason, much too strong for phantasy.
> Therefore thou waked'st me wisely; yet
> My dream thou brok'st not, but continu'st it,
> Thou art so truth, that thoughts of thee suffice
> To make dreams truths; and fables histories;
> Enter these arms, for since thou thought'st it best,
> Not to dream all my dream, let's act the rest. . . .

Specifically, Donne put an end to the conventions of the idealized love which the sixteenth-century sonnet makers repeated *ad nauseam*. He addresses the women in his poems frankly and sometimes rudely. The rough, spoken cadences of his verse contrast with the lyrical sweetness of the Elizabethans. Their structure often follows the pattern of a syllogism in logic so that the mind must be alert to catch the conclusion. Most novel is Donne's delight in introducing any object encountered in his wide reading and varied experience if it will serve for a metaphor or "conceit." Thus he compares the situation of his love and himself at parting to "stiff twin compasses."

> Thy soul the fixed foot, makes no show
> To move, but doth, if the other do.
> And though it in the center sit,
> Yet when the other far doth roam,
> It leans, and hearkens after it,
> And grows erect, as that comes home.

Bizarre as this sort of fantastic image is, one must admit that the one point of similarity is striking and important.

The poetry of Donne and his school has been given the name "metaphysical." Strictly speaking, metaphysical poetry should mean a kind of verse "inspired by a philosophical conception of the universe and the rôle assigned to the human spirit in the great drama of existence" [1]—like Dante's *Divine Comedy* or Lucretius' *De rerum natura*. Donne, George Herbert (1593-1633), and Richard Crashaw (1612-1649) wrote nothing so great, but the term is apt for them in that they think passionately, searching and probing the experience which has given rise to the emotion. This is equally true whether, as in Donne's "The Dream," the experience is the sudden appearance of his love as he is waking or, with Herbert, it is God's curing his rebellious heart ("The Collar") or, with Crashaw, the sight of a picture of Saint Teresa "with a seraphim beside her" ("The Flaming Heart"). After their century their kind of poetry fell into disfavor. The age of Pope thought it absurdly farfetched; the romantic nineteenth century felt that it lacked the passion and sensuousness poetry should have. In our time, the postwar generation poets have taken Donne as their master, and the title "metaphysical" is once again a mark of distinction.

So many of the poets of the years between 1630 and 1650 were adherents of the King that they are called collectively the Cavalier lyrists. They fall sometimes into the metaphysical vein, but most often they sing sweetly of the transitoriness of life and the murdering beauty of a fair one's face. Richard Lovelace (1618-1657) speaks more seriously "To Lucasta, going to the Wars," yet his farewell is said gallantly and lightly:

> I could not love thee, dear, so much,
> Loved I not honor more.

[1] H. J. C. Grierson, *Metaphysical Lyrics and Poems of the Seventeenth Century*, Oxford University Press, 1925, p. xiii.

In spite of the large amount of amatory verse written by the Cavaliers one is soon aware that the greatest poetry of the age is religious. The controversy involving church and state sooner or later affected most of the poets, as it did the other citizens of the realm, and by them all shades of religious belief were put into poetry. Richard Crashaw traveled the whole way to the Roman Catholic church. Donne and George Herbert stood in the middle ground surveyed by Hooker whose *Laws of Ecclesiastical Polity* (1594) defined in admirable prose the Anglican position. Robert Herrick, disciple of Ben Jonson rather than of Donne, refused to be drawn in either direction. In his rural Devon parish he praised the pagan festivals of the countryside—Mayday and the Harvest home— equally with "Ceremonies for Candlemas Eve." But he was orthodox and prayed with a humble piety:

> In the hour of my distress
> When temptations me oppress,
> And when I my sins confess,
> Sweet Spirit, comfort me.

One good came from the controversies between High- and Low-Church parties. At the Hampton Court conference, called by King James in 1604 to consider religious issues, a new translation of the Bible was proposed. Completed in 1611 by the forty-seven revisers, it is the so-called King James or Authorized Version. No other book has so deeply influenced the thinking and imagination of the English-speaking peoples.

At the Puritan extreme stands the greatest literary figure of the century, John Milton (1608-1674). To call him a Puritan is to do him a great injustice because the word cannot suggest the kind of genius he possessed. From his boyhood he was serious and devout. He felt that he was called to be a poet; that in time he would find the great subject which his years of preparation would make him fit to treat in verse. Until the time Milton became the chief pamphleteer of the Puritan groups opposing the King (1641), his career as a writer was that of any learned poet of the day. He imitated the conventions of the elegy in Latin verse and in 1637 essayed an English elegy, "Lycidas," in memory of a Cambridge friend. The poem, perfect as it is, is a kind of exercise, a part of the self-discipline in his art which is also evident in the carefully constructed poems in contrasted moods, "L'Allegro" and "Il Penseroso" (1634). The sonnet he also tried, making it a vehicle for intense personal feeling on a variety of subjects besides love, for which the Elizabethans had employed it almost exclusively. His masques—*Arcades* (1633) and *Comus* (1634)—both written to be performed, show us the youthful Milton, heir of the Elizabethan poets Spenser and Jonson and devotedly in love with classical myth and poetry.

In 1641 begins the long series of prose pamphlets condemning the episcopacy and advocating the synodical form of church government. No Puritan was more scathing in his denunciations of Charles's government or a stronger advocate of extreme measures against him. When Charles was beheaded in 1649 Milton wrote the official defense of the regicidal act. His aid in the cause won him the post of Secretary for Foreign Tongues in the Commonwealth (1649-1660). Of all his prose writings the two most remembered are not directly concerned with the religious struggle: *Areopagitica* (1644), the most eloquent defense of freedom of speech in the language, and *Of Education* (1644), which elaborates the training needed to fit a man "to perform justly, skillfully, and magnanimously all the offices, both public and private, of peace and war."

When the Restoration drove Milton into an apprehensive retirement, he had at last the leisure to devote himself to the great work he had hoped since 1641 to write. To one of Milton's religious views the central problem in life is to understand correctly man's relation to the Almighty. In his search for a solution to this problem he departed from the stern Calvinistic view of the human race as "sinners in the hands of an angry God," for he believed in the moral responsibility of the individual. He wrote *Paradise Lost* (1667) to assert the freedom of man's will. Adam could not have sinned if he had not been free to sin or to obey. If this were not so, then it would be impossible to understand the Divine purpose.

Paradise Lost, like the *Divine Comedy* of Dante, is a synthesis of the beliefs of an age of religious faith—in the case of Milton's poem, of Protestant faith. But Milton was not an orthodox Calvinist as Dante was an orthodox Catholic of the Middle Ages. This fact helps to save the poem for us today, for strict Calvinism is an unlovely religion not now in very good repute. The great battle of the statesmen in Hell in the early part of the poem, the conversations between Adam and Raphael sent down from Heaven to warn him of Satan's wiles, the penetrating psychology of Adam and Eve during the Fall, the vision of Christ's future victory, the expulsion from Paradise are all informed with Milton's passionate convictions about the importance of knowledge as an instrument of virtue. The Adam in us falls whenever passion triumphs over reason in our lives. But what we have lost we may regain. As Michael says to the departing Adam:

> Only add
> Deeds to thy knowledge answerable; add Faith,
> Add Virtue, Patience, Temperance, add Love,
> By name to come called Charity, the soul
> Of all the rest: then wilt thou not be loath
> To leave this Paradise, but shalt possess
> A Paradise within thee, happier far.[2]

The story of *Paradise Lost* remains acceptable to other ages because it is symbolic of the inescapable problem to which all thoughtful men in any time seek an answer: the individual's relationship to the powers which are greater than self. But it is the poetry which makes the epic one of the half-dozen great works of literature. Milton can call forth any strain he desires. He can pass from the sublime description of the War in Heaven in Book VI to the idyllic lines picturing Eve among the flowers in Book IX:

[2] *Paradise Lost,* XII, ll. 581-587. Milton's two last great works, the epic of *Paradise Regained* (1671) and the drama in the form of a Greek tragedy *Samson Agonistes* (1671), are variations on the theme of temptation. Christ in the second epic shows man how to resist; Samson, in the drama, falls through temptation, but after punishment and the probation of new trials, he recovers God's favor, as Adam does in *Paradise Lost.*

> Veiled in a cloud of fragrance where she stood,
> Half-spied, so thick the roses bushing round
> About her glowed, oft stooping to support
> Each flower of slender stalk, whose head though gay
> Carnation, purple, azure, or specked with gold,
> Hung drooping unsustained, them she upstays
> Gently with myrtle band, mindless the while,
> Her self, though fairest unsupported flower,
> From her best prop so far, and storm so nigh.

The epic moves with all the resources of vast learning, passionate belief and a disciplined art, to its appointed end—"to justify the ways of God to men."

2. *France*

The first half of the seventeenth century in France saw the development of that important literary institution, the *salon*. Weary of the swashbuckling court of Henry IV, the young and charming Mme de Rambouillet withdrew to her *hôtel* near the Louvre, redecorated it magnificently, and began to receive there regularly a group of witty and elegant men and women. They met for pleasure but their idea of pleasure was not a supper or a ball but conversation. Conversation, they thought, was the most important thing in life. "Conversation is the bond of humanity, the greatest pleasure of well bred men, the best means of introducing into society not only good manners but also morality of the purest sort and the love of glory and of virtue." That was the dictum of Mlle Madeleine de Scudéry whose novels society—*le monde* they called it—read with enthusiasm. To making of conversation a fine art *le monde* bent all their highest talents.

They were immensely concerned, to begin with, with the perfection of the French language and they laid down the lines along which it has developed ever since: precision, clarity, elegance. The Hôtel de Rambouillet was divided for weeks over the question of the word *car* (*for* or *because*). Should it be approved or banished altogether? They debated the relative merits of Malleville's sonnet, the "Belle Matineuse," and one by Voiture on the same theme. They analyzed emotions and sentiments, made "portraits" in prose of their friends and acquaintances and laid the foundations for the profound character studies of the dramatists Corneille and Racine. They struck off happy phrases which have become a part of the language: *briller dans la conversation* (to shine in conversation), *s'embarquer dans une affaire* (to embark upon an enterprise). They were as exclusive in their choice of words as in their choice of guests for a supper. Any phrase that smacked of commerce, of the stable, or the rude mechanic arts was summarily rejected. They proposed to cast out *poitrine* (breast) because butchers spoke of breasts of veal. They indicated their separation from the grosser sections of the world by speaking of themselves as *Précieux* and *Précieuses*.

What the defects of such a society might be it is easy to imagine and in the scores of minor salons that sprang up in imitation of the Hôtel de Rambouillet the defects were only too apparent. Refinement was overrefined, elegance attenuated to nonsense, metaphors instead of illuminating ideas became elaborate rebuses. "It seems to me, monsieur, that you have paid your debt to love," said the Précieuses when they meant, "Your hair is gray." They became all too worthy of the adjective which Molière's comedy has indissolubly attached to them; they were *Les Précieuses ridicules.*

At their best, however, the *Précieux* were perfectionists and they have more than one tangible achievement to their credit. One can trace their influence directly in the foundation of the French Academy, in the making of its great dictionary, in the creation of French prose by Pascal and of French drama by Corneille.

The founders of the Academy were a group of learned gentlemen whose meetings became so famous that Cardinal Richelieu offered to take them under his protection and organize them into an official body. Their number was increased to forty, they became the Académie Française and they agreed that the best thing they could do for the "embellishment of the language" was to make a dictionary which should formulate and fix the language the salons were creating. They plunged into the labor with vigor but with so much thought and care that not until the end of the century was it ready for publication, presenting then the speech not only of the age in which it was begun but that of the great half-century that flowered in 1661 when Louis XIV began to reign after the death of Mazarin.

The French literature of that golden age is so completely national in character that it is often difficult for the Anglo-Saxon to evaluate it properly. It strikes him on first encounter as stiff, stylized beyond vitality, a little dull. It has, on the surface, none of the exuberance, the richness, the originality of his own best genius. And the modern man of any nationality approaches it with incredulity, for it is the literature of a society which was absolutely certain of its standards. The Catholic religion it accepted without fervor, but as a matter of course. A powerful monarchy, a fixed autocratic society, it took for granted. A long peace made it imperative for the gentleman to establish his reputation with tongue and pen instead of with the sword. For the wretched hordes without its gates the polite world had no care except to make sure that it remained without. It was a narrow world but a bright, a noble, a magnificent one. Reason ruled with taste, and reason and taste are no mean virtues. The experiments, the exaggerations of the *Précieux,* had come to full and glorious flower.

In the early years of the century François Malherbe (1555-1628) had attempted to reform French poetry and the French tongue grown too rich and lush, but he had little success with his contemporaries. For three decades more the poets of France, like the poets of Italy and of Spain, continued to torture similes into hideous acrobatics, to compose acrostics and anagrams and *pointes* that played futilely with the double meaning of words. They paid small heed to Malherbe but the poets of the golden age looked back to him as their master.

The poet in command during the reign of Louis XIV was Boileau (Nicolas Boileau-Despréaux, 1636-1711), a poet of the mind who fled from lyricism to set forth in lucid verse the critical tenets of a rational age. A keen critic he was quick to discern genius in his contemporaries and to force the public to recognize its presence. Racine, Molière, and La Fontaine owed much of their contemporary reputation to him, and much of their fine accomplishment too, for his sound sense and caustic tongue kept his friends working constantly at their highest pitch. In his *L'Art poétique* and in the *Satires* and *Epîtres* which followed, Boileau preached three texts: reason, truth, nature. "Love reason, and let what you write borrow from it alone luster and quality"; and "Rien n'est beau que le vrai; le vrai seul est aimable"—"Beauty is truth, truth beauty," Keats put it two centuries later—to find truth, study nature, and the classic writers who comprehended nature so well, who understood how to extract her essence, the general and universal truth which alone endures. Thus Boileau set forth not the art of poetry only but the whole philosophy of a century.

The greatest poet of that century was Jean de La Fontaine (1621-1695). "In the Middle Ages," says Lytton Strachey in his *Landmarks in French Literature,* "La Fontaine would have been a mendicant friar, or a sainted hermit, or a monk, surreptitiously illuminating the margins of his manuscripts with the images of birds and beasts. In the nineteenth century, one can imagine him drifting among Paris cafés, pouring out his soul in a random lyric or two, and dying before his time. The age of Louis XIV took this dreamer, this idler, this feckless fugitive, spiritual creature, kept him alive by means of patrons in high society, and eventually turned him—not simply into a poet, for he was a poet by nature, but into one of the most subtle, deliberate, patient, and exquisite craftsmen who have ever written in verse." [3] La Fontaine was nearly fifty when his genius matured to the writing of the *Fables* which are moral, and merry as Aesop never was. The little tales are charmingly told and the animals are definitely individual characters. La Fontaine's attitude toward them is by no means that of the naturalist, scientific, romantic, or sentimental. What interested him is the way in which an animal by its habits or appearance epitomizes some human characteristic, exaggerating almost to caricature but more subtly. La Fontaine's feeling for his animals is precisely that of the twentieth-century Walt Disney in his animated cartoons. The fables are close kin to the comedies of Molière.

"The first work of genius in prose" was Voltaire's characterization of the *Lettres provinciales* of Blaise Pascal (1623-1662). Better perhaps than any other writer of the century Pascal demonstrated Boileau's dictum that truth is beauty. His brilliant mind was turned to one single high purpose, the exaltation of the Christian religion as the only true guide for man. Converted as a boy to Jansenism he lived, except for a brief interval of dissipation in the world, the life of a *solitaire* at Port Royal, unbound by vows but devoted to meditation, study and prayer. The "Lettres de Louis de Montalte à un Provincial de ses amis" were a defense of the Jansenist doctrine of grace against the attacks of the powerful Jesuits who regarded them as a heretical sect. Even more magnificent in thought are the *Pensées,* notes for a thesis in defense of Christianity which he did not live to complete. The isolated perfect paragraphs are brilliant examples of what Voltaire meant by genius in prose: "L'homme n'est qu'un roseau . . ."

3 Lytton Strachey, *Landmarks in French Literature,* Oxford University Press, 1912.

Man is only a reed, the feeblest thing in nature, but he is a thinking reed. The universe need not arm itself to crush him. A vapor, a drop of water, is enough to kill him. But even if the universe should crush him, man would still be nobler than his destroyer because he knows that he dies and he knows the advantage which the universe has over him. The universe does not know these things.

All our dignity, then, consists in thought. By thought we must raise ourselves. . . . Let us labor, then, to think well: that is the principle of morality.

This power of distilling wisdom was one of the great attainments of the age. It occurs, in very different form, in another important writer of prose, the Duc de La Rochefoucauld (1613-1680), but there it is the wisdom of a completely disillusioned man of the world. In his *Maximes* La Rochefoucauld put into final form ideas which had been discussed at length in the salons of Mme de Sablé and Mme de Lafayette: "Nous avons tous assez de force pour supporter les maux d'autrui" (We all have enough strength to bear the ills of others). "Quelque bien qu'on nous dise de nous, on ne nous apprend rien de nouveau" (Whatever good anyone tells us about ourselves he tells us nothing new). "Nous pardonnons souvent à ceux qui nous ennuient, mais nous ne pouvons pardonner à ceux que nous ennuyons" (We often forgive those who bore us but we can never forgive those whom we bore). It is scarcely possible to read a line without a disconcerting sense of personal weaknesses laid bare.

Another method of distilling wisdom was the composing of "characters," brief portraits not of individuals but of types. A favorite amusement of the salons, they are preserved for posterity in *Les Caractères ou les mœurs de ce siècle* of Jean de La Bruyère (1645-1696). A well-educated bourgeois who became tutor to the grandson of the great Condé, La Bruyère hated his position but was too fascinated, apparently, by the spectacle of aristocratic and literary France as it passed through the great Hôtel de Condé to think of renouncing it. Instead he watched and set it all down in brilliant bitter disillusionment.

Any society which cared so much for conversation as the seventeenth century produced of necessity great orators, great writers of memoirs and of letters. The oratory of course was pulpit oratory which rose to its greatest height in the magnificent periods of the funeral orations of Jacques-Bénigne Bossuet (1627-1704), preceptor to the dauphin and Bishop of Meaux.

Of the writers of memoirs posterity is most grateful to the Duc de Saint-Simon (1675-1755) who with no attempt to judge or evaluate, merely for the joy of observing and setting down, unrolls before the reader the whole complex fascinating court of Versailles.

Most charming of the letters, perhaps, are those by two women who were in no wise literary by profession, Mme de Sévigné (1626-1696) who so adored her daughter that she could never be happy out of communication with her, and Mme de Maintenon (Françoise d'Augbigné, 1635-1719), that extraordinary woman who by the force of sweet reason dominated the last years of Louis XIV.

The other women who set literary mark upon the century were novelists. Madeleine de Scudéry (1608-1701) was renowned for her "Saturdays" and for her *Clélie* which contained the famous *Carte du Tendre,* a "precious" map where between the sea of Intimacy and the lake of Indifference the river of Inclination flowed by the villages of Billets-Doux, Jolis-Vers, and so forth, to the city of Tendre. Of greater importance is Mme de Lafayette (1634-1693) who in *La Princesse de Clèves* wrote the first great French psychological novel. She reduced the ten volume romances of Mlle de Scudéry to more delicate proportions and wrote in the best "style mondain," intelligent, lively, never sentimental.

Modern French drama, which had begun in 1637 with the production of Corneille's *Le Cid,* came to full flower during Louis XIV's reign in Racine. It was Corneille, however, who set the type. After the decline of the mystery play the French drama had moved in two directions. There were classical tragedies on the model of Seneca, really intended to be read by the scholar in his closet— the typical example is Jodelle's *Cléopâtre* (1552), and there were wild melodramas, notably those of Alexandre Hardy (1569-1630) which delighted the Parisian populace but disgusted the finer spirits. Either genre might have been developed but Pierre Corneille (1606-1684), not deliberately but by instinct, chose to vivify the classic drama. He created a tragedy which was completely expressive of its age and became a model for the theater in Europe for centuries to come.

By his cheerful acceptance of their limitations—though he refused to follow them with absolute literalness—Corneille established permanently in the French theater the power of the famous unities of time, place and action, which Boileau had neatly epitomized. The unities gathered their prestige from a mistranslation of Aristotle's *Poetics* but their power lay in the realism they brought to the stage in a highly rational age. The seventeenth century enjoyed its theater best when it was not called upon to make any great effort of imagination. If the story occupied actually only a few hours and took place in a single room it seemed to the rational spectators far more credible than if they were required to think of the stage now as a room in the king's palace, now as the seacoast of Bohemia. A plot compressed within the limitations of the unities might of course be stiff and artificial but it might, under the hand of a Corneille, become high-charged with passion. *Le Cid* from a complicated story selects for presentation on the stage the scenes where Chimène's love for Rodrigue is at war with her desire for vengeance upon him as the slayer of her father. We see Rodrigue when he presents himself to her hot from the fatal duel and entreats her to kill him in revenge. In a love and honor *tirade,* typical of Corneille and of all classic drama, Rodrigue declares: "I would do it again, if I had it to do" because "A man without honor would not be worthy of you."

With the *Cid* Corneille thus established another important principle of modern drama; the hero creates his destiny by his own will; he is not at the mercy of external forces, human or divine. "I am master of myself as I am master of the universe" cries Auguste in *Cinna.* "And my reason sovereign over my passions" is the phrase of Pauline in *Polyeucte.* Indeed so high are their ideals, so lofty their purposes, that Corneille's characters seem often superhuman. As a matter of fact they are probably quite realistic presentations of the Frenchman of the seventeenth century, still a man of war not yet softened by courtly life, guided not by his heart but by his clear keen mind.

The popular success of the *Cid* was enormous, though Corneille's jealous rivals attacked it and the Academy censured it for plagiarism from its Spanish original. New masterpieces followed swiftly, *Horace, Cinna, Polyeucte,* but with age Corneille's powers weakened and he saw his place in the public favor taken by a younger and a greater man.

Jean Racine (1639-1699) accepted the unities without a second thought. He wrote as a matter of course in conventional alexandrines (the French "blank verse" of twelve syllables) and with the limited vocabulary of the Academy's *Dictionary* but he bent the alexandrine to new powers of passion and of poetry and created dramatic personages who were men and women of the new age. They are, in our sense, modern, near kin to the characters of Shakespeare, though they play their tragic parts within the narrow compass of the classic room. *Bérénice* has three characters, the entire action takes place within a small ante-chamber and lasts scarcely longer than the two and a half hours required for its representation on the stage, but we are left with a sense of the pressure of the great world without as well as of the tumult of individual souls. Racine is a poet who can do much with a single line, a common word or phrase making straight to its mark.

Beginning with *Andromaque* in 1667 this concentrated passion rose to its greatest height ten years later in *Phèdre,* that tragic rôle which every great French actress must play, Phèdre, second wife of Theseus, King of Athens, who, con-sumed by guilty love for her stepson, passes through every shade of jealousy, passion, pride, horror, shame, remorse, until in the fifth act, draining a draft of poison, she dies confessing her crime and the innocence of Hippolyte.

Phèdre, through the machinations of a great lady, was a complete failure on its first presentation and so deeply wounded was Racine that he renounced the stage and returned to the scene of his religious youth. He had been brought up by the Jansenists and his defection to the theater and a worldly life had been a source of scandal and of grief to those who had watched over his promising youth. His repentence was deep and sincere. He was genuinely convinced that as a playwright he had been a poisoner of the public mind and he devoted himself to meditation, to historical writing for the king, and to the duties of a simple family life. It was not until 1689 that Mme de Maintenon induced him to com-pose for pupils in her school at Saint-Cyr a biblical tragedy on the story of *Esther,* followed by one on *Athalie,* daughter of Jezebel. Quietly performed, they made no stir at all during his lifetime but today many critics rank *Athalie* even higher than *Phèdre.*

What Corneille had done for tragedy was done for comedy by Jean-Baptiste Poquelin who called himself Molière (1622-1673). He rescued French comedy from the conventional intrigues of the Italian theater and the extravagant burlesques of Spain and made it realistic, with a strictly classical realism, highly selective and generalized. "The business of comedy," he said (*Impromptu de Versailles,* Sc. IV), "is to represent in general all the defects of men and espe-cially of the men of our time." He believed further that comedy should be both merry and moral. His comedies are exuberant, sometimes even to the point of farce, but they have always a serious purpose and sometimes they cut very deep. The human frailty with which he has least patience is pretentiousness: *Les Précieuses ridicules* who pretend to a refinement and culture they in no wise understand; the ignorant doctors who pretend to skill (*Le Malade imaginaire*); the newly rich tradesman who pretends to fashion (*Le Bourgeois gentilhomme*). All of these people refuse to face facts and that to Molière is the ultimate sin, which is the reason why Frenchmen delight to call him the most thoroughly French of authors.

To his keen powers of observation Molière added a wider experience of human nature than any other literary man of his period. Born in Paris, the son of a carpet-maker, he became the director and principal actor of a company of players who traveled in the provinces until in 1658 they came under the patronage of the king. For the rest of his life Molière stood high in royal favor and Louis could not organize a fête at Versailles or St. Germain without his assistance. Noble, bourgeois, tradesman, peasant, Molière knew them all at first hand, and knew how to use them to make an audience smile or laugh uproariously. He was not himself, though, a happy man. He was continuously in bad health. He was continually overworking, not only directing his company and taking all the principal rôles but turning out in fourteen years twenty-nine comedies, many of them masterpieces. His private life was made difficult by his infatuation for his young and frivolous wife. *Le Misanthrope* is partly autobiography. His literary life was made difficult by jealous critics who complained that he was far from respectful of the unities—Molière replied that the only rule of playwriting was to please. His vocabulary, they said, went beyond the bounds of good taste, for Molière made his lackeys and tradesmen talk in character. *Tartuffe* was thought an insult to the church—for years even Louis did not allow its production, though its satire was directed against hypocrisy, not against true piety. His death was in keeping with his life; playing, though ill, in his own *Malade imaginaire* he was seized with convulsions which his audience took for new comic business added to his rôle.

3. Restoration England

When Charles II returned in triumph to England in May, 1660, after years of exile on the Continent, he and his brilliant court were determined to make the most of his restoration. Life for the majority of Englishmen went on as it always does. Puritan leaders like Milton, so long as they remained in quiet seclusion, were unmolested because Charles was a wise as well as a witty monarch. But at the court the Earl of Rochester, Sir Charles Sedley, and the Earl of Dorset led the revels, scandalizing sober merchants in the city of London. Even Mr. Pepys, the ambitious, diary-writing Secretary to the Admiralty, much as he delighted in recording their amorous intrigues and outrageous escapades, was sometimes appalled.

The comedies of the period are the perfect mirror of its manners. Charles Lamb, in trying to defend them to a stricter age, said of the characters in these plays: "They break through no laws, or conscious restraints. They know of none. They have got out of Christendom into the land—what shall I call it?—of cuckoldry—the Utopia of gallantry, where pleasure is duty, and the manners perfect freedom." This dictum may have persuaded Lamb's contemporaries that they could read Wycherley's *The Country Wife* (1675) or Congreve's *The Way of the World* (1700) without fear of defilement, but the view that these plays are unrealistic is untenable. The comedies of Etherege, Wycherley, Shadwell, Dryden, and Congreve are quite literal transcripts of the life of the small circle about the court, so much so that episodes and characters are often easily identifiable. Their constant theme is the witty pursuit of women, the wit being displayed both in the action and in the dialogue. This generation had decided that there is only one sin—stupidity. Those who deserve punishment are the husbands who through jealousy or complacency allow their beautiful wives to be seduced from them by the gallants who know the art. Not that any woman is really seduced against her will in these plays, for the Restoration had rationalized sex and in the witty warfare between men and women the opponents were equally well equipped for defense.

As the years went by the comedy changed from the brutally coarse plays of the early 1660's to the flashing style of Etherege (1634?-1691?) whose *Sir Fopling Flutter* is the finest expression of the early years of this "pleasant, well-bred, complaisant, free, frolic, good-natured, pretty age." With Wycherley (1640-1716) a serious tone is sometimes heard, for he was essentially a moralist disgusted with the grosser indecencies and hypocrisies of his time. His *The Plain Dealer* (1676) is so outspoken that his attempted cure by way of satire seems to some modern readers more offensive than the disease. In the plays of Congreve (1670-1729), the last of the line, a notable change has come about. The language is completely free of indecency and his heroines, like Angelica in *Love for Love* (1695) and Millamant in *The Way of the World* (1700), are virtuous, lovely, witty women. The old game of hunter and hunted is pursued now in the underplots but the main theme might please even a prude.

While the comic dramatists were bent on producing plays hardly distinguishable in their action from the life of the spectators in the boxes and the pit, the writers of tragedy invented a type which is artificial in the extreme—the heroic play. The standard pattern presents a warrior-monarch, usually from some exotic country like India or Morocco or Turkey, who is passion-torn in a struggle to decide between the imperious demands of Love and Honor. Dryden's *The Conquest of Granada* (1670) is the most notorious example of the type. Doctor Johnson said it was written "with a seeming determination to glut the publick with dramatick wonders; to exhibit in its highest elevation a theatrical meteor of incredible love and impossible valour, and to leave no room for a wilder flight to the extravagance of posterity." Its hero Almanzor (like all these heroes) sweeps everything before him, as a soldier for the Moors who later discovers himself to be the son of a noble Spaniard. But he cannot move Almahide, though she loves him, because Duty binds her to his rival, King Boabdelin, to whom she is married. Dryden resolves this titanic struggle by killing off Boabdelin in the last act.

The heroic play is but one instance of the effort of the authors of the seventeenth century in England and on the Continent to reproduce the classical epic in modern form. Dryden found a precedent for Almanzor's behavior in Homer's Achilles and Tasso's Rinaldo. His essay "Of Heroic Plays" sums up what the age hoped of this form of literature, a hope which D'Avenant and Cowley were believed to have partly realized in their respective verse epics, *Gondibert* (1650) and *Davideis* (1656). The amazing feats of the heroes in these plays, the complex plots involving affairs of high state, the bombastic dialogue, were designed to elevate the drama to the level of epic grandeur. One suspects the Restoration audiences endured rather than enjoyed the heroic play. As a type it soon gave way to the sentimental tragedy of Otway (1652-1685) and Southerne (1660-1746) which was in turn displaced by the arid neoclassical tragedy of the eighteenth century. Addison's *Cato* (1713) is now the only example remembered of this later form.

The deliberate attempt to construct a new kind of drama on a well-considered theoretical basis is only one instance of the effect which the analytical temper of the period had upon its literature. Literary criticism, as one might imagine, flourished. Emulating the examples of the French critics across the water, Englishmen debated in such works as the Earl of Mulgrave's *An Essay upon Poetry* (1682) and Rymer's *Short View of Tragedy* (1692) the comparative advantages and the rank of different sorts of verse, the claims of genius and judgment in poetry, the necessity of preserving the unities in drama, the importance of the fable (plot), the question of decorum (the mode of speech proper to a particular character), the relations between epic and dramatic poetry, the superiority of rhyme over blank verse. Many works were written to the order of the critic, but the native English fondness for abundant action and looseness of construction in a play prevented the best artists from adhering closely to the "rules." Even Dryden, the greatest critic of the age, found good reason for violating every precept he chose not to follow. Certain attempts to import Gallic fashions failed completely, as in the case of the opera. To a common-sense Englishman the mythological fancies of the librettists of Lully and Cambert seemed downright silly and they would have none of them.

The poetry of these forty years which we now read with pleasure is chiefly satire. It was a time when authors were the intimate friends of statesmen and took it upon themselves to defend their patrons against attack. The literary battles were often skirmishes in the larger political war. The greatest license of speech was permitted. The king himself, known to the court poets as "Old Rowley," was the subject of innumerable scurrilous verses in which his bedchamber conquests were well advertised. Most memorable of the political satires are Samuel Butler's *Hudibras* (1663, 1664, 1678) and Dryden's *Absalom and Achitophel* (1681-1682). Butler was a peasant boy, well educated in the classics. His mock epic in four-beat lines about a puritanical knight (Hudibras) convulsed the court, and its author became a favorite with Charles who offered him a pension which he probably never received. The following description of Hudibras' breeches is typical of the style.

His Breeches were of rugged woolen,
And had been at the siege of Bullen,
To old King Harry so well known,
Some writers held they were his own.
Through they were lined with many a piece
Of ammunition—bread and cheese,
And fat black-puddings, proper food
For warriors that delight in blood;
For, as we said, he always chose
To carry victual in his hose.

Dryden's satire on the attempt of the Whig Earl of Shaftesbury to secure the succession to the throne for Charles's illegitimate son, the Duke of Monmouth, under the allegory of the revolt of Absalom (II Samuel, 13-18), is without doubt one of the greatest satires in the language. One by one the opponents of Charles are lashed in verse which has given them an undesired fame. Who now remembers the Earl of Shaftesbury (Achitophel), thrust from the office of Lord Chancellor in 1673, without recalling Dryden's portrait of him?

Of these the false Achitophel was first,
A name to all succeeding ages curst.
For close designs and crooked counsels fit,
Sagacious, bold, and turbulent of wit,
Restless, unfixt in principles and place,
In power unpleased, impatient of disgrace;
A fiery soul, which working out its way, ⎫
Fretted the pigmy body to decay: ⎬
And o'er informed the tenement of clay. ⎭
A daring pilot in extremity;
Pleased with the danger, when the waves went high
He sought the storms; but, for a calm unfit,
Would steer too nigh the sands to boast his wit.
Great wits are sure to madness near allied
And thin partitions do their bounds divide;
Else, why should he, with wealth and honor blessed
Refuse his age the needful hours of rest?
Punish a body which he could not please,
Bankrupt of life, yet prodigal of ease?

The biased judgments of Whig historians like Macaulay have obscured the fact that the years 1660-1700 were a great age for the arts. A society which has Hobbes and Locke for its philosophers, Purcell for its composer, and Wren for its architect has no need to fear posterity's ultimate verdict. The peer in literature of these geniuses is John Dryden (1631-1700), professional man of letters, poet, and critic. Like Jonson before him and Pope in the next generation, he was in the front of every literary battle, admonishing and correcting, always experimenting with new forms, yet ready to abandon whatever proved to be ineffective. There was no branch of literature which he did not adorn.

For twenty years he earned his living by turning out twenty-eight plays in the popular modes of the rhymed heroic drama and the licentious comedy of manners. One play he wrote to please himself, *All for Love* (1678), in which he professed "to imitate the divine Shakespeare" who had treated the same story in *Antony and Cleopatra.* A comparison of the two tragedies illuminates the difference in literary ideals between the two periods. "Dryden has reduced Shakespeare's time from ten years to one day, discarded two thirds of Shakespeare's characters, reduced thirty-seven scenes in almost as many places from Rome to Alexandria, to five single acts. He has renounced the gorgeous, shifting Elizabethan pageantry, but gained in concentration, and has shown the best that the French ideals of the unities and declamation, qualified by English practical common sense, could do for English drama." [4]

Dryden's use of blank verse instead of rhyme in *All for Love,* because this permitted him to "perform more freely," illustrates the way in which he allowed his creative imagination and his common sense to affect his critical opinions. Thoroughly familiar with the dogmatic French critics and often occupied with assimilating their ideas to English practice and theory, he showed a wonderful catholicity of taste beyond any of his contemporaries. His *Of Dramatic Poesy* (1668) defends the older English drama when it was fashionable to consider even Shakespeare's plays barbarous in comparison with the refinements of the new age. Speaking of Jonson, Dryden says boldly: "If I would compare him with Shakespeare, I must acknowledge him the more correct poet, but Shakespeare the greater wit. Shakespeare was the Homer, or father of our dramatic poets; Jonson was the Virgil, the pattern of elaborate writing; I admire him, but I love Shakespeare." Equally unique is his warm praise of Chaucer. "As he is the father of English poetry, so I hold him in the same degree of veneration as the Grecians hold Homer, or the Romans Virgil. He is a perpetual fountain of good sense; learned in all the sciences, and therefore speaks properly on all subjects. As he knew what to say, so he knows also when to leave off—a continence which is practised by few writers, and scarcely by any of the ancients, excepting Virgil and Horace." (Preface to *Fables Ancient and Modern.*)

Dryden's verse satire has already been mentioned. He was equally accomplished in the lyric mode. His plays are jeweled with exquisite songs like "Beneath a myrtle shade" from *The Conquest of Granada* and "Ah fading joy" from *The Indian Emperor.* Dryden's more ambitious lyrics, such as "Alexander's Feast," all have the Baroque qualities of elaborate structure, majestic movement, graceful allusion to classical lore, and melting harmony of sound. They are the last of the great tradition of lyric verse which was established at the court of Henry VIII.

Among all of Dryden's services to his art we have him to thank most especially for inventing the modern prose style. One reads Dryden's essays today with no feeling that he belongs to any particular age. He found English prose built in the marmoreal style of Milton and Sir Thomas Browne; he rebuilt it in utilitarian brick. Eloquent and moving as is Browne's elegiac *Urn Burial* (1658), one cannot imagine how such involuted sentences and gorgeous imagery could be employed

---

4 C. G. Osgood, *The Voice of England,* Harper, 1935 (rev. ed., 1952), p. 277.

in the workaday business of the newspaper and the novel. Dryden forged a new instrument which journalists, biographers, historians, and critics have used ever since.

4. Eighteenth-Century England

When Dryden died in 1700 he was the revered master of a young generation of poets—Prior, Congreve, Addison, and Gay. Swift was thirty-three, Steele twenty-nine, and Pope a boy of twelve. No one was particularly aware that great changes, in society and in literature, were on their way. But closely bound as the two generations were in personal ties and ideals of art, they are in many respects far apart. In the first place a new bourgeois society, made rich by the commercial success during the forty years of comparative peace, had begun to acquire town and country houses, education, and a taste for the arts. They bought books, especially translations of the classics like Dryden's *Virgil* and later Pope's *Iliad* and *Odyssey* (which made Pope a rich man), because by this means at least they could obtain the superficies of the classical culture which had always been the mark of an English gentleman. It was no longer necessary, since this public existed, for a writer to fawn upon his patron. He could now make a living from the books he sold to this new circle of readers. Literature was being democratized.

These new-made gentlemen wanted to know how to behave genteelly—whence the great vogue of the essay dealing with manners, such as Addison and Steele wrote for their *Spectator* (1711-1714), and of courtesy books and complete letter-writers. But with all their zeal for self-culture, these new readers were decent folk. The rakish days of the Restoration receded rapidly into the past. In the 1690's a furious cleaning up of the drama took place, accelerated though not begun by the attack of a nonjuring clergyman, Jeremy Collier, in his *Short View of the Immorality and Profaneness of the English Stage* (1698). This was only one aspect of the general reform of manners which led even to the organization of societies to compel men to be good.

The new age had made up its mind about all the important problems that confront man. The scientific discoveries of Descartes and Newton in the past century gave men confidence that the laws which govern the operation of the great "world machine" could be ascertained by the instruments of mathematics and experimental investigation. Nature obeys her own laws which are invariable in their operation. Let man then study nature if he would bring order into human affairs. Lines 69-71 of Pope's *Essay on Criticism* read:

> First follow Nature, and your judgment frame
> By her just standard, which is still the same:
> Unerring Nature, still divinely bright,
> One clear, unchanged, and universal light.

This reasoning is the origin of the century's worship of nature. Its nature is not that of the romantics, however, but "regular" nature. In religion her worship led to natural religion or Deism which seeks to discover evidence of the First Cause in the physical universe. In political theory it induced men to believe in the social contract because that is the "natural" explanation of the origins of the state. Being true to nature meant in literature to follow the example of the classical poets, for they have most accurately observed her ways. By studying them one might learn the rules by which she can be imitated.

If we whose tastes have been formed in the last years of the romantic era, when temperamental self-expression has been the poet's aim, sometimes grow impatient with the eighteenth century's insistence that poets must know the "rules" for correct writing, we should recall that in Pope's time this was the road to poetic truth. As Pope says in his *Essay on Criticism* (1711):

> Those Rules of old discovered, not devised,
> Are Nature still, but Nature methodized;
> Nature, like liberty, is but restrained
> By the same laws which first herself ordained.

Alexander Pope (1688-1744) was the spokesman of the new generation, a position he rejoiced in because a poet in his day was supposed to voice the general opinions of men and not live remote from the concerns of the hour. A precocious boy, born to parents who were Catholics and so could not give him a university education, he amazed London by his *Pastorals,* published when he was twenty-one and written earlier. Three years later he gave further proof of his genius in his mock epic poem, *The Rape of the Lock* (1712), which satirizes a tempest-in-a-teapot scandal in high places caused by Lord Petre's wanton behavior in snipping off a lock of Arabella Fermor's hair.

But Mr. Pope was preparing himself for greater things. In 1711 he had published a didactic poem, the *Essay on Criticism,* which sums up the literary precepts by which poets and critics were supposed to guide themselves. Derived from Horace's *Ars poetica* and Boileau's *L'Art poétique,* the *Essay* contains little that is Pope's save the wit and the "numbers." The exception is a large one, for here one reads, "What oft was thought, but ne'er so well expressed." There could be no doubt when it appeared that Pope had earned the right to speak for his age.

From 1715 to 1726 he worked at his translations of the *Iliad* and the *Odyssey,* a feat of endurance which brought him a fortune equivalent to $300,000 and preeminence among contemporary writers. The translations are not Homer but Homer transformed by the current ideas about "Nature." As such they appealed to the pseudo-classism of the age and did much, of course, to determine its tone and direction.

In the early 1730's Pope invaded the larger subject of ethics with his *Essay on Man* (1732-1734) and the *Moral Essays* (1731-1735). The optimistic philosophy of his friend Henry St. John, Viscount Bolingbroke, attracted him, without his having assimilated it with any thoroughness, and he was enchanted with the prospect of poetizing it. The result was four verse epistles constituting the *Essay on Man.* They ramble along with little logical order, discoursing on man's relation to God and Virtue. Their purport accords with Deism, the popular religion of the day. The general theme is recapitulated in the last lines, addressed to Bolingbroke as his "guide, philosopher and friend." Urged by him, Pope says:

> I turned the tuneful art
> From sounds to things, from fancy to the heart;
> For Wit's false mirror held up Nature's light;
> Showed erring Pride, Whatever is, is Right;
> That Reason, Passion, answer one great aim;
> That true Self-love and Social are the same;
> That Virtue only makes our Bliss below;
> And all our Knowledge is, ourselves to know.

In these epistles Pope showed himself to be "a very great wit and a very indifferent philosopher," as St. John said of him on another occasion. They are important in the history of popular ideas, as a single fact about them proves: they have furnished more quotable lines to English-speaking people than any other work.

The *Moral Essays* are of another order. In them Pope showed the real bent of his genius. As a means of illustrating his ideas about man's ruling passion, woman's love of sway and the use of riches, he introduces inimitable satirical verse portraits of men and women he disliked. Pope's satire is energized by three qualities in him. Sickly in body and sensitive in mind, he showed towards his enemies, one must admit, the maliciousness of the physically weak. But controlled malice is no detriment to a satirist. More laudable was his acuteness in seeing the typical in the particular in the case of his victims. They are made to sum up all the age could display of the vice or folly they represent. Not of the age only, because Pope makes them universal. The great Duchess of Marlborough, redoubtable Sarah Churchill, the power behind Queen Anne's throne, is remembered as Pope's Atossa.

> Scarce once herself, by turns all Womankind!
> Who, with herself, or others, from her birth
> Finds all her life one warfare upon earth:
> Shines in exposing Knaves, and painting Fools,
> Yet is, whate'er she hates and ridicules.
> No thought advances, but her Eddy Brain
> Whisks it about, and down it goes again.
> Full sixty years the World has been her Trade,
> The wisest Fool much Time has ever made.
> From loveless youth to unrespected age,
> No Passion gratified except her Rage.
> So much the Fury still out-ran the Wit,
> The Pleasure missed her, and the Scandal hit.

These works of his later years, including the *Satires* (1733-1738) and the *Dunciad* which attacked in its two forms two enemies of Pope, are those we read with most delight today.

Pope belonged to the dominant literary coterie of his time. Poets sought society as instinctively as the romantics shunned it. They joined with one another in a common defense against fools and witlings, dined and wined together, published miscellanies and other works together. Until they quarreled in 1717 Pope

and Addison were intimate in the circle of the Queen Anne wits. Addison was
by nature stiff, timid and a little pompous, ready—as Pope spitefully said in his
Epistle to Dr. Arbuthnot, lines 201-202—to

> Damn with faint praise, assent with civil leer,
> And without sneering, teach the rest to sneer.

But the solidity of his character was an excellent balancing weight against mercurial Dick Steele, soldier of fortune, playwright and essayist. A lucky chance
brought them together in the promotion of *The Spectator* and the invention
(Steele's part) and elaboration (Addison's) of the stories and sayings of Sir
Roger de Coverley and his friends. This popular journal exercised a greater influence over the tastes and manners of the new gentleman class than any work
of the day.

In this company too were Matthew Prior (1664-1721) and the genial Dr.
Arbuthnot and John Gay (1685-1732) who made the conventional pastoral ridiculous in his *Shepherd's Week* and set London singing the songs he wrote for his
Beggar's Opera (1728), that travesty of the Italianate opera with highwaymen
and sluts as heroes and heroines.

Most illustrious of Pope's friends was Dean Swift (1667-1745) who left his
cathedral in Dublin now and again to foregather with his old companions in
London. Swift is the most tragic figure in English literature. Doomed as a child
to a poverty which seared his soul, kept a virtual exile in his Irish deanship—
possibly because his *Tale of a Tub* gave offense in high places—cursed with
physical infirmities which resulted finally in deafness, madness, and death, he
was driven to a very gloomy view of humanity. To Pope he wrote: "I hate and
detest that animal called man, although I heartily love John, Peter, Thomas and
so forth." This paradox was uttered in all sincerity. Swift was devoted to the mis-
treated Irish among whom his lot was cast. He labored to arouse England to a
sense of decency about the country she has repeatedly plundered and never understood. When one knows that Swift was tender as well as wrathfully indignant,
convivial, and witty, as well as merciless in his ridicule of fools, it is explicable
that his greatest work, *Gulliver's Travels* (1726), can be at the same time a tale
of wonderful adventure to hold a child rapt and for adults the fiercest indictment of human follies and animalism ever written.

The modern novel is such a familiar part of the lives of most people, even of
those who know nothing of literary origins, that it is difficult to imagine a time
when it did not exist. This is not to say that storytelling in some form has ever
ceased to delight listeners and readers. But the novel is a special kind of story
which came into being in England in 1740 when Samuel Richardson, a London
printer, published *Pamela, or Virtue Rewarded* and became famous in a day.
It is the first real novel because it develops, in prose, a story about ordinary people
and explores motives and works out the solution in accordance with the psychology of the characters.

In the days of Queen Elizabeth two types of stories in prose were produced.

The upper classes read rambling romantic tales, frequently with pastoral themes, like Robert Greene's *Pandosto* (1588) and Thomas Lodge's *Rosalynde* (1590). The most influential of these was Sir Philip Sidney's *Arcadia* (1580-1585) which combines pastoral and chivalric elements in an involved plot that is almost impossible to follow. Written to delight Sidney's sister, the Countess of Pembroke, the *Arcadia* is a reservoir of details imitated from the Greek romances, the old English and French metrical tales of chivalry, mixed with current ideas about morality, the education of the gentleman, language, architecture and even dress.

For the lower classes there were numerous collections of realistic tales like Thomas Deloney's *Jack of Newbury* and *The Gentle Craft* praising the occupations and pastimes of clothiers, weavers, cobblers, and other artisans. Shopkeepers and their wives read also debased prose versions of the medieval romances, the equivalent in their time of the sort of stuff which now crowds the pages of the "pulp" magazines.

In the seventeenth century gentlemen and ladies bought and read the heroic romances of Scudéry and La Calprenède, either in the original French or in translations of intolerable length. They reflect the generation's interest, shown also in the heroic plays, in moral distinctions and in the rules of literary art which were the constant subject of discussion in the French and English salons. Towards the end of the century a reaction took place against this bloodless heroic fiction. *Don Quixote,* frequently republished during the century, and Urquhart's translation of Rabelais (1653) brushed the heroic nonsense out of the heads of the English *précieuses*. Realistic "secret" histories purporting to be the memoirs of persons of quality became popular. "Character books"—collections of brief sketches of illustrious men or of dominant human types—biographies and memoirs increased the desire for prose fiction which was close to reality rather than the description of impossible doings in remote Parthias and Arcadias.

Without John Bunyan's *Pilgrim's Progress* (1678, 1684), one can almost say, there could have been no modern novel. Though a tinker and a simple devout man, he was the first to tell the story of man's struggle "through despair and doubt to the distant and imperfect vision of truth" in colloquial prose. Before Bunyan fiction which dealt with the lives of humble men was "low" and fit to be read only by the lower orders. But it was apparent, even to gentlemen readers, that his book had universal significance, though the hero was not heroic and the style was homely. Only the allegorical framework prevents *Pilgrim's Progress* from being a novel.

The fiction of Daniel Defoe (1660-1731) approaches the definition even closer. Defoe was a journalist whose pamphleteering was for hire by any party which asked his services and could pay. Some 250 works are supposed to have his hand in them but so subtle were his pseudonyms, as he changed from Whig to Tory and back again, that we will never be quite sure what may be called his. In 1719 he luckily hit upon the idea of making fiction out of the adventures of Alexander Selkirk, a Scotsman who had spent five years as a castaway on the island of Juan Fernandez off Chile. It hardly occurred to Defoe, engaged in exploiting for gain the century's taste for travel books, that he was writing what was to be one of the most famous prose works in the language. *Robinson Crusoe* (1719-1720) is notable for the way it induces its readers to believe, by its minute factual detail, that every word is true. Many have supposed it sober fact. Fascinating, too, is Defoe's cleverness, shown in other books, in playing upon two bourgeois traits—acquisitiveness and ingenuity. Who ever tired of watching Crusoe salvage stores from the wreck or invent means for making his life easier?

When Richardson burst upon polite readers with *Pamela* in 1740 they had been taught by these earlier writers to enjoy stories about ordinary mortals who have extraordinary accidents befall them. Richardson's novel is the slow-moving account of the attempts of a gentleman, a Mr. B, to seduce his virtuous servinggirl Pamela. Virtue is triumphant, for Mr. B can win her on no other terms but marriage.

To Richardson and his class this was a highly edifying and quite probable conclusion. To a certain Henry Fielding, dramatist, lawyer, and cosmopolitan, it was hypocritical nonsense and fit subject for burlesque. But *Pamela,* in spite of the ridicule it received in certain quarters, was a mad success and required an immediate sequel. It was translated and imitated in France and Germany. Its importance in the history of the novel arises from a number of innovations for which it was responsible: the story is told mainly by the realistic device of letters which pass between Pamela and her family; the plot unfolds inevitably from the characters of Mr. B and Pamela; motives and emotions are minutely analyzed.

Richardson's next novel, *Clarissa Harlowe* (1748), is the history of the abduction and violation of the heroine by a finished scoundrel Lovelace. In spite of the tears and imploring letters of his female readers, Richardson allowed her to die. In *Sir Charles Grandison* (1753) he atones for Lovelace by creating in the hero a male paragon. The book was, incidentally, a rebuke to Fielding for allowing his hero, Tom Jones, to be a sad sinner with women.

Fielding, whose career as a writer of comedies and political *revues* was ended by the Licensing Act of 1737, tried to put Richardson in his place by burlesquing *Pamela* in his *Joseph Andrews* (1742). The good Joseph, footman to Lady Booby, is a brother of Pamela and suffers wicked importunings from his mistress like those endured by Pamela from Mr. B. Fielding soon forgot the burlesque in his fascination with the picaresque adventures of Joseph (who is no prig but a hard-fisted, curly-headed young Adonis) and his friend Parson Adams, an innocent country clergyman whose natural goodness shames the rogues and hypocrites he encounters.

Joseph Andrews was a prelude to Fielding's masterpiece, *The History of Tom Jones* (1749), by many considered the greatest novel in the language. The complex but deftly constructed story was calculated to show how a warm-blooded, honest English youth really behaves. Repudiated by his foster-father Allworthy, in love with Sophia Western who is destined for another, Tom sets out on his travels. Sophia follows him to London where Tom falls from her favor through his infidelities. All ends happily with the discovery of Tom's identity: he is the natural son of Allworthy's sister. No outline of the plot can give any idea of the panoramic view of English manners displayed by the book; or of its rich humor and the author's sympathy with all kinds of men. Fielding in his next novel, *Amelia* (1751), the story of a long-suffering wife, lapses at times into the sentimentality he derided in Richardson. But *Tom Jones* exemplifies all the best qualities of the century: its tolerance, its common sense, its love of good living.

Two other names must be remembered in connection with the eighteenth-century novel: Laurence Sterne (1713-1768) and Tobias Smollett (1721-1771). Sterne was an eccentric clergyman from a Yorkshire parish whose *Life and Opinions of Tristram Shandy, Gent.* (1760-1767) captivated London and all Europe. The book is indescribable because the book is the man—who once described himself in these words: "His character was,—he loved a jest in his heart. . . . He was as mercurial and sublimated a composition, as heteroclite a creature in all his declensions,—with as much life and whim, and *gaité de cœur* about him, as the kindliest climate could have engendered and put together." The novel (if it is a novel) essays to tell what its title promises, but the hero is not born until near the end of Book III and the opinions expressed are those of everybody but Tristram Shandy. But my Uncle Toby and his servant Corporal Trim and the Widow Wadman are very much alive, and the deliberate confusions and surprises of the narrative make it one of the most fascinating of all whimsical books. Sterne's *A Sentimental Journey through France and Italy* (1768)—characteristically the hero never gets to Italy—involves the narrator in a series of adventures, amorous and other, in which his delicate sensibilities are constantly agitated. But Sterne's sentimentalism is always shaded with a tone of mockery which his many imitators at home and abroad could not catch.

Smollett was cast in a rougher mold. His life at sea as a surgeon's mate gave him materials for the first English novel of the sea, *Roderick Random* (1748). His *Peregrine Pickle* (1751) takes the hero on the Grand Tour; *Humphry Clinker* (1771) relates the adventures of Mr. Matthew Bramble's family party as they journey through England and Scotland. Smollett looks backward to Defoe and forward to Dickens who admired him greatly. His people, especially those of the rougher breed, are vigorously drawn. No English novelist has ever handled with more forthrightness scenes which make the reader hold his nose. One does not forget the nauseating dinner after the Roman manner in *Peregrine Pickle* or the description in *Humphry Clinker* of the King's Bath where all and sundry in various stages of disease swim together.

When Samuel Johnson (1709-1784) journeyed up to London from the provincial city of Litchfield in 1737, a young man of twenty-eight with no assets except a stout heart and a quick pen, Pope was within seven years of his end. Steele and Addison were dead and so were Defoe, Arbuthnot, Gay, and Prior. But it was still the Age of Pope, and poets wrote in the heroic couplet on didactic themes, obeyed the rules, and followed nature.

Johnson was no exception. His *London*, a lively poem in imitation of Juvenal's third satire, won the praise of Pope when it was published in 1738. The critics heralded the arrival of a new poet whose skill with the heroic couplet was hardly less than Pope's and who "followed nature" wisely. The *Vanity of Human*

Wishes (1749) vindicated their judgment. This was another imitation of Juvenal; and some of the lines:

> Deign on the passing world to turn thine eyes,
> And pause a while from learning to be wise;
> There mark what ills the scholar's life assail,
> Toil, envy, want, the patron, and the jail

had the epigrammatic ring of Pope or Dryden and in addition reflected a deeper experience of the lower classes in society.

But Dr. Johnson was not to continue poet. For some years he was constantly engaged in hack-writing for the publishers, which brought him little income but much experience. The authentic voice of the great critic of literature and morals is first heard in his *Rambler*. From *The Spectator* and similar books he had conceived the idea of a series of periodical essays and the *Rambler* (1750-1752) was his first attempt. The elegance of its style and the wisdom of its contents established Johnson's reputation. He followed it later with his *Idler*. At this time, too, he was working on the *Dictionary,* one of the great achievements of the century.

In 1759 Johnson's aged mother died. In order to defray the expense of her funeral he wrote his Oriental tale, *Rasselas*. It is a moral allegory, like Voltaire's *Candide,* in which the prince and his teacher set out from the Happy Valley to find happiness but find only illusion.

The main productions of Johnson's later years were his edition of Shakespeare and his *Lives of the Poets.* For some years there had been barely audible rumblings of dissatisfaction with the artificial polish and urbanity of literature. It was a bit *too* perfect and there was bound to be some sort of reaction. In the *Preface* to Shakespeare Johnson made one of the first attacks upon convention by arguing against the rules of the drama, the so-called "unities." And in the *Lives* he made one of the early contributions to historical criticism by concentrating chiefly upon the "biographical part of literature."

Though he wrote little during the last twenty years of his life, Johnson talked much and his talk was good. In 1764 the Literary Club had been founded, mainly under his leadership. The club met once a week, usually for dinner, at one of the taverns, and there Johnson dominated the conversation of as distinguished a group of men as ever met together. Burke, the great politician; Goldsmith, the poet and playwright; Reynolds, painter and critic; Garrick, the actor and dramatist; Fox, the young orator; Gibbon, the great historian; and many others, not the least of whom was James Boswell, met with Johnson on these evenings for good talk and good food. Boswell had met Johnson in 1762 and soon decided to keep a full record of his acquaintance in order to make a biography of his master.

Johnson died in 1784 and Boswell published his *Life* seven years later. Into it he wrote, with a genius which has often been slighted, the story and above all the personality of one of England's great men of letters. In the conversations of Johnson which Boswell recorded one finds a man who stood four-square for the Christian virtues, but whose occasional doubts of Christian theology and of the conventions of literature and morals make it possible for the discerning reader to sense the coming of radical changes in society and the arts.

Two members of Johnson's circle were responsible for a brief interlude of gaiety in the generally dull dramatic history of the century—Goldsmith and Sheridan. Even before Collier's attack on the immorality of the comedy of the Restoration the drama had shown signs of reform. The astute actor-player-manager Colley Cibber steered into safer waters with his *Love's Last Shift* (1698) which introduces the ingenious trick of a fifth-act conversion to decency so that the audience may enjoy four acts of the rake's progress with a clear conscience, knowing that reform is to follow before the curtain falls.

There were some attempts by playwrights like Mrs. Centlivre to resist the incoming tide of noble renunciations and genteel sentiments dictated by an overflowing heart, but with the vogue created by Steele's *The Conscious Lovers* (1722), "laughing comedy," as Goldsmith later called it, was banished from the stage.

Goldsmith's *Good-Natured Man* (1768) exhibited some of the sentimentalism he so much derided, but it was entirely missing from *She Stoops to Conquer* (1773) which vies with Wilde's *The Importance of Being Earnest* (1895) for the distinction of being the greatest of English farces.

Even Sheridan, especially in the part of Joseph Surface in *The School for Scandal* (1777), shows how difficult it was to escape the sentimental virus. But this play, and *The Critic* (1779), which ridicules professional puff-writers, for a moment restored something like the wit of the Restoration to the theater. Sentimentalism closed in immediately when Sheridan deserted the stage for the House of Commons and discovered still richer fields as the humanitarianism of the age taught the generation to feel for the poor, the enslaved, prisoners, Jews, Methodists and all the rejected of men.

5. *Eighteenth-Century France*

The golden age came to an end with unsuccessful wars and the death of the old king. Louis XV had neither the power nor the wit of his illustrious predecessor Louis XIV and the court sun which had lighted literature set with the Grand Monarque. The world in which the artist had lived was no longer the best of all possible worlds. He began to look about him with a critical eye.

The seventeenth-century writers were realists and rationalists. They were very well aware of the imperfections of mankind, of the misery of the peasant and the hard lot of the bourgeoisie, but it had not occurred to them to do anything about it. As their own lot grew less pleasant the literary men began to comprehend the fundamental sickness of the national life and, as the rational mind made sensitive always does, they became reformers. The literature of the eighteenth century is a literature of propaganda. Its culmination was the French Revolution.

The propaganda began before the death of the king and literary historians are undecided whether to regard the Archbishop of Cambrai, François de Salignac de LaMothe-Fénelon (1651-1715) as belonging to the old age or the new. Fénelon was appointed tutor to the Duc de Bourgogne, grandson to Louis XIV and heir to the throne, though he died too early. For the edification of his charge Fénelon wrote an amusing, fantastical, moral, historical romance, *Télémaque,* which set forth the whole duty of the perfect prince, even to the revolutionary doctrine that a monarch exists for the good of his people. If the little Duke had come to the throne he might well have changed the course of history, for he was genuinely influenced by Fénelon's teaching. A man of the world who was at the same time a Christian mystic, Fénelon had that rare and charming "spiritual coquetry" which was so large an element in the power of George Herbert and of Cardinal Newman. In the letters which he wrote to his host of aristocratic confidants, helping them to live in the world but not of it, one can still feel the force of a sweet and compelling personality.

It is by virtue of his Christianity that Fénelon belongs to the old age rather than the new. The eighteenth century was profoundly skeptical, even to atheism. Its writers were concerned with the well-being of man in this world rather than the next. Just before *Télémaque* there appeared a curious and learned compendium of skepticism, the *Dictionnaire historique et classique* of Pierre Bayle (1647-1706). Bayle had no thesis to set forth. He simply set down the reasons for and against the ideas of the time, especially the religious and theological ideas, but in this dispassionate setting down he established the principle of freedom of individual judgment and set up conscience as the basis of morality. Bayle had no skill as a writer, no ability at all to organize and compose his work— the footnotes occupy ten times as much space as the text—but his *Dictionnaire* was, as the French literary historian Lanson observed, one of the essential books of the eighteenth century; the delight of Voltaire, of Frederick II, of all the unbelievers; the arsenal from which comes almost all the erudition philosophical, historical, philological, theological, with which the philosophers armed themselves against the church and religion.

A succinct expression of the new point of view toward the political, religious, and social ideas on which the state rested was not the province of Bayle. It was made first by Charles de Secondat de Montesquieu (1689-1755). In his *Lettres persanes,* under the guise of a correspondence between two Eastern travelers and their friends at home, he examines the structure of French society, its inequalities, corruption, barbarisms and, indicating what he thinks a good constitution should be, points out the fatal faults of all despotisms. But the *Lettres persanes* is no mere political thesis. Montesquieu was a writer of his time in style as well as matter and the literary man of the eighteenth century was writing for as wide an audience as he could compel. He was no longer content with the select circle of the court. He wanted to force his ideas upon the attention of a frivolous Parisian populace, and to make them palatable he was ready to add not only wit but lush romantic adventures and even a spice of licentiousness. Occasionally Montesquieu's wit ran away with him. It did again and again in his most important work, *L'Esprit des lois,* which Mme du Deffand rechristened neatly *De l'esprit sur les lois.* That book is a curious example of the power of the written word. In describing English political institutions Montesquieu presented them as an illustration of one of his own favorite theories: that the three powers of a government, judicial, legislative, executive, should be separate. He assumed what he wanted to find; as a matter of fact the powers of the English executive and legislative are interlocked but so great was his reputation that his view of the British constitution was accepted as the correct one and it was with that theory that the makers of the American Constitution worked.

The generation of writers who grew up under the influence of Montesquieu were known as the *Philosophes* or *Encyclopédistes*. They were not directly concerned, most of them, with political reform but they were earnest in their desire to enlighten mankind, to sweep away ancient superstitions and let in the clear light of reason. They thought out so carefully the idea of the perfect state and the rights and duties of its citizens that when the Revolution came it found ready an ideal plan on which to work.

Their weapons of learning the *Philosophes* massed for a combined attack on the powers of darkness in the great *Encyclopaedia* whose seventeen volumes were published over a period of twenty years (1751-1772), in the face of constant government opposition. The prospectus, written by Diderot (1713-1784) without whose energy and synthesizing power the work would never have been accomplished, stated that its purpose was "to make a general picture of the accomplishments of the human spirit in all forms and through all the ages."

The roster of the Encyclopaedists is a distinguished one. It includes the naturalist Buffon, the great mathematician d'Alembert, the philosophers, Helvétius, Vauvenargues, Condillac, Condorcet, as well as Montesquieu and Rousseau, but most distinguished of the whole company was François-Marie Arouet who called himself Voltaire (1694-1778).

It is difficult to realize today that Voltaire's contemporaries knew him chiefly as a dramatist and poet, a rhetorical epic poet whose *Henriade* was considered superior to the work of Milton, and a writer of violently exciting melodramatic plays—most famous were *Zaïre* and *Mérope*—so closely calculated to the fashion of the moment that they have almost no interest at all today. Voltaire had genius but it was not until he was more than thirty that he found its true channel. A quarrel with the Chevalier de Rohan made it necessary for him to take refuge for a time in England and his first sight of that country, on which the cultivated Frenchman of the period was not accustomed to expend a second thought, amazed him. Here was a land prosperous, peaceful, cultivated, contented. All the problems under which France labored, England seemed to have solved by virtue of her system of government, her free institutions and the freedom of thought which she permitted. The *Lettres philosophiques* (1734) which Voltaire published shortly after his return were ostensibly a description of 'his sojourn in England; but besides being brilliant journalism they were also brilliant propaganda for the English way of life, so brilliant indeed that the French government swiftly consigned them to the hangman's flames and Voltaire sought a second exile, this time at Cirey in the house of Mme de Châtelet. There he produced his own plays and worked at a universal history, an introductory chapter of which, *Essai sur les mœurs*, was published in 1756. In his *Histoire de Charles XII* and *Le Siècle de*

Louis XIV, Voltaire showed himself the first of modern historians in his painstaking study of documents and sources but chiefly in his conception that history should not be a record of the acts of kings but an explanation and description of the development of civilization.

When Mme de Châtelet died Voltaire accepted the invitation of Frederick the Great, King of Prussia, to visit him at Potsdam. It was an extraordinary friendship but there was on each side so much vitality and egotism that peace was impossible. After some violent quarrels Voltaire took himself off. He could not live in France with any degree of safety but after some miserable wandering he purchased the property of Ferney in Switzerland, close by the French border, and began at sixty the most brilliant period of his life. Voltaire had been born a *petit bourgeois;* by his wit he had become the companion of nobles and princes; by the practical side of his clear-headed materialism he had amassed the largest fortune that, up to that time, had ever been in the hands of a literary man. Now he could begin the work that he had really at heart, teaching to his countrymen the sovereign importance of reason.

The great barrier to enlightenment was in Voltaire's mind the superstition engendered by religion. He comprehended none of the higher qualities of the truly religious mind; he saw only the destructive power of a corrupt church and he fought it with all his phenomenal energy, wit, and irony. There began to pour into Paris a hail of highly amusing and exciting little pamphlets, essays, poems, plays, dialogues, even a *Dictionnaire philosophique.* These appeared over a fantastic variety of signatures—"The Abbé Bazin, and his Nephew," "The Almoners of the King of Prussia," "Hume," "The Emperor of China"—but, though Voltaire took great delight in writing to his friends, speculating as to who some of these mysterious persons might be, no one, of course, had the least difficulty in recognizing the hand of the Patriarch of Ferney. The government was powerless to stop the pamphlets and they sold by the hundreds. Voltaire was fighting against religion, against intolerance, against injustice. If a case arose of the persecution of a Protestant or the excommunication of a comedienne, he cried the facts abroad and would not let injustice rest. He fought, too, against the shallow optimism of so many of his contemporaries and in that cause produced his most famous book, *Candide* (1759), that scintillating tale of horrors which ends with the well-known bit of common sense: "Il faut cultiver notre jardin" (We must cultivate our garden).

His work of enlightenment Voltaire carried on also by means of an enormous correspondence, as keen, as witty, as single in its aim, as his printed works. More than 10,000 letters he is said to have written to correspondents living all about the globe and ranging from cardinals and kings to mathematicians and ladies of the theater. He became a cult, a legend.

When Louis XV died Paris was once more open to Voltaire and his appearance there in February, 1778, was an apotheosis. He was waited upon by delegations from the Academy and the *Comédie Française,* by nobles and princes of the blood. When he presented himself at a performance of his *Irène* the populace went mad with joy. The excitement and emotion of those three months was more than the old man could bear. At the height of his triumph he died.

The tragedies of Voltaire were not his important work and the other tragedians of the age were very minor dramatists, but among the writers of comedy there were two of importance and charm. Marivaux (1688-1763) set upon the stage the exquisitely colored version of contemporary life which we see in the paintings of Watteau and he brought to comedy a new theme. Though Racine had depicted great tragic passions, for Molière love was only a sort of secondary plot complication. Marivaux wrote comedies in which love was the main theme and in which the psychology, especially the feminine psychology, was subtle, charming, and sure. Some thirty-two plays stand to his credit but the two greatest comedies of the century were written by Beaumarchais (1732-1799).

He was a mad, paradoxical, fantastic figure very like his own *Barbier de Séville* who is the principal character also of that still more important play *Le Mariage de Figaro*. Full of rapid witty dialogue and lively action, that play is primarily a political satire in which Figaro, symbol of the rising bourgeoisie, mocks, dupes, and controls all the other artificial characters who represent the doomed aristocracy. "Because you are a great lord you think yourself a great genius; . . . you have taken the trouble to be born, nothing more; . . . while I, good God! . . ." cries Figaro to the count. It is little wonder that for three years the censors declined to permit the production of the play, but popular opinion was with Beaumarchais and when it finally came to the stage there was virtually a riot of enthusiasm.

The realism which the theater, partly because of technical deficiencies in stage setting, was not able to attain, was the great achievement of the eighteenth-century novel. Though it had been held in slight esteem by the classicists of the golden age the novel precisely suited the new century's worldliness (*esprit mondain*). Readers were delighted with details of character, manners, dress, furniture, and they could devour at the same time large doses of sentiment and morality. Marivaux was far more realistic in his novels than in his plays and though in the greater freedom of space his psychology was sometimes rather tiresomely minute, the principal characters in the *Vie de Marianne* and the *Paysan parvenu* are no longer types but real individuals. They mark a definite advance over LeSage's (1668-1747) *Gil Blas,* who had to go through so many variegated adventures that he needed a very flexible personality. LeSage himself is a landmark, however, as the first important man of letters who, without patron or sinecure, undertook to support himself by his pen. LeSage was strongly influenced in the construction of his tales by the picaresque novel of Spain. The other strong current of influence, from England, is most clearly discernible in the Abbé Prévost (1697-1763), who translated *Pamela* and *Clarissa Harlowe*. Once, however, he freed himself entirely from the power of Richardson and wrote in his own vein a little masterpiece, *Manon Lescaut.*

Almost the only real poet in a prose age was André Chénier (1762-1794), a true classicist who took Malherbe and the Greek and Latin writers for his models. He was in sympathy with the Revolution but opposed to the Terror and was sent to the guillotine two days before the fall of Robespierre. By a curious twist of fate his work was "discovered" some twenty years after his death by the romanticists of the nineteenth century who hailed him as a precursor because, born in Constantinople and half Greek, he wrote with genuine emotion on themes which the pseudo-classicists of his day approached by way of books and of pure reason.

Jean-Jacques Rousseau (1712-1778) was a novelist, an encyclopedist, a revolutionary, yet it is impossible to fit him into any of those categories, for he was in revolt not merely against French society as it was constituted in his day but against the whole structure of civilization. Man, Rousseau believed, was by nature free, innocent, and happy; his wickedness, his unhappiness, his slavery are all products of the artificial structure he has built up around him.

An elaborate demonstration of his thesis Rousseau made in a remarkable book, his *Confessions* (1781-1788), a completely frank, outspoken, analytical autobiography such as the world up to that time had never seen. He described himself as the natural man corrupted by civilization. He was born in Switzerland where he was brought up by his father, a watch-maker with an inordinate love for romantic novels, who eventually abandoned his son. Rousseau's schooling and apprenticeship were heterogeneous, his attempts to earn a living spasmodic. He drifted about France as a penniless adventurer, returning now and again to the patronage of the beneficent Mme de Warens who had had him taught music and converted, temporarily, to Catholicism. Arriving in Paris in 1741 with fifteen louis in his pocket Rousseau wrote articles on music for the Encyclopedia, established literary and court connections and began to make his fortune. When the Academy of Dijon announced a competition on the question: Has the progress of the sciences and the arts corrupted or purified society? Rousseau wrote an answer which made him famous overnight. There followed ten years of fame and brilliant literary achievement, unsuccessful attempts to find congenial solitudes in which to write, and an endless series of difficulties with patrons, mistresses, and friends, precipitated by a jealous instability of temperament which became at last absolute madness. The natural man, according to his thesis, was ruined by the pressure of a corrupting society.

The *Confessions* were revolutionary not only in their doctrine and in their frankness; they were completely novel in their introspection, their analysis of sentiments and intimate emotions which the rest of the rational eighteenth century would never have thought worth noting, much less describing in detail. What seemed to Rousseau's contemporaries an extraordinary, though they found it a fascinating, document seems to us the first chapter in a long, rich record of the human soul which we are still writing today. And the style in which the emotions and sentiments are analyzed is as romantic, as lyric, as a poem of the nineteenth century.

Rousseau did not believe that one could really get back to the complete innocence of the natural man, the noble savage whom he unscientifically imagined, but he thought that human happiness might be greatly increased by an approximation to that primitive ideal. He wrote his *La Nouvelle Héloïse* (1761) to show that each of us can re-create in himself the natural man. He wrote *Émile* (1762) to show how the natural man may be developed by education. He wrote *Le Contrat social* (1762) to show how society can restore itself by reversion to the principles on which it was originally built.

La Nouvelle Héloïse was the first of a long line of novels about the natural man which were immensely popular with the romantics of the early nineteenth century. The other important eighteenth-century example is Bernardin de Saint-Pierre's *Paul et Virginie* (1787).

Émile, which scandalized the eighteenth century, seems to the graduate of a modern progressive school only slightly exaggerated. Émile is kept until the age of twelve a little savage, his bodily strength and skill developed, his senses trained, no paternal discipline exerted upon him, his mind left quite virgin of cultivation. And then his mind is trained for years before his preceptor presents to him the idea of God, Rousseau's Providence-God who is the basis of all truly social morality.

In *Le Contrat social* Rousseau demonstrated an ideal, to which he thought the small state like his native Switzerland might most readily attain, a society in which the individual finds freedom by submitting to the central authority created by all the citizens for their mutual protection and guidance, but "The right which the social pact gives to sovereigns over their subjects does not extend beyond the bounds of public usefulness." A simple phrase but, when one interprets "usefulness" in the highest sense, a phrase that ushers in the Revolution.

6. *The Beginnings of Romanticism*

The gradations by which the ideas and attitudes of one age pass over into a quite different set of responses in the next age are so slight, when viewed closely, as to be almost imperceptible. Yet it is perfectly apparent that the literary and artistic tastes of an English gentleman of 1790 were vastly different from those of his great-grandfather flourishing in 1700. Gradually an attitude towards art and life which we now call Romantic had supplanted the neoclassical preferences of the age of Pope.

There are innumerable ways of perceiving this change because it was so pervasive. The earlier age believed that to display emotion was vulgar. The new age thought sensibility the mark of true refinement. In the drama, in poetry, in fiction, the author's aim was now to arouse pity for the poor, the hopeless, and the weak. Tears flow freely and abundantly. The heart rules the head. The most popular novel of one season was Mackenzie's *The Man of Feeling* (1771), in which the hero is possessed of so delicate a sensibility that only on his deathbed does he deem it proper to speak of his passion for the lady of his heart. The words "sentimental, sentimentality, sensibility," are now honorable just as "reasonable, common sense, regular," were fifty years earlier.

This desire to be harrowed by one's feelings until tears of joy or compassion or sorrow flow gave birth to new literary forms. A large group of melancholy poems appeared, the work of the so-called "graveyard school," to give readers the pleasant thrill of meditative grief. Blair's *The Grave* (1743), Young's *Night*

Thoughts (1741-1745), and the most widely known English poem, Gray's *Elegy in a Country Churchyard* (1751), are the chief examples. A whole literature of the sublime emerges, for sublimity is the noblest of the emotions.

In their search for more violent sensations with which to please their readers, authors discovered the possibilities of gothic horror. Earlier in the century "gothick" had been an synonym for barbarous. Gothic architecture was the product of the "Dark Ages," as unfit as the literature contemporary with it for an enlightened society. Cathedral chapters busily tore out priceless stained glass and replaced it with clear panes, broke down altar tombs and carried off chapels to the junk pile. Noblemen refaced their Tudor houses with neoclassical façades.

But that day was past. Now the murky gloom of great crumbling ruins supplied an atmosphere full of delicious sensations of melanacholy and apprehension. Instigated by the dilettante Horace Walpole who built himself a lath and plaster gothic castle on his estate at Strawberry Hill near London, a craze for building in the gothic style swept the country. If you could not have a castle, you could at least afford a sham ruined hermit's cell in your garden. Walpole initiated the vogue of the gothic romance with his *Castle of Otranto* in 1764. A paltry tale, in which portraits walk from their frames and a ghostly giant in medieval armor terrifies and mystifies the inhabitants of the castle, it was so horrible that it made Walpole's friend the poet Gray and his fellow dons at Cambridge "to cry a little" and to be "afraid to go to bed o' nights." A flood of gothic tales of terror poured out. The public was not appeased until the nineteenth century was half over, as Poe's *Fall of the House of Usher* witnesses. The most influential of these novels was Anne Radcliffe's *The Mysteries of Udolpho*. As a sample of Mrs. Radcliffe's style when she is being most effectively harrowing, listen to the following.

> It seemed to conceal a recess of the chamber; she wished, yet dreaded, to lift it, and to discover what it veiled; twice she was withheld by a recollection of the terrible spectacle her daring hand had formerly unveiled in an apartment of the castle, till, suddenly conjecturing that it concealed the body of her murdered aunt, she seized it in a fit of desperation, and drew it aside. Beyond appeared a corpse stretched on a kind of low couch which was crimsoned with human blood, as was the floor beneath. The features, deformed by death, were ghastly and horrible, and more than one livid wound appeared in the face. Emily, bending over the body, gazed, for a moment, with an eager, frenzied eye; but, in the next, the lamp dropped from her hand, and she fell senseless at the foot of the couch.

What delicious nonsense Gay or Addison would have thought this!

The gothic romance is only one indication of the tendency during these years to look backward into the Middle Ages instead of to classical times for ideas and inspiration. Chaucer and the sixteenth-century poets, especially Spenser, were rehabilitated. Their faults were now readily excused because they possessed something greater than a knowledge of the rules, namely "original genius." Young in his *Conjectures on Original Composition* (1759) boldly asserts that the imitation of the classics has crushed original genius and attacks many of the revered works of the neoclassical years, like Addison's *Cato*. This preference for originality led to a search for undiscovered geniuses especially among humble poets—"mute, inglorious Miltons"—and made possible the two great literary hoaxes of the time: Macpherson's *Ossian* (1760) which purported to be translations of primitive Gaelic poems, and the Rowley Poems (1764 ff.) of the marvelous boy Thomas Chatterton. This lad of eighteen, who took his life with poison when faced with starvation in London, deceived some into believing that his imitations of Chaucer were actual medieval verses. Most important was the beginning of the romantic enthusiasm for the old English ballads, instigated by Bishop Percy's publication in *Reliques of Ancient English Poetry* (1765) of a collection of them which he put together from various sources.

As the century moved on a remarkable change in the poet's attitude towards external nature evolved. In spite of their constant arguments about "Nature," meaning the "world machine," the reason and order which prevails everywhere in the universe, the poets of Pope's day saw little in the fields and streams except a pleasant background to man's activities. When Addison crossed the Alps on the Grand Tour he was in haste to get to Italy and was quite unmoved by the sublime scenery. James Thomson (1700-1748) disguises under the traditional generalized language used in descriptions of nature his often genuine appreciation of the mystery of the changing seasons. Shenstone (1714-1763) was one of the first to watch the moods of nature with the eye of a lover. He is in a way comparable to the Barbizon painters of the next century who took their easels into the open air.

The time had to come when poets, impressed by what Wordsworth calls "the infinite variety of natural appearances," would wish and would dare in their verse to dwell on the individual aspects of nature, to describe a particular bird of a known species singing on a particular branch instead of speaking always of the "feathered choir" or—when condescending to the fish—of the "finny tribe." This time arrived with the poetry of William Cowper (1731-1800) whose six books of *The Task* celebrate the delights of his secluded rural life at Olney in Buckinghamshire. Goldsmith in his *Deserted Village* (1770) made familiar the sights and sounds of Auburn, "loveliest village of the plain."

In the poetry of Robert Burns (1759-1796), the original genius the age had long awaited, the new feeling for nature reached its highest expression. Whether he writes of the "twa dogs" Luath and Caesar or of a mountain daisy or of the old farmer saluting on New Year's morning his old mare Maggie or of a field mouse—"wee, sleekit, cow'rin, tim'rous beastie"—turned up by his plowshare, Burns makes man feel "Nature's social union."

So the stream widened and deepened. Each new poet found new occasion for poetic inspiration until the worship of nature—for that is what it came to—became involved in the democratic tendencies of the age, in the nostalgia for the golden age, the admiration for primitive man, the tender regard for dumb animals, and the belief in the superiority of poets who lived in the time of man's innocence.

7. Eighteenth-Century Germany

German literature in the eighteenth century is of little importance until the last quarter is reached. Earlier the patrons of the art affected to prefer English and French works to those of native writers. While Frederick the Great was speaking French with his distinguished protégé Voltaire at Potsdam, the greatest German epicist Klopstock (1724-1803) was supported by a pension given him by the King of Denmark. Schiller in 1800 lamented in "The German Muse" that in Frederick's reign German poetry had turned "away from his throne all unheeded and scorned."

Gottfried Lessing (1729-1781) deserves the title of the second founder of German literature, Luther being the first. By his vigorous criticism of French neoclassical tragedy and his advocacy of the freedom of Shakespearean type in a series of weekly articles, collected under the title *Hamburgische Dramaturgie* (1767-1768), he broke down the tyranny of the rules. His own dramas, especially *Nathan der Weise* (1779) which pleads for tolerance towards the Jews, exemplify his theories. His fine comedy *Minna von Barnhelm* (1767) is the first landmark in the nascent German drama to which Lessing, Goethe, and Schiller contributed their most enduring work.

In 1776 a now forgotten dramatist named Klinger named one of his plays *Sturm und Drang (Storm and Stress)*. It was an ill-made, extravagant affair about a deadly Scottish feud but the title provided a rallying cry for a generation of writers determined to recover German culture from foreign domination. J. G. Herder (1744-1803), poet and critic, the young Schiller (1759-1805), and Johann Wolfgang von Goethe (1749-1832) were ardent supporters of the movement. Students of the universities flocked to it. At Göttingen a "Dichterbund" (Poets' Club) was formed with the aim of making German poetry anew by bringing it close to the people in style and spirit.

Friedrich Schiller was by temperament a lover of heroic deeds and generous actions. All his historical dramas evince his romantic passion for liberty. The youthful *Die Räuber (The Robbers)* (1781) defends the brigandage of Karl Moor, driven from home by a cruel brother, and captain of a band of voluntary outlaws who are sick of the knavery of civilized society. When the girl he loves refuses to marry him because of the blood on his hands, Karl does one final generous act by allowing himself to be captured so that that blood-money may be given to a poor workman with a family of eleven. The Duke of Württemberg commanded Schiller, because of the outspokenness of his play, to write no more dramas and to stay out of Mannheim where the play was produced—neither of which injunctions Schiller obeyed.

From 1789 Schiller was under the patronage of the great Karl August, Duke of Weimar, first as Professor of History at Jena and after 1799 as a court dramatist, residing in Weimar to be near the duke and Goethe. The plays of these last years are full of eloquent defenses of civil liberty and have for their principal character usually some historical personage who championed and suffered in a great cause. The Wallenstein trilogy, a favorite with Coleridge who translated it into English (1800), deals with the attempted revolt during the Thirty Years' War of the Austrian general who, disgusted with the stupidity and ingratitude of his superiors, is on the point of going over to the enemy when assassins stab him to death. *Die Jungfrau von Orleans* (*The Maid of Orléans*) (1802) was written to rehabilitate Joan of Arc whose glorious memory, Schiller felt, had been defamed by Shakespeare's *Henry VI* and Voltaire's *La Pucelle*. So tender is he with his altogether heroic and superhuman Joan that he cannot bear to let her die as history records she did, at the stake. Schiller's Maid of Orléans must perish on the field of battle after having broken from prison and once more rescued her king from danger.

Wilhelm Tell (1804), the last play, depicts the attempts of the Swiss to escape from the Austrian oppression. Schiller was not alone in directing his dramas towards historical examples of struggles against tyranny. Patriotic uprisings, imprisonments, martyrdoms, and popular riots form the principal scenes of the state dramas of the period.

When Schiller came to reside for the last six years of his life in Weimar, Goethe had already been the chief ornament of the ducal court since 1775. From that date until his death in 1832 he lived near the palace, either in his garden house in the park or in the mansion in the Frauenplan, now a Goethe museum. Born to a Frankfort family in easy circumstances, the young Goethe found the fine arts and natural sciences more to his liking than the law which he went to the University of Leipzig to study. In this city occurred the first of those affairs of the heart which from eighteen to eighty furnished so much of the material for his writing.

He took his law degree but turned at once to authorship at the moment when the cry of "Sturm und Drang" was ringing through the country. His *Götz von Berlichingen* (1773) is the second play of importance in the new German theater, following ten years after Lessing's *Minna von Barnhelm*. The public greeted it with wild enthusiasm, for in its medieval pageantry of knights and emperor they saw revived the glories of their past. Chivalric plays and novels were all the rage for several years thereafter.

In 1774 followed *Die Leiden des jungen Werthers* (*The Sorrows of Young Werther*), a sentimental novel in epistolary form about a love-sick youth who finally kills himself with the pistol of his friend and rival. Goethe united in the story a recent sensational suicide with his admiration for Charlotte Buff whose care of her motherless younger brothers and sisters he had observed in her father's house. The book was a furious success, not only in Germany but abroad. Wertherism was the fashionable pose of the hour. The first English translation was made from the French in 1779. Other translations from the original followed in 1786, 1799, 1801, 1802. The *Sorrows* appeared in chapbook form and was hawked about the streets by peddlers. It was imitated in plays and poems which were translated back into German. For years after Goethe had moved on to greater accomplishments he was known in England only as the author of *Werther*.

After his removal to Weimar, where he held a nominal post as councilor of state, Goethe produced nothing for eleven years. Following his return from his Italian journey in 1788 there began to appear a series of dramas which had lain in an unfinished state for some time. *Iphigenia in Tauris* (1787) attempts to reproduce in German the form and style of Greek tragedy. *Egmont* (1788) dramatizes the martyrdom of that Dutch Count, idol of the populace, whom the Duke of Alba put to death for permitting the Protestants to live unmolested. The fine and stirring drama is weakened at the end by a scene in which Egmont in a trance beholds his Clara lifted to heaven as the genius of liberty. *Torquato Tasso* (1790) dwells on the loneliness of the poet. Goethe undoubtedly intended the play as a compliment to his patron, the Duke of Weimar, in whose court poets fared far better than Tasso did at the court of Ferrara.

Goethe's greatest work, the two-part drama *Faust,* was first sketched in 1774. A portion of the final version of Part I was published in 1790, remodeled in 1797, and finished in 1808. The second part Goethe did not complete until 1831, one year before his death. *Faust* is based on the sixteenth-century Germanic legends which grew up around a scholar who, in order to gain knowledge of the supernatural realms, made a compact with the devil. Goethe's Faust agrees to become the servant of Mephistopheles if the delights procured for him ever induce him to exclaim, "Stay, thou art so fair." The revels in Part I culminate in Faust's seduction of Marguerite and end in her miserable death. Part II is symbolistically obscure and vaster in its theme and scenic scope. It is so difficult to produce that it is seldom seen on the stage. Two almost separate ideas are bound together to make the play. In the first section Mephistopheles conjures up Helen of Troy from the shades to be Faust's love (representing the union of the classical and the romantic) and to bear him a son named Euphorion. This youth stands in the allegory for poetry, but also is meant by Goethe to suggest Lord Byron whose death is lamented in Euphorion's.

Faust then turns to devote himself to the welfare of mankind. Delighted with the prospect of the happiness which will come to all the future inhabitants of the waste lands he has reclaimed, he impetuously says the fatal words: "Then to the moment might I say, Linger a while, thou art so lovely" and Mephistopheles has him in duress.

Goethe is undoubtedly the greatest writer Germany has contributed to the world. In every form which he attempted he excelled his predecessors and contemporaries—the drama, the short tale, the novel *Wilhelm Meisters Lehrjahre* (*The Apprenticeship of Wilhelm Meister,* 1795-1796), lyric poetry, autobiography. Though his work incarnates the best of the new spirit animating Germany and is stamped with his own wisdom and passion, yet it belongs to the cosmopolitan world literature which he worked to bring into being. The delightful *Conversations with Goethe,* recorded by his secretary Eckermann from 1823 to 1832, reveal his great familiarity with the best that was being written in Europe. He was proud that Byron and Manzoni and Carlyle and Theophile Gautier looked upon him as their master and that the younger generation—Madame de Staël and the Russian Zhukovsky and the Pole Mickiewicz—came to Weimar as pilgrims go to Mecca.

To the world at large . . . German literature betokened above all two works, *Werther* and *Faust,* primarily because no other two are so imbued with the German spirit. The former is a symbol of dissatisfaction with the world, the starting point of that boundless individualism of which Byron was to become the chief representative; *Faust* represents the spirit of perpetual unrest, of striving and seeking which seized hold of Europe with such force in the first decades of the nineteenth century.[5]

II. BAROQUE AND ROCOCO ART

1. *The Seventeenth Century*

Although it is customary to treat the seventeenth and eighteenth centuries as separate epochs, they are closely related in many ways, the latter period deriving a great many of its ideas from the former. Generally speaking, the seventeenth century in art is more positive and powerful than the eighteenth. Both periods reflect the rise of capitalism and the transition from a primarily aristocratic society to one in which the middle classes played an increasingly important rôle. We shall discuss these epochs in sequence as well as by countries, bearing in mind the exchange of influences and ideas from one part of Europe to another.

To evaluate the predominantly emotional art of the seventeenth century (usually called *Baroque*) we must consider the part played by religious events. As early as the first quarter of the sixteenth century the revolt against the constituted authority of the church (the Reformation) in Germany, England, and the Scandinavian countries had brought about a feeling of disturbance even in the plastic arts. The great success of the revolting Protestant countries made it necessary for the Church of Rome to take definite action toward winning back lost adherents or toward finding new fields for religious activity and revenue. Popular education, therefore, became one of the most important activities of the church. The piety and coöperation of the communicants could no longer be taken for granted; the church had to preach to them firmly and fervently. Churches had to be built with a maximum of floor space—audience space—and church decorations took on an emotional character. In fact, the very form of the buildings intended for worship was emotionalized.

The typical fifteenth-century church or palace when compared with a seventeenth-century building is very simple indeed, with its unbroken surfaces and simple geometric plan. When classical ornaments were used during the earlier period, they were chastely applied. The Baroque (seventeenth-century) church or public building assumes a broken-up and agitated character in keeping with the agitation of the times. Much sculptural protruding surface ornament was applied and the simple lines of the fifteenth-century building now became twisted and curved. The church of *Il Gesù* in Rome, designed by della Porta and Vignola in the late sixteenth century, uses enormous curved volutes to cap the façade. The various parts of front main portal protrude and catch so much light and shade that the building gives the impression of being carved like sculpture. Here, as in Gothic architecture (and both periods have their religious analogies), the di-

[5] L. A. Willoughby, *The Romantic Movement in Germany,* 1930, p. 165.

visionbetween architecture and sculpture is not always clearly drawn. In fact, we often find, as in the *Ecstasy of St. Theresa* by Gian Lorenzo Bernini (1590-1680), that a broken architectural background has been combined with strongly emotional sculpture, and the entire effect augmented by the addition of gilding and other color devices in the stone. A work of this kind reminds us of the colored altar backs of the late Middle Ages in their combination of painting, sculpture, and architecture.

This mixture of media holds true of a great deal of Baroque architectural decoration in villas and town houses as well. Among the finest examples of the unorthodox effects of the Baroque are the monumental fountains of Rome, which even today are a most impressive feature of the city. The *Trevi Fountain* by N. Salvi, with its colossal adaptation of the classical arch of triumph and its elaborately pictorial sculptured figures and ornaments, is one of the most typical products of this period. For the great Cathedral of St. Peter Bernini designed a majestic colonnade which confronts the building at either side of the entrance and an elaborate bronze altar canopy with twisted columns. It is significant that even in his adaptations from classical antiquity, this typically Baroque artist should borrow from the unrestrained Hellenistic art. In such a work as the *Apollo and Daphne* he takes the elegance of the late Greek *Apollo Belvedere* and combines it with the emotional quality of his own period. As a technician in stone, and in his striking portrait busts, Bernini is the outstanding sculptor of the seventeenth century.

If the religious sculpture of Bernini showed a characteristic tendency toward the overwrought and the emotional, the painting of Caravaggio (1569-1609) at the very beginning of this epoch strikes the same note. He displays the typical Baroque interest in the emotional effects made possible by the use of light. Influential in turning artists' minds away from classical subject matter toward a strong everyday type of material, he became the source for many art ideas of the seventeenth century. It is revealing that such a modern Impressionist painter as Manet had a great deal of respect for his work, for it foreshadowed the modern concern in a painting with what the eye can see and not what it knows to be in the scene. This visual approach of Caravaggio was significant of the mental attitude of a period in which realism played an important part. His conception of religious art held out a simple and obvious appeal to the sympathies of the lower classes, for in them he visualized the characters of the Bible. Such a painting as *The Death of the Virgin* brings out the peculiar theatricality which became typical of the religious painting of this epoch; but it does not use the elaborately costumed characters of Venetian painting; it portrays instead a figure whose sorrow is not complicated by a consciousness of aristocratic grandeur.

Technically, the most interesting feature of this painting is its arbitary system of lighting: the sources of illumination are controlled by the artist who arranges them to achieve a dramatic realism. His consciousness of the function of light in a painting makes him a worthy predecessor of Velásquez in Spain.

A not to be neglected element in Caravaggio's work is his genre painting. Such works as his *Lute Player, Fortune Teller,* and *Card Players* show a clear anticipation of the favorite subjects of the Dutch painters in the seventeenth century proper. There is no real distinction to be made between his religious works and his everyday subjects, for both deal with the same people and their emotions; and it is an interesting revelation of the newer attitude of religion that this art should be more humanly interesting and sympathetic.

Italian painting of the seventeenth century is finally important for the creation of a type of romantic landscape best represented in the work of Salvatore Rosa (1615-1673), a versatile artist who was also a poet and musician. He preferred rocky and broken scenes in his landscapes or seascapes, insisting on the contrast between the smallness of man and the largeness of nature. Many of his paintings show a typical Baroque diagonality of composition, a phenomenon we shall encounter again.

Although there are reasons for the great intensity of earlier Spanish re-

St. Peter's Cathedral

ligious art, as in the work of El Greco, the mannerist, it is more important for us to consider the development of a specifically aristocratic strain. This is best expressed in portraiture. The greatest exponent of this type of painting is Diego Velásquez (1599-1660), painter and official at the court of Philip IV. Not only one of the greatest portraitists in history, Velásquez is the outstanding modern example of the realistic seventeenth-century point of view. In his work for the royal family the curiously formalized court of Spain brought forth a stiffness and an unemotional quality which were augmented by the artist's own objective point of view. No other painter during this period concerned himself so exclusively with the external phenomena of reality as Velásquez. His exploitation of its possibilities made light the "main character" in his paintings, and he constructed the figure as the contrast between light and dark. Whether indoors or in the open air, Velásquez was able to show that the figure appeared in space as the result of the light coming up to it and then stopping to create a shadow. His technique mirrored the same point of view, for he painted from outside the figure up to it and stopped where the figure was supposed to begin, thus working from the outside inward rather than the reverse which is the traditional procedure. No more scientific approach could have existed at this time, and so preoccupied did he become with this manner of visualization that he arbitrarily neglected such things as expression and psychology. His portraits of *Philip IV* or of the *Infanta* show us what the eye sees and nothing more; but what the eye sees, Velásquez realized, was the momentary and general silhouette of the figure, only the exposed parts of the body being clearly seen, i.e., the face and hands. In *genre,* however, Velásquez let himself go and expressed a viewpoint, e.g., *The Dwarf,* a picture in which the painter shows his sympathetic understanding.

The portraits of Velásquez, then, are a distinct reflection of the aristocratic society in which he moved; they convey the character of the Hapsburg kings more accurately than the art of Titian who was more concerned with the splendor of his medium and the beauty of the color in which he bathed his sitters. This does not mean that Velásquez' color is comparably lacking, for no more subtle colorist exists in the whole range of painting, particularly in the silvery quality he imparts to his tones. There is unquestionable charm in the landscape backgrounds of such works as *Don Balthasar Carlos* (where, incidentally, the horse, in attempting to dash forward, looks like a rocking-horse model). It is in such interiors as *The Tapestry Weavers* or the *Maids of Honor* that we see his full strength in conveying atmosphere and a convincingly tangible background. Finally, we may say that the portraits of Velásquez were typical of the international European tradition of the seventeenth century in developing the aristocratic picture, particularly in those countries where royal absolutism was in force. In all these countries we can observe the relationship to the earlier efforts of Titian.

If the art of Velásquez lacked religious emotionalism, that of Murillo, Zurbarán, and Ribera made up for this in full measure. It is their work which joins Spain with the general Jesuit outlook of the century. Murillo (1617-

1682), for example, represented the Baroque effort to bring religious subject matter down to an everyday level. Such paintings as his *Holy Family with the Bird,* the *Infant St. John with the Lamb,* or the *St. Joseph and the Infant Christ* reveal a wealth of tender religious sentiment which must have been very attractive to the Spaniards of that day, although to us they appear more than exaggerated. The familiarity and "hominess" with which he has invested these scenes is not only typical of his art, but also of the general southern Catholic casualness in its relation to both religion and its representatives. Another typical seventeenth-century aspect of Murillo's art appears in his numerous genre paintings, such as the *Dice Players, Melon Eaters, Young Beggar,* and *Young Fish Seller,* where he has charmingly shown a series of street types, well composed and humorously expressed.

Zurbarán (1598-1662), the painter of monks, is one of the most typical manifestations of the religious history of the seventeenth century, for in his delineation of an almost fanatical monastic type, he shows the attempt of the church to whip up a religious enthusiasm. Today we can recognize the arbitrary lighting effects he used and his exaggerated emotionality, exemplified by his *Kneeling Franciscan with a Skull.*

With Jusepe de Ribera (1588-1656) we meet a Spanish-born painter who was the founder of the school of Naples and one of the most typically Baroque and typically religious of all the painters of the southern Catholic tradition. A follower of Caravaggio, he dedicated himself to highly dramatic representations of scenes of martyrdom (*Martyrdom of St. Bartholomew*), with a naturalistic interpretation of details of flesh, torture, cloth, and light.

In Flanders in the north, we deal with a vassal state of Spain, whose art was certain to take on some of the courtly and aristocratic character of the mother country as well as its intense religiosity. The first aspect is best represented in the work of Anthony Van Dyck (1599-1641), son of the prosperous upper middle class of Antwerp and a pupil of Peter Paul Rubens. After considerable traveling he settled in England where, with a few interruptions, he remained until his death and where he set the style of fashionable portrait painting for all subsequent English painters. As court portraitist to Charles I, he had the opportunity to indulge his aristocratic style to the full in such efforts as *Charles I in Hunting Costume* and *The Children of Charles I.* Logically his style is descended from Titian in its broad color effects and its warmth. Most striking is his charming handling of fabrics which sets the standard for the best English painters of the following century. Van Dyck's reliance upon the Venetian tradition is apparent in some of his religious paintings, in the elaborate compositional effects and the broad coloring. However, it is in portraiture that Van Dyck has made his greatest contribution, for, as will be seen later, the entire English portrait school of the eighteenth century depended upon him.

A much greater painter and a more universal personality was Peter Paul Rubens (1577-1640). Just as Raphael was the most typical representative of the sixteenth-century golden age, Rubens was the most brilliant exemplar of the Catholic Baroque. He was also the first painter to re-create the marble gods and goddesses of antiquity in a living and breathing form. No painter except Raphael was as eclectic as he, and yet he managed to fuse the various influences into an extremely individual art. Combining the subtle light and dark effects of Leonardo, the drawing of Michelangelo, the color of Titian, and the melodramatic effects of Caravaggio, he produced the strongest painting of the seventeenth century aristocratic tradition. His love of color reminds us of Titian or of the Van Eycks in his native Flanders; his pathos makes us think of Tintoretto.

The most striking artistic personality in the Baroque tradition, Rubens was supreme in Flanders, just as Raphael had dominated the artistic society of Rome in the early sixteenth century. He had an enormous school of pupils, many of whom assisted him, so that a great number of the paintings signed with his name are really "school" efforts in which various specialists in landscape, dead game, flowers, fruit, etc., combined their efforts to produce the final work which was finally retouched by the master who had furnished the design and the supervision. Obviously a man of Rubens' popularity, with so many demands on his time, could not have done otherwise; but he was conscientious enough to admit to his patrons just how much he had painted in a particular work and stated his prices accordingly. He supervised a large number of woodcuts made from his designs (by Jegher) as well as many popular elaborate altarpieces of the period, ceremonial decorations, designs for tapestries, silver reliefs, ivory carvings, etc.

The scope of his genius was as universal as that of any of the great Italian artists of the "High Renaissance"; in addition to his accomplishment as an artist, he was a fine linguist, a classical scholar, an ambassador, and a much loved personality. His activity embraces all the subject matters of painting. Even to choose only one example of each type would prove a lengthy process. The most famous of his religious paintings is the *Descent from the Cross* wherein his general relationship to the Baroque period is clearly seen. In this work, however, we are no longer dealing with the humble folk of Caravaggio or Murillo, but with a specifically aristocratic point of view which will bear much fruit in the following period. The lighting is melodramatic in the best tradition of this time, the foreshortening of the various figures and their arrangement within the picture space are masterfully accomplished, while the contrast between the simple and the sublime places Rubens among the most expressive artists of the seventeenth century.

Rubens, as we have said before, is important for the degree of vitality which all his figures possess; this is particularly interesting in his treatment of classical subjects—of all fields the one which tends to become pompous and stuffy. In such a painting as the *Judgment of Paris* a pagan shepherd type (Paris) sits upon the ground while three typically ample beauties stand waiting to be judged. Their flesh is blond and pink and the warm blood seems to be pounding furiously through their full bodies. Here, as well as in his famous *The Rape of the Daughters of Leucippus,* Rubens brings to life all the lusty joys and strength of the pagan world.

In portraiture Rubens naturally espoused the aristocratic tradition as it appeared in the work of his pupil Van Dyck, but in a more robust fashion. *Anne of Austria,* a characteristic example, shows a clear relationship to the Venetian tradition in the elaborate background, architecture, and draperies. The flesh of the Queen of France is plump and smooth in the Rubenesque manner—it almost glistens, so richly was the paint applied.

Diagonal composition had begun to appear during the second half of the sixteenth century with Titian and Tintoretto and reached its apex in the hands of Baroque painters such as Rubens. It appears not only in religious pictures but in others as well; for example, Rubens' magnificent hunting picture, *The Fox and Wolf Hunt.* Here is the typical example of the diagonally arranged composition of the seventeenth century whose sharp angles in themselves convey a high degree of excitement, the horses charging out of the corners and the lances flashing in diagonal lines. The furious energy of this type of picture is, of course, quite compatible not only with the tremendous vitality of Rubens' own art, but with the general tumultuousness of the seventeenth-century style he represents.

There remains for us to consider only his decorative painting as represented in his famous work for the Queen of France, Marie de Médicis, who commissioned him to do a series of biographical panels in her Luxembourg Palace in Paris. Here he gave his imagination full play in a most elaborate treatment of allegory and mythology. These panels together with his portraits of the Queen, her husband Henri IV, and others summed up the important elements of his style— the full blown nudes of the *Fates Spinning* with their pink flesh and blond hair, the courtliness of *Henri IV Receiving the Portrait of Marie,* the impressive architectural background of *Henri Leaving for the Wars,* etc. These paintings became an academy for the French artists of the following century, and if their work too is pink and blond, if their colors are bright and vivacious, it is because of Rubens' influence. The scope of this artist included every conceivable type—the portrait, the landscape, the allegory, the historical scene, the hunting scene, the genre picture—painted with such mastery that his brightness and energy remained as a source of inspiration for the painters of both the eighteenth and nineteenth centuries. Even the muted love conversations in gardens, so popular in the eighteenth century, stemmed from Rubens. His *Garden of Love* appears to be the first example of this type wherein elegant ladies and gentlemen dally and converse about the trivia of existence against a garden background.

Close to Flanders geographically but as distant spiritually was seventeenth-century Holland. Democratic in politics and Calvinist in religion, it had freed itself of the yoke of the pompous Spanish court and its Catholic implications while Flanders remained a tributary. Such elaborate altarpieces as the *Descent from the Cross* of Rubens had no place in its severe religious system. By the same token, the aristocratic portrait had to be changed to accommodate itself to the more self-conscious ideal of Holland's powerful upper middle class. As a cultural center, Holland was less outstanding than nearby Flanders, yet in certain instances it produced extremely fine characteristically seventeenth-century painting.

The Dutch school of painting, lasting only one short century as a productive force, was dedicated to representing the environment in which the artist happened to find himself. For a time, the wealthy merchants and traders bought many landscapes, portraits, and genre works to hang on their walls, but soon there were so many painters that there was hardly enough work to go around and artists began to starve. Production was tremendous, consumption relatively small. For an artist to live by his brush, he had to be either extremely popular or extremely conservative which meant about the same thing. Thus the Dutch artist during this period was busy making faithful likenesses of the country in its varied aspects. Once that task was completed (a hundred years was not too long for this), there was nothing more to say and the school died.

The typical Dutch painting of the seventeenth century was a completely secular manifestation, yet its robust emotional content cannot be ignored, even in the case of the lesser masters. Naturally we expect it in Rembrandt and Frans Hals, who are the obviously Baroque artists of the Dutch school, but emotional power is evident in others as well. Since there are so many artists in this school and so many examples of their work, we must restrict ourselves to the most typical masters.

For simple genre, we may cite Adriaen van Ostade (1610-1685), one of the most important peasant painters of the school. He is one of those "little masters" so frequently met with in Holland, little in both format and subject matter. Ostade veers from a type of caricaturized interpretation, with his peasants ugly and hateful creatures, to an expression closer to the spirit of Brueghel, in which the subjects become friendlier and more inviting—people eating and drinking at an inn, beggars fiddling for pennies and laughing peasants. Adriaen Brouwer, whose painting is looser and more impressionistic, painted even more casual scenes than Ostade.

A tremendous number of town scenes were done at this time. For the most part, they are meticulously painted and thus reminiscent of the Netherlandish painting of the fifteenth century from which they undoubtedly descended. The colors are bright and clear, accenting the texture of materials. More than ever before, the painter of the Low Countries interests himself in the "touch" quality of satin, wood, glass, metal, and attempts to give the spectator a physical reaction which will be vivid enough for him to believe in the existence of the materials portrayed. This, we might think, would lead to a neglect of the emotional aspects, but it is far from true. Most of these "town" pictures reflect an interesting quietness of mood. Another frequent subject with the Dutch masters was the aristocratic interior groupings. The most important artist of this predilection is undoubtedly Jan Vermeer of Delft (1632-1675) whose perspective, subtle color, fine sense of texture, and restrained mood sum up, in a superior fashion, the qualities of the entire school of town painters. In his *The Young Woman at a Casement* we are able to see the importance of the Dutch tradition as a materialist phenomenon of the seventeenth century. As the young woman stands before the window with one hand resting upon its ledge and the other holding the top of a chair, we see the blue glass of the window casting a bluish light on her face and on her starched collar and cuffs. The silver bowl on the table (a miracle of convincing shininess) reflects the blue of the cushion lying near it as well as the varied colors of the tablecloth on which it stands. Such details of the color effects of adjacent objects upon one another is clearly an anticipation of modern impressionist practice in the late nineteenth century.

Another member of this school, Pieter de Hooch (1629-1678?), preferred to place his sitters out of doors in front of a house. An interest in deep perspectives is characteristic of most of his pictures, but they are really significant for the creation of a most aristocratic and refined mood wherein people are seriously engaged in testing a drink, smoking, or playing cards.

We can pass over still life paintings, architectural pictures, street perspectives, to one of the most important types of Dutch painting, the landscape. The flatness of the Dutch terrain, the immense sky never interrupted by undulating hills as in other countries, forced the artist consciously to arrange his composition for interest. He had to include a large tree or some interesting architectural feature. But even so Dutch landscape still has at least two thirds sky and one third ground, even though it follows the Baroque tradition in composition moving diagonally from corner to corner. The Dutch painter is much interested in the effect of light upon objects, but he is not yet well enough equipped to realize fully the many subtle variations in the modulations of light in a modern landscape. Still, he is an ancestor of the English landscapists of the late eighteenth and early nineteenth centuries and thus the father of modern landscape painting as well.

The most interesting quality of the Dutch landscape is mood. Such painters as Albert Cuyp (1620-1691) show this well. His *Evening Landscape* in which people sit or stand quietly in the setting sun is a fine example. Other painters, such as Jakob van Ruysdael (1628-1682), manifest a fine emotional and even romantic quality. Van Ruysdael's *Waterfall* with its broken contours and generally disturbed effects, and his *Jewish Cemetery* with the strange, gnarled and twisted trees, broken headstones, and melancholy lighting, are as exaggerated as the most romantic nineteenth-century English novel. A definitely Italianate school of landscape existed in Holland in the work of Jan Both, Nicholas Berghem, etc. Dutch painting of the seventeenth century was not untouched by foreign influences, for an entire school of Caravaggists existed there. We are not surprised therefore at the unusually Baroque character of the painting of Frans Hals and Rembrandt, the two greatest masters of the century among the Dutch.

Frans Hals (c.1580-1666) who, together with Rembrandt, represents the more tragic side of Dutch painting, is preëminently a modern artist in his direct approach to the technique of painting and to its subject matter. It is true that like Rembrandt he began as a conventional portrait painter, doing individual portraits (such as *Willem van Huythuysen*) and group portraits (such as *The Governors of the Hospital*), both characterized by a silkiness of handling and a conventional emotional approach. The group portrait was most popular in Dutch society of the seventeenth century; the directors of its many charitable and social groups loved to have themselves painted much as a banquet or picnic group today calls in the local photographer. Hals was as much a rebel artistically as Rembrandt

and insisted on forsaking this genteel atmosphere and choosing his subjects where
he wished. Such pictures as *The Smoker* and the *Yonker Ramp and His Sweet-heart* indicate this change as well as the loosening of his color technique in favor
of bolder and freer dashes of paint and less meticulous drawing. Though Hals's
Bohemian Girl and the *Hille Bobbe, Witch of Haarlem* convinced his con-temporaries that he was rolling in the gutter, he had gained immensely in direct-ness of approach to reality. Without making any preliminary drawings (not a
single Hals drawing exists today) he attacked his canvas in vivid and abruptly
applied colors, giving his subjects a sense of immediacy which the academic and
meticulous painter never achieves.

In Rembrandt van Rijn (1606-1669), the greatest of the Dutchmen and one of
the greatest painters of all time, we find a master whose popularity has changed
with the centuries but who is, today, the best known of all. It is one of the curious
facts of cultural history that his name is known even to the completely unin-formed; in the minds of the public his name has become synonymous with paint-ing.

Part of the explanation lies in the tremendous appeal of his art for the ro-mantic artists of the early nineteenth century who first created the cult of Rem-brandt in modern times; but the real reason for his popularity is the breadth
and universality of his appeal. One of the marked tendencies of the Baroque,
as we have already seen in the religious art of Italy and Spain, was to reduce
doctrinal truth to everyday terms. In this sense, Rembrandt exceeded both the
Italians and the Spaniards, for his religious art consists not merely in clothing
his characters in the costumes of his own time; he clothed them in a profound
sympathy and understanding of the sufferings of humanity which brings him
within the reach of even those who understand nothing of art. To be sure, many
people are won over by his picturesque types, his solemn and impressive rabbis,
his tattered beggars, his people clothed in elaborate Oriental garments; but be-neath this is the kernel of compassion and warmth painted in a dark and mys-terious light from which the figures emerge slowly but powerfully. His art is
perhaps an everyday thing judging by the characters he uses and the environment
in which he usually places them, but like his fifteenth-century Flemish predeces-sors, he has transfigured this simple realism into a universal and eternal truth.

Rembrandt had the advantage of a religious training which intimately familiar-ized him with the facts of the Bible. Living in Amsterdam, where there was a
populous Jewish ghetto, he was struck by the fact that here was the race of which
the Bible spoke—what more appropriate than to paint these people as his heroes
and villains? Thus the primary inspiration did not necessarily come from his
imagination but rather from living beings in the poor houses of the Holland of
his own time. Such characters as Tobias, Susannah, Jacob, and Daniel became his
subjects and it is about them that his greatest paintings revolved. The New
Testament, in his hands, became a convincing flesh and blood drama. His re-ligious paintings thus were no mere collection of cult images but stories told in
most understandable terms. These ideas did not spring into being full grown;

they were the result of his own painful evolution.

The early part of Rembrandt's career, like that of Frans Hals, was very much a success story; his conventional, if superior, portraits made him wealthy. But in his famous *Night Watch* his style underwent a serious change from the glossy, tightly painted method of his early manhood. Instead of rendering the conventional aspects of a number of inactive Dutch heroes, Rembrandt makes of this group portrait something mysterious, something seen at night and bathed in luminous shadows.

From this point on (1642) his work became more introspective; orders naturally fell off, but the artist's power increased mightily. It is only after this date that were born the characteristically "Rembrandtesque" works for which he is famous today. He made a great many self-portraits in both painting and etching (he is the greatest etcher of all time), and as he moved farther into the ghetto of Amsterdam he began to produce the stirring epic conceptions of religious history that make him incomparable. The sheer bulk of Rembrandt's productions up to the very year of his death is staggering to us today. And it is difficult indeed to single out any particular work as more important than the others in his vast number of etchings, drawings, and paintings. In religious art, we may contrast the joyous lustiness of his *Wedding Feast of Samson* with *The Blind Tobit and His Wife* which is the essence of his sympathy for suffering humanity. Among his many portraits he produced such enduring works as *The Man with the Golden Helmet*, possibly a portrait of his brother, which is so imbued with his own sadness that it becomes a symbol of the inherent woes of mankind. In this work we are particularly aware of the unusual quality of his technique; in addition to the heavy and thickly laid-on paint (in such details as the engraving on the golden helmet), the portrait is characteristic of his handling of light and dark. Through the use of many layers of paint and a subtly modulated relationship between them, the painter causes the light from outside to penetrate the shadows as deeply as he wishes and to be reflected back to the eye of the spectator in the same controlled degree. This technique gives his figures a type of modeling whose many possibilities do not fully emerge until we have stood before the painting a long time and allowed the light from our eyes to reach the work and to be reflected back. The longer we stand before these paintings, the firmer the figure becomes and the more we see; we are thus drawn into a visual participation in the painter's efforts.

Among his numerous etchings the most celebrated is the so-called *Hundred Guilders Print,* a representation of Christ healing the lame and halt. Here, as in many other versions of the Christ story, he has shown a universally appealing and human Savior. The halt and the lame who come unto Him for comfort are the poor people of the Amsterdam ghetto. In a powerful transition from light to dark as we move from one side of the etching to the other, the figures emerge with greater clarity and strength to create one of the most compassionate religious narratives of all time.

The final seventeenth-century school we shall consider developed under the monarchical absolutism of Louis XIV in France. Here art, like literature, had a peculiar formality and academicism, reflecting the ceremonial character of its background. Just as Louis pretended to be the state itself (*L'état, c'est moi!*) so the art of the time, for those desiring official favor, was a closely controlled and supervised business dedicated to the glory of the king and court.

The most important architectural products of this school are the royal palaces, the Louvre and Versailles. A tremendous amount of effort and money was lavished on these buildings, elaborately designed as the apartments for the king and his numerous courtiers. As an example of seventeenth-century architecture, such a building as the Louvre (today the national museum of France) shows a centralized five-part composition in each section, with parts of the edifice protruding and others receding. The surface is covered with the monumental type of decoration found elsewhere in Europe at that time. The total effect is one of broken surfaces—an effect which became the basis of much civil architecture in Europe and America. Both the Metropolitan Museum of Art and the Public Library of New York reproduce the spirit of the monumental architecture of the seventeenth century in France.

French sculpture of this period is more characteristically Baroque than the architecture: it is as nervous and emotional as the contemporary efforts of Bernini who was at that time highly esteemed in France. One of the most famous French sculptors was Coysevox (1640-1720) whose portrait bust of the *Great Condé* is reminiscent of Bernini's portrait of *Louis XIV*. Coysevox's *Tomb of Mazarin* is a typical example of the elaborate and exaggerated Baroque sepulcher.

Among the official painters, most important was Charles Le Brun (1619-1690) who was also the director of the royal architectural enterprises. His was a veritable dictatorship over the arts, for he was in a position to supervise practically every type of work. Like the contemparary Italians, he favored combinations of architecture, sculpture, and painting in a typical Baroque manner. His own painting is eclectic in the current academic French sense, for he was influenced by many of the best features of earlier Italian art as they were then preferred. Typical are Le Brun frescoes in the Hotel Lambert in Paris—classical allegories and triumphs (*The Wedding of Hercules and Hebe, The Battle of the Centaurs*) which bring to mind the work of Raphael, Titian, and other sixteenth-century Italians.

The academic and aristocratic character of French art during this period is evident in the large quantity of official portraits. Representative is the work of Philippe de Champaigne (1602-1671). Its suavity and emphasis upon nobility is parallel to the efforts of contemporaneous portraitists in Flanders and Spain.

Nicolas Poussin (1594-1665), one of the most typical academic artists of the French seventeenth century, spent most of his life in Rome, where he studied antique remains and the art of Raphael. A painter of landscape and figure compositions, his conception of nature was a controlled and logical one, quite in keeping with the current French rationalism. We may approach his typical classical landscape much as we view the stage in a theater. The frame of the painting is the "proscenium arch," while at right and left we find a block of landscape coming out of the "wings" and cutting off our view. Between these "flats" the actors in the narrative (which is Poussin's excuse for practicing landscape) move "downstage" parallel with the "footlights" and stay there. The background, a flat conception of nature, is studded with antique ruins. Like a stage backdrop this landscape gives an artificial impression which hardly invites us to walk into the scene and look about. The figures of Poussin show a distinct reliance upon the technique of Raphael whom he worshiped. In his *Two Saints Healing a Cripple* one of the two majestically draped figures points a finger upward in the manner of the Plato in Raphael's *School of Athens* and its carefully balanced composition, with heavy Italianate architecture at right and left and a number of figures covering the steps, is reminiscent. The degree of conscious posturing in this work makes us think of the rhetorical speeches in the contemporary plays of Racine and Corneille.

Another important French artist of this period, Claude Gellée Lorrain (1600-1682), was similarly given to carefully balanced compositions; but his work is more typically Baroque than Poussin's in its insistence on mood. Claude is an outstanding painter of light, and most of his paintings either create a romantic mood or show us subtle sunlight or sunset effects in a beautiful streak of light across water. The influence of Claude in the field of light will be seen later in the work of Turner in England.

One of the most interesting manifestations of seventeenth-century France was the art of the Le Nain family who worked in Paris on a series of city and country genre paintings. Although they are believed to have been under the influence of the school of Frans Hals, the emotional content of these works is entirely different from his, but it compares with some of the effects of restraint and dignity in Dutch upper middle-class and aristocratic genre paintings and portraits. Such pictures as *The Mendicants, Bread Women,* and the *Peasants in Front of Their House* are characteristic examples of the amazing reticence and gently introspective mood which the Le Nain family infused into everyday subject matter. In Holland the poor were portrayed with a certain honest ugliness, but in these French examples they have become dignified and monumental by Christian sympathy. We shall find this strain repeated during the eighteenth century in the work of Chardin and during the nineteenth in that of Millet.

The last significant artist for us to consider is Jacques Callot (1592-1635), one of the most fruitful draughtsmen, etchers and engravers of the French group. He was an extremely prolific illustrator of the everyday life of the people, particularly of soldiers who were wandering about Europe at that time. His figures are often unusually thin and long and with small heads lending themselves to the depiction of fantastic and imaginative themes. His most famous work is the series of eighteen plates known as *The Great Miseries of War,* a realistic and socially conscious portrayal of the horrors of war of that day, particularly in Lorraine. No other artist of this period was as much aware of the burden placed upon the civilian populations of Europe by wars of aggression as Callot.

2. *The Eighteenth Century*

The most important eighteenth-century school of art was undoubtedly the French. Italy became distinctly secondary as a direct source of influence, although the persistence of an academic (i.e., imitative) point of view in both France and England made a certain amount of borrowing from Italy inevitable. French architecture and sculpture had less significance than painting. Fewer building enterprises were undertaken, and these could not begin to compare with the lavishness of the Louvre or Versailles.

Instead of an art revolving exclusively about the court, we find the growth of an urban point of view in the development of the town house for the nobility as well as for the increasingly important commercial groups. Smaller wall spaces called for a small type of painting and we find none of the elaborate "machines" that had been executed by Le Brun during the epoch of Louis XIV. We have to take into account during this period not only the continuation of the aristocratic point of view, but also the growth of the upper middle class with its simpler and more direct form of expression.

The most typical and "French" phenomenon of the eighteenth century was the art developed at the court of Louis XV, which soon spread to all parts of Europe. The lightness and apparent gaiety of this rococo (profusely decorated) art was the keynote of the newer decoration of the palace at Versailles. Ornament became lighter and more replete with gilded surfaces. Curves and countercurves in moldings and furniture appeared in profusion; wall surfaces were more often decorated with mirrors than with paintings. The heaviness and royal pomp of the age of Louis XIV yielded to the new style which proved popular in all parts of the Continent. Every European court of any importance emulated the royal residence of France and tried to build for itself a miniature Versailles in all its details. Frederick the Great of Prussia built the palace of Sans-Souci at Potsdam, Maria Theresa her Schönbrunn in Vienna, Catherine the Great her Hermitage in St. Petersburg, Sweden its Drottningholm on the outskirts of Stockholm. The portrait painters of France were imported into these countries and filled those palaces with entirely typical French portraits. We may take for granted that French fashions in dress and its courtly and elegant behavior found their parallels in the other courts of Europe.

It is rather difficult to explain this new feeling in the art of eighteenth-century France except in terms of a certain moral, physical, and economic lassitude which followed the tremendous expansion and the imperialist wars of the Louis XIV period. Certainly his successor, Louis XV, was a far less powerful or dominant personality, but this scarcely accounts for the change. We must look rather to the fact that the aristocracy had been permitted to remain away from its estates for a long period and that the agrarian resources of France were being sucked dry by the oppressive taxes which had become necessary to support the swollen courts of the French kings. As the aristocracy weakened and as the countryside declined, the already important commercial interests increased in power. By the end of the century they would replace the aristocracy as the rulers of France.

The first important painter of the French aristocratic, rococo tradition was Antoine Watteau (1684-1721) whose art was an interesting transition from the lush vivid colors of the Flemings of the seventeenth century to the more delicate and feminine tones of the new period. Though his early works sometimes borrowed from the genre paintings of the Flemish tradition, his fame rests upon scenes from court life and from the theater. His manner is always restrained and never overtly gay, even when painting the most charming subject in the world. Like the eighteenth-century minuets, his paintings were a curious combination of external beauty and surface gaiety, and over all a restrained and even melancholy refinement. How much of this was owing to his illness and how much to the period itself is difficult to judge, but it is true that the apparent licentiousness of the French court (of which the literature tells enough) never quite registers in its painting. This may be because a cloak of manners and refinement is thrown about the various scenes represented, and on the unconvincing and too delicately characterized nudes.

We may use the painting of Watteau to illustrate the first, and that of Boucher for the second. In such a work as the famous *Embarkation for the Island of Cythera,* Watteau has brought together a series of amorous couples in the "successive steps" of love-making. At our right, we see on a gently sloping hill a couple seated before a statue of Venus, the satin-clothed gentleman whispering sweet nothings into the ear of the equally elegant lady. The second episode shows the lover (really a second couple now) raising the lady to her feet; in the next scene she casts a final glance backward. Finally they descend the grassy slope to join a number of other couples waiting before the elaborately carved boat which is to carry them away. The background here is misty in the typical silvery gray and atmospheric colors which Watteau handles so skillfully and which Corot in the nineteenth century will revive so romantically. As a delicate pageant of love, this picture is one of the most appealing and restrained of the works of Watteau who is primarily a painter of mood. His mood is not as vital as that of the artists of the previous century, but it is just as real. We observe his relationship to the school of Flanders not only in his early genre works mentioned above but in the general blondness of his women (derived from Rubens) and in the silky quality of their garments (recalling the technique of Van Dyck).

If Watteau is characteristic of the more emotional restraint of this period, François Boucher (1703-1770) is perhaps the most typically rococo of the school. Light in sentiment and gay in color, he reproduces mythologies, allegories, pastorals, etc., in a readily recognizable style. He is a fine decorator and his works were eminently suited to the brightly arranged interiors of the time with their curved mirrors and delicate furniture. Typical of his painting is the *Toilet of Venus* in which the pink-fleshed goddess is shown arranging her hair while little Cupids sport about her in an elaborately furnished eighteenth-century interior. The rosiness of her flesh is fully comparable to the pinkness so often found in the work of Rubens from which it is undoubtedly derived, but the flesh here is no longer as firm and appealing as in Rubens. It is more delicate, in the fashion of the small Sèvres porcelain figurines of the period. Boucher's nudes, if this can be taken as an example, are scarcely erotic, for the pinkness is not so much an indication of strongly flowing blood as of a superficial and charming color.

A gifted, refreshing painter whose style and choice of themes are likewise characteristic of the rococo is Fragonard (1732-1806). His delicacy of touch and sometimes risqué subjects say much of the late eighteenth century.

The rococo spirit is also evident in portrait painting. Although there were a considerable number of portraitists working both in France and other parts of Europe from 1700-1750, we may choose one as typical, Nattier (1685-1766), famous for his court portraits. His *Portrait of the Princess de Condé as Diana* best expresses the spirit of rococo portraiture, for in addition to the characteristic pinkness and delicacy of feature we find a striking degree of formality and artificiality. This is not a straightforward representation by any means, but one in which a court lady (powdered hair, satin dress, etc.) is tricked out in a tiger skin intended to suggest the goddess of the hunt, Diana. Holding the bow in one hand and pointing self-consciously with the other, this lady shows a typical eighteenth-century desire to be something she is not.

One of the most important portrait manifestations of the eighteenth century is the pastel (colored chalk), whose great exponent is Quentin de La Tour (1704-1788). In his most famous work, the portrait of *Mme de Pompadour,* the famous lady is surrounded by books and other cultural paraphernalia as evidence that she was a patroness of the arts. With the work of de La Tour, French portrait painting appears to enter a more purposeful and realistic phase, already evident in this work, since the great lady is not posing as Venus or Minerva but is shown merely with her favorite books, music, etc. This type of "occupational" portrait carries us into the next period, the second half of the century. At this time (Louis XVI) the middle-class genre picture and portrait begin to develop with a real interest in naturalistic phenomena and with color effects opposed to the artificiality of the previous epoch.

The great representative of this middle-class art is Chardin (1699-1779), famous for his serious and simple portraits, genre scenes, and still lifes. His *Portrait of the Artist* shows his direct and powerful evaluation of a natural personality entirely devoid of the artificiality of the rococo period. In its ruggedness and realism this self-portrait with the glasses and eyeshade reproduces the unpretentious monumentality of the self-portraits of Rembrandt. Chardin's genre interiors stand in distinct contrast to the fluffy interiors of the rococo painters, for they are not only full of a quiet and tender mood but sometimes, as in *The Blessing,* they show a certain simple Christian sentiment reminiscent of Le Nain in the seventeenth century.

His greatest contribution to art, however, is his monumental type of still life. Using inanimate subject matter such as pots and pans and fruit, he magnified their importance (with such miraculous representation of the bright glow of copper and the dull sheen of pewter) to such a point that they became much more impressive and overpowering than any mere humans ever could be. Once in a while we find that an earlier artist, for example, Rembrandt, had been able to do this. But Chardin is really a predecessor of the monumental still life which we shall find later in the work of Cézanne.

Toward the development of a middle-class point of view, the most important painter of the second half of the century is Greuze (1725-1805). He was a living example of the maxim laid down by the encyclopedist, Diderot, that a painting to have merit must teach a lesson or moral. Beginning in the academic rococo atmosphere of the first half of the century, Greuze began to change the direction of his interests by painting appealing young girls (many in pastoral costume) expressing the new bourgeois sentiment. Although these girls are still painted with the softness of rococo women, a certain sickly and characteristically Greuze sentiment has begun to change them into the sentimental exaggerations which will later be necessary to express his moral and ethical point of view. Two large, poorly painted pictures called *The Father's Curse* and *The Prodigal Son* in their very titles tell us something of the character of this new bourgeois art. The first tells of a son who has sinfully disobeyed his father and joined the army! This fact is turned into an emotional orgy in which the father drives his son out of the house with the usual injunction never to cross the threshold again, while the equally excited female members of the family forcibly restrain the two males. Everyone waves his arms and the excitement is terrific as an arbitrary and melodramatic Baroque light falls upon the scene. In the second episode the prodigal returns from the wars to find his father at death's door. As he slinks into the hushed chamber, he sees the broken, gray figure lying on the bed surrounded by violently weeping women who disturb the quiet of the scene and place this picture definitely in the category of bathos with the moral sticking out all over it. Such pictures as these were characteristic of an age when writers such as Rousseau, Richardson, and the young Goethe insisted upon good middle-class behavior and virtue. As a contrast to the amoral rococo art which was only interested in pleasing the eye, this sentimental art takes on the character of a reform movement which will become stronger as the conflict in society becomes more sharply defined during the period of the French Revolution.

In England during the eighteenth century we have a similar division into two points of view, the academic aristocratic art of the portrait painters and the more severe realism of such a middle-class artist as William Hogarth. England had gone through its revolution. The temporary triumph of the middle classes and the violent reaction of the so-called aristocracy during the Restoration after Cromwell had made the differences sharper. Stringent moral prohibitions under Cromwell gave way before a licentiousness that affected all classes of society. The art of Hogarth (1697-1764), the first great native English painter, may be regarded as a reaction against the looseness of his time. As a reformer he was infinitely superior to his French contemporary Greuze, for it was not merely the accentuation of simple and homely virtues which attracted him but the preaching of hell-fire and punishment for sins. If much of his art can be looked upon as so much pulpit pounding, he still remains important as one of the first social critics in painting produced by the modern period. His various paintings, *The Harlot's Progress, The Rake's Progress, Marriage à la Mode,* are all indictments of the customs of his time. It is interesting that the public of his day liked them so much that they were reproduced in engravings and sold all over England. We find him inveighing against intemperance, licentiousness, the aping of foreigners in manners and art, hypocrisy, and political frauds. It was the period of Addison and Steele with their *Tatler* and *Spectator* papers, the age of Swift and Defoe, and in general an epoch of extreme social consciousness. As a painter, Hogarth founded the native English naturalistic school, particularly in the portrait and genre scene. His *Shrimp Girl,* a spontaneous interpretation of a street character, is loosely painted in bright colors to convey the momentary activity in which she is engaged. The *Portrait of the Artist* is comparable to that of Chardin in simplicity and middle-class seriousness. It may be classed in the group of "accessory" or occupational portraits mentioned before, since it shows the artist with the materials of his profession about him.

The eighteenth century in England is particularly important for the founding of a school of landscape. Beginning with the classical efforts of Richard Wilson (1713-1782) (which remind us of Claude Lorrain), it developed in an individual manner in the work of John Crome (1768-1821) whose *View of Mousehold Heath* was the starting point for the evolution of the school. The approach of the English was naturally conditioned by their great predecessors, the Dutch, since they were similarly interested in an emotional interpretation of nature. Their superiority over the painters of the seventeenth century resides in the fact that they were much more aware of the effects of light and better able to execute their aims. Crome, for example, although interested in the grandeur of nature, is still able to concentrate upon small light effects as they come through the branches of his huge trees. The full development of the English school of landscape properly belongs to the early nineteenth century where it is closely related to the later developments in France.

England, like France, also had its academic (or backward-looking) point of view at this time. This was solidified in the establishment of the Royal Academy under the presidency of Sir Joshua Reynolds (1723-1792) whose *Graces Decorating a Figure of Hymen* is the eighteenth-century equivalent of the sixteenth-century painting of Venice (*The Three Sisters* of Palma Vecchio). Although, like most English portrait painting of this period, Reynolds' work was conditioned by Venice, we can also observe a kinship with the contemporary rococo painting of France in the artificiality of portraying matronly Englishwomen trying desperately to be something else.

English academic portraiture of the eighteenth century reaches its height in Thomas Gainsborough (1727-1788), whose style, like that of many of his contemporaries, results partly from the influence of the Fleming, Van Dyck (of Venetian artistic background) who had lived in England in the previous century. The relationship between Gainsborough and Van Dyck is made clear in such technical details as the silky smooth handling of colors (particularly for fabrics) and psychologically in the fact that Gainsborough's subjects (and by the same token, those of Hoppner, Raeburn, Romney) are represented with a certain degree of glibness and aristocratization. Gainsborough is more important artistically for the type of landscape which he painted, wherein English eighteenth-century sentiment (compare the poetry of the time) emerges in a particularly attractive manner (*The Market Cart* and *The Cow in the Meadow*). The national landscape school of Great Britain evolved in the wake of this painter, even though he was more a romantic than a realist. After him come such figures as John Crome, Constable, and others, whose work carries us into the nineteenth century.

III. APPLICATION OF MUSIC TO THE DRAMA: NEW INSTRUMENTAL FORMS

1. *The Beginnings of Opera and Oratorio*

Between 1580 and 1589 it was the custom of a group of Florentine gentlemen to meet regularly at the home of a wealthy scholar, Count Giovanni dei Bardi. The members of this group, now known as the *camerata* (Italian for "group"), were Vincenzo Galilei, a fine performer on the lute and father of the celebrated astronomer Galileo Galilei, Jacopo Peri and Giulio Caccini, musicians, and Ottavio Rinuccini, a poet. In the course of their discussions, which were largely concerned with the drama of classical antiquity, these men formulated the theory that the texts of the Greek dramas had been sung in a declamatory manner. There was, to be sure, but little Greek music available to these Florentine scholars; but they were quick to see that the emphasis on one voice which apparently had been one of the features of Greek music, possessed potentialities far more fitted for dramatic expression than the complex polyphony of the sixteenth century. In an endeavor to restore what they deemed to be the style of Greek drama these Florentine scholars brought forth a new form and a new style. The new form was the opera, the new style a homophonic one (that is, with an emphasis on one melody against a harmonic background); and their appearance marked the advent of a new musical era.

The *camerata* believed that the sole purpose of music as applied to dramatic poetry was an expressive one, that is, music's function was to intensify the spoken word. In the comparatively short time that has elapsed since its inception, the opera as an art form has experienced many vicissitudes. At various times certain individuals have attempted to "reform" the opera; but all of their efforts have in general amounted merely to a return to the original ideal of the *camerata*: to combine music with the spoken word producing a form of musical speech superior in expressiveness to either of its component parts used individually.

The *camerata* called this new musical speech *recitativo* (recitative), the name indicating that the text was recited or declaimed. The musical accompaniment consisted of a rather simple progression of chords, which, by proper manipulation of dissonance, might be used to bring out certain words into high relief.

The chords underlying the *recitativo* were sounded by a small concealed orchestra consisting of a keyboard instrument and a few stringed instruments. The players freely constructed their own chords from the lowest part, the bass. The interpretation of this bass later became more specific, however, through the use of numbers beneath its notes. The bass itself was called *basso continuo* (continuous bass), then merely *continuo*. English equivalents are *figured bass* and *thorough bass*.

This custom of writing a bass and merely indicating the harmonic superstructure is evidence that musicians had now commenced to emphasize the vertical, that is, the harmonic aspects of music. The chord, a musical unit composed of simultaneously sounding tones, now became an important element of musical speech. The figured bass played a vital part in almost all the ensemble music written between 1600 and 1750; and it was not until the era of Joseph Haydn (1732-1809) that this extemporaneous method of harmonic "filling in" was dispensed with.

That the style of this type of musical performance differed markedly from the older polyphonic procedures was evident to its enthusiastic advocates. In 1602 Caccini published a set of arias and madrigals with *basso continuo* entitled *Nuove musiche (New Music)*. Other musicians of the period not only emphasized the progressive nature of their efforts, but also made slighting comments about the polyphonic style.

Another outcome of the early opera was the creation of the orchestra, a group of instruments which takes its name from its location next to the stage. With the rapid development of the opera went an increase in the size and the resources of the orchestra, and, in fact, the history of the orchestra up to 1700 involves primarily its activities in the opera theater.

The earliest opera preserved is Peri's setting of Rinuccini's dramatic poem *Euridice*, performed in 1600 in Florence as part of the nuptial festivities of Henry IV of France and Marie de Médicis. The work was elaborately mounted and the composer himself took the role of Orpheus. The orchestra consisted of a gravicembalo (a keyboard instrument) and three stringed instruments. Trumpet fanfares announced the beginning of the play, for in the first few years of its existence the opera possessed no formal overture. Three flutes were used to give appropriate color to a pastoral scene. Thanks to the success of *Euridice* the opera became an accepted and established form.

The first truly great operatic composer, Claudio Monteverdi (1567-1643), had achieved fame as a composer of madrigals of considerable harmonic daring before turning his attention to the opera. His *Orfeo,* produced at Mantua in 1607, marked a signal advance in operatic composition. Monteverdi brought all of his harmonic gift to bear in the writing of the work, with a consequent enrichment of the expressive power of his recitative; *Orfeo* abounds in bold dissonances. The orchestra was considerably strengthened and its scope enlarged. No longer confined merely to supplying harmonic background for recitatives, it painted the color for various scenes and furnished meaningful interludes, *Orfeo* containing no less than twenty-six orchestral episodes. Most important, however, was Monteverdi's writing of an orchestral prelude to the work, constituting the first operatic overture in musical history.

Monteverdi's opera *Arianna,* produced at Mantua in 1608, contains the celebrated *Lament,* probably the composer's finest piece of dramatic writing. His fame eventually won him the post of *maestro di capella* at the Cathedral of St. Mark in Venice; but he still found time to compose operas, notably for the newly opened Venetian theaters.

Venetian Opera.—Up to the year 1637 opera represented a diversion for the nobility exclusively. Operas were mounted as part of court festivities and were presented before a limited number of invited guests. The opening of public opera theaters in Venice in 1637, however, introduced a new and influential factor in the development of opera, namely the admission-paying audience. Admission to the performances being cheap, the public flocked to them to such a degree that it was found profitable to build many theaters. Between 1637 and 1700 sixteen opera houses were opened in Venice, of which four would often be giving performances on the same night, at one time as many as eight being open simultaneously.

The theaters were built by the wealthier nobles who usually owned the boxes. Seats in the hall were not reserved and the members of the audience had to content themselves with wooden benches from which they noisily expressed their opinions of the vocal skill of the performers with applause or catcalls.

The operas themselves were mounted in great splendor, huge sums being expended on scenery and costumes. Works were performed with extravagant settings and spectacular stage effects, including shipwrecks, aerial flights, storms. The awe-inspiring stage machine was an indispensable part of the performance. The English diarist John Evelyn visited Venice in 1645 and made this entry in his notebook: "This night . . . went to the opera, where comedies and other plays are represented in recitative musiq, by the most excellent musicians, vocal and instrumental, with variety of sceanes painted and contrived with no lesse arte of perspective, and machines for flying in the air, and other wonderful motions; taken together it is one of the most magnificent and expensive diversions the wit of man can invent. . . . This held us by the ears until two in the morning."

The plots of the operas, while ostensibly based on mythology or classical history, merely utilized classical names in actions rich in contemporary political intrigue, usurpations, and murders.

From the opening of the first public opera theaters important changes had been taking place in the opera. The dramatic purpose which had brought it into being and characterized the first few decades of its existence was now allied with various procedures aiming to entertain or edify an admission-paying audience. Among the musical results were the gradual elimination of the chorus, and a growing emphasis on solo song and on pure melody. Since the day of the early Venetian theaters Italian operatic composers have hardly ever failed to provide their audiences with ingratiating melodies designed to be sung by accomplished vocalists.

Of the many composers occupied in meeting the insatiable demands of the Venetian opera houses, the two most significant were Francesco Cavalli (1602-1676) and Marc' Antonio Cesti (1623-1669). Cavalli, who was Monteverdi's pupil and later his successor as *maestro di capella* at St. Mark's, instilled melodic interest into his recitatives and displayed a fine feeling for form in his arias. Many of these arias were simple tunes in triple rhythm resembling the barcarolles of the Venetian gondoliers. Cavalli was one of the first of the numerous Italian opera composers to be invited to foreign courts. In 1660 he journeyed to Paris to direct the performance of his *Serse* (*Xerxes*), given in the Palais du Louvre as part of the wedding festivities of Louis XIV. Cavalli practically dominated the Venetian opera stages for almost thirty years and the frequent performances of his works brought him great riches.

Cavalli's younger contemporary, Cesti, wrote tuneful operas in a popular vein. His melodies possessed a rather tender, almost feminine charm achieved, however, not without some loss of expressiveness. Cesti was also invited to a foreign court, in this instance Vienna, where his *Il Pomo d'oro* (*The Golden Apple*) was mounted in 1666 with great pomp.

The Oratorio.—The development of the opera was paralleled by the development of its sacred analogue, the oratorio. The oratorio, like the opera, was not a strictly new form, preceded as it was by a long line of sacred dramas in which music had been employed. The first work composed in the new style popularized by the *camerata* was a sacred drama, *La rappresentazione di anima e di corpo* (*The Representation of the Soul and the Body*), performed in the *oratorio* (oratory, hence the name given to the form) of a Roman church in 1600, the year in which Peri's *Euridice* was first presented. The music was composed by Emilio Cavalieri (c. 1550-1602), a friend of Count Bardi's circle. The Italian oratorio developed concurrently with the Italian opera. Certain elements of the Italian style were later taken over by German composers in whose hands the oratorio evolved into an entirely different type of work.

Neapolitan Opera.—Towards the end of the seventeenth century, the center of Italian operatic activity shifted from Venice to Naples, thanks to the presence in that city of the gifted composer, Alessandro Scarlatti (1659-1725). Scarlatti's works set the standards for almost all European operatic composition during the first half of the eighteenth century. The outstanding feature of Scarlatti's operas was their emphasis on vocal melody of a considerable range of expressiveness. His arias, however, were not obviously tuneful; nor can it be said that Scarlatti, like many other composers, was indifferent to the demands of his texts.

By his almost exclusive use of the *da capo* form as a pattern for the organization of his arias, Scarlatti established it as an operatic convention which later became a deadly stereotype. The *da capo* form is a three-part (ternary) form consisting of three sections, the second contrasting with and the last repeating the first. Inasmuch as the third section duplicated the first, composers did not bother to write it out and merely wrote "da capo," meaning "from the beginning" at the end of the second section, thereby producing the pattern A-B-A. A great many musical forms are based on this formula.

Scarlatti was also progressive in his use of the orchestra. But his striking contribution in this field was the prefacing of his operas not with one instrumental movement, but with three short ones played in succession. These three movements, each in a measure independent, were contrasted in tempo and were arranged as follows: fast-slow-fast. It is from this type of overture that our modern symphony evolved. The Scarlatti overture had no bearing on the opera which followed, and it was to all intents and purposes a concert-piece played before the curtain was raised.

Italian opera at the death of Scarlatti constituted more of a vocal concert than a dramatic performance. Choral passages were rarely introduced and the typical opera consisted of a string of arias separated by recitatives. While the burden of the action fell on the recitatives, audiences considered them dull and usually chatted while they were being rendered. Interest was shown only during the tuneful episodes—the arias.

The human voice came to the fore as the musical instrument *par excellence*. Accomplished singers became popular favorites who were not loath to make capital of their hold on the public. They earned fabulous fees and tyrannized impresarios and composers with impunity. Elaborate "embellishment" of what the composer had written formed an invariable part of the rendition of any skilled performer, the most complex type of ornamentation being reserved for the *da capo* sections. This type of extemporaneous variation on what the composer had written was the direct forerunner of the free variation technique employed in modern "swing" music.

Up to the middle of the eighteenth century, the most favored operatic singers were eunuchs, the so-called *castrati*. They possessed soprano voices of great power, for the vocal cords of a boy were combined with the lungs of a man. The important role played by the *castrati* in operas of this period places almost insurmountable difficulties in the way of restoring them to the stage today. Nor does mere examination of a score give a complete aural image of any work, for the eventual shape of almost every aria was subject to the singer's whims and to his skill in embellishment.

The type of opera described above was known as *opera seria* (serious opera). Between the three acts of the *opera seria* it was the custom usually to present a two act *opera buffa* (comic opera). The *opera buffa* served as a perfect contrast to its associated *opera seria,* for its text was often written in a local dialect, and its plot dealt with events in the lives of the common people. A survival of the sixteenth-century *commedia dell' arte,* its action moved swiftly, emphasis being placed on effectiveness of characterization, on tuneful sparkling arias and lively ensembles. The world's greatest *opera buffa* is Giovanni Pergolesi's *La serva padrona* (*The Maid as Mistress*) presented in Naples in 1733. This charming little work, which has had many performances in America, enjoys the distinction of being the oldest opera regularly to be performed in the principal opera houses of the world.

French Opera.—Opera in France has always been under the influence of the age-old national preference for brilliant spectacle and sumptuous presentation. The origins of the form in France are traceable to the ballets which had been given at French courts since the Middle Ages. French opera did not come into its own, however, until comparatively late, and as has often happened in the history of French music, the prime mover was a foreigner, in this instance, the

Italian Jean-Baptiste Lully (1632-1687). In a certain sense Lully perpetuated the tradition of the *camerata* by his faithful adherence to a dramatic purpose. While none of his operas is found in the modern repertoire, the fructifying aspects of his work manifest themselves in instrumental music. Lully possessed an excellent orchestra, comparable in constitution to the orchestra of today. The celebrated *les vingt-quatre violons du roi* (the twenty-four violins of the king) formed a valuable part of this orchestra.

A not inconsiderable portion of a typical Lully opera was given over to ballet divertissements, and for these episodes Lully contributed many dances of great variety, characterized by skillful orchestration and a fine feeling for form. These Lully dances exerted a tremendous influence on later composers in the dance forms, both French and German.

Lully prefaced his operas with an overture which consisted of three consecutive sections. This so-called "French" overture is a three-part (A-B-A) form whose first section is slow, dignified, and majestic in character, and whose second section is lively in pace and polyphonic in texture. It, too, became a prototype for subsequent composers.

In 1664 Lully became friendly with the dramatist Molière (1622-1673) and became associated with him in the presentation of the numerous ballets given before Louis XIV. Lully also wrote music for the divertissements of several Molière plays, notably *Le Mariage forcé* and *Le Bourgeois gentilhomme.*

German Opera.—As in France, the operatic activities of Germany were for a long time in the hands of Italians. Opera houses under the management of Italian musicians, presenting works by Italian composers, were established comparatively early at the many small German courts. Opera written in the German language with music by German composers appeared sporadically; but the history of the form in Germany until late in the eighteenth century was largely a chronicle of Italian music.

The principal center of operatic activity in Germany was the thriving seaport of Hamburg, a city whose position in the maritime world paralleled that of Venice. The Hamburg school achieved its greatest brilliance in the days of the highly talented composer Reinhard Keiser (1673-1739), the German compeer of Alessandro Scarlatti. While contemporary composers admired Keiser's work, its influence was ephemeral, and great as his melodic gifts were, practically none of his music is heard today.

English Opera.—The precursor of opera in England was that peculiarly English type of presentation known as the *masque,* an allegorical entertainment combining poetry, music, and dancing, lavishly produced at the private houses of the nobility.

English opera came into its own with the return of Charles II in 1660 and the subsequent reopening of the theaters. It reached a high point in the works of Henry Purcell (1659-1695) whom many rightfully claim to be England's greatest composer. Thanks to him English opera far outstripped anything that was being written on the Continent during that period.

The opera of the English Restoration was a curiously assembled sequence of scenes, some of which were spoken, others sung. As on the Continent, emphasis was placed on extravagant costuming, representation of supernatural phenomena, and breath-taking stage machines. Thus music was only one of the incidental features of a performance.

Despite the limitations imposed on him by the conventions of his time, Purcell created a great amount of music of singular melodic appeal and invariable dramatic effectiveness, totally free from empty display and pomposity. Well-acquainted with both the French and Italian styles, Purcell did not hesitate to incorporate their better features into his own works. His operas constitute the most remarkable musical products of the seventeenth century, witness such almost perfect creations as the "Lament" of Dido from *Dido and Aeneas,* and the song "Fairest Isle" from *King Arthur,* the text for which opera was supplied by an admiring contemporary of Purcell, the poet John Dryden.

The promise of Purcell remained unfulfilled, however, for shortly after his death in 1695, English music lost its native stamp and eventually succumbed entirely to German influence, a restraining force which was not thrown off until early in the twentieth century.

2. *Instrumental Music of the Seventeenth Century*

The development of both instrumental music and the opera would have been greatly hindered if composers had been limited exclusively to the use of the comparatively weak-toned viols. Happily, however, the infinitely more versatile violin family came into being at this time, and like the opera, was a product of seventeenth-century Italy. Activity in the fashioning of violins centered at Cremona, with Nicolò Amati (1596-1684) as the outstanding maker. Amati's pupil, Antonio Stradivarius (1644-1737), firmly established the art of violin-making, and practically no improvements in the construction of this group of instruments have been initiated since his day.

The development of music for the violin family proceeded along two paths, works for groups of instruments and works for a solo instrument. The foundations of the modern school of violin playing were laid by Arcangelo Corelli (1653-1713) whose *Concerto Grosso* for string orchestra, usually known as the *Christmas Concerto* (1712), enjoys the distinction of being the oldest orchestral composition regularly played today.

The two instrumental forms which crystallized under Corelli's hands were the *sonata* and the *concerto.* The term *sonata* had been loosely used during the sixteenth century to differentiate music to be played (*suonare*) from music to be sung (*cantare*). By Corelli's day, however, the function of the term *sonata* had narrowed down to being a label for pieces for a keyboard instrument or for a solo instrument accompanied by a keyboard instrument. While almost any type of solo instrument might be used, the violin was the favorite.

The sonatas of Corelli fall into two categories, the church sonata (*sonata da chiesa*) and the chamber sonata (*sonata da camera*). The church sonata usually had four movements (slow-fast-slow-fast) and exhibited a polyphonic texture.

The chamber sonata usually consisted of a series of dance pieces in alternating fast or slow tempi.

The *concerto grosso,* an instrumental form in whose development Corelli played no inconsiderable part, is a composition for a band of instrumentalists, in which certain passages are played by all the performers, while others are assigned either to a solo performer or to a small group of performers. Ths large group was called the *ripieno* or *concerto grosso* (large concerto); the smaller group was known as the *concertino* (small concerto). The underlying principle of the *concerto grosso* was that of contrast between passages alternately delivered by groups differing in strength and tone-color. The concerto style, which as has been mentioned before was first fostered by Gabrieli in Venice, permeated almost all ensemble music written in the first half of the eighteenth century.

Keyboard instruments were also undergoing rapid development. Two types of sounding mechanisms, plucking and striking, were employed for the stringed instruments of this group. The instrument with the plucking mechanism was known to the Italians as the *clavicembalo* or *cembalo,* to the French as the *clavecin,* to the Germans as the *Flügel,* and to the English as the *harpsichord.* The strings of the harpsichord were actuated by quills. While deficient in nuance, this instrument gave forth a precise, powerful, and brilliant tone.

The strings of the *clavichord* were struck by brass tangents. The tone of the instrument was thin and somewhat lacking in brilliance; but it possessed a far greater expressive power than its relative, the harpsichord.

The brilliant organ playing of the Venetian masters was imported into northern Europe by a Dutch composer, Jean Pieterszoon Sweelinck (1562-1621), a pupil of Gabrieli. The extent of his influence was wide, many pupils coming to him from all parts of Germany. It is Sweelinck who may be credited with having conferred maturity on the *fugue* as an art form, as well as having laid the foundations of the great German school of organ playing.

The chorale exerted a distinctive influence on the organ music of Germany, for the creation of variations—called *Chorale-vorspiele* (Chorale-preludes)—on the chorale-melodies was a special concern of German organ composers. The methods of treating the chorale-melody varied. The great Nuremberg organist, Johann Pachelbel (1653-1706), habitually used the chorale-melody as the subject of an elaborate fugue. Georg Böhm (1661-1733) of Luneburg subjected the chorale-melody to elaborate embellishment. The celebrated Dietrich Buxtehude (1637-1707) of Lübeck made the chorale-melody serve as the framework for a brilliant display piece. Pachelbel, Böhm and Buxtehude are the three masters who preceded the great Johann Sebastian Bach.

Another Gabrieli pupil, Heinrich Schütz (1585-1672), transplanted the style of the early Italian opera to German sacred music. In his works the eloquent recitative, the independent functioning of the orchestra and the impressive polychoric effects so beloved by the Italians were combined, but with an impressive earnestness. Schütz, undoubtedly the greatest German composer of his epoch, is best represented by his moving settings of the Passion.

3. *The Age of Bach and Handel*

The seventeenth century was largely a period of experimentation. New styles, new instruments, new forms, were all in the process of evolution. The many diverse trends of the period—sacred and secular, instrumental and vocal—reached their culmination at the hands of Johann Sebastian Bach and George Frideric Handel, two German composers who flourished during the first half of the eighteenth century, a period which may be named after them, "The Age of Bach and Handel."

Johann Sebastian Bach, the greatest member of a line of over fifty Thuringian musicians who bore this family name, was born in Eisenach, March, 1685, and died in Leipzig, July, 1750. With the exception of the few years which he spent in the service of a young prince, Bach's life was devoted almost entirely to the playing of the organ in various churches and to the composition of a vast quantity of truly inspired music. The complete edition of his works comprises sixty volumes.

Bach was recognized during his lifetime primarily as an organ composer. He traveled but little and was content to remain an obscure cantor in Leipzig, a city which was a commercial rather than an artistic center. The majority of his compositions were not printed during his lifetime, and consequently many have been lost. The awakening of interest in Bach's music did not take place till seventy-nine years after his death when Felix Mendelssohn revived the *St. Matthew Passion* in 1829.

With the exception of the opera there is hardly a seventeenth-century form on which Bach did not lay a perfecting hand. In fact he brought all of the numerous forms in which he wrote to such heights that they entirely overshadow the efforts of his contemporaries. Thus like many other great composers, Bach placed the keystone on an arch in whose erection many lesser geniuses had participated.

The compositions of Bach are permeated throughout with a Baroque spirit. Baroque art, lively and emotional, laid emphasis on movement, on expressiveness, and on the representation of the picturesque. In music the Baroque style inclined toward the larger forms and infused considerable dramatic interest in them through the use of vital thematic material and effective contrasts. Realistic treatments of texts were common, and the abilities of well-placed dissonant chords to create dramatic surprises were continually utilized.

Bach's tonal creations continually evoke a state of tension, so vital is their expressive purpose and so surcharged are they with emotional content. Popular as his name may be today, Bach is in a sense an unknown composer, for his greatest works, the one hundred and ninety-five church cantatas, have suffered wholly unwarranted neglect.

The works of Bach summed up the past and anticipated the future. The majority of his compositions were written in a polyphonic style, laying great emphasis on imitation. But the polyphony of Bach, unlike that of earlier masters such as Palestrina and de Lassus, was a baroque product, laid out along harmonic lines; and it was primarily in his use of harmonic materials that Bach left a strong impress on subsequent music. The older polyphonic style died with him, having finally been ousted by the homophonic idiom which the rapidly developing opera had fostered.

Although Bach was an organist himself, his organ works form only a small part of his output. They are, however, the nucleus of the repertory of the modern organist. In addition to many chorale-preludes, intensely subjective treatments of the chorale-melodies, Bach wrote a great series of organ fugues, each of which is usually coupled to a prefatory piece of an improvisational character called a *toccata, prelude,* or *fantasia.* (A fugue is a polyphonic form whose prime purpose is the development of a melodic idea called the *fugue-subject.*) Bach is universally conceded to have been the world's greatest writer of fugues.

Bach's works for keyboard stringed instruments are probably his best-known compositions. The influence of French composers is shown in the several series of pieces in dance forms called *suites* or *partitas.* The most important work in this category is the collection of forty-eight preludes and fugues entitled *The Well-Tempered Clavichord,* the name referring to the system in which the strings of the instrument were tuned.

Bach greatly admired the works of the Italian writers of *concerti grossi* and transcribed for the organ several compositions by his contemporary Antonio Vivaldi (c. 1680-1743). About sixteen solo concertos by Bach may be heard today. His finest works in this form are the six *Brandenburg Concertos,* compositions which represent the highest point of development of the *concerto grosso.*

The major part of Bach's contribution is summed up in his choral music, and it was in music of this type that he achieved his greatest heights of inspiration. As cantor of the St. Thomas' Church in Leipzig from 1723 until his death, Bach was charged with the composition of the music required for fifty-nine annual occasions. Of this music the outstanding works in addition to the church cantatas are the *St. John Passion, The St. Matthew Passion* and the *Mass in B Minor.*

George Frideric Handel, father of the modern oratorio, was born in the same year as Bach, 1685, and survived him by nine years, passing away in 1759. The two men never met and their careers and creative accomplishments stand in sharp contrast to each other. From 1712 until his death Handel lived in London, becoming a naturalized British subject.

Handel was an eminently practical musician: while never debasing his art, he continually kept it within the range of popular appreciation. His forty-six operas written for the London theaters followed the style formulated by Alessandro Scarlatti at Naples and consequently are difficult to produce on the stage today. Handel's celebrated *Largo* was in its original form an aria in one of these operas. Most of the variegated instrumental and choral transcriptions of this simple tune, which are heard today, are in questionable taste.

The formulation of a type of musical entertainment to which Handel gave the name *oratorio* constitutes his most significant contribution. The Handel oratorio, however, had little in common with the Italian form bearing the same name. The oratorio in Handel's usage was an extensive work for chorus, soloists, and orchestra based on a text of biblical origin, but nonliturgical, and presented in the concert hall without action, scenery, or costume. Of Handel's thirty-two oratorios the better known are *Israel in Egypt, Samson, Judas Maccabaeus,* and *The Messiah.* The last-named work is probably the world's most frequently performed choral composition.

Of the host of minor composers active in this period the two most worthy of mention here were the Frenchman François Couperin (1660-1733) and the Italian Domenico Scarlatti (1685-1757), famous son of a famous father. Both these composers significantly enriched the literature of the harpsichord. The dance forms which comprised Couperin's suites were assiduously studied by Bach. Scarlatti's brilliant compositions, among the first to employ the crossing of the hands, introduced important technical devices into the art of playing the harpsichord. His numerous *sonatas* foreshadowed a form which later became dominant in instrumental music.

Meanwhile the Italian opera had not been allowed to pursue its artificial course without criticism. Addison and Steele in the *Spectator* lampooned certain features of Handel's operas, for example. One of the most original protests against the mannerisms of the Italian opera appeared in the form of *The Beggar's Opera,* the text by John Gay and the music by John Pepusch (1667-1752). *The Beggar's Opera,* which was produced in London in 1728 and enjoyed a long run, thoroughly caricatured its pretentious Italian relative. Couched in a popular vein, its music was a compilation of well-known songs augmented by several melodies borrowed from the works of Purcell and Handel.

A much more serious protest was raised by the German opera composer, Christoph Willibald Gluck (1714-1787), who, in an elaborate preface to his opera *Alceste,* vigorously condemned the indifference to dramatic necessities found in most of the operas of the Italian school. Gluck's musical, monument is the opera *Orfeo ed Euridice,* produced in Vienna in 1762. It is the oldest serious opera to hold the stage today. Among his reforms Gluck raised the overture to a position of dramatic importance. His overture to the opera *Iphigénie en Aulide* (*Iphigenia in Aulis*), still a part of the modern orchestral repertory, represents a perfect example of the dignity, the grandeur and the classical restraint which characterized Gluck's style. The reforms which Gluck advocated did not take firm hold, however, and it was not until the day of his great disciple, Richard Wagner, that the original dramatic purpose of the opera was completely restored.

4. The Age of Haydn and Mozart

The second half of the seventeenth century witnessed what to all intents and purposes was a revolution in the art of music. Both the forms and the style employed by Bach and Handel were supplanted by a new instrumental form and a new instrumental style, the evolution of which had been accelerated by the feverish activity in the field of opera. This newly established instrumental form was the sonata, to which are related the string quartet, the symphony, the concerto, and the overture. The new instrumental style was the homophonic one initially fostered by the opera and now applied to orchestral music.

Since about 1750 the term *sonata* has designated an instrumental work for a solo instrument, usually consisting of three or four contrasting pieces known as movements. The form of the first of these movements, and only the first, is the characteristic feature of the sonata and hence is called the *sonata form*. A movement in sonata form usually consist of four sections—exposition, development, recapitulation, and coda. The exposition presents the subject matter—two theme groups in contrasting keys. The development, which follows no prescribed rule, allows the composer to manipulate the material of the exposition as his fancy dictates and his technical facility permits. The recapitulation is largely a restatement of the exposition. The coda functions as the summing-up or epilogue.

Many instrumental forms employed the sonata pattern, although the name attached to these forms varied according to the instruments or instrumental combinations for which they were written. For works for a solo instrument such as the piano, or for two instruments in combination such as the violin and piano, the term *sonata* was used. A composition for violin, violoncello, and piano was called a *trio,* and for two violins, viola and violoncello, a *string quartet.* A work for orchestra was called a *symphony,* while a composition for a solo instrument and orchestra was entitled *concerto.* An orchestral work in sonata form which served as preface to a drama or opera was called an *overture.*

The limitless range of contrasts within a unifying scheme of keys which the sonata and its related forms permit, made it the dominant instrumental form of the late eighteenth and early nineteenth centuries. The sonata, like the suite, constitutes another musical form constructed by arranging in a series a number of shorter works which, while entities in themselves, are only parts of a larger whole, a sort of loosely knitted federation. The sonata pattern serves as an excellent solution of the problem of organizing larger musical structures. The average symphony of Haydn or Mozart, for example, fills about twenty-five minutes with meaningful sound.

The second half of the seventeenth century marked the beginning of the active concert life which we today associate with the art of music, for up to this time the performance of music had been almost exclusively confined to the homes of the noble classes, to the church, and to the opera house. The credit for having given the first public concert, that is, a purely musical performance to which an audience is admitted on payment of a fee, goes to an English musician, John Banister, who in 1672 advertised in the *London Gazette* that a performance open to the general public would be given at his house. Full-scale orchestral concerts came into being in a rather curious manner, for initially they were only substitutes for operatic performances. Opera theaters being closed during Holy Week, orchestral concerts were given on their stages instead. Our modern concert life is of recent origin, for the first genuine orchestral concert did not take place until 1725, when the French composer Philidor (1681-1728) founded the *Concerts spirituels* in Paris. Later concert institutions were the *Tonkünstler Societät* founded in Vienna in 1772, and the *Gewandhaus* concerts established in Leipzig in 1781. Beginning with a performance in Charleston, S. C., in 1731, concerts in which the foremost European composers were liberally represented were regularly given in the English colonies in America.

The rapid growth in Germany of amateur musical societies drawn from the middle classes served to make music an important part of middle-class life and hence to create a large musical public. These amateur groups usually gathered at the local inns for their music-making. Although the enthusiasm of these amateurs greatly exceeded their proficiency, they managed to give public concerts which included orchestral works by contemporary composers. These town concerts had a social purpose as well, for they were usually followed by a dinner and ball.

The traveling instrumental virtuoso also became an indispensable part of concert life at this time. Unlike our present-day procedure of giving a solo recital, the virtuoso of the eighteenth century always appeared with an orchestra and almost invariably played music of his own composition. The difficulties in the way of giving a concert were considerable. When arriving in a town the traveling virtuoso had first to curry favor with the local amateur musicians so that he might acquire the use of a hall and an accompanying orchestra. Prosperous citizens were then solicited to buy tickets. At the concert itself the virtuoso appeared in the dual rôle of performer and composer.

Thanks to its inherently musical population and to the presence in it of three great composers, Haydn, Mozart, and Beethoven, Vienna was the musical capital of Europe from about 1760 to 1827. While none of these composers was actually born in Vienna, the three are usually referred to as the "Viennese School" and their epoch as the "Viennese Period," the most significant period in the development of modern instrumental music.

The splendid private orchestras maintained by the art-loving nobility constituted the principal feature of Viennese musical life. These orchestras were composed of versatile servants who could function as liverymen or cooks by day and as competent orchestral musicians at night. The conductor of the orchestra, the *Kapellmeister,* created the music necessary for the various performances of the orchestra. All the music so composed remained the property of the employer, unless express permission could be obtained for its sale to some other nobleman or to a publisher.

Many members of the nobility were themselves competent performers. In fact the Austrian Royal House, the members of which both composed music and participated in its performance, took a leading rôle in fostering musical events. The middle classes were also extremely musical, and orchestras composed almost entirely of amateurs were a regular part of Vienna's musical activity.

Musical tastes at the time were the reverse of those current today. The Viennese were interested primarily in the music of their epoch and continually demanded to hear *new* music. The concerts which were given seem inordinately long according to modern standards; and the demand for music to be performed at them was insatiable. Compositions were regarded as commodities to be furnished either by a purveyor in one's employ, the *Kapellmeister,* or by a publisher. It was usually the custom for purchasers to commission works in batches of six.

Haydn, for example, sent an order of six symphonies to a Parisian concert group, and created six quartets for a wholesale merchant who wished to entertain prospective buyers of his wares.

The system had its advantages, however, for the incessant demand for music greatly accelerated the progress of the art. Haydn's finest orchestral music came into being only because of the concerts which he was paid to give in London. The composer of the period suffered a certain social inferiority, it is true, but unlike a modern composer, he could at least be sure that everything he wrote would be performed.

The Croatian Joseph Haydn (1732-1809) was the first composer to play an important part in Vienna's musical activity. From 1761 to 1790 he was in the employ of the distinguished Esterhazy family, who valued Haydn's gifts highly and placed no obstacles in the path of his development. So great did his fame become that on the death of Prince Nicholas Esterhazy in 1790, Haydn was invited to London to give a series of orchestral concerts. This invitation was again extended to him in 1794. His London concerts were heavily patronized, and honors were heaped upon his head, Oxford University conferring on him the degree of Doctor of Music. The last years of Haydn's life were spent in retirement in Vienna. The affection in which he was universally held won for him the name "Papa Haydn."

Haydn has often been called "father of the sonata," "father of the string quartet," "father of the symphony," "father of the orchestra." While these appellations contain a measure of truth, they are exaggerations, for Haydn invented no new forms. Like many other great composers, he gave a definitive mold to musical forms which had existed previously in an incompletely developed state.

One of Haydn's great contributions was the final formulation of the constitution of the orchestra. His one hundred and four symphonies proved the effectiveness of the particular instrumental combination which he preferred. The Haydn orchestra, to which subsequent composers have only made additions, consisted of: (1) strings—first violins, second violins, violas, violoncellos, basses; (2) woodwinds—one flute, two clarinets (in the last symphonies), two oboes, two bassoons; (3) brass and percussion—two trumpets, two horns, and kettledrums. Haydn wrote for this instrumental ensemble with considerable coloristic skill; and it is in his works that the art of orchestration received its first important impetus.

Of the one hundred and four Haydn symphonies, only about six are heard today, and of these six all but one were written for the London concerts. Well-meaning admirers have tagged these symphonies with imaginative titles such as *The Surprise, The Bear, The Clock, The Hen;* but in no sense are the Haydn symphonies descriptive music.

Of the four movements of a Haydn symphony, the first and last, both fast movements, are usually in sonata form. The second movement is frequently a set of variations on a song-like theme. The third movement, a *minuet,* represents the survival in symphonic music of an older dance form.

Haydn was also one of the first composers to realize the artistic potentialities of the string quartet, and to formulate the particular idiom of this instrumental combination. Every contemporary musician praised Haydn's quartets, Mozart having gone so far as to say, "I learned string-quartet writing from him." Of Haydn's eighty-three quartets about twelve may be heard today.

Wolfgang Amadeus Mozart (1756-1791) was a younger contemporary and dear friend of Haydn. We should not overlook the fact that Mozart died eighteen years before Haydn, and that the majority of Haydn's great works were of later origin than those of Mozart.

The tragedy of Mozart's life was that he never succeeded in finding a position commensurate with his gifts. For a time he was in the service of the Archbishop of Salzburg who unfortunately, like most men of his day, was partial to Italian musicians. From 1781 until his death Mozart was a free-lance in Vienna, earning a miserable living by giving lessons, writing operas, and appearing as soloist and composer at orchestral concerts managed by himself.

Unlike Haydn, Mozart's creativeness extended to all types of composition and in every field he has left significant works. Primarily, however, he was an operatic composer, and his extraordinary melodic gift manifested itself in all the music which he wrote.

Of Mozart's twenty-two operas, five, written in the last ten years of his life, hold the stage today. They are: *Die Entführung aus dem Serail* (*The Abduction from the Seraglio*), *Le Nozze di Figaro* (*The Marriage of Figaro*), *Don Giovanni* (*Don Juan*), *Così fan tutte* (*So Do They All*) and *Die Zauberflöte* (*The Magic Flute*). As the first and last titles on this list indicate, Mozart has the distinction of having composed the first great operas in the German language. Apart from his melodic fluency, Mozart possessed a talent for bringing to life by means of musical characterization the stereotyped personages of his texts.

Mozart, who composed with almost unbelievable ease and was extremely prolific, has left a large amount of chamber music, of which his twenty-seven string quartets form the nucleus. About ten of these quartets are heard today, six of them making a set affectionately dedicated to Haydn.

Four of Mozart's forty-nine symphonies remain as part of the repertory of modern symphony orchestras. They are characterized by a wealth of expressive melody and a great facility in instrumentation, and like almost all of Mozart's instrumental compositions, they contain many striking chordal progressions.

Mozart's contribution to the world's store of musical forms was the concerto, which differed from the *concerto grosso* of Bach's day in being largely a symphony with a prominent part for a solo instrument, usually the piano or violin. Two features of the concerto deserve mention. First, the solo part was written for a virtuoso performer, and consequently the performance of a concerto had as an incidental purpose the display of virtuosity. Second, at a designated point in the first movement, and often in the second and third as well, the orchestra ceases playing and the soloist performs a brilliant display section called the *cadenza*. Before the day of Beethoven the soloist was expected to improvise his cadenza. When Mozart concertos are performed today, the soloist plays a cadenza of his own choice, which he has memorized beforehand.

Mozart composed twenty-seven piano concertos and six violin concertos, of which the former are the more significant. During his sojourn in Vienna, it was his custom to give regular orchestral concerts at which he would play a piano concerto freshly composed for the occasion. The distinctive features of the concertos are the carefully contrived balance of importance between orchestra and solo instrument and the profusion of beautiful melodies. In no sense are the Mozart concertos empty display pieces.

The strong religious tendencies of Mozart, a pious Catholic, found musical expression in the sixty-eight choral works which he composed. While the beautiful motet *Ave Verum Corpus* is probably his best-known work in this form, his greatest accomplishment is the imposing Requiem Mass, on whose composition he was engaged at the time of his premature death. During the writing of this work, which had been commissioned by a mysterious stranger, Mozart was haunted by the idea that he was writing his own Requiem.

SELECTED READINGS

Bernstein, Martin, *Introduction to Music,* Prentice-Hall, 1951.

Blunt, Anthony, *Art and Architecture in France, 1500-1700,* Penguin Books, 1954.

Bukofzer, M. F., *Music in the Baroque Era,* Norton, 1947.

Dobrée, Bonamy, *Essays in Biography,* Oxford University Press, 1925.

———— ed., *From Anne to Victoria,* Scribner, 1937.

DuPont, Jacques, and Mathey, François, *The Seventeenth Century: From Caravaggio to Vermeer,* Skira, 1951.

Einstein, Alfred, *Mozart, His Character, His Work,* Oxford University Press, 1962.

Flower, Newman, *George Frideric Handel, His Personality and His Times,* Scribner, 1959.

Geiringer, Karl, *Haydn, a Creative Life in Music,* Norton, 1946.

Gilbert, K. E., and Kuhn, Helmut, *A History of Esthetics,* Indiana University Press, 1953.

Green, F. C., *Minuet,* Dent, 1935.

Grierson, H. J. C., *Cross Currents in Seventeenth-Century English Literature,* Harper, 1958.

Grout, D. J., *A Short History of Opera,* Columbia University Press, 1947.

Kerman, Joseph, *Opera as Drama,* Vintage Books, 1956.

Kimball, S. F., *The Creation of the Rococo,* Philadelphia Museum of Art, 1943.

Myers, B. S., *Art and Civilization,* McGraw-Hill, 1957.

Osgood, C. G., *The Voice of England,* Harper, 1952.

Pevsner, Nikolaus, *Outline of European Architecture,* Penguin Books, 1960.

Robertson, J. G., *A History of German Literature,* British Book Centre, 1956.

Sachs, Curt, *The Commonwealth of Art,* Norton, 1946.

Schrade, Leo, *Monteverdi,* Norton, 1950.

Spitta, Philipp, *Johann Sebastian Bach,* Dover Publications, Inc., 1951.

Strachey, Lytton, *Landmarks in French Literature,* Oxford University Press, 1912.

Terry, C. S., *The Music of Bach,* Dover Publications, Inc., 1963.

Traz, Georges de, and Fosca, F., *The Eighteenth Century: From Watteau to Tiepolo,* Skira, 1952.

Upjohn, E. M., et al., *History of World Art,* Oxford University Press, 1958.

Vaughan, C. E., *The Romantic Revolt,* Scribner, 1907.

Waterhouse, E. K., *Painting in Britain, 1530-1790,* Penguin Books, 1953.

Wilenski, R. H., *Dutch Painting,* Faber and Faber, 1955.

Wittkower, Rudolf, *Art and Architecture in Italy, 1600-1750,* Penguin Books, 1958.

Wright, C. H. C., *French Classicism,* Harvard University Press, 1920.